Students and Exter

[

Management of Energy/Environment Systems
Methods and Case Studies

Wiley IIASA International Series on Applied Systems Analysis

5 International Series on
Applied Systems Analysis

Management of Energy/Environment Systems
Methods and Case Studies

Edited by

Wesley K. Foell
Energy Research Center,
University of Wisconsin – Madison

A Wiley–Interscience Publication
International Institute for Applied Systems Analysis

JOHN WILEY & SONS
Chichester – New York – Brisbane – Toronto

Library of Congress Cataloging in Publication Data:

Main entry under title:

Management of energy/environment systems.

    (Wiley IIASA International series on applied systems analysis; 5)
    'The IIASA research study on management of regional energy/environment
systems was formally initiated in January 1975.'
    'A Wiley–Interscience publication.'
    Includes index.
    1. Environmental policy–Case studies. 2. Energy policy–Case studies.
3. International cooperation. I. Foell, Wesley K. II. International Institute for
Applied Systems Analysis. III. Series: Wiley IIASA international series on
applied systems analysis; 5.
HC79.E5M345   333.7   78-13617
ISBN 0 471 99721 8

Typeset at the Alden Press, Oxford, London, and Northampton
Printed and bound in Great Britain at The Pitman Press, Bath

To the spirit of cooperation and to the expansion of the IIASA network of institutions and individuals from diverse countries of the world, a network devoted to the improved management of energy and environmental systems

Foreword

Achieving social, political, economic, and environmental stability on a global scale is an elusive but important objective for the benefit of future generations. The size and complexity of the world's society, the increasing demands of human population, and the finite character of the earth and its resources are forcing us to adjust to new realities. Yet, the inertia in our social system is such that it could take several generations to effect orderly changes that culminate in a sustainable balance among the earth's population, its environment, and its principal renewable or recyclable resources. Scientists and statesmen, leaders, and laymen are striving to understand the complexities of this balance.

Few of us interpret the signposts of civilization in the same way; consequently, prophesies for the future span a wide range of possibilities. No one will dispute, however, that to design and follow an orderly course to a stable, sustainable and prosperous world society will require understanding and cooperation among the diverse nations of the world. If such understanding and cooperation are to be adequately developed, international institutions will be needed in which a body of useful experience can be accumulated and ideas can evolve, mature, and become available to the world community. The International Institute for Applied Systems Analysis (IIASA) is becoming one such institution.

IIASA has defined two types of world problems — those that are universal and those that are global. Universal problems are those that many nations have in common, but that each must solve separately. These problems can be worked on by countries individually or collectively and suggested solutions made available to other interested nations. The solution of global problems, on the other hand, requires that the many nations act as one. IIASA is pursuing the understanding of and solutions to both types of problems.

The IIASA research study, Management of Regional Energy/Environment Systems, begun in 1975, has demonstrated how IIASA can assemble a multinational, multidisciplinary team to identify and analyze a given universal problem and its solutions. Such studies increase the understanding of nations on critical issues, surely a necessary step toward achieving a healthier and more stable world community.

RUSSELL W. PETERSON
Director
Office of Technology Assessment
United States Congress

Preface

This book describes an international experiment in East–West collaborative research. The study upon which it is based grew out of a conviction that one vital component of any solution to our increasingly critical global energy problems will be more effective energy system management at the *regional* and *subnational* levels. Furthermore, because of the universality of energy problems among most industrialized societies, the appraisal and further development of these management approaches could greatly benefit from an international setting that spanned economic, political, and social differences between East and West. The International Institute for Applied Systems Analysis (IIASA) in Laxenburg, Austria, provided exactly that setting.[*]

The IIASA research study, Management of Regional Energy/Environmental Systems, was formally initiated in January 1975. Taking advantage of IIASA's access to scientists and institutions in a range of countries in both the socialist and market economy groups, three distinct regions with greatly different political, economic, and social frameworks were chosen for a comparative study. The regions chosen were the German Democratic Republic (GDR), Rhone-Alpes in France, and Wisconsin in the United States. An international IIASA core team conducted in-house research in collaboration with a research institution in each of the three regions: the Institut für Energetik, Leipzig, GDR; the Institut Economique et Juridique de l'Energie, Grenoble, France; and the University of Wisconsin — Madison, Madison, Wisconsin, United States.

Since 1975, IIASA and the three research institutions have formed the nucleus of a small and informal research network coordinated by IIASA. Although IIASA provided the bulk of the financial support through its core research team, each of the three regional institutions also contributed substantially through the time and efforts of its scientific staff, both at their home base and during frequent

---

[*] For information on IIASA, please see the inside of the front cover.

informal meetings and workshops at IIASA. Each regional representative brought with him a significant background of experience in energy systems and policy analysis in his own country. I believe that the interinstitutional arrangements within which this study was conducted served not only to improve our approaches to energy and environmental system management, but also promoted improved understanding between the countries themselves and provided a basis for further cooperation.

In the process of describing and disseminating the results of this research, we have become aware of the breadth of interests and expertise of our audience. We have structured our reporting to meet the needs of four audiences:

1. Policymakers
2. Energy/environment managers, planners, and technical advisors
3. Modelers and analysts
4. Computer systems specialists and programmers

This book is addressed primarily to groups 2 and 3. It focuses on the building and description of long-term energy scenarios for each of the regions as well as on the description of each region's current energy system and the procedures used to manage it. Although the research results provided insight into the energy systems of the regions, the research teams feel that the research *process* was of equal importance.

Because our concept of the energy/environment system of a region is broadly defined to include socioeconomic, technological, and ecological components, we believe the book offers something to the staff of energy enterprises, urban and regional planners, staff and administrators of energy regulatory agencies, environmental and energy researchers, and not least importantly, some interested members of the public. We also hope that the international perspective of this study will make it of interest to countries in both East and West.

For groups 1 and 4 above, other documentation has been or is being prepared. A short set of executive reports is under preparation; and IIASA research reports and memoranda (listed in the chapter references) provide documentation of data and models for the use of modelers and computer-oriented specialists.

The IIASA research team takes responsibility for the conclusions stated here. Although the collaborating institutions did participate extensively in all phases of the research, including the specification and definition of the alternative energy/environment scenarios, the final form of the results and the documentation has not been subject to their detailed review.

WESLEY K. FOELL

Acknowledgments

The material in this book resulted from the contributions of many individuals at IIASA and the collaborating institutions. More detailed descriptions of some of the individual contributions can be found in the references and in other publications resulting from the study. Although all the participants cannot be acknowledged here, the following individuals were associated in a major way with the research:

International Institute for Applied Systems Analysis (IIASA)
    Jacqueline Buehring
    William Buehring
    Jean-Pierre Charpentier
    Robin Dennis
    Loretta Hervey
    Alois Hölzl
    Koichi Ito
    Ralph Keeney
    Bruno Lapillonne
    Harald Stehfest
    Ralf Yorque
Institut für Energetik, Leipzig, German Democratic Republic
    Willy Hätscher
    Peter Hedrich
    Wolfgang Kluge
    Dietmar Ufer
Institut Economique et Juridique de l'Energie (IEJE), Centre National de la Recherche Scientifique (CNRS), Grenoble, France
    Bertrand Chateau
    Dominique Finon

Jean-Marie Martin
University of Wisconsin — Madison, Madison, Wisconsin, United States

Wesley K. Foell, Study Director
Mark Hanson
John Mitchell
James Pappas

Howard Raiffa, IIASA's first director, and Buzz Holling, initial leader of the IIASA Ecology/Environment Project, acted as catalysts for the study and were greatly supportive in the fragile early stages. Roger Levien, current director of IIASA, gave much encouragement in the subsequent stages of the work.

Denise Cavard and Ivano Renzetti of the IEJE, Grenoble, expertly and industriously gathered and analyzed the French data used as a basis for the Rhone-Alpes scenarios. Elizabeth Ampt, Jordanka Dimitrova, Hilary Lee, and Judy Ray of IIASA also provided substantial and dedicated assistance during the course of the research. Jerome Weingart of IIASA gave valuable advice on a reference solar energy system.

The research described in Chapters 1–7 can be attributed to the entire IIASA core group with principal contributions by the chapter authors listed below. The appendixes contain work by IIASA staff as well as specific papers by individuals from institutions in the regions. These authors are also listed below.

Chapter 1   Wesley K. Foell — Energy Research Center, University of Wisconsin — Madison
Chapter 2   Loretta Hervey, Alois Hölzl — IIASA
Chapter 3   William Buehring — IIASA,   Wesley K. Foell — Energy Research Center, University of Wisconsin — Madison
Chapter 4   Robin Dennis — IIASA
Chapter 5   Bruno Lapillonne — IIASA
Chapter 6   William Buehring — IIASA
Chapter 7   Jacqueline Buehring, William Buehring — IIASA; Wesley K. Foell — Energy Research Center, University of Wisconsin — Madison
Appendix A
    Section I   Alois Hölzl — IIASA
    Section II   Alois Hölzl — IIASA
    Section III   William Buehring — IIASA
    Section IV   Jean-Pierre Charpentier — International Atomic Energy Agency (IAEA)
Appendix B
    Section I   Dietmar Ufer — Institut für Energetik, Leipzig
    Section II   Jean-Marie Martin, Dominique Finon — Institut Economique et Juridique de l'Energie (IEJE), Grenoble
    Section III   Stephen Born — Wisconsin State Planning Office, Charles Cicchetti — Wisconsin Office of Emergency Energy Assistance, Richard Cudahy — Wisconsin Public Service Commission

Appendix C
   Section I   Loretta Hervey, Robin Dennis – IIASA
   Section II.A.   Alfred Wischnat – Institut für Energetik, Leipzig
   Section II.B.   Bertrand Chateau – Institut Economique et Juridique de l'Energie (IEJE), Grenoble
   Section II.C.   J. Mitchell – University of Wisconsin – Madison
   Section III.A.   L. Jordan – Institut für Energetik, Leipzig
   Section III.B.   Daniel Blain – Délégation Générale à l'Energie, Ministère de l'Industrie, Paris
   Section III.C.   Charles Cicchetti – Wisconsin Office of Emergency Energy Assistance
Appendix D
   Section I.A.   Peter Hedrich – Institut für Energetik, Leipzig
   Section I.B.   Dominique Finon, Jean-Marie Martin – Institut Economique et Juridique de l'Energie (IEJE), Grenoble
   Section I.C.   Wesley K. Foell – Energy Research Center, University of Wisconsin – Madison; James Pappas – University of Wisconsin – Madison
   Section II.A.   Jean-Marie Martin, Dominique Finon – Institut Economique et Juridique de l'Energie (IEJE), Grenoble
   Section II.B.   Peter Hedrich, Dietmar Ufer – Institut für Energetik, Leipzig
   Section II.C.   Wesley K. Foell – Energy Research Center, University of Wisconsin – Madison; James Pappas – University of Wisconsin – Madison
   Section III.A.   James Pappas – University of Wisconsin – Madison
   Section III.B.   Peter Hedrich, Dietmar Ufer – Institut für Energetik, Leipzig
   Section III.C.   Dominique Finon – Institut Economique et Juridique de l'Energie (IEJE), Grenoble
Appendix E   William Buehring, Ralph Keeney – IIASA; Wesley K. Foell – Energy Research Center, University of Wisconsin – Madison

Contents

1 Introduction

I. BACKGROUND AND OBJECTIVES OF THE STUDY

Energy and environmental problems first became front-page news in the late 1960s and early 1970s. In 1972, the first report commissioned by the Club of Rome, *The Limits to Growth* by Meadows *et al.*, burst upon the world scene, generating tremendous attention and debate in many industrialized countries, not only in academic, government, and business circles, but also by the general public. The possible long-term impacts of environmental degradation and resource depletion reached the public awareness. In autumn, 1973, the cutoff of Mideast oil supplies dramatically demonstrated to the industrialized world the central role played by energy in our society and the maze of interdependencies through which it is linked to the economic and technological fabric of the human enterprise. Since that time, energy planning has become more important at all levels of government in most industrialized countries.

The above events, in concert with a number of other resource-related issues, have brought about the following:

- Increasingly often, society is *explicitly* incorporating energy into its important decision processes.
- A recognition has developed of the major role that energy plays in the quality of the environment.
- Energy and environmental management are becoming recognized as important components of national and regional planning.

This book examines the method and the practice of energy and environmental

---

Chapter 1 was written by Wesley K. Foell – Energy Research Center, University of Wisconsin – Madison.

management — from the perspective of different regions of the world. It is based upon a research program initiated in January 1975 by the International Institute for Applied Systems Analysis (IIASA). The study, designed to integrate energy and environmental management from a systems perspective, had four primary objectives:

1. To describe and analyze patterns of regional energy use and to develop insight into their relationships to socioeconomic and technical variables
2. To compare and appraise alternative methodologies for regional energy and environmental forecasting, planning, and policy design
3. To extend and develop concepts and methodologies for energy/environment management and policy design
4. To use the above methodologies to examine alternative energy policies and strategies for specific regions, to explore their implications from various perspectives using indicators related to environmental impact, energy use, and the like, and to investigate whether these strategies represent a viable choice for a given society

"Regional," as used here, is not defined as either subnational or as a specific part of the world; rather, it refers to a geographic region, appropriately bounded so that it is possible to speak of energy and environmental systems, either from a physical, socioeconomic, or administrative perspective, or from all three. A regional rather than global perspective is employed because many of the significant social and environmental consequences of energy systems are best analyzed within the context of a specific region. In the language of the systems analyst, this is referred to as "embedding" the system in a specific human environment.

What are some of the major regional issues to be addressed? To be sure, they differ according to the region, but there are, nevertheless, several concerns common to many regions. Representative of these are:

Energy Use Patterns: What are the energy implications of continuing the present evolution of energy use patterns? How are these modified by the penetration of alternative energy use technologies, e.g., mass transit systems in the transportation sector?

Energy Supply: What are the resource and environmental implications of satisfying future energy demand by the various alternative energy sources? What additions will be required in the coming decades to the electricity generating, transmission, and distribution facilities?

Human Settlements: How is energy use related to settlement density, size, types of housing, and energy supply technology? What role should these factors play in land-use planning, zoning, and building regulations? How will alternative land development patterns affect environmental quality?

Environmental Protection: What are potential environmental limits associated with alternative patterns of energy demand and supply within a region? What effects

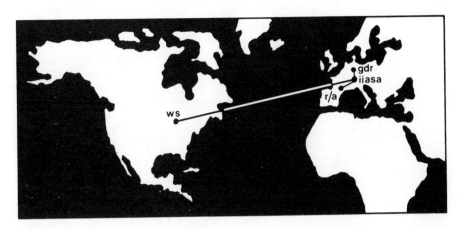

FIGURE 1.1 The 1975 international network of the IIASA Regional Energy/ Environment Project. gdr = the German Democratic Republic; r/a = Rhone-Alpes; ws = Wisconsin; iiasa = International Institute for Applied Systems Analysis, Laxenburg, Austria.

would various pollution control policies have on environmental impacts associated with alternative energy strategies?

Several "world" or "global" energy studies have been conducted within the past few years, e.g., the Workshop on Alternative Energy Strategies (WAES),[1] The Second Club of Rome Report,[2] and the Organisation for Economic Co-operation and Development (OECD) energy forecast (*World Energy Outlook*).[3] These international studies play an important role in providing a broad perspective to evaluate the combined global effect of various national strategies and technological choices. In contrast, in the research described in this book, a regional rather than global approach was employed. To provide a broader view of both theory and practice, the IIASA research was organized on a comparative basis. It focuses on energy/ environment management in three greatly differing regions – the German Democratic Republic (GDR), the Rhone-Alpes region in southern France, and the state of Wisconsin in the United States (Figure 1.1). These regions were chosen primarily because of their greatly differing socioeconomic and political structures, their technological base, their geographic and environmental properties, and their current institutional approaches to energy and environmental management. Comparative studies of differing systems are valuable in that they can help formulate a more generalized understanding of system behavior, as well as an appreciation of the techniques commonly used to study them. For example, it is possible to examine the applicability of a specific energy demand analysis technique to all three of the regions. Two important previous comparative studies are those of Darmstadter[4] and Schippers and Lichtenberg.[5]

The research was oriented toward methodology and policy in an effort to narrow

4

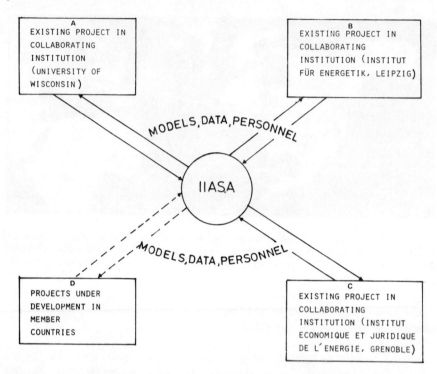

FIGURE 1.2 Interinstitutional relations within the energy/environment system study. "Member Countries" in the lower left-hand box refers to countries that support IIASA.

the gap between the practitioner and the client of applied systems analysis. The management approaches described here are aimed toward long-term management rather than day-to-day operational questions; that is, they are within a strategic rather than an operational or tactical framework.

II. ORGANIZATION OF THE STUDY

II.A. A RESEARCH NETWORK

One of IIASA's strengths is its access to research institutions and scientists throughout the world — and its ability to interact with them in applied and policy-oriented research projects. The IIASA Regional Energy/Environment Study was conducted in close cooperation with research institutions in the three regions under study. In order to be considered in the study, each region had to have an institution with a policy-oriented research program examining energy/environment systems from a broad resource management perspective.

A small core team of IIASA scientists, from several internal research projects, conducted the in-house research in collaboration with the following institutions in the regions under study:

- The Institut für Energetik, Leipzig, GDR
- The Institut Economique et Juridique de l'Energie (IEJE) in Grenoble, France, a part of the Centre National de la Recherche Scientifique (CNRS)
- The Energy Systems and Policy Research Group (ESPRG) of the Institute for Environmental Studies and the College of Engineering, University of Wisconsin – Madison, in the United States

Each of these institutions plays an active role in its country or region in conducting applied policy-oriented energy research and in advising policymakers. The interaction between IIASA and the collaborating institutions is illustrated in Figure 1.2. There was a vigorous flow of models, data, and personnel between IIASA and the institutions. These flows are outlined in more detail in the following section on research components and in Chapter 3 in conjunction with the description of the alternative scenarios developed for each region. The dotted line in Figure 1.2 represents preparations undertaken in 1976 for participation by additional countries in a follow-up study.*

II.B. COMPONENTS OF THE RESEARCH

The research activities can be broken down into six main components. These components, which more or less coincide with the divisions of this book, are as follows.

II.B.1. Description of Energy Systems in the Regions

A descriptive analysis was developed for each of the three energy systems. Included were geography, economic activity, demography, human settlement patterns, past and current energy use, and energy supply modes. The analysis was compiled in a comparative format that demonstrated some striking differences between the regions. For example, the GDR currently exhibits zero population growth – which is expected to persist at least to the end of this century. In contrast, continued population growth in the other regions will have a strong influence on their energy use (Chapters 4, 5, and 6). As a second example, Wisconsin relies heavily on the automobile in comparison with Rhone-Alpes and the GDR; however, auto ownership in the GDR is increasing at an annual rate of 12 percent in comparison with a 4-percent growth in Wisconsin. Also striking is the heavy GDR reliance on mass transit.

---

* In September 1976 IIASA undertook a similar study on regional energy/environment management in Austria. It was completed in 1978.

II.B.2.   Description of Regional Institutional Structure for Energy/Environment Management

Early in the research it became apparent that a strong relationship exists between the institutional and decision structures of a region and the formal models and planning tools that are used. In view of today's growing interest in new government structures and approaches to energy management, the focus on these structures as part of the research intensified as the study progressed. The stark contrasts between planning procedures and tools in the three regions ranged from the highly centralized and formalized GDR system to the extreme diffuseness of decision making and planning in Wisconsin. In contrast to these two, Rhone-Alpes exists primarily as a unit for statistical and information-gathering activities.

II.B.3.   Comparison of Selected Energy and Environment Management Practices

Management practices in the environmental, technical, and economic fields were selected for comparison between the three regions. The topics chosen were

- Air quality management
- Energy-related building practices
- Energy pricing practices

Specialists in each of the regions provided descriptions of the approaches employed, and a comparison was developed by the IIASA team.

II.B.4.   Description of System Models in the Regions

One of the objectives of the project was to appraise and compare the energy and environmental models of the three regions. This appraisal was valuable to each region in assessing the possibility of using models from other regions and revealed how the models are tied to characteristics of the regions. To promote an examination of the transferability of the models, the appraisal was divided into two parts. Each collaborating institution described its own system of energy/environmental models, and each appraised the models of the other two groups from the perspective of its own system and methodological requirements for planning and policy analysis. For example, the Wisconsin group identified the types of information it desires and examined whether the French models treat those areas adequately.

II.B.5.   Development of Alternative Energy/Environment Futures for Each Region as a Policy Analysis Tool

Scenario building, i.e., the development of alternative futures, was employed by the IIASA core research team as a device for analyzing alternative energy and environment policies and strategies in the regions. It is a convenient tool for studying the interaction of complex and uncertain factors. Broadly described, scenario building is a detailed examination of the possible futures and the consequences of the assumptions made to produce the futures. It provides a formal quantitative framework for the examination and discussion of policy options.

The process employed was one of

1. Imposing given policies, i.e., sets of "rules," on the regions, within the framework of their initial conditions and constraints
2. Evaluating the resulting development and evolution of the region

The policy issues were jointly chosen by IIASA and the collaborating institutions in the regions and included transportation systems, energy supply systems, settlement design, and environmental protection. The assumptions underlying the scenarios were developed from lengthy interactions with specialists in the regions, and, in some cases, exogenous inputs to the scenarios were supplied directly by the collaborating institutions. Rather than national scenarios, regional scenarios were studied because of their value in addressing environmental issues, often regional in nature. A 50-year time span was chosen so as to permit the introduction of speculative technologies into the scenarios as well as modest changes in life-styles.

Three detailed energy/environment scenarios were developed for each region. Scenario 1, the "Base Case," represents a continuation of current socioeconomic trends and policies (e.g., the "Plan" in the GDR). Scenario 2 results from policies encouraging a high-energy future and is based on presumed low or moderate energy costs. It places little or no emphasis on improving efficiencies of energy use. Scenario 3 is a lower-energy future resulting from policies encouraging energy-saving technologies in transport, heating, and industry. It assumes increased environmental quality through conservation and stricter pollution controls.

The scenarios displayed a dramatically wide range of energy/environment futures for the regions. The process of evaluation of these scenarios, through workshops with specialists and policymakers (and, in some cases, members of the public) in the regions, also demonstrated a dramatic diversity of opinion about the likelihood of taking any given path into the future.

The success of the use of scenarios in design or managment depends on feedback between the scenario builders and the managers and designers of the energy system itself. Feedback in scenario writing is similar to the mechanism by which man's knowledge grows. The cycling rarely stops for long; new knowledge evolves continuously, and scenario writing is never finished! New scenarios were developed after those described here; the scenarios themselves are perhaps of less importance than the resulting examination of the assumptions and policies embodied in them.

*II.B.6.   A Method for Communicating and Evaluating Energy/Environment
Strategies and Options*

One of the major tasks of this research was to describe the systems and their possible evolution in the three regions. In this respect, the scenario-writing process was
purely *descriptive*. To explicitly transform the scenario output into *prescriptive*
forms, additional steps are obviously required. One of these is the embedding of the
scenarios into an institutional and decision framework where *preferences* and *values*
must be applied to the results. This process differs considerably across the three
regions because of their very different social and institutional structures.

Decision analysis was applied in this research as one approach to the evaluation
of alternative policy designs and to aid in the communication of the value trade-off
alternatives. In this approach, a type of preference model is introduced into the
evaluation process. This preference model provides a formalization of an individual's
(e.g., an energy policymaker's) subjective preferences for various attributes of the
energy system, for example, alternative environmental impacts. For that individual
it allows the calculation of the relative desirability of a given scenario or policy.

III.   TRANSFER OF RESEARCH RESULTS

Although each research component described in the preceding sections has the
potential to contribute to improved management of regional energy/environment
systems, none of them should stand alone. It is essential that each be used as a com-
plement to the others and, more importantly, that they be linked in a coherent
research format that promotes frequent interaction with the institutional and
decision clients for whom it is intended.

Interaction with policymakers was therefore given particular emphasis in the
research. From the inception of the program, information was solicited from the
appropriate potential users of the research, and at the conclusion of the scenario-
building process, they were asked to evaluate the results. Frequent workshops
encouraged this interaction. The workshop process, shown schematically in Figure
1.3, was perhaps the key element in integrating the several components of the
research program, and in facilitating communication between modelers in the three
regions. There are many indications that the scenarios and the personal interactions
have played a role in energy/environment planning in the regions.*

---

* At the second conference, Management of Regional Energy/Environment Systems, held at
IIASA, 16–19 May 1978, retrospective presentations on the scenarios were given by energy
specialists or policymakers from the three regions. To provide perspective on the scenarios,
summaries of the presentations are included immediately before the chapters describing the
scenarios for the regions (Chapters 4, 5 and 6). They will be published in full as part of the
proceedings of the conference: W. K. Foell (ed.), Proceedings of the Conference on Management of Regional Energy/Environment Systems (Laxenburg, Austria: International Institute
for Applied Systems Analysis, in press).

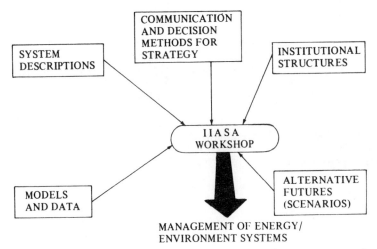

FIGURE 1.3   Diagram of the research components in the IIASA energy/environment system study.

IV.   ORGANIZATION OF THE BOOK

This volume focuses upon the comparative three-region study as outlined in the previous section, within a conceptual framework for management from an energy and environmental perspective. It represents a combination of original material written by the IIASA core research team, and papers contributed to IIASA workshops by specialists from the regions.

The main part of the book focuses on the building and description of energy scenarios for each of the regions. Included is a brief comparison of the three regions (Chapter 2); a summary of the basis and methods underlying the scenario building (Chapter 3); a description of the long-term scenarios developed for each region (Chapters 4, 5, and 6); and lastly, a cross-regional comparison of the resulting scenarios (Chapter 7).

The appendixes begin with a more detailed picture of the regions, including socioeconomic, geographic, and energy-use characteristics (Appendix A). They present an overview of the administrative and institutional structure of energy management in the regions as well as a description of selected energy and environmental management practices in each of the three regions (Appendixes B and C). Appendix D discusses system models employed in each of the regions and has an appraisal of these models by specialists from each of the other two regions. Appendix E describes an approach used in the study for evaluation and choice of alternative energy/environment strategies.

REFERENCES

1. Wilson, Carroll. *Energy: Global Prospects 1985–2000, Report of the Workshop on Alternative Energy Strategies* (WAES). McGraw-Hill, New York, 1977.
2. Mesarovic, M., and E. Pestel. *Mankind at the Turning Point, The Second Report of the Club of Rome.* E. P. Dutton and Co., New York, 1974.
3. *World Energy Outlook.* Organisation for Economic Co-operation and Development, Paris, 1977.
4. Darmstadter, J., J. Dunkerley, and J. Alterman. *How Industrial Societies Use Energy: A Comparative Analysis.* Johns Hopkins University Press, Baltimore, 1977.
5. Schippers, L., and A. J. Lichtenberg. "Efficient Energy Use and Well Being: The Swedish Example," *Science* 194 (4269), Dec. 3, 1976.

2 Summary Comparison of the German Democratic Republic, Rhone-Alpes, and Wisconsin

This chapter contains a comparative summary of selected socioeconomic characteristics and energy systems in the German Democratic Republic (GDR), Rhone-Alpes, and Wisconsin as a prelude to the alternative energy futures developed in the next chapters. The characteristics presented here are among those which have a strong influence upon the evolution of the energy systems in the regions. They are an important part of the initial conditions for the scenarios described in subsequent chapters.* Appendix A presents a more detailed picture of each of the regions.

I. GENERAL CHARACTERISTICS

The location and boundaries of the three regions are shown in the maps in Figures 2.1 and 2.2. Table 2.1 gives a comparison of their sizes, populations and population densities. Wisconsin is by far the largest of the regions. The contrast between the overall densities of sparsely settled Wisconsin and the heavily populated GDR is striking; the GDR population density is more than 5 times greater. Figure 2.3, a comparison of recent population figures in the regions, shows the current zero-population-growth behavior of the GDR, in contrast to the continuing, although modest, growth rates in Rhone-Alpes and Wisconsin (currently approximately 1 percent and 0.8 percent). The contrasting population dynamics had a strong influence on the scenarios presented in later chapters, despite the fact that Wisconsin's population is expected to stop growing shortly after the first quarter of the twenty-first century.

Chapter 2 was written by Loretta Hervey and Alois Hölzl – IIASA.

* 1972 was chosen as the reference year because for later years consistent data could not be obtained for all three regions.

TABLE 2.1   Population and Area of the Three Regions (1972)

	GDR	Rhone-Alpes	Wisconsin
Population ($\times 10^6$)	17.0	4.7	4.5
Area (km²)	108,178	43,634	145,370
Population density (people/km²)	157	108	31

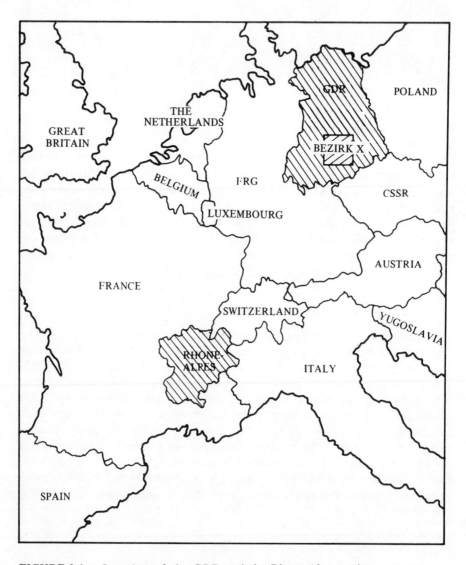

FIGURE 2.1   Location of the GDR and the Rhone-Alpes region.

FIGURE 2.2.   Wisconsin and bordering states in the United States.

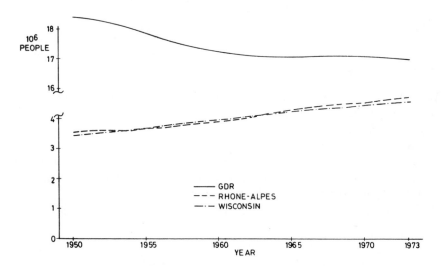

FIGURE 2.3   Cross-regional comparison of population (1950–1973).

Table 2.3 shows cities and towns in the three regions by population categories. These data make it possible to see the structure as well as the degree of urbanization in the study regions. A high percentage (40) of the Rhone-Alpes population live in large cities of 100,000 or more inhabitants. The percentage of the population in Wisconsin and the GDR living in cities of this size is only half as large.

TABLE 2.2   Selected Population Statistics

		GDR[a]	Rhone-Alpes[b]	Wisconsin[c]
Total population (× 10³)	1960	17,241	3,722	3,952
	1972	17,011	4,685	4,526
Median age	1960	32.4[d]		29.4
	1972	36.8[d]	33[e]	27.2[f]
Birth rate per 1,000 residents (births/yr)	1960	17.0		25.1
	1972	11.8	17.1	14.3
Death rate per 1,000 residents (deaths/yr)	1960	13.6		9.6
	1972	13.8	10.0	9.3
Percent urban population (communities	1960	50	53[d]	53[d]
with 1,000 residents or more)	1972	54	68[d]	51[d]
Average household size	1960	2.8[d]		
	1972	2.7[d]	3.1	3.1

[a] SOURCE: *Statistisches Jahrbuch 1974 der DDR*. Staatsverlag der Deutschen Demokratischen Republik, Berlin, 1974.
[b] SOURCE: *Annuaire Rhône-Alpes*, 1974, Principaux Résultats Statistiques en 1973, Supplément de no. 9 de la revue, "Points d'Appui pour l'Economie Rhône-Alpes."
[c] SOURCE: *The State of Wisconsin 1973 Blue Book*. Wisconsin Legislative Reference Bureau, Madison, Wisconsin, 1973.
[d] Estimated.
[e] Average for France.
[f] 1970 value.

II. TRANSPORTATION

Table 2.4 gives a comparison of motor vehicles in the regions in 1972. Here the heavy reliance on the automobile in Wisconsin is vividly demonstrated. Furthermore, the number of registered motor vehicles in Wisconsin has increased approximately 3 times faster than population since 1960. However, recent time series studies show that the auto ownership in the GDR is increasing at an annual rate of 12 percent, in comparison with a 4 percent growth in Wisconsin. Still, in the GDR there is a strikingly heavy reliance on mass transit.

III. ECONOMIC CHARACTERISTICS

Both the GDR and the Rhone-Alpes are more industrialized than Wisconsin. The industrial infrastructures of the three regions also differ significantly. Table 2.5 shows the estimated percentages of total working population in each region by economic sector in 1972. Although there may be some inconsistencies in sector definition, Wisconsin has a significantly smaller percentage of workers in the industrial sector.*

* Wisconsin nevertheless ranks twelfth in total industrial output among the 50 states in the United States.

TABLE 2.3 Cities and Towns by Population Categories

Size	GDR[a] Number of Municipalities	GDR[a] % of Total Population	Rhone-Alpes[b] Number of Municipalities	Rhone-Alpes[b] % of Total Population	Wisconsin[c] Number of Municipalities	Wisconsin[c] % of Total Population
1,000,000 or more	1	6.4 ⎫	1	24.3 ⎫	1	16.2 ⎫
500,000 to 999,999	2	6.4 ⎬ 23.3		⎬ 39.3	1	3.9 ⎬ 19.1
100,000 to 499,999	10	10.5 ⎭	2	15.0 ⎭	8	12.5
50,000 to 99,999	18	7.1	5	9.1	17	12.6
20,000 to 49,999	82	15.1	15	10.8 ⎫	28	8.7 ⎫
10,000 to 19,999	107	8.9		⎬ 40.8		⎬ 54.7
Less than 10,000		45.6		⎭	565	46.0 ⎭
Total		100.0		100.0		100.0

[a] Data from 1973; SOURCE: *Statistisches Jahrbuch 1974 der DDR.* Staatsverlag der Deutschen Demokratischen Republik, Berlin, 1974.
[b] Data from 1968; SOURCE: *Annuaire Rhône-Alpes*, 1974, Principaux Résultats Statistiques en 1973, Supplément de no. 9 de la revue, "Points d'Appui pour l'Economie Rhône-Alpes."
[c] Data from 1970; SOURCE: *The State of Wisconsin 1973 Blue Book.* Wisconsin Legislative Reference Bureau, Madison, Wisconsin, 1973.

TABLE 2.4   Cross-Regional Comparison of Motor Vehicles (1972)

	GDR		Rhone-Alpes		Wisconsin	
	Total (× 10⁶)	Per 1,000 people	Total (× 10⁶)	Per 1,000 people	Total (× 10⁶)	Per 1,000 people
Autos	1.400	82	1.259	270	1.969	436
Motorcycles	1.373	81	0.502	106	0.070	15
Buses	0.018	1.1	0.007	1.5	0.010	2.2
Trams and trolleys	0.0048	0.28	0.0003	0.07		
Trucks	0.256	15	0.328	69	0.376	83
Tractors	0.203	12	0.011	2	0.230	51

TABLE 2.5   Total Working Population by Economic Sector (1972)

	GDR (%)	Rhone-Alpes (%)	Wisconsin (%)
Agriculture	11.6	9.0	8.4
Industry	38.5	36.0	25.5
Building, public works	7.4	9.3	3.3
Commerce, services, administration	42.5	45.7	62.8
Total	100.0	100.0	100.0
Percentage of total population	48.6	43.4	40.8

TABLE 2.6   Industrial Sector by Activity (1972)

	GDR (% of Net Industrial Product)	Rhone-Alpes (% of Industrial Value-Added)	Wisconsin (% of Industrial Value-Added)
Food	11.6	8.7	15.8
Building materials	2.1	3.5	1.3
Primary metals	4.7	5.8	5.6
Machinery[a]	42.0	44.5	49.0
Chemicals and rubber	17.0	14.7	6.0
Light industry	22.6	22.8	22.3
Total	100.0	100.0	100.0

[a] Mechanical, electrical, and transportation equipment.

Table 2.6 presents a cross-regional comparison of fractional industrial activity by sector. The greatest relative differences occur in the food and chemical sectors. Wisconsin ranks high in the United States in food production, particularly in dairy products. On the other hand, it has relatively little activity in the chemical and rubber sectors, both of which are important in the GDR and Rhone-Alpes.

TABLE 2.7   Primary Energy Use (1972)

	Annual Energy Use (10^{15} cal/yr)	Annual Energy Use Per Capita (10^9 cal/person/yr)	Density of Annual Energy Use (10^9 cal/km^2)
GDR	749	44	6.9
Rhone-Alpes	168	35.7	3.8
Wisconsin	319	70.9	2.2

TABLE 2.8   Annual Sectoral End-Use Energy Consumption (1972)

	GDR		Rhone-Alpes		Wisconsin	
	10^{15} cal	% electrical	10^{15} cal	% electrical	10^{15} cal	% electrical
Industrial	312	13	48	28	77	10
Residential and Service	139	12	52	8	106	16
Transportation	55	2	20	3	79	0
Other	15	31			8	11
Total	521	12	120	15	270	9

IV. ENERGY CONSUMPTION

A comparison of energy use in the three regions has revealed some interesting differences, most of which are discussed in detail in connection with the alternative energy futures in the following chapters. Table 2.7 summarizes primary energy use in the regions in 1972. Wisconsin has by far the greatest per capita energy use, whereas, on a density basis, the GDR has almost twice that of Rhone-Alpes and three times that of Wisconsin. Although the energy density varies considerably within a region, the overall density for the region is nevertheless indicative of the concentration of energy-related activities. Table 2.8 shows a comparison of end-use energy consumption by economic sectors in the three regions.

The percentage of end-use energy consumed by the industrial sector is far greater in the GDR (60 percent) than in either Rhone-Alpes (40 percent) or Wisconsin (29 percent). This in part reflects the more industrialized structure of the GDR economy, but also is related to the less energy-intensive character of the residential and transportation sectors. For example, in Wisconsin, the heavy reliance on autos and trucks as modes of transport results in the transportation sector's being responsible for 29 percent of total end-use energy. This contrasts with 17 and 11 percent in the Rhone-Alpes and the GDR. The relatively high percentage of end-use energy in Rhone-Alpes industry supplied by electricity is also striking, although not surprising if one is aware of the heavy concentration of industry that is located near the mountains to take advantage of inexpensive hydropower there.

TABLE 2.9   Electricity Use (1972)

	GDR	Rhone-Alpes	Wisconsin
Electricity consumption (10^9 kWh)	74.0	20.0	28.0
Per capita electricity consumption (kWh/person)	4.3	4.3	6.2
Average annual growth (%/yr) in			
Total consumption	4.8^a	5.3^b	7.2^c
Consumption per capita	4.9^a	3.7^b	6.1^c

^{a} Average for 1960 to 1972.
^{b} Average for 1969 to 1972.
^{c} Average for 1961 to 1972.

One of the important issues investigated in this research program was the potential need for additional electricity generation capacity in the regions. Table 2.9 gives a cross-regional comparison of total and per capita electricity use and growth rates. Although data limitations prevented comparisons for the same time period, the total growth rates are similar. The slightly lower rate of the GDR may in part reflect its relatively stable population during the period.

A comparison of fuel mixes for electricity generation in 1972, shown in Figure 2.4, illustrates the dominance of lignite in the GDR, hydropower in Rhone-Alpes, and coal in Wisconsin. During the past few years, the reliance upon coal has greatly decreased in Wisconsin; in 1976, nuclear plants contributed more than 30 percent of the electricity generated.

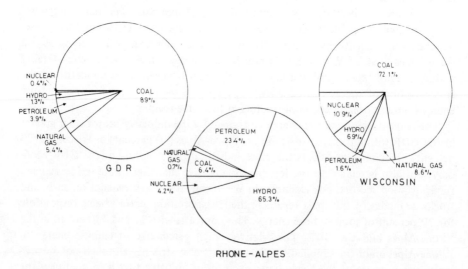

FIGURE 2.4   Cross-regional comparison of fuel use for electricity generation (1972).

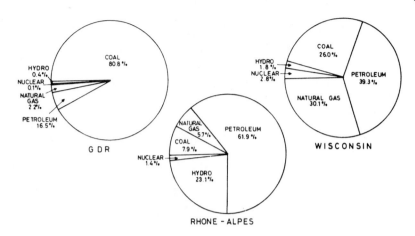

FIGURE 2.5   Cross-regional comparison of primary energy by source (1972).

V. ENERGY SUPPLY

The primary energy sources for the three regions differ significantly, as illustrated in Figure 2.5. The GDR relies heavily on coal (mainly domestic, strip-mined lignite), whereas Rhone-Alpes is heavily dependent on petroleum and hydropower. Wisconsin, although having no naturally occurring fuel resources within its boundaries, has a diverse supply mix mainly of petroleum, natural gas, and coal; uranium is providing a growing percentage of its energy (2.8 percent in 1972 and 8 percent in 1976).

VI. IMPORTING AND EXPORTING IN THE THREE REGIONS

GDR   Hard coal, petroleum, and natural gas is practically all imported; these energy forms represented in 1972 approximately one third of the primary energy supply. There is some export of refined petroleum products (gasoline and diesel fuel), and of lignite products. Electricity imports and exports are almost balanced.

Rhone-Alpes   Rhone-Alpes has to import all energy sources except coal and hydropower for electricity generation. Because of the declining use of coal, petroleum imports are an increasing percentage of the primary energy supply. About 50 percent of the petroleum products are refined within the region. Rhone-Alpes has historically been exporting electricity to other regions. (It had a 20 percent surplus in 1972), but the export surplus is declining.

Wisconsin   Wisconsin has to import practically all of its primary energy supply. There are some small refineries within the region. Electricity imports and exports are almost balanced.

3 A Methodology for Constructing and Modeling Energy/Environment Futures

Views about the future — scenarios, forecasts, or predictions — constitute the language of policy debate, the frames of reference of decision makers, and the bases of assumptions about what is or what is not inevitable. The "tools" used to develop these views are vital to managers and political leaders. They may range from the application of pure intuition, on the one hand, to complex and data intensive computer models, as described in Appendix D. The future with regard to energy is particularly difficult to forecast because of the intricate manner in which energy is interwoven among virtually all of man's activities. What will energy demand be in the coming years? How much of the demand can be satisfied by electricity and at what prices? What rates of growth will be experienced in those industrial sectors that are very energy-intensive? What effect will the dispersion of energy-related pollutants have on human health?

This chapter focuses upon writing alternative energy and environmental futures, i.e., scenario writing, as a tool for policy analysis. It describes a concept, process, and models for writing alternative energy/environment futures for the three regions studied in the IIASA research program, and serves as a prelude to Chapters 4, 5, and 6, which present the scenarios themselves. Although the three regions for which the futures have been written are very different in their socioeconomic, geographic, and technological structures, an attempt has been made to apply a consistent approach.

Section I of the chapter defines the general approach and outlines the objectives of writing alternative scenarios. Section II describes the issues chosen for study and their role in each of the regions. Section III presents the energy system structures used as a basis for writing these futures, and is followed in Section IV by a summary

Chapter 3 was written by William Buehring — IIASA, and Wesley K. Foell — Energy Research Center, University of Wisconsin — Madison.

description of the models, data bases, and general methodology used. These models are described in more detail in a large number of reports published by IIASA and other institutions collaborating in the study.

I. OBJECTIVES

The writing of alternative futures, often referred to as scenario building, is a convenient tool for studying the interaction of complex and uncertain factors. Broadly described, scenario building is a detailed examination of the possible futures and the consequences of the assumptions made about them. This set of futures may provide a better view of what is to be avoided or facilitated, the types of decisions that are important, and the points in time after which various decision branches will have been passed.

In a strict sense, the term "alternative futures" better describes the products of our writing efforts than does the term "scenarios." Scenarios are hypothetical sequences of events constructed for the purpose of focusing attention on causal processes and crucial times for decisions. In general they answer two types of questions:

1. Precisely *how* might some hypothetical situations come about?
2. What *alternatives* exist for each actor at each step for preventing, diverting, or facilitating the process? Scenarios are in some ways like the plot of a stage play.

Alternative futures place more emphasis on setting forth and discussing criteria for the systematic comparison of various alternative policies or alternative combinations of assumptions and objectives. They place less emphasis on the study of the evolution of a system. Nevertheless, in this study we have used the terms "scenarios" and "alternative futures" interchangeably.

In more explicit terms, the primary objectives of the scenario writing in this study are:

● To illuminate significant structural differences or similarities between the energy/environmental characteristics of the three regions
● To describe the sensitivity of energy use and environmental impact to the natural, socioeconomic, and technical infrastructure of a region
● To investigate possible energy-related limits of development in the regions
● To describe and analyze the consequences of specific energy/environmental policy options

The greatest value of writing these alternative futures may be their contribution to inducing fresh thinking. *It must be stressed that these futures should in no way be considered as forecasts.*

II. POLICY ISSUES

Scenario building was employed as a device for analyzing alternative energy and environment policies and strategies in the regions. The process was one of (a) imposing given policies on the regions, within the framework of their initial conditions and constraints, and then (b) evaluating the resulting development and evolution of the regions.

The policy issues were chosen on the basis of two criteria. They had to be of special interest to at least one region and of general interest to the other two; and they had to have sufficient focus and data that they could be approached in at least a semiquantitative manner with the methods available to the IIASA scientists. They also had to be relevant to medium- and long-term policy analysis (5–50 years).

The procedure for choosing policy issues satisfying the above criteria was an iterative one, beginning with discussions with the collaborating institutes in the regions. After several issues were identified, they were explored by the IIASA team to see whether they could be approached within the time frame of the project and with the expertise available at IIASA. After general decisions were made on these policy issues and on the types of scenarios that would help illuminate important policy questions, some months were spent gathering data and developing quantitative relationships with which to describe the alternative futures. The issues chosen for study as a result of the above procedure are described in the following section.

II.A. HUMAN SETTLEMENTS

The structure of human settlements and, in particular, urban settlements, plays a major role in determining man's use of energy and the nature of the influence of energy use upon both the man-made and the natural environment. Urbanization, as a by-product of industrialization, is to a large extent responsible for excessive concentrations of wastes with which man must cope. Many of these wastes are directly or indirectly related to energy. The environmental impacts that accompany man's use of energy are a function of the design of human settlements, of their locations and sizes within a region, and of the embedding of energy production and consumption devices within them. Each of the three regions studied showed a strong interest in investigating these interrelationships, with the goal of improving their design and planning of human settlements. The following areas of interest were identified.

How is energy use and environmental impact related to urban density and size, types of housing, and energy supply technology and type? In all three regions the answers to these questions are useful for policy discussions related to land-use planning, zoning, building codes, and so on. In the GDR, significant portions of the populace live in large housing districts with central district heating systems.[1] There is interest in assessing the tradeoffs between district heating, direct burning of lignite or lignite briquettes, and electric space heating. Such district heating systems are also being constructed in Rhone-Alpes; clearly, however, their feasibility depends upon urban patterns; in the Lyon and Grenoble areas new compact cities are being planned — the so-called *cités dortoirs*. In Wisconsin, land-use planning is becoming a major issue, and the State Planning Office has been studying several strategies for development patterns.[2]

II.B.   TRANSPORTATION SYSTEMS

In each of the three regions, transportation is responsible for a major portion of energy consumption, particularly in Wisconsin and Rhone-Alpes, where transportation accounts for 17 and 29 percent of end-use energy consumption, respectively. In addition, as urban concentrations of people and automobiles continue to grow, the effects of the automobile upon the environment are becoming increasingly evident. Consequently, an examination of issues associated with transportation was of interest to all three regions. The following issues are of particular interest:

• What are the energy and environmental implications of present trends of intercity and intracity passenger transportation? How are these modified by the introduction of alternative modes, including mass transit systems? These are of special interest in the Rhone-Alpes region where there is some experimentation with increased mass transit in the larger cities, as well as development of a large system of high-speed trains between Paris and Grenoble and Lyon. In Wisconsin the state government has proposed a complete reorganization of the administration of the state transportation system to give much higher priority to mass transit systems and to assign a larger fraction of the automobile's social costs to the users. The GDR already provides a large fraction of its passenger transportation without using automobiles,[3] but is moving toward a greater reliance on the automobile.

• What will be the energy and environmental implications of higher efficiency automobiles? This question is closely linked to the reliance of each region on imported petroleum. In Wisconsin this is a major policy issue, addressed in part through proposed legislation to increase license fees for low-efficiency autos.

II.C.   ENERGY SUPPLY

Concern about reliability of a region's energy supply has increased in recent years. For example, Wisconsin is at the "end of the pipeline" in the United States, and, having no indigenous energy sources except for bright sunshine (usually), is very concerned about future availability and prices of its current energy sources. Although Rhone-Alpes and the GDR obtain significant fractions of their energy from sources within their borders, these sources will not supply future demand, according to most long-term demand forecasts. New technologies could play major roles over a 50-year period, but great uncertainties exist about their costs and reliability.

Several policy issues related to energy supply were suggested for inclusion in the study:

• What are the implications of satisfying future energy demand from alternative energy sources? In Rhone-Alpes coal now plays a minor role; the major potential sources are hydroelectric energy, nuclear energy, petroleum and gas, and possibly solar and geothermal energy. In the GDR, lignite currently plays a major role, nuclear energy may have potential for the middle- and long-term; solar and fusion energy are feasible to a lesser degree and only in the long-term. In Wisconsin the energy mix is currently very diverse, and all the energy sources appear to be major contenders for heavy use in the future; emphasis on gas could continue if coal gasification were technically and economically feasible. Solar energy is under considerable discussion in Wisconsin, and various proposals are being studied for legislation which would help this source of energy achieve economic viability. One of the most discussed supply issues is substitution of electricity for other energy sources to provide end-use energy.

• What is the feasibility of the introduction or expanded use of alternative technologies, including district heating, combined thermal–electric plants (cogeneration), and systems that use waste heat? These energy conversion strategies are of interest in all three regions. Some of them have already been implemented in the GDR, and therefore form an interesting comparative subject for study in the other two regions.

II.D. ENVIRONMENTAL PROTECTION AND RESOURCE CONSERVATION

Energy-related environmental issues are of major importance in the three regions. In each of the regions, energy problems and environmental problems are viewed as inseparably linked. Environmental considerations are important in urban settlement, economic growth, transportation, and energy supply systems. Several specific environmental issues were identified:

• Are there environmental limits associated with various patterns of energy demand and supply? What would the impact of the energy futures be on the man-made and the natural environment?

• What are the effects of various pollution control policies associated with alternative energy system strategies? Are these control measures sufficient to permit the implementation of otherwise infeasible energy systems? In Wisconsin this issue is related to the problem of meeting air pollution standards as specified by federal regulations. An analogous situation exists in the other two regions. In the GDR, a serious concern is the use of scarce cooling water in the most efficient manner possible. Within the Rhone-Alpes region, the Rhone river is under major environmental scrutiny because of the plans of Electricité de France to locate most of their nuclear plants on it.

• What are the major environmental trade-offs associated with alternative fuels for the production of electricity? In both the Rhone-Alpes and Wisconsin, the effect of nuclear power plants is an important issue.

• How will a policy encouraging expansion of district heating influence air quality?

III. STRUCTURE OF THE SCENARIOS

The policy issues described in section II were addressed by two specific paths. First, three alternative "policy sets" were developed for application in each region. In selecting a limited number of scenarios for study, rationales were chosen that were applicable to all of the regions, combined the majority of the above policy issues, and could conveniently be compared with one another. The second approach was the development of *sensitivity studies* to evaluate the effects of variations in one policy variable while holding the others constant.

In order to specify a policy set within which a scenario could be built, it was necessary to develop a means for expressing a policy in terms of a limited number of characteristics. The framework for a given scenario was described using the following terms:

- Population
- Economic growth and structure
- Human (urban) settlement location and form
- Technologies of energy use
- Transport systems for people and goods
- Primary energy conversion and supply technology (including electricity generation)
- Environmental control and protection

The general framework then was used to provide the exogenous functions, boundary conditions, and constraints for the models used to build the scenarios.

The above process can be summarized by three main steps:

1. Identification and choice of the *issues*
2. Definition of the scenario *framework* and the *assumptions*
3. Use of the models to build and evaluate the alternative futures

Figure 3.1 shows this process schematically. The models produce "system-indicators," e.g., energy requirements and environmental impacts, which are useful in evaluating alternative strategies.

As emphasized earlier, scenario building was employed as a device for analyzing alternative energy and environment policies and strategies in the regions. The resulting scenarios were not developed as predictions. They are intended to help test and compare the consequences of different policy choices. It is obvious that each of the regions has many energy futures open to it; the scenarios chosen for the research highlight only three of them in order to improve our understanding of energy and environmental management.

It should be emphasized here that the assumptions underlying the scenarios were not chosen arbitrarily by the IIASA research team. They were developed after

26

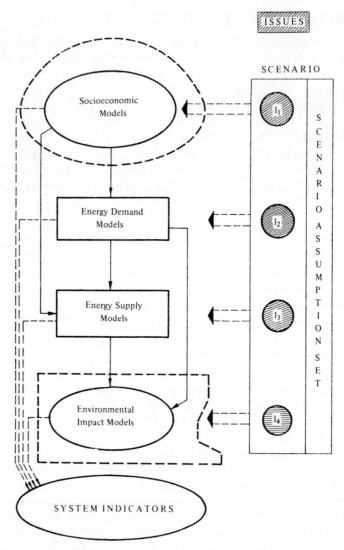

FIGURE 3.1   Relationship between issues, scenarios, and models.

lengthy and repeated interactions with collaborating specialists in the respective regions; in some cases exogenous inputs to the scenarios were supplied directly by the collaborating institutions. Whenever possible, these were tested by reference to other economic or technical studies, e.g., the Energy Policy Project of the Ford Foundation,[4] the GDR long-term energy outlook,[5] and national energy assessments in France.[6] Where feasible, the *WIS*consin Regional *E*nergy (WISE) Model (discussed in more detail later in this chapter) was used to construct sectoral energy demand descriptions, based upon data and parameters from the respective regions. However, the 50-year time span of the scenarios clearly introduces major uncertainty into many of the underlying assumptions and parameters. In all cases, care was taken that the regional socioeconomic development scenarios were consistent with the national or global patterns or both; possible national or global resource constraints were also taken into account.

Because the studies were conducted simultaneously, some scenario characteristics could be specified common to all three of the regions, e.g., stronger conservation measures, or greater emphasis on renewable energy sources. For all regions the energy scenarios could be categorized as high, medium, or low cases. The scenario characteristics are summarized by the following:

- *Scenario S1*, the "Base Case," assumes in general a continuation of past or current trends (at the time the scenarios were constructed) and assumes no dramatic changes in energy prices. For example, in the GDR, it follows the objectives of the 20-year plan* and its expectation of future socioeconomic developments.
- *Scenario S2*, "High-Energy Case," results from combinations of policies favoring higher growth in energy use than S1. It is based on an assumption of decreasing energy costs and few incentives for improved efficiency of energy use.
- *Scenario S3* is based on an assumption of higher energy costs and on the desirability of energy-saving measures; emphasis is placed on conservation of energy resources. However, it does not depict the lowest energy consumption future that could be reasonably constructed.

The policy areas explicitly addressed in the scenarios are:

- Urban form
- Energy-use technology
- Transportation system design
- Energy supply technologies
- Environmental control

Alternatives were formulated in each of these areas and were arranged in groups of consistent policies corresponding to the scenarios.

Tables 3.1, 3.2, and 3.3 give an overview of the scenarios for the three regions. The overall framework comprises socioeconomic structure, lifestyle, technology, and environment. Within each of these general areas, more specific aspects of the scenarios were addressed, namely:

---

* An official "20-year plan" is not developed in the GDR. (See section I. in Appendix B). We use this term to describe what the Leipzig Institut für Energetik refers to as "long-term development over 20 years."

TABLE 3.1   Scenario Overview for Bezirk X (GDR)

Summary Characteristics		Scenario S1 (Base Case)	Scenario S2 (High case)	Scenario S3 (Low Case)
Socioeconomic structure	Population	Slight decrease to zero population growth by 1990	Same as S1	Same as S1
	Human settlements	Urban containment with no growth	Same as S1	Same as S1
	Economy	Linear growth of service sector (factor of 1.67 by 2025); exponential growth in industry (8.3% per year)	Same as S1	Same as S1
Lifestyle	Personal consumption	Current patterns	Same as S1	Same as S1
	Transportation	Car ownership: Increase in cars/household from 0.173 in 1970 to 0.65 in 2025; only slight decrease in km/yr driven	Car ownership increase to 1.0/household by 2025	Same as S1
	Housing	Emphasis on basic electrical appliances. Low penetration of dish washers, freezers, clothes dryers; 66% of dwelling units apartments	Same as S1	Same as S1
Technology	Industry	Large decrease in industrial energy-intensiveness	Smaller decrease in industrial energy intensiveness relative to S1	Industrial energy intensiveness for electricity decreases faster than S1 (20% lower than S1)
	Transportation	Increase in efficiency of freight transport and mass transit due to electrification; only small improvements in auto energy efficiency	Emphasis on truck freight transport (68% by 2025)	Penetration of electric auto to 10% by 2025; lower auto use per capita

Housing	No change in insulation patterns; Apartments 25% more energy efficient than 1-family houses; High use of DH[b]	Same as S1	15% of 1- and 2-family houses meet strict insulation standards by 2000; 60% by 2025
Energy supply	Electricity 100% coal-based until 1995; thereafter nuclear penetration (1,228 MW by 2020) Export of electricity and coal briquettes Emphasis on coal-based district heating Electricity grows faster than total energy consumption (6.6% per year)	No nuclear power; Large electricity imports Less rapid penetration of district heating in residential sector	Penetration of solar-electric plants (20% of capacity is solar by 2025) Nuclear penetration 818 MW by 2025 Large penetration of solar in residential sector: by 2025, 50% of new 1- and 2-family houses constructed with solar units
Environment Environmental regulations	Present trends in control of PM[a] and SO_2 By 2025: SO_2: 60% control, electricity; 35% control, DH; 20% control, industry coal PM: 99% control, electricity; 95% control, DH; 95% control, industry coal	No control of PM and SO_2 beyond present-day practices	High control of PM and SO_2 By 2025: SO_2: 90% control, electricity; 60% control, DH; 30% control, industry coal PM: 99% control, electricity; 99% control, DH; 99% control, industry coal

[a] PM ≡ Particulate matter.
[b] DH ≡ district heat.

Table 3.2 Scenario Overview for Rhone-Alpes

Summary Characteristics		Scenario S1 (Base Case)	Scenario S2 (High Case)	Scenario S3 (Low Case)
Socioeconomic structure	Population	Decline in growth rates: 1.3%/yr in 1970s to 0.4%/yr after 2000	Same as S1	Same as S1
	Human settlements	Continuation of current patterns of urbanization	Dispersed urban settlement patterns	Growth in small-scale compact cities
	Economy	Growth rate of GRP/yr.[a] 1971–1985 5% 1985–2000 4.2% 2000–2025 3.5%	Same as S1	Same as S1
Lifestyle	Personal consumption	Continuation of current trends	Same as S1	Same as S1
	Transportation	Predominance of autos	Same as S1	Same as S1
	Housing	60% of new houses are apartments	Same as S1	Same as S1

		S1	S2	S3
Technology	Industry	Large decreases in energy intensiveness Large penetration of electricity	Reduction of energy intensiveness for nonelectric use slightly lower than for S1	Heating energy intensiveness decreases 35% by 1985; 15% between 1985 and 2000 Furnace energy intensiveness decreases 15% by 1985 and 10% between 1985 and 2000 Steam energy intensiveness decreases 25% by 1985 and 20% between 1985 and 2000
	Transportation	Continuation of current auto and truck fuel efficiencies	Same as S1	Efficiency gains for autos and trucks Shift from truck to train for freight
	Housing	Stringent insulation standards	Same as S1	Same as S1
	Energy supply	Electricity generation from nuclear; large penetration of electric space heating	Mix of nuclear, oil, coal for electricity generation	Maximum feasible hydroelectricity Solar electric No new nuclear plants
Environment	Environmental regulations	Increasing controls: continuation of present trends	Low control (maintenance of current levels)	Strict control

[a] GRP ≡ Gross regional product.

TABLE 3.3 Scenario Overview for Wisconsin

Summary Characteristics		Scenario S1 (Base Case)	Scenario S2 (High Case)	Scenario S3 (Low Case)
Socioeconomic structure	Population	Declining growth rate from 1%/yr to 0.4%/yr; average approximately 0.75%/yr from 1970–2025; slow decline in average family size to a level in 2025 that is 30% below 1970 level of 3.3	Same as S1	Same as S1
	Human settlements	Suburban extension, continuation of present trends	Exurban dispersal, growth in low density areas distant from cities	Small compact cities of 20,000–100,000
	Economy	Continued expansion of service in relation to industry. Service growth averages 4.0%/yr; industrial 2.25%/yr	Same as S1	Same as S1
Lifestyle	Personal consumption	Current trends in personal consumption, e.g., appliance ownership	Current trends with preference for electrical energy supply	Current trends with emphasis on conservation measures
	Transportation	Trend to compact and small cars Ownership at current levels of about 430 autos/1,000 people	1975 auto size distribution continues into the future Ownership as in S1	Mass transit doubles from S1 Increased load factors Accelerated trend to small cars, including small urban car
	Housing	25% of new dwellings are apartments	10% of new dwellings are apartments	50% of new dwellings are apartments
Technology	Industry	Almost constant energy use per unit value-added in service and industry	Increasing energy use per unit value-added Emphasis on electricity	Decline in both electrical and nonelectrical use per unit value-added Conservation measures
	Transportation	Auto efficiency gain; by 1980, 12 liters /100 km 75% of freight by truck	No auto efficiency gain Introduction of urban electric auto 75% of freight by truck	Large auto efficiency gain; by 1985, 8.5 liters/100 km 50% of freight by truck

	Housing	Gas heat in most new residences. Appliance saturation	Almost all new residences use electric heat	Improved insulation reduces heating needs per house by 30 to 40%. Solar space and water heating
	Energy supply	Synthetic fuels from coal. Mix of coal and nuclear for electricity. Increased coal use in industry	Synthetic fuels from coal. Mostly nuclear for electricity. Emphasis on electricity	Solar for heating and electricity; solar supplies 30% of electricity by 2025. No new nuclear. Synthetic fuel from coal
Environment	Environmental regulations	Present trends of increasing controls for SO_2 and particulates. Emission standards for electrical generating plants. 30% of SO_2 removed from industrial coal emissions	Low controls for SO_2 and particulates except for electrical generation. No SO_2 removal from industrial coal emissions	Stringent controls for SO_2 and particulates for electrical and nonelectrical generating plants. 70% removal of SO_2 for industrial coal use
		Dust standards enforced in underground coal mines	Same as S1	Same as S1
		Mostly closed-cycle evaporative cooling at power plant	Same as S1	Same as S1

33

- Socioeconomic structure: demography, human settlements, and the economy
- Lifestyle: personal consumption, transportation use, housing types, and appliances
- Technology: industrial technology, transportation systems, housing climate control and fuels, and energy supply and conversion technologies
- Environment: environmental controls and environmental regulations

For several of the regions, some of the factors were not varied between the scenarios. For example, the level of economic activity in Wisconsin was not varied between scenarios. In addition, the mix of manufacturing and service activity was not varied from scenario to scenario, although it changed over time. Population growth for a given region was also in general the same for all scenarios. Examples of contrasts in the scenarios are the assumed evolutions of human settlement patterns in Wisconsin (Table 3.3). Population growth and spatial distribution affects virtually all components of the energy system. For example, travel patterns and distances are strongly related to city size; the location of pollution sources relative to population strongly influences associated health impacts. Several alternative settlement patterns have been postulated and quantitatively incorporated into these scenarios.

In addition to the scenarios, many sensitivity studies were conducted in which only a single parameter is varied in a given scenario. Typical of the parameters varied are housing type, penetration of solar home and water heating, insulation standards, electricity supply alternatives, and SO_2 control regulations.

The scenarios for the GDR were constructed for "Bezirk X," a composite region typical of the heavily industrialized southeastern GDR.* A detailed comparison of the socioeconomic and energy characteristics of Bezirk X and the GDR as a whole is given in Chapter 4. The IIASA research team felt the Bezirk was very representative and that an analysis of its energy system did indeed provide considerable insight into that of the entire country.

As pointed out earlier, regional rather than national scenarios were studied because many significant social and environmental consequences of energy systems are best analyzed within the context of a specific region. However, because none of the regions are politically or economically autonomous, it is not possible to discuss regional scenarios while ignoring the evolution of the national systems. The scenarios were based upon policies that could be implemented, albeit in varying degrees, both nationally and regionally; the resulting energy patterns and environmental consequences were then evaluated for the regions.

IV. MODELS AND METHODOLOGY

The objectives of this section are to provide the reader with a picture of some of the broad aspects of scenario building, and of the specific approach used in the

---

* *Bezirk* can mean *district* or *region* in English.

IIASA research. Further descriptions of models and data bases are provided in the references.*

One of the main tools used for scenario writing was a family of simulation models, originally developed at the University of Wisconsin[7] and extended at IIASA to treat regional energy/environment systems with characteristics differing from Wisconsin. The Wisconsin Regional Energy Model (WISE) simulates a region's energy system within a framework that includes energy demand, regional supply systems, and environmental impacts. Most of the models are based on engineering process descriptions. Socioeconomic aspects of the regions, e.g., population, settlement patterns, and economic activity, were modeled differently in each of the regions.[†]

A simulation structure was chosen for several reasons. First, simulation is a convenient method of integrating the variety of analytical techniques likely to be employed in a multidisciplinary effort of this type. Second, a simulation structure provides a great deal of flexibility in both the modeling process and the application of the model to systems analysis. For example, it enables one to modify selected components of the system without the necessity of reworking the entire model, and to focus attention on specific areas of the energy system as well as on the system as a whole. Finally, the simulation structure lends itself to the scenario-generating approach that is extremely useful in the analysis of major policy issues and alternatives. That is, simulation facilitates the application of the model to questions of the "what if" type.

In addition to the significant extension of the Wisconsin model, some new models and quantitative approaches were developed at IIASA during the course of this research. Among these are energy/environment preference models,[8,9,10] and methods for analyzing regional air pollution impacts on human health.[11,12]

The general structure used to describe the energy/environment system is shown in Figure 3.2. The major components are:

- Socioeconomic activities
- Energy demand
- Energy conversion and supply
- Primary energy sources
- Environment

* A general description of the family of models used in the IIASA Regional Energy/Environment Studies is given in W.K. Foell, J.S. Buehring, W.A. Buehring, R.L. Dennis, M.E. Hanson, L.A. Hervey, A. Hölzl, K. Ito, R.L. Keeney, J.P. Peerenboom, E. Pönitz, J. Richter, and A. Toifelhardt, A Family of Models for Regional Energy/Environment Analysis (Laxenburg, Austria: International Institute for Applied Systems Analysis, in press).
† In the recent application of this model to Austria, a demand-oriented input–output model (AUSTRIA II) provided economic scenarios for the study; see W.K. Foell, R.L. Dennis, M.E. Hanson, L.A. Hervey, A. Hölzl, J.P. Peerenboom, and E. Pönitz, Assessment of Alternative Energy/Environment Futures for Austria: 1977–2015 (Laxenburg, Austria: International Institute for Applied Systems Analysis, in press).

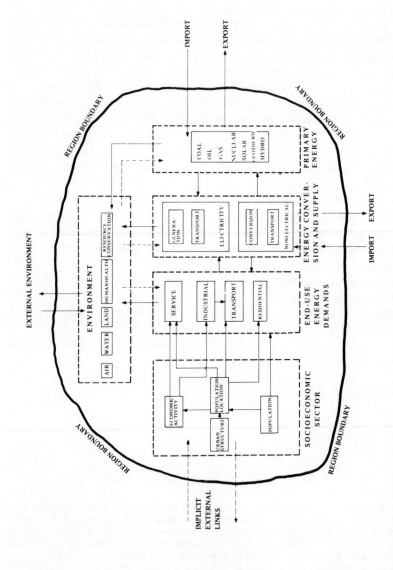

FIGURE 3.2   Structure of the energy/environment system for scenario development.

36

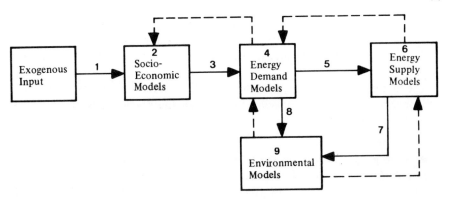

FIGURE 3.3   Simplified diagram of the overall information flow between model components.

This structure was based primarily upon the Wisconsin energy model. For the most part, the following description of the modeling that was used in the scenario-building process is based upon the Wisconsin model with significant modifications for the GDR and Rhone-Alpes where required.

The overall flow of information between these components is shown in a highly simplified manner in Figure 3.3; it can be summarized as follows:*

1. Regional socioeconomic information (e.g., population, settlement patterns, economic activity) is provided exogenously [1] or by models, or both exogenously and by models [2].

2. The socioeconomic information serves as input [3] to energy demand models [4], which are structured according to economic sector (e.g., industry, service, or agriculture) or by technological process (e.g., heating, cooling, or lighting). In general the outputs of the energy demand models are in the form of annual demand, usually specified by fuel.

3. The outputs of the energy demand models form the inputs [5] to energy supply models, which in turn are used to calculate primary energy requirements, needed conversion and transport facilities, supply system costs, and so on. In most of the analysis conducted with these models, supply was directly matched to demand or related to demand within a framework of constraints.

4. The energy flows in the supply system [6] and the end-use energy serve as inputs [7, 8] to the environmental impact models [9]. These models calculate impacts on a broad spectrum of areas, including human health and safety, on a systemwide and localized basis.

* The numbers in the brackets correspond to indicated flows or components in Figure 3.3.

The additional flows of information between the major components are indicated by the dashed lines in Figure 3.3. In general, although not in all cases, the dashed flows are implemented by human intervention and not by formal mathematical links.

The methods originally used for modeling the Wisconsin system had to be modified for some aspects of the modeling for the GDR and Rhone-Alpes mainly because of the following considerations:

- Since a "plan" exists in the GDR (through the year 1990) that the government intends to implement by exerting a great deal of control, the range of options was more narrowly perceived by GDR planners than by planners in Wisconsin. In addition, the role of the WISE end-use demand models was greatly diminished because energy use is one of the variables in the economy that is explicitly specified in the plan.
- The Rhone-Alpes region of France is not a distinct political or administrative unit. Therefore, only limited data are available and in many cases the models had to be simplified to take advantage of the data that could be obtained.

The following sections describe the modeling procedures according to the system components of Figure 3.2.

IV.A. SOCIOECONOMIC MODELS

The socioeconomic models provide demographic and economic data that are used as input to the end-use demand models and the human health and safety aspects of the environmental impact models.

IV.A.1. Population Size and Distribution

Population is a main driving force in the end-use demand models and has an important effect on the environmental impact models as well, particularly in the area of air pollution and its effect on health. In order to provide sufficient spatial resolution, the region being studied is divided into *districts*.* Population size and distribution within each district are described in terms of community size and geographic relationship to urban centers. This degree of disaggregation is required for several reasons:

---

* These areas are called districts or regions in the GDR, departments in Rhone-Alpes, and counties in Wisconsin.

- Urban structure affects the number of passenger trips in the transportation sector.
- Population density affects the feasibility of urban mass transportation systems.
- Urban structure affects the percentages of single-family and multiple-family houses that will be constructed.
- Population density affects the potential market for district heat and solar heat.
- Geographic distribution affects the population's exposure to emissions of air pollutants.

The first level of disaggregation is the *districts*, mentioned above. Population is further divided into four *subdistricts*. An area is classified according to whether

- It lies within 30 miles of a large urban center (greater than 500,000 people).
- It lies within 30 miles of a medium-sized urban center (100,000 to 500,000 people).
- It lies within 30 miles of a small urban center (20,000 to 100,000 people).
- It is nonurban.

Areas within 30 miles of an urban center with more than 20,000 people are then subdivided into 6 *sectors*:

1. Central city and mature suburbs
2. Suburbs and fringes
3. Exurban areas
4. Rural and small communities (less than 2,500 people)
5. Adjacent communities (2,500 to 5,000 people)
6. Satellites (5,000 to 20,000 people)

Areas lying 30 miles or more outside an urban center are called nonurban areas and are categorized as either sector 4, 5, or 6. Each sector is then described in terms of total population, land area, and population growth rate.

Within the above descriptive framework, 4 distinctly different spatial development patterns were specified for use in the scenarios:

1. Suburban extension: The growth rate is equal in all sectors.
2. Small compact cities: Growth occurs in the central city and mature suburbs of cities with less than 90,000 people, and in satellites, and brings the population in these cities to between 40,000 and 90,000.
3. Urban containment: Growth occurs in the central city and in the mature suburbs of large cities of over 100,000 people.
4. Exurban dispersal: Growth occurs in exurban areas, rural and small communities, and in adjacent communities.

It must be realized that urban structure represents a long-term commitment, and that even a severe change in growth patterns will only very slowly modify the existing structure.

IV.A.2. *Economic Activity*

Because of the links between economic activity and energy use, a description of economic growth is an important component of energy studies for each of the regions. In the studies described here, collaborating institutions in each of the regions provided descriptions (alternative forecasts) of economic activity that could be linked with models for end-use energy demand. This approach was far more practical than any efforts by the IIASA research group to develop independent economic models for the regions.

In this study, economic activity was represented by exogenous variables, e.g., value added or value of output, that represent the level of economic activity in the three regions. The exact description of the indicators, the delineation of the industrial and service sectors in each of the regions, and the techniques to project the indicators into the future will be discussed for each region in the scenario descriptions. In all cases the level of economic activity is expressed in constant monetary terms to remove the effects of inflation and is disaggregated by industry and by district.

Regional economic activity was generally expressed in relative rather than absolute terms. That is, economic activity is described relative to a base year in the regions. Comparisons of alternative energy futures were then analyzed in terms of economic development after the base year. This approach avoided the difficulties associated with the development of a consensus on appropriate currency exchange rates. Although it does not permit direct comparisons of the ratio of energy consumption to gross domestic product (E/GDP), as examined in detail by Darmstadter *et al.*[28] and others, it does allow examination of some of the energy-related consequences of changes in the relative economic indicators.

Employment is also recognized as an important factor in the service and industrial sectors. Depending upon the availability and reliability of the data, either employment or other economic indicators (expressed in monetary terms) are the driving forces behind the development of the service sector.

IV.B. END-USE ENERGY DEMAND

The purpose of the end-use demand models is to provide annual end-use energy demand by fuel type for the transportation, residential, service, and industrial sectors of the economy. In general, the socioeconomic models described above are the driving forces behind the sectoral end-use demand models. An economic approach is used in the industrial model; the other models are based on a combination of economic and technical or engineering approaches.

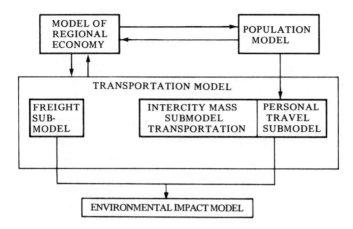

FIGURE 3.4   Overall structure of the transportation model (Source: Hanson and Mitchell[13]).

IV.B.1.   *Transportation Sector*

The transportation model is divided into two submodeis; the passenger transport submodel and the freight transport submodel.[13] Energy use and emissions are calculated by district and subdistrict within the region. A schematic representation of the transportation model is shown in Figure 3.4. The number of trips required is a major component of the passenger transport submodel. The population model provides population data by district and subdistrict. Person-trips per day have been found to be a function of population density and automobile ownership. Trips are split between local and intercity trips as a function of city size, and into urban passenger auto travel and urban mass transit. Average trip length has been found to be a function of city population. A load factor (persons per vehicle) may be determined from available data; passenger trips can then be converted to vehicle-kilometers.

The second major factor in the passenger transportation calculation is the vehicle population characteristics. Automobiles are disaggregated by year of manufacture and class (conventional, compact, and subcompact or electric). Average intercity and intracity energy intensiveness (energy required per unit distance traveled) is specified for each class and year of manufacture; kilometers per vehicle are calculated as a function of class and age. Then total energy use for passenger auto transport can be calculated. Vehicle characteristics for intracity and intercity mass transit are also specified externally, allowing energy use for mass transit to be calculated.

Demand for freight transportation and its distribution by mode of transport are inputs to the freight transportation model. The demand over time is usually linked with the level and type of industrial production in the region. Energy intensiveness for truck, rail, and air transport are estimated from available data.

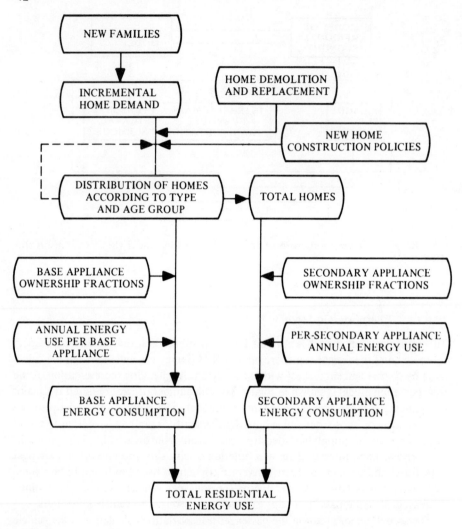

FIGURE 3.5   Block diagram of the residential submodel (Source: Frey[14]).

The methodology used for the transportation sector in Bezirk X and Rhone-Alpes was essentially the same as the approach used for Wisconsin. Data from Bezirk X were provided by the Institut für Energetik in Leipzig and reflected goals in terms of automobiles per household, intercity and intracity travel, and energy intensiveness. For mass transit, projected passenger-kilometers and energy use per passenger-kilometer were estimated from variables such as load factor. This resulted in some simplification of the transportation model for Bezirk X.

IV.B.2.   Residential Sector

A schematic diagram of the residential model[14] is shown in Figure 3.5. The general approach is to calculate total energy demand based upon the number of households in the region and the characteristics of those households, such as the percentage that are in multifamily dwelling units or the number of appliances owned. New dwelling units will be constructed to meet the demand created by new families and the demolition of old homes. The demolition function represents the probability that a dwelling unit of a certain age will be destroyed in any year. The percentages of new dwelling units that are single family and multifamily units are inputs to the model and are determined in part by the "urban scenario" selected. Since apartments are usually smaller and have some common walls, the energy required to heat the average apartment is less than that required to heat the average single-family home.*

Space heating, water heating, and central air conditioning are called "base" appliances. The percentage of new dwellings that contain a base appliance of each fuel type and the average yearly energy consumption of such applicances are forecast for each category of appliance.

The fraction of homes with a particular secondary appliance (i.e. dishwasher, television, washing machine) is independent of the construction of new homes and follows a saturation curve defined by input parameters.

The demolition and construction parts of the residential model were not appropriate for either Rhone-Alpes or Bezirk X. The plan for Bezirk X provided the number of units demolished and built as well as the fraction of total units that were multifamily housing units. Energy use for space heating per housing unit by fuel type and housing type and the fraction of each type of housing unit heated by each type of fuel were also provided. Since the data required for the demolition function were not available for Rhone-Alpes, the number of pre-1970 homes demolished and the number of new homes build in each 10-year period to the year 2025 were estimated.

IV.B.3.   Service Sector†

The service sector model[15] is based upon engineering design of service sector buildings and a forecast of floor area. Energy use is broken down into four physical end-use processes: illumination, space heating, air conditioning, and process energy. The basic relationship for all final consumption calculations is

---

* J.W. Mitchell and G. Venkataro, Energy Use in a Sample of Homes in Madison, Wisconsin, Institute for Environmental Studies Report No. 72 (Madison, Wisconsin: University of Wisconsin, Feb. 1977) provides a detailed empirical description of these heating requirements for typical Wisconsin households.
† In this study, *service sector* refers also to the commercial sector, unless the commercial sector is mentioned explicitly.

$$E_{i,j} = \frac{EI_i\,AP_{i,j}}{N_{i,j}C_j}$$

where

$E_{i,j}$ = the annual energy consumption for end-use i and fuel type j

EI_i = the annual energy intensity for end use i

A = the total service floor area

$P_{i,j}$ = the fraction of A assignable to end use i using fuel type j

$N_{i,j}$ = the mechanical equipment efficiency corresponding to end use i and fuel type j

C_j = the conversion factor for consistency in energy units

The fraction of the floor area assignable to each fuel type by end-use ($P_{i,j}$) and the mechanical equipment efficiencies ($N_{i,j}$) are input parameters. For illumination, the intensity ($E_{i,j}$) is based upon the illumination intensity (watts per square meter) and the equivalent operating hours per year. Space heating and space cooling energy intensity depends upon the engineering design of the buildings: the weighted heat transmission coefficients, the wall-to-floor and roof-to-floor area ratios, and an overall temperature difference. The analysis also accounts for the internal heat contributions provided by people, lights, and commercial equipment as well as heat loss from the introduction of outside ventilation air and natural infiltration. Process energy is energy for restaurant kitchen equipment, office machines, elevators, and other commercial equipment.

The GDR has no statistics on floor space but has very good data on employment. Their plan gives the fraction over time of the population working in the service sector by subregion and the average end-use energy (both total and for space heating) by fuel type per worker in the service sector.

Floor area data as well as the technical engineering information necessary for the energy intensity calculation were also lacking for the Rhone-Alpes. Employment projections in the service sector were available, however. Therefore employment was used as the basic driving force of the model and a conversion factor was used to obtain floor area. Energy intensity for space heating and cooling was estimated since the technical data were not available.

IV.B.4.   Solar Heat and District Heat

The penetration of solar heating and district space and water heating into the residential and service sectors creates a special modeling problem. In the case of solar heating, the ultimate *market capture potential* is a fixed percentage of the total market. For residential heating in particular, the market capture potential declines in high-density areas. Since there will also be periods with no sunlight that will last longer than the economically feasible supply of stored energy, a backup oil, gas, or electric system must be provided that will typically be required to supply 30 to

50 percent of the total energy depending upon local climate.[16] In the case of district heat, the feasibility increases with density and is usually only available for multi-family dwelling units and service sector establishments.

The penetration of a new product into a market usually follows a logistic curve[17]

$$\ln \frac{f}{1-f} = c(t - t_0)$$

where

f = the fractional penetration into the total potential market, $0 < f < 1$

c = a constant

t = time

t_0 = the time at which $f = 0.5$

If the fractional penetration is known at two times, the constants are determined and f at any time t can be calculated. This approach was implemented for solar penetration into the residential sector.

IV.B.5.   Industrial Sector

The industrial model[18] is based upon economic activity indicators rather than engineering design. Its primary input is the forecast of economic activity by industry. Energy intensiveness (energy per unit of output) projections, by type of industry, are based upon a study of past trends and judgment about future trends. The basic demand equation is

$$E_{i,j} = VA_i EI_{i,j}$$

where

$E_{i,j}$ = the annual energy consumption in industry i of fuel type j

VA_i = the annual value added (in constant monetary terms) in industry i

$EI_{i,j}$ = the energy intensiveness (energy per unit of value added) in industry i of fuel type j

A schematic diagram of the industrial calculations is shown in Figure 3.6. The calculations for all three regions were similar.

IV.C.   ENERGY SUPPLY

The energy supply system in the scenarios was based upon the end-use energy demands and was specified by the introduction of alternative assumptions about the supply system. Although no formal supply model was used in the development of these scenarios, a broad spectrum of policy issues was investigated.* It was not

---

* In addition to the approach described here, a formal resource allocation model was used in an energy/environment study of Austria: Foell *et al.*, Energy/Environment Futures for Austria.

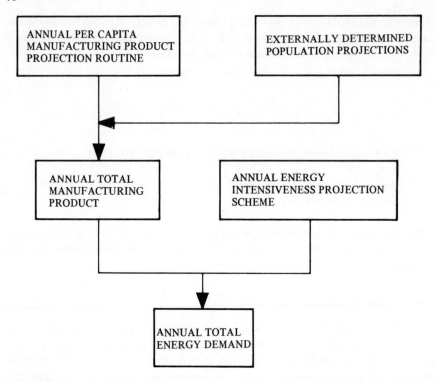

FIGURE 3.6   Schematic representation of the industrial submodel (Source: Shaver et al.[18]).

assumed that any one of the alternative supply scenarios had a higher probability of realization than any other. However, the scenarios do present a helpful picture of some of the consequences of alternative energy supply strategies that result from the considerations treated here.

IV.C.1   Definitions and General Concepts for Energy Supply

The energy system as defined in this study includes the complete fuel system, from resource extraction, transportation, and energy conversion, through waste disposal. The specification of the energy supply not only includes the quantity of energy obtained from each of the supply options, but also the location of the original resource extraction. Such information is used as input to the environmental impact models in order that systemwide environmental impacts can be identified and, to some degree, their locations specified.

Energy supply can be divided into several categories. The main division is between *nonelectrical* and *electrical* energy. The demand models provide the end-use needs for each of the supply options in the nonelectrical sector and the kilowatt-hours of electricity consumed. Another important distinction is between *end-use* energy and *primary* energy. The primary energy is determined from the end-use demands by accounting for losses, such as in electricity transmission, and the efficiency of conversion from primary fuels to another energy form, such as from coal to electricity or district heat. The primary sources considered were coal, petroleum, natural gas, nuclear fuel, hydropower, solar energy, and geothermal energy.

The calculations became somewhat more complicated when *import* and *export* of energy were considered. In all scenarios for all regions, some importing of primary fuels from other regions is required. In some scenarios, secondary energy forms, such as electricity or gas made from coal, are imported or exported. In no scenario in these studies is primary fuel export considered. Therefore, the total primary energy requirement for the region depends not only on the end-use demands, losses, and conversion efficiencies, but also on the amount of electricity exported and the corresponding conversion efficiency. The primary energy requirement is given by

$$P = E + L + C + P'$$

where

P = primary energy requirement
E = end-use demands
L = losses, such as in electricity transmission
C = energy used in conversion of energy forms, such as from coal to electricity
P' = primary energy used to produce electricity for export

The energy derived from the sun was defined as primary energy after absorption by a collection device. Thus, the reflected portion of the solar energy falling on a collector is not included in the primary energy. The energy rejected as waste heat at a solar power plant that uses a conventional steam cycle is included in the primary energy.

Geothermal energy used for space heating in the Rhone-Alpes region was defined as primary energy when removed from the ground. The losses in transmission then had to be subtracted to obtain end-use geothermal energy.

Hydroelectricity was assumed to be produced at an efficiency of 85 percent. The corresponding primary energy is representative of the energy actually used, not the fossil fuel energy that would have been used as a substitute.

IV.C.2. Nonelectrical Energy Supply Systems

In most scenarios the end-use demand calculations specify the nonelectric energy supply from the alternative sources to some degree. For example, transportation energy demand is strongly linked to petroleum. In some cases, however, substitution among some fuels to carry out the same function, or the use of synthetic fuels, is possible.

The nonelectrical supply options are represented by a reference system for each alternative. Typical reference system characteristics were used that are representative of the particular situation in each region. The importance of the individual nonelectrical energy sources varied considerably among the regions; this will become evident in the scenario comparisons (Chapter 7).

The nonelectrical energy sources are assumed to be able to supply the needs of each region; no detailed model of world energy markets or reserves has been used.* In some cases special constraints were used that required some substitution among supply options. However, in general, either the supplies or synthetic substitutes are assumed to be available. Energy imports are important in all three regions considered in these studies, and therefore the energy supply within each region is strongly dependent on conditions outside the region.

The nonelectrical supply options and some basic considerations are listed below. Other potential supply options were not included because the probability of major penetration by 2025 was felt to be low or because reasonably well-defined system descriptions were unavailable.

Coal   Bezirk X is the only region that has significant coal reserves within its borders.

Petroleum   Petroleum must be imported in all three regions.

Natural Gas   Natural gas must be imported in all three regions.

District Heat from a Central Plant   District heat obtained from coal- or oil-fueled plants was assumed at various levels in the Rhone-Alpes and Bezirk X scenarios. The district heat is used for both space heating and process energy.

Solar Space Heating and Water Heating   Solar energy was assumed to provide space heating and water heating in some scenarios for all three regions. A solar system on a building is assumed to provide a significant percentage of the energy needs for space heating and water heating; the remaining energy requirement is assumed to be provided by an auxiliary system.

Synthetic Fuels   Synthetic fuels were assumed to be available in some scenarios for Bezirk X and Wisconsin. The synthetic fuel for Bezirk X is *Stadtgas*,† used primarily for residential and commercial purposes in cities. The synthetic fuels for Wisconsin are assumed to be made from coal and to be substitutable for natural gas and petroleum.

Geothermal Energy   Some geothermal energy is assumed to be available for heating purposes in Rhone Alpes.

---

* The recent IIASA study of Austria (Foell *et al.*, Energy/Environment Futures for Austria) used a world petroleum forecast developed by the Workshop on Alternative Energy Strategies (WAES).[29]
† Literally, *Stadtgas* means "*city gas*;" it is usually coal gas.

IV.C.3.   *Electrical Energy Supply Systems*

In contrast to nonelectrical energy, the end-use demand calculations for electricity do little to specify the mix in electrical energy supply from the alternative sources. The end-use demands, exports,* and transmission losses determine the *total* generation requirement. Because of time-varying electricity loads, an appropriate mix of types of generating capacity is needed, e.g., base-load, intermediate-load, and peaking plants. In these studies the focus of the analysis was on generation (kilowatt-hour) requirements; typical load characteristics were assumed to apply in order to determine capacity needs (kilowatts).

The relative potential for each of the alternative generation sources to be installed when new capacity is needed is specified exogenously. The generation and capacity by fuel type as a function of time is input to the electricity impact model.

The alternative electrical generating systems are represented by individual reference systems that can change over time because of technology advances or changes in regulation. The reference systems include those options that had well-defined system descriptions available in the literature and that were felt to have a reasonable probability of major market penetration by 2025.[†] The electrical supply options and some basic considerations are listed below.

Hydropower   Although hydropower is currently the major source of electricity in Rhone-Alpes, this option does not have a potential for major expansion in that region. Hydropower is a minor source of electricity generation in the GDR and in Wisconsin, and the potential for further development is small.

Coal   Coal is expected to continue as a major fuel source for electrical generation in Bezirk X, with its extensive reserves, and in Wisconsin, where the coal must be imported from other states.

Petroleum   It is unlikely that significant quantities of new electrical generating capacity will be oil-fired in any of the three regions. Relatively small amounts of high-priced petroleum may be used for peaking plants.

Natural Gas   Natural gas supplies and prices will probably prevent this fuel from being a significant factor in future electrical generation in any of the three regions.

Nuclear Fission   The pressurized water reactor (PWR), because of its current operating capacity and according to announced plans, is the preferred type of nuclear plant in all regions.[19] Although the boiling water reactor (BWR) makes up about one-third of all operating and ordered nuclear capacity in the United States, only one small 50-MWe BWR is among the nuclear plants (with a capacity of 4,500 MW) that are operating or have been announced for Wisconsin. No BWRs are in the announced plans for the Rhone-Alpes or the GDR. However, the BWR is a viable nuclear alternative and has been included as a supply option. The high-temperature

---

* Electricity export is an important policy issue. For these studies it was assumed to be specified exogenously and to be supplied within resource constraints.

† Some system descriptions are provided in the Appendix of this chapter.

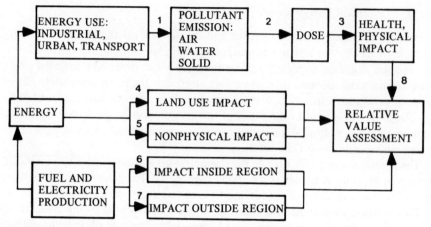

FIGURE 3.7   Pathways for environmental impact analysis. This structure is essentially identical to that used in the Wisconsin Regional Energy Model.[7] 1 – Emission; 2 – Dispersion; 3 – Dose–response, 4 – Direct land use, 5 – Direct economic effects, 6 – Fuel chain impacts within region, 7 – Fuel chain impacts outside region, 8 – Value assessment of alternatives. These pathways encompass three geographic scales: local impacts, regional impacts, and impacts outside the region due to use of energy in the region.

gas-cooled reactor (HTGR) may become an attractive advanced reactor; it has not yet received the general acceptance that the PWR and BWR have. The liquid-metal fast-breeder reactor (LMFBR) has been included although, unlike the other nuclear systems included in the model, it clearly is not a current alternative. Since detailed information on its expected performance and fuel cycle are available,[20] the LMFBR has been included as a *future* alternative.

   Solar Energy   Solar thermal electric plants were assumed to be available and to be a favored type of electric generation in one scenario for each region.

IV.D.   ENVIRONMENTAL IMPACT

The energy supply systems discussed in the previous section form the basis for the environmental impact calculations. In this section the methods employed for impact estimation are summarized along with some of the problems and limitations of this type of analysis.

IV.D.1.   Systemwide Impacts

The impacts associated with any particular energy scenario have been estimated from a *systemwide* perspective. Therefore, some impacts are included that occur outside the region because of energy use inside the region. Some general considerations involved in the environmental impact analysis are displayed in the pathway diagram (Figure 3.7). Energy use may cause pollutant emission, pollutant transport, and exposure of living organisms, and corresponding health impacts. Obtaining the

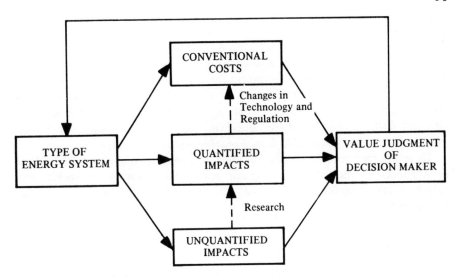

FIGURE 3.8   Factors in energy decision making.

primary fuels may result in impacts outside the region, such as land disturbed for coal mining, as well as impacts within the region where the energy is finally used.

For these studies the system boundary was defined to include all end-use energy activities and associated fuel supply industries. Therefore, impacts resulting from the mining of coal to produce electricity are included, but the impacts associated with the production of coal-mining machines are not included.

IV.D.2.   Quantified and Unquantified Impacts

All impacts cannot be quantified in a satisfactory manner. Therefore, the quantified impacts as estimated by the models that are described in the following sections are by no means the "total" environmental impact. Other environmental impacts not included in the models are defined as "unquantified" impacts. Some environmental concerns are recognized as falling in the unquantified category. Further research may allow some of the unquantified impacts to enter the quantified category as suggested in Figure 3.8. However, some impacts will most likely always remain unquantified. This may be because the impact has just been recognized as potentially important and no research has been devoted to it, or because the impact quantification is based almost entirely on value judgment.

Quantified impacts are the focus of the impact models to be described. They include systemwide effects such as water consumption and pollutants emitted. When new control technologies become available or new standards are set, some quantified impacts are generally reduced or eliminated while conventional costs usually increase. Thus, transfers between the categories in Figure 3.8 may take place as a function of time.

IV.D.3. Value Judgments and Preferences

When decisions must be made on alternative energy sources, at least three important sets of information need to be considered: (1) conventional costs, (2) quantified impacts, and (3) unquantified impacts. These impacts and costs are, in general, combined through the value judgment of decision makers, who may be utility executives, government regulators, or average citizens (Figure 3.8). This is a complex and difficult task, but these value judgments are being carried out, though perhaps not explicitly, since decisions on energy matters are being made.

These complex problems related to value judgments are discussed in some detail in Appendix E; multiattribute decision analysis is presented to provide some help in thinking about complex trade-offs involving costs and both quantified and unquantified impacts.

IV.D.4. Characterizing Impacts

Categorization of impacts is itself a form of value judgment and would differ among individuals. However, for the purposes of organization, the quantified impacts have been classified into five broad categories:

1. Human health and safety
2. Air quality
3. Water quality
4. Land
5. Fuel resource, efficiency

Human health and safety includes both public and occupational effects. Typically, the impacts are measured as premature fatalities, nonfatal injuries, or illness. In an attempt to measure the severity of these accidents and health effects in a single unit, results are sometimes displayed in terms of person-days lost (PDL). In the United States the number of disability days associated with various accidental injuries is determined by tables developed by the American National Standards Institute.[21] These tables have been used here and extended to all human health and safety impacts, including deaths or total disability (6,000 PDL), and nonfatal injuries and illnesses at correspondingly lower PDL per occurrence.

Impacts that fall in the other categories are not readily combinable in most cases. Therefore, only representative impacts from the other categories have been selected for display.

Another problem of characterization is the location of impacts and their associated causes. The four classifications selected were:

1. Impacts that occur within the region because of energy use within the region
2. Impacts that occur outside the region because of energy use within the region

3. Impacts that occur within the region because of energy export to other regions

4. Impacts that occur outside the region because of energy export to other regions

These classifications show the degree to which impacts are exported to other regions because of energy use within the region. In the case of energy export (exclusively electricity export in these studies), the region suffers some impacts in order to supply the export energy. Impacts within the region because of energy production outside the region are included in the models as a background contribution.

IV.D.5.   Description of the Models

The four main models used in these studies were related to thermal pollution, emission and dispersion of air pollutants, air pollution health effects, and general systemwide impacts. A brief description of each of these models follows.

Waste Heat Disposal   The regional environmental impacts of waste heat disposal from electric power plants have been examined. Two direct consequences of disposal of heat into a water body are (1) a temperature increase of the water body, and (2) evaporation of water. Since these consequences have several different impacts themselves, most of which are difficult to quantify, artificial water temperature increase and evaporation have been used as indicators of the environmental impact of waste heat disposal from electric power plants.

The cooling options considered in this analysis were once-through cooling on rivers (water passes from the river, through the condenser, and back to the river), wet (evaporative) cooling towers, and dry (nonevaporative) cooling towers. Waste heat is fed into water bodies with once-through cooling water and blow-down water* from cooling towers. Water is evaporated artificially from both wet cooling towers and the heated surfaces of bodies of water.

The increase in river temperature is calculated as a function of distance along the river, waste heat rejected, width of the river, and wind speed. Radiative, evaporative, and convective heat losses are included in the calculation.†

The amount of waste heat included in the blow-down from the cooling towers is a function of the water flow rate, water evaporation from the cooling tower, and the salinity of makeup water. For rivers with high salinity the temperature increase of the river rather than the amount of water available may be the limiting factor for wet cooling towers.

The impact on the weather is measured by the artificial increase in relative

---

* Blow-down is the intermittent release of water from a cooling tower system in order to prevent the buildup of salts.

† Some details for the calculation of water temperature, waste heat from blow-down, and weather effects of evaporation are given in the Appendix of this chapter.

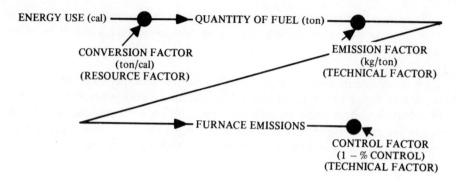

ENERGY USE (cal) ⟶ ● ⟶ QUANTITY OF FUEL (ton) ⟶ ●

CONVERSION FACTOR
(ton/cal)
(RESOURCE FACTOR)

EMISSION FACTOR
(kg/ton)
(TECHNICAL FACTOR)

⟶ FURNACE EMISSIONS ⟶ ●

CONTROL FACTOR
(1 − % CONTROL)
(TECHNICAL FACTOR)

FIGURE 3.9   Emission submodel.

humidity. Disregarding local phenomena from single towers or single warm water plumes, the increase in humidity over a region can be calculated approximately. A Gaussian plume model is used for the dispersion calculation that provides an estimate of the increase in relative humidity at ground level.

Air Pollution and Health Effects   This section describes the methodology used in the top pathway of Figure 3.7, energy use → emissions → dose → health impact. The models for calculating emissions, dispersion, and dose-response are briefly outlined below. More detailed accounts are available in other publications. [11,12]

Pollutant emission   The purpose of the emission submodel is to calculate emissions of air pollutants that result from energy use; the calculations are performed on an annual basis over a given study period at the subregional level. The total emission submodel consists of five sectors (i.e., residential, service, industrial, transportation, and power plant sectors), and emissions of five critical air pollutants are calculated, namely, particulates, sulfur oxides (SO_x), nitrogen oxides (NO_x), hydrocarbons (HC), and carbon monoxide (CO). The structure of the submodel is shown in Figure 3.9; a brief overview of each important sector follows.

RESIDENTIAL, SERVICE, AND INDUSTRIAL SECTORS   As input data to the emission submodel, annual sectoral energy demand is given for each fuel type. These data come from the demand models for various scenarios over the study time period. Fuel is divided into four categories: coal (anthracite, bituminous, coke), oil, gas (coal and natural), and district heating. Taking into account the calorific content of each fuel used in the region, the energy value is converted into the quantity of fuel consumed. By multiplying the fuel consumption by emission factors and control factors as shown in Figure 3.9, subregional emissions of air pollutants (particulates, SO_x, NO_x, CO, HC) are estimated. Emission factors depend significantly on the fuel characteristics (e.g., percent ash and sulfur content) and furnace characteristics (e.g., type, size, and fuel preparation). Therefore, emission factors will be different in the different sectors for the same fuel type. Emission factors must generally be considered in a time series to reflect changes of fuel combustion technology. Control factors are estimated in a time series taking into account the possible advances of future emission control technology. For SO_x and particulates, three emission control policies for the future (low, middle, and high controls) are assumed by sector and by fuel type for each region. No pollution control is assumed for air pollutants of NO_x, CO, and HC. It is desirable to use the regional average emission and control factors, but national average values have been used in most cases.

TRANSPORTATION SECTOR   The emission computations are directly tied to the vehicle mileage by class and year. The emission factors are based on U.S. Environmental Protection Agency surveillance data of current vehicles. Future emission factors are estimated from potential emission control and vehicle age. The model assumes emissions to increase linearly with vehicle age for hydrocarbons and CO, and exponentially with vehicle age for NO_x. Emissions are determined separately for urban and rural areas.[13]

POWER PLANT SECTOR   Power plant emissions are determined as part of the general environmental impact model, which is described later in this section. Emissions of carbon dioxide (CO_2), aldehydes, and various trace elements of coal, such as mercury and arsenic, are included, as well as SO_x, NO_x, particulates, hydrocarbons, and CO. Important control policy options can be examined by the model with respect to SO_x and particulates. Radioactive emissions from nuclear plants are also computed by the model.

Pollutant dispersion   The geographic detail of the dispersion model is at the level of urban areas of the region. The model is divided into two parts, urban and rural — urban areas are treated specifically and rural areas are treated generally. Emissions must be split into urban and rural components as part of the input to the dispersion model. The dispersion model is based on a mix of empirical monitoring data, physical dispersion models, and meteorological data.

URBAN COMPONENT   The urban component of the model requires that emissions be given in three classes: (1) tall stacks (power plants), (2) medium stacks (industry and district heat), and (3) low-level sources (residential sector, service sector, transportation sector). For each source class a dispersion scaling parameter is calculated using the detailed dispersion models at Wisconsin and IIASA[27] to convert tons of pollutant emitted to an annual ambient concentration, or dose, in micrograms per cubic meter ($\mu g/m^3$). The three classes of doses add together to give the total dose from the energy use considered.

$$UD = \alpha(E_T D_T + E_M D_M + E_L D_L)$$

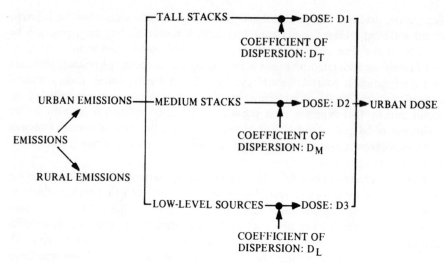

FIGURE 3.10   Dispersion submodel.

where

   UD = urban dose.
    α = calibration constant determined from empirical data.
   E_T = emission from tall stacks.
   E_M = emission from medium stacks.
   E_L = emission from low-level sources.
   D_T = dispersion coefficient for tall stacks.
   D_M = dispersion coefficient for medium stacks.
   D_L = dispersion coefficient for low-level sources.

This is schematically shown in Figure 3.10. The dispersion coefficients are based on the assumption that the population is mobile and that, on the average, individuals encounter the arithmetic mean of the dose calculated for the entire urban area; that is, gradients across the urban areas are averaged by population mobility. As a result of this averaging, the dispersion coefficient for industry is independent of the location of the industrial sources and of the industrial density over several orders of magnitude for a constant number of sources. For low-level sources, the scaling factor is dependent on city size.[27] For Wisconsin the coefficients are in the ratio $1:11:57$ $(D_T:D_M:D_L)$. These ratios show the importance of dispersion and indicate that impact is not directly proportional to emissions.

Most of the calibrations for the dispersion coefficients were based on detailed modeling and empirical data for Wisconsin. The dispersion coefficients were then

adjusted for the other regions, primarily using meteorological data on wind roses*
and atmospheric stability characteristics. Only those adjustments were made that
could be inferred from the data available.

The health impact model discussed on the following pages requires a geometric
standard deviation (GSD) in addition to the annual average pollution concentration.
The GSD is obtained from empirical data relating GSD and city size; in general the
GSD decreases with increasing city size.

This methodology could be used for other pollutants, but has only been applied
in this set of models to SO_2 because SO_2 has the most extensive data set and damage
functions are available. The problems associated with partial quantification of
impacts and value judgments have been mentioned earlier (Sections IV.D.2 and 3).

The health impacts associated with emissions from electric power plants are
treated separately and are based on detailed calculations for reference plants. The
reference plant concept assumes a distribution of air pollution and GSD divided
into quadrants that extend 80 km from the plant. The distribution is then combined with different population distributions to arrive at an average dose-impact to
the population.

RURAL COMPONENT   The rural impact is treated in a more general manner
using empirical data from each of the regions to set the 1970 value. The rural values
are proportional to total regional emissions, because all of the emissions influence
the rural values; relative contributions are determined by dispersion models. The
rural dose is then given by:

$$RD = \beta(E_R + E_L + E_M + 0.1E_T)$$

where

RD = the rural dose.

β = 1970 proportionality constant between rural dose and total emissions.

E_R = emissions from the rural area.

E_L = emissions from low-level sources.

E_M = emissions from medium stacks.

E_T = emissions from tall stacks.

0.1 = factor accounting for elevated releases and dispersion from very tall stacks.

For the pollutant calculation, it is assumed (1) that the climate of the region
does not change over time, and (2) that the emissions from surrounding areas change
proportionately to the emissions within the region.

To calculate the impact on health of pollutant emission and dispersion, a health
impact model, based on an EPA model of health effects[22] was used. At the time
this study was carried out, the EPA model provided the best estimation of health

---

* A wind rose is a diagram that gives the percentage of occurrence for all combinations of wind
direction and wind velocity.

58

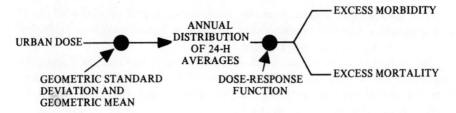

FIGURE 3.11   Health model relating pollution dose to damage.

impacts associated with acid sulfates produced from the conversion of SO_2.* However, the model does not include all health effects thought to be related to air pollution.

Central to the model are two assumptions: acid sulfates, not SO_2, are the cause of SO_2-related health effects, and the important averaging time is one day (24 h). The 24-h distribution is obtained by using the GSD and by taking into account the fact that the frequency of occurrence of different levels of pollution in the course of a year is distributed log-normally.

Dose-response functions related to acid sulfates are given for:

- Excess daily mortality (with a threshold effect)
- Excess aggravation of heart and lung disease (no threshold)
- Excess aggravation of asthma (no threshold)
- Excess acute lower respiratory disease in children (with a threshold effect)
- Excess risk of chronic bronchitis for smokers (with a threshold effect) and for nonsmokers (with a threshold effect)

The dose–response functions give an excess mortality and excess morbidity in the population resulting from air pollution (Figure 3.11) This is not the total impact, but only an indication. These are then converted to person-days lost, as defined earlier (section IV.D.4.) and combined with the other energy-related impacts as a human health effect.

Features of the Environmental Impact Submodel (EIS)   The Environmental Impact Submodel (EIS)† was used in addition to the detailed waste heat and air pollution calculations described in the previous sections. The EIS provides a broad view of selected quantified impacts that occur throughout the energy supply system as a result of energy use. Both nonelectric and electric supply systems are included in the model. An overview of the model follows.

---

* Although acid sulfates may not be the causal agent of the health impacts, they are considered to be a good indicator of the impacts.
† This model is an extension of the Electricity Impact Model (EIM).[23]

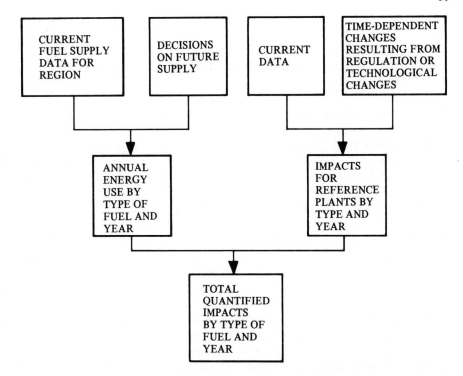

FIGURE 3.12   Basic structure of the Environmental Impact Submodel.

The input required by EIS is the year and the quantity of energy use by fuel source. Additional input is required to change any of the numerous parameters that describe the reference systems. The output from EIS is quantified environmental effects that result from the energy use and the supporting fuel system activities.

The basic structure of EIS is shown in Figure 3.12. The fuel supply data for each year of computer simulation are combined with impacts associated with reference plants to obtain total quantified impacts by fuel type and year. A reference system for a particular year may have different impacts from the reference system for the same fuel type in another year because of time-dependent factors, such as a reduction in SO_2 emissions per unit electrical generation because of sulfur removal systems or increased use of low-sulfur coal.

"Impact factors" are associated with each type of fuel supply. The factors have been determined from collection and analysis of relevant data; they are calculated in the model as a function of energy (kcal or kWh) or, in some cases, electrical capacity (kW).

The impacts are calculated by multiplying the matrix of impact factors for a particular year and a particular energy source by the energy use from that source. The quantified impacts are given by:

$$Q_{ijk} = E_{jk}I_{ijk}$$

where

Q_{ijk} = quantified environmental impacts of type i in year j resulting from energy source k.

E_{jk} = quantity of energy source k used in year j.

I_{ijk} = impact factor of type i in year j for energy source k.

The quantified impacts can be summed over index j to obtain cumulative impacts for a particular energy source. Impacts with similar units can be summed over index i to obtain totals for a particular year and energy source, and over index k to obtain totals for all energy sources in a particular year.

The impact factors were determined from reviews of impact quantification in the literature as well as independent analysis of the specific regional situation. Many of the factors determined in this manner were directly applicable only to current energy systems. However, modification of impact factors in the future can simulate effects of changes in technology, regulation, population, or other considerations. The impacts associated with annual electrical generation of a 1,000-MWe unit in 1970 are not necessarily the same as for annual generation from that same unit in 1980.

As an example, underground coal miners face the well-known health hazard of black lung disease, also known as coal workers' pneumoconiosis (CWP). In the advanced stages, CWP spreads even without exposure to coal dust, which is the original cause of the problem, and may lead to death or total disability. A fraction of the underground coal miner labor force became disabled in 1970 from this disease. If their disability rate could be shown to be related to coal production over a period of time, a certain quantity of coal miners' disability could be associated with each unit of coal obtained by underground mining. However, the CWP disability rate should diminish as new standards are instituted and new miners join the miner work force. By studying the data and the statements of appropriate experts, an estimate can be made for a CWP impact factor that decreases as a function of time. Thus, as a result of a new regulation, the impact factor, total disability from CWP per unit of underground coal, is a function of time.

A general characteristic of EIS is that impacts are associated with the energy use that caused them. Therefore, uranium mining accidents that may have occurred two or three years before the electrical generation, and exposure to krypton-85 and tritium that may occur many years after the generation, are tabulated in the year of the energy use. A mathematical expression that describes the impacts at time t' because of electrical generation at time t is

$$Q(t) = E(t) \int_{t'} I(t, t')dt'$$

where

$Q(t)$ = quantified environmental impacts associated with energy use at time t.

$E(t)$ = energy use at time t.
$I(t, t')$ = impacts that occur at time t' per unit energy use at time t.

It should be noted that the time that the impacts occur is not specified in EIS. $I(t, t')$ is not provided. The impacts are associated with the energy use that caused them.

APPENDIX

ELECTRICAL ENERGY SYSTEM CHARACTERISTICS

There is not sufficient space to list all the important assumptions associated with each reference system. However, a few of the characteristics for the reference coal, PWR, and solar electric systems for Wisconsin are listed in Tables 3A.1–3A.3.

Characteristics of the coal plant that uses bituminous coal are listed in Table 3A.1 separately from the characteristics for a plant using sub-bituminous coal because the plants and associated impacts are significantly different. Thus, one of the important parameters is the fraction of coal delivered to Wisconsin power plants that is sub-bituminous from western states. This fraction is assumed to increase from its 1970 value of only 0.01 to 0.25 by the year 2000. The 1970 reference coal system and the annual flow rates of coal to support the annual operation of a 1,000 MWe plant at 70 percent capacity factor are displayed in Figure 3A.1.

The characteristics for the Wisconsin coal systems are in general not applicable to reference systems for Rhone-Alpes or Bezirk X. For example, the heating value in 1975 for typical coal (lignite) for Bezirk X was only 2,300 kcal/kg; the sulfur content was 1.4 percent by weight; and the typical shipping distance was only 10 km. Therefore, different reference systems were used in the other regions only when the appropriate data were available.

The reference PWR system for Wisconsin (Table 3A.2 and Figure 3A.2) and the other reference nuclear systems for Wisconsin were assumed to hold equally well for the other two regions. Some data obtained for the PWRs used in the GDR indicated that a lower equilibrium burnup and lower fresh fuel enrichments would be appropriate.

The reference solar electric system for Wisconsin (Table 3A.3) was only adjusted in the following characteristics for the other regions

- Assumed average solar input
- Power per unit area
- Land area per 100 MWe

The assumed solar input was 3 kWh/m^2/day for Bezirk X, based on observations

TABLE 3A.1   Reference Coal-Fired Electrical Generation Systems for Wisconsin

	Bituminous Coal from Midwestern States	Sub-bituminous Coal from Western States
Fraction of coal used in Wisconsin	0.99[a]	0.01[a]
Coal heat content per unit mass (kcal/kg)	6,670	4,720
Sulfur content (weight %)	2.5	0.6
Ash content (weight %)	10.0	10.0
Source of coal	outside region	outside region
Percent surface mined	50[a]	100[a]
Surface area disturbed by surface mining (m^2/metric ton)	1.4	0.089
Coal mining fatalities per million metric tons mined:		
Underground mining	0.72[a]	
Surface mining	0.13	0.13
Coal shipping distance (km)	640	2,240
Metric tons coal per train	9,100	9,100
Public fatalities per million train-kilometers	2.3	2.3
Power plant heat rate with once-through cooling (kcal/kWh)	2,220	2,370
Capacity at a single site (MWe)	2,000	2,000
Millions of people within 80 km:		
Urban site	6.30	6.30
Average site	2.25	2.25
Rural site	0.30	0.30
Fraction of ash collected	0.99[a]	0.99[a]
Fraction of SO_2 collected	0.0[a]	0.0[a]
Trace-element emissions	proportional to ash	proportional to ash
Percent of coal cleaned:		
underground mining	70	
surface mining	30	0.0
Disabling cases of black lung disease per million metric tons coal mined underground	0.47[a]	

SOURCE: Buehring[23]
[a] Assumed to vary as a function of time. Only initial conditions (1970) are listed.

for Leipzig and Dresden. A reasonable average solar input for Rhone-Alpes was approximately the same as for Wisconsin, so the same reference plant was used for these two regions.[24]

ENVIRONMENTAL IMPACT OF WASTE HEAT DISPOSAL

The alternatives for disposal of waste heat produced by electric power plants considered were

TABLE 3A.2   Some Characteristics of the Reference Pressurized Water Reactor System for Wisconsin

Percentage of uranium from surface mines	54[a]
Grade of the ore (percent U_3O_8 in ore)	0.2
Uranium mining fatalities per thousand metric tons U_3O_8:	
Underground mining	0.79
Surface mining	0.20
Land disturbed for surface mining of uranium (m²/metric ton of ore)	0.75
Source of Uranium	outside region
Percentage of ^{235}U in enrichment tailings	0.25
Uranium recycled	yes
Plutonium recycled	no
Fresh fuel enrichment (percent ^{235}U)	3.3
Spent fuel enrichment (percent ^{235}U)	0.89
Equilibrium burnup (MW-days/metric ton)	33,000
^{85}Kr in spent fuel (Ci/MW-day)	0.34
Tritium in spent fuel (Ci/MW-day)	0.021
Average capacity factor for reactor[b]	0.70
Power plant heat rate with once-through cooling (kcal/kWh)	2,670
Noble gas release at reactor (μCi/kWh)[c]	0.45
Tritium release at reactor (μCi/kWh)	0.045
Occupational exposure at reactor (person-rem/1,000 MWe-yr)[d]	450

SOURCE: Buehring[23]
[a] Assumed to vary as a function of time. Only initial conditions (1970) are listed.
[b] Capacity factor is the actual generation (kWh) divided by the maximum possible generation of the unit continuously operated at full power.
[c] μCi = 10^{-6} Ci
[d] The value listed is associated with annual operation of each 1,000 MWe of capacity regardless of capacity factor. A person-rem (or man-rem) is a measure of population exposure to radiation.

TABLE 3A.3   Reference Solar Electrical Generation System for Wisconsin

Maximum rated capacity of a module (MWe)[a]	333
Average output capacity from solar (MWe)	100
Annual solar capacity factor[b]	0.30
Power plant heat rate with once-through cooling (kcal/kWh)	2,150
Assumed average solar input for Madison, Wisconsin (kWh/m²-day)	4
Collection efficiency (electricity/solar input)[c]	12.5%
Power per unit area (W/m²)	20
Land area per 100 MWe (km²)	5.0

SOURCE: Weingart[24]
[a] This may be a hybrid fossil–solar plant so that excess steam cycle capacity will not be idle most of the time. Another parameter is the number of hours of storage capacity for the solar plant.
[b] Capacity factor is the actual generation (kWh) divided by the maximum possible generation of the unit continuously operated at full power.
[c] The efficiency represents the percentage of the solar input falling on the entire land area that is converted to electricity. It is estimated that less than half of the land area will be covered by collectors.

64

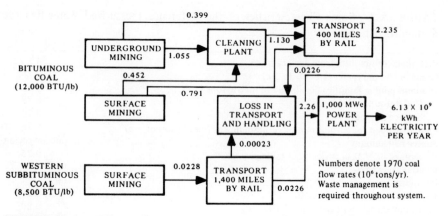

FIGURE 3A.1 The coal electrical energy system in Wisconsin (Source: Buehring[23]).

- Once-through cooling on rivers
- Wet cooling towers
- Dry cooling towers

The monetary cost increases from the first to the third.

The regional environmental impacts of the first and second alternatives result mainly from two direct consequences of the waste heat disposal:

- Increase of the temperature of the water body to which the heat is discharged
- Evaporation of water

Both consequences occur with both alternatives: waste heat is fed into water bodies with both cooling water and blow-down water; water is evaporated artificially from both cooling towers and heated surfaces of water bodies. Since the two consequences have several different impacts, most of which cannot be quantified satisfactorily at present, artificial water temperature increases and evaporation are taken as indicators for environmental impact and analyzed quantitatively.

An artificial increase of water temperature influences mainly aquatic flora and fauna and drinking water production. In polluted water the main influence is through acceleration of self-purification, which may in rare cases be beneficial.

Artificial evaporation means less water is available for other purposes (drinking water, navigation), and there is an increase of fog frequency, clouding, icing, rainfall, and plant diseases.

Relatively little is known about the environmental impacts of dry cooling towers. They can increase cloudiness and they may facilitate the formation of thunderstorms. However, it is felt that their environmental impacts are small compared to those of the other cooling alternatives, and therefore these impacts are not considered here.

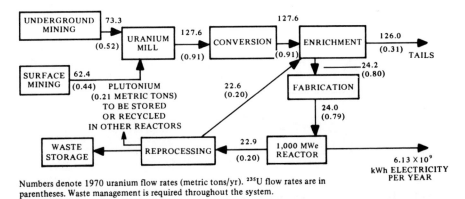

Numbers denote 1970 uranium flow rates (metric tons/yr). ^{235}U flow rates are in parentheses. Waste management is required throughout the system.

FIGURE 3A.2   Pressurized water reactor reference system in Wisconsin (Source: Buehring[23]).

The increase ΔT of the natural river water temperature due to sources of waste heat depends on the river flow rate Q and some meteorological parameters, which affect the heat transport through the water–air interface. It can be calculated approximately from an easily solvable differential equation of the form[25]

$$\frac{d\Delta T}{ds} = \frac{\chi(s)}{cQ} - \frac{Y_0(s)}{cQ}\phi(w, T)\Delta T$$

where

  s = distance along the river
  χ = waste heat ejected per unit distance and time
  c = specific heat of water
  Y_0 = width of the river
  w = wind speed
  T = water temperature

The function ϕ is made up of three terms which account for radiative, evaporative, and convective heat losses. ϕ does not depend on air temperature and humidity, although the natural water temperature is influenced by those parameters.

The total amount of water evaporated in the region is of interest. For evaporation from water surfaces it can easily be calculated using the appropriate term in $\phi(w, T)$. For evaporation from cooling towers it is sufficient to assume that the waste heat is removed exclusively by evaporation and blow-down water discharge.

With regard to meteorological effects of artificial evaporation, the artificial increase of relative humidity is a more useful measure of impact than the total amount of water evaporated. Disregarding local phenomena from single towers or single warm water plumes, the increase in humidity in the region can be calculated approximately. Each river is looked upon as two line sources of humidity emission:

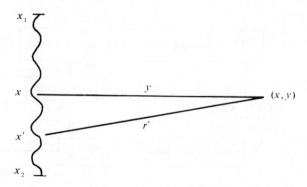

FIGURE 3A.3   Increase in humidity at (x, y) from a line source of evaporation.

one at ground level (evaporation from river surface) and one at a height h equal to cooling tower height plus plume rise (evaporation from cooling towers on the river). For the dispersion of humidity from these line sources, the Gaussian plume model can be used. If uniform, isotropic winds of velocity w, constant thickness H of the dispersion layer, and a stability class are assumed, the increase $\Delta\epsilon$ of humidity at ground level at point (x, y) (in Figure 3A.3) can be calculated according to

$$\Delta\epsilon(x, y) = \frac{1}{2\pi wH} \left(\int_{x_1}^{x_2} \frac{e_1(x')f(0, H, r')}{r'} dx' + \int_{x_1}^{x_2} \frac{e_2(x')f(h, H, r')}{r'} dx' \right) \quad (1)$$

where

e_1 = water evaporated from river per unit distance and time
e_2 = water evaporated from cooling towers per unit distance and time
$r' = \sqrt{(x - x')^2 + y^2}$

The function f is the ratio between actual ground level concentration and concentration in the case of complete vertical mixing within the dispersion layer. (This means $f \to 1$ for $r' \to \infty$.) The function f is analytically known.[25] If there are many rivers in the region one can assume a homogeneous area source instead of many line sources and derive a formula analogous to Eq. (1).

The amount of waste heat carried to rivers with blow-down water is determined by the maximum permissible salinity C_m of the water which enters the condenser. The amount W_d of blow-down water can easily be derived from the balance equations of the cooling system.

$$W_d = \frac{W_0 - W_e}{1 + \frac{W_0}{W_e}\left(\frac{C_m}{C_i} - 1\right)} \quad (2)$$

where

W_0 = water flow through the condenser
W_e = water evaporated in the cooling water
C_i = salinity of makeup water

For calculating the heat discharge into the river, one can assume that for fixed weather conditions the temperature of the blow-down water does not depend on the temperature of the makeup water.[26] One can see from Eq. (2) that for rivers with high salinity the temperature increase of the river rather than the amount of water available, may be limiting for wet cooling towers.

The cooling options discussed above are of different importance for the different regions. Rhone-Alpes and Wisconsin have good water resources per capita, and therefore once-through cooling and wet cooling towers will be the only cooling options of interest for the next decades. For the GDR the water resources per capita are so small that once-through cooling is out of the question now and even cooling with wet cooling towers will be limited in the near future.

REFERENCES

1.   Surber, Helmut, "Die Entwicklung der Fernwärmeversorgung in der Deutschen Demokratischen Republik." Paper presented at the International District Heating Convention, 6–9 Apr. 1976, Warsaw.
2.   Wisconsin State Planning Office. *Wisconsin's Development Alternatives.* Madison, Wisconsin, 1975. Appendix III.
3.   *Statistisches Jahrbuch 1974 der DDR.* Staatsverlag der Deutschen Demokratischen Republik, Berlin, 1974.
4.   Energy Policy Project of the Ford Foundation, *A Time to Choose: America's Energy Future.* Ballinger, Cambridge, Massachusetts, 1974.
5.   Hedrich, P., and D. Ufer, Institut für Energetik, Leipzig, German Democratic Republic. 1975: Personal communication.
6.   Chateau, B., and B. Lapillonne. "Prévisions à long-terme de la consommation d'energie: pour une nouvelle approche méthodologique." Synthetic report, Institut Economique et Juridique de l'Energie (IEJE), Grenoble, 1976.
7.   Foell, W.K., J.W. Mitchell, and J.L. Pappas. The WISconsin Regional Energy Model: A Systems Approach to Regional Energy Analysis. Institute for Environmental Studies Report No. 56, University of Wisconsin – Madison, Sept. 1975.
8.   Keeney, R.L. Energy Policy and Value Tradeoffs. Report No. RM-75-76, International Institute for Applied Systems Analysis, Laxenburg, Austria, 1975.
9.   Buehring, W.A., W.K. Foell, and R.L. Keeney. Energy/Environment Management: Application of Decision Analysis. Report No. RR-76-14, International Institute for Applied Systems Analysis, Laxenburg, Austria, 1976.
10.   Buehring, W.A., W.K. Foell, and R.L. Keeney. "Examining Energy/Environment Policy Using Decision Analysis." *Energy Systems and Policy* 2(3), 1978.
11.   Dennis, R.L. Regional Air Pollution Impact: Dispersion Methodology Developed and Applied to Energy Systems. Report No. RM-76-22, International Institute for Applied Systems Analysis, Laxenburg, Austria, 1976.

68

12. Buehring, W.A., R.L. Dennis, and A. Hölzl. Evaluation of Health Effects from Sulfur Dioxide Emissions for a Reference Coal-Fired Power Plant. Report No. RM-76-23, International Institute for Applied Systems Analysis, Laxenburg, Austria, Sept. 1976.

13. Hanson, M.E., and J.W. Mitchell. A Model of Transportation Energy Use in Wisconsin: Demographic Considerations and Alternative Scenarios. Institute for Environmental Studies Report No. 57, University of Wisconsin – Madison, Dec. 1975.

14. Frey, D.A. A Model of Residential Energy Use in Wisconsin. Institute for Environmental Studies Report No. 37, University of Wisconsin – Madison, Dec. 1974.

15. Jacobsen, D.A., J.W. Mitchell, and J.L. Pappas. A Model of Commercial Energy Use in Wisconsin. Institute for Environmental Studies Report No. 36, University of Wisconsin – Madison, Nov. 1974.

16. The Aerospace Corporation. *Penetration Analysis and Margin Requirements Associated with Large-Scale Utilization of Solar Power Plants.* Report prepared for Electric Power Research Institute (Report No. ER-198), Palo Alto, California, Aug. 1976.

17. Marchetti, C. Second Status Report of the IIASA Project on Energy Systems. Report No. RR-76-1, International Institute for Applied Systems Analysis, Laxenburg, Austria, 1975. p. 207.

18. Shaver, D.B., J.L. Pappas, and W.K. Foell, A Model of Industrial Energy Use in Wisconsin. Institute for Environmental Studies Report No. 33, University of Wisconsin – Madison, Nov. 1974.

19. "World List of Nuclear Power Plants." *Nuclear News* 20: 73–90, Aug. 1977.

20. See, for example, U.S. Atomic Energy Commission. *Proposed Final Environmental Statement on the Liquid Metal Fast Breeder Reactor Program.* WASH-1535, Dec. 1974.

21. American National Standards Institute. The American National Standard Method of Recording and Measuring Work Injury Experience. Report No. Z16. 1-1967.

22. Finklea, J.F., G.G. Akland, W.C. Nelson, R.I. Larsen, D.B. Turner, and W.F. Wilson. *Health Effects of Increasing Sulfur Oxide Emissions.* USEPA Draft Report, Mar. 6, 1975.

23. Buehring, W.A. "A Model of Environmental Impacts from Electrical Generation in Wisconsin." Ph.D. dissertation, Department of Nuclear Engineering, University of Wisconsin – Madison, 1975.

24. Weingart, J., International Institute for Applied Systems Analysis, 1976: Laxenburg, Austria, 1976: Personal communication.

25. Faude, D., A. Bayer, G. Halbritter, G. Spannagel, H. Stehfest, and D. Wintzer. "Energie und Umwelt in Baden-Württemberg." KFK (Kernforschungszentrum Karlsruhe), 1966 UF Gesellschaft für Kernforschung, Karlsruhe, 1974.

26. Zathureczky, A. *Bau und Betrieb von Kühltürmen.* Budapest, 1972.

27. Dennis, R.L., The Smeared Concentration Approximation Method: A Simplified Air Pollution Dispersion Methodology for Regional Analysis. Report No. RR-78-9, International Institute for Applied Systems Analysis, Laxenburg, Austria, 1978.

28. Darmstadter, J., J. Dunkerley, and J. Alterman. *How Industrial Societies Use Energy: A Comparative Analysis.* Johns Hopkins University Press, Baltimore, 1977.

29. Wilson, Carroll. *Energy: Global Prospects 1985–2000,* Report of the Workshop on Alternative Energy Strategy (WAES). McGraw-Hill, New York, 1977.

Prologue to Chapter 4
The GDR Scenarios
in Retrospect

Wolfgang Kluge and *Dietmar Ufer*
Institut für Energetik, Leipzig
May 1978

During the past few years, intensive work has been carried out in the GDR on long-term energy planning. The precision of the planning has been increased and the planning horizon has been extended.

One important innovation in planning has been a move from national-level to district-(Bezirk) level planning. Appropriate models have been developed and applied for this purpose. Regional authorities are now responsible for the statistical registration of energy demand and for providing the necessary energy supply. These authorities can also exercise some influence upon energy supply strategies in their regions.

The institution of regional planning has shown the necessity of coordinating regional plans with central plans. Regional plans are only acceptable if they conform to the provisions of the national plan. For instance, within the long-term planning context, the per capita residential electricity demand was calculated for all 15 districts of the GDR. The results showed that the demand in 1990 in 1 district was 4 times higher than in another district, although both had comparable economic and population structures. No explanation could be found for this large difference. The problem of regional inequalities is being resolved through planning restrictions that the regional authorities receive from the central planning agencies.

At the second conference, Management of Regional Energy/Environment Systems, held at IIASA, 16–19 May 1978, retrospective presentations on the scenarios were given by energy specialists or policymakers from the three regions. To provide perspective on the scenarios, summaries of the presentations are included immediately before the chapters describing the scenarios for the regions (Chapters 4, 5, and 6). They will be published in full as part of the proceedings of the conference: W.K. Foell (ed.), Proceedings of the Conference on Management of Regional Energy/Environment Systems (Laxenburg, Austria: International Institute for Applied Systems Analysis, in press).

It is hoped that in the future a more satisfactory correspondence between regional and central planning will be achieved.

Our collaboration with IIASA, especially in preparing for and attending the 1975 Three-Region Workshop, has brought us new knowledge that is of great value for our work in energy planning. For instance, we fully agree with the conclusions presented at the 1975 Workshop on the benefits of district heating, and we are going to continue to develop this energy technology in the GDR. Four rationales underlie our expansion plans. We want to (1) utilize our lignite in the most efficient way, (2) protect the environment, (3) offer the population a maximum of convenience, and (4) help the economy. Currently, district heating is being developed to as great an extent as the nation can afford economically. At the present time about 75 percent of all new flats are connected to district heating. During modernization, existing residential districts are also being partially adapted to district heating. To achieve economy, standardized heating power stations with steam generators of 320 tons/h and 60 MW turbines (and larger) have been developed and will become operational within the next few years.

Our interaction with IIASA also encouraged us to examine the potential for developing solar power in the GDR. We have concluded that, due to the geographic conditions of our country, the solar electric option cannot be seriously considered for the near future. Only the production of low-temperature heat for hot water and space heating seems promising. For this purpose, the GDR has begun large-scale production of solar collectors. Despite our plans for the development of solar power, it appears that the contribution made to total primary energy requirements by this energy source by the year 2000 will be very small. Economic reasons underlie this rather pessimistic estimation. At present, the costs of supplying heat from solar energy are twice as high as the costs of supplying heat from oil and six times higher than the costs of supplying heat from lignite briquettes. The cost of solar collectors must be lowered, and their efficiency must be increased. In addition, efficient heat storage systems must be developed for times when solar energy is not available.

The application of the IIASA models to Wisconsin, Rhone-Alpes, and Bezirk X is very promising for long time horizons. However, for shorter horizons, like the year 2000, it is necessary to investigate the effect of the energy scenarios on the economy, as well as on the environment. Such an analysis would make decisions possible that serve society as a whole. Even the scenario that is best in terms of environmental control is worthless if the society is not able to pay for it.

A last note on the question of industrial energy intensiveness in the GDR: At the 1975 Workshop there were vehement discussions about the great decreases in industrial energy intensiveness which were assumed to take place in the scenarios until 2025. In the GDR, an annual rate of decrease of five percent in energy intensiveness is used as a basis for planning for the next one to two decades. This corresponds to past trends. However, an extrapolation beyond the year 1990 is not possible. Over longer time periods, significant changes in economic structure may occur which could affect energy demand. In order to make realistic estimates of industrial energy intensiveness for years after 1990, complex economic analyses are needed.

Now let us turn to the environmental sphere. At the time that our collaborative venture with IIASA began, we were aware that environmental problems would have to be integrated into the energy models, but it had not yet been done. Therefore, this aspect of the IIASA research was of special interest to us. At the present time, two important environmental factors, land use for open pit lignite mining and its reclamation, and SO_2 emissions and ground level concentrations (as criteria for air quality), have been built into our model, and soon we expect to include water, as a limited resource, as a third environmental factor. Through a vigorous land reclamation program, the adverse effects of land use for mining have been almost completely eliminated in the GDR.

The work carried out by the IIASA team on pollution levels in the GDR has led us to compare ground level SO_2 exposures as calculated by our own models with the exposures calculated by the IIASA models. The comparison revealed a good correspondence for low- and medium-level sources, but for point sources with tall stacks (120 m or taller), the figures calculated by our models were larger than those calculated by the IIASA models. The explanation may lie in differences in the stack heights, differences in the meteorological conditions, or differences in the allocation of emissions from large point sources (that actually lie 10–20 km away from the city center) to the urban area.

As a next step, we studied large emitting sources in more detail, and disaggregated SO_2 emissions in a district capital into those caused by industry, district heating, and low-level heating sources — classes similar to those used in the IIASA work. The emissions and resulting ambient concentrations associated with these sources were projected until 2025; then, in an extension of the IIASA sensitivity analysis of the environmental implications of district heating, the effect of a flue-gas desulfurization policy on pollution levels from industry and district heating emission sources was studied. The results indicated that under our conditions of primary energy supply, district heating and flue-gas desulfurization must be used together in order to improve air quality in the future. In presenting such findings to decision makers, it is very helpful to have evidence from other research teams, like IIASA's and our own.

Finally, we have made an analysis of the economic implications of several SO_2 emission control strategies. A comparison was made of the costs of improvements in ambient air quality in urban areas because of urban sources and surrounding large point sources of emissions. It was found that increasing the stack heights of district heating plants outside the urban area from 180 to 300 m would be effective, but not possible because some stacks would interfere with air traffic. Although flue-gas desulfurization is more costly than increasing stack heights, it must be used for these stacks. For existing plants within an urban area, costs being equal, one would prefer flue-gas desulfurization to increases in stack heights for environmental reasons. For industrial emitters situated in the urban area, a change-over to district heating produced from a combined cycle plant situated 20 km from the city center is clearly a cost-effective way to reduce exposure in the urban area. For more distant new power plants (i.e. over 30 km from a city center), it is more economical to assure that stacks are sufficiently tall (300 m) than to use flue-gas desulfurization.

As these remarks suggest, our collaboration with the IIASA regional energy/ environment management study has proved to be of notable relevance to our own planning. The IIASA work has underscored our interest in the expansion of district heating networks and the integration of environmental factors into energy planning, and spurred the development of the solar option. Our planning is now reaching new levels of precision, through a regional focus on energy demand and supply, through specification of sources of pollution, and through the testing of pollution control strategies.

4 Alternative Energy/Environment Futures for the German Democratic Republic

I. INTRODUCTION

This chapter describes the background, assumptions, character, and results of the three alternative futures developed for a region within the German Democratic Republic (GDR). The concept and objectives of writing alternative futures are discussed in detail in Chapter 3. Major emphasis is given in this chapter to what is termed the "Base Case" to provide a framework for comparison with the other two alternative futures (scenarios).

The rest of this introduction describes the character of the region studied, the character of the data, the policy questions of concern within the region and an overview of the three scenarios. Section II presents the base case in detail. Section III describes the two other scenarios, compares them with the base case scenario, and then presents some sensitivity studies that relate to certain policy issues. Finally, some overall conclusions are presented in Section IV.

An overview of the GDR is contained in Appendix A, and we need only describe here three major aspects:[1]

- Human geography — the majority of the population ($\sim$ 63 percent) resides in the lower one-third of the country.
- Economic geography — most of the industrial production (68 percent) occurs in the lower third of the country.
- Resource geography — almost all of the lignite is produced in five of eight Bezirks in this lower third of the country.

Chapter 4 was written by Robin Dennis – IIASA.

74

TABLE 4.1   Comparison of Bezirk X and the GDR

	Bezirk X (1970)	GDR (1972)
Population ($\times 10^6$)	1.425	16.95
Rural population (%)	46.2	45.6
Land area (km^2)	4,820	108,000
Population per km^2	290	157
Industrial net goods per capita (mark)	9,831[a]	4,495
Freight (rail and truck) per capita (ton-km)	3,789	3,443
Passenger cars per capita	0.063	0.083
Per capita end-use energy consumption		
(10^9 cal)	20.31	24.8
Electricity (kWh)		
Per capita generation	9,430	4,103
Per capita net export and losses	5,937	319
Per capita consumption	3,493	3,794
Primary energy per capita		
(including exported energy) (10^9 cal)	110.7	42.4
Primary energy use per capita		
(excluding exported energy) (10^9 cal)	37.8	~ 42.4

SOURCES: *Statistisches Jahrbuch 1974 der DDR;*[1] Institut für Energetik;[3] United Nations Economic Commission for Europe;[4] Doblin;[5] United Nations Economic Commision for Europe.[6]
[a] 1975 value.

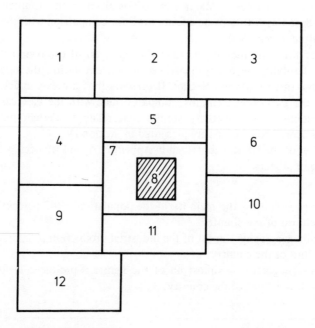

FIGURE 4.1   Map of Bezirk X.

I.A. BEZIRK X

Difficulty in obtaining official data of the breadth and depth needed and in the short time required by the research program necessitated the construction of a fictitious Bezirk, or administrative region, named Bezirk X. The alternative was to model the entire GDR or a part of it. Bezirk X, shown in Figure 4.1, is a regional composite of a typical industrial Bezirk of the lower third of the country, such as Leipzig, Halle, Karl-Marx-Stadt, or Dresden.[2] The main features of Bezirk X are:[3]

● Human geography − Subregion eight is a major city of 535,000 people surrounded by a rural area (subregion seven). Each other subregion has a single town; the average population per town is 23,000. This characteristic of having a single major city in the region is similar to Wisconsin and Rhone-Alpes, although the population of the Bezirk's main city is half that of Milwaukee, Wisconsin, or Lyon, France.

● Industry − Bezirk X represents a highly industrialized region of the GDR; the Bezirk produces industrial goods for the rest of the country, as is evident in Table 4.1. This industrial character is comparable with the relation of Rhone-Alpes to France, but not so much with the relation of Wisconsin to the United States.

● Resources − Large amounts of strip mining occur in Bezirk X and account for 20 to 25 percent of the GDR total.[1] This makes Bezirk X unique among the three regions; Rhone-Alpes and Wisconsin have insignificant mineral fuel resources.

● Energy − Coal is the main energy source; there is significant use of district heating for space heat and industrial processes.[7] This contrasts greatly with Wisconsin and significantly with Rhone-Alpes. The Bezirk is also an energy exporter.

● Environment − Bezirk X was defined to represent Bezirks with SO_2 pollution problems.[2]

For any results to be meaningful in this research context, Bezirk X must be realistic and representative. Several indices are compared with the GDR published statistics in Table 4.1 to demonstrate that this is indeed the case, and to show the industrial character of Bezirk X. The Bezirk, in strong contrast to Wisconsin, and to a lesser degree to Rhone-Alpes, is a major energy source for the GDR; in 1970 it exported 66 percent of its primary energy flow to the rest of the country.

I.B. THE DATA

I.B.1.   General Characteristics

The framework for the data to be compiled for Bezirk X was defined by collaborative efforts of the IIASA and Leipzig researchers based on the methodology presented in Chapter 3. Values for many variables that span the 55-year study period were compiled in Leipzig and sent to IIASA where the models were run.[3] Through the year 1995 these data represent the outlook of the "20-year plan"* of the GDR for industrial Bezirks; from 1995 to 2025 they are an extra-polation of the trends exhibited by the 20-year plan.[2] For all of the demand sectors and the supply sector, the data were supplied for the twelve Bezirk X subregions (*Kreise*). In some cases, statistics available in the GDR did not fit the detailed Wisconsin Regional Energy (WISE) model requirements, and alternative means were defined to obtain the needed results.

I.B.2. Special Constraints

Several factors, in addition to the ones mentioned above, make this composite GDR Bezirk stand apart from the other two regions. First, the GDR *planning process* takes a relatively long (20-year) detailed planning horizon with a high emphasis on plan implementation. Thus, the near future is fairly tightly constrained in the scenario development. Second, the *population* of the GDR is expected to decrease slightly and then remain constant. This removes a major force for the increase in energy demand, so that the GDR represents an industrial zero population growth (ZPG) society. Third, the unique features of *lignite* as the energy base, with its low energy content, high water content, and high transportation costs, played an important role in the composite Bezirk.

I.C. SCENARIO DEVELOPMENT

I.C.1. Rationale

As discussed in Chapter 3, scenarios have several objectives. The most important is their use in addressing policy questions of interest to the region. Policy questions of special concern to the GDR include:

● Urban Setting — How is the energy use and environmental impact connected to the urban setting, especially with high use of district heat?[7,8,9]

● Transportation — What are the consequences of present trends for intercity and intracity transport and of a greater dependence on automobiles than desired?[2,10]

● Energy Supply — What are the demands on the present resource base of lignite in view of energy self-sufficiency and what new fuels might help to meet the demand for energy?[2,10]

● Economic Growth — What is the relationship between energy use and supply and desired economic growth?[2,7,10]

● Environment — There is a very strong interest in connecting energy use and environmental impacts and a strong interest in environmental control, especially cooling-water requirements and air pollution.[2,7,8,9,11]

---

* An official "20-year plan" is not developed in the GDR. (See Section I. of Appendix B). We use this term to describe what the Leipzig Institut für Energetik refers to as "long-term development over 20 years."

The scenario methodology calls for the systematic comparison of various alternative futures. Several discussions were held between the IIASA and Leipzig researchers to discuss criteria for combinations of interests, assumptions, and boundary conditions for different scenarios. With the backdrop of the above interests, the requirements of the WISE models, and the GDR planning process, it was decided that Bezirk X should be defined by the Leipzig researchers and that the objectives of the GDR 20-year plan should form the foundation for the Base Case scenario. The input data to the year 2025 for the Base Case, described in detail below, were to be provided by the Leipzig researchers, along with any special constraints or boundary conditions for other scenarios.[3] The IIASA team and the Leipzig group felt that following the 20-year plan for the Base Case would best reflect the GDR's interests and concerns.

Two other scenarios were also chosen to illuminate regional structure, policy questions, and various sensitivities to energy and environment. The writing of these scenarios was begun in the meetings between the Leipzig and IIASA staffs; after the Base Case was received from Leipzig, the other two scenarios were further defined at IIASA and completed there. A concerted attempt was made at IIASA to remain in the spirit of the boundary conditions developed with Leipzig. Thus, certain basic socioeconomic variables, such as population, industrial growth, service sector growth, and housing were not varied from scenario to scenario. In a few instances the IIASA team felt that parameters should be varied over a greater range than that recommended by the Leipzig team. Such judgment was used sparingly in the two scenarios which were developed in addition to the Base Case.

I.C.2.   Sketch of the Scenarios

The three scenarios can be briefly characterized as follows:

• S1: Base Case — This scenario follows the objectives of the long-term GDR plan until 1995 and represents an extrapolation of the trends from 1995 to 2025. A considerable industrial growth shapes the character of this scenario.

• S2: High-Energy Case — The assumptions for this scenario tend to result in higher energy use in the transportation and industrial sectors. Supply options are highlighted in sensitivity studies. An objective is to elucidate impacts of industrial efficiencies and demands on the Bezirk's resource base as well as on the environment. Lax environmental controls are assumed.

• S3: Conservation Case — This scenario includes some technical conservation policies, with emphasis on solar energy and energy efficiencies in automobiles and homes. Strict pollution control is assumed.

Factors that remain constant across scenarios are

• Population growth

TABLE 4.2 Policies and Assumptions for the Three Bezirk-X Scenarios

Growth Assumptions	Scenario S1	S2	S3
Population	• Slight decrease to ZPG[1] by 1990	• Same as S1	• Same as S1
Economy	• Linear growth in service : factor of 1.67 by 2025	• Same as S1	• Same as S1
	• Exponential growth in industry : factor of 60 by 2025 over 1975	• Same as S1	• Same as S1
Policy Areas			
Technology	• Large decrease in industrial energy intensiveness	• Smaller decrease in industrial energy intensiveness relative to S1	• Industrial energy intensiveness for electricity decreases faster than S1
	• High penetration of district heating	• Medium penetration of district heat	• Very high penetration of district heat plus penetration of solar-thermal and solar-electric energy
Transportation	• Low automobile use	• Greater auto use relative to S1	• Lower auto use than S1 with more mass transit
	• Efficient freight mode	• Much less efficient freight relative to S1	• Freight same as S1
Energy Supply	• Electricity almost all coal, some nuclear after 2000	• Must imported electricity due to increased direct demand for coal	• Less nuclear energy than S1
			• Solar-electric energy penetrates
Environment	• Present trends in control of particulates and SO_2	• Low control of particulates and SO_2 control	• High control of particulates and SO_2

[1] Zero Population Growth.

78

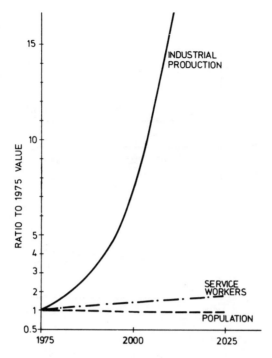

FIGURE 4.2   Basic economic indicators of Bezirk X (Source: Institut für Energetik[3]).

- Housing growth and ratio of single-family homes to apartments
- Industrial growth

In Chapter 3, the breakdown of the scenarios into building blocks was discussed. Table 4.2 presents a key-word overview of the three scenarios in this form.

II.   BASE CASE SCENARIO

II.A.   BASIC ASSUMPTIONS

The most important socioeconomic data provided by Leipzig[3] are shown in Figure 4.2 (normalized to 1975) and Figure 4.3.* The dominant feature is that the industrial growth is extreme, an exponential growth of 8.3 percent per year. This is much faster than Wisconsin's or Rhone-Alpes' growth; and furthermore the Bezirk's industrial growth does not taper off and shift into the service sector as it does in the

---

* These socioeconomic indicators are the same in the three scenarios.

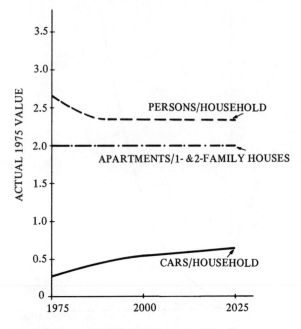

FIGURE 4.3   Additional indicators for Bezirk X.

other two regions. Bezirk X differs appreciably from Wisconsin and Rhone-Alpes in that it has no population growth; car ownership in 1975 was one-seventh that in Wisconsin. However, the occupancy per housing unit is nearly the same as the other two regions. By 2025 car ownership per capita will have increased in Bezirk X by a factor of 2.66; although this increase in car ownership is much greater than in Wisconsin or Rhone-Alpes, there will be fewer cars per capita in the GDR in 2025 than in Wisconsin and Rhone-Alpes.

Assumptions that are important to the Base Case are shown in Figures 4.4 to 4.7. The figures are self-explanatory, but it is worth pointing out in Figures 4.4 and 4.5 the dominance of coal in service and residential space heating in 1970, the emerging dominance of district heating by 2025, and the relatively low penetration of electricity and gas by 2025. Coal is still important in 2025 because of Bezirk X's resource base; the low penetration of electricity by 2025 reflects an attitude of careful use of primary energy to remain as nearly energy-sufficient as possible.

The Leipzig research group provided dwelling unit demolition and construction projections for each subregion; these vary across the Bezirk. Space heating requirements for a given fuel type for old and new homes were also provided, but since the difference was only 6 percent, the same value was used for old and new homes. In the residential sector, one- and two-family houses are 20 percent more energy intensive than apartment units. The space heat requirements for the service sector were provided on a per worker basis. By 2025 there was a 1 percent decrease in the

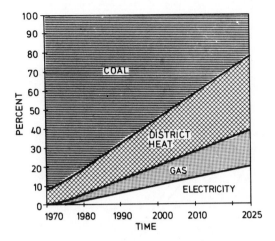

FIGURE 4.4   Contributions to residential heating by fuel type for subdistrict 9 (Bezirk X).

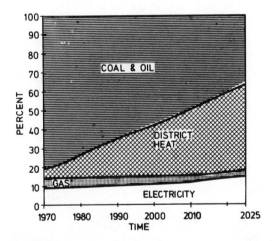

FIGURE 4.5   Representative contributions to service sector heating by fuel type for the small cities in Bezirk X.

average space heat required per worker. For these two sectors the fraction of the space heat demand met by a given fuel type was provided until the year 2025 as shown in Figures 4.4 and 4.5.

Saturation curves until 2025 were provided for all of the major secondary appliances. A sample is shown in Figure 4.7 where it can be seen that selected major electric appliances, such as clothes driers and single-room air conditioners, have a low priority in Bezirk X's plans for the future.[2]

The industrial sector was divided into six categories: metals, metal processing

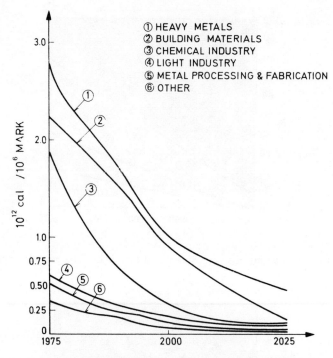

FIGURE 4.6   Energy intensiveness for each industrial subsector in Bezirk X.

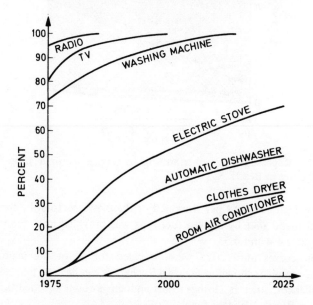

FIGURE 4.7   Saturation curves for selected appliances in households in Bezirk X.

TABLE 4.3   Base Case Transportation Indices for Bezirk X

	1970	2000	2025
Cars per household	0.173	0.54	0.65
Auto use (km/yr)	9,000	9,500	8,700
Mass transit (10^6 passenger-km/yr)			
Intercity	4,420	6,100	6,100
Intracity	1,240	1,225	1,190
Freight (10^9 ton-km)	5.4	36.0	215

TABLE 4.4   Characteristics of Bezirk-X Fuels

	% Sulfur	% Ash	Heat Value
Lignite	1.35	10	2,300 kcal/kg
Briquettes[a]	2.7	5	4,700 kcal/kg
Coal gas			3,380 kcal/m^3

[a] A 1-kg briquette requires 1.9 kg of lignite.

and fabrication, chemicals, building materials, light industry, and other. The industries in Bezirk X of major importance for energy are chemicals and metal processing and fabrication. Industrial and service activity are different in each of the Bezirk's subregions; three subregions dominate the industrial activity (much like Rhone-Alpes). The industrial energy intensiveness shown in Figure 4.6 drops quite steeply in accordance with GDR historical trends of the past several years.[2] (France also has a declining industrial energy intensiveness, but the decline is not as rapid.)

A view of the Base Case transportation picture is given in Table 4.3. Mass transit is high, but does not grow significantly; automobiles triple in number, but ownership remains at half the current U.S. value; freight transport, following industry, increases dramatically.

In the energy supply sector, coal-fired power plants produce 100 percent of the electricity through 1995, after which nuclear power is allowed to penetrate. By 2025 three pressurized water reactors (PWR) with a total capacity of 1,228 MW are assumed to exist in the Bezirk.[10, 12] No other fuels are assumed for electricity production. It is important to note that the Bezirk is an electricity exporter and remains so through 2025. A lignite strip-mining capacity of 60 million tons per year was specified for Bezirk X by the Leipzig researchers; this was interpreted as a resource limit and desired mining capacity limit. This limit, maintained through the year 2025, represents about 20 percent of the present GDR coal tonnage and about 20 percent of the expected sustained peak of GDR coal tonnage for future years.[1, 2]

A significant amount of lignite production goes into briquette export from the Bezirk: 27.9 million tons in 1970 (49 percent of total coal production in the Bezirk); 19 million tons in 2000 (32.4 percent of the total); and 1.9 million tons in

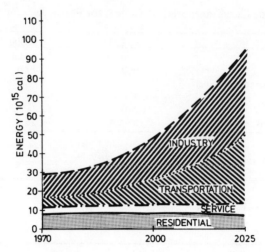

FIGURE 4.8   Annual end-use energy demand by sector (Base Case scenario for Bezirk X).

2025 (3.2 percent of the total). The export of briquettes makes up 86.5 percent, 84.7 percent and 42.4 percent of the briquette production in 1970, 2000, and 2025, respectively. Table 4.4 presents some important characteristics of Bezirk X fuels. Bezirk X imports oil, small amounts of anthracite coal, and natural gas.

II.B.   ENERGY DEMAND RESULTS

II.B.I.   End-Use Energy

Figure 4.8 shows the total annual energy demand calculated by the models for the Base Case scenario developed by Leipzig and IIASA. Figure 4.9 presents the annual per capita end-use energy by sector for the years 1970, 2000, and 2025.

Residential demand hardly changes, because coal is being replaced by more efficient district heat and demand-efficient electricity. The service sector grows steadily, but the energy demand per worker remains almost constant. Industry and transportation energy demands increase rapidly even with the large improvements in energy intensiveness in industry. Figure 4.10 shows the industrial end-use demand by sector, and Figure 4.11 shows this same industrial demand by fuel type. District heat is dominant in industry in 1970 and remains so; the demand for electricity makes up most of the remainder of the total demand by 2025. To keep the industrial energy demand at its present growth rate of 2.38 percent per year, the energy intensiveness of district heat use in the industry decreased by more than a factor of 10, while electricity energy intensiveness decreased overall by less than a factor of 3 in 55 years. This great increase in the efficiency of low-temperature district heat is difficult to explain.

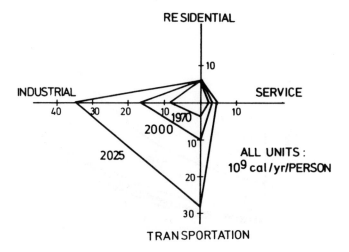

FIGURE 4.9   Annual per capita end-use energy demand by sector (Base Case for Bezirk X).

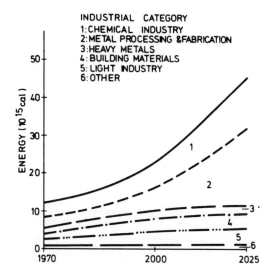

FIGURE 4.10   Industrial end-use energy demand by fuel type (Base Case scenario for Bezirk X).

Figure 4.12 shows the transportation demand disaggregated into its components. The effect of the increase in car ownership is apparent; the freight component is tied to the industrial growth. Associated with freight and intercity mass transit end-use energy demands are increases in efficiency due to significant shifts from coal and diesel trains in 1970 to electric-powered trains by 2025 (diesel efficiency is

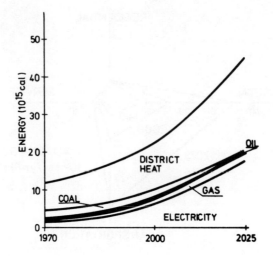

FIGURE 4.11   Industrial end-use energy demand by fuel type (Base Case scenario for Bezirk X).

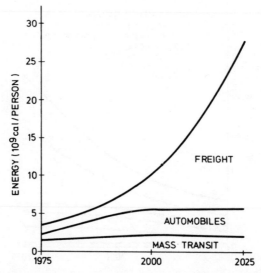

FIGURE 4.12   Per capita transportation end-use demand by mode (Base Case scenario for Bezirk X).

284 kcal/ton-km and electricity is 44 kcal/ton-km*. Mass transit in the Bezirk is more important than in the other regions, because of intercity use of trains. Energy

---

* This is end-use energy and does not account for waste heat in electrical generation or transmission losses. However, the electrical transport remains more efficient even after accounting for these factors.

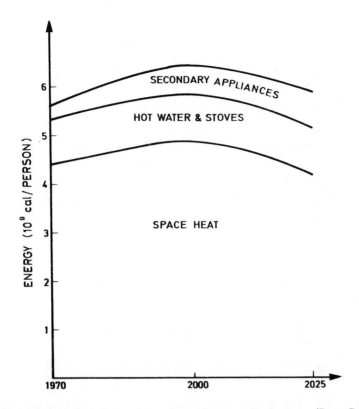

FIGURE 4.13a Residential end-use demand per capita by type (Base Case scenario for Bezirk X).

use per capita in transportation increases more rapidly than the other two regions because of the dominance of freight. Residential end-use demand per capita for base appliances and secondary appliances is shown in Figure 4.13a (secondary appliances are 100 percent electric). By 2025 district heat accounts for 35 percent of the residential space heating demand. Since the number of dwelling units stabilizes by 2000, the replacement of the more energy-intensive coal by district heat and electricity (Figure 4.13b) causes the end-use energy demand for space heating to drop between 2000 and 2025. These are the main demand sector results for the Base Case.

II.B.2. Supply Sector Results

Table 4.5 shows the total primary energy supply by fuel type calculated to meet the end-use energy demands of Scenario S1, the Base Case. The total lignite production by category of use in Bezirk X is given in Table 4.6. In 1970, 48 percent of the lignite produced was exported as briquettes. The total coal produced per year in

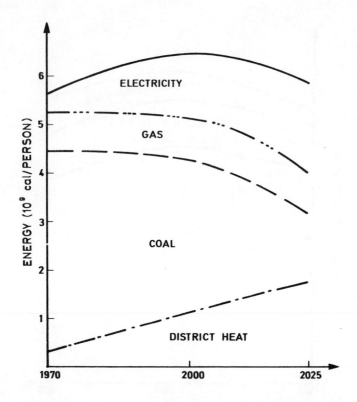

FIGURE 4.13b   Residential end-use demand per capita by fuel (Base Case scenario for Bezirk X).

the Bezirk remains rather constant, according to long-term planning for the Bezirk as specified by the Leipzig researchers. Resource base longevity was a major reason for this constraint on coal production in the scenario.

The two largest components of the supply sector in 1970 are the export of briquettes (43.8 percent of the total primary energy) and the export of electricity (14 percent of the total primary energy). Table 4.6 shows that electricity production and briquette export required most of the coal in 1970 (84 percent of the total). In 2025 these two still require 82 percent of the total; however, almost all of the coal is now going to electricity production and very little to briquette export; a trade-off has occurred as a result of the industrial demand for electricity in Bezirk X. District heat requires the second largest amount of coal by 2025, but it still requires a minor amount compared with electricity.

While energy exports are 58 percent of the Bezirk's primary energy flow in 1970, they are only 14.8 percent of the total primary energy flow in 2025. The Bezirk is a strong energy supplier for the rest of the country in 1970, but it is unable to maintain this after 2000 because of its own industrial energy demand and the limit

TABLE 4.5   Primary Annual Energy Flow in the Supply Sector for Bezirk X (10^{15} cal/yr)

	Coal						
		Briquettes		Electricity[a]		District heat[a]	
	Nonbriquette	Bezirk	Export	Bezirk	Export	Briquettes	other
1970	3.41	10.9	69.1	17.0	22.0	13.5	10.5
2025	1.20	6.4	4.7	66.2	22.6	0.7	36.6

	Gas	Oil	Nuclear	Other
1970	0.90	4.4	0.0	6.3
2025	3.2	30.2	19.5	0.0

[a] Includes efficiency losses.

TABLE 4.6   Annual Lignite Coal Demand in Bezirk X (10^6 tons/yr)

	Direct Use		Indirect Use Via Briquettes			
	Electricity	District Heat	Direct Demand	District Heat	Export	Total
1970	21.1	4.7	3.4	1.1	27.9	58.2
2025	42.6	7.2	1.1	1.7	1.9	54.5

placed on annual lignite production. This could have important consequences for the energy supply for the rest of the country. The GDR will most likely have to begin importing significant quantities of energy if it maintains the high industrial growth represented in the Base Case.

II.C. ENVIRONMENTAL IMPACTS

A limited number of quantified impacts have been chosen to highlight different aspects of the chain of energy-related environmental impacts that have been calculated by the environmental impact models. The overall methods for calculation are described in Chapter 3. The environmental effects selected for presentation here are representative of impacts that are judged important to the Bezirk or to the GDR.[2, 7, 8, 10, 11] They highlight important aspects but by no means form a complete set of information. As mentioned in the discussion of the evaluation of options (Appendix E at the back of the book), not all impacts have been quantified; therefore, some individuals may feel that other quantified impacts or selected unquantified impacts are more important. The emphasis in this section is on quantified human health and safety impacts and particularly on air pollution effects.[13, 14, 15]

The emission control factors for fossil fuels assumed for the Base Case are shown in Table 4.7.[10] Emissions of SO_2 are shown in Figures 4.14–4.16. Figure 4.14 presents different measures of emissions for the entire Bezirk; Figure 4.15 gives the total SO_2 emissions by sector for 1970, 2000, and 2025. The large decline in the

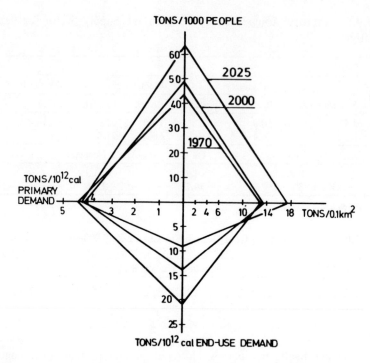

FIGURE 4.14   Selected indicators of total SO_2 emissions (Base Case scenario for Bezirk X).

TABLE 4.7   Assumed Control Factors for Particulates and SO_2 for the Base Case in Bezirk X (percentage removed prior to emission)[a]

	1970		2000		2025	
	P.M.[b]	SO_2	P.M.	SO_2	P.M.	SO_2
District heat						
Coal	70	0	95	35	95	35
Industry						
Coal	60	0	95	6	95	20
Oil	0	0	0	50	0	50
Gas	0	0	0	20	0	40
Electricity generation						
Coal	80	0	99	30	99	60

[a] The service and residential sectors had no controls, except for a refinery-produced 50% reduction in the sulfur content of oil by 2000. The district heat SO_2 control in 2000 was assumed to be a combination of SO_2 control at the plant and a reduction of sulfur content of the coal and oil used.
[b] Particulate matter.

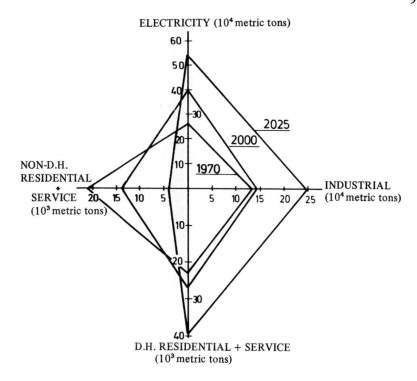

FIGURE 4.15   Demand sector and electricity SO$_2$ emissions (Base Case scenario for Bezirk X). *D.H.* stands for district heat.

non-district heat emissions in the residential and service sectors is striking. Figure 4.16 shows the emission by subregion and by residential, service, and industrial sectors for 1970 and 2025. The large variation in emission among subregions is an important factor in the calculation of selected health impacts associated with SO$_2$. Subregion 9 has a very large emission relative to the other subregions, primarily because all briquette production is in Subregion 9 and because a large quantity of low-temperature heat is used in that district. Of the 206,000 tons of SO$_2$ emitted in Subregion 9 in 1970, 81 percent is associated with the briquette factory.

The electrical generation and industrial sectors account for most of the SO$_2$ emissions. However, health effects are not directly proportional to emissions; the character of the emission sources must be taken into account. For example, the percentage of the emissions in each emission class (sources with high, medium, and ground-level release heights) and their respective percentage of the calculated average ground-level concentration (average dose) are shown in Figure 4.17 for two Bezirk cities. Clearly, the near-ground-level emissions from the residential and service sectors are much more important for human health impact than the relative magnitude

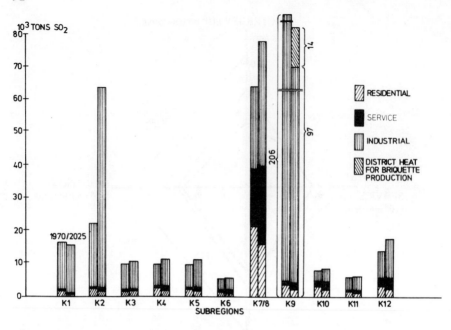

FIGURE 4.16   SO$_2$ emissions by subregion (Base Case for Bezirk X).

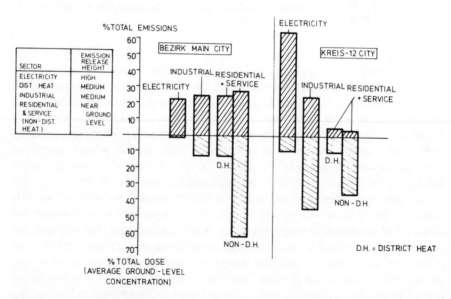

FIGURE 4.17   1970 Bezirk X SO$_2$ emissions and SO$_2$ doses.

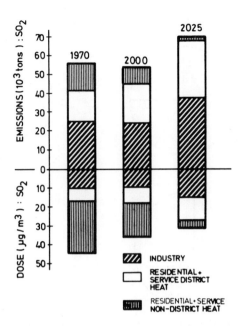

FIGURE 4.18   SO$_2$ emission and dose by source in the main city of Bezirk X (Base Case).

of their emission would indicate. This is primarily attributable to differences in dispersion for the three types of emission sources.[15]

Even though the calculated results indicate that SO$_2$ emissions will increase with time in the Bezirk main city, the average ground-level concentration (dose) declines (Figure 4.18). The increasing use of district heat in the residential and service sectors causes the decreasing ambient air concentrations. The district heat plants have tall stacks, while the individual heating units that district heat replaces have near-ground-level release heights.

The calculated dose can be used with the SO$_2$ health impact model[14] to provide an indication of premature mortality and excess morbidity related to air pollution. The premature mortality and excess morbidity are expressed in terms of person-days lost (PDL). Health impacts and accidents of different severity have various quantities of PDL associated with them. For example, excess asthma attacks and aggravation of heart and lung disease in the elderly have one PDL per event, and each premature fatality has 6000 PDL associated with it. PDL from accidents, morbidity, and mortality related to energy use can be aggregated to obtain a measure of the total quantified human health and safety impact.*

---

* Because some impacts are not quantified, the total quantified health and safety impact clearly cannot be equated to the total health and safety impact.

94

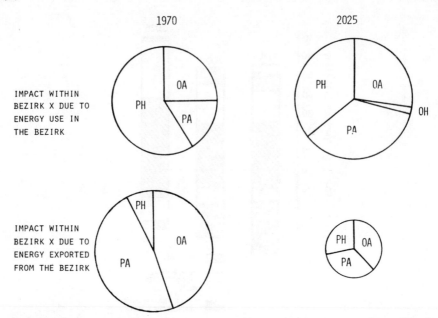

IMPACT WITHIN
BEZIRK X DUE TO
ENERGY USE IN
THE BEZIRK

IMPACT WITHIN
BEZIRK X DUE TO
ENERGY EXPORTED
FROM THE BEZIRK

FIGURE 4.19   Human health impact in terms of person-days lost (Base Case for
Bezirk X). OA – occupational accidents; OH – occupational health; PA – public
accidents; PH – public health.

The total PDL within Bezirk X for energy production and use in 1970 and 2025
is shown in Figure 4.19; the total PDL is divided into components of accident and
health for both occupational and general public impacts. In 1970 the Bezirk suffers
a major human health and safety impact associated with energy export. The largest
share of the PDL resulting from energy export is public accidents, i.e., accidents
resulting from the transport of the energy sources, such as lignite and briquettes. In
contrast, the largest quantified impact within the Bezirk due to the Bezirk's own
energy use is public health PDL from air pollution. In 2025 the public health impact
from energy use within the Bezirk is approximately equivalent to the sum of PDL
from energy-related occupational accidents and public accidents. Although SO_2
emissions increased from 1970 to 2025 (Figure 4.14), the public health impact
within the Bezirk in 2025 is slightly less than in 1970 mainly because of SO_2 controls and shifts to district heat. The small occupational health impact in 2025 is the
radiation health impact on nuclear power plant personnel. Human health and safety
impacts in the Bezirk associated with energy export in 2025 are significantly reduced
from the 1970 level because energy export is reduced (Table 4.5).

Table 4.8 shows the quantified PDL, classified by the cause of the person-days-
lost (occupational accidents, public accidents, occupational health, or public health),
the location of the impact (inside or outside the Bezirk), the source of the impact
(electrical or nonelectrical system), and whether the energy associated with the

TABLE 4.8   Quantified Person-Days Lost Resulting from Energy Flow in Bezirk X for the Base Case[a]

| | 1970 | | | | | 2025 | | | | |
| | Electrical | | Nonelectrical | | | Electrical | | Nonelectrical | | |
	Bezirk	Export	Bezirk	Export	Total	Bezirk	Export	Bezirk	Export	Total
Impacts within Bezirk X										
Occupational accidents	9,600	12,000	9,600	34,000	66,000	21,000	7,100	6,100	1,500	36,000
Occupational health	0	0	0	0	0	600	0	0	0	600
Public accidents	3,300	4,300	6,700	26,000	40,000	13,000	4,400	6,700	1,800	26,000
Public health	12,000	16,000	37,000	2,200	66,000	21,000	6,800	25,000	58	52,000
Impacts outside Bezirk X										
Occupational accidents	0	0	700	3,800	4,500	1,300	0	4,800	270	6,400
Occupational health	0	0	0	0	0	170	0	0	0	170
Public accidents	0	0	3,000	32,000	35,000	120	0	21,000	2,200	23,000
Public health	0	0	0	0	0	510	0	0	0	510
Totals										
Occupational accidents	9,600	12,000	10,000	38,000	70,000	23,000	7,100	11,000	1,700	42,000
Occupational health	0	0	0	0	0	770	0	0	0	770
Public accidents	3,300	4,300	9,700	57,000	75,000	13,000	4,400	27,000	4,000	49,000
Public health	12,000	16,000	37,000	2,200	66,000	21,000	6,800	25,000	58	52,000
Grand total	25,000	32,000	57,000	97,000	211,000	58,000	18,000	63,000	5,800	140,000

[a] One death or case of total disability is equated with 6,000 person-days lost (PDL). Columns and rows may not add to totals because of rounding.

impact is used inside the Bezirk or exported. The quantified impacts outside the Bezirk that result from energy use within the Bezirk are not as large as impacts within the Bezirk; yet, these effects outside the Bezirk are not insignificant. The total PDL inside the Bezirk, categorized according to energy use within the Bezirk and energy export, form the basis for Figure 4.19. Public health and public accidents that result from involuntary exposure are responsible for a sizeable majority of the total PDL both within and outside the Bezirk. The total PDL resulting from energy use in 2025 are equivalent to 24 premature deaths.

Human health and safety has been emphasized here because it is generally considered one of the most important categories of quantified impacts. Other environmental impacts associated with the GDR scenarios are presented in later sections and in Chapter 7.

II.D.   IMPORTANT ASPECTS OF THE BASE CASE SCENARIO

Several important features of Bezirk X emerge from the Base Case. The first of these is the extreme dominance of the energy use by industry and the freight component of transportation, two sectors that are closely connected. The high energy use of freight transport is also associated with the large energy export foreseen by the scenario. Essentially, three factors underlie the energy growth in these sectors:

• Zero population growth removes a cause of increased energy use from the other sectors.

• The Bezirk is a major industrial area that must produce goods for the rest of the country as well as for itself.

• The planning of the GDR has a strong emphasis on high industrial growth compared with present trends in free-market countries.

The possibility of continuing industrial growth and decreasing industrial energy intensiveness even after the year 1995 in the Bezirk was the subject of much discussion during the workshop; some participants from the other two regions expressed great doubts that the industrial projections could be realized. The GDR participants pointed out that Bezirk X is embedded in the country and is not independent of the whole in its production. In addition, the assumed decreases in energy intensiveness for industry, as anticipated by the Leipzig researchers, are in fact historical trends of the past 10 years.

The nonfreight components of transportation deserve attention. The increase in energy use for automobiles is solely due to an increase in car ownership per household (only a small improvement in fuel economy per car can be expected). The total mass transit energy use is dominated by long-distance train and bus travel, 78 percent and 84 percent of the passenger-km in 1970 and 2025, respectively. This implies an extensive use of trains and buses for intercity travel. As in 1970, trains account for three-fourths of the intercity mass transit passenger-km in 2025 and become increasingly energy-efficient as steam engines are replaced by diesel engines and then diesel engines by electric engines. Freight transport is very energy-efficient in this scenario because all intercity freight hauling is by rail (there is no trucking).

In the residential sector after the year 1990, there is a decrease in end-use energy per capita, clearly noticeable in Figure 4.13a.* This decrease is the result of a shift from coal to district heat, electricity, and gas, each of which requires less end-use energy than coal. No changes in housing structure or insulation patterns occur. Among appliances, penetration of dishwashers, deep freezers and clothes dryers is low; room air conditioners penetrate even less, and central air conditioning is not introduced. These projections reflect an official GDR attitude toward the best use of resources.

From an environmental perspective, district heat is quite significant; it results in lower ground-level air pollution concentrations in the urban area than does normal space heating with equivalent emissions. This health impact advantage disappears when the air pollutants disperse from the urban area to the rural areas because the effect of space-heating emissions is roughly the same, whether they come from a district heating plant or household units.

Bezirk X, unlike Wisconsin and Rhone-Alpes, not only absorbs environmental impacts due to its own consumption of energy and goods, but it also absorbs large impacts, especially before the year 2000, associated with demands outside the region. Bezirk X exports a lot of its electricity and coal briquettes, and its industry produces for the rest of the country. The impacts associated with energy production for industrial exports and energy export occur mostly within the Bezirk because lignite is the basic fuel and no lignite is imported into the Bezirk, even by 2025.

II.E.   OBSERVATIONS ON THE BASE CASE SCENARIO

The Base Case for Bezirk X represents an extrapolation of the GDR's 20-year outlook for industrial regions of the country. This 20-year outlook provided a consistent set of socioeconomic and technical assumptions for the scenario development. Extrapolating the trends in the GDR outlook had inherent uncertainty associated with it; no claim is made about the likelihood that the Base Case will be realized. The Base Case did point up several problem areas, which is one of the reasons that the scenario approach is useful.

One major area of concern was the likelihood of a high rate of industrial growth continuing over such a long time-span. By 2025 the industrial output per worker must increase by a factor of 80 over the output in 1970, a heroic achievement to say the least.

A closely related area of concern was the continuing decrease in industrial energy intensiveness over the entire 55 years. The projected tenfold increase in the efficiency of the use of low-temperature heat (district heat) in industry is difficult

---

* The average number of people per household is constant after 1990 (Figure 4.3).

to justify. The decreasing intensiveness coefficients do represent recent historical trends; however, analysis of their correctness is complex because both space heat and process heat demands are combined in the coefficients.

The Base Case indicated that the twin objectives of energy export and material export (industrial goods) could not be maintained, even with the large increases in industrial energy efficiency posited. An increase in mining capacity would be required to do both, reducing the lifetime of the GDR's resource base and forcing an earlier relinquishing of energy self-sufficiency in coal.

Growth rates of end-use demand and total electricity produced, 4.3 percent and 6 percent, respectively, were quite representative of current European experience[4] and for electricity, representative of earlier Wisconsin experience. Electricity, as in other countries, grows somewhat faster than total energy consumption.

The Base Case indicates that the population living in Bezirk X accepts a large environmental burden for the welfare of the rest of the country. In the beginning years the burden is the result of energy export, and in the final years of the scenario, it is the result of material export.

Other observations on the Base Case are made in the following comparison with the other two scenarios and in sensitivity studies. Comments concerning modeling difficulties are presented in the conclusion of this chapter.

III.   OTHER SCENARIOS

Two additional scenarios will be presented here and compared with the Base Case. There will also be a selection of sensitivity studies that highlight features of Bezirk X. The two additional scenarios have been simply labeled as the High-Energy Case, S2, and the Energy-Conservation Case, S3. The rationales for their development is as follows:

• High-Energy Case (S2): Some energy aspects of the Base Case appeared questionable over the long term. These were (1) the industrial energy intensiveness, (2) long-distance freight hauling only by rail, and (3) the low number of cars per household through 2025. Changes in these characteristics were the primary basis for definition of the high case. No economic parameters were changed.

• Energy-Conservation Case (S3): Here energy-saving technological modifications were introduced into a Base Case that was already quite energy conserving. Major changes were (1) improved fuel economies, (2) stricter insulation standards, and (3) the penetration of solar thermal and solar-electric alternatives. Again, no economic changes were introduced.

TABLE 4.9   Policies and Assumptions for Scenarios S2 and S3 for Bezirk X

Bezirk X: Scenario S2

Industrial energy-intensiveness decreases only 1/3 as much by 2025 as in Scenario S1 (similar to the Rhone-Alpes Base Case).

By 2025, 80 percent of the long-distance freight (ton-km) is transported by truck.

The number of cars per household increases to 1.0 in 2025.

District heat penetrates less rapidly in the residential sector.

Supply: No nuclear power; large import of electricity.

No sulfur controls for fuels before 2025.

Bezirk X: Scenario S3

Insulation standards reduce 1- and 2-family house space heat requirements by 20%:

- By 2000, 15% of the 1- and 2-family houses meet the new standards.
- By 2025, 60% of the 1- and 2-family houses meet the new standards.

Low-temperature solar space heat units that can replace 50% of the space heat demand in 1- and 2-family houses are made available beginning in 1980:

By 2025, 50% of 1- and 2-family houses constructed in that year have the new solar units.

The penetration of the solar units for space heat for the service sector matches the penetration in the residential sector.

Industrial electricity energy-intensiveness is 20% lower than in S1.

Transportation
- Penetration of electric auto is 10% by 2025.
- There is lower auto use per capita.
- Trains are 100% electric by 2025.

Supply
- 20% of electricity capacity is solar by 2025.
- There are two nuclear pressurized water reactors (PWRs) (818 MW) by 2025.
There are strict sulfur and particulate matter controls.

III.A.   SCENARIO COMPARISONS

Table 4.9 gives the most important parameter changes for S2 and S3. Tables giving energy supply, demand, and sources for the three scenarios can be found in the Appendix to this chapter.

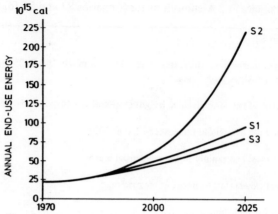

FIGURE 4.20   Total end-use energy demand by scenario for Bezirk X.

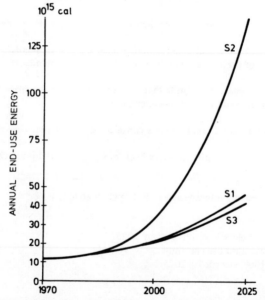

FIGURE 4.21   Industrial end-use energy demand by scenario for Bezirk X.

Figure 4.20 shows a comparison of the total end-use energy demand for the three scenarios. As expected, Scenario S3 is quite similar to S1; the small differences are mostly attributable to industry and transportation. The industrial end-use demand and the transportation end-use demand are shown in Figures 4.21 and 4.22. The change in industrial demand is due only to a change in energy intensiveness; for transportation the change is due to a change in transport mode and fuel economy. Interestingly enough, the shift in favor of trucks for long-distance freight had about

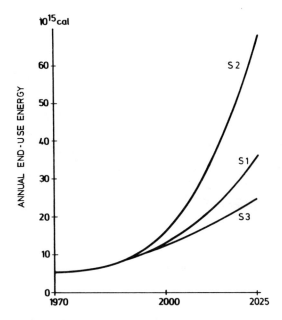

FIGURE 4.22   Transportation end-use energy demand by scenario for Bezirk X.

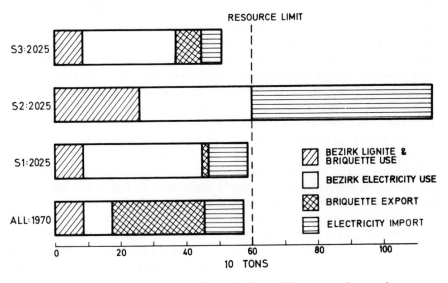

FIGURE 4.23   Total lignite coal demand in Bezirk X by use and scenario.

the same effect on the energy demand as changing the energy intensiveness for industry. This has important implications for the Bezirk and the GDR, because Scenario S2 provides for industrial energy conservation efforts similar to those cur-

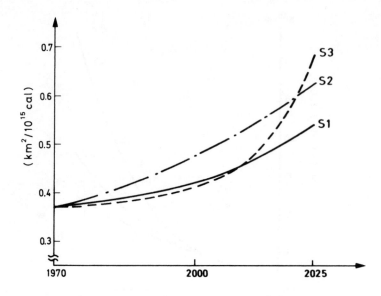

FIGURE 4.24   Land intensiveness of end-use and export energy production for Bezirk X.

rently underway in the United States and Western Europe. However, the decrease in industrial energy intensiveness for S2 is larger than even the Wisconsin conservation case. This indicates that, with its postulated high industrial growth and with current world industrial energy intensiveness trends (rather than the postulated efficiency improvements), the GDR would have no hope of being energy self-sufficient past the year 2000. In the residential and service sectors, there was no significant change in the energy end-use demand for the three scenarios. Of interest is the use of district heat and the penetration of solar-thermal; these will be discussed for the residential sector in the sensitivity studies described in section III.B.

There are several significant differences in the environmental impacts for the three scenarios. Some of these differences result from the fact that in Scenario S1, the Bezirk is an exporter of an appreciable fraction of its electricity production, whereas in S2, it imports a significant fraction of its electricity demand. This is illustrated in Figure 4.23. Interestingly enough, for S1, almost all of the coal production initially used for briquette export is required to satisfy the Bezirk's own demand for electricity by 2025. To be achieved, S2 would require a major mining activity outside the Bezirk for the importation of electricity. Electricity rather than coal would be imported because of the high lignite transportation costs in the GDR. The large increase in mining activity (in the country as a whole) required by S2 would imply an earlier dependence on imports of primary energy for the GDR.

Total land disturbed (by coal mining, power plants, or nuclear reprocessing plants) is shown in Figure 4.24 for the three scenarios; it is expressed in units of land area per unit of end-use energy (including energy exported). In all scenarios,

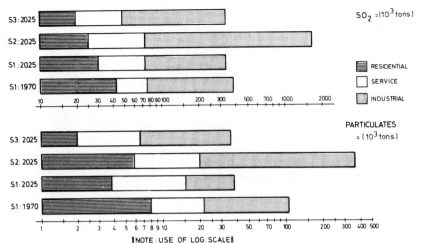

FIGURE 4.25   Demand sector emissions of particulates and SO$_2$ due to energy use.

increasingly more land per unit of energy is required because of the continuing shift to electricity and district heat (an increase of almost 50 percent by 2025 for Scenario S1). In S1, mining accounts for 60 percent ($\sim$ 21.8 km^2/yr) of the land disturbed in 1970 and 38 percent ($\sim$ 22.4 km^2/yr) in 2025; the rest of the energy-related land use is for energy facilities. The shift to electricity does not require more land for mining (because briquette export decreases at the same rate as the associated mining) but does require more land for the additional power plants. The same applies to district heat. In S3, the land intensiveness increases significantly in later years because of more use of solar energy. By 2025, even though solar energy provides only 20 percent of total electrical capacity, it requires about 50 percent of the land needed for all energy facilities (power plants, for example); in fact, solar energy facilities account for 35 percent of the total quantified land used for energy, including mining.

Sulfur dioxide and particulate matter emissions are shown for 1970 and 2025 by sector and by scenario in Figure 4.25 (it should be noted that the emissions are displayed on a logarithmic scale). The differences among scenarios are due not only to changes in energy use, but to differences in assumed pollution control. In general, however, the fact that in Scenario S1 the emissions in 2025 are less than in 1970, even though total primary energy use is greater, can be attributed to emission controls.

When these emissions are translated into ambient air concentrations, health impacts can be calculated. As presented in Table 4.10, one indicator of differences in the health impacts for the three scenarios is a comparison of the calculated number of days the standards are exceeded in selected cities. These numbers represent ambient concentrations calculated by a dispersion model.[15] Although the calculated results are somewhat low compared to small samples of actual data, the relative magnitudes are adequate for comparative purposes. Calibration with empirical data is not possible because Bezirk X is a composite region.

TABLE 4.10   Estimate of the Number of Days That SO_2 Standards in the GDR Are Exceeded in Selected Bezirk Cities (GDR Standard $= 150\,\mu g/m^3$)

Subregion Number for the City[a]	Number of Days			
	1970	2025		
	S1	S1	S2	S3
2	3	10	108	10
8	24	13	90	9
9	59	20	140	25
12	2	2	27	1

[a] See Figure 4.1 for a map of the Bezirk and its numbered subregions.

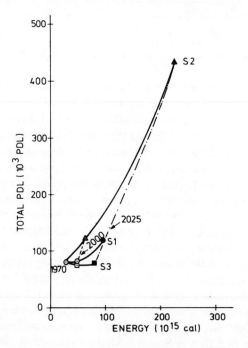

FIGURE 4.26   Total PDL due to end-use energy demand in Bezirk X over time for S1, S2, and S3.

As mentioned earlier, one indicator of human health impact is person-days lost (PDL). It is of interest to examine the total PDL in the Bezirk as a function of its own energy demand. As shown in Figure 4.26, this indicator is a nonlinear function of energy, mainly because there are mortality threshold effects in the air pollution health impact model.

In 1970, only 30 percent of the Bezirk's PDL is attributable to electricity

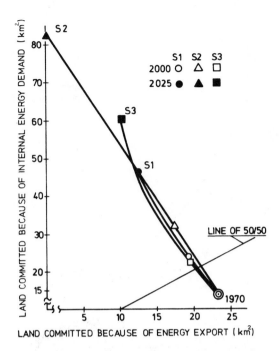

FIGURE 4.27   Land use for Bezirk demand versus land use for export demand.

production. In all but S3, the share of the Bezirk's PDL due to electricity production increases significantly during the time frame of the scenarios. This increase in electricity's contribution to total PDL has three main causes: (1) the fraction of space heat demand met by district heat continually increases; (2) briquette production for export dramatically decreases; and (3) electricity production increases. However, if SO_2 controls are instituted as in S3, then there is no significant increase in electricity's share of total PDL. Thus controls on SO_2 emissions from electricity generation could have importance in terms of health impacts.

Since the Bezirk exports so much energy, it is of interest to see what kinds of export-related impacts occur. Figure 4.27 compares the land in the Bezirk committed to meet its own energy demand with land related to energy export. For S1 and S3, not until about 1990 does the land used for the Bezirk's own energy needs equal the land used for exported energy. For export, the land use is almost entirely strip mining, which necessitates land reclamation efforts in the Bezirk. By 2025 in S1 and S3, much of the strip mining activity must support the Bezirk's own energy demands.

In Figure 4.28 the human health impacts of energy export and internal energy use are displayed. In 1970, over half the human health impact is due to the export of energy. Health impact due to energy export in S3 remains low because of stringent pollution control on electric power plants (95-percent SO_2 control is assumed).

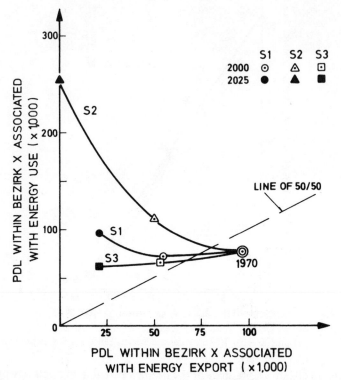

FIGURE 4.28   PDL in Bezirk X due to internal energy use and export.

Health impact due to energy export in S1 initially decreases due to the introduction of improved SO_2 controls through 2000; from then until 2025, no significant improvement in controls occurs, and any increase in energy use produces an increased impact on health. S2 indicates the consequences of uncontrolled SO_2 emissions and high energy use. In the year 2000 differences between S1 and S2 are largely due to the difference in pollution control measures (compare with Figure 4.20), mostly instituted in the electricity sector.

Various emission controls were included in the three scenarios. Scenario S1 had moderate controls; S2 had low or no controls; and S3 had stringent controls. The sensitivity of the SO_2 and particulate emissions from coal to these control assumptions is shown in Figure 4.29. The controls are specified according to five different groupings; the difference between the groups is the ease (both technological and economic) of implementation. They are normalized to the low control case (S2), and expressed in terms of the percent of control greater than in S2. For example, in the case of particulate emissions from electricity generation plants, there was 95 percent particulate control in S2 and 99 percent in both S1 and S3. Thus the control in S1 and S3 allowed release of only 20 percent as many particulates as in S2, as

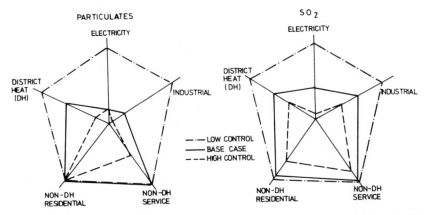

FIGURE 4.29   Sensitivity of the particulates and SO$_2$ emissions in Bezirk X in 2025 to different control levels.

can be seen in Figure 4.29. One may also conclude from this figure that controls are most easily applied to electricity generation facilities because they are highly centralized; controls on industry are the next easiest because industry is also relatively centralized and has money to spend on controls; buildings in the residential and service sectors are the most difficult to control.

III.B.   SENSITIVITY STUDIES

Several studies were conducted to examine how sensitive various scenario results were to alternative assumptions. The results of four representative studies are presented in this section.

III.B.1.   *Electricity Supply and Emission Control*

As expected, changes in types of electrical generation and emission controls affect quantified environmental impacts both inside and outside the Bezirk. Study of the effect of such changes on health was the objective of a sensitivity analysis (based on S2) for 2025, which considered the following supply and control options:

- All electricity generated to meet Bezirk demand (62 percent must be imported) is from coal-fired power plants; no control of SO$_2$ emissions is assumed. These are the assumptions of Scenario S2.
- All electricity generated to meet Bezirk demand (62 percent must be imported) is from coal-fired power plants; 90 percent control of SO$_2$ emissions is assumed.
- All electricity generated to meet Bezirk demand is produced within the Bezirk.

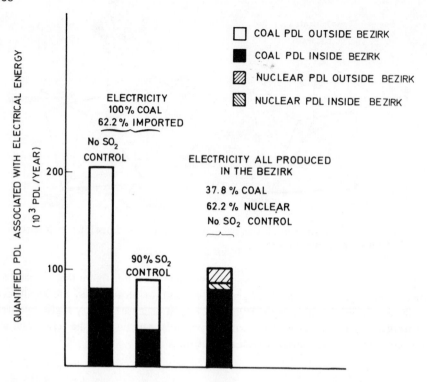

FIGURE 4.30   Quantified PDL for S2 with different electrical supply options in Bezirk X.

Nuclear power (six pressurized water reactors) is used to generate the electricity that otherwise would have to be imported. No control of SO_2 emissions from coal-fired power plants is assumed.

The results in terms of quantified PDL related to electrical generation are displayed in Figure 4.30. The case with 90 percent SO_2 control and the case with nuclear generation each result in slightly more than a 50-percent reduction in PDL compared with the S2 results. The case with nuclear generation has almost all the PDL within the Bezirk, while the non-nuclear cases have a significant share of the PDL in regions outside the Bezirk (because most of the coal mining and electricity generation to supply the Bezirk occurs in other regions).

If both SO_2 controls and nuclear generation were available, then a further reduction in human health impact due to electricity generation could be achieved, a reduction of approximately 75 percent compared with S2. In this case the majority of the PDL would also occur in the region of energy use, Bezirk X.

TABLE 4.11 Annual Space Heating Consumption in the Residential Sector in Bezirk X (10^{12} cal).

	S1		S3		
	Total	Electric	Total	Electric	Solar
1970	6,260	4.5	6,260	4.5	0
2000	6,370	452	6,260	426	26.5
2025	5,480	785	5,070	453	332

III.B.2. Solar Penetration in the Residential Sector

It was of interest to know how much potential saving there might be in space heating using solar thermal energy. Current estimates indicate that solar heating could provide 50 percent of the space heat requirements of a single-family house in the southern part of the GDR[16] and electricity would provide the rest. In the sensitivity study, solar heating was substituted for electricity in an increasing percentage of new one- and two-family rural houses; the percentage increased from 0 to 50 between 1980 and 2025 (see Table 4.11).

The potential saving in 2025 from solar energy is 42 percent of the residential space heat electricity demand. Of the total residential electricity demand (with appliances) and the total residential space heat demand in 2025, solar energy represents a saving of 22 percent and 6 percent, respectively. Solar energy can replace a significant portion of the space heat electricity demand in Bezirk X, but the amount of energy it represents is relatively low, even by 2025.

Seventy-five percent of the difference in the total energy for space heating between S1 (Base Case) and S3 (Conservation Case) is due to the insulation standards and 25 percent to the increased use of district heating. The same amount of energy was saved in 2025 with better insulation in 60 percent of the one- and two-family houses (20 percent reduction in space heat requirement per home) as with solar space heat. Of course the number of houses with solar space heat was much smaller, but the cost for a solar house would be much larger than for a well-insulated house. Thus, for the 55-year period of the scenario, the use of solar energy for residential space heating does not appear to be as economical as providing better insulation in houses. Solar heating, however, would compare more favorably with a longer time horizon.

III.B.3. District Heat versus SO_2 Dose

There is a great interest in the GDR industrial districts in reducing the SO_2 air pollution that now exists. The ground-level air pollution concentration (dose) due to the emission of a given amount of pollutant depends on the type of source that emits the pollutant.[15] There is a large difference between the dose due to pollutants emitted from a house chimney (a low-level source) and the dose due to pollutants emitted from a district heating plant (a medium-level source with a stack). One

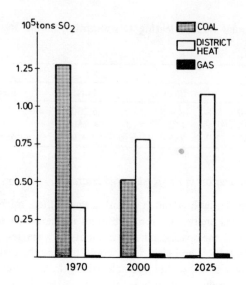

FIGURE 4.31   Residential SO_2 emissions by source in the main city of Bezirk X.

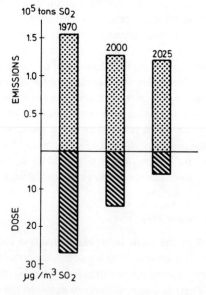

FIGURE 4.32 SO_2 emissions and dose from district heat used for space heat for the residential sector in the main city of Bezirk X.

method to reduce the SO_2 dose is to use district heat rather than house or apartment furnaces to supply space heat needs. It was of interest to investigate what effect district heat could have on SO_2 dose.

The Bezirk-X main city was chosen for this sensitivity study because it has almost complete penetration of district heat for residential space heating by 2025. Figure 4.31 shows residential emissions as a function of space heat source in the Bezirk X main city. By 2025 the main source of emissions has shifted from direct coal burning to district heat. Direct coal and gas burning are low-level sources.

The sensitivity of the dose due to residential space heating to the increase in district heat use for space heat is shown in Figure 4.32 for the data of Figure 4.31. The total SO_2 emissions decrease slightly because better SO_2 control at district heat plants is assumed (30 percent SO_2 removal before emission). Importantly, the dose per unit of SO_2 emitted in 1970 is much less than in 2025, 17.1 $\mu g/m^3$ per 10^5 tons SO_2 and 4.9 $\mu g/m^3$ per 10^5 tons SO_2, respectively. By switching from the direct burning of coal to district heat, the dose per ton of SO_2 emitted decreased by a factor of 3.5. The dose itself decreased by a factor of 4.5 because of the pollution controls at the district heating plants. With better SO_2 controls than assumed, the reduction in dose attributable to residential space heating could be reduced even further. It is clear that the use of district heat can provide a good means to reduce the SO_2 air pollution that now exists in the urban areas of regions like Bezirk X.

IV.   CONCLUSION

Some general conclusions can be drawn from the scenarios. These are grouped around issues that were thought important in the region. It should be re-emphasized that Bezirk X represents a major industrial center in the GDR; its zero population growth provided an interesting ingredient in the study by removing a powerful driving force from the scenarios.

Socioeconomic Aspects

• The planned growth in the industrial sectors after the year 2000 is extremely optimistic. Because the population is not increasing, the projected growth assumes a seemingly unrealistic increase in labor productivity.

• Industrial growth, together with its associated freight transportation, was the dominant driving factor for energy demand in Bezirk X. This growth will be of major concern if energy prices continue to increase.

Energy Intensiveness

• The postulated strong reduction in energy use per unit of output resulted in a manageable growth in industrial energy demand despite the high industrial growth.

The reduction in industrial energy intensiveness was extrapolated from a strong historical emphasis on energy saving. If this decline does not continue, a much larger increase in energy demand will occur. This should be an area for more investigation.

Transportation

• Freight was the dominant driving force behind transportation energy demand. Changes in the freight sector will strongly influence energy demand.

• Freight transport was relatively efficient, with the emphasis on trains for long hauls. If more freight were shifted to trucks for long hauls, the energy demand for freight would greatly increase.

• Passenger transport was also relatively efficient because of emphasis on mass transit. Obviously an increase in auto use would significantly increase gasoline demand. There is, however, room for improved auto fuel efficiency.

Energy Supply

• Bezirk X is self-sufficient in coal, the fuel that powers most of its activity.

• Failures in achieving the assumed increases in energy efficiencies will result in great pressure on the energy supply system in the future. This will have an effect on the entire GDR because Bezirk X is a significant exporter to the rest of the country at present. Such failures, if industrial growth does not slow down, could mean that the rest of the country would have to shift to energy sources other than coal. Any major shift to trucks for freight would increase the demand for imported oil.

• The use of district heat both for process heat in industry and for space heat in all sectors allows the region to exploit its coal resources better and to depend less on imports.

• The primary electricity supply option today is coal, and in the future, nuclear and possibly solar energy.

• Solar space heat does not have a large impact in terms of relative number of units installed. However, its impact could be greater if it could be installed in areas whose population density is too low to justify district heating economically.

Environment

• Coal is better utilized, from an environmental perspective, in district heating plants and electricity generating plants. In the first place, this reduces pollution concentrations in the urban areas. Second, total emissions, which affect the rural areas, can be more easily controlled at central facilities such as district heating plants.

• A significant environmental impact is being absorbed by the Bezirk because of its export of energy. Impacts in the Bezirk due to export of energy decrease over time because the Bezirk requires more and more of its own energy resources, leaving less for export.

● A significant decrease in human health impacts would be effected through the application of SO_2 emission controls. Impacts due to SO_2 air pollution are the fastest growing human health impact considered in this study.

APPENDIX: ENERGY TABLES FOR BEZIRK-X SCENARIOS

SCENARIO S1

TABLE 4A.1 Primary Energy Supply (10^{15} cal)

	1970	2000	2025
Petroleum	5.5	14.0	32.1
Natural gas	2.0	2.7	3.3
Coal	143.0	139.1	135.5
Nuclear energy	0.0	0.0	19.5
Hydropower	0.0	0.0	0.0
Other	0.0	0.0	0.0
Total	150.5	155.8	190.4

TABLE 4A.2 End-Use Energy Consumption (10^{15} cal)

1970	Coal	Gas	Oil	Electricity	District Heat	Solar	Total
Industrial	2.1	0.6	0.6	1.7	7.2	0	12.2
Residential	5.9	1.1	0	0.6	0.4	0	8.0
Service	2.0	0.3	0	0.3	1.0	0	3.6
Transportation	1.3	0	3.8	0.1	0	0	5.2
Total	11.3	2.0	4.4	2.7	8.6	0	29.0
2000							
Industrial	1.7	1.3	0.5	6.0	12.5	0	2.0
Residential	4.1	1.1	0	1.7	1.5	0	8.4
Service	2.0	0.3	0	0.6	1.6	0	4.5
Transportation	0	0	12.0	1.1	0	0	13.1
Total	7.8	2.7	12.5	9.4	15.6	0	48.0
2025							
Industrial	0	2.0	0.5	17.7	25.3	0	45.5
Residential	1.9	1.1	0	2.4	2.3	0	7.8
Service	2.2	0.2	0	1.0	2.4	0	5.8
Transportation	0	0	29.7	6.7	0	0	36.4
Total	4.1	3.3	30.2	27.8	30.0	0	95.5

114

TABLE 4A.3   Sources of Electricity

	Generation (10^9 kWh)			Primary Energy (10^{15} cal)		
	1970	2000	2025	1970	2000	2025
Coal	16.3	24.9	42.2	48.8	64.8	105.4
Nuclear energy	0	0	7.5	0	0	19.5
Solar energy	0	0	0	0	0	0
Total	16.3	24.9	49.7	48.8	64.8	124.9

SCENARIO S2

TABLE 4A.4   Primary Energy Supply (10^{15} cal)

	1970	2000	2025
Petroleum	5.5	17.4	70.1
Natural gas	2.0	3.4	7.4
Coal	143.0	146.2	143.7
Nuclear energy	0	0	0
Hydropower	0	0	0
Other	0	0	0
Total	150.5	167.0	221.2

TABLE 4A.5   End-Use Energy Consumption (10^{15} cal)

1970	Coal	Gas	Oil	Electricity	District Heat	Solar	Total
Industrial	2.1	0.6	0.6	1.7	7.1	0	12.2
Residential	5.9	1.1	0	0.6	0.4	0	8.0
Service	2.0	0.3	0	0.3	1.0	0	3.6
Transportation	1.3	0	3.8	0.1	0	0	5.2
Total	11.3	2.0	4.4	2.7	8.5	0	29.0
2000							
Industrial	2.1	2.0	0.6	8.7	19.7	0	33.1
Residential	3.2	1.1	0	2.8	1.2	0	8.4
Service	1.7	0.3	0	0.9	1.6	0	4.4
Transportation	0	0	15.4	0.8	0	0	16.1
Total	7.0	3.4	16.0	13.2	22.5	0	62.0
2025							
Industrial	0	6.1	1.6	35.5	97.7	0	140.8
Residential	0	1.1	0	5.4	1.9	0	8.4
Service	1.2	0.2	0	2.1	2.4	0	5.9
Transportation	0	0	66.5	1.4	0	0	67.9
Total	1.2	7.4	68.1	44.4	102.0	0	223.0

TABLE 4A.6   Sources of Electricity

	Generation (10^9 kWh)			Primary Energy (10^{15} cal)		
	1970	2000	2025	1970	2000	2025
Coal	16.3	30.5	26.1	48.8	79.3	67.9
Nuclear energy	0	0	0	0	0	0
Solar energy	0	0	0	0	0	0
Total	16.3	30.5	26.1	48.8	79.3	67.9

SCENARIO S3

TABLE 4A.7   Primary Energy Supply (10^{15} cal)

	1970	2000	2025
Petroleum	5.5	13.5	19.4
Natural gas	2.0	2.6	3.3
Coal	143.0	136.9	124.7
Nuclear energy	0	0	15.8
Hydropower	0	0	0
Solar energy	0	0	7.1
Other	9.6	0	0
Total	160.1	153.0	170.3

TABLE 4A.8   End-Use Energy Consumption (10^{15} cal)

1970	Coal	Gas	Oil	Electricity	District Heat	Solar	Total
Industrial	2.1	0.6	0.6	1.7	7.2	0	12.2
Residential	5.9	1.1	0	0.6	0.4	0	8.0
Service	2.0	0.3	0	0.3	1.0	0	3.6
Transportation	1.3	0	3.8	0.1	0	0	5.2
Total	11.3	2.0	4.4	2.7	8.6	0	29.0
2000							
Industrial	1.7	1.3	0.5	5.4	12.5	0	21.4
Residential	3.9	1.1	0	1.7	1.6	0.03	8.3
Service	1.9	0.3	0	0.6	1.6	0.03	4.4
Transportation	0	0	11.6	1.1	0	0	12.7
Total	7.5	2.7	12.1	8.8	15.7	0.06	46.8
2025							
Industrial	0	2.0	0.5	13.3	25.3	0	41.1
Residential	1.3	1.1	0	2.1	2.6	0.3	7.4
Service	1.9	0.2	0	1.1	2.4	0.3	5.9
Transportation	0	0	17.0	8.2	0	0	25.2
Total	3.2	3.3	17.5	24.7	30.3	0.6	79.6

116

TABLE 4A.9   Sources of Electricity

	Generation (10^9 kWh)			Primary Energy (10^{15} cal)		
	1970	2000	2025	1970	2000	2025
Coal	16.3	24.2	33.0	48.8	62.9	85.8
Nuclear energy	0	0	5.0	0	0	13.0
Solar energy	0	0	3.0	0	0	7.8
Total	16.3	24.2	41.0	48.8	62.9	106.6

REFERENCES

1. *Statistisches Jahrbuch 1974 der DDR*. Staatsverlag der Deutschen Demokratischen Republik, Berlin, 1974.
2. Hedrich, P., and D. Ufer, Institut für Energetik, Leipzig, 1975: Personal communication.
3. Institut für Energetik. Data Set for a Composite Region in the GDR. Leipzig, 1975.
4. United Nations Economic Commission for Europe. Annual Bulletin of General Energy Statistics for Europe. Geneva, Vol. VII, 1974.
5. Doblin, Claire P. German Democratic Republic: Energy Demand Data. Report No. RM-76-43, International Institute for Applied Systems Analysis, Laxenburg, Austria, June 1976.
6. United Nations Economic Commission for Europe. Annual Bulletin of General Energy Statistics for Europe. Geneva, vol. V, 1972; vol. VI, 1973.
7. "IX. Weltenergiekonferenz." (Detroit, 22–27 Sept. 1974), *Energietechnik*, vol. 25. No. 2, Leipzig, Feb. 1975.
8. "Aktuelle Fragen des Umweltschutzes in der DDR." *Die Wirtschaft*, No. 17, Aug. 20, 1975.
9. "Messtechnische und Rechnerische Ermittlungen von Immissionskonzentrationen im Einflussbereich von Grossemittenten als Bewertungsgrundlage für die Territorialplanung." *Energietechnik*, vol. 25, No. 3, Leipzig, Mar. 1975.
10. IIASA Research Team 1975: Personal communication.
11. Kommission für Umweltschutz. *Technik und Umweltschutz*. VEB Deutscher Verlag für Grundstoffindustrie, Leipzig, 1972–1975.
12. "World List of Nuclear Power Plants." *Nuclear News* 20: 73–90 Aug. 1977.
13. Buehring, W.A., and W.K. Foell. Environmental Impacts of Electrical Generation: A Systemwide Approach. Report No. RR-76-13, International Institute for Applied Systems Analysis, Laxenburg, Austria, Apr. 1976.
14. Buehring, W.A., R.L. Dennis, and A. Hölzl. Evaluation of Health Effects from Sulfur Dioxide Emissions for a Reference Coal-Fired Power Plant. Report No. RM-76-23, International Institute for Applied Systems Analysis, Laxenburg, Austria, Sept. 1976.
15. Dennis, R.L. Regional Air Pollution Impact: A Dispersion Methodology Developed and Applied to Energy Systems. Report No. RM-76-22, International Institute for Applied Systems Analysis, Laxenburg, Austria, Feb. 1977.
16. Weingart, J. International Institute for Applied Systems Analysis, Laxenburg, Austria, 1975: Personal communication.

Prologue to Chapter 5
The Rhone-Alpes Scenarios
in Retrospect

Bertrand Chateau
Institut Economique et Juridique de l'Energie, Grenoble
May 1978

Since the scenarios were written in 1975, several significant changes have occurred in the economic and energy sectors of France. First, Rhone-Alpes, and France as a whole, has been experiencing rising unemployment and low economic growth. GNP growth has averaged 3 percent annually, instead of the 5.5 percent annual growth rate assumed in the scenarios. The industries most affected include the steel industry and the textile industry. In the energy sector, the ambitious national nuclear development program, which called for 6 new 1,000 MW plants per year, has been delayed by 18 months, mostly for technical reasons. This should not have major consequences since a slowing in the growth of electricity demand accompanied the slowing of economic growth. At the same time, however, research priorities have shifted from the development of nuclear technologies to energy conservation measures. Important studies have been conducted on the recovery of waste heat from conventional and nuclear power plants for use in district heating in the residential sector and for provision of process heat in the industrial sector. New standards for equipment efficiency and building insulation in the residential, service, and industrial sectors are also being developed.

Several institutional changes have also occurred in the energy sector since 1975. The *Agence pour l'Economie de l'Energie*, which is concerned with energy conservation, and the *Commissariat de l'Energie solaire*, which deals with solar energy,

---

At the second conference, Management of Regional Energy/Environment Systems, held at IIASA, 16–19 May 1978, retrospective presentations on the scenarios were given by energy specialists or policymakers from the three regions. To provide perspective on the scenarios, summaries of the presentations are included immediately before the chapters describing the scenarios for the regions (Chapters 4, 5, and 6). They will be published in full as part of the proceedings of the conference: W.K. Foell (ed.), Proceedings of the Conference on Management of Regional Energy/Environment Systems, (Laxenburg, Austria: International Institute for Applied Systems Analysis, in press).

have been set up. Concurrent with the creation of these agencies, there has been a surge of interest in the local determination of energy policies. Energy matters in France are under the jurisdiction of the central government, and regional authorities do not possess real decision-making power in this sphere. However, in the past three to four years local authorities have acquired more "bargaining power." The "Agency for Energy Conservation," for instance, has a budget which is allocated at the regional level for promotion of waste heat recovery, for the study of power plants for the combined production of electricity and heat, and for similar activities. The regional representative of the energy conservation agency has authority to make the allocations, and his dynamism determines to a great degree the freedom of a region in pursuing its own energy strategies. Perhaps such developments indicate the beginning of a new type of decision-making at the regional level in France.

Turning to the usefulness of the scenarios, one must carefully distinguish the areas in which they are applicable to the real decision-making process. The scenario approach may be used to reveal the future point in time when disruptions may occur, and to explore policies which could be implemented to avoid such disruptions. The long time horizon of the scenarios – the year 2025 – is also appropriate for the definition of research and development strategies. The time scale makes it possible to build a consistent energy/economic future and to identify the actions that would have to be taken to reach such a future.

On the other hand, the scenario approach cannot be used to make predictions. It also has limited usefulness for short- or medium-term decision making. Finally, it is very important to avoid the pitfalls of extrapolating the trends of the past 10–15 years to the 2000–2025 time period. For example, it is clear that new solar technologies and other innovations may be developed during the next several years that could greatly affect the energy situation in 2025. If it is possible to produce inexpensive solar cells in the next 20 years, the energy picture for the next 50 years could be completely changed.

If a scenario stressing strong development of nuclear power were to be written today, it would be important to include construction of combined power plants. It appears that in France such plants will be more and more frequently built, and, in addition, existing plants could be converted for the coproduction of electricity and steam or heat. The results of studies carried out in Rhone-Alpes indicate that the steam or heat that could be produced by nuclear plants is almost competitive with steam or heat produced from conventional fuels (oil or coal). Last year, a consulting commission in Paris, convened by the "Ministry of Industry", held numerous hearings on the topic of heat recovery and combined heat and power production. Though a real policy decision has not yet been made, the conclusions of the commission were favorable to the development of such plants.

5 Alternative Energy/Environment Futures for Rhone-Alpes

I. INTRODUCTION

As background to the three scenarios for Rhone-Alpes, there will be a brief description of the current economic condition of the region and of the trends or phenomena that could have an influence on the evolution of the region.

Although this study focused on one region in France, most of the data and scenario assumptions are relevant to France as a whole. The use of Rhone-Alpes as a focus of study allowed analysis at a local level and clearly showed the environmental implications of the scenarios in a small geographic area.

II. INITIAL CONDITIONS AND CURRENT PLANS*

II.A. SOCIOECONOMIC ASPECTS

Rhone-Alpes is one of the most dynamic regions in France. The growth rate of the population is one of the highest of the 21 regions; the region's economic activity contributes about 10 percent of the French gross national product (GNP); the region employs about 10 percent of the French labor force and uses about 10 percent of the energy consumed in France. Rhone-Alpes is not uniformly developed, however, since three departments dominate the economy.† Rhone, Isere, and Loire provide 70 percent of the employment in the industrial sector and even more in the service sector. The largest city in Rhone is Lyon (1,130,000 people). In

---

Chapter 5 was written by Bruno Lapillonne – IIASA.
* More detailed information on the initial conditions is given in Chapter 2.
† There are 8 departments in Rhone-Alpes: Ain, Ardeche, Drome, Isere, Loire, Rhone, Savoie, and Haute-Savoie (see Chapter 2).

Isere the largest city is Grenoble (330,000 people), and in Loire the largest city is St. Etienne (330,000 people).

Rhone-Alpes is primarily an industrial region; industry provides 45 percent of the employment and contributes 60 percent of the gross regional product (GRP, defined here as the sum of value-added of all sectors). Heavy industries (steel, aluminum, and pulp and paper) are concentrated in the Alps because of the low price of hydroelectricity, but chemical industries are concentrated around the three main cities of Lyon, Grenoble, and St. Etienne. The other industries (see Table 5.8) are more evenly distributed, but they are predominantly in the three most productive districts.

Transportation in France is mainly by automobile and truck. Automobiles are used for 75 percent of the passenger transport and trucks are used for 40 percent of the freight transport. The connections between Rhone-Alpes, the Paris area, and neighboring European countries (particularly Italy, the FRG and Switzerland) are being improved by

- The completion of the highway network connecting the largest cities of Rhone-Alpes (St. Etienne, Lyon, Valence, Annecy, Grenoble, and Chambery) with Paris, Geneva, and Marseille
- High-speed trains between Paris and the largest cities in Rhone-Alpes. The trains should be running by 1980
- The Rhone-Rhine canal
- The development of Lyon International Airport

Because of communication and transportation difficulties elsewhere, French companies are now concentrated in Paris. Improvements in the transportation network in Rhone-Alpes will encourage them to move some of their offices to places like Lyon and Grenoble.

II.B. ENERGY SUPPLY

Although Rhone-Alpes is a net exporter of electricity, energy production in the region is very low. All the oil used in the region is imported. It is refined in the large refinery of Lyon-Feyzin which has a capacity of 6 million tons per year. In 1972, sixty percent of the electricity generated in Rhone-Alpes was from hydropower, 24 percent from oil, 4 percent from nuclear power, and 6 percent each from coal and gas. There are 2 coal mines in Rhone-Alpes. They do not contribute significantly to the energy supply and were scheduled to be closed in 1980. But the rise in oil prices may keep the mines open.

There is geothermal energy in Rhone-Alpes, but little is known about it. What is known was learned as a by-product of oil prospecting. The French government is now using financial incentives to stimulate research on the use of geothermal energy, though on a small scale. In Rhone-Alpes, the use of geothermal district heating in

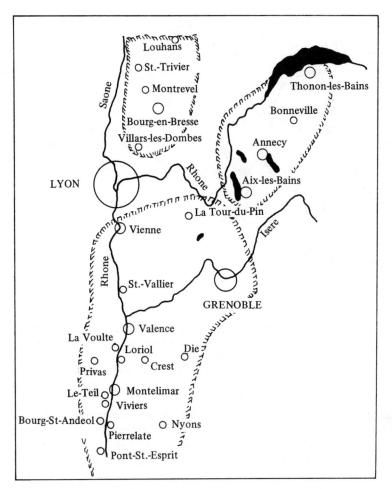

FIGURE 5.1   Regional geothermal reserves (Rhone-Alpes). In the area of Bourg-en-Bresse, the average geothermal gradient is estimated at $3.3°C/100\,m$. For the other areas (Grenoble, Valence) the figure could be of the same order of magnitude. Under Bourg-en-Bresse the water temperature reaches $90°C$ at $2,000\,m$.

Bourg-en-Bresse is being contemplated. Figure 5.1 shows the location and extent of geothermal fields in the region.

The Rhone-Alpes is a good area for nuclear plants since they could be cooled with the water of the Rhone River. Figure 5.2 shows the locations of the existing and planned reactors. Immediately following the oil crisis in 1972, the French government decided to develop nuclear energy as the basis for the energy supply of France. An initial long-term program provided for the construction of six nuclear plants each year until 1977 and the construction of an enrichment plant and a reactor to supply it in the south of the region at Tricastin. But the implementation

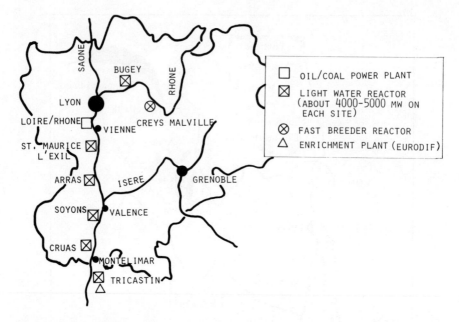

FIGURE 5.2   Nuclear sites in Rhone-Alpes. One plant in Bugey went into operation in 1973. The planned dates of other plants to go into operation are: Cruas — 1984 (2 plants), 1985 (1 plant); Bugey — 1978 (1 plant), 1979 (3 plants); St. Maurice l'Exil — 1985 (1 plant); Tricastin — 1979 (2 plants), 1980 (1 plant), 1981 (1 plant). The other sites are tentative.

of the plans of *Electricité de France* (EDF), the government-run company responsible for electricity production, that are shown in Figure 5.2 has been delayed.[*]

The possibility of building an experimental solar plant is now being studied. Solar houses are being built in the south of France, and official reports estimate that the number of solar houses built every year will grow to 50,000 by 1985, or 10 percent of total housing construction.

III.   GENERAL CONSIDERATIONS FOR THE SCENARIOS

III.A.   PRESENTATION OF THE SCENARIOS

Rhone-Alpes is a more financially and politically dependent region than the GDR or Wisconsin. A discussion of Rhone-Alpes cannot take place without a discussion of France as a whole, so the scenarios that will be described include policies for both Rhone-Alpes and France.

[*] See EDF Enerpresse No. 1994, Jan 19, 1978.

III.A.1.   Urban Policy

Besides the current trends of urban development, two other alternatives were considered.

• Very concentrated urbanization in the form of new compact cities like the ones built around Paris (*"villes nouvelles"*) and the rapid growth of small existing towns with between 20,000 and 50,000 inhabitants. These kinds of urbanization are now being tested on a small scale in France. L'Isle d'Abeau near Grenoble is an example of a new compact city in Rhone-Alpes. The new compact cities are thoroughly planned and include low-cost mass transportation and space heating for the entire community. All of the new towns near Grenoble, for example, will be served by a district heating system already connected to about 10,000 housing units. It is planned to heat L'Isle d'Abeau from the nuclear plants now under construction in Bugey.

• Growth of the population in small cities or in rural areas. Such growth could result from a modification of urban trends within the current economic framework, in which people continue to work in cities but live outside of them (urbanization similar to that in the United States). Or, such growth could result from a decentralization of the economy.

III.A.2.   Transportation Policy

In addition to the current situation described in section II.A., one other alternative has been considered for transportation: A shift from cars and trucks to railways and other forms of mass transit brought about through intervention by municipalities, the regional administration, and especially the central government. Such an interventionist policy, radically different from the current one, could be implemented to save energy or to stimulate the development of public transportation.

III.A.3.   Energy Policy

With respect to energy supply, the current plans emphasize nuclear energy. As Rhone-Alpes is very much involved in the current nuclear energy program, it seemed very interesting to explore in the Base Case the environmental impacts of implementation of a long-term policy based on nuclear energy. In contrast to such a policy, two alternatives were considered.

• The first was based on a large-scale development of new sources of energy (solar and geothermal) in order to examine the fraction of the energy markets that could be penetrated over a long period of time and to compare the resultant environmental impacts with those associated with nuclear energy.

• The second policy corresponds to an intermediate nuclear energy policy in

TABLE 5.1   Policies and Assumptions for the Three Rhone-Alpes Scenarios

Growth Assumptions

Growth rate of GRP/year	1971–1985	5%
	1985–2000	4.2%
	2000–2025	3.5%

Population growth: Gradual decrease from 1.3% per year in the 1970s to 0.4% after 2000.

| Policy Areas | Scenario | | |
	S1	S2	S3
Urban form	• Continuation of current patterns	• Dispersal; emphasis on single family houses (80% of post-1975 houses)	• Growth in small-scale compact cities • Multifamily buildings
Technology	• High level of conventional fuel prices – high penetration of electricity for space heating and industrial uses – large decrease in energy intensiveness	• Low level of fuel prices – smaller decrease in energy intensiveness than for S1 – low penetration of electricity for thermal uses	• Low penetration of electricity in industry • Large reduction of energy intensiveness • High penetration of solar and geothermal heating
Transportation	• Predominance of auto • Slight increase of intercity mass transportation	• Same as S1	• Mass transit increase • Efficiency gains for autos and trucks • Shift from truck to train for freight
Energy supply	• Electricity generation from nuclear energy	• Mix of nuclear, oil, and coal for electricity generation	• Maximum feasible hydroelectricity • Solar electric • No new nuclear plants
Environment	• Present trends of increasing controls	• Low control (current levels)	• Strict controls

which nuclear energy would be used only for electricity generation and not to replace conventional fuel for space heating and industrial thermal uses.

With respect to energy demand, several trends were considered based on the rate of growth of energy prices and on energy conservation. All the options were combined into consistent policies from the point of view of a decision maker, and from these policies three scenarios were selected. Those scenarios were selected that had meaning for the other regions and could be easily compared. At the same time, each scenario assumes a different level of energy consumption (high, medium, and low).

- S1, the Base Case, assumes the continuation of current socioeconomic trends and the extension of the current nuclear program because of high conventional fuel prices.
- S2 assumes the implementation of an exurban dispersal policy. Such a policy can only be considered in a context of low fuel prices, which would lead to a smaller reduction of energy intensities than in the other scenarios, and a transportation system still based on cars and trucks.
- S3 assumes the implementation of an urban policy based upon the development of compact cities. A shift of economic activity from industry to the service sector is also assumed. This scenario can only be realized with an interventionist policy by the government to develop mass transit and district heating, require lower pollution levels, and implement energy-saving measures.

S3 assumes low energy use, S2 assumes high energy use, and S1 assumes medium energy use. The three scenarios are summarized in Table 5.1.

III.B. CHARACTER OF THE DATA

Data collection at the regional level is very difficult since the French regions were only recently created and have no real political independence. Data gathering in Rhone-Alpes is done by the *Institut National de la Statistique et des Etudes Economiques* (INSEE), which has an office in Lyon. The INSEE data is far from complete, and is mainly on the residential sector.* With respect to economic activity, only employment data are available.† We therefore tried to estimate the value-added of Rhone-Alpes economic sectors from the Rhone-Alpes employment data and from national data on labor productivity. For some aggregated sectors, the estimates have been corrected to account for the difference in structure between France and Rhone-Alpes. In the transportation sector, there are data on internal traffic, but information on the flows of passengers and freight through the region was incomplete. All the data on energy intensiveness were taken from national data. For space heating and hot water heating in the residential and service sectors, data were drawn from Chateau.[3] For the transportation and industrial sectors the data came from the *Centre d'Etudes Regionales sur l'Economie de l'Energie* (CEREN).[4]

---

* When the results of the last census have been analyzed, data on Rhone-Alpes will be much better than they are now.
† An unsuccessful survey was organized by INSEE – Rhone-Alpes to evaluate the value-added of the major economic sectors. It was thwarted because of the centralization of the French economy and because most of the companies in Rhone-Alpes are run from outside of the region – mostly from the Paris area.

TABLE 5.2 Estimated Population, Households, and Working Population for Rhone-Alpes

Year	Population ($\times 10^3$)[a]	Average Growth Rate per Year in Each Period[a]	Number of Households ($\times 10^3$)[a]	Average Number of Persons per Household[a]	Working Population ($\times 10^3$)[a]	Percentage of Working Population in Total Population
1972	4,660 }		1,500	3.1	2,030	44%
1980	5,130 }	1.2%	1,730	3.0	2,160 }	
1985	5,410 }	1.1%	1,870	2.9	2,270 }	42%
1990	5,630 }	0.8%	2,000	2.8	2,300 }	
1995	5,800 }	0.6%	2,150	2.7	2,380 }	41%
2000	5,980 }		2,350	2.7	2,400 }	
2025	6,600 }	0.4%	2,640	2.5	2,640 }	40%

[a] Data based upon INSEE estimates for France up to the year 2000 and corrected so as to take into consideration the particularities of the region; after 2000, as no demographic estimates have been made, a growth rate of 0.4% per year is assumed.

TABLE 5.3 Dynamics of Housing in Rhone-Alpes

Period	Annual Increase of Housing Units[a]	Number of Housing Units Demolished Each Year[b]	Number of Housing Units Built Each Year
1962–1968	23,500	12,700	36,200[c]
1968–1970	25,000	19,200	44,200[c]
1970–1980	28,000	20,000	48,000
1980–1990	27,000	30,000	57,000
1990–2000	25,000	29,000	54,000
2000–2025	13,600	12,400	26,000

[a] See Table 5.1 for the assumptions about housing used in the scenarios.
[b] Until 1970, the number of demolitions is calculated from the number of housing units built and from the number of new households; from 1970 until 1985, we assume the demolition of all substandard, pre-1949 houses; demolition of all 1949–1961 houses is assumed to take place between 1985 and 2000 (houses built after the Second World War and corresponding to very low standards). The necessity of maintaining the activity of the building industry at a high level was taken into consideration (because of the high fraction of total employment in this sector and its importance in the economic growth).
[c] Actual figures according to INSEE.[1]

Up to the year 2000, the scenarios were constructed with the help of studies made of France at the University of Grenoble.[5] For 2000 to 2025, rough extrapolations were made that assumed a slowing of the previous trends.

Two assumptions are shared by all the scenarios.

• Projections of population growth, number of households, and working population (see Table 5.2).
• Projections of number of housing units built and demolished during each period. This implies that the housing policy of the government is identical for all the

TABLE 5.4   Single-Family Housing in Rhone-Alpes by Date of Construction $(\times 10^3)^{a, b}$

	Single-Family Housing Occupied In				
	1970	1980	1990	2000	2025
Pre-1949	915 (51%)[b,c]	715 (51%)	495 (51%)	350 (51%)	250 (51%)
1949–1961	225 (46%)	225 (46%)	145 (46%)		
1962–1970	310 (36%)	310 (36%)	310 (36%)	310 (36%)	150 (36%)
Total pre-1975	1,450 (47%)	1,490 (46%)	1,190 (45%)	900 (44%)	640 (45%)
1975–1980		240	240	240	240
1980–1990			570	570	570
1990–2000				540	540
2000–2025					650
Total post-1975		240	810	1,350	2,000

[a] For the dynamics of housing see Table 5.3.
[b] Percentage of housing that is single houses and percentage that is apartments is drawn from national data[1] (excluding Paris and its metropolitan area) and corrected with the help of estimates for the distribution of current housing in Rhone-Alpes.
[c] Percentage of total number of single-family houses.

scenarios (see Table 5.3). The percentages of pre-1975 and post-1975 housing have been calculated using the assumptions detailed in Table 5.4. These percentages are important because after 1975, all new housing units have to be well insulated to standards close to those of electrically heated housing units.

IV.   BASE CASE SCENARIO

IV.A.   SOCIOECONOMIC ASSUMPTIONS: CONTINUATION OF CURRENT TRENDS

IV.A.1.   Economic Growth

Scenario S1 can be characterized (a) by a slight shift from the heavy industries to the service sector, (b) by a continuing decrease in agricultural activities, and (c) by an increase in light industry activity (at approximately the same rate as the service sector). The contribution of the major economic sectors over time to the GRP is shown in Table 5.5a. Table 5.5b shows annual growth rates of the GRP. Table 5.6 shows the changing distribution of the working population by sector.

IV.A.2.   Urban Growth

Each population density class will grow roughly the same as it grows now; the 6 density classes are 0–2000 inhabitants/km^2, 2000–3,000, 3000–5,000, 5,000–8,000, 8,000–15,000, and more than 15,000. Forty percent of new housing units have been assumed to be single-family houses.

TABLE 5.5a Breakdown of Rhone-Alpes Gross Regional Product by Economic Sector

			1985		2000		2025	
	1968[a]	1971[a]	S1, S2	S3	S1, S2	S3	S1, S2	S3
Agriculture	7%	5%	4%	4%	3.5%	3.5%	3%	2.5%
Industry								
Heavy	51%	10%	9.5%	9%	8%	7.5%	6%	5%
Light		41.5%	42%	39.5%	43.5%	37%	45%	35.5%
Building,								
public works	10%	10%	10%	10%	10%	10%	10%	10%
Service sector	32%	33.5%	34.5%	38%	35%	42%	36%	47%
GRP								
(10^6 francs)[b]		56.4	115	100	215	160	495	290
GRP/capita								
(10^3 francs)		12.3	21.3	18.5	36	27	75	44
GRP/capita								
(10^3 dollars)		2.5	4.4	3.8	7.4	5.5	15.3	9.0

[a] These are estimates (see section III.B. of this chapter).
[b] 1963 francs. $1 = 4.9 francs.

TABLE 5.5b Annual Growth Rates of GRP and GRP/Capita by Period

	1971–85	1985–2000	2025
GRP	5%	4.2%	3.5%
GRP/capita	4%	3.5%	3%

IV.A.3. Transportation

Table 5.7 summarizes the main assumptions used for the Rhone-Alpes freight transportation sector for energy intensiveness, distribution of transportation modes, and total freight demand. For passenger transportation, it is assumed that, as a result of the urban pattern, the number of trips per capita will remain approximately constant. Moreover, it has been assumed that the distribution of cars, mass transit systems, and railways remains constant over time.

IV.B. TECHNOLOGICAL ASSUMPTIONS

IV.B.1. Industrial Sector

The rise in oil prices will have two effects on the energy intensiveness of French industry.

- Electricity will be used instead of other fuels for thermal uses and space heating. Table 5.8 shows the distribution of industrial energy consumption in 1971.

TABLE 5.6   Distribution of Working Population by Economic Sector

	1962	1968	1972	1985		1990		2000		2025	
				S1, S2	S3	S1, S2	S3	S1, S2	S3	S1, S2	S3
Agriculture	18%	12%	9%	6.5%	6.5%[d]	6%	6%[d]	5.5%	5.5%	4.5%	4%
Heavy industries[a]	}36%	6%	5.5%	5%	5%	5%	4%	5%	4%	4%	3%
Light industries[b]		30%	30.5%	31.5%	30.5%	32%	28%	32.5%	26%	34.5%	24%
Building, public works	9.5%	10%	9.5%	9%	9%	9%	9%	9%	9%	9%	9%
Service sector[c]	36.5%	42%	45.5%	48%	49%	48%	53%	48%	55.5%	48%	60%
Total employment (thousands)	1,710	1,819	2,032	2,270		2,300		2,400		2,640	

NOTE: We assumed a slight decrease of the current level of employment in the primary metal industry as well as in the chemical industry, and for the building materials industry a growth rate of employment close to the present trend.
[a] Primary metals, chemicals and building materials industries (energy industries included).
[b] Other than heavy industry, building, and public works.
[c] Commercial, tertiary, and transportation sectors.
[d] The estimate of the working population in agriculture in 1985 is 145,000 persons, after 1985 a slight reduction of working population in this sector has been assumed (120,000 persons by 2025).

TABLE 5.7　Freight Transportation in Rhone-Alpes for Scenario S1

	1970	2000	2025
Fraction of total ton-km by mode of transport			
Rail	.38	.35	.30
Truck	.54	.58	.64
Barge	.08	.07	.06
Energy intensiveness (kcal/ton-km)[a]			
Rail	110	110	110
Truck	710[b]	710	710
Barge	160	160	160
Total energy for freight transport (10^{15} cal)	6	20	37

a From Lapillonne.[2]
b 400 kcal/ton-km for transportation over distances of more than 150 km.

TABLE 5.8　Distribution of the Industrial Energy Consumption in France by Main Processes

	Electrical Uses		Fuel Uses		
Industrial Sector	Lighting and Process Energy (%)	Thermal Processes and Electrolysis (%)	Steam (%)	Direct Uses of Fuel (Furnaces) (%)	Heating (%)
Food industry	97	3	74	13	13
Building material	90	10	5	95	
Primary metals			low[a]	> 90[a]	low
Manufactured goods	60	40	20	43	37
Chemical industry	65	35	50	45	5
Paper	98	2	90	4	6
Miscellaneous	90	10	60	20	20
Percentage of total used by each process	65	35	40	50	10

NOTE: Data are estimated from the CEREN survey of 1971.[4]
a The main consumption is the use of coke in the steel industry; in this sector no substitution for one fuel by another can be envisaged.

●　Energy intensiveness will decrease. The amount of the decrease will vary from sector to sector depending on the importance of energy costs in the production cost and on the distribution of energy consumption among space heat, furnaces, steam, and so on. The distribution among the different processes determines the economic and technological limits on the decrease of energy intensiveness.

In order to calculate the degree to which electricity will be used instead of other fuels, we:

TABLE 5.9   Change Over Time in the Rhone-Alpes Industrial Energy Intensiveness for Scenario S1[a]

	Reduction of Energy Intensiveness (%)		
	1970–1985	1985–2000	2000–2025
Heating (nonelectric)	25	15	0
Furnaces (nonelectric)	10	10	0
Steam	15	15	0

[a] Values for all electric processes for each sector are extrapolated from past trends and vary from one sector to another.

1. Calculated the energy intensiveness by fuel for nonelectric use. Fuels for space heating, all steam generation, and most of the furnaces (the three make up more than 90 percent of the thermal uses) were considered.

2. Evaluated the overall energy intensiveness; all fuels were aggregated in terms of useful energy by considering the efficiency of the fuel in comparison with electricity.

3. Calculated the distribution of this useful energy intensiveness by process. Three processes were considered — space heating, steam, and furnaces. Table 5.8 indicates the values used for each sector.

4. Identified for each sector the market competition between electricity and conventional fuels. It was assumed that this market includes space heating and furnaces.

5. Specified the rate of penetration of electricity into this market: 20 percent in 1985, 50 percent in 2000, and 80 percent in 2025.

6. Calculated the electric and nonelectric intensiveness.

For each process the assumed reductions in energy intensiveness are indicated in Table 5.9.

IV.B.2.   Service Sector

Initial data on energy use in the service sector are shown in Figure 5.3.* The following assumptions have been made:

● Oil and gas heating efficiencies are improved from 60 to 75 percent and from 70 to 80 percent, respectively, by the year 2000.

● The energy use per worker for heating and hot water is assumed to decrease in the following way: 15 percent between 1972 and 1985, 25 percent between 1985 and 2000, and 30 percent thereafter. This reduction can be justified by the consideration of two phenomena: (a) Buildings constructed now are much more

* Data on energy use are from the IEJE study.[5]

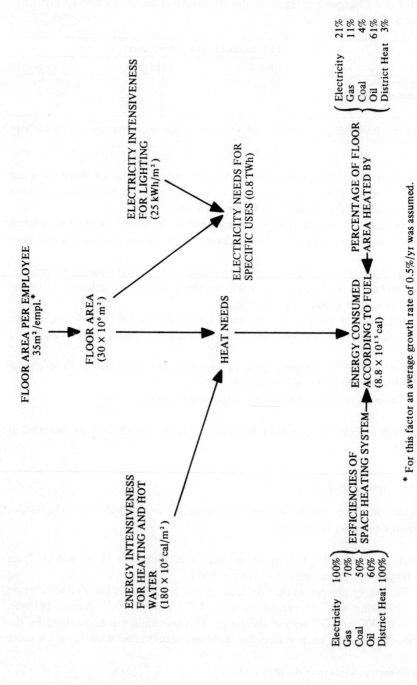

FIGURE 5.3 Energy use in the French service sector (1972) (Source: Chateau and Lapillonne[5]).

FLOOR AREA PER EMPLOYEE
35m²/empl.*

FLOOR AREA
(30 × 10⁶ m²)

ELECTRICITY INTENSIVENESS
FOR LIGHTING
(25 kWh/m²)

ELECTRICITY NEEDS FOR
SPECIFIC USES (0.8 TWh)

HEAT NEEDS

ENERGY INTENSIVENESS
FOR HEATING AND HOT
WATER
(180 × 10⁶ cal/m²)

Electricity   100%
Gas   70%
Coal   50%
Oil   60%
District Heat 100%

EFFICIENCIES OF
SPACE HEATING SYSTEM

ENERGY CONSUMED
ACCORDING TO FUEL
(8.8 × 10¹⁵ cal)

PERCENTAGE OF FLOOR
AREA HEATED BY

Electricity   21%
Gas   11%
Coal   4%
Oil   61%
District Heat 3%

* For this factor an average growth rate of 0.5%/yr was assumed.

132

TABLE 5.10   Fuel Mix in the Service Sector

	Percentage of Floor Area Heated by				Percentage of Floor Area Cooled by Electricity
	Electricity	Gas	Oil	Oil District Heating	
1985	35%	20%	40%	5%	5%
2000	50%	15%	30%	5%	20%
2025	80%	10%	5%	5%	50%

TABLE 5.11   Average Energy Used in Space Heating in France (10^9 cal)

	Pre-1975 Housing Units						Post-1975 Housing Units[d]	
	1970^a		1985^b		2000 and 2025^c		1975–2025	
	Single House	Apartment	Single House	Apartment	Single House	Apartment	Single House	Apartment
Electricity	16.4	9.4	16.4	9.4	16.4	9.4	16.4	9.4
Gas	26.0	15.0	34.0	20.0	32.0	18.8	20.5	11.8
Oil	30.3	17.5	36.4	23.1	34.0	20.0	21.9	12.5
Coal	36.4	21.0						
District Heat^e		10.5		15.0		15.0		9.4
Solar							16.4	

^{a} Data are based upon the following assumptions: average heat requirements of about 14.2 $\times$ 10^9 cal/house (18.2 for single houses and 10.5 for apartments — actual data for France in 1970); average efficiencies for space heating: coal 55%, oil 60%, gas 70%; number of housing units with space heating appliances: 1.1 million (out of 1.4 million).
^{b} All houses are supposed to be equipped with space heating appliances; average heat requirements: 25.5 $\times$ 10^9 cal/yr for a single house and 15.0 $\times$ 10^9 cal/yr for an apartment; average efficiencies: oil 65%; gas 75%.
^{c} Average efficiencies are oil 75% and gas 85%; these are the efficiencies of the most efficient current heating system.
^{d} Housing units to which new insulation standards must be applied. For the specification of these standards, France has been divided into three areas (A, B, C): A, the coldest one, includes mainly two districts, Savoie and Haute-Savoie, plus some mountainous areas in other departements (about 20% of Rhone-Alpes population); all the other places in Rhone-Alpes are in the second area. B. The standards are as follows in terms of the insulation parameter $G \equiv$ kcal/m^3/ h/$^{\circ}$C: area A — single houses ($G = 1.25$), aparments ($G = 0.85$); area B — $G = 1.38$, and 0.90, respectively.
^{e} End-use energy of district heat in the housing units.

energy efficient than old buildings because there is now recovery of some thermal loss from electric lighting and elevators: and (b) the percentage of buildings in the service sector constructed after 1975 increases rapidly from 40 percent in 1985 to 85 percent in 2000.

• Demand for electricity is assumed to increase at a rate of 1.5 percent per year.

The assumptions for the changes over time in the fuel mix for heating and cooling are listed in Table 5.10.

TABLE 5.12   Average Energy Use for Hot Water in France (10^9 cal/yr/household)

Electricity, district heat, and	
solar energy	2.3
Gas	2.9
Oil	3.7
Coal	4.6

SOURCE: Chateau.[3]

TABLE 5.13   Annual Electricity Consumption for Basic Secondary Appliances in Rhone-Alpes (1972)

	Annual Electricity Consumption per Housing Unit[a]	Percentage of Housing Units Owning these Appliances[b]
Refrigerator	350 kWh	85%
Television	300 kWh	74%
Washing machine	100 kWh	69%
Dishwasher	360 kWh	3%

[a] Data based on U.S. consumption estimates for television, washing machine, and dishwasher and checked with the consumption in Rhone-Alpes.
[b] Data from INSEE study.[1]

IV.B.3.   Residential Sector

Table 5.11 shows the change over time in the average energy use for space heating in France by fuel and type of housing unit.* About 77 percent of French households own hot water heaters. The distribution by source of energy was approximately the following in 1972: electricity 23 percent, gas 20 percent, oil 21 percent, coal 10 percent, district heat 3 percent. We assumed that the average energy use for hot water would be 1.5 times higher in 2000 than in 1970 and twice as high in 2025. The current average energy use for hot water in households is indicated in Table 5.12.

Only four secondary "appliances" were considered. Their average consumptions are listed in Table 5.13.

Other electrical energy consumption for lighting, dryers, and so on has been summed and in 1972 was an average of 270 kWh per family. The change over time of total electrical consumption by this category of appliances has been calculated from past trends. Past trends have also been used as a basis for predicting penetration rates of new appliances. Figure 5.4 gives the expected rate for equiping households with these appliances. The form of the curves was taken from observations in more developed countries such as the United States.

* Because no data on "base appliances" (space heaters and hot water heaters) were available for Rhone-Alpes, national data were used from the IEJE study.[5]

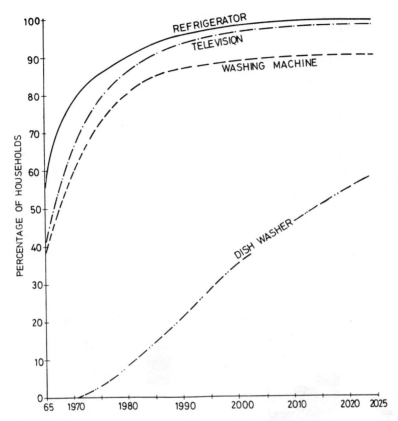

FIGURE 5.4   Evolution of the percentage of households owning major secondary appliances in Rhone-Alpes (Source: INSEE[1] before 1972; later estimates based upon the experience of other countries).

The following assumptions underlie the choice of a fuel mix for space heating and hot water heating in Scenario S1:

- Maximum penetration of electric heating.
- The share of gas increases to about 40 percent of the market in 2025. Now it has 5 percent of the market.
- No pre-1975 housing units could be converted to electric heating because of the very strict insulation standards required for this type of heating, and the difficulties of implementation at a reasonable cost in existing housing units (in 2025, 5 percent of the housing units would be heated using electricity).
- In 1985 all housing units would be equipped with space heating and hot water appliances.

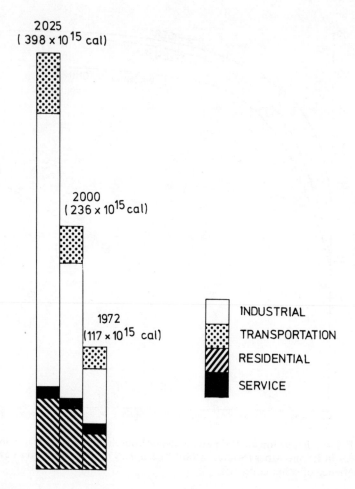

FIGURE 5.5   Distribution of the total end-use energy by sector in Rhone-Alpes (Scenario S1).

type of housing, would be the last ones to be demolished. Consequently, 10 percent of the housing units will be heated by district heat in 2025.

IV.C.   RESULTS FOR SCENARIO S1

IV.C.1.   End-Use Energy

Figures 5.5 and 5.6 show the distribution of the total end-use energy over time by economic sectors and fuel type, respectively, as calculated for S1 by the demand models. These results correspond roughly to an average demand growth rate of 2.3 percent per year (1.7 percent per year per capita). The share of the industrial sector

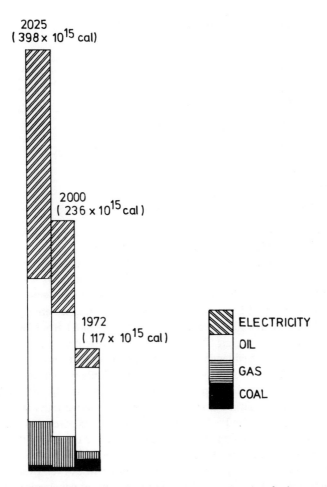

FIGURE 5.6   Distribution of the total end-use energy by fuel types in Rhone-Alpes (Scenario S1).

in the total demand increases very rapidly, since, according to these projections, this sector would account for about 65 percent of the total energy consumption in 2025 (compared with 45 percent currently). The demand of the residential sector decreases from 30 percent to about 15 percent of total demand. This can be easily explained by the combination of two phenomena: (1) the population, which is the driving force behind the residential energy demand, grows slower than the industrial value-added, and (2) a saturation effect of the energy needs seems to appear in the residential sector after 2000.

The latter phenomenon is due to the increase in the number of well-insulated housing units and the saturation of appliances such as televisions, refrigerators, and washing machines between 1985 and 2000 (see Figure 5.4). This is reflected in the

TABLE 5.14   Fuels for Space Heating and Hot Water Heating for Post-1975 Housing Units in Rhone-Alpes (S1 Assumptions)

	1975–1985		1985–2000		2000–2025	
	Single Houses	Apartments	Single Houses	Apartments	Single Houses	Apartments
Electricity	30%	30%	75%	40%	95%	60%
Gas		30%		30%		20%
Oil	70%	40%	20%	25%		5%
Oil district heat				5%		10%
Geothermal district heat						5%
Solar energy			5%		5%	

consumption per capita which only increases from 9.8×10^9 cal in 2000 to 10.4×10^9 cal in 2025. In 1970 it was about 7.0×10^9 cal.

The importance of electricity increases significantly, although in 2025 only 54 percent of the total end-use energy demand is for electricity. It was assumed that decision makers would rapidly reduce dependence on conventional fuels, particularly oil, by replacing them with electricity produced from nuclear energy. But the percentage of electricity in end-use energy only increases in S1 from 16 to 54 percent in approximately 50 years, an illustration of the difficulty of achieving this aim. The reduction of the dependence on oil and gas can only be envisioned over a very long time period. In the change over time of the fuel mix in each sector, two major constraints partly explain this dependence phenomenon. (1) In the residential and service sectors, it was assumed that most of the new housing units would be heated by electricity (Tables 5.10 and 5.14). Nevertheless, only 48 percent of the residential heating demand in 2025 is actually supplied by means of electricity (80 percent for the service sector) because pre-1975 housing units, which were assumed not to be convertible to electric heating, remain in the housing stock even over a long period of time (Table 5.4). (2) In the industrial sector, the rate of penetration of electricity is constrained by the size of the market because electricity cannot replace conventional fuels used in industrial furnaces and space heating, for example.

IV.C.2.   Environmental Impacts

The following discussion will deal only with impacts from nuclear energy since Scenario S1 is based primarily on the use of nuclear energy. The evaluation of nuclear impacts raises some difficulties, because some important ones are unquantified (e.g. aesthetic impacts of high cooling towers or wide transmission line corridors, the risk of theft of radioactive products), or because others are not well known and hence very often debated. Special care has therefore been taken to avoid the aggregation of impacts about which knowledge is uncertain. The importance of each impact that is described is left to the judgment of the reader.

Number of sites   The nuclear capacity can be calculated from the level of electricity generation (95×10^9 kWh and 255×10^9 kWh in 2000 and 2025 and from the average load factor of all the nuclear plants. The latter factor is difficult to evaluate because it depends on technical considerations (improvements in reactor availability) and on the structure of the load curve of electricity demand. As a basis, we have assumed an average capacity factor of 60 percent to account for the fact that all these plants could not be used for the base load. Hence the nuclear capacity would be about 18,000 MWe in 2000 and 48,500 MWe in 2025 (15,500 MWe and 42,000 MWe if a 70 percent capacity factor was assumed).

Although currently four to six 900 MWe reactors are constructed on each site, 1,200 MWe light water reactors are expected to be used before 1980. The fast breeder reactor now under construction will have a capacity of 1,200 MWe. If 1,200 MWe reactors are used, Rhone-Alpes would have 4 or 5 sites in 2000.* The number of sites in 2025 will depend on the strategy followed by EDF. If the capacity on each site is 5,000 MWe, then 4 new sites would have to be constructed between 2000 and 2025. If 10,000 MWe sites are developed, then the initial 5 sites would be enough.

The latter strategy would avoid the public opposition to the opening of new sites, reduce the number of radioactive shipments and hence the risk of theft, and take advantage of economies of scale. But some environmental impacts would be greater. For example, thermal pollution would be very concentrated. The characteristics of the nuclear potential in 2025 are summarized below.

- Capacity in 2025: 42,000 MWe (70 percent load factor) to 48,500 MWe (60 percent load factor)
- Number of sites: 9 sites of about 5,000 MWe or 4–5 sites of about 10,000 MWe
- Percentage of light water reactors (LWR) in 2025: 60 percent (fast breeder reactor: 40 percent)

Thermal Discharges   Only once-through cooling and wet cooling towers were considered as cooling techniques for nuclear power plants in Rhone-Alpes. Once-through cooling was assumed to be limited by a maximum permissible increase of Rhone River temperature (ΔT) under unfavorable conditions: minimum flow in a dry year and minimum natural cooling. Table 5.15 shows the possibilities for the disposal of waste heat for two control policies. The resultant water evaporation has also been included.

Figure 5.7 shows the probability density functions of a ΔT increase in the river water temperature at the southern border of the region by seasons if the less restrictive standard applies. (See Chapter 3, section IV.D.5 for the method of calculation.) This figure shows that, in the south of the region, the normal temperature of the Rhone river increases 5°C during 50 to 60 days per year and 4°C during about 140

---

* Bugey, Tricastin, St-Maurice-l'Exil, Arras, Soyons, Cruas. See Figure 5.2 for location of these sites.

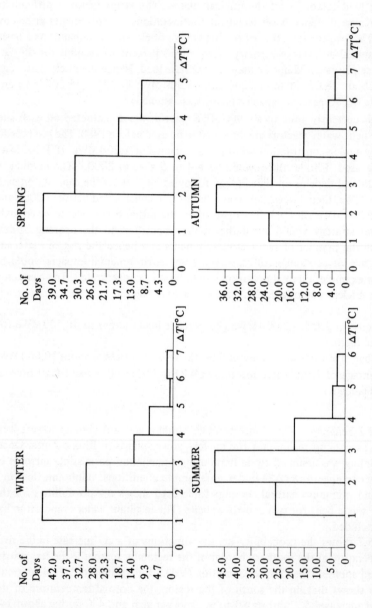

FIGURE 5.7   Probability density function of a ΔT increase of the river temperature at the southern border of the Rhone-Alpes region.

TABLE 5.15 Cooling System Requirements in Rhone-Alpes for Scenario S1 in 2025

	Maximum Waste Heat Dischargeable into Rhone River (Gigawatts)	Percentage of Nuclear Capacity Using Once-Through Cooling[b]	Water Evaporated Artificially (m^3/sec)[c]
Low control ($\Delta T \leqslant 5°C$)[a]	21	41	15
High control ($\Delta T \leqslant 3°C$)[a]	14	27	18

[a] ΔT is used here instead of a maximum permissible temperature T_{max} of the Rhone River because the limitation by a maximum permissible temperature is not very reasonable. With hybrid cooling the water temperature could be close to T_{max} throughout the year, which would affect the aquatic flora and fauna that are adapted to an annual temperature cycle.
[b] The remaining capacity uses cooling towers.
[c] From cooling towers and heated surfaces of water bodies. The average flow of the Rhone is about 1,100 m^3/sec in the south of Lyon (recorded minimum: 200 m^3/sec; average yearly minimum: 700 m^3/sec) and 500 m^3/sec in the north.

days per year. Nevertheless, it is clear that the average temperature increase below each nuclear site is higher, since the above figures account for some dilution of the waste heat in the river.

The limitation on the temperature increase of the Rhone River requires the utilization of closed-cycle cooling systems. In this study only wet cooling towers were considered. The cooling of a light water reactor of 1,000 MWe requires a tower approximately 150 m high with a diameter between 120 and 140 m in the case of natural draft systems.[10] According to the level of control of thermal discharges (high or low; see Table 5.15), the number of such towers would be between 28 and 34 in 2025, corresponding to an average of 3 towers on each site (considering a 5,000 MWe site). In the case of 10,000 MWe about 6 or 7 such towers would be needed on each site. In the case of mechanical draft systems, the towers are smaller, but each 1,200 MWe reactor requires 2 towers 30 to 50 meters high.[11]

Each light water reactor cooled with a wet cooling tower causes an evaporation of approximately 0.8 m^3/sec.* Some water containing salt and chemicals is discharged into the river (blow-down water discharge of about 0.8 m^3/sec). Because of the heat discharged into the atmosphere (1.7×10^{12} cal/h/tower), these cooling towers may induce climatic perturbations (artificial rain, modification of the local insolation, or increase of foggy days). These impacts were not quantified because of the very site-specific nature of the impacts and the detailed analysis required for their quantification.

Table 5.16 shows the amount of water evaporated by cooling towers at typical sites. Once-through cooling causes about 25 percent less evaporation than natural draft wet cooling towers.

* Average of U.S.[8,9] and French[7] data for a 1,000 MWe reactor. For comparison, the average annual volume of water flowing in the Rhone at Bugey is 10^9 m^3/yr.

TABLE 5.16   Water Evaporated by Cooling Towers at Typical Nuclear Sites

Site Type	Capacity Cooled with Wet Cooling Tower	Water Evaporated by Cooling Towers	
		m^3/sec^a	$10^6 \, m^3/yr$
5,000 MWe	Low control 3,000 MWe	2.4	45
	High control 4,000 MWe	3.2	60
10,000 MWe	Low control 6,000 MWe	4.8	91
	High control 7,000 MWe	5.6	106

a The assumption was made that the reactors operate at full power and that $0.8 \, m^3/sec$ evaporates per 1,000 MWe reactor.

Right-of-Way for Transmission Lines   For each 5,000 MWe site, a corridor 200 m wide would be necessary to "evacuate" the electricity generated.[10] If the average capacity at a site were 10,000 MWe, the width of the transmission corridors would be 500 m representing a very intensive network of wires and pylons. (The total corridor is actually divided into 4 or 5 smaller corridors.)

Land Use   The land used for reactor sites in the Base Case is 55 km^2 in 2000 and 150 km^2 in 2025. It was assumed that each 1,000 MWe reactor uses about 3 km^2, regardless of the number of reactors on a site.[9,10] A large part of Rhone-Alpes is covered by the Alps, a part of the Jura, and the Massif Central, so the land used for reactors is not insignificant. Nuclear sites in 2025 will occupy approximately one quarter of the area in Rhone-Alpes on which buildings are standing in 1970. Part of this land for reactor sites is a long-term commitment, since it will be set aside when the reactors are no longer in service. From 5.3 to 7.3 km^2 in Rhone-Alpes, 50 to 70 km^2 at the national level, will be set aside for retired reactors and will be occupied for a very long time.

Table 5.17 indicates the annual and cumulative land use in 2025 for uranium mining and radioactive waste storage. The land disturbed for the nuclear fuel supply of all power plants from 1970 to 2025 is about 40 percent of the land occupied by the power plants themselves. There is no uranium in Rhone-Alpes, so the mining is outside the region and probably outside of France. At the national level, about 25 km^2 will be used for radioactive waste and, like the land used for retired reactors, it will not be available for other uses for a long time.

Annual Radioactive Shipments from Power Plants to Reprocessing Plants   The only reprocessing plant in France is located on Cape La Hague, about 1,000 km from the Rhone-Alpes plants. It seems difficult, from both technical and environmental considerations, to locate another reprocessing plant near Rhone-Alpes, or even in another part of France. It has therefore been assumed that all additional reprocessing plants would be located near the existing one. Calculations based on the Impact Model,[9,10] show that 50 percent of the radioactive shipments would be by train at a

TABLE 5.17   Land Associated with Nuclear Energy Use in Rhone-Alpes for Scenario S1

	2025	Cumulative Requirements 1970–2025
Surface mining (km²)[a]	1.5	35
Radioactive waste storage (km²)[b]	0.1	2.5
Retired reactors (km²)[c]		
18 Reactors (25-yr lifetime)	7.3	
13 Reactors (30-yr lifetime)	5.3	

NOTE: Figures are based on the Environmental Impact Model.[9,10]
[a] Assumes 100% of uranium from surface mining, with an ore grade of 0.2%. Mining of very low-grade ores would increase the total land disturbed. No reclamation has been assumed.
[b] All types of wastes: low level (such as packaging) through high level.
[c] Assumes 0.4 km²/reactor.

TABLE 5.18   Impacts Associated with Electricity Generated by Nuclear Plants in 2025 for Scenario S1

	65% Surface Mining	100% Surface Mining
Accidents (PDL)[a]	13,000	5,500
Health (PDL)	2,500	

[a] 1 PDL ≡ one person-day lost (6,000 PDL are equivalent to 1 death).

rate of 3.0 tons of fuel per shipment, and fifty percent would be by truck at 0.5 tons of fuel per shipment. The number of shipments in 2000 and 2025 would be 471 and 1,250.

Health Impacts from Uranium Mining   These impacts depend heavily on how much of the mining is underground and how much is on the surface. The impacts from uranium mining associated with electricity are listed in Table 5.18. The cumulative quantified impacts of the nuclear energy program from 1970 to 2025 show that 1,600,000 person days would be lost if 65 percent of the uranium mining were done on the surface. If all the uranium mining were done on the surface, 15 percent fewer person days, 1,350,000, would be lost. Approximately 75 percent of these PDL are occupational impacts and the remaining 25 percent are public impacts.

Selected quantified impacts, including those caused by sources other than nuclear energy, are listed in the scenario comparison section that follows. But since the consumption of conventional fuel is small, a significant share of these impacts has to be associated with nuclear energy.

V.   OTHER SCENARIOS

The major socioeconomic assumptions for the three scenarios have already been mentioned (see Tables 5.1 to 5.6). Therefore only the technological assumptions will be described here, usually in relation to the Base Case.

TABLE 5.19   Reduction in Intensiveness for Nonelectric Industrial Energy Use in Scenario S3 (%)

	1970–1985	1985–2000	2000–2025
Heating	35	15	0
Furnaces	15	10	0
Steam	25	20	0

TABLE 5.20   Fuels used for Space Heating and Cooling in the Rhone-Alpes Service Sector

| | Percentage of Total Floor Area Heated | | | | | | | | |
| | 1985 | | | 2000 | | | 2025 | | |
	S1	S2	S3	S1	S2	S3	S1	S2	S3
Electricity	35	15	15	50	10	12	80	5	10
Gas	20	30	35	15	40	45	10	45	60
Oil	40	50	40	30	45	25	5	30	10
District heating	5	5	10	5	5	18	5	20	20
Percentage of floor area cooled	5	5	5	20	20	10	50	50	25

NOTE: In S3, solar substitutes in part for each heating fuel.

V.A.   TECHNOLOGICAL ASSUMPTIONS

V.A.1.   Industrial Sector

The penetration of electricity into the industrial sector is the same for S2 and S3: 5 percent in 1985, 15 percent in 2000, 30 percent in 2025. The reduction of energy intensiveness for nonelectric use in S2 is slightly lower than in S1. For S3 see Table 5.19.

V.A.2.   Service Sector

Energy use per employee in the service sector is slightly higher for S2 than for S1. For S3 it is assumed that the energy efficiency for space heating or hot water heating could be improved by the addition of solar collectors with a resultant dramatic decrease in end-use energy of 30 percent between 1972 and 1985, 45 percent between 1985 and 2000, and 30 percent thereafter. For the fuels used in space heating and cooling, see Table 5.20.

V.A.3.   Residential Sector

Space heating uses the same amount of energy for all the scenarios. The current insulation standards are already very stringent and cannot be increased significantly because the marginal cost of investment to improve insulation is very high compared

TABLE 5.21   Energy Sources Assumed for Space Heating in Housing Constructed After 1975 in Rhone-Alpes

	1975–1985				1985–2000			
	Single Houses		Apartments		Single Houses		Apartments	
	S2	S3	S2	S3	S2	S3	S2	S3
Electricity	5%	5%	5%		15%	5%	15%	
Gas			40%	35%			35%	15%
Oil	95%	90%	50%	35%	80%	65%	30%	15%
Oil district heat			5%	22%			15%	25%
Geothermal heat[a]				8%			5%	15%
Solar energy		5%			5%	30%		30%
	2000–2010				2010–2025			
	Single Houses		Apartments		Single Houses		Apartments	
	S2	S3	S2	S3	S2	S3	S2	S3
Electricity	30%		20%		30%		20%	
Gas			20%				20%	
Oil	55%	25%	10%		45%	25%	10%	
Oil district heat			35%	10%			30%	
Geothermal heat[a]			15%	30%			20%	30%
Solar energy	15%	75%		60%	25%	75%		70%

NOTE: Percentage of single houses: S2 − 80%, S3 − 20%.
[a] In S3 it has been estimated that about 30% of the new flats built between 1975 and 1985 would be located above geothermal fields, 30% in the period between 1985 and 2000, and 60% thereafter.

with the marginal fuel savings. For the energy sources for space heating, see Table 5.21.

The assumptions about hot water heating for S2 are the same as for S1. For S3, there is a small increase in consumption over that of 1970.

V.A.4.   Transportation Sector

Freight Transportation   Freight transportation in S2 is the same as in S1. In S3 there is a shift from trucks (53 percent of the traffic in 1970) to railways (37 percent) and barges (10 percent). It has been assumed that the truck traffic will stay constant after 1985, resulting in an increase of the percentage of freight carried by train to 60 percent in 2000 and 65 percent in 2025, and a corresponding decrease in the percentage for trucks to 30 percent and 25 percent. Moreover, a 20 percent increase in the energy efficiency of trucks has been assumed. Consumption of motor fuel drops from 710 kcal/ton, which is the S1 average, to 600 kcal/ton.

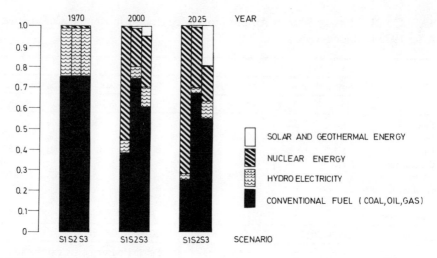

FIGURE 5.8   Primary energy use: the fraction of different energy sources used for the three Rhone-Alpes scenarios.

Passenger Transportation   For S2 and S3 the effects of the changing urban pattern on the transport demand per capita were based on American studies (see the assumptions made for Wisconsin in Chapter 6, section III.C.6.). In addition, an increase in the efficiency of cars and a shift to mass transit systems have been assumed for S3.

V.A.5.   Energy Supply Sector

For electricity generation, in S2 there will be a mix of oil, coal, and nuclear energy. For S3 there will be an increase of the hydroelectric capacity. There will be no construction of new nuclear plants, but the plants already built or under construction will be used. Solar electricity plants will be developed after 1990 and will provide 1 gigawatt electric (GWe) peak power in 2000. In 2025 they will provide 13 GWe peak power or 4 GWe average power (the power produced if the plant were running all year) and generate 35×10^9 kWh per year. A mix of oil and coal will supply the rest of the demand.

V.B.   ENERGY SUPPLY AND END-USE ENERGY CONSUMPTION

V.B.1.   Primary Energy

The change over time of the distribution of primary energy consumption by energy source in the three scenarios is displayed in Figure 5.8. In Scenario S1, the penetration of nuclear energy is clearly the highest and seems the maximum feasible because of requirements for conventional fuels for cars and trucks and in some industrial processes. Even with very favorable assumptions about the rate of development

TABLE 5.22   Primary Energy Consumption in Rhone-Alpes for the Three Scenarios (10^{15} cal/yr)[a]

	Coal	Gas	Oil	Hydroelectricity	Nuclear Energy	Geothermal Energy	Solar Energy	Total
2000								
S1	14 (11)	29	130 (11)	25 (25 TWh)[b]	252 (95 TWh)			450
S2	47 (44)	38	215 (44)	25 (25 TWh)	80 (30 TWh)			405
S3	29 (26)	38	135 (26)	35 (35 TWh)	80 (30 TWh)	4	14 (3 TWh + 7 × 10^{15} cal)	339
2025								
S1	25 (22)	44	159 (22)	25 (25 TWh)	645 (255 TWh)	1.5	0.5	900
S2	113 (110)	73.5	375 (110)	25 (25 TWh)	265 (100 TWh)	1.5	2	855
S3	68 (65)	100 (55)	149 (65)	35 (35 TWh)	80 (30 TWh)	7.0	83 (35 TWh + 11 × 10^{15} cal)	522

[a] For coal and oil, the numbers in parentheses represent the quantity of fuel used for electricity generation.
[b] TWh $\equiv$ terawatt hour.

147

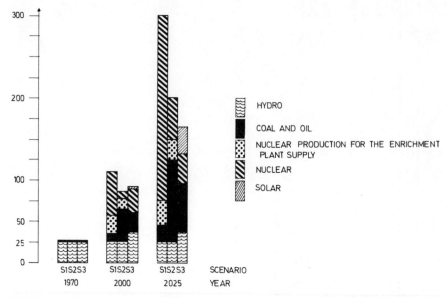

FIGURE 5.9 Fuel mix for electricity generation for the three Rhone-Alpes scenarios.

of new energy sources (solar and geothermal energy), their contribution to the total primary energy is rather limited — no more than 20 percent after a 50-year period. For Scenario S2, the important conventional fuel requirements will have to be supplied with imports. Table 5.22 indicates primary energy consumption by energy source and scenario. In 2025, the total primary energy consumption is almost twice as high in the highest cases (S1 and S2) as in the lowest case (S3). Energy consumption is very sensitive to policy option. The fuel mix for electricity generation in the three scenarios is displayed in Figure 5.9.

V.B.2.   End-Use Energy

The change over time of the total end-use energy per capita is displayed in Figure 5.10. Scenario S2 has the highest final consumption, which is consistent with the assumptions made for this scenario (more single housing units, urban patterns requiring more transportation, high energy intensiveness). In S3, despite the drastic energy conservation policy there is still growth of end-use energy per capita mainly because of the energy requirements of the industrial and service sectors.

The energy use per capita in the residential sector is graphed in Figure 5.11. The decrease of the final energy consumption in S3 is a result of the increase in the housing stock of the percentage of apartments, whose energy requirements are lower than single houses. In addition, electric and district heating are used, which are very

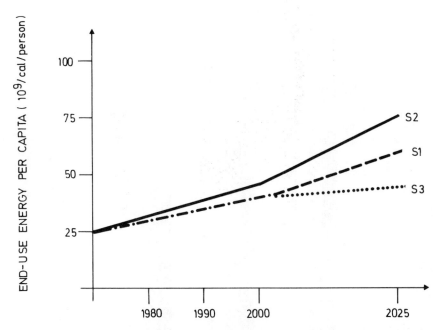

FIGURE 5.10   Total end-use energy per capita for the three Rhone-Alpes scenarios.

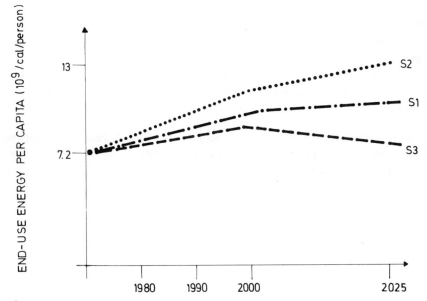

FIGURE 5.11   End-use energy use per capita in the residential sector for the three Rhone-Alpes scenarios.

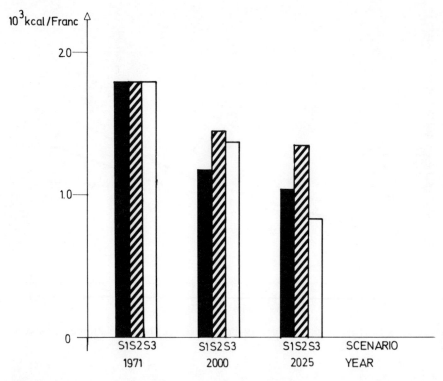

FIGURE 5.12   Energy intensiveness in the industrial sector for the three Rhone-Alpes scenarios.

efficient. The values plotted in Figure 5.11 correspond to the end-use process, for which electric and district heating are 100 percent efficient. A corresponding curve for primary energy per capita would be different because of energy losses before end use.

Energy intensiveness in the industrial sector is displayed in Figure 5.12, personal transportation energy use per capita in Figure 5.13, and energy use in freight transportation in Figure 5.14. No comments are necessary since these figures illustrate clearly the assumptions underlying the scenarios.

V.B.3.   Environmental Impacts

Three impacts have been selected to characterize the environmental consequences associated with each scenario. The quantification of these impacts was achieved by means of the impact model described in Chapter 3, section IV.D.5. Other impacts could be presented, but, in order to simplify the presentation of the results, we restricted the scenario comparison to

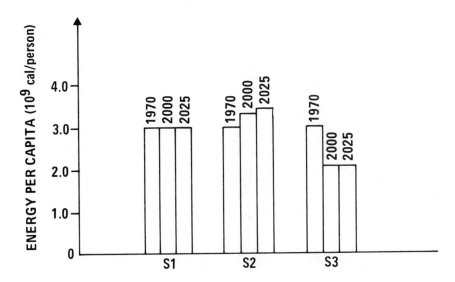

FIGURE 5.13   Personal transportation energy use per capita for the three Rhone-Alpes scenarios.

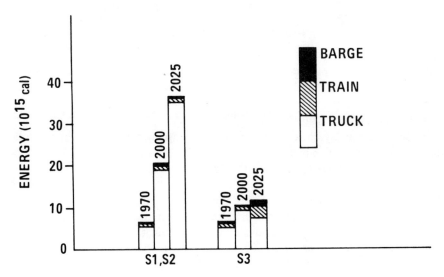

FIGURE 5.14   Energy use by freight transportation for the three Rhone-Alpes scenarios.

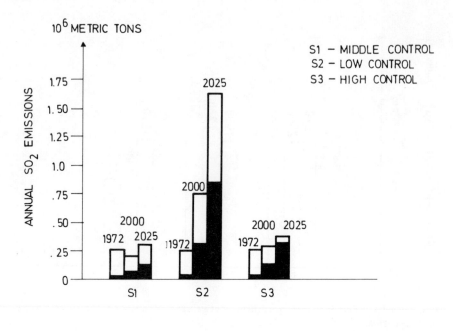

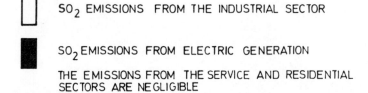

FIGURE 5.15   Comparison of the total SO_2 emissions for the three Rhone-Alpes scenarios.

- SO_2 emissions (Figure 5.15)
- Total person-days lost (Figure 5.16) as an aggregated measure of the total unquantified impact on human health
- Land use for energy generation (Table 5.23)

Table 5.24 summarizes all the quantified impacts.

If we only consider the first two impacts, the second scenario, which assumes a low level of nuclear energy development and a continuation of the use of conventional fuel, has the highest environmental impact. In the case of Scenario S1, in which there is a rapid development of nuclear energy, the total PDL in 2025 is about 215,000. This is roughly equivalent to 36 fatalities, if all PDL were from fatalities, and might appear to be too small an estimate to individuals opposed to

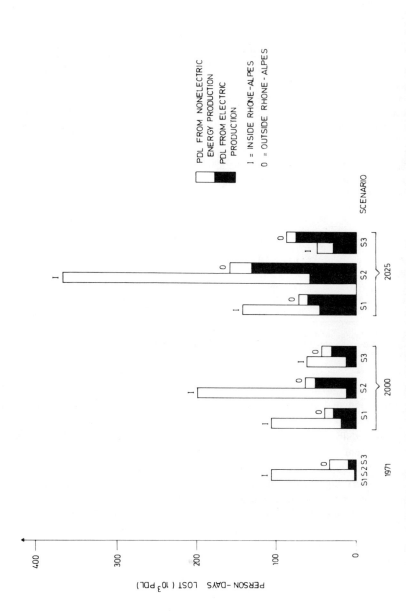

FIGURE 5.16 Total quantified person-days lost (PDL) for the three Rhone-Alpes scenarios. (Note: Air pollution health impact from nonelectric energy use is calculated using a different SO$_2$ removal policy in each of the scenarios.)

TABLE 5.23   Annual and Cumulative Land Use Associated with Energy Production in Rhone-Alpes

	Facilities (km²)	Resource Extraction (km²)[a]		Total (km²)	
S1	2025	2025	1970–2025	2025	1970–2025
Electricity (nuclear energy)	154.0	1.5	49.0	155.6	203.0
Electricity (coal)	3.2	3.0	79.0	6.2	82.0
Electricity (oil)	2.9	0.5	0.5	3.4	3.4
Nonelectrical energy	2.8	4.0	4.0	6.8	6.8
Total	162.9	9.0	132.5	172.0	295.0
S2					
Electricity (nuclear energy)	60.0	0.8	21.0	60.8	81.0
Electricity (coal)	16.0	15.4	352.0	31.4	368.0
Electricity (oil)	14.0	2.7	2.7	16.7	16.7
Nonelectrical energy	5.0	7.1	7.1	12.1	12.1
Total	95.0	26.0	382.8	121.0	477.8
S3					
Electricity (nuclear energy)	18.0	0.3	12.0	18.3	30.0
Electricity (coal)	10.0	10.0	205.0	20.0	215.0
Electricity (solar)	200.0			200.0	200.0
Electricity (oil)	9.0	2.0	2.0	11.0	11.0
Nonelectrical energy	2.0	2.0	2.0	4.0	4.0
Total	239.0	14.3	221.0	253.3	460.0

SOURCE: Buehring,[9] and Buehring and Foell.[10]
[a] Surface uranium mining and surface coal mining exclusively; extraction occurs both inside and outside the region; no reclamation.

nuclear energy who emphasize its unlikely but dangerous risks. Not all impacts have been quantified in terms of human health because of lack of information about some of them, and above all because there is divergent opinion among experts about others. The nuclear health impact calculations utilize the Rasmussen report[11] for reactor accidents and the linear dose–response relationships used by the U.S. National Academy of Sciences for routine exposures.[12]

S2 has a very high health impact because of SO_2 emissions. It was not based on stringent environmental conservation policies. SO_2 emissions for S2 in 2025 are about 1.7×10^6 tons, which is more than 60 percent of emissions for France in 1970. SO_2 emission at the national level in 1970 was 2.9×10^6 tons, of which the Rhone-Alpes region contributed 8 percent.[15] In 1970 in France, electricity generation was only responsible for 20 percent of the total emission. In Scenario S2 in 2025, the percentage of emission from electricity generation is almost half the total emission from Rhone-Alpes. In all of France, this scenario would produce a total SO_2 emission of about 20×10^6 tons in 2025 – a factor of 8 larger than the current emission levels.

Because of the large land requirements for solar electricity generation, S3 uses the most land of all the scenarios. Land use for S3 is 50 percent higher than for S1 in

TABLE 5.24   Scenario Comparison of Selected Quantified Environmental Impacts

	1970	2025 S1	S2	S3
Inside Rhone-Alpes				
Health impacts				
Total fatalities		6	6	2
Occupational accidents (PDL)[a]	1,100	13,000	9,500	7,200
Accidents affecting the public				
(PDL)		1,300	4,600	2,800
Occupational health (PDL)		24,000	9,300	2,800
Public health	100,000	100,000	340,000	43,000
Land use (km^2)				
Facilities land use	1	150	87	240
Long-term commitment	0	0.7	0.3	0.1
Air pollution				
SO$_2$ Emissions (10^6 metric tons)	0.25	0.30	1.7	0.35
CO$_2$ Emissions (10^6 metric tons)	26.0	57.0	130.0	88.0
Outside Rhone-Alpes				
Health Impacts				
Total fatalities	4.6	9	17	9
Accidents and health impacts				
(PDL)	33,000	74,000	150,000	88,000
Land use				
Resources extractions and				
related facilities (km^2)	5	19	34	16
Total				
Fatalities	5	15	23	11
Health (PDL)	140,000	210,000	510,000	140,000
Land (km^2)	6	170	120	250

NOTE: Impacts due to electricity generation and end-use energy consumption are calculated from the Impact Model.[9,10] All figures are rounded.
[a] PDL ≡ person-days lost.

2025. For comparison with the land use figures in Table 5.24, see the comments on land use in the Base Case in section IV.C.2.

With regard to cumulative land use from 1970 to 2025, S1 requires much less land than S3. But if we change Scenario S3 so that the coal used to produce electricity is replaced by gas or oil, for example, than S3 requires only 250 km^2. S1 requires 295 km^2. In the nuclear energy scenario, however, about 70 percent of the land is disturbed outside the region, whereas the solar energy scenario uses a huge area within the region. Moreover, some of the land disturbed for uranium mining can be reclaimed.

All these comments show that the land use for each scenario depends on a great number of factors and that in each case the assumptions underlying the figures for land use should be carefully considered.

VI.   SENSITIVITY STUDIES

Two variants of the Base Case have been selected to show the influence of changes in the energy supply on the environmental impacts.

$S1_L$: Little development of fast breeder reactors. In the Base Case, 40 percent of the electrical capacity in 2025 is from fast breeder reactors. In this sensitivity study, only 10 percent is from fast breeder reactors in order to show the difference between light water reactors and fast breeder reactors from an environmental standpoint.

$S1_H$: Development of hybrid reactors producing electricity, and hot water or steam. Since hybrid reactors have little waste heat and high efficiency, fewer hybrid reactors than fast breeder reactors would be required to supply energy demands. Hybrid reactors can supply heat either by way of the electricity they produce or by way of district heat. This analysis shows the sensitivity of selected environmental impacts to district heating from nuclear energy as compared with heating with electricity from nuclear energy. The analysis does not take into account the economic feasibility of the hybrid reactors.

The assumptions made about the technical characteristics of the hybrid reactor, as well as about the integration of these reactors into the total energy supply system (number of housing units that can be supplied, storage requirements, and so forth) are based on the preliminary research of B. Bourgeois and B. Chateau.[13] The potential market for district heating from nuclear energy was roughly calculated from the investigations carried out for Scenarios S2 and S3. It was assumed that 30 percent of the industrial and residential heat demand could be supplied by nuclear district heat and that 40 percent of the floor area in the service sector could be heated by nuclear district heat. The total consumption of nuclear district heat would then be 90×10^{15} cal.

In summary, the energy supply of Rhone-Alpes in this sensitivity study has:

- An electricity production of 190×10^9 kWh instead of 225×10^9 kWh as in S1
- Fifteen hybrid reactors producing 90×10^{15} cal and 70×10^9 kWh. The study by Bourgeois and Chateau[13] refers to a standard 900 MWe reactor where 20 percent of the heat produced is withdrawn to supply district heat. The real electric capacity is then 720 MWe. Each hybrid power plant could supply the needs of about 340,000 housing units.
- A 20 percent reduction of oil consumption by industry. Some of the oil used for steam generation is replaced by nuclear heat.
- A total nuclear capacity of 39,500 MWe, of which 10 percent is supplied by breeder reactors

Table 5.25 shows selected impacts for S1 and its two variants. With regard to $S1_L$, the reduction in the penetration of the liquid metal fast breeder reactor (LMFBR) and the corresponding increase in the pressurized water reactor (PWR) capacity, with everything else held constant, does not really affect the quantified

TABLE 5.25   Comparison of Environmental Impacts for Three Nuclear Development Variants in 2025.

	S1 – 2025[a]	S1$_H$ – 2025[b]	S1$_L$ – 2025[c]
Impacts from nuclear power			
Annual global health impact[d]			
Person-rem to public	12,000	11,900	14,600
Expected excess cancer deaths	2.2	2.1	2.6
Expected excess genetic effects	1.8	1.8	2.2
Total annual public fatalities (health and accident)	3.2	2.9	3.6
Uranium miners (annual impact)			
Accidental fatalities	1.7	2.1	0.6
Excess cancers	0.4	0.5	0.6
Total annual occupational fatalities (Health and Accident)	7.9	7.4	9.1
Total quantified person-days lost (annual)	75,100	70,000	86,100
Thermal discharge			
Annual heat discharge to condenser water (10^{12} kWht)	0.49	0.40	0.53
Annual water evaporated (10^6 m³)	564	457	614
Annual land use for mining and milling of uranium (km²)	1.0	1.2	1.5
Annual radioactive shipments	6,700	4,820	5,920
Shipments of plutonium and high level waste	152	52	64
Radioactive cesium released as liquid waste at reactors[e] (Ci/yr)	11.4	14.1	17.3
Electricity needed for gaseous diffusion to supply fuel for PWR[f] (10^9 kWh/yr)	6.9	8.5	10.4
Nonelectric impacts			
Health impacts (PDL)	87,500	67,500	87,500

NOTE: Figures are based on the Impact Model.[9,10]
[a] S1: Development of fast breeders (40% of the total electric capacity).
[b] S1$_H$: Development of nuclear district heating.
[c] S1$_L$: Low penetration of fast breeders (10% of the total electric capacity).
[d] Only global doses from complete release of ^{85}Kr and ^{3}H at reprocessing are included.
[e] Radioactive strontium releases are much lower than cesium.
[f] Pu produced at pressurized water reactors (PWRs) is not taken into account.

health and safety impacts. There is a slight increase of the total person-days lost from 75,000 to 86,000 mainly because of public exposure to radioactivity and because of uranium mining. The total quantity of water evaporated increases by less than 10 percent. However the annual land use for uranium mining is 50 percent higher than in S1 and the annual quantity of radioactive cesium released by the reactors is more than 50 percent higher. The limitation on the development of breeder reactors yields a 60 percent decrease in the annual shipments of plutonium and highly radioactive waste.

All the conclusions about the differences between the environmental consequences of S1 and $S1_L$ are uncertain and above all subjective. Some impacts of $S1_L$
may be less severe than those of S1, but others may be more severe and more
important, and outweigh those that were less severe.

In relation to S1, $S1_H$ leads to a

- 20 percent decrease in the total health impacts (from nuclear and nonelectric use)
- 25 percent decrease in the annual quantity of water evaporated, and of the total waste heat rejected, which means fewer climatic impacts and less water drawn from the regional resources
- 20 percent decrease in the land disturbed by uranium mining
- 20 percent decrease in the annual radioactive shipments
- 20 percent reduction of the radioactive cesium released as a liquid waste

These sensitivity studies show that the environmental impacts of the hybrid
reactors are less severe than those of the fast breeder reactor. Even if it is more
economical to heat with electricity produced from nuclear reactors than to heat
with nuclear district heat, the low social cost of nuclear district heating must also
be taken into account.

VII.   CONCLUSIONS

The following comments and observations do not apply just to Rhone-Alpes. Rather,
they are more characteristic of the energy strategies than of the region.

VII.A.   ENERGY DEMAND

Each of the alternative futures has a different level of energy use. For a given growth
rate of the GNP, the level of energy demand will depend on the nature of the economic growth.* Therefore, since the energy consumption of a region does not have a
linear relationship with GNP or any other macroeconomic indicator, forecasts of
energy consumption should be based on detailed investigations of the technological
and societal changes and the main political options (human settlement policy, transportation policy, industrial policy, and so on.

VII.B   DEPENDENCE ON OIL

Most countries are trying to develop nuclear energy as fast as possible to reduce
their dependence on oil, and France is one of the countries trying the hardest. But

---

* Energy Policy Project of the Ford Foundation, *A Time to Choose: America's Energy Future*
(Cambridge, Massachusetts: Ballinger, 1974).

Scenario S1, the nuclear energy scenario, shows that dependence on oil cannot be reduced significantly or as fast as might be expected. The rate of penetration of electricity from nuclear plants is constrained by the time needed for installation of electrical end-use equipment and by the rate of increase in demand for electrical end-use energy. At the upper limit, only about 50 to 60 percent of end-use energy demand is for electricity. Electricity cannot yet be economically used in place of motor fuels, in steam production, or in some large capacity kilns, for example. Obviously, technological innovations may raise the limit on electrical end-use energy. A drastic reduction of oil consumption through the development of nuclear energy can only be achieved by using nuclear energy to produce other sources of energy such as hydrogen, hot water, or steam.

VII.C. RATE OF DEVELOPMENT OF NEW ENERGY SOURCES

For similar reasons, though on a different scale, the rate of penetration of solar and geothermal energy is very slow. In Scenario S3, which has very favorable assumptions about the development of these two energy sources, their contribution to the total end-use energy is not more than 20 percent after a 50-year period.

VII.D. ENVIRONMENTAL IMPACTS

Based on the judgment of the IIASA team, the most significant environmental impacts have been selected. But it is certain that some impacts have been neglected or that too much emphasis has been placed on others. Unlike the description and interpretation of energy patterns, the evaluation of environmental impacts is very controversial. We will try to summarize the important results for four major impacts considered in this study: waste heat, land use, SO_2 emissions, and human health impacts.

VII.D.1. Waste Heat

Whatever the cooling system, waste heat is discharged into the environment: into a water source if once-through cooling is used, or into the air with cooling towers. In the nuclear energy scenario, S1, light water reactors discharge 66 percent of their primary energy as waste heat, and liquid metal fast breeder reactors discharge 60 percent of their primary energy as waste heat. In Scenario S1, the high amount of electricity produced leads to a lot of waste heat. In the other scenarios the thermal wastes are low compared with their level in S1.

The utilization of once-through cooling is limited by the acceptable temperature increase of the water source. In the case of the Rhone River, two levels of control were considered, one allowing a maximum temperature increase of 5°C (a maximum of 40 percent of the nuclear capacity could use once-through cooling) and the other allowing a temperature increase of only 3°C (less than 30 percent of the nuclear capacity could use once-through cooling). In the case of the less restrictive control policy, the temperature of the Rhone River in the southern part of the region would be artificially increased by 4°C for approximately 140 days per year, and by 5°C for 50 to 60 days. If the remainder of the capacity uses wet cooling towers, there will be two major environmental impacts: 28 to 34 towers each 150 m high with a diameter between 120 and 140 m, and an estimated artificial evaporation between 0.5 and 0.6 × 10⁹ m³/yr. The evaporation might create local climatic perturbations and cause a loss of water from the Rhone, an important water source.

VII.D.2.   Land Use

It is beyond all question that solar electricity generation requires a lot of land. If we compare, for instance, the "nuclear scenario" (S1) and the "solar scenario" (S3), the land occupied by energy facilities is 1.5 times higher for S3 than for S1 (239 km² for S3 compared with 163 km² for S1).

The land use for resource extraction, e.g. coal mining, occurs outside the region and cannot be compared with land use for facilities. The consumption of coal requires a lot of land especially if the coal comes from surface mines.

In the case of S1, the high increase of electricity consumption requires the development of transmission networks and wide corridors for the transmission lines throughout the region. The aesthetic impact of the transmission networks may be greater than the land-use impact.

VII.D.3.   SO₂ Emissions

The "conventional fuel scenario," S2, has high SO_2 emissions. With the current emission standards, this scenario would be unacceptable for most people because of the very high level of SO_2 emissions: eight times higher in 2025 than in 1970. The high level causes human health impacts which were quantified as far as possible, but also damage to flora and fauna which was not evaluated. In S1 and S3, SO_2 air pollution is almost negligible since the total emissions in 2025 are only slightly higher than in 1970 (see Table 5.24).

VII.D.4.   Health Impacts

The health impacts have been quantified for the three scenarios and expressed in person-days lost for accidents and diseases and in number of deaths for fatalities. It should be noted that health impacts that are not recognized or recognized but unquantified were not included in the health impact estimates. Because of the large SO_2 emissions, S2 has the highest health impacts. The development of solar energy in Scenario S3 results in very few health impacts. However, it was assumed that more than 20 percent of the electricity in Scenario S3 is generated from coal, and the human health impacts from coal mining are high. If oil or gas were used instead of coal, the impacts would be lower.

The sensitivity studies on the Base Case show the difficulty of differentiating from an environmental standpoint between nuclear energy development with the liquid metal fast breeder reactor and nuclear energy development without it. They show that using waste heat from nuclear plants has less of an impact on the environment than simply discharging it into a body of water. The use of waste heat also reduces the amount of uranium needed.

A very interesting technique based on multiattribute decision analysis has been developed to deal with the complexity of judging environmental impacts and has already been applied in the case of Wisconsin.[14, 16] The technique is summarized in Appendix E at the end of the book.

APPENDIX: ENERGY CONSUMPTION AND END-USE ENERGY TABLES FOR RHONE-ALPES

TABLE 5A.1   Energy Consumption in 1970 (10^{15} cal)

	Coal	Gas	Oil	Electricity	District Heating[a]	Total	Total Electricity (TWh)[b]
Industrial	5.6	5.0	29.0	13.5		53.1	15.7
Residential	4.1	2.3	23.8	2.2	1.0	33.4	2.6
Service	0.5	0.9	5.9	2.1	0.3	9.7	2.2
Transportation			20.0	0.4		20.4	0.5
Total	10.2	8.2	78.7	18.2	1.3	116.6	21.0

SOURCE: CEREN.[4]
[a] Estimate from national data.
[b] TWh ≡ terawatt hours.

TABLE 5A.2   End-Use Energy in Scenario S1 (10^{15} cal)

	Coal	Gas	Oil	Electricity	Oil District Heating	Geothermal	Solar	Total	Total Electricity (TWh)
2000									
Industrial	2.6	16.2	45.7	65.4				129.9	76.0
Residential		11.4	32.1	14.0	1.0			58.5	16.5
Service		1.0	2.1	5.6	0.5			9.2	6.5
Transportation			37.3	0.9				38.2	1.0
Total	2.6	28.6	117.2	85.9	1.5			235.8	100.0
2025									
Industrial	3.1	29.5	56.7	171.1				260.4	199
Residential		13.4	19.5	32.7	2.0	0.5	0.5	68.6	38
Service		0.6	0.3	9.5	1.0	0.5		11.9	11
Transportation			55.6	1.7				57.3	2.0
Total	3.1	43.5	132.1	215	3.0	1.0	0.5	398.2	250

TABLE 5A.3   End-Use Energy in Scenario S2 (10^{15} cal)

	Coal	Gas	Oil	Elec-tricity	Oil District Heating	Geo-thermal	Solar	Total	Total Electricity (TWh)
2000									
Industrial	2.6	25.4	77.0	55.0				160.0	64.0
Residential		9.4	47.8	7.2	1.4	11.0	0.4	66.2	8.4
Service		3.0	3.5	3.5	0.5			10.5	4.1
Transportation			39.3	0.9				40.2	1.1
Total	2.6	37.8	167.6	66.6	1.9	11.0	0.4	276.9	77.6
2025									
Industrial	3.1	60.9	146.0	130.7				340.7	152.0
Residential		9.4	51.3	19.6	2.5	0.7	2.0	85.5	22.8
Service		3.1	2.9	6.3	1.2	0.4		13.9	7.3
Transportation			58.7	1.2				59.9	1.4
Total	3.1	73.4	258.9	157.8	3.7	1.1	2.0	500	183.5

TABLE 5A.4   End-Use Energy in Scenario S3 (10^{15} cal)

	Coal	Gas	Oil	Elec-tricity	Oil District Heating	Geo-thermal	Solar	Total	Total Electricity (TWh)
2000									
Industrial	2.6	20.4	61.1	65.3				149.4	75.9
Residential		15.2	23.2	5.2	5.0	2.9	2.2	53.7	0.6
Service		2.5	1.5	2.1	0.5		4.6	11.2	2.4
Transportation			22.0	1.2				23.2	1.4
Total	2.6	38.1	107.8	73.8	5.5	2.9	6.8	237.5	85.7
2025									
Industrial	3.0	34.0	30.0	138.0				205.0	160.4
Residential		9.0	17.6	7.9	8.0	4.9	5.0	52.5	9.2
Service		2.0	1.0	3.5	1.0	0.6	5.6	13.7	4.1
Transportation			23.6	2.2				25.8	2.6
Total	3.0	45.0	72.2	151.6	9.0	5.5	10.6	297.0	176.3

REFERENCES

1.   Institut National de la Statistique et des Etudes Economiques (INSEE) Rhône-Alpes. *Tableaux de l'Economie, les Conditions de Logement des Ménages en 1970.* Paris, 1971.

2.   Lapillonne, B. Les Consommations d'Energie des Transports de Marchandises en France: Facteurs d'évolution à long terme. Institut Economique et Juridique de l'Energie (IEJE), Grenoble, Mar. 1975.

3.   Chateau, B. Prévision à Long Terme de la Demande d'Energie Finale pour le Chauffage, l'Eau Chaude Sanitaire et la Cuisson, des Ménages du Système Urbain. Insitut Economique et Juridique de l'Energie (IEJE), Grenoble, Sept. 1975.

4.   Centre d'Etudes Regionales sur l'Economie de l'Energie (CEREN). *Consommations Apparentes d'Energie par Branches en 1972,* Paris, 1973.

5.   Chateau, B. and B. Lapillonne. Projection à Long Terme de la Demande d'Energie en France. Institut Economique et Juridique de l'Energie (IEJE), Grenoble, 1976.

6.   Institut National de la Statistique et des Etudes Economiques (INSEE). L'Economie de la Région Rhône-Alpes, Notes et Etudes Documentaires. No. 3491, 1968.

7.   Lapillonne, B. Centrales Nucléaires et Environnement: le Point de Vue des Pouvoirs Publics et d'EDF, Institut Economique et Juridique de l'Energie (IEJE), Grenoble, 1973.

8.   U.S. Nuclear Regulatory Commission, Office of Nuclear Reactor Regulation. Draft Environmental Statement related to the proposed A.R. Barton Nuclear Plant, Apr. 1975.

9.   Buehring, W.A. "A Model of Environmental Impacts from Electrical Generation in Wisconsin," Ph.D. dissertation, Department of Nuclear Engineering, University of Wisconsin, Madison, 1975.

10.   Buehring, W.A., and W.K. Foell. Environmental Impacts of Electrical Generation: A Systemwide Approach, Report No. RR-76-13, International Institute of Applied Systems Analysis, Laxenburg, Austria, 1976.

11.   Reactor Safety Study. An Assessment of Accident Risks in U.S. Commercial Nuclear Power Plants. (Rasmussen Report). WASH-1400-MR, U.S. Atomic Energy Commission, Washington, D.C., Oct. 1975.

12.   National Academy of Sciences, National Research Council, Division of Medical Sciences. The Effects on Population of Exposure to Low Levels of Ionizing Radiation, Report of the Advisory Committee on the Biological Effects of Ionizing Radiation (BEIR), Nov. 1972.

13.   Bourgeois, B., and B. Chateau. Note sur la Recuperation de la Chaleur Basse Temperature dans les Centrales Thermiques Combinées et son Stockage. Institut Economique et Juridique de l'Energie (IEJE), Grenoble, Feb., 1976.

14.   Buehring, W.A., W.K. Foell, and R.L. Keeney. Energy/Environment Management: Application of Decision Analysis. Report No. RR-76-14, International Institute for Applied Systems Analysis, Laxenburg, Austria, May 1976.

15.   Centre Interprofessionnel Technique d'Etudes de la Pollution Atmosphérique (CITEPA). "Statistiques françaises de la Pollution due à la Combustion." Etude Documentaire No. 40.

16.   Buehring, W.A., W.K. Foell, and R.L. Keeney. "Examining Energy/Environment Policy Using Decision Analysis." *Energy Systems and Policy* 2(3), 1978.

Prologue to Chapter 6
The Wisconsin Scenarios
in Retrospect

Charles Cicchetti
Wisconsin Public Service Commission
May 1978

Comparisons between the GDR, Rhone-Alpes, and Wisconsin suggest that Wisconsin has perhaps the farthest to go in improving its efficiency of energy use, strengthening its conservation policies, and reducing its rates of energy growth. Since the Wisconsin scenarios were written in 1975, some progress has been made in these areas; many ideas for energy-related reforms in Wisconsin have grown out of interactions with our colleagues in the GDR and Rhone-Alpes during the three-region study.

Energy use in Wisconsin has been marked by high growth during the 1960s and a leveling off in the 1970s. The growth experienced during the 1960s can be traced to several factors. First, the cost of end-use energy fell by 50 percent between 1960 and 1970. Second, the implementation of environmental protection measures began during the 1960s; improved pollution control required increases in energy use. Finally, in the early 1960s Wisconsin industries were characterized by a high level of energy intensiveness. All of these factors contributed to the dramatic growth in energy-use figures of the 1962–1970 period.

This exponential growth did not continue into the 1970s, however. The trade-off between increased energy use and environmental protection did not result in continued high rates of growth in energy use. The mix of industries also shifted toward those that are less energy intensive. In fact, since the oil embargo of 1973–

At the second conference, Management of Regional Energy/Environment Systems, held at IIASA, 16–19 May 1978, retrospective presentations on the scenarios were given by energy specialists or policymakers from the three regions. To provide perspective on the scenarios, summaries of the presentations are included immediately before the chapters describing the scenarios for the regions (Chapters 4, 5, and 6). They will be published in full as part of the proceedings of the conference: W.K. Foell (ed.), Proceedings of the Conference on Management of Regional Energy/Environment Systems (Laxenburg, Austria: International Institute for Applied Systems Analysis, in press).

1974, there has been virtually no increase in energy consumption in Wisconsin. During some years there has been a modest 2–3 percent increase in electricity consumption, but this has been offset by decreases in natural gas use. This is a great change from the 7–10 percent annual increases in electricity consumption in the early 1970s. In light of these developments, the projections of continued exponential growth made in the Wisconsin Base Case scenario seem to be outdated. Actually, the State of Wisconsin has set itself the goal of reducing its energy use by 10 percent by 1985.

One way in which it is hoped that this goal will be achieved is through government regulations designed for energy conservation. In suggesting areas in which reforms were needed, Wisconsin's collaboration with the GDR and Rhone-Alpes brought us several tangible benefits. For instance, we learned from the French that our technique of pricing electricity was counterproductive. Not only did the French bring to our attention the diseconomy of charging customers less when they buy electricity in bulk, but they also suggested a better pricing mechanism. Following their example, Wisconsin is now adopting a system of marginal cost-pricing for electricity – i.e. the state is instituting a time-of-day variation in tariffs. At the present time, 40 percent of Wisconsin's electricity is sold during high demand hours on a time-of-day pricing system. Also, in a pioneering U.S. effort, it is planned to install residential "time-of-day" meters or load management systems in the city of Milwaukee within one or two years. The natural gas pricing system is beginning to be changed according to the same principle of marginal cost pricing that we learned from our French colleagues.

Our interactions with representatives from the GDR made us aware of the potential of district heating, and we have decided that district heating, as a concept, should be encouraged. We are requiring electric utilities to continue to sell steam to industrial users; new plants built to replace decommissioned plants are required as well by state regulations to sell steam to industries. Whenever any new coal-burning plant is built, all potential industrial users in the surrounding service area must be asked if they would like to purchase the plant's waste heat. Because of the controversy currently surrounding the nuclear question, no decision has been made yet about the use of waste heat from nuclear power plants.

The use of waste heat to increase the temperature of drinking water by about five degrees centigrade is also under consideration in Wisconsin. The water is very cold, so there may be no health problem from bacteria connected with this scheme. Early studies have indicated that use of waste heat in the drinking water system would reduce energy costs and bring tangible savings to residential customers in their bills for water-heating. Until now, heat pumps were not very practical in Wisconsin because of the coldness of the state's water. But if the temperature of the drinking water were to be increased, some engineers believe that efficient heat-pump systems would be feasible. The example the GDR gave us for the utilization of waste heat was a real impetus for better utilization of this energy source on our part.

It has been asked which features of the research results were surprising. No one in Wisconsin was surprised that so much of the state's energy consumption was related to transportation, in comparison with energy use patterns in the GDR and Rhone-Alpes. But it was surprising to see how much more energy Wisconsin was using for residential space heating, even after correcting for differences in degree-days, and excluding energy for air-conditioning purposes. A part of the higher use is due to the larger size of Wisconsin housing units — i.e. floor space per person. But as we learned from the other regions, a much more important factor is heat losses because of poor insulation. This realization convinced us that we ought to be changing the state's building codes. Wisconsin is now one of the few states in the United States that has a complete building code with measures for real enforcement. The Wisconsin Public Service Commission has also developed a set of pricing rules that will penalize people who do not improve insulation in existing housing. Again, the impetus for these changes came from our new awareness of practices in the other regions.

The interregional comparisons also provided us with new insights about energy savings in the transportation sector. We were convinced of the savings that could result if large cars were replaced with small cars, even if distances traveled remained constant. On the basis of our recommendations, the governor of Wisconsin proposed a set of taxes and subsidies that would have made the purchase of new cars vary by as much as $1,000, depending on size. (At the time, a typical car in Wisconsin cost about $4,000.) Because the State of Wisconsin is a major automobile manufacturer, these proposals were politically very risky — especially since most of the discounts would apply to European and Japanese cars and the taxes would be levied on American cars. As might be expected, the governor was not able to win legislative approval. Still, this serious attempt at policy change in the transportation sector resulted from ideas we gained through interaction with representatives from the other regions. As a footnote, it is interesting that even without the benefit of federal regulations and state taxes, people in Wisconsin are buying smaller cars and reducing the amount they drive.

There have been several other events of significance in the energy field in Wisconsin since 1975. State legislation has been passed to give tax credits to people who install solar energy systems. The Public Service Commission has also passed a special set of tariffs for the electric back-up systems needed for solar units. In industry, there has been a significant amount of energy conservation and conversion from natural gas spurred by the oil embargo of 1973 and the gas shortage of 1976. In the residential sector, voluntary conservation measures, such as lowering thermostats, are also being taken. The result of these activities has been the creation of a conservation bubble — i.e. Wisconsin now has excess energy supplies. However, this should not be understood to mean that we can return to "business as usual." Wisconsin is firmly committed to the goal of reducing energy consumption by 10 percent by 1985.

6 Alternative Energy/Environment Futures for Wisconsin

I. INTRODUCTION

I.A. ORGANIZATION AND OBJECTIVES

In this chapter the background, key assumptions, and typical results for three alternative energy/environment futures for Wisconsin are presented. A Base Case scenario is presented in some detail to provide a basis for comparison with assumptions and results of other scenarios. Before the presentation of the details of the scenarios starting in section II, a general overview of the initial conditions, data availability, and the character of the three scenarios is given in the next few pages. Following the scenario presentation in sections II and III, sensitivity studies related to critical parameters are discussed in section IV. Finally, some overall conclusions of the Wisconsin studies are presented in section V.

I.B. GENERAL CHARACTERISTICS AND INITIAL CONDITIONS

Chapter 2 presents an overview of demographic, geographic, and energy characteristics of Wisconsin; that information will not be repeated here. Instead, a brief comparison of a few statistics for Wisconsin and the entire United States is given in Table 6.1. The population of Wisconsin is about 2 percent of the national total. The state has a higher population density, greater manufacturing value-added per capita, lower personal income per capita, and lower energy consumption per capita than the U.S. average; however, of these four indices, only population density deviates more than 25 percent from the national average.

The population of Wisconsin is not spread evenly over the state. The 1970

Chapter 6 was written by William Buehring – IIASA.

TABLE 6.1   Comparison of Selected Statistics for Wisconsin and the United States

	Unit	Wis.	U.S.	Ratio: Wis./U.S.
1970 population ($\times 10^6$)		4.4	203.8	.02
Land area	$10^3\,km^2$	141	9,160	.02
Water area	$10^3\,km^2$	4.4	203	.02
Population density (1970)	people per km^2	31	22	1.41
Farms				
Number (1970)	thousands	99	2,730	.04
Area	1,000 km^2	73	4,317	.02
Fishing licenses sold	licenses per			
(1972)	100 residents	30	12	2.50
Motor vehicle	registrations per			
registrations (1970)	100 residents	50	53	.94
Manufacturing value-				
added per capita	$ (1972)	2,086	1,700	1.23
Personal income per capita	$ (1972)	4,290	4,537	.95
Primary energy per capita				
(1970)	10^9 cal	65	83	.78
Electricity generated per				
capita (1970)[a]	kWh	6,742	8,046	.84

SOURCES: U.S. Bureau of the Census;[1] Bowman et al.;[2] *The World Almanac and Book of Facts*;[3] U.S. Department of the Interior.[4]
[a] Includes industrial generation as well as electric utilities.

population in each of the 8 districts used in these studies is shown in Figure 6.1. About 40 percent of the total population is found in the southeastern district (District 2 in Figure 6.1), which includes Milwaukee and its suburbs. There are 2 other metropolitan areas with population greater than 200,000 (Table 6.2). In addition, 2 other metropolitan areas that are primarily in other states have a portion of their population in Wisconsin. They are Minneapolis–St. Paul, Minnesota, with 1,965,000 total population and 34,000 in Wisconsin (District 6 in Figure 6.1) and Duluth, Minnesota–Superior, Wisconsin, with 265,000 total population and 45,000 in Wisconsin (District 8).

I.C.   THE THREE WISCONSIN SCENARIOS

I.C.1.   *Description of the Scenarios*

Three complete scenarios for Wisconsin, summarized in Table 6.3, have been examined in detail. For purposes of comparison, population growth and economic activity are not varied among these three scenarios. The scenarios can be briefly characterized as follows:

- S1 (Base Case): The assumptions tend to be a continuation of past trends, with

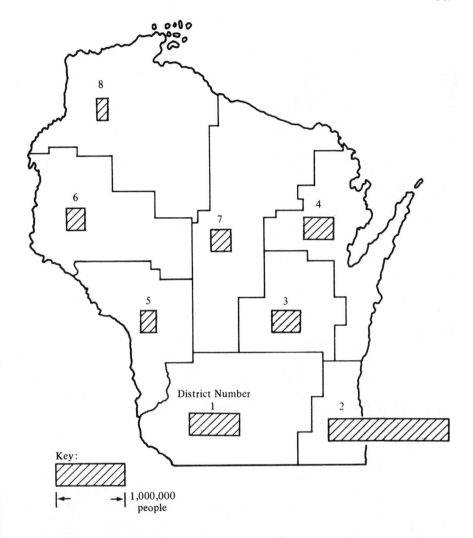

FIGURE 6.1   1970 Wisconsin population by district. The total population of Wisconsin in 1970 was 4.4 million.

some energy-saving methods, such as the construction of more efficient automobiles.

• S2 (High-Energy Case): The assumptions tend to result in significantly higher energy consumption than S1. Electricity is preferred for end-use energy. Emission controls on air pollutants are minimal except for power plants.

• S3 (Low-Energy Case): The assumptions tend to result in lower energy consumption than S1 but by no means the lowest energy consumption that can

TABLE 6.2   Metropolitan Areas in Wisconsin with Over 200,000 People

	Metropolitan Population ($\times 10^3$)	District in Figure 6.1
Milwaukee	1,404	2
Madison	290	1
Appleton-Oshkosh	277	3

TABLE 6.3   Policies and Assumptions for the Three Wisconsin Scenarios

	S1	S2	S3
Growth assumptions			
Population	• Declining growth rate	• Same as S1	• Same as S1
Economy	• Continued expansion of service in relation to industry	• Same as S1	• Same as S1
Policy areas			
Urban Form	• Surburban extension • 25% apartments	• Exurban dispersal • 10% apartments	• Small compact cities • 50% apartments
Energy-Use Technology	• Almost constant energy use per unit value-added in service and industry	• Increasing energy use per unit value-added • Emphasis on electricity	• Declining energy use per unit value-added • Conservation measures
Transportation	• Auto efficiency gain	• No auto efficiency gain	• Large auto efficiency gain • More rail shipment of freight
Energy Supply	• Synthetic fuel from coal • Mix of coal and nuclear for electricity	• Synthetic fuel from coal • Mostly nuclear for electricity	• Solar for heating and electricity • No new nuclear • Synthetic fuel from coal
Environment	• Present trends of increasing controls for SO_2 and particulates	• Low controls of SO_2 and particulates	• Stringent controls of SO_2 and particulates

reasonably be expected. Solar energy is developed for both heating and electrical generation. Conservation measures and pollution control are stressed.

An example of the contrasts in the scenarios is the assumed urban form (Table 6.3). Population growth and spatial distribution affects virtually all areas of the model (e.g., the average trip length for personal transportation is related to city size). Population distribution also affects environmental impacts resulting from

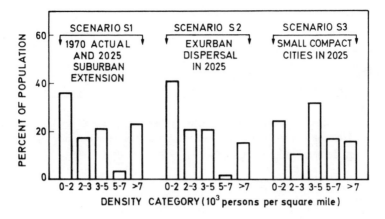

FIGURE 6.2   Wisconsin population by density category.

energy use in ways other than the modification of energy use. For example, the location of pollution sources relative to population is an important consideration in the estimation of associated health impacts.

Several possible future urban forms for Wisconsin have been postulated and quantified for incorporation in the scenarios.[5,6] Three of these urban forms with different population density distributions are shown in Figure 6.2. Suburban extension is a continuation of the 1970 density distribution and was used in Scenario S1. The urban form assumed in S2 is exurban dispersal, which indicates a trend of settlement in low-population areas. Growth occurs in low-density urban areas in S3 (the case of small compact cities).

I.C.2.   Sensitivity Studies

Several representative sensitivity studies, in which only a single parameter is varied, have been selected for presentation from the numerous possibilities afforded by the multitude of assumptions required for a complete scenario description. The particular sensitivity analyses for the Wisconsin studies are related to solar home heating and water heating, housing type and fuel use, sulfur dioxide control in electrical generation, electricity supply alternatives, and transportation energy for alternative urban forms.

I.C.3.   Demand Sectors and Energy Indicators

The energy demand calculations for Wisconsin were based on four demand sectors — residential, service, industrial, and transportation — as described in Chapter 3. The boundaries between these sectors are often not well defined because of some difficulties in data collection procedures. For the scenarios described here, the sectors have been defined as in previous applications of the Wisconsin Regional Energy (WISE) Model,[7] and the period of study has been extended to 2025.

TABLE 6.4 Population Assumptions for Wisconsin Scenarios

	Population ($\times 10^6$)	Average Growth Rate Since 1970 (%/yr)
1970	4.418	
2000	5.78	0.90
2025	6.58	0.73

Some key parameters that have a close relationship with energy consumption in the demand sector models are listed below. Assumptions about population growth affect energy demand in all the models.

Residential
   Type of housing (apartment or single-family home)
   Appliance ownership fractions
   Fuel preference for space heating
Service
   Floor area growth rate
   Energy intensiveness (energy use per unit floor area) by type of fuel
Industrial
   Growth in value-added* for 20 industrial classifications
   Energy intensiveness by type of fuel
Transportation
   Automobile ownership and efficiency
   Distribution of freight between rail and truck

The energy demand results are used to determine total energy supply requirements by fuel type and associated environmental impacts.

I.D.   FACTORS COMMON TO THE THREE SCENARIOS

To allow for easy comparison among scenarios, some factors were not varied among the scenarios. However, it should be emphasized that this does not imply certainty for these parameters. The five general areas in which some parameters were held constant over the three scenarios are population growth, economic growth, transportation, energy supply, and environmental impact.

I.D.1.   *Population Growth*

The population estimates used for Wisconsin through 1990 were based on those provided by the Wisconsin Department of Statistical Services. The average annual

* Value-added is a measure of manufacturing activity derived by subtracting the cost of materials, supplies, containers, fuel, purchased electricity, and contract work from the value of shipments for products manufactured plus receipts for services rendered.

growth rate is approximately 1 percent. From 1990 to 2010, an average annual growth rate of 0.7 percent was used, and from 2010 to 2025, an average annual growth rate of 0.4 percent was used. This approximates the Series X projection of the U.S. Bureau of the Census.[1] Series X reaches zero growth around the middle of the twenty-first century.

The resulting populations for all Wisconsin scenarios are shown in Table 6.4. This estimate is lower than most historical estimates have been[1] but is thought to be a reasonable extension of the recent tendency toward slower population growth. It should also be noted that these growth rates include net migration, which in recent years has increased Wisconsin population by about 0.4 percent annually.

•

I.D.2.   Economic Growth

The scenario methodology required an explicit treatment of economic conditions. Value-added or gross regional product are the typical measures of economic activity. Total value-added includes activity in both the manufacturing and service sectors, which typically have very different energy consumption characteristics.

The level of economic activity in Wisconsin was not varied among scenarios. In addition, the mix of manufacturing and service activity was not varied from scenario to scenario, although it was varied over time. The overall economic growth, measured in terms of total value-added,* used in all Wisconsin scenarios was 3.1 percent per year, which is 2.4 percent per year on a per capita basis.† The overall growth is lower than that of the gross national product since 1950 and is higher than the growth rate since 1910.[1] For comparison, the growth rates used for gross national product in the scenarios developed by the Ford Foundation Energy Policy Project (EPP) for 1975–2000 were 3.3 to 3.4 percent.[8]

The resulting rate of real growth in the Wisconsin manufacturing sector was 2.25 percent per year in the scenarios; this is somewhat lower than the 1958–1971 rate of approximately 3 percent per year.[9] However, the overall growth rate in industry was not a basic assumption; instead, the current rate of change of value-added per capita in 20 industrial classifications was extended into the future,[9] resulting in an overall annual growth rate of 2.25 percent, or 1.5 percent on a per capita basis.

The real rate of growth in the service sector‡ was assumed to be 4.0 percent annually, which was approximately the national growth rate for 1950–1972.[1] Therefore, service value-added represents a larger share of the total value-added as time passes. An additional sector that includes activities such as farming and contract construction is assumed to grow at the same rate as industry. The resultant value-added for all Wisconsin scenarios is shown in Figure 6.3.

---

* All value-added figures are in constant dollars to remove the effect of inflation.
† The overall growth was not an assumption itself; instead, growth rates in specific industrial classifications and service sectors were assumed.
‡ This sector includes wholesale and retail trade; finance, insurance, and real estate; services; and government enterprises.

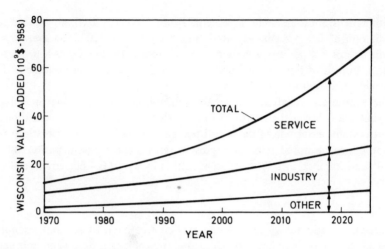

FIGURE 6.3 Assumed value-added in Wisconsin.

For comparison, the Ford Energy Policy Project selected annual growth rates for 1975–2000 of 2.6 percent for U.S. manufacturing and 3.5 percent for service.[8] This is somewhat higher than the assumed rate of growth for Wisconsin industry and somewhat lower than for Wisconsin service. However, the two studies are not easily compared, since time periods, regions, population growth, and the definitions of industry and service are different.

The more recent U.S. National Energy Plan[10] is based on an average growth in GNP of 4.3 percent per year over the period 1976 to 1985. This rate of growth is significantly higher than that used in the scenarios presented here.

I.D.3.   Transportation

The freight transportation model is based upon ton-kilometers of freight transported. In all scenarios the number of ton-km is related to economic activity. Since economic activity is the same for all scenarios, the total number of ton-km is the same for all scenarios. However, variations in the distribution between truck and rail tranport are used in the scenarios.

I.D.4.   Energy Supply

Wisconsin must import its fossil and nuclear fuels from other regions. Thus, Wisconsin is very dependent on conditions in other states. It has been assumed that required fuel supplies are available from these sources, except for natural gas and petroleum. Acceptable synthetic fuels from coal are assumed to be available in unlimited supply by 2025 as natural supplies of oil and gas diminish.

Wisconsin is assumed to generate exactly the amount of electricity required within its own borders. No net import or export of electricity occurs in any scenario. Although export of electricity is a possibility for the state, this was considered unlikely, and it would be an additional complicating factor that would make results of alternative futures more difficult to compare on a consistent basis. From 1970 through 1974, Wisconsin had a net import of electricity that totaled only 2.1 percent of total electrical generation.[2]

I.D.5. Environmental Impact

In general, the assumptions related to environmental impact are a continuation of the trend toward stricter regulations regarding air pollution, radioactive releases, and waste heat disposal. In all Wisconsin scenarios, control devices and use of low-sulfur coal keep SO_2 emissions from coal-fired electrical generation within U.S. emission standards.* Ash control at coal plants is assumed to retain about 99 percent of the mass of ash.

Reprocessing of fuels from nuclear reactors in order to remove the uranium and plutonium is assumed to take place. Radioactive release from nuclear fuel reprocessing plants is assumed to decline after the year 1990, when equipment that prevents the release of 90 percent of the krypton-85 and tritium (^3H) is installed. These two radionuclides have a long half-life and are expected to be produced in large quantities during normal operation of the plants.

Some other important assumptions that affect environmental impacts have been made. For example:

- Cooling systems for new power plants are mostly closed-cycle evaporative cooling, such as natural-draft wet-cooling towers.
- Occupational fatalities per unit of coal mined decline rapidly to a level that is 30 percent of the 1970 U.S. rate for underground mining and 40 percent of the 1970 value for surface mining.
- New cases of total disability from black lung disease per unit of coal mined underground drops to a level that is nearly 100 times below the 1970 rate.
- The energy input for synthetic fuels is 60 percent from surface-mined Western sub-bituminous coal, 20 percent from bituminous surface mines, and 20 percent from bituminous underground mines.
- The average future power plant (coal or nuclear) is sited within 80 km of 2,250,000 people (this assumption affects population exposures to air pollution and radioactivity).

---

* See Appendix C for a discussion of air pollution standards in the three regions.

II. THE BASE CASE SCENARIO

II.A. OVERALL PHILOSOPHY

The primary purpose of the scenario that is presented in some detail in this section is to provide a reference future or Base Case for comparison with the results of other scenarios having different assumptions; the Base Case scenario is not intended to be a prediction of the most likely future for Wisconsin. Assumptions for the near future in the Base Case were established in general by assuming a continuation of current trends, including moderating effects such as slower population growth and more efficient energy use than extrapolation of historical data would indicate. Assumptions over the long run in the Base Case required estimates of what technologies might be available and to what degree they will be used. For example, synthetic fuels that can substitute for some petroleum and natural gas are assumed to be available around the year 2000 in the Base Case. Important assumptions for the Base Case are discussed individually in the following subsections.

II.B. FRAMEWORK FOR SCENARIO S1

In this section the framework for Wisconsin Scenario S1 is presented in some detail. The specific assumptions indicated are the inferred results of implementation of the overall policies shown in Table 6.3.

II.B.1. Assumptions for the Energy Demand Sectors

Transportation Sector   Energy use in transportation is categorized into passenger transport and freight transport.

Passenger Transport   The demographic characteristics of communities affect the calculated average trip length in the model.[5] The urban form in S1 is a continuation of current growth patterns, designated as suburban extension. The population growth is in suburbs and fringes of the urban areas. In the Base Case, average fuel economy is 40 percent better in 1980 than it was in 1974. Thus, the fuel economy for all types of driving of all 1980 models of autos averages slightly over 8.5 km/liter (20 miles/gal). The current trend toward small cars continues; compact and small cars capture 60 percent of the market after 1980.

Rail, air, and bus passenger service continue at low energy consumption levels relative to passenger auto energy consumption. The assumptions for mass transit fuel use are listed in Table 6.5.

The load factor, the average number of people per vehicle, is assumed to be 1.4 for local and 2.4 for intercity automobile trips. The load factors for buses are 10 passengers per bus for urban travel and 22 passengers per bus for intercity travel.

Freight Transport   The freight transport calculations are divided into truck,

TABLE 6.5   Mass Transit Fuel Use

Transport Mode	Energy Use
Urban bus	1.9 km/liter
Intercity bus	2.8 km/liter
Air	555 kcal per passenger-km
Rail	71 kcal per passenger-km
Electric urban bus	645 kcal per passenger-km

SOURCE: Hanson and Mitchell.[5]

TABLE 6.6   Freight Transport Fuel Use

	Energy Use (kcal/metric ton-km)
Truck	485
Rail	118
Air	7,270

SOURCE: Hanson and Mitchell.[5]

rail, and air categories, although air freight is assumed to contribute negligibly to the total energy demand for freight transport. The assumed fuel requirements for the three modes are listed in Table 6.6. Since truck transport requires considerably more energy than rail on a ton-kilometer basis, and since most freight transport is assumed to be by truck, the energy demand for freight shipments by truck is nearly 12 times greater than for rail freight in Scenario S1.

Residential Sector   Energy use in the residential sector depends on the type of housing unit, single family or multiple family (apartment), and ownership of energy-consuming devices. Three types of energy consumption are assumed to be a function of housing type for the Wisconsin scenarios; they are space heating, water heating, and central air conditioning. Annual fuel use for and fraction of households owning these three "base appliances" differ considerably for single-family houses and apartments, as shown in Table 6.7. Ownership of secondary appliances, such as refrigerators and television sets, is assumed to be independent of housing type.

The pattern of ownership for new residences shown in Table 6.7 is not the same as for residences that were built before 1970. Therefore, the new and old residences are treated separately in the calculations.

Secondary appliance ownership is assumed to penetrate as indicated in Table 6.7. Essentially all households are assumed to have a refrigerator, television, lighting, and a mixture of small appliances. The only nonelectric secondary appliances that have been included are gas stoves and gas dryers. In 1970 half the households have a gas stove, and about 10 percent have a gas dryer.

The number of occupied households is determined by dividing the population by average family size. Although population only increases by approximately 50

TABLE 6.7   Key Parameters For Wisconsin Residential Energy Use — Scenario S1

Annual Fuel Use for Pre-1970 Residences[a]

| | Single Family Home | | | Apartment | | |
	Electricity	Gas	Oil	Electricity	Gas	Oil
Space heat	23.1	47.0	47.0	11.0	18.0	18.0
Water heat	4.5	6.9	6.9	3.6	5.6	5.6
Central air conditioning	1.7	3.2		0.66	1.3	

Ownership Fractions for Post-1970 Residences

| | Single Family Home | | | Apartment | | |
	Electricity	Gas	Oil	Electricity	Gas	Oil
Space heat	0.12	0.86	0.02	0.31	0.59	0.10
Water heat	0.62	0.38	0.0	0.80	0.20	0.00
Central air conditioning	0.20	0.05	0.0	0.80	0.10	0.00

Secondary Appliances

| | Fraction of Households That Own Appliance | | Electricity Use (10^3 kWh/yr) |
	1970	2025	
Refrigerator	0.998	0.999	1.3
Freezer	0.40	0.47	1.4
Dishwasher	0.17	0.67	0.36
Clothes washer	0.59	0.88	0.10
Television	0.97	0.99	0.36
Second television	0.31	0.80	0.50
Room air conditioner	0.26	0.50	0.65
Electric stove	0.49	0.54	1.2
Electric dryer	0.44	0.77	1.0
Lighting	1.0	1.0	0.75
Small appliances	1.0	1.0	0.50
Miscellaneous	0.49	0.54	0.50

SOURCES: Buehring et al.[11] and Frey.[12]
[a] Electricity in 10^3 kWh, oil and gas in 10^9 cal.

percent from 1970 through 2025, the number of households nearly doubles over the period because the average family size is assumed to decline from its 1970 value of 3.33.

In 1970, single-family dwellings represented 88 percent of all Wisconsin residences. For Scenario S1, new residences were 75 percent single-family and 25 percent multiple-family dwelling units.

Service Sector   Floor area in the service sector is the primary parameter for calculation of energy demand.[13] Based upon the assumption that the ratio of floor area

TABLE 6.8   Key Energy Demand Parameters for Wisconsin Service Sector Calculations — Scenario S1

	Space Heating System Efficiency	Fraction of Total Floor Area Heated	Fraction of Total Floor Area Cooled	Fraction of Total Floor Area Illuminated
Electricity	0.95	0.02	0.60	1.0
Natural gas	0.60	0.60	0.10	0.0
Coal	0.50	0.05	0.0	0.0
Petroleum	0.60	0.25	0.0	0.0
Average growth in service value-added	4.0%/yr			
Average fraction of each month that buildings are open for business	0.40 for all months			
Average daytime thermostat setting	21.1°C (70°F) for all months			
Average nighttime thermostat setting	21.1°C (70°F) for all months			
Average building ventilation rate	0.046 m³/min/m² floor area for all months			
Wall to floor area ratio for new buildings	0.35			
Glass to floor area ratio for new buildings	0.15			

SOURCE: Buehring.[15]

to service-sector value-added remains constant over time, the service growth was calculated from the value-added growth shown in Figure 6.3.

Some important assumptions by fuel type for Scenario S1 are listed in Table 6.8. In addition to space heating, space cooling, and illumination energy demands, some "process" energy is required for equipment such as elevators, stoves, and water heaters. The calculations have been calibrated to give actual energy demands by fuel type determined from independent analysis of Wisconsin energy use.[14]

Industrial Sector   Population growth (discussed earlier), economic activity, and energy intensiveness are the primary parameters for calculation of energy demand in the industrial sector. The primary assumption about economic activity for the Base Case is that there will be an increase in value-added per capita that averages 1.5 percent per year. The increase in value-added per capita, coupled with the assumed population growth, yields a total industrial value-added growth rate that averages 2.25 percent per year over the 55-year period.

The value-added calculations, however, are not based on the overall industrial growth rate but rather on 20 individual industrial categories as shown in Table 6.9. In terms of value-added, the major industries in Wisconsin are food, pulp, fabricated metals, machinery, and transportation equipment. Each industrial category listed in Table 6.9 has an initial value-added per capita, an annual growth rate in value-added per capita, and a rate of change for that growth rate; these initial values are based on historical data.[9]

The energy intensiveness, or energy use per unit of value-added is calculated for five energy sources for each industrial classification. The five energy sources are

TABLE 6.9   Initial Data for Wisconsin Industrial Energy Use

	1970 Value-Added Per Capita (1958 $)	Annual Growth Rate in Value-Added Per Capita 1958–1970
Food and kindred products	178.82	0.54
Tobacco manufactures	0.11	0.70
Textile mill products	16.68	1.95
Apparel and related products	13.76	1.93
Lumber and wood products	21.46	1.08
Furniture and fixtures	16.55	0.54
Pulp and paper products	129.07	1.49
Printing and publishing	59.76	2.49
Chemicals and allied products	54.37	5.55
Petroleum and coal products	3.73	2.25
Rubber products	30.13	3.78
Leather and leather goods	23.63	0.00
Stone, clay, and glass products	21.28	1.74
Primary metal industries	67.25	1.37
Fabricated metal products	100.19	1.53
Nonelectrical machinery	267.30	2.50
Electrical machinery	114.11	1.46
Transportation equipment	90.25	1.00
Instruments and related products	20.92	0.00
Miscellaneous manufactures	17.97	0.56

SOURCE: Shaver et al.[9]

electricity, natural gas, fuel oil, coal, and other miscellaneous fuels such as wood and gasoline. Historical data were used to specify the initial energy intensiveness and their rates of change. The Base Case uses these historical trends with two exceptions:

● The trend away from coal to natural gas reverses so that coal use in industry rises and natural gas growth is not as rapid as a projection of historical data would indicate.

● The overall energy intensiveness growth rate is assumed to be lower than historical trends.

The reason for shifting some emphasis from natural gas to coal is that it appears that the period of rapid expansion of natural gas use in industry has ended in Wisconsin. The overall energy intensiveness in the Base Case is assumed to be nearly constant, rather than the 1.5 percent per year average increase that occurred up to 1970. A reduction in the energy intensiveness growth rate is expected because of increasing energy costs and related conservation measures.

The growth rates for economic activity and energy intensiveness in Wisconsin industry are summarized in Table 6.10. The overall growth rate for electrical intensiveness is somewhat greater than for nonelectrical intensiveness as indicated by historical data.[9]

TABLE 6.10   Annual Growth Rates for Economic Activity and Energy Intensiveness in Wisconsin Industry for Scenario S1

	1970–2025 Average Annual Growth Rate
Industrial value-added per capita (constant $)	1.5%
Total energy intensiveness for industry (energy per $ value-added)	0.34%
Electrical energy intensiveness for industry	0.72%
Nonelectrical energy intensiveness for industry	0.29%

II.B.2.   Energy Supply

In general, the nonelectrical energy demanded is assumed to be available. Adjustments were made to some of the demand calculations to reflect expected drifts away from historical trends. For example, the aforementioned rapid growth of natural gas in industry is assumed to slow down.

Production of petroleum and natural gas in the United States may be stimulated in coming years by extensive offshore exploration and development of advanced recovery technologies. However, the likelihood that U.S. production of petroleum and natural gas plus a reasonable quantity of imports will be unable to meet domestic demand, especially by the year 2000 and beyond, is generally thought to be high.[8,16] A potential solution to the shortfall in gas and oil production is synthetic oil and gas produced from coal. In the scenarios, synthetic fuels from coal are assumed to supply significant quantities of energy starting at about the turn of the century. By the year 2025, U.S. production of natural gas and petroleum are assumed to provide Wisconsin with only 80 percent of the 1970 levels of oil and gas consumption; the remaining demand is satisfied by synthetic fuels from coal. The assumed efficiencies for conversion of coal to synthetic gas and to oil are 60 percent and 50 percent. These efficiencies are in reasonable agreement with the projections by the Synfuels Interagency Task Force.[16]

Electricity supply in the Base Case is from a mix of nuclear energy and coal. Half of all new nonpeaking electrical generating capacity is arbitrarily assumed to be nuclear energy after 1982. The mix of nuclear energy sources for new capacity after the year 2000 is approximately 46 percent PWR, 23 percent BWR, 25 percent HTGR, and 5 percent LMFBR.* Coal supplies for electrical generation were assumed to be 25 percent sub-bituminous coal from western states and 75 percent bituminous coal. Hydroelectric capacity and energy production were assumed to remain at current levels.

* PWR is the pressurized water reactor; BWR is the boiling water reactor; HTGR is the high temperature gas-cooled reactor; and LMFBR is the liquid metal fast breeder reactor. Since these studies were completed, the likelihood of HTGR and LMFBR use in Wisconsin in the near future has decreased considerably.

TABLE 6.11   Control Factors for SO_2 and Particulates — Scenario S1 (percentage removed)

	SO_2		Particulates	
	2000	2025	2000	2025
Residential				
gas	30	40	0	0
oil	50	60	0	0
Service				
coal	0	0	45	60
gas	30	40	0	0
oil	50	60	0	0
Industrial				
coal	15	30	94	95
gas	30	40	0	0
oil	40	50	12	30
Electric power				
coal	65	67	99	99

II.B.3.   Environmental Impact

In general the assumptions for environmental impact are extensions of the present trend of increasing controls. Control factors, or the percentage of a pollutant that is kept out of the air, for SO_2 and particulates have been estimated for each sector and fuel type. The factors for the Base Case are shown in Table 6.11. The SO_2 control is generally assumed to be the result of fuel cleaning operations before delivery to the end use sector except for SO_2 control for coal in industry and electric power generation, where complex sulfur removal systems are assumed to be available. Other key assumptions on factors that affect the environment were presented in section I.D of this chapter.

II.C.   RESULTS FOR WISCONSIN SCENARIO S1

II.C.1.   End-Use Demands

End-use energy includes only energy consumed in end-use processes; therefore, conversion and transmission losses, such as in electrical generation, are excluded from the end-use total. The total end-use energy for the Wisconsin Base Case increased at an average annual rate of 2.4 percent, from 236×10^{15} cal in 1970 to 856×10^{15} cal in 2025.*

The fraction of total end-use energy in each demand sector did not stay constant over time. The service sector increased its share of the total end-use energy from 13

---

* Detailed tables showing end-use and primary energy for the scenarios can be found in the appendices at the end of this chapter.

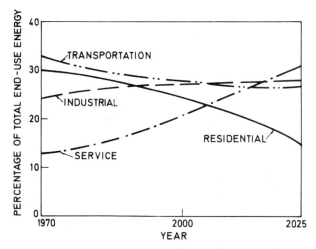

FIGURE 6.4   Distribution of total end-use energy by sector for Wisconsin Scenario S1.

to 31 percent over the 55-year period while the residential sector's share dropped from 30 to 15 percent (Figure 6.4). The percentage of end-use energy in transportation dropped off slightly and the industrial share showed a small increase. The average growth rate in end-use energy varied from a low of only 1.1 percent per year for the residential sector, just slightly higher than the 0.75 percent per year increase in population, to a high of 4.0 percent in the service sector.

The results for end-use energy are shown on a per capita basis in Figure 6.5. The rapid growth of energy use in the service sector relative to the other sectors is evident. Energy consumption per capita in transportation nearly doubles in the 55-year period, although consumption per capita for personal transportation by automobile showed a decline of nearly 18 percent, primarily because of efficiency gains. The energy used for freight transport increased faster than private transportation declined; therefore, total end-use energy in transportation increased as shown in Figure 6.5.

II.C.2.   Primary Energy

Primary energy includes both end-use energy and energy losses that occur in processing and transport, such as conversion and transmission losses for electricity. The primary energy supply results for the years 1970, 2000, and 2025, are listed in Table 6.12. The average rate of increase from 1970 to 2025 for primary energy use is 3.1 percent per year. The higher rate of increase for primary energy than for end-use energy (2.4 percent per year) is the result of shifting to electricity and synthetic

TABLE 6.12 Primary Energy Supply for the Wisconsin Base Case (10^{15} cal)

	1970	2000	2025
Petroleum	114.7	168.8	91.8
Natural gas	90.3	149.1	72.2
Synthetic fuel from coal			
end-use fuel	0.0	35.4	473.9
conversion loss	0.0	29.7	403.2
Total	0.0	65.1	877.1
All other coal sources	80.7	130.4	253.4
Nuclear energy	0.1	145.1	225.1
Hydrolectricity	1.6	2.1	2.1
Total	287.4	660.6	1,521.7

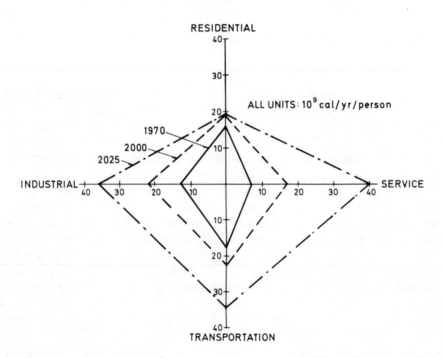

FIGURE 6.5 Annual end-use energy per capita by sector for Wisconsin Scenario S1.

fuels, which both have significant energy losses in conversion. If synthetic fuels from coal were not needed, i.e. if enough petroleum and natural gas were available, the total primary energy use in 2025 would be only about 1,120 × 10^{15} cal, the amount listed in Table 6.12 minus the large conversion loss for synthetic fuels.

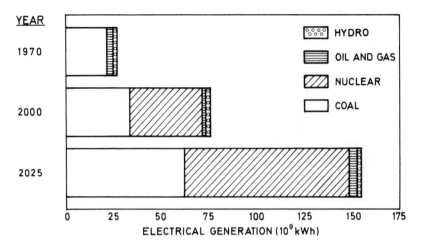

FIGURE 6.6   Sources of electrical generation for Wisconsin Scenario S1.

II.C.3.   Electricity

Energy required for electrical generation increased from 72×10^{15} cal in 1970 to 383×10^{15} cal in the year 2025; this corresponds to an average annual growth rate of 3.1 percent per year. Energy for electricity represented 25 percent of the total primary energy in 1970, 30 percent in 2000, and 25 percent in 2025. The decline is the result of the large energy consumption in the production of synthetic fuels. If enough oil and natural gas were available that the need for synthetic fuels were eliminated, energy for electricity would have been 32 percent of the total energy in 2000 and 34 percent in 2025.

The growth in electrical generation over time and the production of electricity by fuel type is shown in Figure 6.6. Nuclear generation increases from 0.2 percent of all generation in 1970 to 56 percent by the year 2025. Nuclear generation accounted for approximately 25 percent of the electricity in Wisconsin in 1974 and about 33 percent in 1975. However, no new nuclear plants are planned to be operating in Wisconsin before the late 1980s; therefore, the nuclear percentage of total generation will decline until that time if electricity demand continues to increase.

Coal electricity generation in 2025 is nearly three times the 1970 production. Oil and gas do not play major roles in Wisconsin's electricity generation now, nor are these fuels expected to be used as major sources of electrical generation in the future.

The generating capacity in the year 2025 for the Base Case totals approximately 35,000 MW of which 47 percent is coal-fired, 40 percent is from nuclear energy, and 13 percent is hydroelectricity and peaking capacity. Nuclear energy produces more than 40 percent of the electricity (Figure 6.6) because nuclear plants, with their relatively low fuel costs, operate more hours per year than coal plants. Generating capacity in Wisconsin at the end of 1974 was 8,361 MW.[2]

186

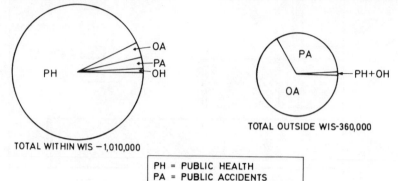

FIGURE 6.7   Quantified human health and safety impact associated with Wisconsin's energy use in 2025 for Scenario S1.

II.C.4.   Environmental Impacts

Certain quantified environmental impacts associated with the Base Case energy use are discussed in this section. The impacts selected are only part of the quantified impacts which in turn are only part of the "total" impact. The models used to estimate quantified impact include a broad range of impacts.[17, 18, 19] Examination of these impacts and comparison among scenarios can provide a general impression for certain categories of impacts. A decision analysis methodology for combining quantified impacts with conventional costs and unquantified impacts is presented in Appendix E.

Human Health and Safety   The quantified impacts relating to human health and safety in the year 2025 are shown in Figure 6.7. Person-days lost (PDL)* are used as a representation of total quantified human health and safety impact, including fatalities, nonfatal injuries, and illnesses.

Human health and safety impacts can be subdivided into several categories such as those indicated in Figure 6.7. Occupational accidents include impacts such as mining accidents and accidents at the power plants; occupational health includes radiation exposure and black lung disease; public accidents include transportation accidents with vehicles involved in the energy system; and public health includes radiation and quantified air pollution health effects. The health impact of air pollution is the primary contributor to the large public health impact shown in Figure

---

* Associating the number of disability days with various accidental injuries is practiced according to methods developed by the American National Standards Institute.[20] This methodology has been extended here to all human health and safety impacts, including death or total disability (6,000 PDL), and nonfatal illnesses.

TABLE 6.13 Quantified Annual Person-Days Lost Resulting From Wisconsin's Energy Use — Base Case Scenario S1[a]

	1970			2025		
	Electric	Nonelectric	Total	Electric	Nonelectric	Total
Within Wisconsin						
Occupational accidents	1,400	5,500	6,900	8,100	21,000	29,000
Occupational health	26	0	26	6,900	0	6,900
Public health	19,000	150,000	170,000	15,000	940,000	950,000
Public accidents	4,400	670	5,100	21,000	6,100	27,000
Total	24,000	160,000	180,000	51,000	960,000	1,000,000
Outside Wisconsin						
Occupational accidents	30,000	50,000	80,000	50,000	190,000	240,000
Occupational health	12,000	4,500	16,000	2,100	1,200	3,300
Public health	7	0	7	680	0	680
Public accidents	13,000	6,100	19,000	62,000	55,000	120,000
Total	55,000	60,000	120,000	120,000	240,000	360,000
Totals						
Occupational accidents	32,000	55,000	87,000	58,000	210,000	270,000
Occupational health	12,000	4,500	16,000	9,000	1,200	10,000
Public health	19,000	150,000	170,000	16,000	940,000	950,000
Public accidents	18,000	6,700	24,000	83,000	61,000	140,000
Grand totals	80,000	220,000	300,000	170,000	1,200,000	1,400,000

[a] One death or case of total disability is associated with 6,000 person-days lost (PDL). Columns and rows may not add to totals because of rounding.

6.7. Occupational accidents are the next largest single category. Two major conclusions may be drawn from Figure 6.7.

- A significant share of the human health and safety impact resulting from energy use in Wisconsin occurs in regions other than Wisconsin.
- Public health impact inside Wisconsin represents nearly all of the total quantified human health and safety impact within Wisconsin.

The quantified human impacts can be further categorized according to whether they are related to electrical or nonelectrical energy and when the energy use occurred. The results for the Base Case for the years 1970 and 2025 are shown in Table 6.13. The PDL calculated by the models are listed in the table in order to avoid rounding difficulties. It is interesting to note that although energy use increases by more than a factor of five from 1970 to 2025 in the Base Case (Table 6.12) the quantified impacts in some categories decline over that period. For example, the PDL in occupational health outside Wisconsin drops from more than 16,000 in 1970 to 3,300* in 2025 primarily because of the assumption that cases

* Radiation exposure accounts for more than half of the occupational health PDL outside Wisconsin in 2025.

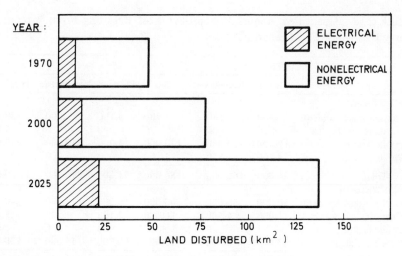

FIGURE 6.8   Land disturbed for fuel resource extraction outside Wisconsin because of energy use within Wisconsin for Scenario S1.

of disability from black lung disease will become rare by 2025. One category that shows a marked increase is public health impact inside Wisconsin from nonelectrical energy use. This is primarily the effect of air pollution on people living in urban areas. Another category that increases over time is occupational health PDL inside Wisconsin from electricity use (26 in 1970; 6,900 in 2025). This is entirely from radiation exposure of workers at nuclear power plants. If all the PDL shown in Table 6.13 were the result of fatalities, the total number of fatalities associated with energy consumption in Wisconsin would have increased from about 50 in 1970 to nearly 230 in 2025.

Land Use for Fuel Resource Extraction   The land area disturbed for extraction of energy resources because of energy use within Wisconsin for Scenario S1 is shown in Figure 6.8. The land use plotted in Figure 6.8 is land disturbed to supply energy in the year shown. In most cases the land can be reclaimed for other uses, although reclamation of land mined in the western United States may be limited because of water scarcity. Twenty-five percent of the coal for electrical generation and 60 percent of the coal for synthetic fuels are assumed to be mined in western states. *All* of the land disturbed for resource extraction occurs outside Wisconsin.

Sulfur Dioxide Emission   The total emissions of sulfur oxides, expressed in metric tons of SO_2, for the eight districts of Wisconsin are shown in Figure 6.9 for the years 1970 and 2025. The future location of electrical plants was assumed to be such that the fraction of coal-fired electrical generation in each district remains constant after taking into account current capacity and announced plans as of 1975. Sulfur emission controls and use of low-sulfur coal in coal-fired electrical plants is

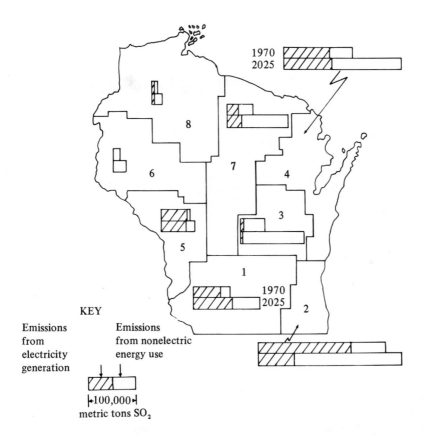

FIGURE 6.9   Total emissions of SO_2 in Wisconsin by district for 1970 and 2025 for Scenario S1.

assumed to reduce the quantity of SO_2 emitted per kilowatt-hour of generation by more than a factor of three over the period 1970 to 2025.

It is obvious from Figure 6.9 that SO_2 emissions in Wisconsin are expected to vary significantly among the eight districts. The corresponding ground-level concentrations can be estimated using the characteristics of the release, such as stack height. Since the ground level concentrations strongly depend on these release characteristics, the average concentrations are not directly proportional to the emissions shown. The effect is clearly shown for Milwaukee, Wisconsin, in Figure 6.10, which has the percentage of emissions on the left half of the chart and the percentage contribution to dose, measured in micrograms per cubic meter ($\mu g/m^3$), on the right half. The relatively low release heights of the residential and service sources result in higher ground-level concentration in the urban area than the emissions from the tall stacks associated with electrical generation plants and industrial sources.

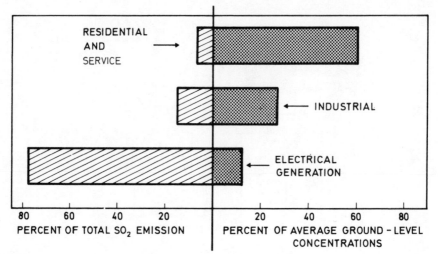

FIGURE 6.10   Sulfur dioxide emissions and concentrations in Milwaukee, Wisconsin, in 1970.

II.D.   SOME CONCLUSIONS FOR THE BASE CASE

It is difficult to assess the validity of any scenario that has a time span of more than 50 years. Scenario S1 for Wisconsin is based on what is believed to be a relatively consistent policy set, as presented in section II.B. The guideline used in selecting assumptions for the Base Case was a continuation of current trends in factors related to energy consumption, and, over the long term, including slower population growth and more efficient energy use than extrapolation of historical trends would indicate. One can speculate as to the validity of numerous assumptions for the Base Case. No claim is made about the likelihood of realization for S1; it does, however, provide a point of comparison for other scenarios with some of the key assumptions changed.

The Base Case has demonstrated the problem of growing demand for petroleum and natural gas in the face of declining ability to supply these fuels for U.S. sources. The synthetic fuel (produced from coal) supplies over half the total end-use energy in the Base Case by the year 2025. A supply alternative to synthetic fuel use is a massive conversion to electricity, where coal can also be the primary energy source.

The growth rate in electrical energy generation in the Base Case is significantly below historical trends and some relatively recent projections for Wisconsin,[11] such as the 7.4-percent-per-year growth that occurred in Wisconsin over the 1942 to 1974 period,[2,21] and the 5-percent-per-year growth rate from 1976 to 1995 that was recently predicted by the large electric utilities in Wisconsin. For the period 1970 through 2000 the electricity generation average growth rate in S1 is 3.6 percent per year. The growth in total primary energy over the same period is only 2.8 percent per year, so electricity continues its historical trend of growing somewhat faster than total energy consumption. However, electricity does not play a dominate role in S1.

The quantified impacts that have been estimated for the Base Case show that regions other than Wisconsin will feel the effect of energy consumption in Wisconsin. For example, more than 25 percent of the quantified human health and safety impact associated with Wisconsin's energy use occurs outside Wisconsin. The degree to which the environmental impacts are "exported" to other states and nations is related to the mix of fuel supply systems.

Another observation for the Base Case is that the residential sector has a dramatic decline in its share of the total end-use energy. The service, transportation, and industrial sectors are all roughly equivalent in end-use energy by 2025. Since the service sector in 1970 is the smallest energy consumer of the end-use sectors, the equality with transportation and industry by 2025 represents a rapid expansion in energy consumption in service relative to all other sectors.

Other observations on the Base Case are presented in the final section of this chapter.

III.   OTHER SCENARIOS

III.A.   THE HIGH ENERGY CONSUMPTION, HIGH ELECTRICITY CASE – SCENARIO S2

The second scenario (S2) has assumptions that tend to result in higher energy consumption in Wisconsin than the Base Case (S1). In addition, electricity is assumed to be preferred for end-use energy. The differences in critical assumptions between Scenarios S1 and S2 are highlighted in Table 6.14.

The growth of population primarily in low-density areas within 20 km of urban areas (exurban dispersal policy) results in more single-family houses (fewer apartments) than the suburban extension policy of the Base Case. Also, the transportation energy is increased because the average trip length is longer with exurban dispersal than with suburban extension.

The use of electricity for space heating and water heating is almost universal in new construction for Scenario S2. Electricity consumption per unit of industrial value-added is assumed to grow even faster than the 2.7 percent annual rate that U.S. industry experienced from 1955 to 1970.[9] The resulting electricity consumption by demand sector for the year 2025 is compared with the Base Case results in Table 6.15 (the 1970 end-use electricity consumption was about 24×10^9 kWh). The assumption changes listed in Table 6.14 caused electricity consumption in 2025 to increase by nearly a factor of three over the Base Case. However, end-use demand for natural gas and petroleum was nearly one-third *less* in the high-energy

TABLE 6.14   Wisconsin Scenario S2 in Relation to S1[a]

	Changes in Policy or Assumptions
Urban form	• Exurban dispersal policy (growth in low population density areas but within 20 km of urban areas) instead of suburban extension growth in suburbs and fringes of urban areas).
Transportation sector	• Average automobile efficiency remains at the 1975 level instead of improving 40%. • An urban electric automobile is introduced in 1980 and accounts for about 7% of personal transportation by 2025.
Residential sector	• New residences are 90% single family houses instead of 75% (the remainder of new residences are apartments). • All water heating in new residences is electric. • More than 90% of new residences use electric heat. • New residences cannot use any natural gas.
Service sector	• Commercial buildings are open 45% of the time instead of 40%. • Electric heat and air conditioning is emphasized so that nonelectric fuel use declines from the 1970 levels.
Industrial sector	• Total energy intensiveness (energy consumed per dollar value-added) grows at 1.3%/yr instead of 0.34%/yr. • Electricity intensiveness grows at a rate of 3.4%/yr instead of 0.72%/yr. • Nonelectrical intensiveness grows at 0.89%/yr instead of 0.29%/yr.
Energy supply	• New nonpeaking electrical generating capacity is 70% nuclear energy instead of 50%.
Environmental impact	• Lax controls for SO_2 and particulates from nonelectric fuel use.

[a] Compare with section II.B of this chapter.

TABLE 6.15   End-Use Electricity Consumption in 2025 for Wisconsin Scenarios S1 and S2 (10^9 kWh)

	Base Case (S1)	High-Energy Case (S2)
Residential sector	29.6	74.6
Service sector	77.1	172.6
Industrial sector	33.1	139.5
Transportation sector	0.0	6.4
Total	139.8	393.1

TABLE 6.16   End-Use Petroleum, Natural Gas, and Synthetic Fuels from Coal in 2025 for Wisconsin Scenarios S1 and S2 (10^{15} cal)

	Base Case (S1)	High-Energy Case (S2)
Residential sector	101.5	24.5
Service sector	189.0	6.3
Industrial sector	108.5	155.1
Transportation sector	228.1	248.8
Total	627.1	434.7

TABLE 6.17   Wisconsin Scenario S3 in Relation to S1[a]

	Changes in Policy or Assumptions
Urban form	• Growth in small compact cities resulting in high population densities.
Transportation sector	• Mass transit use doubles from S1.
	• Urban bus load factor increased to 15 passengers per vehicle.
	• Urban auto load factor increased to 1.7 passengers per auto.
	• An urban car captures 30% of the new car market after 1980. This car has fuel economy of nearly 13 km/liter for urban travel and 17 km/liter for intercity travel (30 and 40 miles/gallon).
	• Compact and small cars capture 45% of the market, leaving only 25% for large and intermediate autos.
	• The distribution between truck and rail freight transport was assumed to shift to rail so that the metric ton-kilometers of freight shipments in 2025 were the same for rail and truck.
Residential sector	• Only 50% of new residences are single family homes.
	• Better insulation and conservation reduces heating requirements per house by 30 to 40%.
	• Solar home heating and water heating, with an electrical auxiliary system, is available starting in 1980. The percentage of new residences using solar increases from 5 in 1980 to 50 in 2000 and stays constant after that. Only new dwelling units use solar energy; no retrofitting of existing units is considered.
Service sector	• Solar energy reduces demand for natural gas and petroleum by 28% in 2025 compared with the same case with no solar energy.
	• Wall to floor area ratio for new buildings is reduced from 0.35 to 0.30.
	• Glass to floor area ratio for new buildings is reduced from 0.15 to 0.10.
	• Better insulation reduces heat transfer through walls and windows.
	• Lower thermostat settings in winter during the day (18.9°C) and night (15.6°C).
	• Higher thermostat settings in summer during the day (23.9°C)
	• Building ventilation rate reduced from 0.046 to 0.037 m^3/min/m^2 floor area for all months.
	• Cooling system efficiencies increase relative to S1.
Industrial sector	• Total energy intensiveness declines at 0.66%/yr.
	• Electricity intensiveness declines at 0.36%/yr.
	• Nonelectric intensiveness declines at 0.70%/yr.
Energy supply	• Solar energy for space heating.
	• Solar electric power plants account for 30% of the generation and 50% of the capacity by 2025.
	• No new nuclear plants; all new capacity is either coal-fired or solar energy.
Environmental impact	• Stringent controls for SO_2 and particulates from nonelectric fuel use. Improved SO_2 removal systems at electric power plants.

[a] Compare with section II.B of this chapter and Table 6.14.

TABLE 6.18   Solar Energy Contribution in S3 (percentage of total energy)

	2000	2025
Residential end-use[a]	3.8	16.9
Service-end-use[a]	1.8	8.8
Electrical generation	4.2	30.0

[a] This does not include the percentage of electricity supplied by solar energy. The energy obtained from solar space heating and water heating is divided by total end-use energy for all purposes to obtain the percentages in the table.

case than in the Base Case (Table 6.16) primarily because of electricity substitution in S2.

Other results of the high-energy case are presented in a later section (III.C) that contains a comparison of all three Wisconsin scenarios.

III.B.   THE LOW ENERGY CONSUMPTION, HIGH SOLAR ENERGY CASE – SCENARIO S3

The third Wisconsin scenario (S3) selected for presentation has assumptions that tend to reduce energy consumption when compared with Scenario S1. Solar energy is assumed to be developed for both electrical and nonelectrical applications. Nuclear power plants remain at the 1975 level of capacity and generation; all new electrical plants use either coal or solar energy; solar energy grows rapidly after the year 2000. Half of all new residences use solar space heating and water heating. Other differences in important assumptions between the Base Case and S3 are listed in Table 6.17.

Transportation energy demand is significantly lower in S3 than in S1 because of the assumption changes listed in Table 6.17. The shift of some freight from truck to train results in nearly a 25-percent energy savings in freight transport when compared with the Base Case although the number of ton-kilometers of freight is constant in all Wisconsin scenarios.

In S3, population growth is in small compact cities that result in high population densities. This limits solar space heating applications since solar energy can supply less of the total space heating energy needs in a high-density area. However, solar energy does contribute significantly to the total energy requirements in this scenario, as indicated in Table 6.18. Development of solar electricity to such a large degree by 2025 would require very favorable circumstances. Other results of S3 are presented in the next section in which all three Wisconsin scenarios are compared.

III.C.   WISCONSIN SCENARIO COMPARISONS

III.C.1.   Primary Energy

Primary energy per capita for the three scenarios is displayed in Figure 6.11. Scenario S3 has a 1.5-percent-per-year average increase in per capita primary energy

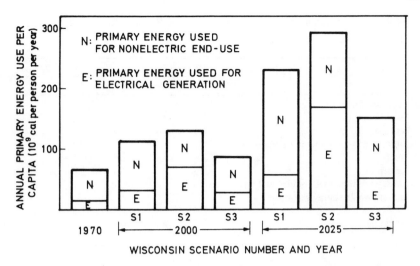

FIGURE 6.11   Primary energy use per capita for the Wisconsin scenarios.

consumption over the period 1970 to 2025. However, if enough oil and gas were available that synthetic fuels from coal were not needed, the per capita primary energy use in 2025 for S3 would be only 120×10^9 cal per person. The rest of the energy is losses associated with conversion of coal to synthetic fuels. As indicated in Table 6.19, the average annual increase in per capita primary energy use would be only 1.1 percent if synthetics are not needed. Furthermore, renewable resources (solar energy and hydropower) contribute 20×10^9 cal per capita to the primary energy in 2025 for Scenario S3. Excluding these renewable resources, primary energy per capita grows at 1.3 percent per year if synthetics are needed, and only 0.8 percent if synthetics are not needed. Primary energy in S3 grows at only 1.8 percent per year from 1970 to 2000 (0.85 percent per capita annually). One reason S3 exhibits a higher growth rate from 2000 to 2025 than from 1970 to 2000 is that some conservation measures have their major impact before the year 2000. For example, the average fuel efficiency of new automobiles is assumed to improve dramatically between 1970 and 1985, and then remain at that level through the year 2025.

Scenarios S1 and S2 show much higher growth rates in primary energy use, as Table 6.19 indicates. Scenario S2 in particular represents a high-energy future with a total growth in primary energy of 3.3 percent per year from 1970 to 2000. This is close to the average growth in primary energy of 3.5 percent per year that took place in the United States between 1950 and 1973.[4, 22] Because of the rise in world oil prices, the rise in other energy prices, economic recession, and general awareness about energy, primary energy consumption in the United States by the year 1976 had not increased above the 1973 level; the average growth rate in U.S. primary energy consumption from 1950 to 1976 was 3.0 percent per year.[23] The Energy

TABLE 6.19   Average Annual Growth Rates in Primary Energy Consumption for the Three Wisconsin Scenarios (%/yr)

	1970–2000			1970–2025		
	S1	S2	S3	S1	S2	S3
Including synthetic fuel conversion losses						
Total	2.6	3.3	1.8	3.1	3.5	2.3
Per capita	1.7	2.4	0.9	2.3	2.8	1.5
Excluding synthetic fuel conversion losses						
Total	2.4	3.2	1.6	2.5	3.3	1.9
Per capita	1.5	2.3	0.7	1.8	2.5	1.1
Excluding synthetic fuel conversion losses and renewable energy resources[a]						
Total	2.4	3.2	1.5	2.5	3.3	1.5
Per capita	1.5	2.3	0.6	1.8	2.5	0.8

[a] Solar energy and hydropower are the only renewable resources in these scenarios.

Policy Project of the Ford Foundation (EPP) found average annual growth rates in primary energy between 1970 and 2000 of 3.5 percent for the high-growth scenario, 2.1 percent for the "Technical Fix" scenario, and 1.3 percent for the zero-energy-growth scenario.[8]* This compares with 3.3 and 1.8 percent per year growth from 1970 to 2000 for the high and low Wisconsin scenarios shown here (see Table 6.19). President Carter's U.S. National Energy Plan called for an annual growth rate of less than 2 percent by 1985.[10]

Primary energy use by fuel type for the three scenarios is shown in Figure 6.12. All scenarios show a significant expansion in coal use. Natural gas and petroleum use declines to 80 percent of the 1970 levels by 2025 because supplies are assumed to be limited. Coal use in 2025 for synthetic fuel production is 78, 62, and 62 percent of the total coal use in S1, S2, and S3.

III.C.2.   End-Use Energy

End-use energy for the years 2000 and 2025 for the three Wisconsin scenarios is listed in Table 6.20. It is interesting to note that although S2 is a high-energy scenario, end-use energy in S2 is less than in S1 in, for example, the residential sector. The increased use of electricity in S2 results in less end-use energy, but the primary energy use in S2 is significantly greater than in S1, as Figures 6.11 and 6.12 show.

---

* These growth rates are average annual percentage changes over the entire period. They may vary considerably during the period. For example, the EPP zero-energy-growth scenario has a constant energy demand after 1990.[8]

TABLE 6.20   End-Use Energy for the Wisconsin Scenarios (10^{15} cal)

	1970	2000			2025		
		S1	S2	S3	S1	S2	S3
Residential	70.8	109	86	87	127	89	85
Service	29.8	97	63	72	264	155	182
Industrial	57.8	127	160	94	237	409	137
Transportation	77.8	129	144	101	228	254	168
Total[a]	236.0	462	453	352	856	907	572

[a] Columns may not add to totals because of rounding.

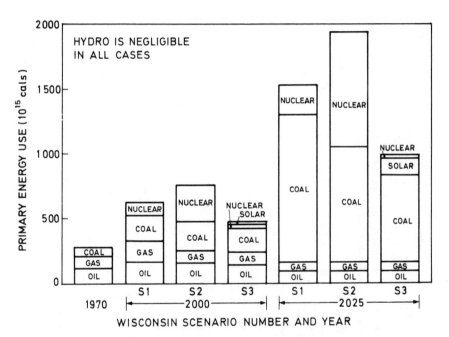

FIGURE 6.12   Primary energy use by fuel type for the Wisconsin scenarios.

The average annual increase in *end-use* energy for the period 1970 to 2000 is

1. 1.4 percent in S1
2. 1.3 percent in S2
3. 0.4 percent in S3

These growth rates increase somewhat after the year 2000, primarily because economic growth continues at the same rate but with lower population growth.

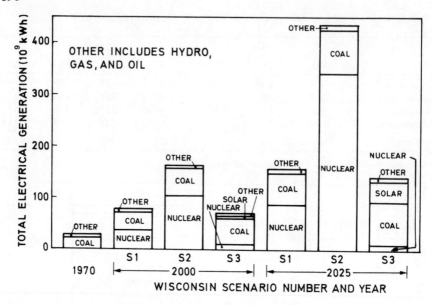

FIGURE 6.13   Electrical generation for the Wisconsin scenarios.

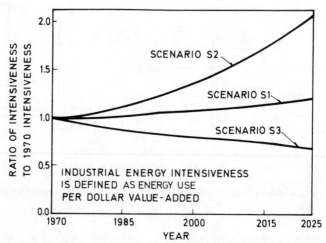

FIGURE 6.14   Wisconsin industrial energy intensiveness for the three scenarios in relation to 1970 intensiveness.

III.C.3.   Electrical Generation

The emphasis on electricity in S2 is strikingly clear in Figure 6.13, which shows generation by fuel type as a function of time. Nuclear and coal sources provide all

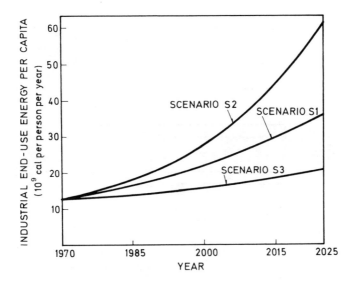

FIGURE 6.15   Industrial end-use energy per capita for the Wisconsin scenarios.

but a small portion of the electricity except in S3 where solar electrical generation provides 30 percent of the total by 2025. The average annual growth rate in electrical generation ranges from 3.1 percent in S3 to 5.2 percent in S2.

III.C.4.   *Energy Intensiveness in Industry*

Each Wisconsin scenario has a different assumption about energy intensiveness in industry, as shown in Figure 6.14. The high-energy scenario assumes that the intensiveness doubles over the 55-year period; the Base Case intensiveness is nearly constant; and the low-energy case has intensiveness declining to about two-thirds of its 1970 value. The average change in intensiveness ranges from − 0.7 percent per year in S3 to + 1.3 percent per year for S2. For comparison, the U.S. industrial energy intensiveness* used by the Energy Policy Project declined at a rate of 0.2 percent per year for the historical growth scenario and decreased at an average rate of 1.5 percent per year in the zero-energy-growth scenario.[8]

The industrial end-use energy per capita for the three Wisconsin scenarios is plotted as a function of time in Figure 6.15. It should be noted that these three scenarios are based on the same population and industrial value-added assumptions. Thus, the curve for S3 in Figure 6.15 indicates that value-added per capita in industry is assumed to increase slightly faster than energy intensiveness declines.

* Industrial energy intensiveness is estimated by dividing energy use in industry by total manufacturing value-added.

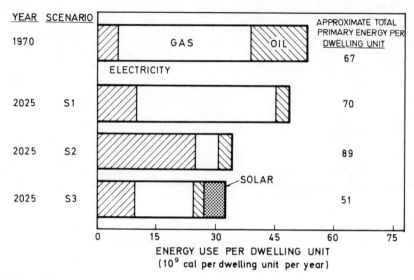

FIGURE 6.16   Annual end-use energy per average dwelling unit for Wisconsin.

III.C.5.   Total Energy Use Per Dwelling Unit

The total end-use energy per dwelling unit for the three Wisconsin scenarios is plotted in Figure 6.16. It may seem surprising that the end-use energy in 2025 in the high-energy scenario (S2) is only slightly greater than in the low-energy scenario (S3) and is significantly lower than in the Base Case. The emphasis on electricity in S2 results in relatively low end-use energy but relatively high primary energy as the numbers on the right of Figure 6.16 indicate. Electrically-heated housing units are assumed to have better insulation than oil- or gas-heated units.

Since Figure 6.16 shows energy per average housing unit, it should be noted that the percentage of apartments is not the same in the three scenarios, as shown in Figure 6.17. Single-family houses require more energy than apartments; therefore, the 2025 primary energy use for S1 and S3 in Figure 6.16 would be somewhat higher, but still less than for S2, if the same percentage of single-family houses were used in all scenarios.

III.C.6.   Personal Transportation

The end-use energy for personal transportation for the three scenarios is shown in Figure 6.18. Even with the assumed population growth from 4.4 million people in 1970 to 6.6 million in 2025, energy use for personal transportation shows a decline in absolute terms in S3 (21 percent over the same period) primarily because of (1) the introduction of a very efficient urban car, (2) increase in load factors, and (3) urban form (Table 6.17). The high-energy scenario (S2) shows a relatively level energy

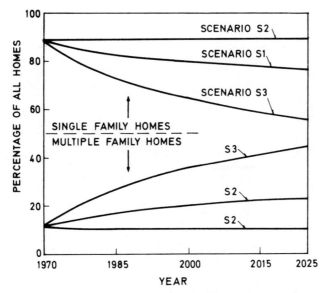

FIGURE 6.17   Type of housing assumed for the Wisconsin scenarios.

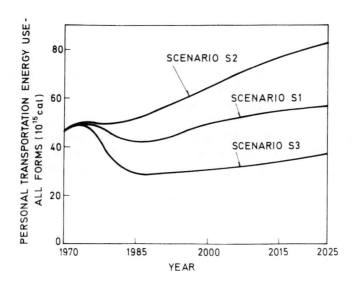

FIGURE 6.18   End-use energy for personal transportation for the Wisconsin scenarios.

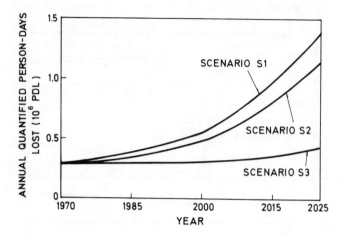

FIGURE 6.19   Quantified human health and safety impacts associated with energy use for the Wisconsin scenarios.

demand in the early years because the compact and small cars are assumed to increase their market share from 40 percent to 60 percent of the new car sales over the period 1970 to 1980.* These results for personal transportation clearly demonstrate that relatively modest measures in the transportation sector may save significant amounts of energy in a supply category where resources are limited.

III.C.7.   Environmental Impacts

A comparison of the impacts among scenarios must of necessity be brief and cover only a few of the quantified impacts from the models. A few representative quantified impacts have been selected for description here. More details about the impacts that have been quantified and the models used can be found in Buehring and Foell.[18]

The quantified impact on human health and safety, as measured in person-days lost (PDL), that results from Wisconsin's energy use for the three scenarios is shown as a function of time in Figure 6.19.† The primary contributor is the quantified health impact on the public of air pollution from nonelectric energy use; this single category represents 68, 54, and 18 percent of the total PDL in the year 2025 for

---

* Scenario S2 includes some electricity use for electric cars. If this electricity is included as primary energy in the transportation energy use of S2 in 2025, the transportation energy use increases from 83×10^{15} cal (Figure 6.18) to 95×10^{15} cal.
† At 6,000 PDL per fatality, the total PDL associated with energy use in S1 for 2025 is equivalent to nearly 230 fatalities. Alternatively, if these PDL are associated only with illness, the level of PDL in S1 is equivalent to one extra day of illness per year for 21 percent of Wisconsin's population in 2025.

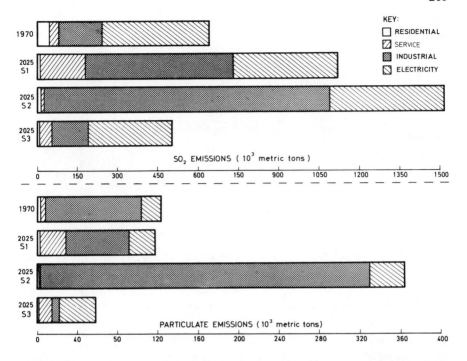

FIGURE 6.20 Sulfur dioxide and particulate emissions by sector for the Wisconsin scenarios.

the three scenarios, respectively.* One surprising result of this analysis is that the total PDL in the Base Case scenario (S1) is greater than the high-energy scenario (S2). One reason that S1 has relatively high PDL is that residential and service SO_2 emissions (Figure 6.20) are relatively high in areas of high population density. As described earlier, residential and service emissions generally have low release heights and therefore cause higher ground-level concentrations per unit emitted than emissions from tall stacks (Figure 6.10).

Residential and service emissions in S2 are less than in S1 because of the substitution of electricity for fossil fuels. Scenario S3 has much lower PDL from air pollution primarily because the industrial emissions are nearly an order of magnitude less than in S2 and the majority of service emissions are away from the main population center of Milwaukee. The quantified health impact of air pollution in the Wisconsin scenarios is strongly related to urban form as well as to the emission characteristics.

In 2025 more than one-fourth of the PDL in each scenario occurred outside

---

* Only a portion of the impacts of air pollution have been quantified; these are primarily the result of short-term exposures to high levels of SO_2.[19]

TABLE 6.21   Control Factor Assumptions for SO_2 and Particulates in 2025 for the Wisconsin Scenarios

| | Potential Emission That is Retained Because of Emission Control or Fuel Treatment (%) | | | | | |
| | SO_2 | | | Particulates | | |
	S1	S2	S3	S1	S2	S3
Residential						
oil	60	30	80	0	0	0
gas	40	20	60	0	0	0
Service						
coal	0	0	40	60	40	80
oil	60	30	80	0	0	0
gas	40	20	60	0	0	0
Industrial						
coal	30	0	70	95	90	99
oil	50	0	80	30	0	50
gas	40	20	60	0	0	0
Electricity						
coal	67	67	75	99	99	99

Wisconsin's boundary; in S3 two-thirds of the total quantifed human health and safety impact is in other regions. Thus, it appears that if human health and safety is an important consideration in energy policy decisions, one must take a systemwide perspective and look beyond the impacts that occur in the immediate vicinity of the energy consumption.

The emissions shown in Figure 6.20 depend not only on the fuel used but also on the assumed control factors (Table 6.21). Thus, the industrial SO_2 emissions in 2025 decline by about a factor of 8 between S2 and S3 because the quantity of coal used drops and because the emission per unit of coal used in S3 is only 30 percent of the emission in S2. Electric power plants are assumed to have relatively good controls in all scenarios because they are such large point sources of pollution that extensive control measures are expected to be required.

Total quantified person-days lost are plotted against primary energy use in Figure 6.21. One observation that can be made from Figure 6.21 is that the quantified human health and safety expenditure per unit of primary energy is considerably less in S3 than S1. For example, in the year 2025, the PDL per 10^{18} cal of primary energy are 0.90, 0.59, and 0.43 in S1, S2, and S3, respectively; in 1970, this ratio was 1.0. Another observation is that S2, with its high electricity use, is less costly in terms of *quantified* human health and safety than the Base Case, in spite of the larger energy requirement. These results are influenced strongly by the quantified air pollution person-days lost, by the selection of alternative energy options, and by the assumed gradual reduction in human health and safety impact per unit of coal mined.

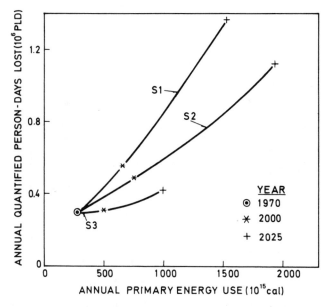

FIGURE 6.21 Quantified person-days lost as a function of primary energy use for the Wisconsin scenarios.

In some categories the low-energy scenario has greater impacts than the other scenarios. For example, land disturbed per unit of primary energy is considerably greater in S3 because of the solar electrical generating plants (Figure 6.22). The land use shown is the sum of all land disturbed, except for electricity transmission,* in order to produce the energy in the year shown. The land use in S3 by 2025 is about 0.3 percent of the area of Wisconsin; however, not all land use is in Wisconsin. The land use for solar energy in 2025 in S3 is 240 km². Solar electrical generation in Scenario S3 accounts for 30 percent of the total in 2025. The total land use in 2025 in Scenario S2 is larger than for S3 however; the primary energy requirement is approximately twice as large for S2 as for S3.

No scenario has the lowest environmental impact in *all* categories considered. Therefore, one must make value judgments concerning the tradeoffs among impacts. Of course, the conventional costs of the alternatives and the unquantified impacts must be included in the analysis along with the quantified impacts as discussed in Appendix E.

* Land for electricity transmission corridors may still be usable, e.g. for agriculture. All land shown in Figure 6.22 is at least temporarily unavailable for other uses. The total land disturbed in 30 yr may be less for a solar plant than for a coal plant since new coal must be mined every year. However, the land used for mining can often be quickly reclaimed for other uses, while the land at the power plant is in use for the lifetime of the plant.

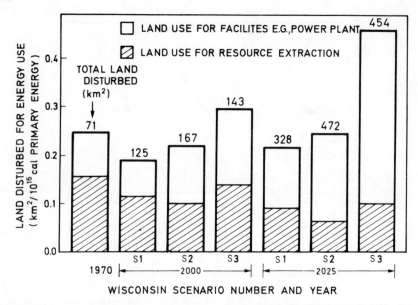

FIGURE 6.22   Land disturbed per unit of primary energy for the Wisconsin scenarios.

IV.   SENSITIVITY STUDIES

A thorough sensitivity ansalysis of the scenarios presented in the previous section would require far more space than is available here. Therefore, several representative sensitivity studies have been selected for presentation. Among the topics discussed in this section are solar home heating and water heating, type of housing and fuel consumption, SO_2 controls on power plants, and transportation energy related to urban form.

IV.A.   SOLAR HOME HEATING AND WATER HEATING

Solar energy is a major supply source for space heating and water heating in the low-energy scenario (S3). Residences that use solar systems with electrical auxiliary systems are assumed to increase from 5 percent of those constructed in 1980 to 50 percent of those constructed in 2000. After the year 2000, 50 percent of all new housing units are assumed to use solar energy.

The results for residential energy demand in the solar energy scenario (S3) are compared with the results for the same scenario with no solar energy in Table 6.22. Elimination of solar space heating and water heating in 2025 for the low-energy scenario would cause residential demand for (1) natural gas to increase by 56 percent, (2) electricity to decline by 13 percent, and (3) nonsolar end-use energy to

TABLE 6.22   Impact of Solar Energy on Wisconsin's Residential Energy Demand

End-use Residential Energy				Nonsolar Energy Use[b]	
With Solar Homes		Without Solar Homes			
Electricity $(10^9 \text{ kWh})^a$	Natural Gas $(10^{15} \text{ cal})^a$	Electricity (10^9 kWh)	Natural Gas (10^{15} cal)	Solar Scenario $(10^{15} \text{ cal})^{a, c}$	No Solar Energy (10^{15} cal)
1970 8.6	44.2	8.6	44.2	70.6	70.6
2000 21.0	50.1	20.2	55.0	81.8	86.0
2025 28.2	39.2	24.4	61.3	70.8	89.6

[a] These columns show results for the S3 low-energy scenario.
[b] Electricity converted at its end-use energy value of 0.86×10^6 cal/kWh.
[c] Solar energy is excluded from the end-use tabulated here. If solar energy absorbed by the collection devices were included, the results would be 85.0×10^{15} cal in 2000 and 85.2×10^{15} cal in 2025.

increase by 27 percent. For the low-energy scenario assumptions, solar energy significantly reduces the residential demand for natural gas, a fuel that is expected to be in short supply. The energy saving associated with solar energy could be even greater if some assumptions listed in Table 6.17 were changed to favor solar energy, e.g. addition of solar facilities to existing homes (retrofitting) could be allowed.

It is interesting to note that the residential nonsolar energy demand in the year 2025 for the case with solar energy is approximately the same as the residential nonsolar energy demand in 1970, in spite of a doubling of the total number of dwelling units over the 55-year period. Other contributing factors are the shift toward apartments with low energy use, better insulation, and other conservation measures.

IV.B.   IMPACTS OF HOUSING TYPE ON FUEL USE

An important parameter in the residential model used is the percentage of single-family houses in new construction. In the Base Case, new housing is assumed to be 75 percent single-family houses and 25 percent multiple-family dwellings. The impact on natural gas use of changing the percentage of single-family houses in new construction is displayed in Figure 6.23; the differences are primarily the result of larger space heating requirements for single family houses. Natural gas demand in the residential sector for the case with 90 percent single-family houses is about 11 percent higher than the Base Case by the year 2025. The shapes of the curves in Figure 6.23 are strongly linked to the need for new housing; this in turn is affected by assumptions about population growth, family size, and replacement of old houses. However, it is evident in Figure 6.23 that a major shift to apartments, with no change in other factors such as insulation, would result in significantly lower demand compared to the Base Case scenario for natural gas demand in the residential sector.

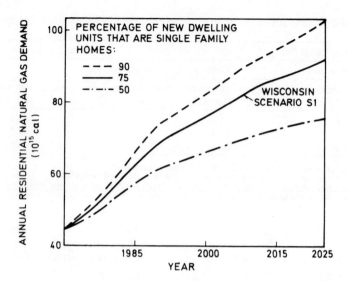

FIGURE 6.23   Effect of the type of housing on residential natural gas use in Wisconsin.

IV.C.   SULFUR DIOXIDE CONTROL FOR ELECTRICAL GENERATION

Electrical generation from coal in Scenario S1 results in sulfur dioxide emissions that are at the maximum level permitted by the U.S. Environmental Protection Agency emission standards* (see section II.A. in Appendix B).

The standard is met by using a combination of low-sulfur coal from western states and SO_2 stack gas removal equipment on plants that use high-sulfur midwestern coal. The impact of eliminating SO_2 emission standards and discontinuing use of western coal in Wisconsin's power plants is the subject of this sensitivity study.

The impact on human health and safety in the year 2025 is indicated in Table 6.23. Eliminating SO_2 controls increases the public health impact in the year 2025 by about 34,000 PDL, but the public accident PDL declines by about the same amount.[†] The increase in public health PDL is primarily increased days of aggravation of heart and lung disease in the elderly. The reduction in public accidents is the result of shifting to coal that must be shipped a shorter distance (midwestern) than the western coal. The overall change in quantified PDL that results is small, but the burden has been shifted somewhat from people who live outside Wisconsin (transportation accidents) to people who live in Wisconsin (public health). The same general conclusions hold for the cumulative totals shown in Table 6.23, except that the magnitudes of the PDL are increased.

---

* 1.2 lb SO_2 per 10^6 Btu heat input.
† This quantity of PDL is approximately equivalent to 6 premature fatalities. Total PDL in 2025 for S1 is 1,400,000.

TABLE 6.23   Quantified Person-Days Lost Related to Electrical Generation from Coal[a]

	2025		Cumulative 1970–2025	
	Base Case (S1)	No SO$_2$ Controls, No Western Coal	Base Case (S1)	No SO$_2$ Controls, No Western Coal
Occupational accidents (10^3 PDL)	47	46	1,600	1,600
Public accidents (10^3 PDL)	82	45	2,600	1,500
Occupational health (10^3 PDL)	0.3	0.4	100	100
Public health (10^3 PDL)	15	49	600	1,600
Total	144	141	4,900	4,800
PDL inside Wisconsin (%)	28	45	29	44
Total coal-fired electrical generation (10^9 kWh)	62	62	2,056	2,056

[a] Six thousand PDL are associated with each fatality or case of total disability. One PDL is associated with each excess asthma attack or excess day of aggravation for elderly people with preexisting heart and lung disease.

TABLE 6.24   Impacts on Land Related to Electrical Generation from Coal (km^2)

	2025		Cumulative 1970–2025	
	Base Case (S1)[a]	No SO$_2$ Controls No Western Coal	Base Case (S1)[a]	No SO$_2$ Controls, No Western Coal
Disturbed by surface mining	12.8	14.6	425	478
Subsidence from underground mining	7.9	9.5	268	312
Ash disposal at power plant	0.22	0.20	7.3	6.6
Sulfur sludge disposal at power plant	0.37	0.0	10.4	0.0
Solid waste from underground mining	0.03	0.03	1.0	1.1
Solid waste from coal cleaning plants	0.11	0.13	3.7	4.3

[a] There also is land disturbed in connection with the limestone needed for the sulfur removal system. In Scenario S1 the limestone needed is 1.3 million metric tons in 2025 and the cumulative (1970 to 2025) total is 38 million metric tons.

The impacts on land in the year 2025 that result from eliminating power plant SO$_2$ controls and discontinuing use of western coal are shown in Table 6.24. Western coal is generally found in much thicker seams than midwestern coal; therefore, more land is disturbed for surface mining and subsidence if midwestern coal is used. Of course, elimination of SO$_2$ controls also eliminates land needed for sulfur sludge disposal. The sludge is the product of the desulfurization system and is assumed to be piled in waste banks approximately 7.5 m high for wet limestone removal systems. The elimination of western coal results in more land disturbed for mining

TABLE 6.25   Impact of Electricity Supply Change for the Wisconsin High-Energy Scenario (S2)

	S2 as presented	S2 with No New Nuclear Plants
Annual electricity generation (10^9 kWh)		
2000 – nuclear energy	106	10
2000 – coal	53	149
2025 – nuclear energy	341	10
2025 – coal	85	416
Annual land use outside Wisconsin for Wisconsin's electricity generation (km²)		
1970	9	9
2000	19	50
2025	31	139
Annual quantified public person-days lost from SO_2 radiation exposure resulting from electrical generation		
1970	10	10
2000	1,500	140
2025	5,700	170
Annual quantified public person-days lost from SO_2 exposure resulting from electrical generation		
1970	19,000	19,000
2000	13,000	37,000
2025	20,000	97,000
Annual water evaporated for electrical generation (10^6 m³)		
1970	27	27
2000	320	250
2025	920	690
Cumulative (1970 through 2025) fuel resource use for electricity (10^6 metric tons)		
Uranium oxide (U_3O_8)	0.140	0.012
Thorium oxide (ThO_2)	0.0017	0.0001
Uranium and Thorium ore		
At 0.2% grade	71.	6.
At 0.01% grade	1,400.	120.
Coal	1,140.	3,340.

in midwestern states. However, the long-term impact may be less because midwestern land generally can be reclaimed faster and with less costly measures.

The difference between the total cumulative impacts for the Base Case and for "No SO_2 Controls" shown in Table 6.24 indicates that nearly 100 km² of additional land would be disturbed for mining if SO_2 controls are eliminated. However over $10 \, km^2$ of land would have sulfur sludge piles by 2025 if the controls remain. The land for sludge piles may have more permanent effects than the nonwestern land disturbed for mining.

In summary, some effects of elimination of SO_2 controls on power plants and discontinuing use of western coal in power plants are:

- Some of the human health and safety impact related to electrical generation in Wisconsin is shifted from people who live in other states to the people who live in Wisconsin and are the electricity consumers.
- Land disturbed for mining is increased in areas where reclamation is easiest, but land for sulfur sludge waste piles is eliminated.

Of course there are many other factors that need to be considered before one can decide whether SO_2 emission standards for Wisconsin power plants are needed.

IV.D.   ELECTRICITY SUPPLY MIX FOR THE HIGH-ENERGY SCENARIO

The electricity supply in the high-energy scenario (S2) is based on the assumption that 70 percent of the new non peaking electrical generating capacity added after 1982 is nuclear and the remainder is coal-fired. Some effects of having all new capacity be coal-fired are reviewed in this section.

The annual electricity generation that is nuclear and coal-fired for the years 2000 and 2025 is listed in Table 6.25 for S2 as presented earlier and for the same scenario with no new nuclear plants. Nuclear generation in the case with no new nuclear plants is about the current level of nuclear generation in Wisconsin.

The annual land use outside Wisconsin that results from electricity generation in Wisconsin includes:

- Land disturbed for surface-mined uranium
- Uranium mill tailings storage area
- Radioactive waste burial area
- Land disturbed by and subsidence from coal mining
- Coal mining waste disposal area
- Coal cleaning plant waste disposal area

Most of the land disturbed by mining can be reclaimed for other uses. The land used for waste disposal is generally a more permanent commitment, especially in the case of radioactive wastes. The land use tabulated here does not include land used for siting fuel industry buildings or any of the land used at the power plant itself (inside Wisconsin). The results shown in Table 6.25 indicate that the switch to coal increases the land use outside Wisconsin by over $100 \, km^2$ in the year 2025. In general, electricity from coal requires more land disturbance than electricity from nuclear energy. However, this conclusion could be reversed by assuming that all coal were mined from very thick western subbituminous seams and all uranium from surface mining of very low-grade ores.*

The quantified public PDL from radiation is reduced approximately in proportion to the reduction in nuclear generation. The PDL level in 2025 in the high nuclear energy case is approximately equivalent to one radiation fatality per year. The quantified occupational PDL from radiation is about six times greater than the public PDL shown in Table 6.25.

When coal-fired plants meet SO_2 emission standards that were announced after 1970, the quantified public PDL from SO_2 exposure increases approximately in proportion to the coal generation. The primary contributors to this category of PDL are excess asthma attacks (one PDL is assumed per attack) and excess days of aggravation of heart and lung disease in the elderly. If there were no SO_2 removal systems assumed in these cases, public PDL from SO_2 would be increased by approximately a factor of three in the years 2000 and 2025.

The total water evaporated from power plant cooling systems is about 30 percent higher in the case with new nuclear plants than in the case with no new nuclear plants. In general, nuclear reactors have a larger quantity of heat to reject to the condenser cooling water than a similarly-sized coal plant because the nuclear plant has a lower thermal efficiency (advanced reactors may have efficiencies about equal to coal plants) and because a coal plant emits some waste heat directly to the atmosphere via the stack. Therefore, a nuclear reactor will evaporate more water than a coal plant of the same size with the same cooling system. The total fresh water consumed for all purposes (evaporated, transpired, or incorporated into products) in Wisconsin in 1970 was only 250 million m^3, so the quantities of water consumption indicated in Table 6.25 may be more than can reasonably be allowed. Some form of dry or nonevaporative cooling system, which usually has a large thermal efficiency penalty and cost, may be required. Even the Base Case scenario (S1), with its lower electricity demand, has about 300 million m^3 of water evaporation for electrical plant cooling in the year 2025.

The cumulative fuel resource consumption for these scenarios with high energy and electricity demands are also shown in Table 6.25. If nuclear power is accepted as the major electricity supplier in other states and electricity demand per capita is about the same all over the United States, then the U.S. cumulative uranium requirements through the year 2025 would be about 7 million tons. The U.S. Energy Research and Development Administration (ERDA) has recently estimated domestic U.S. uranium resources under $30/lb as approximately 3.5 million tons.[24] If this estimate were correct, then the extensive nuclear power development described in the high-energy scenario S2 might have to be more heavily dependent on the breeder reactor, with its extremely low uranium consumption rate; in S2 as currently

---

* Low-grade concentrations of uranium are at levels of 100 or less ppm while high-grade concentration is about 2,000 ppm.

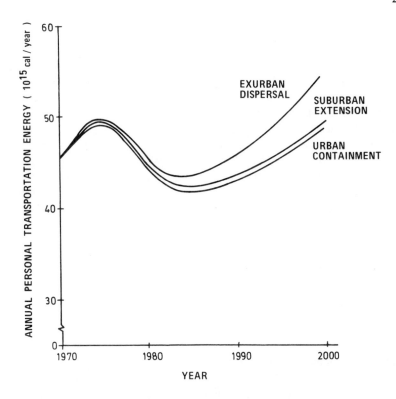

FIGURE 6.24   Urban form and resultant transportation energy use.

described, the breeder was only 5 percent of new nuclear capacity after 1995. On the other hand, if U.S. domestic uranium reserves are considerably more plentiful, and need only additional incentives for exploration and development as argued by the most recent Ford Foundation study,[25] even this high-energy nuclear future might not require significant contributions by the breeder during the time period considered.

The cumulative coal resource requirements are 1.1 billion metric tons in the low nuclear variation of S2. Total recoverable coal resources in the United States have been estimated to be in the range of 1 to 1.8 billion tons.[26] Coal reserves in the United States are sufficient to withstand high-energy growth scenarios for decades, but other factors, such as associated environmental effects, may limit this fuel's use.

Other impacts with long-term implications, such as radioactive waste production by nuclear plants and CO_2 production from the use of coal, increase or decrease approximately in proportion to the energy produced from the respective sources.[27] It is clear that value judgments concerning tradeoffs between impacts and costs are necessary to decide on the most acceptable electricity supply future.[28]

IV.E. TRANSPORTATION ENERGY AND URBAN FORM

The final sensitivity study shows the relationship between alternative population growth patterns and personal transportation energy use.[5] The Base Case scenario uses the suburban extension growth pattern, which is an extension of current trends. The other alternatives shown in Figure 6.24 are an exurban dispersal case, in which the population growth is mainly in rural areas, and an urban containment case with small compact cities, in which growth occurs in small urban areas (20,000–100,000 people). The exurban case results in an 11-percent increase in energy use over the Base Case by the year 2000. Considering that only incremental population is affected, this is a substantial increase that would remove over half the savings resulting from the assumed increase in fuel economy (see the discussion of transportation in section II.B.). The small compact cities case results in a 9-percent energy savings over the Base Case by the year 2000.

These studies have indicated that variation of city size, population density, and the mix of surrounding communities can significantly alter the personal transportation energy demand.

V. OVERALL CONCLUSION FOR THE WISCONSIN SCENARIOS

The process of scenario writing and evaluation is an iterative process in which the scenario writers learn something about inconsistencies, data problems, and what assumptions other people feel are more realistic than the ones in the scenario. During the workshop when the preliminary results of the Wisconsin scenarios were presented for the first time, several workshop participants suggested assumption changes that would result in scenarios they felt would better span the options available for Wisconsin.* Workshop participants also commented on which information was and was not of particular interest; these comments have helped to shape the presentations in the previous sections, and to develop new scenarios that reflected the perceptions of some of these participants and use more recent policies and data.†

A few general conclusions drawn from the Wisconsin scenarios are listed below for each of the policy areas. Needless to say, additional policies related to population growth and economic activity will also affect energy and environmental

---

* Workshop on Integrated Management of Regional Energy/Environment Systems held November 10–14, 1975, at the International Institute for Applied Systems Analysis in Laxenburg, Austria.
† Summary descriptions of such policies and data are given in: The Potential Impact of the National Energy Plan on Wisconsin's Energy Future, Institute for Environmental Studies Report (Madison, Wisconsin: The University of Wisconsin-Madison, June 1977); and J. R. Peerenboom *et al.*, Alternative Energy Futures for Wisconsin, In W. K. Foell (ed.), *Proceedings of the 1978 Conference on Alternative Energy Futures for Wisconsin* (Madison, Wisconsin: Energy Research Center, University of Wisconsin-Madison, 1978).

systems. Several of the following statements are based on value judgments and should be recognized as such.

Urban Settlements

- Energy use and environmental impacts are strongly related to urban form. Land use planning, zoning, and other policy-setting actions need to consider these factors.
- Energy efficient transportation planning must account for future urban forms.

Transportation

- Large energy savings are possible if relatively modest policy shifts are directed toward more efficient automobiles and more rail shipment of freight. This is especially important if saving is needed in petroleum consumption.

Energy Intensity

- Conservation measures or more efficient use of energy per unit of activity in several of the 20 industrial categories and for the service sector would favorably affect Wisconsin's energy/environment future.

Energy Supply

- If a long-term shortage of natural gas and petroleum develops, strong conservation measures, synthetic fuel from coal, solar energy, and a shift to electricity can help alleviate the shortfall.
- Coal and nuclear power, and possibly solar energy after a few decades, are the basic electricity supply options. Each has its long term and short-term advantages and disadvantages.
- Solar space heating and water heating has the potential for significantly reducing natural gas and petroleum demand.
- Electricity supply options are not tied strongly to the growth in demand except through resource limitation and environmental impacts. For example, solar electric power may be developed faster in a high-energy scenario but may be limited by its land requirement.

Environmental Protection

- Coal is better utilized by converting to a low-sulfur form as a synthetic fuel, or for electric generation, than for direct residential and commercial applications that typically result in high ground level pollution concentrations.
- Significant environmental effects from Wisconsin's energy use occur in regions other than Wisconsin.
- Land use may limit solar electric applications.
- Tall stacks are better than no stacks, but reducing sulfur emission is an even better way to reduce health impacts from sulfur dioxide.
- If electricity consumption continues to grow, power plants may have to turn to nonevaporative cooling systems.

- Energy transport systems do not result in insignificant environmental impacts.
- Quantified human health impact from air pollution is a significant consideration in all scenarios examined.
- Quantified environmental impacts cannot be considered in isolation, but must be combined with conventional costs, unquantified impacts, and other factors in the decision process.

The three Wisconsin scenarios selected for presentation are not considered the best or only alternatives facing the state. No judgments have been made on the probability of occurrence for the scenarios. However, the scenarios have demonstrated that there is a spectrum of futures open to Wisconsin and that management related to a small piece of the energy/environment system would be aided by a view of the entire energy system and related environmental impacts. The scenarios also provide an opportunity to study and display the fundamental components of the Wisconsin energy/environment system and contribute to a better basis for choosing among Wisconsin's energy paths into the future.

APPENDIX

ENERGY TABLES FOR WISCONSIN SCENARIO S1

TABLE 6A.1   Primary Energy Supply (10^{15} cal)

	1970 (for comparison)	2000	2025
Petroleum	114.7	168.8	91.8
Natural gas	90.3	149.1	72.2
Synthetic fuel from coal			
End-Use fuel	0.0	35.4	473.9
Conversion loss	0.0	29.7	403.2
Total primary energy	0.0	65.1	877.1
All other coal	80.7	130.4	253.4
Nuclear energy	0.1	100.4	225.1
Hydropower	1.6	2.1	2.1
Total	287.4	615.9	1521.7

TABLE 6A.2   End-Use Energy Consumption (10^{15} cal)

	Coal	Gas	Oil	Electricity	Total	Electricity (10^9 kWh)
2000						
Industrial	48.3	54.6	8.2	15.8	126.9	18.4
Residential		76.4	13.9	19.0	109.3	22.1
Service	3.1	33.8	35.3	24.6	96.8	28.7
Transportation			129.2		129.2	
Total	51.4	164.8	186.6	59.4	462.2	69.2

TABLE 6A.2 – Continued

	Coal	Gas	Oil	Electricity	Total	Electricity (10⁹ kWh)
2025						
Industrial	100.0	95.7	12.8	28.5	237.0	33.1
Residential		92.5	9.0	25.4	126.9	29.6
Service	8.3	90.9	98.1	66.3	263.6	77.1
Transportation			228.1		228.1	
Total	108.3	279.1	348.0	120.2	855.6	139.8

TABLE 6A.3   Fuels for Electricity

	Generation (10⁹ kWh)			Primary Energy (10¹⁵ cal)		
	1970	2000	2025	1970	2000	2025
Hydropower	1.6	2.1	2.1	1.6	2.1	2.1
Petroleum	0.6	0.9	1.7	2.0	2.9	5.6
Gas	2.4	0.9	1.6	7.9	2.9	5.2
Coal	21.8	33.9	62.3	60.3	79.0	145.1
Nuclear energy	0.04	38.7	86.8	0.1	100.4	225.1
Total	26.4	76.5	154.5	71.9	187.3	383.1

TABLE 6A.4   1970 End-Use Energy (10¹⁵ cal)

	Coal	Gas	Oil	Electricity	Total	Electricity (10⁹ kWh)
Industrial	19.5	27.9	4.8	5.6	57.8	6.5
Residential		44.2	19.0	7.4	70.6	8.6
Service	0.9	10.3	11.1	7.5	29.8	8.7
Transportation			77.8		77.8	
Total	20.4	82.4	112.7	20.5	236.0	23.8

ENERGY TABLES FOR WISCONSIN SCENARIO S2

TABLE 6A.5   Primary Energy Supply (10¹⁵ cal)

	2000	2025
Petroleum	155.0	91.8
Natural gas	95.1	72.2
Synthetic fuel from coal		
End-use fuel	27.8	292.3
Conversion loss	24.2	260.6
Total primary energy	52.0	552.9
All other coal	179.7	331.8
Nuclear energy	273.7	879.3
Hydropower	2.1	2.1
Total	757.6	1,930.1

TABLE 6A.6   End-Use Energy Consumption (10^{15} cal)

	Coal	Gas	Oil	Electricity	Total	Electricity (10^9 kWh)
2000						
Industrial	55.8	66.4	9.5	28.8	160.5	33.5
Residential		30.2	13.7	42.3	86.2	49.2
Service	0.5	5.2	5.9	51.4	63.0	59.8
Transportation			138.8	4.8	143.6	5.6
Total	56.3	101.8	167.9	127.3	453.3	148.1
2025						
Industrial	133.5	137.8	17.3	120.0	408.6	139.5
Residential		15.8	8.7	64.2	88.7	74.6
Service	0.3	2.9	3.4	148.4	155.0	172.6
Transportation			248.8	5.5	254.3	6.4
Total	133.8	156.5	278.2	338.1	906.6	393.1

TABLE 6A.7   Fuels for Electricity

	Generation (10^9 kWh)		Primary Energy (10^{15} cal)	
	2000	2025	2000	2025
Hydropower	2.1	2.1	2.1	2.1
Petroleum	1.3	3.3	4.3	10.8
Gas	1.2	3.3	123.4	198.0
Nuclear energy	106.1	340.8	273.7	879.3
Total	163.6	434.4	407.4	1,101.0

ENERGY TABLES FOR WISCONSIN SCENARIO S3

TABLE 6A.8   Primary Energy Supply (10^{15} cal)

	2000		2025
Petroleum	131.0		91.8
Natural gas	105.0		72.2
Synthetic fuel from coal			
End-Use Fuel		26.2	216.3
Conversion Loss		22.3	191.6
Total primary energy	48.5		407.9
All other coal	159.1		254.6
Nuclear energy	27.3		27.3
Hydropower	2.1		2.1
Solar energy	11.3		128.2
Total	484.3		984.1

TABLE 6A.9   End-Use Energy Consumption (10^{15} cal)

	Coal	Gas	Oil	Electricity	Solar	Total	Electricity (10^9 kWh)
2000							
Industrial	34.5	42.5	5.8	11.2	0.0	94.0	13.0
Residential		50.1	13.6	18.1	3.2	85.0	21.0
Service	2.1	21.8	22.8	24.5	1.3	72.5	28.5
Transportation			101.0			101.0	
Total	36.6	114.4	143.2	53.8	4.5	352.6	62.5
2025							
Industrial	55.8	58.2	7.1	15.7	0.0	136.8	18.2
Residential		39.2	7.3	24.3	14.4	85.2	28.2
Service	5.5	44.3	47.0	69.1	16.0	181.9	80.3
Transportation			168.0			168.0	
Total	61.3	141.7	229.4	109.1	30.4	571.9	126.7

TABLE 6A.10   Fuels for Electricity

	Generation (10^9 kWh)		Primary Energy (10^{15} cal)	
	2000	2025	2000	2025
Hydropower	2.1	2.1	2.1	2.1
Petroleum	0.7	1.4	2.3	4.6
Gas	0.7	1.4	2.3	4.6
Coal	52.6	83.0	122.5	193.3
Nuclear energy	10.1	10.1	27.3	27.3
Solar energy	2.9	42.0	6.8	97.8
Total	69.1	140.0	163.3	329.7

	2000	2025
Total capacity (MWe)	15,777	31,964
Solar contribution (MWe)	1,120	15,982

REFERENCES

1.   U.S. Bureau of the Census (USBOC). *Statistical Abstract of the U.S.* U.S. Government Printing Office, Washington D.C.; 1973, 1974, 1975.

2.   Bowman, J.D., R.W. Colley, C.P. Erwin, M.E. Hanson, M.T. Kwast, J.W. Mitchell, and J.L. Pappas. 1975 Survey of Energy Use in Wisconsin. Institute for Environmental Studies Report No. 65, University of Wisconsin-Madison, 1976.

3.   *The World Almanac and Book of Facts.* Newspaper Enterprise Association, 1976, 1977.

4.   U.S. Department of the Interior (USDOI), Bureau of Mines. "U.S. Energy Use at New High in 1971." News Release, Washington D.C., Mar. 31, 1972.

5.   Hanson, M.E., and J.W. Mitchell. A Model of Transportation Energy Use in Wisconsin: Demographic Considerations and Alternative Scenarios. Institute for Environmental Studies Report No. 57, University of Wisconsin-Madison, 1975.

6.   Friedman, S.B. "Public Service Costs and Development: Part of a Study of Wisconsin's Future Development." Wisconsin State Planning Office, Madison, 1975.

7.   Foell, W.K., J.W. Mitchell and J.L. Pappas. The WISconsin Regional Energy Model: A Systems Approach to Regional Energy Analysis. Institute for Environmental Studies Report No. 56, University of Wisconsin-Madison, 1975.

8.   Energy Policy Project of the Ford Foundation (EPP). *A Time to Choose: America's Energy Future*. Ballinger, Cambridge, Massachusetts, 1974.

9.   Shaver, D.B., J.L. Pappas, and W.K. Foell. The Wisconsin Industrial Energy Use Model: Description of the Model and Analysis of Alternative Futures, Institute for Environmental Studies Report No. 43, University of Wisconsin-Madison, June 1975.

10.   Executive Office of the President, Energy Policy and Planning. *The National Energy Plan*, U.S. Government Printing Office, Washington, D.C., 1977.

11.   Buehring, W.A., W.K. Foell, P.H. Hunter, D.A. Jacobsen, P.D. Kishline, J.L. Pappas, and D.B. Shaver. Alternative Future Electricity Generation Requirements for the State of Wisconsin. Institute for Environmental Studies Report No. 26, University of Wisconsin-Madison, 1974.

12.   Frey, D.A. A Model of Residential Energy Use in Wisconsin. Institute for Environmental Studies Report No. 37, University of Wisconsin-Madison, 1974.

13.   Jacobson, D.A., J.L. Pappas, and J.W. Mitchell. A Model of Environmental Studies Report No. University of Wisconsin-Madison, 1974.

14.   Dietz, M.M., and W.K. Foell. 1974 Survey of Energy Use in Wisconsin. Institute for Environmental Studies Report No. 25, University of Wisconsin-Madison, 1974.

15.   Buehring, J.S. User's Guide for the Wisconsin Regional Energy Model (WISE). Institute for Environmental Studies Report, University of Wisconsin-Madison, 1975.

16.   Synfuels Interagency Task Force. "Recommendations for a Synthetic Fuels Commercialization Program," Draft report to the President's Energy Resource Council. 1975.

17.   Dennis, R.L. Regional Air Pollution Impact: A Dispersion Methodology Developed and Applied to Energy Systems. Report No. RM-76-22, International Institute for Applied Systems Analysis, Laxenburg, Austria, 1977.

18.   Buehring, W.A., and W.K. Foell. Environmental Impact of Electrical Generation: A Systemwide Approach, Institute for Environmental Studies Report No. 67, University of Wisconsin-Madison, 1976.

19.   Buehring, W.A., R.L. Dennis and A. Hölzl. Evaluation of Health Effects from Sulfur Dioxide Emissions for a Reference Coal Fired Power Plant. Report No. RM-76-23, International Institute for Applied Systems Analysis, Laxenburg, Austria, 1976.

20.   American National Standards Institute. "The American National Standard Method of Recording and Measuring Work Injury Experience." ANSI 216.1-1967.

21.   Foell, W.K., and J.E. Rushton. Energy Use in Wisconsin. Institute for Environmental Studies Working Paper 4, University of Wisconsin-Madison, 1972.

22.   U.S. Department of the Interior, Bureau of Mines. "U.S. Energy Use Declines in 1974 After Two Decades of Increases." News Release, Washington, D.C., Apr. 3, 1975.

23.   U.S. Department of Interior, Bureau of Mines. "Annual U.S. Energy Use Up in 1976." News Release, Washington D.C., Mar. 14, 1977.

24.   U.S. Energy Research and Development Administration. *Statistical Data of the Uranium Industry*. GJO-100(76), Grand Junction Office, Grand Junction, Colorado, 1976.

25.   Nuclear Energy Policy Study Group, *Nuclear Power: Issues and Choices*, Ballinger, Cambridge, Massachusetts, 1977.

26.   Parent, J.D., and H.R. Linden. A Survey of United States and Total World Production, Proved Reserves and Remaining Recoverable Resources of Fossil Fuels and Uranium as of December 31, 1975. Institute of Gas Technology, Chicago, Illinois, 1977.

27.   Broecker, W.S. "Climatic Change: Are We on the Brink of a Pronounced Global Warming?" *Science* 189(4201): 460–463, Aug. 8, 1975.

28.   Buehring, W.A., W.K. Foell and R.L. Keeney, "Examining Energy/Environment Policy Using Decision Analysis." *Energy Systems and Policy* 2(3), 1978.

7 Cross-Regional Comparison of Energy/Environment Futures

I. INTRODUCTION

I.A. PURPOSE

With so much energy data available from the three regions, it is an irresistible temptation to make comparisons and draw conclusions concerning energy consumption patterns. Although many problems and pitfalls with such comparisons are recognized, this section is an attempt to highlight some cross-regional comparisons that the IIASA research team felt were both meaningful and interesting. Structural differences related to the climate, natural resources, past economic and social development of the region, as well as policy differences are considered in their influence on energy consumption and environmental impact. It is in the expectation of developing a greater understanding of the complex interactions and interdependencies in the energy supply and demand system and socioeconomic development that the comparisons are made, rather than to imply that any region is "better" or "worse" than any other region in total or in any particular respect. We hope this section will be read in the same spirit.

It is only within the framework of the differing political and administrative structures of the three regions and their physical, economic, and social characteristics that comparison can be made and understood. Frequent reference will be made to material discussed previously in the sections describing the regions and their institutional structures. Descriptions of the scenarios being compared can be found in the previous three chapters. This chapter also provides a good opportunity to examine the consistency and plausibility of assumptions made by the research team and to explain the differences.

Chapter 7 was written by Jacqueline Buehring and William Buehring — IIASA; and Wesley K. Foell — Energy Research Centre, University of Wisconsin — Madison.

I.B.   SPECIAL CONSIDERATIONS

The scenarios for the regions are described in detail elsewhere. Briefly, they are: (1) the Base Case, (2) a high-energy case, and (3) a low-energy conservation case.

The German Democratic Republic (GDR) plans long-term development over a 20-year period in a centrally planned economy.* The Base Case for the composite Bezirk X therefore represents the "plan" through 1995 and an extrapolation of the plan from 1995 to 2025. For the state of Wisconsin, on the other hand, with its diffuse decision-making apparatus, no coherent plan is available. The system is complicated not only by decisions made under multiple conflicting objectives but also by decisions made by several decision-makers each with his or her own set of conflicting objectives. The Base Case scenario for Wisconsin is a continuation of present trends with restraints, limits, and new technologies imposed according to the best judgment of the IIASA team. The Base Case for the Rhone-Alpes region is defined from past economic trends and the current energy plans of the government, essentially in the same manner as the Wisconsin Base Case scenario.

The high-energy scenario and the conservation scenario for each region were also written within the constraints imposed by the political and economic systems and physical resources of the regions. The result is that the alternative scenarios are not defined identically across the regions, and care must be taken in drawing conclusions from comparisons of both assumptions and results.

The initial reference year for the scenarios is 1970. This year was chosen because the energy data were more complete than for subsequent years and consequently calibration was more readily achieved. However, data from later years were used in specifying parameters in the scenarios and in the models.

Data were available in varying quantity and with varying reliability from the regions. Wisconsin, Rhone-Alpes, and Bezirk X in the GDR are all regions embedded within a larger political unit. Since the GDR is a centrally planned economy, a large quantity of data is available to the central authorities and planners. Bezirk X is, however, a hypothetical bezirk with characteristics chosen to represent a typical industrial area of the GDR. Appropriate, although composite, data are therefore available, but consistency problems sometimes arise. Wisconsin is a distinct political unit within the United States, with its own legislative, judicial, and administrative apparatus. Many decisions relating to energy are made at the state level, so a great deal of data is available. The planning regions within France, of which Rhone-Alpes is one, are recent creations with no government of their own. Consequently, few data have been collected on a regional basis and much of the Rhone-Alpes data for this study was deduced from data for France as a whole.

Another obvious result of the political structures is that only in Wisconsin are many energy-related decisions made at the regional level. Therefore, one might expect to see more decisions made in Wisconsin "for the good of the region" (rather

---

* As noted in section I. in Appendix B, a 20-year plan is not developed in the same sense of the word as the official 1- and 5-year plans.

than "for the good of the country") than in either Rhone-Alpes or Bezirk X. The goals of the planning process in both Bezirk X and Rhone-Alpes are likely to be the goals of the country as a whole with the region playing the part assigned to it. Wisconsin has much more autonomy with respect to setting its goals and carrying out plans to implement those goals. One result of this may be that Wisconsin is unlikely to tolerate any very large adverse environmental effect, especially one that would harm the very important tourist industry of northern Wisconsin.

Another difference between the regions, possibly influenced by the political structure described above, is the role envisioned for each region within the national economy. Rhone-Alpes and Bezirk X are both heavily industrialized, as is the southeastern area of Wisconsin. Plans for future development show very large expansion of industrial activity in Bezirk X compared with the planned growth for the GDR as a whole. In Rhone-Alpes, both past trends and plans for the future indicate a higher growth rate for Rhone-Alpes than for the whole of France. The Wisconsin economy, on the other hand, is expected to grow at a rate comparable to or slightly less than the growth rate of the United States as a whole. Thus, the anticipated roles of the regions in their countries must be considered when looking at the scenario cross-regional comparisons dealing with industry, transportation, energy supply, and environment.

II. SOCIOECONOMIC COMPARISONS

II.A. POPULATION

The population, the population distribution by size of city, and the population density are important factors in energy demand and the human health impacts of pollution. Population remains nearly constant in Bezirk X and grows slowly in both Rhone-Alpes and Wisconsin for the 55-year period of the study. Total population and overall population density are graphed in Figure 7.1. The projections shown were used for all scenarios. A relatively large proportion of the population is in older age groups in the GDR (see Table 8.2). It is therefore very unlikely that population will grow in the next 55 years and that has been reflected in the hypothetical Bezirk X. The constant population in turn restricts employment.

In addition to the total population, the density distribution and the distribution of the population by city size also have an important impact on per capita energy consumption and health effects of air pollution. The calculation of the population densities is described in Chapter 3. The fractions of the population in high density areas in Rhone-Alpes and the Bezirk are greater than in Wisconsin, the result of differences in historical patterns of growth between the three regions. Obviously, the structure of cities changes only gradually and the urban scenarios presented in the scenario chapters are attempts to explore the possibilities and effects of different types of urban development.

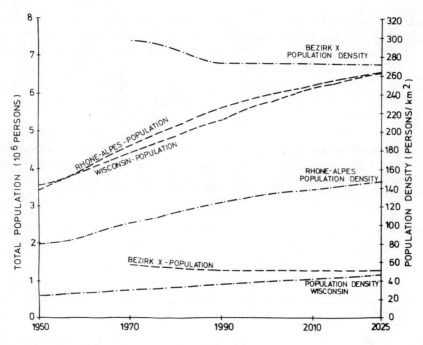

FIGURE 7.1 Population and population density in the three regions (actual figures until 1970, projected thereafter).

II.B.   ECONOMY

Comparison of economic indicators is complicated by a lack of consensus on the proper currency exchange rates and by different definitions of the industrial and service sectors. Therefore, economic activity is described in relationship to the 1970 value in each country rather than analyzed on an absolute basis. Then comparison can be made across the regions on the change in productivity or energy intensiveness per unit of output.

The value-added or net production in a particular year for a particular region did not vary across the scenarios, except for Scenario 3 for Rhone-Alpes. Figure 7.2 shows the change in economic activity per capita in the industrial and service sectors that formed the basis for the scenarios. It must be emphasized that the value-added is a variable exogenous to the energy models. In Rhone-Alpes it is a continuation of current economic trends resulting in growth rates that start at 5 percent per year in 1970 and decline to 3.5 percent per year by 2025. Scenario S3, the low-energy scenario, includes a shift from industrial to service sector activity and a reduction in the value-added growth rate. Total value-added in 2025 for S3 is approximately 60 percent of that used in S1 and S2. In Wisconsin the overall economic growth is

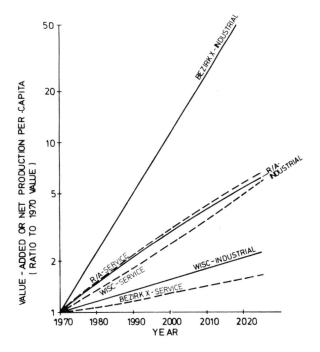

FIGURE 7.2   Economic activity indicators (ratio to 1970 value).

projected at 3.1 percent per year, somewhat lower than historical trends, with a continuing trend toward greater activity in the service sector. Only the southeastern area around Milwaukee is heavily industrialized and Wisconsin is not now, or expected to be in the future, a large industrial center. Industrial activity in Wisconsin more than doubles from 1970 to 2025; service sector activity increases by a factor of approximately 6.

The data from the Bezirk are from the 20-year "plan" through 1995 and from an extrapolation of the plan after 1995. Economic growth is 8.3 percent per year or a factor of 75* over the 55-year time period in the industrial sector, but the service sector grows linearly and grows much less than either Wisconsin or Rhone-Alpes service sectors. Such a large growth in production naturally raises many questions about the corresponding social and political consequences. Unless the increase in production is exported from the region without equivalent compensation for the workers involved, one would expect the personal income in the area to grow commensurately with the increase in production since industrial employment does not increase. Such a large increase in income could be expected to alter the lifestyles and expectations of the people in the areas of personal transportation and housing.

* Somewhat greater on a per capita basis since population declines slightly over the period.

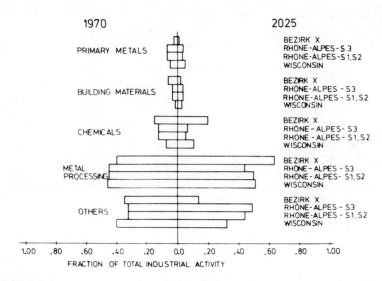

FIGURE 7.3   Industrial activity by industrial sector (all scenarios unless otherwise indicated).

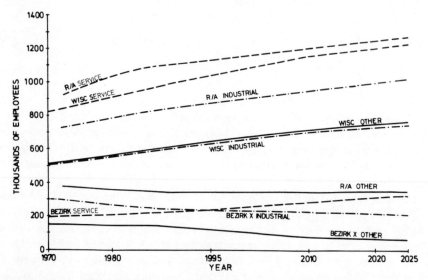

FIGURE 7.4   Employment by economic sector (all scenarios).

Secondary questions may also be asked about the effect on energy demand of the consumer or of the industrial goods produced.[†]

The distribution of industrial activity by industry is shown in Figure 7.3. The

[†] See the Prologue to this chapter for comments on this economic growth.

distribution is quite similar among the three regions in 1970; Wisconsin has a slightly larger fraction of metal fabrication and a smaller fraction of chemicals.

By the year 2025, the fractions of the very energy intensive metal processing and chemical industries have increased slightly in Wisconsin, decreased slightly in Rhone-Alpes, and increased considerably in the Bezirk. This factor would tend to increase overall energy intensiveness in Bezirk X with respect to Wisconsin and Rhone-Alpes. This increase, however, is more than offset in the energy use results of the scenarios by assumed improvements in technology that will be discussed later.

Employment in the service and industrial sectors is compared in Figure 7.4. In the projections for all three regions, the percentage of the population that is employed remains fairly constant; only Rhone-Alpes shows a change of as much as 3 percent. In 1970, approximately 42 percent of the population is employed in Rhone-Alpes and Wisconsin and approximately 46 percent in Bezirk X. In Bezirk X, the population is nearly constant so that the size of the work force is nearly the same in 2025 as in 1970. Rhone-Alpes and Wisconsin with their slowly growing populations have a larger work force at the end of the period. It is interesting to note that although industrial value-added is increasing at a very high rate in Bezirk X, the industrial sector is losing employees to the service sector where productivity (economic activity per employee) is assumed not to increase. In Rhone-Alpes and Wisconsin where activities such as insurance, consulting and computer service companies are increasingly influencing the service sector, that sector is not only assumed to grow faster than the service sector in Bezirk X, but productivity is also assumed to increase. Figure 7.5, with value-added or total production plotted against employment, gives an idea of employment and economic activity changes over the 55-year period, and indicates changes in productivity as well. Reference lines representing constant productivity, a tripling of productivity, and a tenfold increase in productivity, are also plotted. For example, any point, independent of the year, that falls on the line labeled "tripling of productivity" implies a threefold increase in productivity over the 1970 value. Bezirk X industrial productivity crosses that line well before the year 2000. Rhone-Alpes industrial productivity crosses that line about the year 2000, and Wisconsin's industrial productivity does not triple even by the year 2025.*

There are additional factors that must be considered in comparing the assumed productivity changes. One is that the three regions do not start at the same level of productivity, and as no comparison has been made on absolute values of production or value-added, no absolute comparison can be made on productivity. Productivity in the industrial sector by 2025 is projected to increase by factors of over 100 in the Bezirk (calculated from production and employment figures supplies by the Institut für Energetik in the GDR) by a factor of approximately $2\frac{1}{2}$ in Wisconsin, and by a factor of slightly over 6 in Rhone-Alpes. The consensus of the IIASA research group is that the Bezirk-X estimate is probably overly optimistic for the

---

* A tripling of productivity over the 55-year period can be attained by an average annual increase of 2 percent.

228

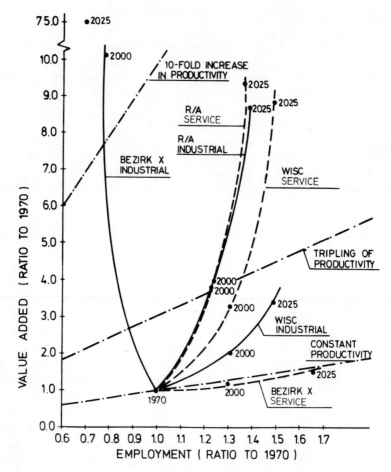

FIGURE 7.5   Value-added plotted against employment (ratio to 1970 value).

period after 2000, and that in any event, the differences in growth rates between the regions in both production and productivity will probably not be as extreme as indicated by these scenarios.

In summary

● Economic activity is assumed to increase at approximately 3.1 percent per year in Wisconsin, 3.5 percent to 5 percent in Rhone-Alpes, and 8.2 percent in Bezirk X, with most of the Bezirk's growth occurring in the industrial sector.

● Employment patterns are not assumed to change drastically in any of the
· regions. In Wisconsin and Rhone-Alpes the service sector is the largest employer; in Bezirk X the industrial sector employs the greatest number of workers in 1970 but by 1995 the service sector passes the industrial sector in number of employees.

TABLE 7.1   Annual End-Use Energy

		Bezirk X			Rhone-Alpes			Wisconsin		
	Scenario	1970	2000	2025	1970	2000	2025	1970	2000	2025
Annual end-use energy	S1	29	48	96	117	236	398	236	462	856
(10^{15} cal/yr)	S2	29	62	223	117	277	500	236	453	907
	S3	29	47	80	117	238	297	236	352	572
Annual end-use	S1	20	37	73	25	39	60	53	80	130
energy/capita	S2	20	48	171	25	46	76	53	78	138
(10^9 cal/person/yr)	S3	20	36	61	25	40	45	53	61	87
Density of annual	S1	6	10	20	3	5	9	2	3	6
end-use energy	S2	6	13	43	3	6	11	2	3	6
(10^{12} cal/km²)	S3	6	10	17	3	5	7	2	3	4

- By 2025, productivity declines in the Bezirk service sector; approximately doubles in the Wisconsin industrial sector; increases by a factor of 5 or 6 in the Rhone-Alpes service and industrial sectors and in the Wisconsin service sector; and increases by a factor of over 100 in the Bezirk industrial sector.

III.   END-USE ENERGY DEMAND*

End-use energy includes only energy consumed in end-use processes; conversion and transmission losses, such as in electrical generation, are excluded from the end-use energy total. Each sector will be discussed in detail in this section, but first a summary of total annual end-use energy for all three scenarios is shown in Table 7.1. For reference, the Wisconsin average annual end-use energy consumption per capita in 1976 was 57×10^9 cal/yr or about 23 percent less than the 1976 U.S. average.[10] Wisconsin uses more than twice as much energy per capita as Rhone-Alpes or Bezirk X in 1970 and this relationship continues to 2025 in the Base Case, although the higher economic growth for Bezirk X provides a greater energy demand increase in that region. Since the population density in Wisconsin is so much lower than in the Bezirk or Rhone-Alpes, the energy use per square kilometer is lower on the average than for the other regions. However, Wisconsin population and industry are clustered in the southeastern corner of the state so that some Wisconsin citizens enjoy no advantage with respect to pollution effects despite the lower average density of energy use. Environmental effects are discussed further in section V.

The broad range of policy measures and/or economic growth assumptions leads to a wide range of future energy use in the regions. Table 7.2 presents the average annual growth rates of end-use energy over time for the scenarios.

Both Wisconsin and Rhone-Alpes experience somewhat less than historical growth

* Purchased fuels and electricity consumed by user.

TABLE 7.2   Average Annual Growth Rates of End-Use Energy Over Time

Scenarios	Bezirk X 1970–2000	2000–2025	Rhone-Alpes 1970–2000	2000–2025	Wisconsin 1970–2000	2000–2025
S1	1.7%	2.8%	2.4%	2.1%	2.3%	2.5%
S2	2.6%	5.2%	2.9%	2.4%	2.2%	2.8%
S3	1.6%	2.2%	2.4%	0.9%	1.3%	2.0%

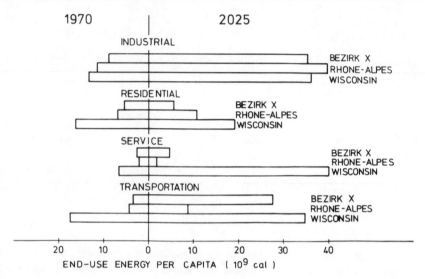

FIGURE 7.6   End-use energy per capita by economic sector (Scenario S1).

rates in the Base Case and high-energy scenario (S1 and S2) through 2000.* In contrast, the end-use energy growth by 2025 in Bezirk X increases by more than a factor of 8 in S2; this growth results primarily from the postulated 8.3 percent per year industrial growth. The dramatic increase in S2 as compared to S1 and S3 is a direct result of a slackening of the rate of improvement of efficiency of industrial use.

End-use energy per capita by economic sector is shown in Figure 7.6. Each sector will be discussed in more detail later; however, it is worth noting now the relative importance of the transportation and residential sectors in Wisconsin compared with the other regions at the beginning of the time period. The difference can in part be attributed to more personal transportation in Wisconsin, especially by less energy efficient means of transportation such as large automobiles, and to larger dwelling units with more appliances. The increasing importance of the transportation sector in energy use in Bezirk X is a result of freight transportation necessitated by

* In Wisconsin, the energy growth rate increases slightly after the year 2000, primarily because economic growth continues at the same rate, despite lower population growth.

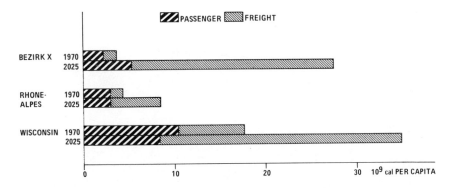

FIGURE 7.7   End-use energy per capita in the transportation sector.

the growth in industrial output. The increase in the demand for transportation in Wisconsin is also related to freight rather than passenger transportation. The energy use in the service sector increases dramatically in Wisconsin, an effect that will be discussed in the service sector comparisons.

The rest of this section contains more specific comparisons of the transportation, residential, service, and industrial sectors of the economy.

III.A.   TRANSPORTATION

The transportation sector is very different in each of the regions. Table 4 in Chapter 2 shows a key reason — the great differences in motor vehicle stocks. The auto ownership comparison is most striking; autos per 1,000 inhabitants in 1972 range from 82 in the GDR, to 270 in Rhone-Alpes, to 436 in Wisconsin.

The transportation sector is divided into two main categories: passenger transport and freight transport. Transportation energy use per capita in each category is shown in Figure 7.7. Freight increasingly dominates transportation in both Bezirk X and Wisconsin. Differences in freight transportation are largely attributable to the location, type, and amount of industrial and service sector activity in the regions. Passenger transportation demand is affected by income and employment as well as city size and structure.

II.A.1.   Passenger Transportation

Intracity personal transportation is generated by the need of transportation for employment, for shopping, and for pleasure. Auto ownership and the number of trips depend in part upon per capita personal income and the amount of income left for pleasure trips after the basic necessities are provided. A less obvious but equally important determinant of personal travel is the size and structure of the cities. Wisconsin cities tend to be less dense with fewer local or neighborhood shopping

232

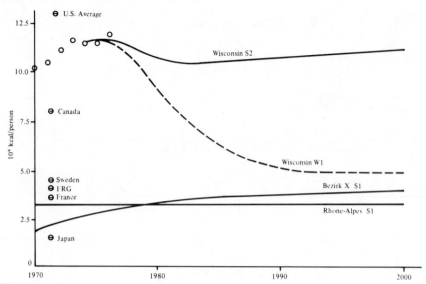

FIGURE 7.8   Personal transportation energy use per capita.

areas than GDR or Rhone-Alpes cities and therefore the average trip length is longer. Thus, although the fraction of the population employed is greatest in the Bezirk, the more energy efficient structure of the cities keeps the urban passenger travel low. To account for possible city structure changes over time, Scenarios S2 and S3 have differing assumptions on the future growth pattern of cities in the three regions. However, a sensitivity study (Chapter 6, section V.F.) indicates that even a strong urban containment policy would not bring per capita energy use for personal transportation in Wisconsin into the range of Bezirk X and Rhone-Alpes.

The penetration of mass transit systems into the city passenger transportation market is also an important determinant of energy demand since most urban mass transit systems are more energy efficient than private automobile transport. The use of mass transit is influenced not only by income and the relative prices of mass and personal transit, but also by the structure of the cities. A high-density area can be served more efficiently by mass transit since there are more potential customers per vehicle-mile; these high-density areas are also less attractive for large numbers of private automobiles because of increased congestion. Hanson and Mitchell[1] have shown, however, that given current city structure, a shift to more energy-efficient automobiles has a greater potential for energy savings in Wisconsin than a shift to mass transit. The trend toward smaller autos has been incorporated into the Wisconsin Scenarios S1 and S3 and explains the decrease in energy use per capita for passenger transportation. Energy intensiveness for private passenger transportation is assumed to remain constant in Bezirk X and in Rhone-Alpes.

Figure 7.8 compares personal transportation energy use per capita for several scenarios. Important characteristics of these are:

• Bezirk X (S1): Car ownership rises to approximately 240 cars per 1,000 persons by 2025; fuel economy remains approximately constant.

• Rhone-Alpes (S1): Ownership and efficiency do not greatly change.

• Wisconsin (S2): Fuel efficiency remains at level of 1975 new cars; ownership and travel level unchanged.

The contrasts are great between both the initial use levels and the scenarios; with no improvements in fuel economy, the Wisconsin values would remain far higher than the other regions. Scenario S2 for Wisconsin does not include the standards of the U.S. Energy Policy and Conservation Act (EPCA) which mandates an average yearly standard that reaches 8.6 liter/100 km for the 1985 model fleet. Scenario W1, shown by a dashed line, has recently been developed at the University of Wisconsin to include EPCA and some additional conservation measures;[13] by the year 2000 the Wisconsin per capita use is only 20 percent greater than in Bezirk X (Scenario S1).

II.A.2. Freight Transportation

Freight transportation is partially the result of industrial and service activity and consumer needs within the region. Bezirk X had a growth in industrial output that is nearly double the growth in freight transportation. This is partially explained by a reduction in the export of briquettes. In Wisconsin, on the other hand, freight transportation was found to grow at a faster rate than industry partly as a result of the large increase in the service sector. Freight transportation increases very slowly in Rhone-Alpes. Freight transportation within the regions is, however, not solely dependent upon the service and industrial activity in the area since freight that passes through the region with both departure point and destination outside the region is also counted as ton-kilometers while within the region. A lower growth rate in freight transportation may also result from a shift to manufactured products with a higher value per unit weight or from a policy to locate factories nearer to their source of raw materials or to the destination of the manufactured goods.

The fraction of freight by each mode of transportation (truck, rail, and barge) with associated energy intensiveness is shown in Table 7.3 for Scenario S1. The present mix of freight transportation is assumed to remain unchanged in Wisconsin, while the trend from rail to truck continues in the Rhone-Alpes. In the Bezirk all intercity freight transport is assumed to be by rail. The energy intensiveness of rail freight transport also improves dramatically because of the gradual replacement of steam locomotives with diesel and eventually electric engines.* Since diesel engines are already in use in Wisconsin and both electric and diesel engines are in use in Rhone-Alpes, the energy intensiveness of rail freight transport is assumed to remain constant in these regions.

An overall picture of the fuel efficiency of the freight transportation systems

TABLE 7.3   Freight Transportation by Mode and Associated Energy Intensiveness

		Fraction of Total Ton-km			Energy Intensiveness (kcal/ton-km)		
		Bezirk X	Rhone-Alpes	Wisconsin	Bezirk X	Rhone-Alpes	Wisconsin
Rail	1970	.77	.38	.26	360	110	118
	2025	.81	.29	.26	80	110	118
Truck	1970	.23	.54	.74	335	710	485
	2025	.19	.64	.74	375	710	485
Barge	1970		.08		160		
	2025		.06		160		

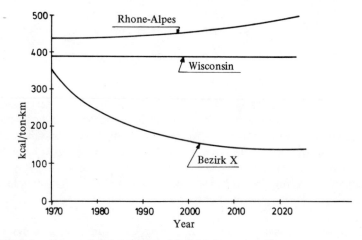

FIGURE 7.9   Energy intensiveness of freight transportation.

in the regions can be obtained from Figure 7.9 showing the energy use per ton-kilometer of freight transportation. If the primary energy used for electricity generated were also included, the overall energy intensiveness for Bezirk X would be about 280 kcal/ton-km. The heavy reliance on rail and the decreasing intensiveness of the new locomotives account for the substantial improvement in Bezirk X. Rhone-Alpes actually increases in overall energy intensiveness per ton-kilometer because of increasing use of truck transport, which is more energy intensive than rail transport.

* The energy intensiveness of electric engines does not include the energy needed to produce electricity. Therefore in terms of primary energy required per ton-kilometer, improvement is not so striking.

TABLE 7.4   Single-Family Dwelling Units in the Three Regions for Each Scenario
(% of total housing stock)

	1970	2025		
	All Scenarios	S1	S2	S3
Bezirk X[a]	62	54	56	48
Rhone-Alpes	47	41	72	26
Wisconsin	88	77	90	56

[a] Two-family dwelling units are counted as single-family dwelling units in the Bezirk-X data.

III.B.   RESIDENTIAL SECTOR

The number, size, and characteristics of the dwelling units in a region as well as the appliances in those dwelling units are major factors determining the energy use in the residential sector. Table 7.4 gives the current and projected percentages of single-family dwelling units in the total housing stock for the three scenarios. Wisconsin has the largest percentage of detached homes in all scenarios, a significant factor since detached homes tend to be larger and to have a greater heat loss through the roof and walls (they do not have common walls with other dwelling units). A discussion of the energy required to heat typical single-family homes and apartments in the three regions may be found in Appendix C, section II, which deals with building practices.

In all three regions, space heating consumes the most residential energy. Wisconsin's larger residential floor area, colder climate, and high fraction of households with many appliances, all contribute to a residential energy use between two and three times larger than in the other regions.

Assumptions about the type of heating system for future dwelling units posed a difficult problem for the IIASA team, particularly in achieving consistency across the regions. Table 7.5 is a summary of the types of energy assumed for use in residential space heating. Very little coal is used for residential space heating in Wisconsin and Rhone-Alpes and use of this fuel is expected to decline even more. In Bezirk X in 1970, direct use of coal is the main source of fuel for residential space heating. In the future, the Bezirk's abundant supply of coal will instead be used for coal district heating where the air pollution problems can be minimized with pollution control equipment and high stacks. In all three regions, oil is considered to be an undesirable alternative because of the need to rely on imports, although a high level of dependence on oil use continued in Scenario S2 for Rhone-Alpes. Gas is also in increasingly short supply although both Rhone-Alpes and Bezirk X plan to introduce it to some extent. Wisconsin is heavily dependent on natural gas in 1970, but all scenarios except the Base Case call for a decrease in use. Where demand for such fuels exceeds what could realistically be expected to be supplied in Wisconsin, the gap is filled by synthetic fuels. High use of electricity for home heating is examined in Scenario S2 for Wisconsin and Scenario S1 for Rhone-Alpes. Some advantages of

TABLE 7.5 Fraction of Housing Units Using Each Type of Energy Source for Space Heating

| | Fractions of Housing Units | | | |
| | | 2025 | | |
	1970	S1	S2	S3
Coal				
Bezirk X	.91	.22	.24	.22
Rhone-Alpes	.055	.0	.0	.0
Wisconsin	.0	.0	.0	.0
Gas				
Bezirk X	.005	.16	.18	.13
Rhone-Alpes	.07	.219	.145	.178
Wisconsin	.64	.74	.20	.48
Oil				
Bezirk X	.0	.0	.0	.0
Rhone-Alpes	.6	.292	.6	.267
Wisconsin	.33	.13	.11	.14
Electricity				
Bezirk X	.001	.16	.17	.08
Rhone-Alpes	.015	.423	.138	.017
Wisconsin	.02	.12	.68	.13
Solar energy				
Bezirk X	.0	.0	.0	.12
Rhone-Alpes	.0	.011	.054	.263
Wisconsin	.0	.0	.0	.25
District heat[a]				
Bezirk X	.08	.46	.4	.45
Rhone-Alpes	.03	.048	.051	.166
Wisconsin	.0	.0	.0	.0
Geothermal district heat				
Bezirk X	.0	.0	.0	.0
Rhone-Alpes	.0	.007	.012	.109
Wisconsin	.0	.0	.0	.0

[a] Primarily oil for Rhone-Alpes and coal for Bezirk X.

electricity use are in moving pollution problems to the power plant and in enabling sources such as nuclear energy to be used for heating; disadvantages include the higher primary energy use resulting from conversion and transmission losses, and the myriad of environmental impacts and social costs involved in generating electricity. However, since the cost per unit of energy is higher for electricity than for most other types of energy, electrically heated homes are usually better insulated (except in Rhone-Alpes where standards are very high for all homes) resulting in decreases in end-use energy. Scenario S3, the energy conservation scenario, also includes solar heating in each of the regions.

Wisconsin is the only region with a significant residential air conditioning load. In addition Wisconsin homes have more "secondary" appliances, i.e. dishwashers,

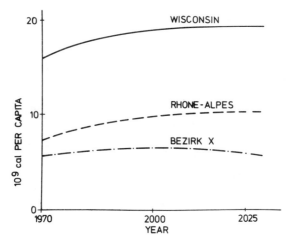

FIGURE 7.10   Residential end-use energy per capita.

washing machines, televisions, refrigerators, and they are in general larger and more energy intensive than the Rhone-Alpes and GDR appliances. In 1970 the average electricity use per home for secondary appliances was approximately 5,200 kWh in Wisconsin, 1,000 kWh in Bezirk X, and 900 kWh in Rhone-Alpes.* By 2025 these figures were projected to be 6,400, 2,000, and 3,100 kWh.

Total residential end-use energy per capita is shown in Figure 7.10. Rhone-Alpes uses only half as much energy per capita as Wisconsin but about 30 percent more than the Bezirk in 1970 and the differences increase by 2025. One of the major conclusions for the residential sector is that demands for energy are not expected to increase significantly over the time period studied, and under some conditions may decrease. Vigorous implementation of improved insulation practices would have major conservation impacts on all regions, particularly in Wisconsin with its larger dwelling size and colder climate.[†]

III.C.   SERVICE SECTOR

Since definitions of service sector activity vary among the regions, comparisons are difficult. In addition, data for the service sector were the most difficult to obtain. Service floor area in both the Bezirk and Rhone-Alpes was assumed to grow proportionately to employment in the service sector. Reasonable projections of employment could be made. In Wisconsin, floor area was assumed to grow proportionately to value-added in the service sector. Since value-added, especially in

* One kWh is equivalent to 0.86 million cal.
† In December 1978, Wisconsin instituted its first building construction code for new 1- and 2-family dwellings. See section II.C. in Appendix C.

TABLE 7.6 Space Heating in the Service Sector by Source of Energy

| | Percentages of Each Fuel Type | | | |
| | | 2025 | | |
	1970	S1	S2	S3
Coal				
Bezirk X	64.2	43	19.5	35.4
Rhone-Alpes	4	0	0	0
Wisconsin	5	5	1	5
Gas				
Bezirk X	1.7	1.7	1.7	1.7
Rhone-Alpes	11	10	45	60
Wisconsin	60	60	2	43
Oil				
Bezirk X	0	0	0	0
Rhone-Alpes	61	5	30	10
Wisconsin	25	25	.8	18
Electricity				
Bezirk X	.2	7.6	31	7.6
Rhone-Alpes	21	80	5	10
Wisconsin	2	2	88	2
Solar energy				
Bezirk X				7.6
Rhone-Alpes (In S3, solar substitutes in part for each heating fuel.)				
Wisconsin				24
District heat				
Bezirk X	33.9	47	47	47
Rhone-Alpes	3	5	20	20
Wisconsin				

the Wisconsin service sector, is growing much faster than employment (Figure 7.5), i.e. productivity is increasing, a much larger growth rate in floor area and consequently in energy use appears in the Wisconsin service sector than in either Rhone-Alpes or Bezirk X. In retrospect, the assumption that floor area grows proportionately to value-added may not have been justified in the Wisconsin case, especially since the larger growth is assumed to take place in insurance companies, consulting firms, and so on, where the ratio of floor area to value-added is less than in more traditional service industries.* If the assumptions had been that floor area grows proportionately to employment as in the other two regions, Wisconsin's consumption in the service sector would have been more similar to the Bezirk's and Rhone-Alpes'. In Rhone-Alpes the assumption was also made that new service sector buildings would be much more energy efficient than existing buildings.

Space heating accounts for most of the energy use in the service sector and, as in the residential sector, the fuel mix (Table 7.6) was a subject of much discussion.

* A more recent study of the impact of the U.S. National Energy Plan on Wisconsin has assumed that floor area grows more slowly than value-added.[11]

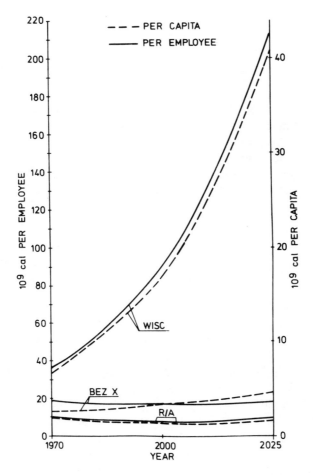

FIGURE 7.11   Service end-use energy per capita and per employee.

Space air conditioning is much more prevalent in Wisconsin in 1970, but by 2025 50 percent of Rhone-Alpes service floor space is also projected to be air conditioned. The GDR does not plan to install air conditioning in service sector buildings.

Results in terms of end-use energy per capita and end-use energy per employee in the service sector are compared in Figure 7.11. The differences between Rhone-Alpes and Bezirk X may be partially attributed to a milder climate in the Rhone-Alpes region that requires less energy for space heating.

III.D.   INDUSTRIAL SECTOR

In all of the three regions, the industrial sector is a major consumer of energy (Table 2.8 in Chapter 2). However, each of the collaborating regional institutions in this study brought widely differing views of future industry development and energy consumption in its region. The alternative industrial energy demand patterns showed a strong divergence in the long run.

The diversity of these patterns can be discussed in terms of three important determining factors:

- The rate of industrial economic growth and the resulting mix of industry between energy-intensive and less energy-intensive activities, i.e. between processes which require more or less energy
- The energy intensiveness in terms of energy per unit of activity (e.g. cal/$ or cal/ton) for individual industrial subsectors
- The distribution of the energy consumption in an industrial subsector among the various energy forms (fuel mix)

Because the economic growth patterns were summarized previously in section II.B, the major attention in this section is devoted to energy intensiveness. The energy intensiveness factor was the focus of our industrial energy demand and conservation analysis. This analysis has been based in part on historical trends in sectoral intensiveness, and in part on examination of conservation potentials and incentives for major technical processes used within these sectors. Among the regions, the energy analysts from the GDR were the most optimistic about the likelihood of continuing long-term reductions in energy intensiveness. Based upon the results of the past two five-year plans, and their long-term planning, they expect a five percent annual decrease in the overall industrial intensiveness. This suggests not only a continued implementation of currently available conservation measures but a constant development of new measures and technologies.

Industrial classifications in the three regions have been consolidated into five categories: (1) building materials, (2) primary metals, (3) metal fabrication, (4) chemicals, and (5) others. Industrial activity by category for the three regions is described in section II.B. above and is summarized in Figure 7.3. Energy intensiveness (end-use energy per unit of output) is shown in Figure 7.12. Bezirk X plans a drastic reduction in energy intensiveness, especially in chemicals and primary metals, combined with an exponential increase in industrial activity during the time period. The change in energy intensiveness and worker productivity (see Figure 7.5) for the Bezirk industrial sector implies that the GDR would far surpass France and the United States in both industrial productivity and efficiency of industrial processes by 2025. The energy intensiveness figures for Wisconsin result from a study of past trends modified by the best judgment of the researchers. Perhaps the current increasing cost of energy was not adequately accounted for in the projections since historical data are from a period of decreasing energy costs. It seems more reasonable that trends that would result from improved industrial processes and shifts to different products would be seen in all three regions. The magnitude of the differences in this case can only be explained by greater optimism on the part of the GDR researchers than the Rhone-Alpes and Wisconsin researchers could muster.

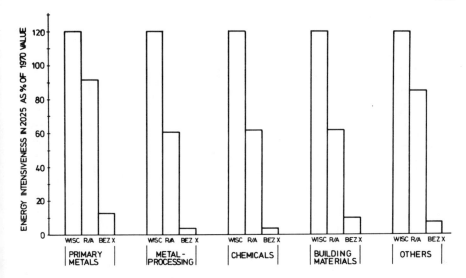

FIGURE 7.12   Energy intensiveness by industry.

Figures 7.13 and 7.14 show the overall industrial energy intensiveness for the Base Case and low-energy Scenario. It must be emphasized that these values incorporate the industrial structures of these scenarios and the associated fuel mixes for each industrial sector. All scenarios shown here except the Wisconsin Base Case show decreasing intensiveness. Subsequent analysis for Wisconsin, based upon more recent data, indicates that the decreases shown for S3 best represent current trends and future potential.[12]

The effects of the decreasing energy intensiveness and increasing production off-set each other in the Bezirk X Base Case scenario, so that the trends in total indus-trial end-use energy per capita (Figure 7.15) are roughly similar to those in Wiscon-sin and Rhone-Alpes. The Base Case scenarios all yield an industrial energy use that grows more slowly than it has historically, except for the GDR, where the high economic growth more than compensated for the continuing decrease in energy intensiveness. The low-energy scenarios all yielded growths in demand that were significantly lower than historical growths; in Wisconsin, the demand in the indus-trial sector grew less rapidly than in the service sector, and by the year 2025, the service sector used more energy than the industrial sector.

Industrial end-use energy is broken down by energy source in Table 7.7. Coal district heat is the primary source of industrial energy in Bezirk X in 1975 and that is expected to continue in all scenarios. Coal is also an important source in Wiscon-sin and, except for scenario S2 where electricity is more heavily used, becomes even more important in the future despite the pollution control problems. Rhone-Alpes, which presently gets 11 percent of its industrial energy from coal, expects coal use in industry to be negligible by 2025 because there is no readily available supply of

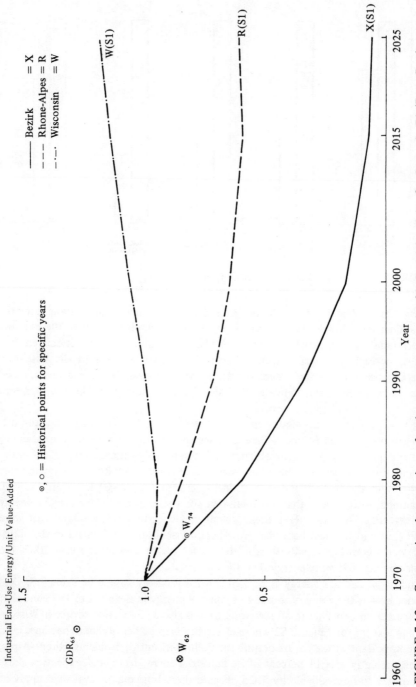

FIGURE 7.13   Cross-regional comparison of end-use energy per unit of industrial activity for Scenario S1 (Base Case). For Bezirk X, the unit of the vertical axis is Industrial End-Use Energy/Unit Net Production.

242

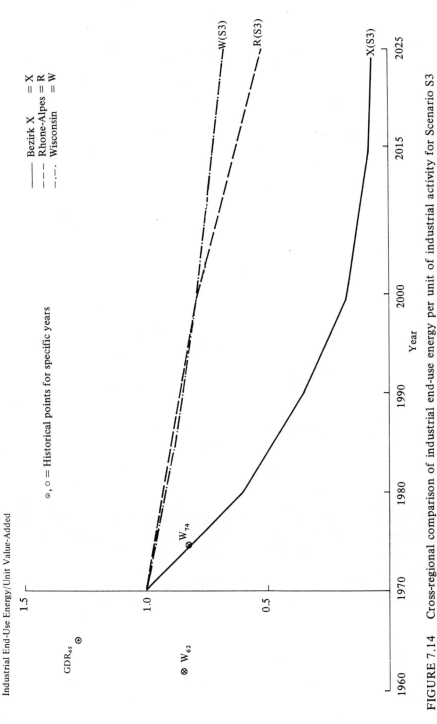

FIGURE 7.14 Cross-regional comparison of industrial end-use energy per unit of industrial activity for Scenario S3 (low-energy scenario). For Bezirk X, the unit of the vertical axis is Industrial End-Use Energy/Unit Net Production.

243

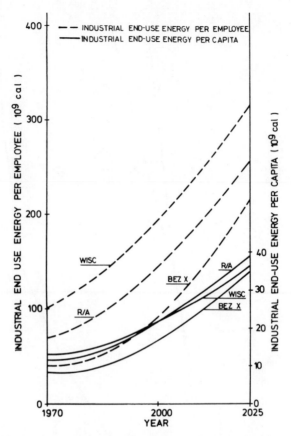

FIGURE 7.15   Industrial end-use energy per capita and per employee.

high-grade coal. Only Wisconsin currently uses a large amount of gas for industrial uses. Natural gas is not expected to be available in those quantities in the future, but gas manufactured from coal has been assumed to be available. Rhone-Alpes is very dependent on imported oil for its industry. Except for Scenario S2, the dependence is decreased but still remains a factor of importance. The decrease in oil and coal use is to be offset by an increase in use of electricity in Rhone-Alpes. Electricity use for industry also increases in all scenarios in Bezirk X and Wisconsin.

IV.   ENERGY SUPPLY

Choices of alternative fuels and supply technologies are among the most important of the long-term strategies being debated in the regions studied. Resource availability and economic considerations played a major role in shaping the end-use energy

TABLE 7.7   Industrial End-use Energy by Source

| | Fraction of Total Industrial Energy Use | | | |
| | | 2025 | | |
	Initial Values[a]	S1	S2	S3
Coal				
Bezirk X	.17	0	0	0
Rhone-Alpes	.11	.01	.01	.01
Wisconsin	.34	.42	.33	.41
Gas				
Bezirk X	.05	.04	.04	.05
Rhone-Alpes	.09	.11	.18	.17
Wisconsin	.48	.40	.34	.43
Oil				
Bezirk X	.05	.01	.01	.01
Rhone-Alpes	.55	.22	.43	.15
Wisconsin	.08	.05	.04	.05
Electricity				
Bezirk X	.14	.39	.25	.32
Rhone-Alpes	.25	.66	.38	.67
Wisconsin	.10	.12	.29	.11
District heat				
Bezirk X	.59	.56	.69	.62
Rhone-Alpes	0	0	0	0
Wisconsin	0	0	0	0

[a] For Rhone-Alpes and Wisconsin, 1970 values; for Bezirk X, 1975.

demands described in the previous section, but perhaps to an even greater degree they influence the energy-supply strategies for a region. This section describes end-use and primary energy flows by fuel type, and discusses other supply considerations such as electricity generation, district heating, and use of renewable resources.

IV.A.   ENERGY BY FUEL TYPE

IV.A.1.   Initial Conditions

A slightly different perspective on end-use energy consumption within the region is given in Figure 7.16. The fraction of end-use energy by fuel type is shown with the fraction of each type of fuel used in each sector of the economy for 1970. Perhaps the distinction between end-use and primary energy should be made again at this point. End-use energy is energy that is consumed within the region for heat, light, or mechanical or chemical processes. Primary energy is the energy in its original form. In practice, in this study, "primary energy consumed within the region" is identical to end-use energy except for district heat, electricity, and synthetic gas and oil. In these cases, the primary energy is the hydropower, solar energy, nuclear

246

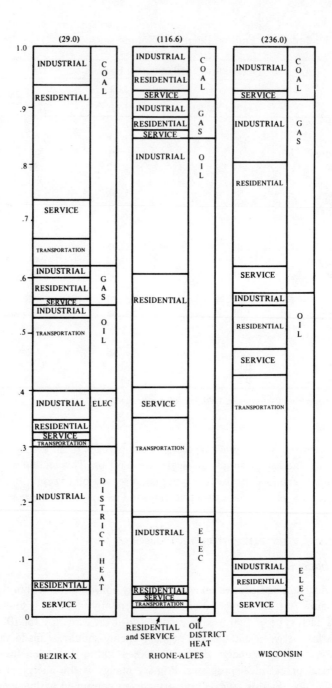

FIGURE 7.16   Annual end-use energy by fuel and economic sector (1970). Numbers in parentheses indicate total end-use energy in 10^{15} cal/yr.

energy, geothermal energy, coal, or oil that produced the district heat, electricity, or synthetic fuel. The end-use energy from these sources does not include losses from conversion at the plant or distribution of the energy. Primary energy that is exported from the region is also tabulated.

In 1970, the only region with a significant fraction of end-use energy supplied by district heat is Bezirk X, where coal district heat is the major source of energy for industry and is also used in small amounts in the residential and service sectors. Rhone-Alpes also has a minor amount of oil district heat for the residential and service sectors. One can theorize that in the GDR economic system, where industry is state-owned, district heat is easier to develop than in France or the United States where different companies would have to cooperate or a new energy supply system, perhaps similar to the American electric utilities or the French state-owned utility, would have to be developed. Because of its primary reliance on coal in a densely populated country, the GDR also has an incentive to make efficient use of its abundant supply of low-grade coal without adversely affecting the health and welfare of its citizens. District heat provides a convenient means of exploiting the coal resource while minimizing the local health impacts.

Direct use of coal provides less than 10 percent of the energy use in Rhone-Alpes and Wisconsin where its main use is for industry; minor amounts are used for space heating in the residential and service sectors. Bezirk X, on the other hand, obtains nearly 40 percent of its end-use energy with the direct combustion of coal. It is the primary fuel for residential space heating (about 50 percent of the total) and is also used for industry, steam locomotives, and space heating of service sector buildings. The direct use of coal in situations where pollution control devices or high stacks are infeasible, especially in densely populated areas, is a major source of concern in the GDR.

Gas is used in minor amounts in the residential, service, and industrial sectors of Bezirk X and Rhone-Alpes. In Wisconsin, however, it is the primary energy source for residential home heating and is also used in the service and industrial sectors, accounting for over one-third of the total end-use energy. Natural gas is expected to be in increasingly short supply at higher prices in the future and presents a problem for Wisconsin's decision-makers. The Wisconsin scenarios have dealt with supply problems in gas and oil by postulating that synthetic fuels from coal will be available.

Oil must be imported into all three regions. Because of well-known political problems, both the supply and prices of oil are unpredictable, although perhaps Wisconsin feels the pressure least since the United States has some oil resources of its own. Oil is used almost exclusively for transportation in Bezirk X and accounts for only about 15 percent of the energy supplied. Oil is the primary fuel for transportation in Wisconsin also. About one-third of Wisconsin's end-use energy is used for transportation and another 15 percent is oil used in the other three sectors; over 45 percent of its end-use energy is from oil. Rhone Alpes has an even worse situation with almost two-thirds of its end-use energy in the form of oil, a result of the

248

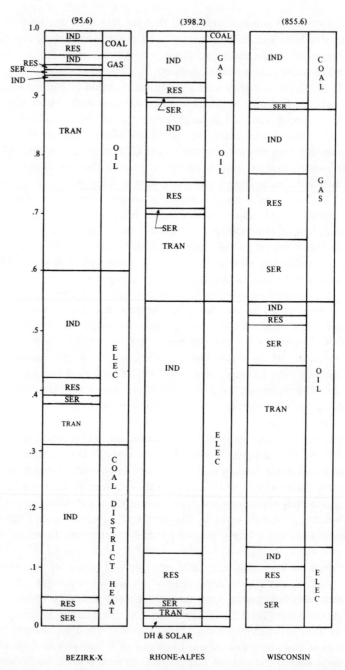

FIGURE 7.17 Annual end-use energy by fuel and economic sector (Scenario S1 — 2025). Numbers in parentheses indicate total end-use energy in 10^{15} cal/yr.

previous easy availability of low-priced Middle-East oil. Oil is not only the primary fuel for transportation, but also is used for residential and service space heating and industrial production.

Electricity accounts for less than 10 percent of end-use energy in Bezirk X and Wisconsin. It is divided among the residential, service, and industrial sectors somewhat evenly in Wisconsin. The industrial sector uses a larger fraction of the total electricity (and total energy) in Bezirk X than in Wisconsin. A small amount of electricity is also used in the transportation sector. Over 15 percent of the end-use energy in Rhone-Alpes is from electricity, the majority of which is used in the industrial sector. Electricity has been a more attractive source of power in Rhone-Alpes than in the other regions because of the availability of hydro power.

IV.A.2.   *Scenario S1*

End-use energy in Scenario S1, shown in Figure 7.17, was defined as a successful implementation of the 20-year plan in the Bezirk and a combination of current plans, present trends, and the judgment of the researchers in Wisconsin and Rhone-Alpes. In Bezirk X the overall strategy is to phase out the direct use of coal, which presents a significant air pollution problem, in favor of coal district heat and electricity, both of which can exploit the coal resource while minimizing the impact of the air pollution. The implied goal in the Rhone-Alpes Scenario S1 is the replacement of imported oil with nuclear generated electricity. The results of the Wisconsin Scenario S1 in 2025 do not differ from the initial conditions as dramatically as either Rhone-Alpes or Bezirk X, perhaps because of a lack of a clearly articulated energy policy in Wisconsin. Gas and oil remain the primary sources of energy although the assumption is that a significant fraction of these will be synthetic fuels produced from coal by 2025.

In all three regions the fraction of energy from coal used directly in the residential, service, and transportation sectors is greatly reduced. Only in Wisconsin is the direct use of coal increased and that is in the industrial sector where the use of high stacks and some pollution control devices is assumed.

Gas is not assumed to significantly increase its share of the market in either Rhone-Alpes or Bezirk X. In Wisconsin its share of the market decreases slightly but is still about a third of the total end-use energy. A decline in the fraction used for residential space heating is nearly offset by the rapidly growing service sector.

One of the most alarming results of Scenario S1 is the heavy dependence on oil in 2025 in all three regions despite efforts to control its use. No satisfactory substitute for oil, except synthetic oil, was foreseen in any of the regions for the transportation sector. One conclusion of this result may be that a high priority should be placed on finding an alternate fuel that can be used for transportation. There are several alternatives of varying degrees of feasibility to supply heat and process energy in the other sectors of the economy, but the research team did not believe that any other form of energy with currently foreseeable technology could reasonably be

250

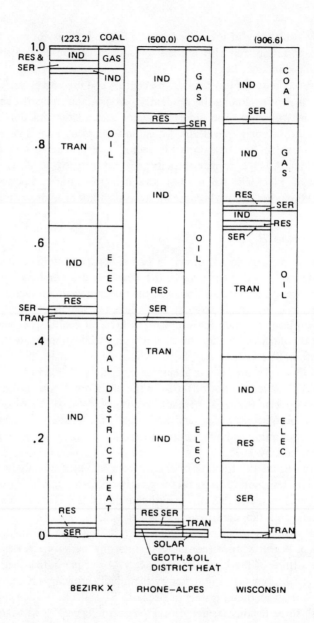

FIGURE 7.18   Annual end-use energy by fuel and economic sector (Scenario S2 — 2025). Numbers in parentheses indicate total end-use energy in 10^{15} cal/yr.

substituted for oil in the transportation sector. The Bezirk nearly eliminates oil for all uses except transportation, but oil still increases to nearly one-third of end-use energy in 2025. Rhone-Alpes decreases the fraction of end-use energy from oil from over two-thirds in 1970 to just over one-third in 2025, mainly by encouraging the use of electricity for industry and for residential and service space heating. The transportation sector uses a smaller fraction of the total end-use energy in Rhone-Alpes than in the other two regions, another factor that keeps oil at only one-third of the end-use energy. In Wisconsin, the fraction of end-use energy from oil decreases only slightly, mainly as a result of a decrease in oil-based residential space heating and a slight decrease in the importance of the transportation sector in end-use energy consumption.

The use of electricity increases greatly in both Bezirk X and Rhone-Alpes, especially in industry; electricity even supplies a significant amount of energy for freight transportation in Bezirk X. In Wisconsin, electricity increases from less than 10 percent to nearly 15 percent of the total end-use energy and the rapidly growing service sector accounts for the increase. More will be said about electricity and about the supply of primary energy in section IV.B.

District heat continues to be developed in the Bezirk and in Rhone-Alpes but its impact on the total end-use energy supply does not change appreciably.

IV.A.3. *Scenario S2*

The results of Scenario S2, defined as a high-energy case, are shown in Figure 7.18, once again in terms of the allocation of total end-use energy among the competing fuels and economic sectors.

The direct use of coal is very similar to Scenario S1 in all three regions. Coal use almost disappears in Rhone-Alpes and Bezirk X and increases slightly in terms of the fraction of total end-use energy in the industrial sector in Wisconsin.

Wisconsin Scenario S2 assumes that gas will not be available in the future to the same extent as in the past, and gas is phased out for service and residential space heating. Energy use in industry, however, grows at a faster rate relative to the other sectors than in Scenario S1, the gas supplies a large fraction of this demand. Perhaps a more likely policy would be that the available supplies of gas are reserved for residential and service space heating, forcing industry to use other fuels. Gas accounts for approximately the same fraction of end-use energy in Bezirk X and Rhone-Alpes in Scenario S2 as in S1.

Use of oil in Bezirk X and Wisconsin does not vary much from Scenario S1, although for space heating in the service sector it is largely replaced by electricity. The Rhone-Alpes Scenario S2, however, is not as successful as S1 in replacing oil with electricity and over half of the end-use energy in 2025 is still supplied by oil. Oil supplies about one-third of the end-use energy in Rhone-Alpes in S1. Since S2 is is also higher in total end-use energy than S1, this represents a substantial additional amount of oil that must be obtained.

252

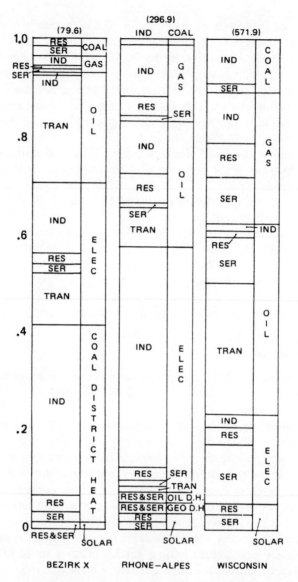

FIGURE 7.19   Annual end-use energy by fuel and economic sector (Scenario S3
– 2025). Numbers in parentheses indicate total end-use energy in 10^{15} cal/yr.

Electricity does not capture as large a fraction of the market in Scenario S2 as in
S1 in Rhone-Alpes and Bezirk X. In the Bezirk, the decrease in the share of electricity in the transportation sector is made up by oil because of the importance of
truck freight transport; in the industrial sector it is made up by coal district heat. In

Rhone-Alpes Scenario S2, the decrease in the share of electricity compared with S1 is from the low penetration of electricity into industry. For Wisconsin, Scenario S2 is the high energy, high electricity case. Electricity captures nearly 40 percent of the total end-use energy including most of the residential and service space heating markets, a large fraction of the industrial energy use, and even a small amount of mass transit.

In Bezirk X, the industrial sector grows even faster in S2 in relation to the other sectors than in S1 and coal district heat provides most of the additional energy required, resulting in 45 percent of the end-use energy being supplied by district heat.

IV.A.4.   Scenario S3

Scenario S3 was defined as an energy-conservation case with emphasis on more speculative sources of energy and a high degree of environmental control. Perhaps one of the most interesting results of Scenario S3 was the demand that could be met by solar and geothermal energy as a result of quite vigorous programs to introduce them (Figure 7.19).

In terms of the fuel mix, Scenario S3 is very similar to S1 in Bezirk X except that coal district heat for industry supplies an even larger share of the total energy. Solar space heating is also introduced but accounts for less than 1 percent of the total by 2025. The Rhone Alpes picture is also very similar to S1. Solar and geothermal district heat together account for slightly over 5 percent of the end-use energy in 2025, a substantial contribution but certainly a long way from solving the energy problem. The result is very much the same in Wisconsin where solar space heating accounts for just over 5 percent of the total end-use energy needs by 2025.

IV.B.   ENERGY FLOWS

IV.B.1.   Initial Conditions

Primary Energy   The primary energy flows in 1970 for the three regions are shown in Figure 7.20. Bezirk X is an energy producer, exporting directly or after conversion over half of the coal mined in the region in 1970. The coal is exported mostly in the form of briquettes, but also as electricity. Of the energy used in the Bezirk, only approximately 12 percent must be imported to supply the needs for coke, gas, and oil. To meet its energy needs, Rhone-Alpes must import about 70 percent of its total requirement, primarily Middle Eastern oil. The abundant supply of hydro power supplies 17 percent of its total primary energy requirement and allows Rhone-Alpes to export nearly 20 percent of the electricity produced in the region. Rhone-Alpes also has a limited amount of coal that provides another 10 percent of the primary energy requirement. The coal reserves, however, are not large and are not expected to be a significant source of energy for Rhone-Alpes in the future.

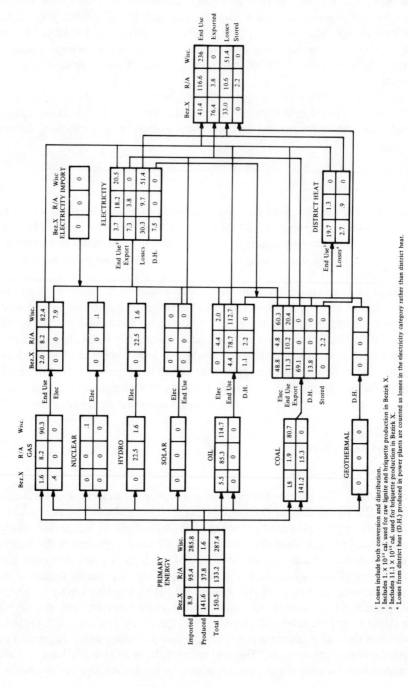

FIGURE 7.20 Primary energy flows for all scenarios: 1970 ($\times$ 10^{15} cal).

Wisconsin is in the worst position; except for about .5 percent of its primary energy supplied by hydro power, its entire supply was imported in 1970.

Electricity Generation and District Heat   Electricity generation and district heat production provide convenient methods of utilizing the low grade, high sulfur lignite that is found in the GDR. Excluding exported briquettes, 60 percent of the primary energy is used in electric power plants that both generate electricity and produce district heat and another 18 percent is used in pure district heating plants. The penalty that must be paid of course is the losses that occur in conversion and in transmission and distribution of the new form of energy. In the Bezirk, conversion, transmission, and distribution losses are 44 percent of the total primary energy, excluding again exported briquettes. Both Wisconsin and Rhone-Alpes use about 25 percent of their primary energy for electricity generation. Rhone-Alpes uses another 3 percent for district heat, resulting in losses in total primary energy of 18 percent for Wisconsin and, because of the high efficiency of hydro power, of only 8 percent for Rhone-Alpes. In all regions, losses associated, for example, with the combustion of fuels in a house furnace are included in end-use energy rather than losses. Losses are defined solely as conversion, transmission, and distribution losses associated with electricity or district heat production.

District heat is a significant energy option in Bezirk X, already supplying 30 percent of the end-use energy; 38 percent of the district heat is produced in electric power plants with an overall efficiency (electricity plus district heat) of 39 percent. The remainder is produced in coal and oil-fueled district heating plants at 82 percent efficiency. Rhone-Alpes also has a limited amount of oil-fueled district heat produced at 60 percent efficiency.

IV.B.2.   The Scenarios

Primary Energy   Figures 7.21 through 7.23 show the primary energy flows in 2025 for the three basic scenarios. Bezirk X remains relatively energy self-sufficient producing between 66 percent and 86 percent of its own energy, again excluding exported briquettes. By 2025, however, in all three scenarios, exports must be drastically curtailed as the Bezirk needs a larger percentage of its coal to supply its own needs. Increasing amounts of foreign oil are also required primarily to meet transportation requirements. The energy self-sufficiency of Rhone-Alpes declines rapidly to only about 3 percent of its primary energy needs by 2025 in Scenarios S1 and S2 as the coal reserves dwindle and no more suitable sites are available for hydro plants. In Scenario S1, however, 70 percent of the energy is nuclear, a source that the French policymakers hope will be cheaper and more reliable than the coal, oil, and gas of Scenario S2. Wisconsin, whose only energy resource is a small amount of hydro power (Wisconsin Scenarios S1 and S2 have no solar energy), can produce only a small fraction of 1 percent of its energy needs by 2025 in S1 and S2. In Scenario S3, with the introduction of energy conservation measures, solar and

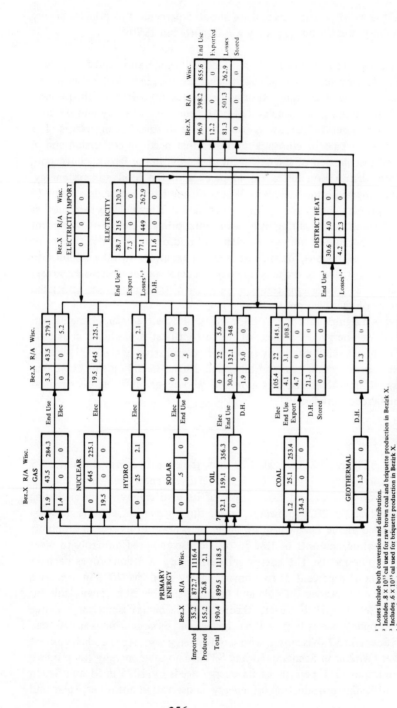

FIGURE 7.21 Primary energy flows in Scenario S1: 2025 ($\times 10^{15}$ cal).

[1] Losses include both conversion and distribution.
[2] Includes .8 × 10¹⁵ cal used for raw brown coal and briquette production in Bezirk X.
[3] Includes .6 × 10¹⁵ cal used for briquette production in Bezirk X.
[4] Losses from district heat produced in power plants are counted as losses under electricity rather than district heat.
[5] 25.8 × 10¹⁵ cal counted as losses in Rhône-Alpes electricity generation is actually used for a uranium enrichment plant that supplies all of France.
[6] Wisconsin gas includes 212.1 × 10¹⁵ cal of imported synthetic gas produced from coal at a conversion efficiency of 60%.
[7] Wisconsin oil includes 261.8 × 10¹⁵ cal of imported synthetic oil produced from coal at a conversion efficiency of 50%.

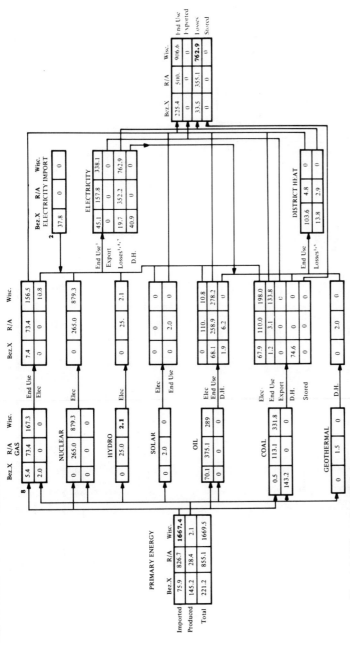

FIGURE 7.22 Primary energy flows in Scenario S2: 2025 ($\times 10^{15}$ cal).

[1] Losses include both conversion and distribution.
[2] Nine percent of imported electricity is counted as losses in transmission and distribution. The electricity is generated at 33% efficiency resulting in a primary energy use of 113×10^{15} cal. This primary energy has *not* been included in the primary energy figure for Bezirk X.
[3] Includes $.8 \times 10^{15}$ cal used for raw lignite and briquette production in Bezirk X.
[4] Note that losses are so low in Bezirk X because most electricity generation is outside the Bezirk and therefore conversions are not accounted for.
[5] Includes 1.6×10^{15} cal used for briquette production in Bezirk X.
[6] Losses from district heat produced in power plants are counted as losses under electricity rather than district heat.
[7] 21.5×10^{15} cal counted as losses in Rhone-Alpes is actually used for a uranium enrichment plant that supplies all France.
[8] Wisconsin gas includes 9.5×10^{15} cal of imported synthetic gas produced from coal at a conversion efficiency of 60%.

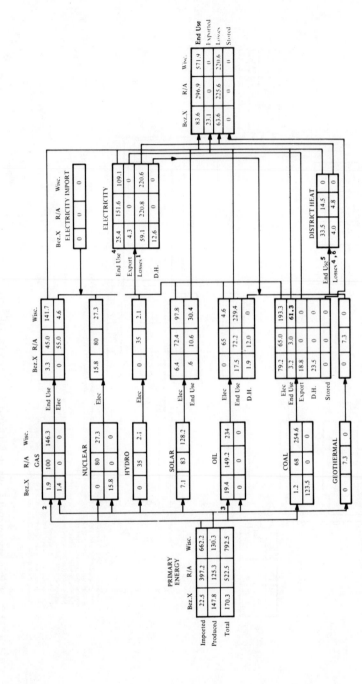

[1] Losses include both conversion and distribution.
[2] Wisconsin gas includes 74.1×10^{15} cal of imported synthetic gas produced from coal at a conversion efficiency of 60 percent.
[3] Wisconsin oil includes 142.2×10^{15} cal of imported synthetic oil produced from coal at a conversion efficiency of 50 percent.
[4] Includes $.7 \times 10^{15}$ cal used for raw lignite and briquette production in Bezirk X.
[5] Includes 3.2×10^{15} cal used for briquette production in Bezirk X.
[6] Losses from district heat produced in power plants are counted as losses under electricity rather than district heat.

FIGURE 7.23   Primary energy flows in Scenario S3: 2025 ($\times 10^{15}$ cal).

TABLE 7.8   Average Annual Increase in Electricity Consumption and Percentage of Total Primary Energy Devoted to Electrical Generation

		1970–2000		
Annual average percentage increase in electricity consumption[a]	1970	S1	S2	S3
Bezirk X	4.8[b]	4.2	5.4	3.9
Rhone-Alpes	5.3[c]	5.3	4.4	4.8
Wisconsin	7.2[d]	3.6	6.3	3.3
		2000		
Percentage of Primary Energy Used for Electrical Generation[e]	1970	S1	S2	S3
Bezirk X	32	42	48	41
Rhone-Alpes	24	66	48	50
Wisconsin	25	30	54	34

[a] Excludes exports and transmission losses; includes electricity import.
[b] Average for 1960–1972 period.
[c] Average for 1969–1972 period.
[d] Average for 1961–1972 period.
[e] Includes primary energy used for electricity export as well as primary energy used for electricity import.

geothermal energy, Wisconsin and Rhone-Alpes manage to supply 6 percent and 24 percent of their own needs.

Electricity Generation and District Heat   Bezirk X continues to rely heavily on electricity and district heat in all three scenarios. The percentage of total primary energy used for electricity and district heat ranges from 66 to 75. Rhone-Alpes and Wisconsin also increase their reliance on electricity in all three scenarios with a corresponding increase in energy lost in conversion, especially in Rhone-Alpes where new power plants must be nuclear or fossil-fueled rather than the very efficient hydro plants.

One of the major conclusions inferred from the range of futures is that future growth of electricity generation will be much lower than historical rates. Table 7.8 shows the average annual growth rates for the selected scenarios in comparison with historical values. Also shown are the percentages of primary energy used for electrical generation. The significant slowing of electricity growth in these industrialized regions indicates the need for a continuous examination of the requirements for future generating facilities.

In terms of efficiencies, district heat is better than electricity and Bezirk X achieves its best overall efficiency of close to 70 percent in Scenario S2 (including the generation losses associated with the imported electricity). The high electricity cases result in low efficiencies, especially Scenario S1 for Rhone-Alpes with 72 percent of its primary energy coming from nuclear energy for electric power plants. However, since nuclear energy is used only for electricity generation, it is not really consistent to compare losses from nuclear energy with losses from fossil fuels, except in the consideration of environmental effects such as the impact of waste heat discharges.

TABLE 7.9   Solar Energy Contribution to Energy Requirements in Bezirk X, Rhone-Alpes, and Wisconsin for Scenario S3 in 2025

	Bezirk X	Rhone-Alpes	Wisconsin
Residential end-use	5%	10%	17%
Service end-use	6%	41%	9%
Total end-use energy[a]	3%	12%	11%
Electricity generation	7%	16%	30%

[a] These figures include solar-generated electricity used in the end-use sectors.

Sources of electricity are primarily coal for all three scenarios in Bezirk X; nuclear energy for Rhone-Alpes Scenarios S1 and S2 and Wisconsin Scenario S1; coal and nuclear energy for Wisconsin Scenario S2; a combination of solar energy, oil, gas, coal, and nuclear energy for Rhone-Alpes Scenario S3; and coal and solar energy for Wisconsin Scenario S3.

Solar Energy   One strategy examined in the scenarios for reducing petroleum requirements was the development of renewable resources such as solar power. Vigorous development of solar power for heating was examined in the residential and service sectors, and to a more limited extent in electricity production. As stressed in the scenario descriptions in the three previous chapters, the scenario assumptions about solar penetration were not meant to be a prediction of technological progress: rather they were included to assess the impact of a given penetration rate on end-use energy demands and on resource requirements in the time frame of the scenarios.

The potential solar contribution to the energy needs of the three regions in 2025 is shown in Table 7.9. Its contribution is significant, especially in Rhone-Alpes where solar energy provides 41 percent of service energy needs and in Wisconsin where it provides 17 percent of residential needs. One must keep in mind that in the scenarios, the utilization of solar power was restricted to new construction, and even during a 50-year period the turnover of a stock of buildings is slow. Should retrofitting of existing buildings with solar equipment become economical, the impact of the solar strategy would be even greater. It must be emphasized too that in the scenarios only technology that is currently operational, such as space heating and water heating, was considered. The scenarios could be radically altered if inexpensive mass production of the photovoltaic cell and solar energy systems for producing intermediate temperatures for industry became feasible.

IV.C.   SOME CONCLUDING COMMENTS ON ENERGY SUPPLY

In concluding the discussion on energy supply systems in the three regions, the following observations can be made:

- Despite vigorous conservation measures and alternative fuel strategies, the scenarios demonstrated the difficulty that could be experienced well before the end of the century in avoiding severe constraints or shortfalls of petroleum supplies if petroleum production begins to decline in that period.

● Although conventional and environmental costs could be appreciable, coal represents a major option for decreasing dependence on scarce petroleum and gas, and is a major competitor to nuclear power.

● In general, future growth of electricity generation in the regions will be much lower than historical rates.

● The potential of energy savings through application of district heating or cogeneration is significant in all of the regions. The GDR is well on its way to the widespread implementation of district heating.

● Solar energy has the potential to appreciably reduce the long-term, nonrenewable energy resource requirements in all of the regions.

V.   SELECTED ENVIRONMENTAL IMPACTS

The analysis of environmental consequences was one of the major objectives of scenario building. A wide range of quantified environmental indicators have been used to characterize the environmental implications. *Quantified* here refers only to those impacts included in the models used in this research. The choice of this set of impacts is to some extent subjective; in addition, some degree of uncertainty (and perhaps controversy) is associated with some of the impact factors. There are also many indicators which are recognized but remain unquantified; there are others that are unrecognized and hence unquantified. An approach to coping with this uncertainty and subjectivity is described in Appendix E.

The impacts presented in this section are only a fraction of those studied with the methodology described in Chapter 3, and described in the scenarios for each of the regions in Chapters 4, 5, and 6. Representative impacts have been selected from several categories as shown below:

● Impacts on water: Water evaporated by power plant waste heat
● Impacts of land: Land use for energy resource extraction and energy-related facilities
● Impacts on air: Sulfur dioxide emissions
● Impacts on people: Quantified human health and safety impacts
● Potential long-term impacts: Carbon dioxide production and radioactive waste production

The first three categories are primarily regional or local impacts. The fourth category, human health and safety impacts, includes some quantified global impacts as well as the local effects. The final category has impacts that are representative of the potential long-term risks that are global in nature.

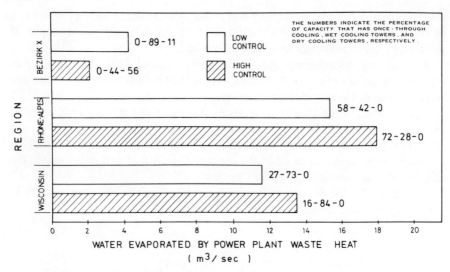

FIGURE 7.24 Water evaporated by power plant waste heat in 2025 for two control options (electrical generation as in Scenario S1).

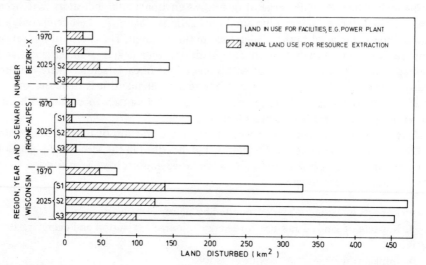

FIGURE 7.25 Cross-regional comparison of annual land use for energy production. Note that land in use for facilities does not include land used for hydropower plants.

V. HEAT DISCHARGE FROM POWER PLANTS

Waste heat from electrical generation presents a problem that varies in magnitude among the three regions. Three categories of cooling options have been considered for power plants: once-through cooling on rivers; evaporative cooling such as provided by wet cooling towers; and dry (nonevaporative) cooling towers. A high control and a low control case for each region were based on different allowable temperature increases for rivers. Since Rhone-Alpes and Wisconsin have sizable water resources, once-through cooling and wet cooling towers are the only options considered. For Bezirk X the water resources are very limited, and once-through cooling is not an option.

Calculation of water evaporated for the 2025 levels of electrical generation in Scenario S1 have been made for each region. The results for low control and high control cases are shown in Figure 7.24. The high control case for Bezirk X has less evaporation (more dry cooling), while the high control case for Rhone-Alpes and Wisconsin requires more evaporation (less once-through cooling). If strict environmental standards are imposed, dry cooling may also eventually be required in Rhone-Alpes and Wisconsin. Current designs for dry cooling systems are avoided because of large efficiency penalties and costs.

The total fresh water consumed for all purposes (evaporated, transpired, or incorporated into products) in Wisconsin in 1970 averaged approximately $9.5 \, m^3/sec$. This is less than the evaporation from Wisconsin power plants for either control option shown in Figure 7.24.

V.B. LAND USE

The annual land use for energy production is shown in Figure 7.25. The land being used may be divided into facilities land use, such as at power plant sites, and resource extraction land use, such as at uranium or coal surface mines (land use for hydropower plants was not included in this study). Therefore, not all the land use shown in Figure 7.25 is within the region since some fuels are imported and some fuel system facilities, such as uranium mills, are located in other regions.

Even if it is assumed that all land disturbed for past resource extraction is reclaimed so that the total quantity of land disturbed because of energy activities is just what is shown in Figure 7.25, the quantities of land use are not insignificant. For example, the scenario with the largest land use in 2025 amounts to the following percentage of total land areas in each region:

- Bezirk X – 2.9 percent (S2)
- Rhone-Alpes – 0.6 percent (S3)
- Wisconsin – 0.3 percent (S2)

V.C. SO₂ EMISSIONS

Sulfur dioxide (SO_2) is generally thought to have unfavorable effects on human health, vegetation, and structures. Coal is a major source of SO_2 emissions in Bezirk X and Wisconsin, and to a lesser degree, in Rhone-Alpes. Table 7.10 indicates typical

TABLE 7.10   Assumed Typical Coal Characteristics for Electricity Impact Calculations

	Heating Value (kcal/kg)	Percent Sulfur	Grams SO_2 per 10^6 cal (No Control)	Percent Ash	Grams Ash per 10^6 cal (99% Control)
Bezirk X					
lignite (thru 1985)	2,300	1.4	12.2	10	0.43
lignite (after 1985)	2,200	1.4	12.7	10	0.45
Rhone-Alpes					
bituminous	7,000	0.7	2.0	10	0.14
Wisconsin[a]					
bituminous	6,650	2.5	7.5	10	0.15
subbituminous	4,700	0.6	2.6	10	0.21

[a] United States Environmental Protection Agency (USEPA) emission standard for SO_2 from power plants is 1.2 lb/10^6 Btu, or 2.2 g/10^6 cal.

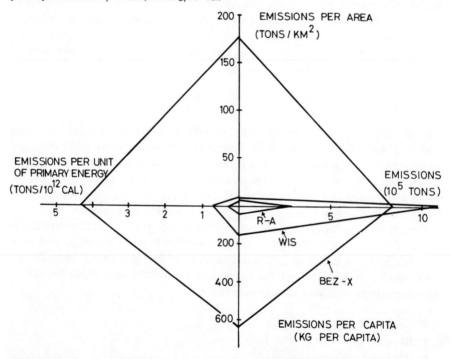

FIGURE 7.26   Sulfur dioxide emissions in 2025 for Scenario S1.

coal characteristics assumed for the three regions. With no SO_2 control measures, the Bezirk coal produces about twice as much SO_2 per unit energy as a blended U.S. coal, or nearly 5 times as much as low-sulfur western subbituminous coal. The table demonstrates the wide variability in energy resource characteristics in the three regions.

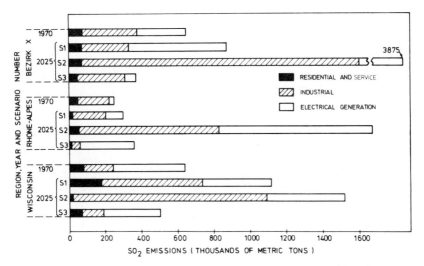

FIGURE 7.27   Cross-regional comparison of SO₂ emission resulting from energy use and energy export.

The SO$_2$ emissions for Scenario S1 in the year 2025 are compared for the three regions in Figure 7.26. Four different indices for the emissions are shown: total absolute emissions, emissions per unit area, emissions per capita, and emissions per unit of primary energy use. Wisconsin has the largest total emissions, but Bezirk X has the greatest impact on the other three scales. The Bezirk is a highly industrialized region that uses lignite for most of its energy.

The SO$_2$ emissions for the years 1970 and 2025 for all scenarios are compared in Figure 7.27. It is clear that residential and service sector emissions are a small fraction of total emissions in all scenarios considered. The very large total emission for the Bezirk in Scenario S2 is the result of expansion of energy-intensive industry, emphasis on electricity, and no SO$_2$ emission controls. Some of the emission for Bezirk X in S2 occurs in other regions because the Bezirk imports a significant quantity of electricity.

In general, the SO$_2$ emission controls were assumed to be minimal in S2, maximum in S3, and in the middle for S1. These assumptions, coupled with the widely varying energy demands in some scenarios, result in total SO$_2$ emissions in 2025 that are near 1970 levels (Rhone-Alpes S1 and S3) or even decline from 1970 levels (Bezirk-X S3 and Wisconsin S3).

Expected emissions of particulates, nitrogen oxides, carbon monoxide, and hydrocarbons have also been computed for the scenarios. Only SO$_2$ is presented because it is the only pollutant with which some quantified health effects have been associated in the models used here. However, it should be noted that the transportation sector, which includes private autos, is a large contributor of some of these other pollutants but is not a significant contributor of SO$_2$.

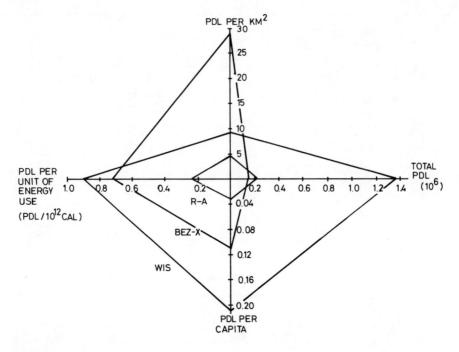

FIGURE 7.28 "Quantified" human health and safety impacts (Scenario S1 – 2025; PDL = person-day lost).

V.D. HUMAN HEALTH AND SAFETY

The total "quantified" human health and safety impacts in the year 2025 for Scenario S1 are shown in Figure 7.28, which is similar in format to Figure 7.26. Person-days lost (PDL) are used to combine the effects of mortality and morbidity. The quantified totals shown in the figure include health and accidental impacts on the general public and those people employed throughout the energy system, from resource extraction to waste disposal. In contrast to SO_2 emissions for Scenario S1, Bezirk X has the largest impact only on the scale showing PDL per unit area. Quantified impacts of air pollution are a major share of the total PDL for Wisconsin.

To provide some perspective on these numbers, the PDL per capita in Figure 7.28 are compared with the PDL per capita that result from all accidental fatalities in the United States. The risk of fatality from all accidents (autos, falls, burns, drowning, firearms, and so forth) was 49 per 100,000 in the United States in 1974.[2] This is equivalent to 2.9 PDL per person per year.* The quantified PDL per capita in 2025 that results from Wisconsin energy use in Scenario S1 is about 7 percent of the PDL per capita from all fatal accidents at current incidence levels.

* One accidental fatality is equivalent to 6,000 PDL in this accounting system.

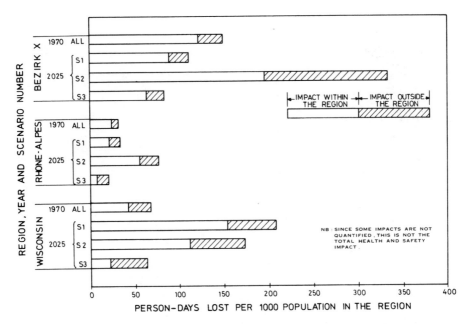

FIGURE 7.29   Cross-regional comparison of quantified human health impacts.

The quantified health and safety impacts are not spread evenly over all population groups. For example, nearly 30 percent of the quantified PDL in 2025 for Wisconsin Scenario S1 are imposed on less than 1 percent of the total population, namely, 53,000 elderly people who live in the industrialized Milwaukee area and had heart or lung disease before the period of the study.

The total PDL per 1,000 people in the region is displayed in Figure 7.29 for the years 1970 and 2025 for all scenarios. It is interesting to note that there is at least one scenario in each region that has fewer PDL per capita in 2025 than in 1970. Also, it is clear from the figure that a significant fraction of the total PDL is imposed on regions other than where the energy is consumed. Impacts in other regions result from consumption of fuels that must be mined elsewhere and transported into the regions, or from the expected global health effects from radioactive releases and so on. The quantified health impacts of air pollution are a significant consideration in all scenarios examined in this study.

V.E.   CARBON DIOXIDE EMISSIONS

Carbon dioxide emissions are of concern on a global scale since the atmospheric concentration of CO_2 affects average global temperature.[3,4,5,14] Burning of fossil fuels has produced enormous quantities of CO_2, about 10.8×10^9 metric tons in 1960,[3] for which there are three main reservoirs: the oceans, the biosphere (defined

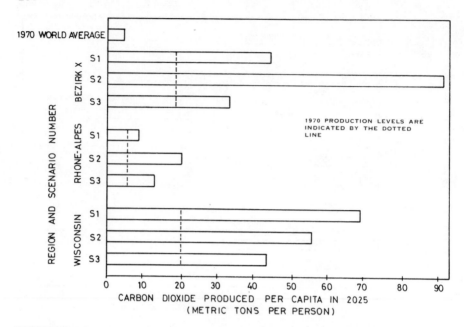

FIGURE 7.30   Carbon dioxide production per capita in 1970 and 2025.

as the mass of living and nonliving organic matter), and the atmosphere. About half of the CO_2 liberated by fossil fuel combustion has remained in the atmosphere.[3,4] Calculations have shown that the CO_2 concentration in the atmosphere may increase from about 320 parts per million (ppm) by volume in 1970 to from 370 to 380 ppm in 2000; the resulting global temperature increase may be nearly one degree Celsius. Global temperature changes of this magnitude may have serious implications for agriculture, global sea level, and global precipitation patterns. Thus, CO_2 emissions that result from burning of fossil fuels may involve a significant long-term risk to future generations.

The per capita CO_2 emissions in the year 2025 for the three scenarios in each region are shown in Figure 7.30 along with the 1970 emission levels. All three regions have greater CO_2 emissions in 2025 for all three scenarios than they had in 1970. The total CO_2 emissions in Wisconsin in 2025 for Scenario S1 are more than a factor of 5 greater than the 1970 emissions (population increases by about 50 percent from 1970 to 2025). Bezirk X relies on coal for a large fraction of its energy in all scenarios; the total emissions for the high-energy scenario (S2) in the Bezirk are nearly 5 times greater than the 1970 emissions. In Rhone-Alpes, the availability of fossil fuels is more limited and a significant fraction of the energy comes from other sources, such as hydropower or nuclear energy.

The emissions resulting from Wisconsin's energy use in 2025 for S1 are approximately 4 percent of the total emissions for the world in 1960. If all regions of the

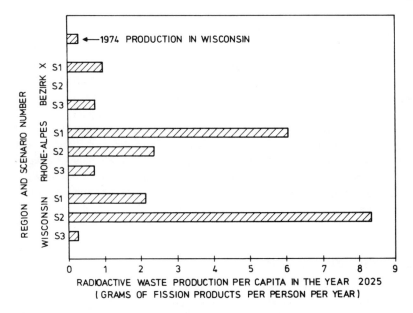

FIGURE 7.31   Radioactive waste production per capita in 2025 for all scenarios.

world were to increase their CO_2 emissions as in these scenarios, methods for reducing CO_2 emissions to the atmosphere, e.g., Marchetti's disposal method,[6] or even CO_2 removal from the atmosphere, may be required, or the fossil fuel option might be unacceptable.

V.F.   RADIOACTIVE WASTE

Radioactive wastes produced during reprocessing of nuclear fuel are highly radioactive and must be stored in isolation for long time periods.[7,8] The safety and reliability of waste management alternatives are among the recognized potential long-term risks related to nuclear power.

The mass of radioactive waste that is produced annually to provide nuclear electricity in each of the three regions is shown in Figure 7.31 for the three scenarios. The large commitment to nuclear power in Rhone-Alpes Scenario S1 and Wisconsin Scenario S2 is evident. The Bezirk relies heavily on coal (lignite) for its electricity, and nuclear power is not introduced until after the year 2000 in Scenarios S1 and S3; there is no nuclear power at all in Scenario S2. Wisconsin has a significant quantity of nuclear energy in Scenario S1 but nuclear generation in Wisconsin Scenario S1 is only about one-third of the production in Rhone-Alpes Scenario S1. The 2025 nuclear generation in Rhone-Alpes Scenario S1 is greater than 3 times the 83×10^9 kWh (gross) produced from nuclear plants in the United States in 1973.[2]

Radioactive wastes could have both global and regional impacts. Accidents at reprocessing plants, waste storage facilities, or during transportation could cause severe local radioactive contamination. A worldwide heavy commitment to nuclear power, such as in Scenario S1 for Rhone-Alpes, would present a formidable waste management problem, one that would require global cooperation. In concluding this section on the environment, it should be noted that no scenario has the lowest environmental impacts in all categories considered. Therefore, one must make value judgments concerning tradeoffs between impacts. Some impacts are local and short-term, while others are global and long-term. Some are quantified, others are recognized but unquantified, still others are unrecognized and therefore unquantified. Local government controls over the localized impacts may be adequate to keep local impacts at a tolerable level; in contrast, some of the potential long-term impacts may require cooperation among nations to avoid "the tragedy of the commons"[9] on a global scale.

VI. CONCLUDING COMMENTS

The alternative futures compared in this chapter are clearly not intended as forecasts; no probabilities of occurrence have been associated with them. In the time since the scenarios were written, it has become clear that some of the parameters, assumptions, and policies embodied in them would have to be changed, were the scenarios to be rewritten. However, because of their emphasis on the mid- to long-term, the examination of these futures is a valuable process for analysis of the policy issues treated here; if anything, these issues are of even more importance today than at the beginning of the research project.

The preceding sections have only highlighted some of the results of the comparative analysis. One of the important aspects not described here is an analysis of the relationship between the decision structures of a region and the formal models and planning tools that are used. This work is presented in Appendixes B and C of this book.

In closing, it should be emphasized that this study was made with the objective of developing a greater understanding of the regions and their futures. No region should be judged as "better" or "worse." We hope that our results are read in that spirit and that they contribute to improved management of energy and environmental systems.

REFERENCES

1.   Hanson, M.E., and J.W. Mitchell. A Model of Transportation Energy Use in Wisconsin: Demographic Considerations and Alternative Scenarios. Institute for Environmental Studies report No. 57, University of Wisconsin-Madison, Dec. 1975.
2.   U.S. Bureau of the Census. *Statistical Abstract of the U.S.* U.S. Government Printing Office, Washington, D.C., 1975 (also previous editions of this annual publication).

3.   Matthews, W.H., W.W. Kellogg, and G.D. Robinson (eds.). *Man's Impact on the Climate*. MIT Press, Cambridge, Massachusetts, 1971.

4.   Broecker, W.S. "Climatic Change: Are We on the Brink of a Pronounced Global Warming?" *Science* 189(4201): 460–463, Aug. 8, 1975.

5.   Niehaus, Friedrich. A Nonlinear Eight Level Tandem Model to Calculate the Future CO_2 and C-14 Burden to the Atmosphere. Report No. RM-76-35, International Institute for Applied Systems Analysis, Laxenburg, Austria, 1976.

6.   Marchetti, Cesare. On Geoengineering and the CO_2 Problem. Report No. RM-76-17, International Institute for Applied Systems Analysis, Laxenburg, Austria, 1976.

7.   Avenhaus, R., W. Häfele, and P.E. McGrath. Considerations on the Large Scale Deployment of the Nuclear Fuel Cycle. Report No. RR-75-36, International Institute for Applied Systems Analysis, Laxenburg, Austria, 1975.

8.   U.S. Atomic Energy Commission. *High Level Radioactive Waste Management Alternatives*. WASH-1297, 1974.

9.   Hardin, Garrett. "The Tragedy of the Commons." *Science* 162: 1243–1248.

10.   Aigner, V.W., C.P. Erwin, and M.J. Osborne. "Wisconsin Energy Use: 1972–1976." Wisconsin Office of State Planning and Energy, Madison, Wisconsin, 1977.

11.   Energy Systems and Policy Research Group. "The Potential Impact of the National Energy Plan on Wisconsin's Future." University of Wisconsin, Madison, Wisconsin, 1977.

12.   Hanson, M.E., and J.M. Lang. "Conservation and Fuel Strategies in the Industrial Sector." In W.K. Foell (ed,), *Proceedings of the 1978 Conference on Alternative Energy Futures for Wisconsin*. University of Wisconsin, Madison, Wisconsin, 1978.

13.   Hanson, M.E. "Energy Conservation and Alternative Transportation Strategies," In W.K. Foell (ed.), *Proceedings of the 1978 Conference on Alternative Energy Futures for Wisconsin*. University of Wisconsin, Madison, Wisconsin, 1978.

14.   Williams, Jill (ed.). *Carbon Dioxide, Climate, and Society*, IIASA Conference Series. Pergamon Press, Oxford, 1978.

Appendixes

BACKGROUND PAPERS

The appendixes of this book provide a detailed picture of the three regions. Appendix A, which contains a description of socioeconomic, geographic, and energy-use characteristics of the regions, has much more detail than Chapter 2. Appendixes B and C provide an overview of the administrative and institutional structure of energy management as well as a description of selected energy and environmental practices in each of the three regions. Appendix D describes energy system models employed in each of the regions and an appraisal of these models by specialists from the two other regions. Finally, Appendix E presents an approach used by IIASA to find the preferences of decision makers with regard to energy/environment strategies.

A Description of the Three Regions

I. THE GERMAN DEMOCRATIC REPUBLIC

Alois Hölzl – IIASA

I.A. PHYSICAL CHARACTERISTICS

I.A.1. Geography

The German Democratic Republic (GDR) is a middle European country; in the north it borders on the Baltic Sea (Its coastline is 901 km.) and it has common boundaries with the Federal Republic of Germany (FRG) in the west and southwest (1,381 km), with Czechoslovakia in the southeast (430 km), and with Poland in the east (456 km). The area of the GDR is 108,178 km^2, and its population was about 17.1 million in 1970. The capital is Berlin, which had about 1.1 million residents in 1970. Figure 1 gives an idea of the size and location of the GDR.

Geographically, the country consists of two regions: the northern part of the GDR is part of the North German lowland, while the southern part belongs to the German low mountain area. The highest elevation in this area is the Fichtelberg (1,214 m) in the Erzgebirge. The main river of the GDR is the Elbe which enters the country from Czechoslovakia at the southeast border and leaves the country in the northwest (at the border with the FRG). The length of the GDR section of the river is 566 km (49 percent of the total length of the river), and its drainage area covers 77 percent of the total land area of the GDR. The second important river is the Oder which forms part of the border with Poland. Here, the GDR section is 162 km (18 percent of the total length of the river). Including a number of smaller rivers and several canals (such as the Oder–Spree Kanal) the inland water-way system of the GDR has a total length of approximately 2,500 km.

Natural resources in the GDR are very scarce. The most important minerals mined are iron, uranium, and potassium; even taking these into consideration, the country is not self-sufficient. Within the energy sector, lignite is practically the only primary energy source supplied in the country itself; it supplied about 75 percent of the total energy demand in 1970. Other fossil fuels, such as hard coal, crude oil, and natural gas, have to be supplied almost exclusively by imports. Due to the

275

276

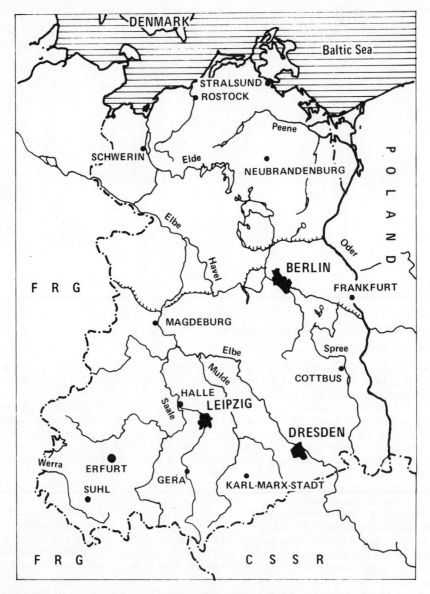

FIGURE A.1   Map of the German Democratic Republic.

geographic characteristics, the climate, the location of raw materials, and historical factors, the northern part of the GDR is dominated by agriculture, whereas the southern part is highly industrialized. The most important branches of industry are the lignite industry, the chemical industry, iron and steel, construction of machinery

TABLE A.1   Area, Population, and Population Density of the Regions in the GDR

	Area (km²)	1970 Population (× 10³)	1970 Population Density (people/km²)
Berlin	403	1,086	2,695
Cottbus	8,262	863	104
Dresden	6,738	1,877	279
Erfurt	7,348	1,256	171
Frankfurt/Oder	7,185	681	95
Gera	4,004	739	185
Halle	8,771	1,925	219
Karl-Marx-Stadt	6,009	2,047	341
Leipzig	4,966	1,491	298
Magdeburg	11,525	1,320	115
Neubrandenburg	10,793	638	59
Potsdam	12,572	1,133	90
Rostock	7,074	859	121
Schwerin	8,672	598	69
Suhl	3,856	553	143

SOURCE: *Statistisches Jahrbuch 1974 der DDR*[1]; pp. 3, 77–106.

and equipment, the fine mechanical and optical industry, and the textile industry. In the north, the only industrial centers are Berlin (electrical equipment) and the seaports Rostock and Stralsund (shipbuilding).

I.A.2.   Climate

The GDR has a moderate continental climate. The temperature ranges are slightly less in the north due to the influence of the Baltic Sea. For instance, the average annual minimum and maximum temperatures in Cottbus (69 m above sea level in the southern part of the GDR) are $-10.4°C$ and $4.9°C$ in January, and $15.8°C$ and $20.7°C$ in July. The corresponding values for Schwerin (59 m above sea level, near the Baltic Sea) are $-8.6°C$ and $4.5°C$ in January, and $14.2°C$ and $19.9°C$ in July. The figures are average values over the period 1901 to 1973. The number of degree-days calculated on the basis of these data give a measure of the heating requirements. A degree-day is defined as the difference between the average of the daily maximum and minimum temperatures and the normal room temperature ($18.3°C$), accumulated during the heating season. Assuming that the heating season lasts from October through April, the average number of degree-days is 3,342 for Cottbus and 3,335 for Schwerin. Apart from the coastline and a few elevated points, the climate is rather dry. The average annual amount of precipitation ranges between 500 mm and 650 mm.

I.B.   POPULATION CHARACTERISTICS

The GDR is divided into 15 regions (*Bezirke*) broken down into 27 urban and 191 rural districts (*Kreise*), which in turn consist of 8,868 communities (*Gemeinden*). Table 1 gives a listing of the 15 regions along with their area, population, and density (see Figures A.2a and A.2b).

The population changes in the GDR have been very unusual. In 1939, 16.7 million

National Border
Region Borders (*Bezirke*)
District Borders (*Kreise*)
Cities

Bezirke:

1 *Berlin*
2 *Cottbus*
3 *Dresden*
4 *Erfurt*
5 *Frankfurt*
6 *Gera*
7 *Halle*
8 *Karl-Marx-Stadt*
9 *Leipzig*
10 *Magdeburg*
11 *Neubrandenburg*
12 *Potsdam*
13 *Rostock*
14 *Schwerin*
15 *Suhl*

1 : 3,000,000   0 20 40 60 80 km

FIGURE A.2a   Regions (*Bezirke*) and districts (*Kreise*) of the GDR — 1974.

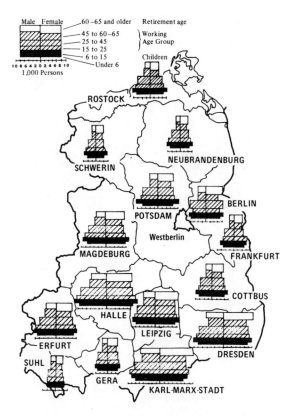

FIGURE A.2b   Population of the GDR regions by age and sex — 1972.

people lived in the GDR area. Due to the inflow of refugees, this number increased to 18.6 million by 1946. From 1946 to 1964, the population dropped to 17.0 million. Currently, the population is stable. The major reasons for the stability are an extremely high proportion of older people, a surplus of women in the total population due to war losses, and migration of many in the labor force to the FRG before 1961 (Table A.2). The labor shortage is compensated in part by the rather large number of working women and by a high number of people working beyond the retirement age.

The regional distribution of the population within the GDR is not very homogeneous. Roughly speaking, the line Magdeburg-Dessau-Görlitz is the boundary between the densely populated southern part, with average densities between 100 and 500 persons/km^2, and the more sparsely populated northern part, with densities of less than 100 persons/km^2. In the southern part of the GDR there are three urban areas with densities higher than 475 persons/km^2. These areas are

- Halle-Leipzig (2 million people)
- Karl-Marx-Stadt (1.6 million people)
- Dresden (1 million people)

TABLE A.2   Structure of the GDR Population by Age and Sex (%)

Age group	1950	1960	1973
A ≤ 6	7.0	9.4	7.6
6 < A ≤ 15	15.9	12.0	14.7
15 < A ≤ 25	13.7	14.9	15.1
25 < A ≤ 45	25.4	22.2	26.2
45 < A ≤ 65	27.5	27.7	20.3
65 < A	10.5	13.8	16.1
Total	100.0	100.0	100.0
Male	44.4	45.1	46.3
Female	55.6	54.9	53.7

SOURCE: *Statistisches Jahrbuch 1974 der DDR*[1]; p. 419,

TABLE A.3   GDR Population by Size of Community

	Percentage of Total Population			
	1950	1960	1970	1973
Rural communities (< 2,000 people)	29.0	28.0	26.2	25.3
Urban communities				
2,000 < R ≤ 20,000	31.9	31.5	29.7	29.2
20,000 < R ≤ 100,000	18.4	19.1	22.1	22.2
100,000 < R	20.7	21.4	20.0	23.3
Total	100.0	100.0	100.0	100.0

SOURCE: *Statistisches Jahrbuch 1974 der DDR*[1]; p. 10.

One-third of the total GDR population lives in Berlin or one of these three urban areas, which account for one-tenth of the total land area. The natural population change is negatively correlated with the density: in the northern part, there are more births than deaths, whereas in the southern part there are more deaths than births (especially in Dresden and Karl-Marx-Stadt). In the middle of the country there is a stable zone. This stability is modified by the migration to the industrialized areas in the south, and to the east-central part of the GDR, where new chemical factories are being built.

The distribution of the GDR population by community size reveals a shift from rural and small urban communities to medium-size cities; the percentage of the population living in cities with more than 100,000 residents has remained fairly constant since 1950 (see Table A.3).

I.C.   TRANSPORTATION CHARACTERISTICS

Before World War II, the main transportation routes in the GDR area were constructed from east to west. Therefore, basic changes in the traffic network were necessary in order to connect the industrial centers in the south with the agricultural areas and seaports of the northern GDR after the separation from the western part of Germany.

The railway network of the GDR is fairly dense (14,317 km in 1973), despite the

TABLE A.4   Motor Vehicles in the GDR

| | Absolute Figures (10^3 vehicles) | | | | Average Annual Growth Rate (%) | | |
	1950	1960	1970	1973	1950–1960	1960–1970	1970–1973
Autos	75.7	298.6	1,159.8	1,539.0	14.7	14.5	9.9
Motorcycles	197.5	848.0	1,374.0	1,360.9	15.7	4.9	–0.3
Mopeds		477.4	1,538.0	1,813.3		12.5	5.6
Buses	1.9	9.3	16.7	19.1	4.9	6.0	4.6
Trucks	93.5	117.8	185.9	216.3	2.3	4.7	5.2
Special-purpose vehicles	3.3	13.9	43.0	53.5	15.5	12.0	7.6
Traction vehicles	11.6	85.6	194.0	204.1	22.1	8.5	1.7
Trailers		163.5	491.3	633.0		11.6	8.8

SOURCES: *Statistisches Jahrbuch 1974 der DDR*[1]; p. 245.

closing of several lines in the last few years. The main railway lines are the connections between Berlin and the seaports Rostock and Stralsund in the north, and those connecting Berlin with the industrial centers in the south (Dresden, Halle/ Saale, Leipzig, Frankfurt/Oder). Currently, about 10 percent of the railroad networks are electrified (especially the main routes). In 1973 the rail service (measured in gross ton-kilometers and including both passenger and freight transportation) was divided among the three traction types as follows: steam — 33 percent, electricity — 16 percent, diesel — 51 percent. Currently, steam engines are being replaced mainly by diesel engines.

Expansion of the road system began on a large scale in 1968; the total length of roadways in the GDR in 1973 was 126,667 km. The number of private cars in the GDR is still rather low, but is increasing very rapidly. Although there is apparently a strong trend towards more private transportation, as can be seen in Table A.4, the official plans are to emphasize public transportation.

In the public transportation sphere, a significant trend is a shift away from the tramway in favor of buses in intracity mass transit. Buses are also becoming increasingly important in intercity mass transit, replacing the train as a favored mode of travel. Summary statistics on the volume (number of passengers) and service (number of passenger kilometers) of mass transportation by mode are given in Tables A.5 and A.6. The data reflect the continued importance of public transportation in the GDR. In 1973, for example, the average number of trips per person on public transportation facilities was 218 (17 percent rail, 33 percent intercity buses, 49 percent intracity mass transit), and the average distance traveled was 2,864 km (43 percent rail, 37 percent intercity buses, 14 percent intracity mass transit).

In the freight transportation sector, one can observe a shift from railways to trucks, but the relative decline of the railway service is not as strong as in the case of mass transportation. An overview of the volume (number of tons) and service (number of ton-kilometers) of freight transportation by mode is given in Tables A.7 and A.8. The items "factory vehicles" and "sea boats" cause some distortion in the statistics: the former category accounts for a large fraction of the total tonnage transported, but since the average length of a haul is very short, its contribution to the total freight transportation service is rather small; conversely, the latter category represents only a small percentage of the total tonnage transported but a large part of the total freight service.

I.D. ECONOMIC STRUCTURE

The GDR has a centrally planned economy, making the concept of measuring economic activity (net material product) different from the concept used in free-market economies. The main difference is the fact that the definition of the net material product (NMP) excludes economic activities not contributing directly to material production, such as public administration and defense, personal and professional services, and similar activities. An estimation of the gross national product (GNP) of the GDR made by the West German Institute for Economic Research (DIW), by calculating the contribution of the "nonproductive" services, indicates that the GNP in 1960 was about 18 percent higher than the NMP in that year. In 1970 the GNP was about 15 percent above the NMP. Tables A.9 and A.10 show the difference between the two concepts; it affects mainly the so-called service sector.

The percentage of the labor force employed in the most important sectors is given in Table A.11. One may note a decline in the percentage of people working in agriculture, and an increase in the percentage of people in the service sectors.

TABLE A.5 Volume of Mass Transportation by Mode

	Percentage of Total Passengers				Number of Passengers (× 10⁶)	Annual Average Rate of Change (%)		
	1950	1960	1970	1973	1973	1950–1960	1960–1970	1970–1973
Rail	33.7	26.1	18.0	17.1	633	− 0.1	− 4.0	0.4
Bus intercity	3.9	18.5	31.8	32.7	1,213	19.7	5.2	3.1
intracity	62.1	54.5	49.2	48.9	1,814	1.1	− 1.4	1.9
Riverboat	0.2	0.2	0.2	0.2	8	1.3	0.0	0.0
Ship		0	0	0	.0105		5.8	− 12.7
Airplane		0	0	0	.09117		12.6	2.7
Subtotal[a]	100.0	99.4	99.1	98.9	3,669	2.4	− 0.4	2.0
Factory vehicles		0.6	0.9	1.1	40		4.1	10.1
Total %	100.0	100.0	100.0	100.0		2.5	− 0.3	2.1
10⁶ passengers	2,830	3,607	3,486	3,709	3,709			

SOURCE: *Statistisches Jahrbuch 1974 der DDR*[1]; p. 239.
[a] Columns may not sum to totals because of rounding.

283

TABLE A.6 Mass Transportation Service by Mode

	Percentage of Total Passenger-kilometers				Number of Passenger-kilometers (× 10⁶)	Annual Average Rate of Change (%)		
	1950	1960	1970	1973	1973	1950–1960	1960–1970	1970–1973
Rail	68.2	54.6	41.5	42.8	20,851	1.4	– 1.8	5.7
Bus intercity	7.0	24.0	38.3	37.4	18,228	17.2	5.7	3.8
intracity	24.2	18.9	14.8	14.1	6,863	1.1	– 1.5	2.9
Riverboat	0.6	0.5	0.5	0.5	234	2.7	1.6	0.3
Ship		0.1	0.2	0.1	48		[a]	[a]
Airplane		0.4	2.2	2.3	1,120		19.1	5.8
Subtotal[b]	100.0	98.5	97.7	97.2	47,344	3.5	0.8	4.5
Factory vehicles		1.5	2.3	2.8	1,345		5.6	10.5
Total %	100.0	100.0	100.0	100.0				
10⁶ passenger-km	27,234	39,004	42,525	48,689	48,689	3.7	0.9	4.6

SOURCE: *Statistisches Jahrbuch 1974 der DDR*[1]; p. 239.
[a] Because of the strong fluctuations it is not meaningful to give average growth rates.
[b] Columns may not sum to totals because of rounding.

284

TABLE A.7 Volume of Freight Transportation by Mode

	Percentage of Total Tonnage				Total Tonnage (10⁶ tons)	Annual Average Rate of Change (%)		
	1950	1960	1970	1973	1973	1950–1960	1960–1970	1970–1973
Rail	56.9	45.5	34.4	32.9	280.6	6.3	1.0	2.2
Truck	19.6	25.2	23.6	20.9	178.5	11.5	3.2	— 0.3
River barge	4.4	2.4	1.8	1.5	12.7	2.4	0.8	— 2.5
Ship		0.3	1.1	1.3	11.5		20.0	10.5
Airplane		0	0	0			14.2	4.6
Pipeline			2.0	2.9	24.5			16.8
Subtotal[a]	81.0	73.4	62.9	59.6	507.8	7.7	2.3	1.9
Factory vehicles	19.0	26.6	37.1	40.4	344.9	12.4	7.4	6.7
Total %	100.0	100.0	100.0	100.0		8.7	3.9	3.7
10⁶ tons	225.8	522.1	764.0	852.6	852.6			

SOURCE: *Statistisches Jahrbuch 1974 der DDR*[1]; p. 237.
[a] Columns may not sum to totals because of rounding.

TABLE A.8   Freight Transport Service by Mode

	Percentage of Total Ton-kilometers				Total Ton-kilometers (10^6)	Annual Average Rate of Change (%)		
	1950	1960	1970	1973	1973	1950–1960	1960–1970	1970–1973
Rail	81.0	64.9	32.4	32.3	46,829	8.1	2.4	4.1
Truck	5.2	5.2	4.8	4.8	6,980	10.5	8.9	4.0
River barge	8.5	4.4	1.8	1.3	1,884	3.6	0.5	− 7.2
Ship		20.8	54.5	54.1	78,542		20.8	4.1
Airplane		0	0	0	30.8		18.9	5.0
Pipeline			1.7	2.4	3,512			17.7
Subtotal[a]	94.8	95.3	95.3	95.0	137,778	10.6	9.7	4.1
Factory vehicles	5.2	4.7	4.7	5.0	7,317	9.3	9.8	6.6
Total %	100.0	100.0	100.0	100.0	145.095	10.5	9.7	4.3
10^9 ton-km	18.6	50.6	128.0	145.1				

SOURCE: *Statistisches Jahrbuch 1974 der DDR*[1]; p. 238.
[a] Columns may not sum to totals because of rounding.

286

TABLE A.9   Contributions by Sector in the GDR to the Net Material Product (NMP)[a] (%)

	1960	1970	Average Annual Growth Rate, 1960–1970 (%)
Agriculture	16.4	11.7	0.96
Industry	56.4	60.7	5.26
Construction	7.0	8.2	6.19
Trade, catering	13.0	12.6	4.17
Transport, communication	5.5	5.2	3.96
Other activities[b]	1.6	1.6	4.14
Total %	100	100	4.35
10^6 marks	73.0	113.3	

SOURCE: *United Nations Yearbook of National Accounts Statistics.*[4]
[a] Prices in 1967 used as basis.
[b] Excluding economic activities not contributing directly to material production.

TABLE A.10   Contributions by Sector in the GDR to the "Gross National Product"[a] (%)

	1960	1970	Average Annual Growth Rate, 1960–1970 (%)
Agriculture	13.1	9.7	1.50
Industry	47.1	50.6	5.35
Construction	5.7	6.6	6.14
Trade, catering	9.9	10.0	4.70
Transport, communication	5.1	5.0	4.39
Other activities[b]	18.8	18.1	4.20
Total %	100	100	4.60
10^6 marks	92.8	145.0	

SOURCE: *Meyers Enzyklopädisches Lexikon*[2]; p. 509.
[a] Prices in 1967 used as a basis.
[b] Including economic activities not contributing directly to material production (public administration and defense, personal and professional services, and so on).

Currently, a high proportion (48 percent) of the total population is employed (including apprentices). Further information about each economic sector is provided in the following sections.

Agriculture   The agricultural acreage of the GDR is about 10.83 million hectare (58 percent of the total land area of the GDR); a further 27 percent of the land area is woodland. Of the agricultural acreage, 73 percent is arable land and 27 percent are pastures and meadows. Due to geographic characteristics and soil properties, arable farming is dominant in the northern part of the country, whereas in the south there are mainly stock breeding farms. Self-sufficiency has been achieved in livestock products, but not yet in crops. The dominant legal form of farms is the agricultural cooperative, in which all means of production, including domestic cattle, are used in common. These farms occupied 86 percent of the total land area in 1970. Additional agricultural statistics are given in Table A.12.

TABLE A.11   GDR Working Population by Economic Sector

	Percentage of Total Working Population[a]		
	1955	1960	1973
Agriculture	22.3	17.0	11.7
Industry[b]	39.5	41.4	42.0
Construction	5.6	6.1	6.9
Transport, communications	6.9	7.2	7.6
Trade, catering	10.9	11.6	10.7
Other sectors	15.2	16.7	21.1
productive[c]		1.2	2.7
nonproductive[c]		15.5	18.4
Total %	100	100	100
10^6 workers	7.7	7.7	7.8

SOURCE: *Statistisches Jahrbuch 1974 der DDR*[1]; p. 57.
[a] Excluding trainees; in 1973 the total number of trainees was about 0.46 million, and their distribution among the sectors reported above was as follows: agriculture — 5 percent, industry — 50 percent, construction — 14 percent, transport and communications — 8 percent, trade and catering — 9 percent, other productive sectors — 2 percent, nonproductive sectors — 11 percent.
[b] Including minor (craft) industry.
[c] This distinction is made with respect to their contribution to the net material product.

TABLE A.12   Agricultural Activity in the GDR

	1965	1970	1973
Employment (10^3 people)	1,178	997	918
Total land area (10^3 ha)	6,358	6,286	6,287
Arable land (10^3 ha)	4,718	4,618	4,634
Livestock (10^3 tons)	1,578	1,800	2,094
Milk (10^3 tons)	6,371	7,091	7,738
Eggs (10^6)	3,935	4,442	4,554
Corn (10^3 tons)	6,730	6,456	8,503
Potatoes (10^3 tons)	12,857	13,054	11,401
Sugar beets (10^3 tons)	5,804	6,135	6,682

SOURCE: *Statistisches Jahrbuch 1974 der DDR*[1]; pp. 187 ff.

Industry   In the industrial sector, almost all production is by nationalized enterprises or cooperatives, as is evident from Table A.13. Industrial gross production in the GDR grew by 80 percent during the period 1960–1970, which is equivalent to an annual growth rate of 6 percent. As is seen from Figure A.3, the fastest growing branches are

- Electrical, fine mechanical, and optical products
- Chemicals
- Machinery and transportation equipment

The building materials sector is growing at approximately the same rate as the industrial sector as a whole. The growth rates of the other branches are below

TABLE A.13   GDR Industry by Legal Form of Property

	Percentage of All Plants			Percentage of Total Industrial Gross Production[a]			
	1950	1960	1970	1950	1960	1970	1973
Nationalized enter- prises and cooperatives	25.6	31.8	23.6	76.5	88.7	88.7	99.9
Semigovernmental		27.8	48.7		7.5	9.9	
Private	74.4	40.4	27.5	23.5	3.8	1.4	0.1
Total	100.0	100.0	100.0	100.0	100.0	100.0	100.0

SOURCE: *Meyers Enzyklopädisches Lexikon*[2]; p. 509.
[a] At constant prices.

TABLE A.14   Gross Production of GDR Industry by Branch

	Percentage of Total Industrial Gross Production			Percentage of Total Employment in Industry
	1960[a]	1970[a]	1970[b]	1973[b]
Energy sector	6.8	5.6	5.0	6.4
Chemicals	12.1	14.5	15.0	11.0
Primary metals	8.4	7.8	8.0	4.2
Building materials	2.0	2.1	2.1	3.0
Machinery and transport- ation equipment	22.1	24.9	24.6	28.5
Electrical machinery and equipment, elec- tronics instruments	6.8	9.5	10.5	14.0
Consumer goods (excluding textiles)	12.0	11.2	11.0	16.6
Textiles	8.8	7.0	6.7	8.3
Food	21.0	17.4	17.2	7.9
Total	100	100	100	100

SOURCES: [a] *Meyers Enzyklopädisches Lexikon*[2], p. 509; [b] *Statistisches Jahrbuch 1974 der DDR*[1], pp. 116, 118.

average. Table A.14 shows the relative importance of the individual branches in various years.

The regional distribution of industrial production is markedly uneven. In 1973, the most important regions in terms of gross industrial production were Karl-Marx-Stadt (14.6 percent), Halle (14.4 percent), and Dresden (12.3 percent). The contribution of the other southern regions varied between 5 and 9 percent, whereas the share of the northern regions was only on the order of 1 to 4 percent, with the exception of Berlin (5.9 percent).

Service Sector   The major branches included in the service sector are

- Construction
- Transportation, communication
- Trade, catering (hotels and restaurants)

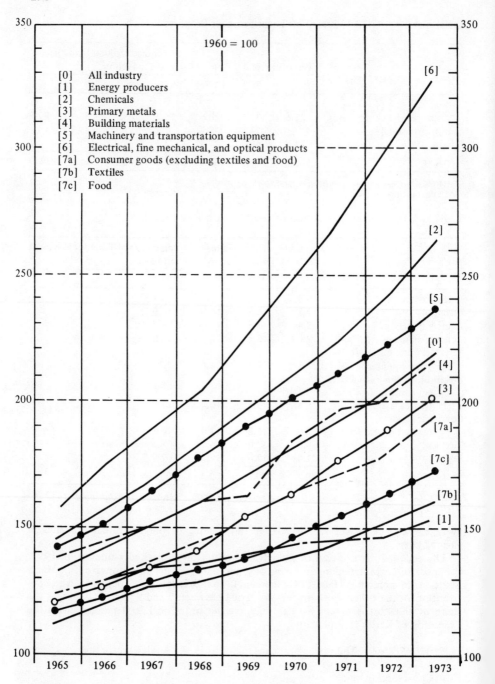

FIGURE A.3   Index of the industrial gross production by sector.

TABLE A.15   Summary Statistics for the GDR Service Sector

	1965	1970	1973
Construction[a]			
Establishments	22,795	18,618	16,234
Employment (10^3 people)	446	533	549
Total production (10^6 mark)	11,371	16,979	19,169
Industrial production (10^6 mark)[d]	8,377	11,735	14,818

	1968	1973
Production subcategories		
Industrial complexes	25.0%	28.7%
Water supply	9.5%	8.2%
Agriculture	6.0%	3.1%
Communication	15.1%	12.1%
Construction of new houses	17.3%	18.2%
Retrofitting of houses		0.7%
Cultural buildings	13.8%	16.3%
Repair work	12.5%	12.1%
Demolition	0.9%	0.5%

Trade, Catering[b]	
Employment (10^3 people)	
Wholesale (nationalized) (1973)	100
Retail trade (nationalized) (1973)	403
Total sales in retail trade (10^6 mark)	
– 1965	51,086
– 1970	64,059
– 1973	74,601
Shops (1971)	97,269
Total floor space (10^3 m^2) (1971)	4,705
Restaurants (1968)	34,035
Total sales in restaurants (10^6 mark)	
(1968)	5,721

Other services[c] [e]	Expenditure (10^6 mark)			
	1950	1960	1970	1973
Education	1,136	3,613	5,812	7,275
Culture	312	649	1,082	1,451
Public health and social security	1,394	4,240	5,877	6,940
Social insurance	4,575	9,600	14,976	19,848

SOURCE: *Statistisches Jahrbuch 1974 der DDR*[1]; [a] pp. 144 ff.; [b] pp. 261 ff.; [c] p. 310.
[d] Refers to the legal form.
[e] The employment figures in Table A.11 show that this is a rapidly growing sector. It includes both productive services and services for education, social security, and administration. Government expenditures indicate the importance of such services.

• Other services (education, culture, public health and social security, social insurance)

The activities of the transportation sector were described in section IV.A.4. Summary statistics about the other branches are given in Table A.15.

TABLE A.16   Electricity Generation by Source in the GDR

	Percentage of Total Generated Electricity		
	1960	1970	1973
Hard coal	4.4	1.4	1.2
Lignite	72.7	83.2	83.0
Lignite briquettes	6.8	1.8	1.0
Hydropower	1.5	1.8	1.6
Fuel oil	0.1	2.6	3.6
Gas, nuclear energy	14.5	9.1	9.6
Total %	100	100	100
10^6 kWh	40,304.8	67,650.0	76,908.0

SOURCE: *Statistisches Jahrbuch 1974 der DDR*[1], p. 141.

I.E.   ENERGY SYSTEM

The energy supply of the GDR is based mainly on lignite. There are rich deposits in the southern part of the country i.e. in the regions Halle-Leipzig-Cottbus. The annual lignite production increased continuously until 1964; since that time the production level varied between 240 and 260 million tons per year. Because of the low heat content, the lignite is practically all converted. In 1973, for instance, 40.8 percent of the total lignite available for home consumption was converted to briquettes, and 57.4 percent was used for electricity generation and/or district heating. Other fossil fuels such as hard coal, crude oil, and natural gas have to be supplied almost exclusively by imports. In the case of hard coal, the percentage supplied by home production dropped from 22 in 1963 to 10 in 1973, while the consumption level remained fairly constant. The annual supply of crude oil is almost exclusively imported; however, a large fraction of refined products, especially light products, is exported. Natural gas was introduced only in the late 1960's, but since that time the annual consumption has been increasing at a very high rate. Until 1972, natural gas was supplied entirely by home production. In 1973 however, 23 percent of the natural gas was imported and this fraction will increase due to the scarcity of home deposits and their low energy content. Other forms of primary energy such as electricity from hydropower or nuclear plants, are rather insignificant. In 1970, only about 0.4 percent of the total primary energy supply was provided in these forms.

In the energy conversion sector, the most important types of conversion are the generation of electricity and district heat. According to an energy flow chart for 1970 provided by the Institut für Energetik in Leipzig, 29 percent of the total primary energy was converted to electricity or, in combined cycle plants, to steam and hot water. Table A.16 shows the fuel mix for electricity generation. The most important energy source is lignite; gases (coke-oven gas and natural gas) and fuel oil are also used to some extent.

The growth rate of electricity production is declining: between 1960 and 1970, the average annual growth rate was 5.3 percent; between 1970 and 1973 it was only 4.4 percent.

Manufactured gas is becoming less important. The production of coke-oven gas and blast furnace gas is decreasing and the production of city gas (mainly from lignite gasification) is increasing slightly.

To summarize these remarks, primary energy consumption and end-use energy

TABLE A.17   Primary and End-Use Energy Consumption in the GDR

Primary Energy Consumption in 1970 (%)[a]

	Coal	Petroleum	Natural Gas	Other	Total
Electrical generation	27.3	0.9	0.3	0.4	28.9
Other consumption	58.3	12.1	0.5	0.0	71.1
Total	85.6	13.0	0.8	0.4	100.0

End-use energy consumption in 1970 (%)

	Residential Sector	Transportation	Industry and Internal Consumption	Total
Electricity	2.0	0.2	4.5	6.7
Other fuels	27.0	4.2	19.8	51.0
Total	29.0	4.4	24.3	57.7

Energy losses (% of total production)

Production and transportation of electricity	22.5
Fuel use	
Residential sector	10.4
Transportation sector	1.7
Industry, internal uses	7.7
Total	42.3

[a] The total consumption in 1970 was 714 × 10^{12} kcal.

consumption (after conversion losses) are presented in Table A.17. The figures were taken from the 1970 energy balance prepared by the Institut für Energetik in Leipzig. Finally, end-use energy consumption is provided in detail for 1973 in Table A.18.

II.   RHONE-ALPES

Alois Hölzl – IIASA

II.A.   PHYSICAL CHARACTERISTICS

II.A.1.   Geography

Rhone-Alpes is one of the 22 regions into which France is divided. It is located in the eastern part of the country and is surrounded by the regions Franche-Comté and Bourgogne in the north, Auvergne and Languedoc-Roussillon in the west, and the Mediterranean region Provence-Cote d'Azur in the south; in the northeast, Rhone-Alpes borders on Switzerland (between Lake Geneva and Mont Blanc), and in the east it has a border with Italy (see Figure A.4). With an area of 43,694 km^2 or 8 percent of the total area of France, it is the second largest region; it also ranks second with respect to population (4.5 million people or about 9 percent of the entire population of France in 1970).

TABLE A.18   End-Use Energy Consumption in the GDR in 1973 by Sector and Fuel Type (10⁹ kcal)

	Energy Production	Other Industries	Transportation	Residential Sector	Distribution Losses	Total
Hard coal		7,504	10,297	3,500	14	21,315
Lignite	3,199	4,410		2,205	217	10,031
Peat	28	602		399	7	1,036
Lignite briquettes	1,617	26,551	1,493	101,290	476	131,432
Coke-over-coke		20,503		875	14	19,250
Gas coke	84	4,431	105	2,706	7	6,594
Total solid fuels	4,928	64,001	11,900	110,971	735	189,658
Crude oil					1,526	1,526
Light petroleum products[a]	56	14,658	8,981	8,981	182	55,461
Heavy petroleum products[b]		21,462	5,145	3,857		30,464
Refinery fuel[c]					308	308
Total liquid fuels	56	36,120	14,126	12,838	2,751	87,759
Natural gas	1,071	4,494		35	455	6,055
Derived gases	6,062	17,456	28	8,362	841	33,055
Total gases	7,133	21,959	28	8,407	2,296	39,796
Total electricity	13,349	29,099	1,155	18,949	4,501	67,051
Total steam, hot water	57,302	76,272	2,401	12,712	6,426	155,120
Grand total	82,768	227,451	29,610	163,912	16,709	539,441
Estimated conversion losses[d]						205,219
Estimated primary energy consumption						744,660

SOURCE: *Annual Bulletin of General Energy Statistics for Europe 1973.*[5]
a Light products: gasoline, jet fuel, kerosene, naphtha.
b Heavy products: diesel, residual fuel oil.
c Refinery fuel: total consumption of petroleum products at refineries.
d The losses were calculated from data on total energy converted by applying the following efficiency factors: coal–gas: 0.6; coal–briquettes: 0.95; fossil fuels–steam: 0.8; steam–electricity: 0.4; gas reforming: 0.9.

FIGURE A.4 Regions and departments in France.

The Rhone-Alpes region is composed of three very distinct geological formations: the Saone-Rhone plain (which crosses the region from north to south), the area to the west of this plain (which belongs to the Massif Central), and the eastern part of the region which contains the western spur of the Alps (Europe's highest mountain, Mont Blanc, with an elevation of 4,807 m, is located in this section).

In the French economy, mining and quarrying plays an important role. There is mining of minerals such as coal, iron, salt, potassium, bauxite, and sulfur from methane deposits. However, only two relatively poor coal mines, the so-called Bassin de la Loire (near St. Etienne) and Bassin du Dauphine (south of Lyon) are located in Rhone-Alpes. Since 1967, production in these mines has been reduced considerably in favor of richer deposits in the north of France, which are also advantageously located near iron deposits. Important for the economy of Rhone-Alpes are the bauxite deposits in the south of France, i.e., in the region Provence-Cote d'Azur. To a large extent, this bauxite is refined in Rhone-Alpes because of the abundance of sources of electricity in this region.

The South European Pipeline (Marseille–Strasbourg–Karlsruhe) passes through Rhone-Alpes and provides the refinery Feyzin (near Lyon) with crude oil. The output of this refinery amounts to about 5 percent of the total French production. A fact that may be important for the economic situation of Rhone-Alpes in the future is that the abundance of cooling water provided by the Rhone River makes the region a desirable site for nuclear power plants (currently the uranium production in France is about 10 percent of the total production in the western hemisphere). The water resources of Rhone-Alpes have also been exploited by numerous hydro-power plants.

II.A.2. Climate

Due to the diversity of the geographical formations, the climate of Rhone-Alpes is also very heterogeneous, ranging from alpine in the northern and eastern parts of the region, to continental in the western section, and nearly Mediterranean in the south-central part. In Lyon, which may be considered the capital of Rhone-Alpes, the average daily minimum and maximum temperatures are $-0.9°C$ and $5.4°C$ in January; the corresponding figures for July are $14.8°C$ and $26.6°C$. The annual average precipitation in Lyon is 813 mm. The number of degree days (which is a measure of heating requirements), is 2,664 for Lyon (the number has been calculated using 30-year average figures); it is higher for all other parts of the region with the exception of Drome, which has a more Mediterranean climate, i.e. the number of frost days (days with a minimum below $0°C$) is only around 30 in the capital of Drome, compared with about 50 in Lyon, and approximately 70 in the capitals of the other departments.

II.B. POPULATION CHARACTERISTICS

France was subdivided into regions comparatively recently. A region is not yet an administrative entity but rather an aggregation of departments; only the latter have administrative authority. It must be said, however, that the Rhone-Alpes region has a clearly dominant economic center, the metropolitan area of Lyon.

On the other hand, the departmental structure is rather old: these administrative entities were established in the year 1789 and have remained almost unchanged. Currently there are 94 departments in France of which eight are in Rhone-Alpes. A department is further subdivided into *arrondissements* (25 in Rhone-Alpes) and *cantons* (268 in Rhone-Alpes). The smallest administrative unit is called a *commune* (there are 2,372 of them in Rhone-Alpes). For each department, the capital city, the land, the population and the population density are listed in Table A.19. The figures show that the population is distributed very unevenly within Rhone-Alpes: almost 60 percent of the total population is concentrated in the 3 industrial regions of Loire, Isere, and particularly Rhone, which together cover only 35 percent of the total area.

Population change in Rhone-Alpes and its departments is summarized in Table A.20. The average annual growth rate (1.61 percent between 1962 and 1968, and 1.67 percent between 1968 and 1974) is higher than in France, mainly because of immigration. Of the total increase in the population between 1965 and 1974 (460,000 people) about 30 percent can be attributed to immigration, 20 percent to the interregional migration surplus, and the rest to the excess of births over deaths. In 1971, for example, the birth rate was 1.74 percent and the death rate was 1.02 percent.

TABLE A.19   Area and Population of the Rhone-Alpes Departments

	Capital	Area (km²)	Population (1970; 10³ people)	Density (persons/km²)
Ain (01)[a]	Bourg-en-Bresse	5,797	343.8	59
Ardeche (07)	Privas	5,523	258.1	47
Drome (26)	Valence	6,525	352.2	54
Isere (38)	Grenoble	7,789	782.4	100
Loire (42)	St. Etienne	4,774	725.7	152
Rhone (69)	Lyon	2,859	1,372.4	480
Savoie (73)	Chambery	6,036	294.6	49
Haute-Savoie (74)	Annecy	4,391	392.8	89
Rhone-Alpes		43,694	4,522.0	103

SOURCE: *Meyers Enzyklopädisches Lexikon²*, vol. 9, p. 256.
[a] Numbers in parentheses refer to the number of the department.

TABLE A.20   Population Change in Rhone-Alpes

	Population (10³ people)			Average Annual Growth Rate (%)	
	1962	1968	1974	1962 to 1968	1968 to 1974
Ain	314.5	339.3	366	1.27	1.27
Ardeche	248.5	256.9	261	0.56	0.26
Drome	304.2	342.9	371	2.02	1.32
Isere	678.0	768.5	855	2.11	1.79
Loire	696.3	722.4	745	0.62	0.51
Rhone	1,181.1	1,325.5	1,435	1.94	1.33
Savoie	266.7	288.9	307	1.34	1.02
Haute-Savoie	329.2	378.6	427	2.36	2.03
Rhone-Alpes	4,018.6	4,423.0	4,767	1.61	1.26
France	46,459.0	49,755.8	52,340	1.15	0.85
Rhone-Alpes as % of France	8.65	8.89	9.3		

SOURCE: *Annuaire Rhône-Alpes 1974*[7], p. 25.

TABLE A.21   Urban Population in Rhone-Alpes

	Population in 1968 (10³ people)	Average Annual Growth Rate, 1962–1968 (%)
Lyon	1,074.8	2.2
Grenoble	332.4	4.0
St.-Etienne	331.4	0.8
city size > 100,000 people	1,738.6	2.3
Valence	92.1	3.4
Annecy	81.5	4.2
Roanne	77.9	1.0
St.-Chamoud	77.0	0.8
Chambery	75.5	3.0
city size > 50,000 people	404.0	2.5
city size > 20,000 people	476.9	2.9
other population	1,803.5	0.5
Total	4,423.0	1.6

SOURCE: *Annuaire Rhône-Alpes 1974*[7], pp. 25, 27.

Some other population statistics reflecting the urban–rural split and average family size and their historical trends are given in Tables A.21 and A.22 and Figure A.5; these factors exert an important influence upon energy demand in the residential and transportation sectors.

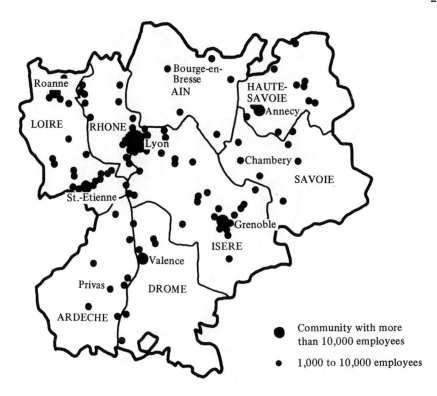

FIGURE A.5   Industrial locations in the Rhone-Alpes region (1964).

TABLE A22   Average Family Size in the Departments of Rhone-Alpes and in Their Capital Cities

Department	1962	1968	1974	Capital City	1968
Ain	3.09	3.14	2.87	Bourg-en-Bresse	3.31
Ardeche	3.27	3.19	3.06	Privas	a
Drome	3.27	3.22	3.11	Valence	3.14
Isere	3.09	3.26	3.15	Grenoble	3.28
Loire	3.01	3.00	2.91	St.-Etienne	2.89
Rhone	3.23	3.09	2.98	Lyon	2.68
Savoie	3.40	3.33	3.09	Chambery	3.31
Haute-Savoie	3.47	3.33	3.17	Annecy	3.24
Rhone-Alpes	3.19	3.16	3.03		

SOURCE: *Annuaire Rhône-Alpes 1974*[7], pp. 25–28.
[a] Not available.

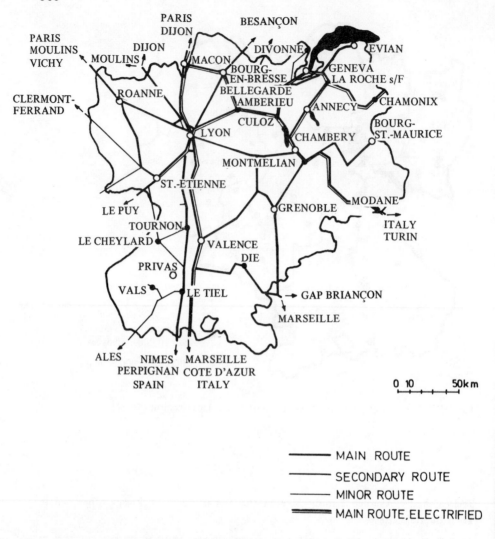

PARIS
DIJON
BESANÇON
PARIS
MOULINS
VICHY
DIJON
MOULINS
DIVONNE
EVIAN
MACON
BOURG-
EN-BRESSE
GENEVA
LA ROCHE s/F
CLERMONT-
FERRAND
ROANNE
BELLEGARDE
AMBERIEU
ANNECY
CHAMONIX
CULOZ
BOURG-
ST.-MAURICE
LYON
CHAMBERY
MONTMELIAN
ST.-ETIENNE
MODANE
LE PUY
GRENOBLE
ITALY
TURIN
TOURNON
LE CHEYLARD
VALENCE
DIE
PRIVAS
VALS
LE TIEL
GAP BRIANÇON
MARSEILLE
ALES
PERPIGNAN
SPAIN
NIMES
MARSEILLE
COTE D'AZUR
ITALY

0 10   50km

⸻⸻ MAIN ROUTE
⸻⸻ SECONDARY ROUTE
⸻⸻ MINOR ROUTE
═══ MAIN ROUTE, ELECTRIFIED

FIGURE A.6   Railway network in Rhone-Alpes.

II.C.   TRANSPORTATION CHARACTERISTICS

The traffic system of Rhone-Alpes is determined by the region's geographical characteristics. Most important is the Saone-Rhone valley, which forms one part of the main traffic artery of France, the connection Paris–Dijon–Lyon–Marseille. Another important connection is the Lyon–St.-Etienne–Roanne–Paris route in the west of the Saone-Rhone valley; in addition, the Lyon–Geneva, Lyon–Turin, and the Grenoble–Marseille routes in the eastern part of the province cross the Alps

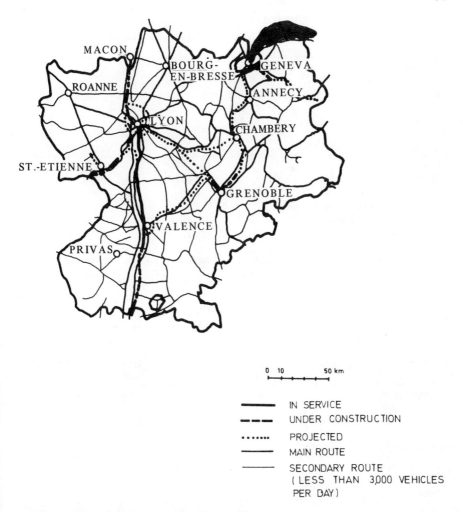

0 10   50 km

——— IN SERVICE
– – – UNDER CONSTRUCTION
••••••• PROJECTED
——— MAIN ROUTE
——— SECONDARY ROUTE
(LESS THAN 3,000 VEHICLES
PER DAY)

FIGURE A.7   Road network in Rhone-Alpes.

from west to east and north to south. All these connections are in the form of major railway lines and roads. The rivers Saone (north of Lyon) and Rhone (south of Lyon) also form an important inland waterway. In addition, air traffic has shown a significant increase during the 1960s in the whole of France, especially in Rhone-Alpes. Here, interregional rather than international traffic is important. The main airport is Lyon-Bron. Figures A.6 and A.7 show the rail and road network in Rhone-Alpes.

One factor which influences the energy demand for personal transportation in the Rhone-Alpes region is car (and motorcycle) ownership. In the year 1972, about 260 cars (private and commercial) and 95 motorcycles/1,000 people were registered in France as a whole. These figures can be used as an approximation of the private vehicle ownership level in Rhone-Alpes. In the same year, about 32 new cars per

TABLE A.23 Selected Transportation Statistics for Rhone-Alpes

Road system (km; 1972)[a]

Limited access highways	322
Other highways	6,844
Provincial roads	22,353
Urban roads	42,584
Rural roads	51,203

Motor vehicle registration (1972)[b]	10^3 Vehicles	Vehicles/10^3 people
Cars	1,214.2[i]	259[i]
Motorcycles	438.6[i]	94[i]
Buses	8.8	
Trucks and special transport vehicles	315.8	
Other transport vehicles	36.4	
Tractors for nonroad use	128.7[i]	27[i]

Intraurban public transportation (1971)[c,j]	Length of Network (km)	Number of Passengers (10^6)
Bus	851	162
Trolley bus	93	69
Tramway	7.5	22
Total	951.5	253

Interurban public transportation (1971)[d,k]	Length of Network (km)	Number of Bus Kilometers (10^6)
Regular service	66,000	72.8
Occasional service		25.4
Transport of school children		15.2

Truck transportation (10^6 tons)[e]	1967	1971
Intraregional	129.6	120.3
Interregional	17.3	21.7
International	3.6	4.2
Total	150.5	146.2[m]

Railway transportation (1971)[f]

Total length of network (km)	1,746
with electricity	914
Passenger transportation (10^6 passengers)	
Normal tickets	9.2
Commuter tickets	5.3
Freight transportation (10^6 tons)	
Intraregional	1.6
Interregional	11.4
International	3.2

TABLE A.23 – Continued

River barges (1971)[g]

Length of waterways (km)	454
Freight transportation (10^6 tons)	
Intraregional	2.8
Interregional	1.4
International	0.4

Air transportation (1970)[h]	Passengers ($\times 10^3$)	Freight (10^3 tons)	Mail (10^3 tons)
Lyon–Bron	870.6	6.8	8.3
Grenoble–St. Geoirs	105.5	0.1	
St.-Etienne–Bouthion	43.8	0.1	

SOURCES: *Annuaire Statistique de la France 1974*[6]; [a] p. 368; [b] pp. 377, 379. *Annuaire Statistique Régional des Transports*[8], [c] pp. 58; [d] pp. 70, 71; [e] pp. 147, 148, 156, 157; [f] pp. 44, 46, 52, 53, 156, 157; [g] pp. 20, 36, 37, 156, 157; [h] pp. 8, 13.
[i] Estimated from average figures for France.
[j] Includes the cities Annecy, Annemasse, Bourg-en-Bresse, Chambery, Grenoble, Lyon, Roanne, St.-Chamond, St.-Etienne, and Valence.
[k] Does not include railway transportation.
[m] The corresponding figure for 1970 is 162.4 million tons. The 1971 figure is exceptionally low.

1,000 people were registered in Rhone-Alpes. To give a quantitative picture, selected statistics about the transportation systems in Rhone-Alpes, as well as the volume of freight and mass transportation, are listed in Table A.23. It should be noted, however, that these data reflect only the transportation related to the economic activity within the region; transit traffic is not included unless otherwise noted. The actual traffic density is therefore considerably higher than indicated by these figures.

II.D.   ECONOMIC CHARACTERISTICS

Because of the centralized structure of the French economy, it is necessary to use employment as an indicator of economic activity within Rhone-Alpes. Table A.24 shows changes in the distribution of the working population in 3 major economic sectors in France and Rhone-Alpes. One notes a heavy decline in the population engaged in agriculture and forestry; this is compensated for by growth in the so-called "secondary" sectors (industry in the narrowest sense, electricity, gas and water supply, construction, transportation) as well as in the "tertiary" (commercial and service) sectors. The regional distribution of the working population in 1968 is displayed in Figure A.8. The aggregation used here and in the following statistics differs from the one used in Table A.24: electricity, gas and water supply is included in industry, transportation and construction are considered as service sectors (the construction sector is sometimes accounted for separately). This aggregation is based on the classification called *"Nomenclature des Branches de la Comptabilité Nationale,"*[11] which distinguishes 37 sectors (1: agriculture; 2–23: industry; 24: construction; 25–37: commerce and services).

Figure A.8 shows that in 1968 about 63 percent of the working population of Rhone-Alpes was concentrated in the 3 departments of Rhone (30 percent), Isere (17 percent) and Loire (16 percent). The departments Isere and Loire are more industry-oriented (over 40 percent of the working population is employed in industry) whereas the commerce and service sector is dominant in Rhone (50

TABLE A.24   Changes in the Working Population in Rhone-Alpes

| | Percentage of Total Working Population | | | |
	1954^a	1962^a	1968^b	1974^b
Agriculture	24.8	17.2	12.2	8.5
Industry, building,				
transportation	47.7	51.5	49.9	49.5
Commerce, services	27.5	31.3	37.9	42.0
Total	100.0	100.0	100.0	100.0
10^3 people	(1,960)	(1,710)	(1,819)	(2,071)
(% of total population)	(46.6%)	(42.8%)	(41.1%)	(42.4%)

SOURCES: *L'Economie de la Région Rhône-Alpes*[9], p. 14, *Annuaire Rhône-Alpes 1974*[7], pp. 37—38.

percent of the working population is employed in this sector). Selected statistics about the activity level in these sectors and the importance of the sectors in the national economy are presented in Tables A.25 and A.26. The industrial output data in Table A.24 show that Rhone-Alpes leads in the production of aluminum (38 percent of French production) iron-alloys (56 percent of national production), as well as in the production of some fabricated metal products such as hydroturbines and mechanical tools. The employment data also indicate the significance of some other industrial branches (textiles and apparel, chemicals, and electrical devices and fine machinery) in the Rhone-Alpes economy.

To give an idea of the amount of value-added which can be attributed to economic activities within Rhone-Alpes, national productivity figures (value-added in a given sector divided by the number of people employed in this sector) are presented along with regional employment data for 4 major sectors in Table A.27. By using this presentation, one may obtain a rough estimate of the value added in these sectors in Rhone-Alpes.

The implied growth rates (7 percent per year for the total value-added, 7.25 percent for industry, 8 percent for commerce and services) are much higher than the growth rates in the national economy (5.7 percent per year for the total value-added between 1963 and 1972, 6.4 percent for industry, and 5.4 percent for commerce and services). Currently, Rhone-Alpes contributes between 10 percent and 11 percent of the GNP of France.

II.E.   ENERGY SYSTEM

In the following description of the energy use in Rhone-Alpes, only 4 fuel types will be considered: solid mineral fuels, gas, electricity, and petroleum products. The disaggregation of energy use by consumer corresponds in principle to the categories which are generally used in the statistics of France, i.e., industry, household and small consumers (*foyers domestiques et petite industrie*), transportation; agriculture is included in the household and small consumer sector. Table A.28 shows the share of each energy source over time in the final energy consumption, or end-use energy (this term is used when the conversion losses in the generation of electricity are not counted). The change in the fuel mix is typical: there is a movement away from solid mineral fuels in favor of petroleum products. While the share of gas and electricity is decreasing slightly, it is important to note the high level of electricity

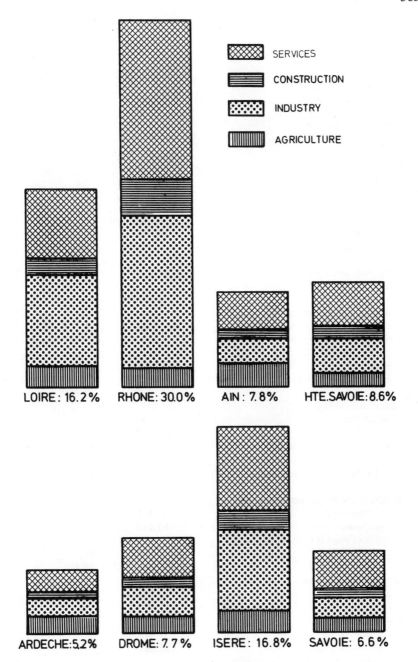

FIGURE A.8   Regional distribution of the working population in Rhone-Alpes (1968).

TABLE A.25   Selected Statistics on Economic Activities in Rhone-Alpes

	Rhone-Alpes	Percentage of France	Year
Agriculture[a]			
Establishments ($\times 10^3$)	141.7	8.9	1973
Agricultural land (10^3 km^2)	1,754.4	5.8	1973
Value of products (10^9 F)			
Livestock and by-products	3.3	6.6	1972
Crops	1.8	5.1	1972
Agricultural working population (10^3 people)	175		1974
Percentage of total working population	8.5		1974
Industry[b]			
Iron and steel production			
Establishments	33		1973
Employees	16,000		1973
Steel production (10^3 tons)	585	3.0	1966
	736	3.1	1972
Nonferrous metal production			
Establishments	37		1973
Employees	6,676		1973
Aluminum production (10^3 tons)	145	39.9	1966
	150	37.8	1972
Primary transformation of metals			
Establishments	165		1973
Employees	32,083		1973
Production of iron-base alloy (10^3 tons)	149	54.0	1966
	219	55.6	1972
Forging and casting			
Establishments	1,006		1973
Employees	45,147		1973
Value of hydroturbine production (10^6 F)	91	60.6	1966
	108	78.9	1972
Value of water pipe production (10^6 F)	54	22.9	1966
	100	25.6	1972
Machinery and mechanical equipment			
Establishments	977		1973
Employees	50,890		1973
Value of mechanical tool production (10^6 F)	170	31.1	1966
	340	39.8	1972
Diverse metal products:			
Establishements	3,092		1973
Employees	59,900		1973
Production of vehicles:			
Establishments	2,422		1973
Employees	57,342		1973
Electrical, fine mechanical, and optical equipment			
Establishments	1,503		1973
Employees	84,049		1973

TABLE A.25 — Continued

Chemical, rubber and plastics		
Establishments	1,178	1973
Employees	73,029	1973
Textiles and apparel (including shoes)		
Establishments	4,127	1973
Employees	139,795	1973

Commerce and Services (1974)[c]	Employment (10^3 people)	Percentage of Total Working Population
Construction	192.3	9.3
Transportation	70.6	3.4
Communication	32.4	1.6
Trade	233.2	11.3
Banking, insurance	32.4	1.6
Hotels, restaurants, housing	288.2	13.9
Government	153.4	7.4
Public services	131.4	6.3
Total	1,133.9	54.8

SOURCE: *Annuaire Rhône-Alpes 1974*[7], [a] pp. 5, 12; [b] pp. 76–105; [c] p. 37.

consumption: more than 30 percent of the total end-use energy is consumed in the form of electricity (the corresponding figure for France as a whole is only 20 percent). In Table A.29, the actual energy consumption is listed for the year 1972 by sector and by fuel type. In the following sections, the consumption of each source of energy will be considered in more detail.

II.E.1.   Electricity

In French statistics, the electricity consumption is recorded for 2 categories: low voltage (mainly for residential use) and high voltage (for industry and transportation).

In the low-voltage category, Rhone-Alpes accounted for about 10 percent of the total national consumption in 1972. This is slightly more than its share of the total population (9 percent). But the growth rate in low-voltage consumption in Rhone-Alpes (8.22 percent per year between 1966 and 1972) was significantly lower than that which occurred in France as a whole during that period (10.07 percent). Therefore, it seems reasonably certain that per capita residential energy use in Rhone-Alpes will approach the national average in the near future. The breakdown of total low-voltage electricity consumption in Rhone-Alpes in 1971 is shown in Table A.30.

The level of high-voltage electricity consumption in Rhone-Alpes is extremely high; the province accounted for 18.3 percent of total national consumption in 1971. The growth rate in consumption in Rhone-Alpes was between 5 percent and 6 percent per year between 1966 and 1972 (the growth rate for France as a whole was 5.49 percent per year within this period). The breakdown of the total high-voltage electricity consumption in Rhone-Alpes by major sectors in 1971 is listed in Table A.31.

TABLE A.26   Industrial and Service Enterprises in Rhone-Alpes (1971)

Companies

Size (Employees)	Enterprises	Percentage of all French companies
0 or not declared	85,382 (48.99%)	10.22
1–2	50,775 (29.13%)	9.39
3–5	17,105 (9.81%)	9.63
6–9	7,957 (4.57%)	10.26
10–19	10,632 (6.10%)	10.52
50–199	1,910 (1.10%)	9.58
200–999	471 (0.27%)	9.26
1,000 and over	53 (0.03%)	5.99
Total	174,285(100.00%)	9.91

Plants

Size (Employees)	Plants	Percentage of all French plants
0 or not declared	87,937 (46.30%)	10.15
1–2	57,393 (30.22%)	9.49
3–5	19,385 (10.21%)	9.69
6–9	9,200 (4.84%)	10.27
10–19	12,818 (6.75%)	10.51
50–199	2,469 (1.30%)	9.80
200–999	659 (0.35%)	10.91
1,000 and over	49 (0.03%)	8.18
Total	189,910(100.00%)	9.92

SOURCE: *Annuaire Statistique de la France 1974*[6], pp. 608, 609.

II.E.2.   Gas

In 1972 the Rhone-Alpes industries consumed about $5,497 \times 10^9$ kcal of gas. The largest consumers were the chemical industry (52 percent), the iron and steel industry (11.3 percent), producers of mechanical and electrical machinery (10.6 percent) and the textile, leather and apparel sectors (7.5 percent). The total gas consumption by industry in Rhone-Alpes in that year was only 5.3 percent of the total industrial gas consumption in France. The gas consumption in the residential and commercial and service sectors was $3,790 \times 10^9$ kcal in 1972; from this amount, about 60 percent was consumed by households, 25 percent by commercial establishments, and the remaining 15 percent by small industrial establishments. The level of gas consumption in the residential sector of Rhone-Alpes is low relative to the national consumption level (it accounts for only 4.5 percent of total non-industrial gas consumption in France).

II.E.3.   Petroleum

A preliminary breakdown of consumption of petroleum products by major sector can be based on the product mix. This is given in Table A.32 for the year 1972. Statistics about fuel oil consumption by industry sector are only available at the national level. An estimation using national fuel oil intensiveness figures (defined as

TABLE A.27   Employment and Value-Added in France and Estimation for Rhone-Alpes

France

	Employment (10³ Workers)			Value-Added (10⁹ F – 1963)		
	Mar. 1962	Mar. 1968	Dec. 1971	1963	1968	1972
Agriculture	3,793.2	2,998.7	2,576.1	34.6	40.0	40.8
Industry	5,749.8	5,869.8	6,126.2	156.9	210.3	274.8
Construction	1,533.9	1,910.9	1,925.6	34.0	49.7	61.8
Commerce, service	7,979.0	9,182.4	10,204.9	134.8	169.3	216.3
Total	19,055.9	19,961.8	20,832.8	360.3	469.3	593.7

Rhone-Alpes

	Employment (10³ Workers)			Value-Added (10⁹ F – 1963)		
	Mar. 1962	Mar. 1968	Dec. 1973	1963	1968	1972
Agriculture	294.5	221.6	175.5	(2.7)	(3.0)	(2.8)
Industry	667.7	667.5	761.5	(18.2)	(23.9)	(34.2)
Construction	156.2	176.5	192.3	(3.5)	(4.6)	(6.2)
Commerce, service	591.6	753.3	941.7	(10.0)	(13.9)	(20.0)
Total	1,710.0	1,818.9	2,071.0	(34.4)	(45.4)	(63.2)

SOURCES: *Annuaire Statistique de la France 1974*[6], pp. 54, 55, 596; *Annuaire Rhône-Alpes 1974*[7], p. 37; *L'Economie de la Région Rhône-Alpes*[9], pp. 13–15.

TABLE A.28   Final Energy Consumption in Rhone-Alpes and France by Fuel (%)

	1966		1970		1972	
	Rhone-Alpes	France	Rhone-Alpes-	France	Rhone-Alpes	France
Solid mineral fuels	17.8	27.9	9.6	17.4	6.2	12.4
Gas	6.4	6.8	6.1	6.9	5.9	8.0
Electricity	34.9	20.9	33.9	20.6	33.7	21.1
Petroleum products	40.9	44.4	50.4	54.1	54.2	58.5
Total	100.0	100.0	100.0	100.0	100.0	100.0

SOURCE: *Annuaire Rhône-Alpes 1974*[7], p. 53.

fuel oil consumption per unit of value added) and regional value-added figures for each industry sector, indicates the following consumption pattern for Rhone-Alpes: building materials — 26 percent; mechanical and electrical machinery and equipment — 22 percent; chemicals — 14 percent; food production — 11 percent; paper and pulp — 4 percent; primary metals — 2 percent; other industry sectors — 22 percent.

TABLE A.29   Final Energy Consumption in Rhone-Alpes in 1972 by Sector and Fuel Type (10^{15} cal)

Industry	
Solid fuels	4.6
Gas	5.7
Electricity	38.7
Petroleum	20.5
Total	69.6
Households and Small consumers	
Solid fuels	4.8
Gas	3.3
Electricity	11.5
Petroleum	41.9
Total	61.5
Transportation	
Solid fuels	0.0
Electricity	1.5
Petroleum	20.7
Total	22.2
Total of all sectors by fuel type	
Solid fuels	9.5
Gas	9.1
Electricity	51.7
Petroleum	83.1
All fuels	153.3
Total of all fuels by sector	
Industry	69.6
Households and small consumers	61.5
Transportation	22.2
All sectors	153.3

SOURCE: *Annuaire Rhône-Alpes 1974*[7], p. 53.

II.E.4.   Solid Mineral Fuels

Coal is the second most important indigenous primary energy resource in Rhone-Alpes (hydropower is first), but the output of the region's two mines (Bassin de la Loire and Bassin du Dauphine) has gone down drastically since 1967; this is in line with the decreasing demand for coal, as shown in Table A.33. The total coal consumption by Rhone-Alpes industries in 1972 was 700,000 tons; the most important consumers were the electrometallurgical industry (28 percent), building industry (24 percent), chemical industry (18 percent), and the textiles, leather and apparel

TABLE A.30 Distribution of Total Low-Voltage Electricity Consumption in Rhone-Alpes (1971)

	Consumption in Rhone-Alpes (10^6 kWh)	Percentage of National Consumption
Residential and agricultural sectors	2,379.2	10.07
Trade and business	982.1	10.38
Public lighting	201.7	12.34
Local public services	85.6	8.78
Internal consumption (distribution losses)	22.6	8.65
Total	2,671.2	10.21

SOURCE: *Annuaire Statistique de la France 1974*[6], pp. 190, 191.

311

TABLE A.31 Breakdown of Total High-Voltage Electricity Consumption in Rhone-Alpes (1971)

	Consumption in Rhone-Alpes (10^6 kWh)	Percentage of National Consumption
Railways	580.0	9.93
Mines	248.8	11.19
Coal	159.9	5.84
Other minerals	88.9	5.35
Electrochemical and electrometallurgical industry	5,074.5	46.72
Iron alloys	1,877.6	61.13
Aluminum	2,323.1	35.72
General metal industry and other industries	12,586.4	15.77
Iron, Steel	805.9	8.73
Paper, pulp	723.5	14.81
Textile, leather, apparel	1,168.6	24.50
Total	18,489.7	18.32

SOURCE: *Annuaire Statistique de la France 1974*[6], pp. 188, 189.

TABLE A.32 Consumption of Petroleum Products by Major Sectors (1972)

	Consumption in Rhone-Alpes	Percentage of National Consumption
Gasoline (10^3 m^3)	1,839.7	9.40
Diesel (10^3 m^3)	679.7	9.82
Domestic fuel oil (10^3 m^3)	3,606.9	10.72
Light fuel oil (10^3 tons)	181.8	8.52
Heavy fuel oil (10^3 tons)[a]	1,970.4	10.56
Propane and butane (10^3 tons)[b]	180.2	8.49

SOURCE: *Annuaire Statistique de la France 1974*[6].
[a] Excluding sales to the national railway company, Société nationale des Chemins de fer Français (SNCF), to the national electricity company, Electricité de France (EDF), and to builders.
[b] Excluding sales to gas plants.

313

TABLE A.33   Coal Demand in Rhone-Alpes

	1966	1970	1972
Production (10^3 tons)	2,899	2,184	1,533
Percentage of national production	5.5	5.4	4.7
Deliveries (10^3 tons)	1,898	1,865	856
EDF power plants; (10^3 tons)	469	705	201
Industry (10^3 tons)	959	651	371
Households, small consumers (10^3 tons)	456	244	165

SOURCE: *Annuaire Rhône-Alpes 1974*[7], p. 54.

TABLE A.34   Production of Electricity in Rhone-Alpes and France (10^6 kWh)

	Rhone-Alpes			France		
	1966	1970	1972	1966	1970	1972
Hydropower plants	20,184	22,471	16,650	51,695	56,612	48,657
Thermal power plants	1,908	4,187	8,741	54,416	84,096	114,995
Total	22,092	26,658	25,391	106,111	140,708	163,652
Proportion of hydropower in total electricity production	91%	84%	66%	49%	40%	30%
Proportion of French electricity produced in Rhone-Alpes	20.8%	19.0%	15.5%			

SOURCE: *Annuaire Rhône-Alpes 1974*[7], p. 57.

industry (15 percent), which together account for 85 percent of the total coal consumption.

To obtain the primary energy consumption in Rhone-Alpes, the fuel mix used for electric generation must be taken into account. Table A.34 shows the electricity production in Rhone-Alpes and, for comparison, in France as a whole. The data show the importance of hydropower for the energy supply of Rhone-Alpes.* Adding the conversion losses in thermal power plants (about 15×10^{15} cal in 1972) to the final energy consumption, the total primary energy consumption in the Rhone-Alpes region in 1972 is estimated to be about 171.2×10^{15} cal, which is 11.7 percent higher than the final energy consumption.

* The amount of hydropower which remains to be exploited in Rhone-Alpes is currently being examined. Between 1974 and 1979 construction of new plants should result in an additional annual generation of 2077 GWh (9.5 percent of total 1973 generation). Potential sites which could yield as much as 9,015 GWh are also being surveyed.[10]

FIGURE A.9   Wisconsin and surrounding area in the United States.

III.   WISCONSIN

William Buehring – IIASA

III.A.   PHYSICAL CHARACTERISTICS

III.A.1.   Geography

Wisconsin is located in the north-central United States and has common borders with the states of Minnesota, Iowa, Illinois, and Michigan and with two of the Great Lakes, Lake Superior and Lake Michigan (Figure A.9). The total area of Wisconsin is 145,439 km² of which 4,377 km² is water.* There are over 8,500 lakes, of which Winnebago with an area of 557 km² is the largest. Major rivers include the Wisconsin River and the Mississippi River, which forms Wisconsin's border with Iowa and southern Minnesota. Public parks and forests occupy one-seventh of the land area; and there are 49 state parks, 9 state forests, and 2 national forests.

Wisconsin is a state of diverse physical features. The northern topography is relatively irregular with moderate or few changes in elevation. In the southwestern portion of the state the tributaries of the Mississippi River have cut into the sandstone to provide local relief approaching 150 m. The upland portion of this area is gently rolling. The central and eastern portions are predominately rolling plains. Elevation in the state ranges from 177 m above sea level along the Lake Michigan shoreline to a maximum of only 595 m at Tim's Hill.

Mineral production in Wisconsin is relatively small. The total value of all minerals produced in 1972 was $89 million; only 12 of the other 49 states had a lower dollar

---

* Unless otherwise noted, data in the text are from *The World Almanac and Book of Facts* and *Statistical Abstract of the United States*.[12,13]

FIGURE A.10   Wisconsin counties and their 1970 population (× 1,000).

value production. Sand and gravel, stone, cement, iron ore, and zinc are the principal minerals produced. Recently, copper deposits have been discovered in the northern part of the state. There are no known mineral fuel resources.

III.A.2.   Climate

Wisconsin's humid continental climate results in great variation in seasonal average temperatures. For example, an average January day in Madison has a maximum temperature of − 3°C and an average minimum temperature of − 13°C; in July the average daily maximum is 28°C and the average minimum is 16°C. An important

---

* The number of heating degree-days for any day is computed by averaging the daily high and low temperatures and then subtracting the average from 18.3°C, the standard used for comfortable room temperature. The degree-days are accumulated over the heating season to obtain annual values.

TABLE A.35   Major Cities in Wisconsin

	County[a]	1970 Population (10^3 people)
Milwaukee	Milwaukee	717
Madison	Dane	169
Racine	Racine	95
Green Bay	Brown	88
Kenosha	Kenosha	79
West Allis	Milwaukee	72
Wauwatosa	Milwaukee	59
Appleton	Outagamie	56
Oshkosh	Winnebago	53
LaCrosse	LaCrosse	51

SOURCE: Newspaper Enterprise Association, Inc.[13]
[a] See Figure A.10.

TABLE A.36   Selected Population Statistics for Wisconsin

Total population	1960	3,952,000
	1973	4,569,000
Total employment	1973	1,979,000
Manufacturing	1973	529,000
Trade	1973	364,000
Government	1973	276,000
Services	1973	264,000
Median age	1970	27.4 yr
Birth rate/1,000 residents	1960	25.2/yr
	1973	13.7/yr
Death rate/1,000 residents	1960	9.7/yr
	1973	9.0/yr
Heart diseases	1973	3.7/yr
Malignant neoplasm	1973	1.6/yr
Cerebrovascular diseases	1973	1.0/yr
Accidents	1973	0.5/yr
Urban population	1970	2,910,000
Rural population	1970	1,507,000

SOURCE: U.S. Bureau of the Census.[12]

consideration for heating requirements is the number of degree-days* Madison has had an annual average of 4,150 degree-days in recent years. Average precipitation at Madison is 77 cm/yr. Snowfall in Milwaukee averages 111 cm/yr.

III.B.   POPULATION CHARACTERISTICS

Wisconsin's population, which totaled 4,568,000 in 1973, has exhibited a declining growth rate in recent years. The average annual percentage change was 1.4 from 1950 to 1960, 1.1 from 1960 to 1970, and 1.0 from 1970 through 1973. Net migration into the state accounted for nearly 40 percent of the net increase in population of 152,000 from 1970 to 1973.

318

TABLE A.37   Selected Transportation Data for Wisconsin

Motor vehicle registrations		
Autos, Trucks, and Buses	1960	1,600,000
	1970	2,181,000
	1975	2,591,000
Automobiles	1974	2,084,000
Trucks	1974	408,000
Motorcycles	1974	106,000
Trailers	1974	86,000
Buses	1974	11,000
Road network (km)		
Rural	1974	145,000
Urban	1974	24,000
Total	1974	169,000
Surfaced	1974	160,000
Auto, truck, and bus drivers	1975	2,721,000
Commerce at principal Wisconsin ports (tons)		
Duluth-Superior (Minnesota and Wisconsin)	1974	36,677,000
Milwaukee	1974	3,876,000
Green Bay	1974	2,301,000
Kewaunee	1974	1,165,000
Railroad network (km)	1972	14,314

SOURCES: U.S. Bureau of the Census,[12] Newspaper Enterprise Association, Inc.,[13] Wisconsin Legislative Reference Bureau,[15] Bowman et al.[16]

The state is divided into 72 counties, as indicated in Figure A.10. The 1970 population of each county is also shown in the figure; it is evident that the southeastern area (Milwaukee) has relatively high population densities and that the northern part of the state has relatively low densities. The 1970 population density for the state as a whole was 31 people per km^2, for Milwaukee County it was 1,718 people per km^2, and for Florence County, which borders on Upper Michigan, only 2.6 people per km^2.

The Wisconsin cities with 1970 populations greater than 50,000 are listed in Table A.35. Milwaukee is by far the largest city with 16 percent of the state population and nearly one-third of the state total in the metropolitan area. Approximately half of Wisconsin's 1970 population lived in cities and towns of 10,000 population or more.

Other population statistics for Wisconsin are listed in Table A.36. The birth rate dropped 44 percent from 1960 to 1972, while the death rate showed a decline of only a few percent over that period.

III.C.   TRANSPORTATION CHARACTERISTICS

The number of registered motor vehicles has increased approximately 3 times faster than the population since 1960 (Table A.37). The dominance of the automobile in Wisconsin's transportation system can be demonstrated by dividing the registration by total population; there are approximately 450 autos per 1,000 people.

TABLE A.38   Service Sector Activity in Wisconsin

	1963	1967	1972
Retail trade			
Establishments ($\times 10^3$)	44.3	45.1	47.2
Sales (10^9 \$)	5.2	6.6	9.7
Percentage of U.S. sales	2.1	2.1	2.1
Employees ($\times 10^3$)		214.7	259.4
Wholesale trade			
Establishments ($\times 10^3$)	6.74	6.63	7.20
Sales (10^9 \$)	5.5	7.3	10.4
Percentage of U.S. sales	1.8	1.6	1.5
Employees ($\times 10^3$)	55.1	63.1	69.5
Services (establishments with payroll)			
Establishments ($\times 10^3$)		10.4	11.1
Total receipts (10^9 \$)	0.57	0.73	1.16
Percentage of U.S. receipts	1.4	1.3	1.4
Employees ($\times 10^3$)	50.2	57.2	76.0
Consumer Price Index (1967 = 100)	91.7	100.0	125.3
Government			
Employees, total ($\times 10^3$)			288
Employees, federal ($\times 10^3$)			26
Employees, state ($\times 10^3$)			67
Employees, local ($\times 10^3$)			195
Payroll (10^9 \$)			0.16
State and local government expenditures (10^9 \$)			3.76
Percentage of total for all states			2.3

SOURCE: U.S. Bureau of the Census.[12]

III.D.   ECONOMIC CHARACTERISTICS

For this discussion of the Wisconsin economy, *service* denotes the service, retail, wholesale, and public sectors; *industrial* refers essentially to the entire manufacturing sector. A brief overview of these two sectors and agriculture follows.

III.D.1.   Service Sector

The diverse activities that are classified under the service sector accounted for approximately 1.2 million of Wisconsin's total employment of 1.9 million in 1972.[16] Some other statistics for the retail trade, wholesale trade, selected services (e.g. hotels, auto repair, amusement, and recreation services), and government are listed in Table A.38. The rapid growth of these sectors is demonstrated by the growth rates in sales and receipts from 1963 through 1972: 7.2 percent per year for retail trade, 7.3 percent for wholesale trade, and 8.2 percent for selected services. Since the rate of inflation, as measured by the consumer price index, was 3.5 percent per year over this period, real growth for these sectors was approximately 4 percent per year.

Employment also increased over this period but not as rapidly as sales. Total employment in Wisconsin, excluding manufacturing and farming, increased at 5.2 percent per year from 1968 through 1973.[15]

TABLE A.39   Industrial Activity in Wisconsin

	1963	1967	1972
Establishments ($\times 10^3$)	7.94	7.84	7.84
Employees ($\times 10^3$)	462	512	501
Payroll (10^9 \$)	2.78	3.58	4.72
Value added by manufacturing (10^9 \$)	5.36	7.01	9.44
Ranking of value-added among the 50 states	11	11	12
Largest industries in terms of value-added (10^9 \$)			
Machinery, except electrical	1.40	1.59	2.01
Food and kindred products	0.75	0.91	1.32
Fabricated metal products	0.38	0.57	0.95
Paper and allied products	0.50	0.66	0.82
Electrical equipment	0.60	0.70	0.80
Transportation equipment	0.73	0.56	0.79
Percentage of total for these 6 industries	78	71	71

SOURCES: U.S. Bureau of the Census,[12] Wisconsin Legislative Reference Bureau.[15]

III.D.2.   Industrial Sector

Wisconsin has considerable industrial activity, as indicated in Table A.39. The total industrial output, as measured by value-added, ranks Wisconsin twelfth among the 50 states. The growth in Wisconsin's total value-added by manufacturing from 1963 to 1972 was 6.5 percent per year. The wholesale price index for industrial commodities increased 2.5 percent per year over this period, so real industrial growth was about 4 percent per year over this period. Employment increased at only 0.9 percent per year, somewhat less than the 1.1 percent per year growth of total population over this period.

Industrial activities are often categorized into 20 Standard Industrial Classifications (SIC). The 6 categories with the largest value-added account for more than 70 percent of the total in all 3 years shown in Table A.39. Other categories that have shown rapid growth in recent years include printing and publishing (7.3 percent per year from 1963 to 1972), chemicals and allied products (9.9), lumber and wood products (10.4), rubber and plastic products (13.6), and furniture and fixtures (10.6). These 5 rapid-growth industries accounted for 15 percent of the total value-added in 1972.

III.D.3.   Agriculture

Agriculture is an important part of Wisconsin's economy, as indicated in Table A.40. Total cash receipts from farm marketing of over \$2 billion in 1973 placed Wisconsin eleventh among the 50 states. Total workers on Wisconsin farms have dropped steadily from 282,000 in 1960 to 173,000 in 1973.

Known as America's Dairyland, Wisconsin produces more bulk milk and cheese than any other state.[13] Dairy products account for \$1.2 billion of the \$1.9 billion receipts from livestock and products in 1973. Wisconsin is also a leading producer of butter, beets, snap beans, corn, oats, peas, cranberries, alfalfa hay, honey, and maple syrup.

TABLE A.40   Agricultural Activity in Wisconsin

	1964	1970	1973
Employment, farm (10^3 people)	246	193	173
Total cash receipts (10^9 \$)	1.18	1.60	2.29
Livestock and products	1.01	1.38	1.89
Crops	0.17	0.22	0.40
Land area of farms (10^3 km^2)	82.5		79.7

Leading agricultural products (% of U.S. production)	1968	1971	1973
Butter	19.4	17.7	19.5
Cheese	43.6[a]	41.6[a]	39.9[a]
Milk	15.5[a]	15.9[a]	16.0[a]
Beets for processing	34.3[a]	35.7	30.2
Snap beans for processing	14.5	21.8[a]	18.6
Cabbage	7.7	17.4	11.6
Sweet corn for processing	22.2	26.3[a]	23.5
Cranberries	29.8	31.7	36.4
Green peas for processing	26.7	28.1[a]	24.8[a]

SOURCE: Wisconsin Legislative Reference Bureau.[15]
[a] Wisconsin ranked first among the 50 states for these products.

III.E.   ENERGY DEMAND

In this section, end-use energy is tabulated by fuel type and sector. The difference between end-use and primary energy (given in the next section) is that energy losses in electricity generation and transmission are not included in end-use energy. It should also be noted that the definition of the sectors (service, industrial and so on) used here because of the data recording traditions are not the same definitions as for the demand models that were used in the scenario development.

The end-use energy by sector for the years 1970 through 1974 are shown in Figure A.11 and Table A.41. A few comments on each sector follow.

III.E.1.   Industrial Sector

Industry consumed 28 percent of Wisconsin's end-use energy in 1974. The breakdown by fuel type shows that industrial coal use in 1974 was only one-third of the 1970 use. Many firms have switched from coal to alternate fuels, such as natural gas or electricity, because of air quality regulations, prices and availability. It should be noted that the industrial coal data for 1970 to 1972 include service coal use, but this was probably a small fraction of the industrial coal use, as the 1974 data indicate.

Industrial natural gas use reached a peak in 1972 and declined about 7 percent in the next 2 years. Economic conditions, conservation, fuel availability, weather conditions and other factors all contributed to the decline in gas use.

Industrial electricity consumption increased at an average rate of 6.0 percent per year over the 5-year period. However, the 1973–74 increase was only 1.4 percent. Industrial electricity accounted for 38 percent of Wisconsin's total electricity consumption in 1974.

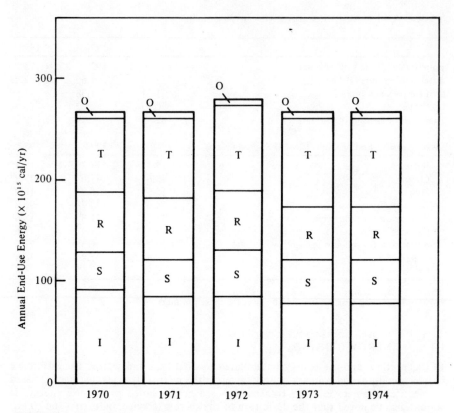

FIGURE A.11 Total end-use energy by sector. I = industrial; S = service; R = residential; T = transportation; O = other. (After Bowman et al.[16])

III.E.2.   Service Sector

The service sector has been increasing its consumption of total end-use energy and used 15 percent of Wisconsin's end-use energy in 1974. The tabulation of fuel use in Table A.41 indicates that natural gas demand increased by 28 percent over the 5-year period. This may be partly attributable to the inclusion in the service sector of some multifamily dwellings with more than 4 units; this classification problem occurs because of natural gas tariff structures.

Electricity use in the service sector increased at nearly the same rate as natural gas use, and petroleum consumption remained nearly constant.

III.E.3.   Residential Sector

The residential sector consumed 25 percent of Wisconsin's end-use energy in 1974. The residential energy consumption remained almost constant over the 5-year period (Table A.41), while the state's population increased by 2.4 percent. Natural gas accounted for about half of the total residential consumption in 1974. Petroleum

TABLE A.41 End-Use Energy in Wisconsin (10^{15} cal)

	1970	1972	1974
Industry			
Natural gas	34.2	44.1	41.1
Coal	35.7[a]	21.8[a]	11.4
Petroleum	5.4	5.5	5.1
Electricity	7.9	9.0	9.9
Total end-use energy	83.2	80.4	67.5
Service			
Natural gas	13.2	13.9	16.9
Coal	b	b	b
Petroleum	15.2	15.6	15.0
Electricity	4.4	5.1	5.6
Total end-use energy	32.8	34.6	38.1
Residential			
Natural gas	27.4	31.6	30.1
Coal	1.2	0.6	0.3
Petroleum	24.4	23.0	21.2
Electricity	8.2	9.2	9.7
Total end-use energy	61.2	64.4	61.3
Transportation			
Gasoline	56.5	62.7	63.9
Diesel	6.9	8.2	10.0
Other petroleum	2.0	2.3	2.5
Total end-use energy	65.4	73.2	76.4
Total end-use energy by sector			
Industrial	83.2	80.4	67.5
Service	32.8	34.6	38.1
Residential	61.2	64.4	61.3
Transportation	65.4	73.2	76.4
Miscellaneous	5.6	5.4	4.8
Total	248.2	258.0	248.1
Total end-use energy by fuel			
Natural gas	74.8	89.6	88.1
Coal	36.9	22.4	12.3
Petroleum	115.4	121.9	121.7
Electricity	21.1	24.1	26.0
Total	248.2	258.0	248.1

SOURCE: Bowman et al.[16]
[a] Includes service coal use.
[b] Included in industrial coal use.

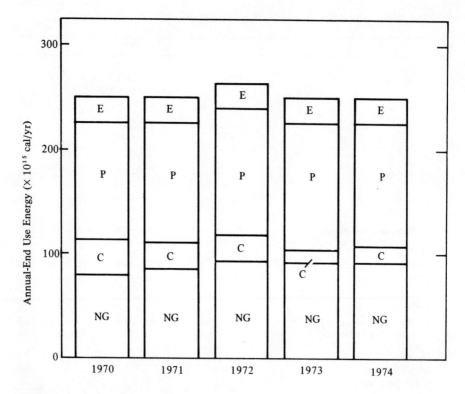

FIGURE A.12   Total end-use energy by fuel. NG = natural gas; C = coal; P = petroleum; E = electricity. (After Bowman *et al.*[16])

consumption steadily declined over this period as electricity and natural gas became more widely used. Electricity increased by 18 percent from 1970 to 1974; this corresponds to an annual growth rate of 4.2 percent. Residential electricity consumption was 37 percent of Wisconsin's electricity use in 1974.

III.E.4.   *Transportation*

Transportation had the largest energy consumption of any sector in 1974; it amounted to 31 percent of Wisconsin's total energy consumption. Furthermore, petroleum consumption for transport in 1974 was 62 percent of Wisconsin's total consumption of petroleum. Personal travel resulted in 56 percent of the total transportation energy use and 17 percent of all end-use energy in the state.[16]

The overall rate of growth in transportation energy use has been large since World War II and the trend continued in the years 1970–1973 at a rate of 5.5 percent.[16] In 1974, however, the increase in gasoline prices, the economic recession, and conservation efforts resulted in a small decline in transportation energy use.

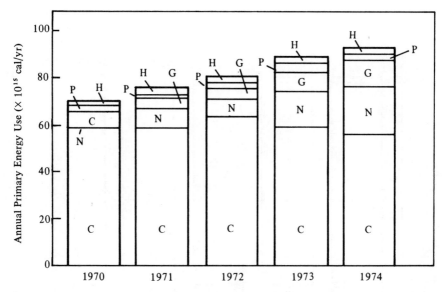

FIGURE A.13   Primary energy use in Wisconsin for electrical generation. C = coal; N = nuclear energy; G = gas; P = petroleum; H = hydropower. Hydropower is used at approximately 100 kcal/kWh; this is *not* equivalent to the fossil fuel that would have been consumed if hydropower were not available. (After Bowman *et al.*[16])

III.E.5.   Total End-Use Energy

As shown in Figure A.11, Wisconsin's total end-use energy was nearly the same in 1974 as in 1970. The transportation and service sectors increased end-use energy consumption from 1970 to 1974, while the residential sector had stable consumption and the industrial sector consumed less.

The end-use energy by fuel type in Figure A.12 shows a steady growth in electricity consumption, a rapid decline in coal use, and a leveling of natural gas and petroleum use.

III.F.   ENERGY SUPPLY

In order to determine the total primary energy, the electricity fuel supply and losses must be combined with the end-use energy discussed in the previous section. The use of fuels used for electricity generation, shown in Figure A.13, increased at an average annual rate of slightly over 6 percent, while total generation increased from 27.4 to 32.6 × 10⁹ kWh. Coal and nuclear power account for nearly 90 percent of the total fuel use. Nuclear power's contribution grew from virtually nothing in 1970 to 26 percent in 1974. However, the 1974 nuclear energy totals are approaching the maximum that can be expected from the state's 1,600 MW nuclear capacity.* All major new facilities for the next few years are planned to be coal-

---

* Nuclear generation in 1975 was about 20 percent above generation in 1974.[17]

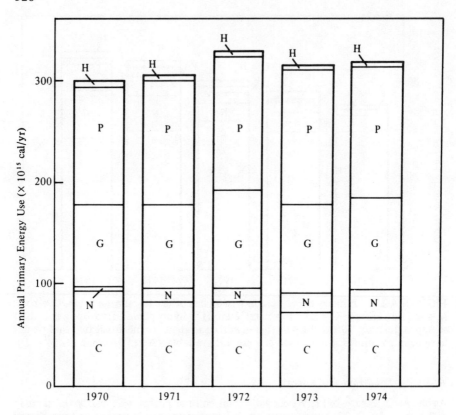

FIGURE A.14   Total primary energy use in Wisconsin by fuel type. C = coal; N = nuclear energy; G = gas; P = petroleum; H = hydropower. (After Bowman *et al.*[16])

fired. No new nuclear capacity is planned before the mid-1980s. Therefore, coal can be expected to increase its share of the total electrical fuel supply if electricity demand continues to grow.

Natural gas and petroleum are not major sources of fuel for electricity nor are they expected to be in the future. Use of hydropower is relatively small and is expected to remain almost constant.

Total primary energy consumption is obtained by adding the electrical fuel supply results in Figure A.13 to the end-use fuel results in Figure A.12. The total primary energy use in Figure A.14 shows a slight increase of approximately 1.1 percent per year over the period. As noted previously, the end-use energy remained almost constant over this period; the slight increase in primary energy use is attributable to the increased use of electricity during the period.[16]

With the exception of coal, there were increases in all of Wisconsin's energy sources from 1970 to 1974. Natural gas and petroleum provided over 70 percent of the state's primary energy use. Wisconsin has no fuel resources, other than hydropower, so all these fuels must be imported.

IV. ENERGY FLOWS IN THE THREE REGIONS

Jean-Pierre Charpentier — International Atomic Energy Agency (IAEA)

Before describing energy flows in the GDR, France, and Wisconsin, their respective average energy consumption per capita, and relative position in world energy consumption will be summarized. Figure A.15 gives the distribution of world energy consumption per capita in kilowatt-year-thermal per year (kWy_{th}/y). This distribution, using data from 178 countries throughout the world shows that countries can be divided into 3 classes:

• The first class includes countries which consume more than $7\ kWy_{th}/y$. Only 3 percent of the countries belong to this class. It is essentially composed of the United States, Canada, and some exceptional consuming countries such as Kuwait.
• The second class includes all European countries. It is composed of those countries in which the average level of energy consumption per capita is between 2 and $7\ kWy_{th}/y$. This group represents 22 percent of the countries of the world.
• The third group includes all developing countries or countries consuming less than $2\ kWy_{th}$ per capita per year. This last group is the largest one, in which are 75 percent of the countries of the world.

It is also worthwhile mentioning that if population, rather than the number of countries, is taken as the studied variable, the distribution remains roughly the same. The first class has 6 percent of the world population instead of 3 percent of the countries; the second class has the same percentage of people and countries, and the third class has 72 percent of the population in comparison with 75 percent of countries.

The mean value of this energy distribution per capita in the world for 1971 is $1.64\ kWy_{th}/y$. The GDR, Rhone-Alpes, and Wisconsin, are *three "rich" energy con-*

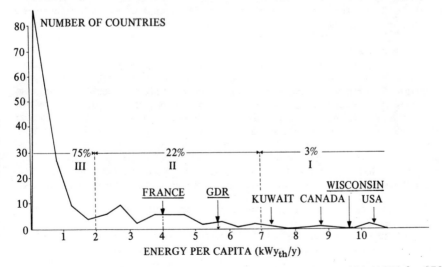

FIGURE A.15   Distribution of energy consumption in the world in 1971 for 178 countries. (After *Statistical Yearbook*[20])

328

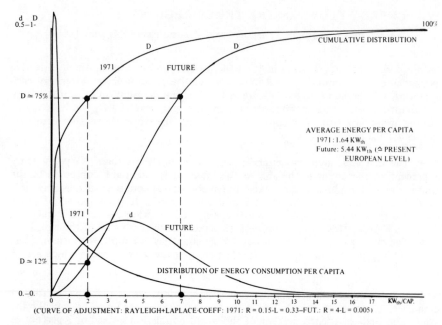

FIGURE A.16   1971 and possible future distribution of energy consumption per capita in the world.

sumers because their average energy consumptions for 1970–71 were, respectively, 5.6 kWy$_{th}$/yr., 4.0 kWy$_{th}$/yr. and 9.3 kWy$_{th}$/yr. Therefore, the conclusions drawn about the 3 countries are applicable to only 25 percent of the countries of the world. This clearly shows the necessity of continuing development and implementation of this kind of study in order to improve our knowledge of energy consumption at the global level.

Figure A.16 shows the first step in what seems a promising method of research for analyzing the development of energy consumption both globally and within countries.[18] The general idea is to analyze how a country (or people) shifts from one class of consumer to another through time. This mainly requires analysis of how technological knowledge spreads and is applied from country to country over time. The analysis has not progressed past the preliminary stage. For Figure A.16 it was assumed that the distribution of energy per capita in the world will remain the same in the future, and only its parameters will change. Roughly speaking, this could mean that the historical trends related to the speed of technological progress in countries will remain the same. There are, however, two normative assumptions:

● The average world energy consumption per capita will reach the present European level.
● Of the countries of the world, 75 percent will reach the upper limit of the second class of consumers and use 7 kWy$_{th}$ per year and per capita.

Based on these assumptions, the "future" distribution of energy consumption per capita in the world will have the form of curve D.

In order to determine a date for this so-called future energy distribution, it was necessary to study the growth rates of this energy consumption per capita. This situation could occur by the year 2040 if the growth rate of energy per capita is around 2 percent per year, or the year 2000 if the annual growth rate per capita is 4 percent.

If the average energy growth rate per capita were 2 percent per year, the energy consumption in the three regions would be 7.5 kWy$_{th}$/yr for the GDR, 5.5 kWy$_{th}$/yr for France, and 12.5 kWy$_{th}$/yr for Wisconsin.

It would be worthwhile to carry out the same kind of study within each country in order to have a better understanding of energy distribution across the population and among its different groups: those living in urban areas, those in rural areas, and so on.

Figures A.17, A.18, and A.19 summarize in a standard form, the energy flows of the 3 regions for the year 1970. All numbers indicated on these energy patterns are in percentages either of total energy consumed or by sector. The relative orders of magnitude are interesting to note. It is clear that only Wisconsin's consumption of primary energy fuel is well balanced among natural gas (28.5 percent), coal (31.5 percent), and liquid fuels (38.9 percent). The other two countries are mainly dependent on only one primary fuel: coal for the GDR (85.8 percent) and fuel oil for France (62 percent). These great dependencies on one primary fuel lead to less flexibility and could lead to great difficulties for the country if any shortage in this fuel appears. In addition, in such a country, any kind of replacement by another fuel would need more time because the technical structure related to this primary fuel is extensive and more difficult to change.

If we now look at electricity production, the ranking of the countries appears quite different. We see that the GDR is a high electricity producer; approximately 30 percent of its primary fuels are devoted to electricity production. Roughly 20 percent of primary fuels are for electricity production in each of the other two regions.

In all 3 regions there is a highly unbalanced distribution among the primary fuels used for this electricity production. The GDR produces 94.5 percent of its electricity from coal, Wisconsin 79 percent from coal, and in France 46 percent of its electricity is from fuel oil. In the case of France, it is interesting to note that 20 percent of the electricity was supplied from hydropower in 1970, in comparison with a very small percentage in the other two countries.

In all countries, nuclear energy did not play a major role in 1970, generally accounting for less than 1 percent in the primary energy balance.*

If we look at end uses by economic sector, industry, transport, and "other sectors" (household, commercial, service, and agricultural), 3 totally different structures appear. Table A.42 summarizes this structure of end uses. Wisconsin has the characteristics of an agricultural area with only 29 percent of its energy used in the industrial sector in contrast to more than 40 percent in the GDR and France. The part of its total energy used by the GDR in transport is very small compared with the 2 other regions: 8 percent in the GDR and 20 and 25 percent in France and Wisconsin.

The energy structure for the 3 regions is presented in a triangular graph in Figure A.20. These 3 regions follow 3 *totally different energetic developments* when compared with other countries. By cross-section analysis, one sees that according to their economic evolution, countries are moving along the line *ABCD* in Figure A.20.

---

* In 1976, nuclear energy supplied approximately 9 percent of Wisconsin's primary energy use.

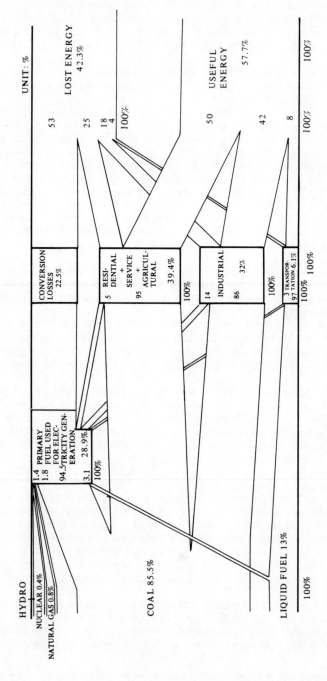

FIGURE A.17 Energy flows in the GDR (1970).

{ TOTAL PRIMARY ENERGY USED IN 1970: 95·10⁶ kWy_th

{ ENERGY PER CAPITA IN 1970: 5.6 kWy_th

330

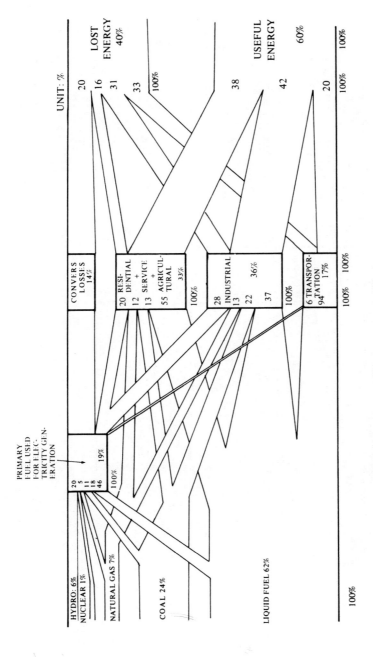

FIGURE A.18   Energy flows in France (1970).

331

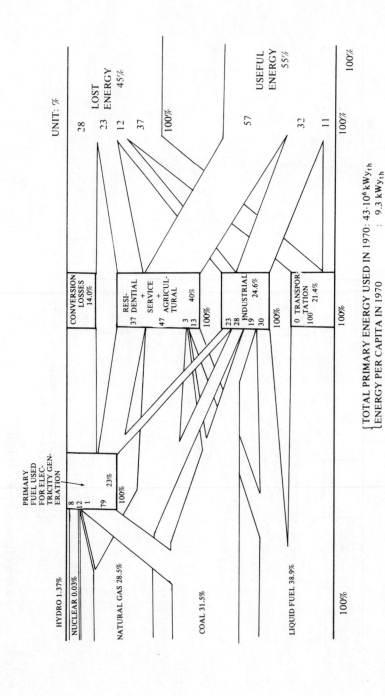

FIGURE A.19   Energy flows in Wisconsin (1970).

332

TABLE A.42   End-Use Energy by Sector (%)

	Wisconsin	GDR	France
Industry	29	41	42
Transportation	25	8	20
Other sectors	46	51	38
Total	100	100	100

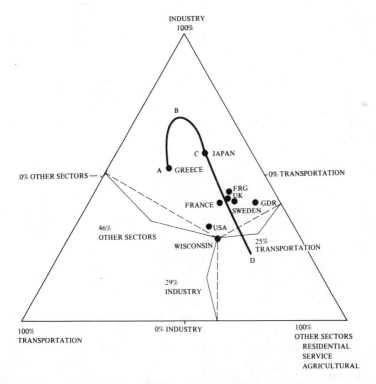

FIGURE A.20   Structure of energy consumed by sector (1970).

The line *AB* corresponds to such countries as Greece, Portugal, and Turkey which used a disproportionally large amount of energy in transport, with corresponding development of their industry. The line *BC* refers to such countries as Japan or Spain which are engaged in a rapid development of their industry. But after a given point *C* (corresponding to the present Japanese situation) it seems that countries are moving on parallel lines which correspond to:

- A fixed proportion of energy used in the transportation sector
- A decreasing proportion of energy used in industry and more energy used in the tertiary and residential sectors

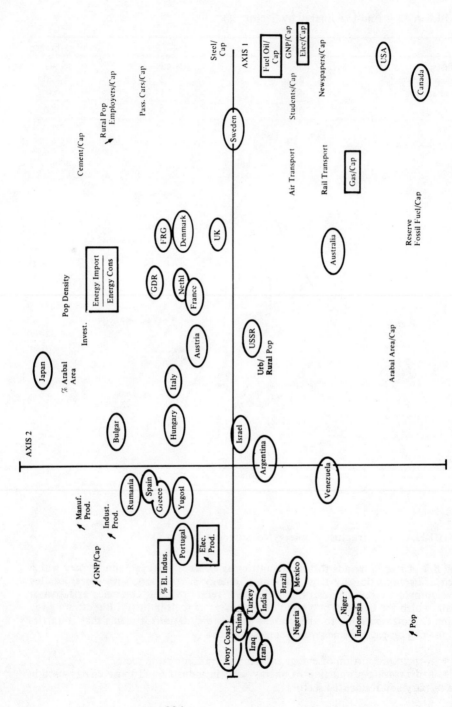

FIGURE A.21 Factor analysis: energy versus growth (1971).

Most of the European countries are moving along a straight line which shows that roughly 20 percent of their energy is consumed in the transport sector. For 10 years the United States has also moved on a parallel line but with a greater amount of energy used in transport (25 percent), and Wisconsin seems to be on the same line. The GDR used a much lower share of its energy for transportation (8 percent).

Examining the fuel mix at the level of end-use, the GDR's link to coal is noted: 86 percent of fuels used in industry come from coal and 95 percent of energy consumed in the service and residential sectors is also supplied by coal. For the 3 regions, 55 to 60 percent of primary energy is transformed into useful energy.

To conclude, there will be a description of the results of a factor analysis made not only with these 3 countries but with 35 countries, each characterized by a vector of 27 parameters (dimensions).[19] Factor analysis is a method for summarizing and clarifying a set of data. In order to give a general idea of its objective, consider the following example: You are living in Austria and you want boxes of a certain size built by people in an industrialized country such as Japan. Let us suppose that neither you nor your agent in Japan have any knowledge of geometry, so in order to obtain your boxes you must send to your contact person a great deal of information (perhaps too much; e.g. volume of boxes, external surface area, length of each side, angle of each corner). If your Japanese agent has a knowledge of factor analysis (though he is ignorant of geometry!) he will find that only three factors are needed: length, width, and height. No single parameter determines a factor or axis, rather they are determined by the combined influence of the parameters which characterize the 35 countries. The first two axes, typically restricted to be at right angles, indicate the strongest common "directions" or patterns in the data.* The coordinate of a given variable, with respect to an axis, is proportional to the correlation coefficient between the variable and the axis. The variables (either parameter or countries) that are grouped along an axis must be interpreted so as to identify what the axis represents.

In this study, the first axis (or factor), which corresponds to the economic level of development, explains 41 percent of the variance of the initial information (the matrix of 35 countries and 27 parameters).

Figure A.21 shows a summary of a factor analysis. Axis 1, corresponding to economic development, depicts the high correlation between such variables as steel consumption, electricity consumption, primary energy consumption, newspapers, and cars per capita. The United States is clearly at a high level of economic development, followed closely by Canada and Sweden; then come the FRG, Denmark, the United Kingdom, followed by the GDR, the Netherlands and France. The second axis is related more to the notion of space and population density. This analysis is described in more detail by Charpentier and Beaujean.[19]

REFERENCES

1. *Statistisches Jahrbuch 1974 der DDR*. Staatsverlag, Berlin, 1974.
2. *Meyers Enzyklopädisches Lexikon*, Bibliographisches Institut Mannheim, 1972.
3. *The World Factbook 1974*. Publishing Sciences Group, Inc., Acton, Massachusetts, pp. 119–120.

* The axes are the eigenvectors of the variance–covariance matrix between the different parameters. It can be shown that the most important factor loadings are given by the eigenvectors corresponding to the longest eigenroots of the variance–covariance matrix.

336

4.   *United Nations Yearbook of National Accounts Statistics*, Vol. I., 1973, p. 393.

5.   *Annual Bulletin of General Energy Statistics for Europe 1973*, Economic Commission for Europe, Geneva.

6.   *Annuaire Statistique de la France 1974* (Résultats de 1972) Institut National de la Statistique et des Etudes Economiques (INSEE), Paris.

7.   *Annuaire Rhône-Alpes 1974* (Principaux Résultats Statistiques en 1973) Supplément de no. 9 de la revue "Points d'Appui pour l'Économie Rhône-Alpes."

8.   *Annuare Statistique Régional des Transports, Région Rhône-Alpes, Années 1969–1970–1971*. Service Régional de l'Équipment, Division Transports, Lyon, 1973.

9.   "L'Economie de la Région Rhone-Alpes", *Notes et Etudes Documentaires*, Nos. 3491–3492, May 20, 1968.

10.   Martin, J.M., CNRS, Grenoble, Oct. 14, 1977: Personal Communication.

11.   Ministere de L'Economie et des Finances. *Nomenclature D'activités et de Produits 1973*. Journaux Officiels, Paris, 1976.

12.   U.S. Bureau of the Census. *Statistical Abstract of the United States* (annual publication). Washington, D.C., 1973, 1974, 1975.

13.   Newspaper Enterprise Association, Inc. *The World Almanac and Book of Facts* (annual publication). New York, 1977.

14.   Mitchell, John W., and Gann Venkataro. Energy Use in a Selected Sample of Homes in Madison, Wisconsin. Institute for Environmental Studies Report No. 72, University of Wisconsin-Madison, 1977.

15.   Wisconsin Legislative Reference Bureau. *The State of Wisconsin Blue Book* (published biennially on odd-numbered years). Madison, Wisconsin, 1971, 1973, 1975.

16.   Bowman, J.D., Colley, R.W., Erwin, C.P., Hanson, M.E., Kwast, M.T., Mitchell, J.W. and Pappas J.L. 1975 Survey of Energy Use in Wisconsin. Institute for Environmental Studies Report No. 65, University of Wisconsin-Madison, 1976.

17.   Public Service Commission of Wisconsin. "Generating Plants Operated by Wisconsin Electric Utilities," Bulletin No. 46, Aug. 1976.

18.   Charpentier, J.P. *"Toward a Better Understanding of Energy Consumption,"* Part I – "The Distribution of per Capita Energy Consumption in the World" In *Energy*, Vol. I., Pergamon Press, Oxford, Apr. 1976, pp. 325–334.

19.   Charpentier, J.P., and Beaujean, J.M. "Toward a Better Understanding of Energy Consumption," Part II – "Factor Analysis: A New Approach to Energy Demand?" In *Energy*, Vol. 1, Pergamon Press, Oxford, July 1976, pp. 413–428.

20.   *Statistical Yearbook*. United Nations, New York, 1972. Table 140, pp. 353–356.

B Institutional Structures of the Three Regions

An analysis of energy and environment management tools in a region cannot be undertaken without an understanding of the institutional framework within which they are used. This framework, in turn, is best viewed within the overall economic and political framework of the region. The socioeconomic and political structures have shaped the quantitative tools and the planning and decision practices used in the three regions. The following three sections briefly describe the institutional settings for energy (and in some cases environmental) planning and decision making in the three regions. The contrasts are vivid and revealing.

I. THE GERMAN DEMOCRATIC REPUBLIC*

Dietmar Ufer – Institut für Energetik

In the German Democratic Republic (GDR) the people own the productive equipment in all industries. The fact that the socialist title to the means of production is undivided, renders product-line planning possible by the public, but it makes it necessary, at the same time, to organize, plan, and control the socialist development according to consistent principles. The energy sector must also be planned. Full particulars about the energy industry in the GDR will be given. First, however, the organizational chart of the energy industries will be outlined to give a better understanding of the planning policy applied.

The energy economy covers all the utilities and facilities for the production, conversion, transportation and use of all forms of energy (see Figure B.1). The energy systems penetrate all processes in public life, in production, and consumption, and are therefore planned with great care. The Ministry for Coal and Energy

---

* This section describes planning in the energy sector only; a description of practices in air pollution control is given in section I of Appendix C. For further information on the GDR, see also K. Hanf's report, "Policy and Planning in the German Democratic Republic – an Interorganizational Perspective," (Internationales Institut für Management und Verwaltung, Berlin, 1975) – ED.

338

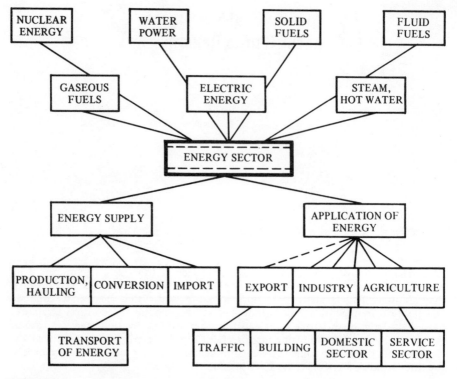

FIGURE B.1   The energy sector in the GDR.

is held responsible for working out and implementing the national energy policy. The decisions made by the United Socialist Party of Germany are the basis of these activities. The Ministry for Coal and Energy operates according to the principles of the national economic policy accepted by the Council of Ministers and is subordinate to this Council. The structure of the GDR hierarchy is shown in Figure B.2. The State Planning Commission, also subordinate to the Council of Ministers, is the most important staff organization which outlines the strategy of development of national industry and is therefore considered to be an important partner in the process of planning the energy industry.

All the authorities that regulate the economy are subordinate to the Ministry of Industries. In the case of the Ministry of Coal and Energy, the authorities concerned are the Association of Nationally-Owned Enterprises (VVB) for Hard Coal, Brown Coal, Power Plants, and Energy Supply, as well as the Gas Manufacturing Group (Gaskombinat Schwarze Pumpe; see Figure B.3). The Institute of Energetics is also under the direct control of the Ministry for Coal and Energy.

The single-product factories, scientific centers, and, to some extent, the planned enterprises are also under the control of the Association of Nationally-Owned Enterprises. For example, as shown in Figure B.4, the Association of Nationally-Owned Enterprises for Power Plants controls the large-scale power plants operated with lignite, the nuclear power stations, the gas turbine power plants, the storage pumping stations, and the Institute of Power Stations. The Association of

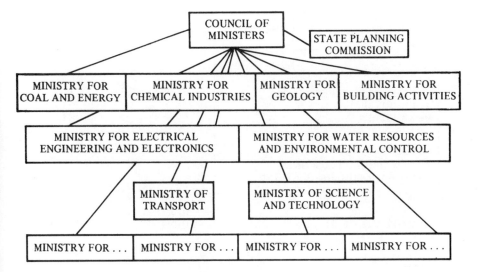

FIGURE B.2   The structure of the government in the GDR.

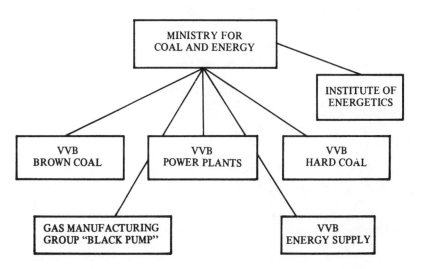

FIGURE B.3   The GDR Ministry for Coal and Energy and its subordinates. VVB is the Association of Nationally Owned Enterprises.

Nationally-Owned Enterprises for Brown Coal and the Gas Manufacturing Group have been organized analogously. In contrast, the Association of Nationally-Owned Enterprises for Energy Supply has been divided into territories. The energy supply authorities in the districts comprise the combined heating and power stations, larger heating stations, gas works, and the stations for the distribution of electricity, gas,

340

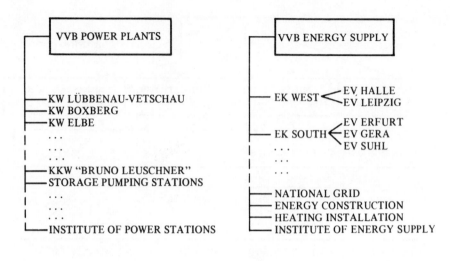

KW = POWER STATION   EK = ENERGY SUPPLYING GROUP
KKW = NUCLEAR POWER STATION   EV = ENERGY SUPPLY UNDERTAKING

FIGURE B.4   The structure of the Associations of Nationally Owned Enterprises (VVB).

and district heat. They constitute the marketing units in the energy industries for these forms of energy.

Thus the Ministry for Coal and Energy is responsible for the greatest part of the energy supply. The only exceptions are (1) the primary processing of petroleum, which falls within the sphere of the Ministry of Chemical Industry; (2) the extraction of natural gas, which is controlled by the Ministry of Geology; and (3) the industrial power plants in the different branches of industry as well as the municipally-owned heating plants and other plants of only local significance. With regard to the responsibility for the development strategies for the energy industry, the Ministry for Coal and Energy has to fulfill a double function:

● It is responsible for the supply of energy by the economic units under its control, i.e. about 78 percent of total primary energy.
● It is responsible for the realization of rational principles of energy use, and thus for energy policy in all spheres of national industry and social life (with respect to all forms of energy).

In order to translate the latter function into practice, a whole system of executive bodies has been set up in recent years:

● In all the Ministries controlling industry, and in the authorities controlling the economy, there are energy specialists supervising the economical use of energy who are responsible for the development of energy plans. This, of course, includes the responsibility assumed in the overall operating management by the managers and ministers for the energy consumption in their own sectors.

- Under the direction of a deputy chairman of the District Council, county energy commissions which take care of the national energy policy in the political regions have been established. They cooperate closely with the regional energy supply authorities and central government authorities.

The most important instrument for the implementation of energy policy is the Plan, more particularly, the Energy Plan. This Plan has been worked out for ten years by all energy intensive large-scale enterprises and facilities in conjunction with the one-year and five-year Plans. The Plans are coordinated centrally and an account is given annually. The implementation of the policy for efficient energy use is given support by a pricing policy as scheduled for the various forms of energy.

It is not possible here to describe the overall planning process in detail. Some principles in socialist planning, and some phases of long-range energy planning will be outlined. The planning of the energy economy forms part of the overall planning of the national economy. Its goal is the consolidation and steady development of the socialist community as well as the continual supply of the growing necessities of life, and the fulfillment of the intellectual desires of its members by a continuous and rapid rise in production in all sectors. Since the objectives in the planning process are important interests of the whole community, the process is controlled centrally by the government. It is reviewed at all levels of the government up to the Enterprise Associations, where the people employed participate in the determination of the indices in the Plans of the Enterprises.

The GDR is a member of the Council for Mutual Economic Assistance (CMEA). The Plans of the member countries, especially the five-year plans, are closely coordinated in order to gain a steady and quick development of national industries in all socialist countries.

Planning is carried out by means of coordination over different periods: annual planning, five-year planning, and long-term planning, which usually covers several decades and is especially important in the energy industry. The forecasting of the scientific and technical development of single processes and procedures within them is presupposed to be of great importance. The planning for one and five year Plans is done according to a centrally designed practice which also applies to energy planning. The methods of long-range planning vary and depend on which economic sphere and which time period are to be examined. However, three methodological principles apply in each case:

- The starting point is the demand, either national or subnational, depending on the planning.
- The leading consideration in planning is balancing, i.e. to balance the demand and supply capacity, the economic requirements, and the economic potentials.
- Planning is carried out with consideration for all essential interrelations with other activities.

With reference to the energy sector this means that the forecasting of the demand for energy is the starting point for energy planning. The quantity and the structure of the energy supplied depends closely on the development of the national economy and on living standards. The forecasting of energy supply requires, on the one hand, the awareness of the future economic trends, especially the production volume of energy-intensive products, such as steel, aluminum, and glass, not to mention railway transportation service, the number of flats requiring heating, and so on. On the other hand, it is necessary to have information on the specific energy consumption trends for these products and services. For this purpose, investigations into the technological and economic development of the individual processes are made in cooperation with the experts from the appropriate sectors. In certain cases, suggestions are made by the energy economists, suggestions appropriate to an advanced technological development promising exceptionally efficient consumption of energy, or which permit the use of domestic energy instead of imported sources. In long-range planning for 1 to 2 decades, approximately 40 percent of the total demand for energy is estimated with the aid of detailed indices on specific consumption. This percentage, of course, will decrease with a longer planning period. The remaining consumption of energy is assessed by applying global methods such as trend and correlation calculations.

The selection of the most effective alternative is of special significance in the long-range planning of energy supply. With the advanced development of production techniques such as those applied in the steel or cement industries, there is always a great variety of technological capabilities and possibilities for employing energy. The sole intention is not to realize the alternative representing the least demand for energy. Together with the appropriate branch, we hope to find technological solutions that facilitate the required results at the lowest social expenditure. This will also be in the interest of the entire national economy.

Such isolated calculations of alternatives for the individual processes show the drawback that an energy structure which cannot be realized for economic reasons may be established (e.g. the calculation of the excessive consumption of natural gas or another limited energy source). For this reason we have developed a model that takes into consideration the substitution of energy forms. Thus, it has been rendered possible to distribute the forms of energy among the individual processes such that there will be maximum economic benefit not for the individual processes, but for the processes together. The model in question is the so-called substitution optimization model (SOM).

Apart from these detailed techniques for the determination of energy consumption arising from the individual products and services, global methods are also used in order to calculate the total consumption and demand of the individual sectors. Such methods have priority over mere trend determinations resulting from the correlation between production, national income, other economic variables, and energy consumption. These global methods are best applied to the consumption figures and then verified by applying other methods. They must also be considered as the only methods suitable for the calculation of consumption variables for very long periods.

In the next phase of the planning process, the total production and importation of all energy forms and the primary energy is calculated. In long-range planning for a period of around two decades, an optimization model that takes into account the interdependence of the various forms of energy is used. Application of this model, the so-called production optimization model (POM), provides for the selection of alternative combinations of energy forms and extraction and conversion systems by which the demand for energy can be met at the lowest social expenditure. These calculations are supplemented by computations with global methods (methods for handling the totality of energy-related problems), especially beyond the year 2000. Experience has shown that at least rough investigations must be made when interdependence is assumed. As an example, a pure trend extrapolation for electricity will show results which are untenable for technological and economic reasons.

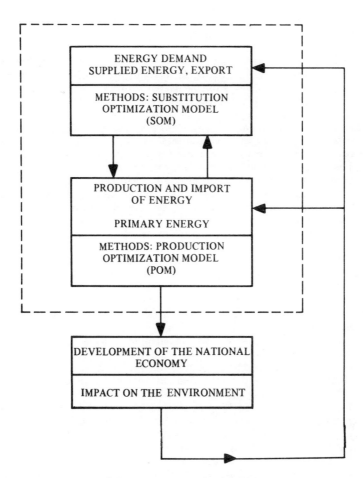

FIGURE B.5   Planning of the energy sector in the GDR.

This phase in the planning process is linked with studies of the scientific and technological development of energy production, transportation, and power conversion. The computations require a great deal of knowledge about available energy resources, both domestic and foreign. Economic variables such as the amount invested, wages, and prices for imported energy are of significance for the computations involved. The process of long-range energy planning is nowhere near completion so the computation of an optimum structure of the energy industry is not yet possible. The two phases of the planning process — the calculation of the energy demand, and subsequently the calculation of the consumption of primary energy — must be constantly repeated (Figure B.5). This is indispensable for two reasons:

● The basic data of these two planning phases change, in particular due to the experience gained with long-range planning in other sectors of the national economy.

● The results obtained in long-range energy planning must be screened for their ability to be adapted to national economic planning.

In other words, the first computations by means of the production optimization mode, or similar computations from other methods, frequently give rise to invest- ment or man-power requirements for the energy industry which cannot be satisfied by the national economy. There might also be an amount and a structure of energy demand which cannot be supplied at the proper time, e.g. if the power capacity required up to that time cannot be attained, or if a certain quantity of crude oil can- not be imported. The case may also arise in which the structure of the energy demand resulting from the first calculation would have such an adverse effect on the biosphere that it could not be realized if environmental controls are also sought.

The studies performed after the optimization calculation constitute an extremely significant stage of long-range planning for energy systems. Since a balance between the energy/economic requirements can rarely be reached immediately, it is necessary to eliminate any discrepancies. The solution may be to consider a higher efficiency relative to energy conversion with the aid of new or advanced systems and tech- niques, to consider the replacement of imported fuels with those from the indus- tries, to provide for development of new or advanced techniques of energy use, to lower the pollutant emission, or finally, to change the national economic structure by not developing certain energy-intensive processes. This, at any rate, implies repeating the two phases in energy planning. Such an iteration process must be repeated until the degree of correspondence between requirement and potential can be considered adequate.

Some part of the feedback can be simulated by making use of mathematical models. For instance, the substitution optimization model can be linked with the production optimization model. Optimum distribution of fuel resources available only to a limited extent are then obtained not only in the field of energy use and conversion but also in the energy sector as a whole.

Special attention is paid to the relationship between the energy industry and environmental protection. Environmental control is not considered the necessary evil that places a great strain on the national economy. Measures for environmental protection are systematically included in the development of the national economy, as an effective safeguard of the social welfare. An example is the possibility of extensive reuse of waste products. The Ministry of Environmental Protection and Water Economy has outlined the main directives for environmental protection measures up to 1980. With these directives as a starting point, concrete concepts for districts of industrial conurbation are created on the basis of socialist legislation for environmental conservation. Such a program has been implemented by the County Council of the District of Leipzig.

In 1975, two-thirds of the investments in environmental protection were con- centrated in districts of industrial conurbation which are assumed to be the most important areas for the energy industry. Their importance is shown by the fact that 19 percent of the particulate emissions in the GDR are from the power plants located in the districts of Halle and Cottbus. In 1975, 34 percent of the investments for environmental control were spent for air pollution control measures, 47 percent for water pollution control measures (a vital problem in the energy industry since the GDR has a lack of surface waters), 15 percent for the utilization and removal of trade refuse, and 4 percent for noise abatement measures. Altogether, environ- mental control in the GDR is planned in such a way that it will serve for the immediate improvement of the living conditions.

Summarizing, there has been some good experience in the methods applied to long-range energy planning in the GDR in recent years. The strategy for energy-industrial development derived from long-range planning is the starting point for working out the five-year plans. The good results obtained in achieving the target of these plans speak for the benefits of long-range planning. Here are some facts demonstrating the level of development in the GDR.

● The GDR is one of the countries in the world whose energy industries must be considered highly developed. It ranks third in Europe in the case of primary energy with about 44 Gcal/per capita, and ninth in Europe in electric power with about 4,000 kWh/per capita. The GDR is the largest producer of lignite in the world.

● Planning of energy intensiveness has been entirely successful. This is witnessed by the 4.5 percent average annual reduction in the intensity of supplied energy in recent years.

● The percentage of high-grade forms of supplied energy was corrected so that electric power, for instance, is about 12 percent of the total supply at the present.

● Policy has been consistently based on maximum utilization of primary energy, especially in the case of lignite. More than 90 percent of domestic imported energy comes from socialist countries (mainly from the Soviet Union). The fact that energy industries were not directly affected by the oil crisis demonstrates the success of such a policy.

● The energy technology is developed according to plan. Modern methods are applied and use is being made of modern equipment. The nuclear power stations, the 500 MW turbogenerators (developed by the Soviet Union) and the 60 m over-burden conveyor gantry are examples.

In the planning of the GDR energy industry we will keep our course true to the target. We are confident that good results will be obtained by improving joint planning activities with other socialist countries within the Council of Mutual Economic Aid. This will receive further emphasis in our future activities.

II. RHONE-ALPES

Jean-Marie Martin and Dominique Finon – Institut Economique et Juridique de l'Energie (IEJE)

Two aspects of the French economic and political organization are of importance for an understanding of the energy and environmental decisions in the Rhone-Alpes region.

First, for historical reasons, the entire French decision system is extremely centralized. This is true both for the state decision making apparatus which is centralized in high-level administrative agencies (the ministries) geographically clustered in the capital, and also for the important firms whose power is also centralized within headquarters located in the capital. Government and corporate administrations (their overlapping will be discussed later) may be represented by bodies with greatly expanded heads and atrophied limbs that are reduced to executing orders coming from the top.* For a long time, the departments formed the framework

* If any difficulty arises on a given occasion, the department or region refers to its central agency which indicates how the obstacle may be overcome. If this is not sufficient, the central agency sends a high official who settles the problem on the spot.

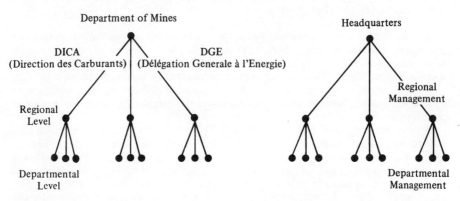

PUBLIC ADMINISTRATION   ENTERPRISE

Ministry of Industry

Department of Mines   Headquarters

DICA   DGE
(Direction des Carburants) (Délégation Generale à l'Energie)

Regional Management

Regional Level

Departmental Level   Departmental Management

FIGURE B.6   Simplified decision structures of the French public administration and individual enterprise.

for executing orders. They were purposely small (about 90 in France) so that they could not compete with the central authority. Recently, a shift has occurred: Regions consisting of several departments (from 4 to 10, depending on the specific case), have been created but they have not yet acquired true autonomy.

Consider the two simplified decision structures in Figure B.6. In the realm of public administration and planning, monitoring and regulation are carried out only at the national level; in other words, they are uniform for the group of regions. The regional and departmental bodies collect information for the central agencies, promulgate the decisions of these agencies and supervise the application of the decisions.*

In the area of energy and environment, the central agencies do not have any unified model. They limit themselves to ruling on decisions made by the firms which, as will be clear later, produce good national models.

The second important feature of French institutions is the status of corporations in the energy sector. The structure of this sector (e.g., the relations between firms) differs from that of other sectors of economic activity. Most sectors usually consist of a greater or lesser number of private French firms. Corporations of this type have practically disappeared from the energy sector to the extent that there are only 2 types of firms:†

---

* This structure is so resourceful that it is capable of shaping all innovations to its needs. A recent study has pointed out, for example, that contrary to all expectation, the generalization of information processing in French enterprises is favorable to centralization. See: Balle, Catherine. "The computer, a break in the reforms of structure of enterprises," *Le Monde*, September 18, 1975.
† The emergence of nuclear energy tends, however, to change this situation. Pechiney-Ugine-Kuhlman, one of the largest French firms, is now being aided in taking control of a part of the fuel cycle.

- branches of multinational firms which control about 50 percent of the French petroleum market
- public enterprises or mixed industry, either competing (CFP and ERAP in the oil branch)* or monopolistic (EDF, CDF, GDF, CEA, CNR) †

Branches of multinational firms have a variable degree of autonomy, according to the structure and the strategy of the firm upon which they depend. At any rate, these firms never make decisions on their own, since the stakes are of some importance (large investment in refining or in transport, for example).

In the eyes of such firms, a region is at most a subgroup of consumers whose characteristics (quantity, density, growth rate) it is advisable to consider in a model representing the conditions of development of future sales. The results of such a model can influence the policies of the firm, for instance, in the placing of investments.

Public enterprises or mixed industries enjoy a larger degree of power; however, this power is far from complete because the public status of such firms makes them subordinate to the state authority. The amount of subordination varies, however, according to the extent to which the enterprise is a monopoly (the guardianship of the state is less constraining for the firms like CFP and ERAP which compete with the branches of the multinational oil companies) and to the extent to which it can defray its investment expenses (EDF, which has become more than 50 percent self-financing, has acquired much more autonomy than CDF or GDF). No matter what their weight is in final decisions — especially those which concern new investments — all these firms resort to models in order to diminish the uncertainty in the evolution of their market, in the prices of their imported raw materials, and in the technologies which they adopt. But these models are conceived both by and for the central agencies. Regional specifications are only taken into consideration in the form of exogeneous data and constraints such as

- the probable evolution of the energy consumption
- the availability of sources of energy
- opportunities of sites and water cooling for the large power plants

Some comments should be made about the ties between the 2 decision-making structures. The national government is of paramount importance because it is a legacy of the history of a nation dominated by a struggle between the Centre (the monarchy) and the provinces (the feudal system). The structure of the firms closely approximates that of the central government for reasons easy to understand. Since the foreign oil firms first opened branches in France at the beginning of the century, they have tried to influence legislation which has not always been favorable to them; in order to do this, they have installed representatives as close as possible to the center of the national power. Later on, since the great wave of nationalization in 1945, rationalization has been synonymous with standardization and centralization. This was in reaction to the disintegration of the mechanism of production (especially electricity and gas), which resulted from undynamic and diffuse capitalism. The osmosis between government administration and energy firms has been made considerably easier and has been speeded up by another aspect of French

---

* Compagnie Française des Petroles; Enterprise de Recherche et d'Applications Petrolières.
† Electricité de France; Charbonnages de France; Gaz de France; Commisariat à l'Energie Atomique; Compagnie Nationale du Rhône.

centralization, the uniform production of managers in the *"Grandes Ecoles"* of engineers also concentrated in the Paris region. Through a well-known and often-studied phenomenon, the same people go from the directorship of government agencies to that of public and sometimes private firms.

III. WISCONSIN

Stephen Born – Wisconsin State Planning Office; Charles Cicchetti – Wisconsin Office of Emergency Energy Assistance; and Richard Cudahy – Wisconsin Public Service Commission

Energy and environmental decision-making and planning in the United States is highly diffused; there is no single centralized planning or decision-making body. Not only are Federal responsibilities widely distributed, but various areas of jurisdiction are either the province of or shared with state and local governments. At the Federal level, power and responsibility for energy/environmental policy matters, as for other public policy areas, is "balanced" between the executive and legislative branches of government. The judicial branch serves as an interpreter and arbiter of the process. Substantial authority for energy and environmental matters rests with the traditional cabinet agencies in the executive branch – the Departments of Interior, Commerce, and Agriculture. In recent years more and more power has been placed within a number of relatively independent agencies and other governmental bodies. These independent offices include the Energy Research and Development Administration (ERDA); Federal Energy Administration (FEA); Environmental Protection Agency (EPA); Federal Power Commission (FPC); National Science Foundation (NSF); Nuclear Regulatory Commission (NRC); and the Tennesee Valley Authority (TVA). In 1977 a cabinet-level office called the Department of Energy (DOE) was formed from a combination of the Energy Research and Development Administration (ERDA), the Federal Energy Administration (FEA), and a number of other smaller agencies. This listing is a partial one, and simply illustrates that there are many institutional factors that affect energy decisions and administer energy-related programs at the Federal level.

A few states in the United States have been able to consolidate energy-related functions within a relatively few, or even a single agency; examples are Connecticut, California, and Kentucky. Most states, however, have a rather dispersed institutional framework for energy/environmental planning and decision-making. Wisconsin is fairly typical. State executive agencies are responsible for planning and administration of legislated programs at the state level. However, many state authorities and actions result from federally-mandated programs and requirements. In Wisconsin, emphasis has been placed on strong functional planning by line agencies, such as the Departments of Transportation and Natural Resources. To coordinate these functional planning efforts and to provide an independent policy analysis capability to the executive office, a comprehensive State Planning Office exists within the State Department of Administration. The following brief overview suggests the complexity of these arrangements.

The Department of Transportation (DOT) has the responsibility for all major energy consequences. At present, planning and operating programs are largely segregated by mode. It has not been organizationally or fiscally possible to examine transportation decisions from a multi-modal viewpoint, or to fully evaluate economic development or energy use "tradeoffs" associated with various modal choices.

State legislation is now pending that would reorganize DOT and its planning/ decision-making functions into an integrated, genuinely multi-modal transportation department.

The Department of Natural Resources (DNR) is charged with planning for and management of the state's air, water, recreational, and biologic resources. Its environmental protection planning and management responsibilities exert great influence on a number of energy-related issues. The agency's air pollution control regulatory responsibility furnishes an excellent example.

For several years, even before passage of the Federal Clean Air Act in 1970, a national debate has been underway in the United States regarding air pollution and the issue of "nondegradation." The Supreme Court has upheld the position that state air quality plans must prevent significant deterioration of air quality. Much of the controversy has centered on the impact of such a policy on economic growth. States are charged with developing the requisite air quality implementation plans, and in Wisconsin DNR has primary responsibility.

In May 1975, three utilities submitted plans and specifications for the construction of Columbia II, a 527-MW power plant to be built in south-central Wisconsin at a location adjacent to its twin, Columbia I. Wisconsin's air pollution control regulations required DNR to review these plans for air quality implications. DNR found that although the proposed plant would not violate air quality standards and would meet federal emission requirements, it would cause significant degradation of air quality that would in effect preclude additional growth. The data showed that Columbia II would pollute to 97 percent of one SO_2 standard and to 68 percent of another standard. DNR determined that this was a significant degradation of air quality and halted construction of the power plant in June. A hearing in the affected area to assess the public attitude on permitting construction of the power plant was held in July. Over 1,000 people attended the hearing, but hearing testimony along with other letters, resolutions, and petitions submitted to the DNR reflected an almost even split between supporters and opponents of construction. Since the assessment of public attitude was inconclusive, DNR decided that construction of Columbia II could not be prohibited. Construction is proceeding under requirements that are to keep Columbia II's emissions at an absolute minimum. The Columbia II incident not only demonstrates the development implications of air quality regulations, but the intimate relationship between air quality and energy decisions and the powerful role of the state DNR in such matters.

The Public Service Commission (PSC) is a three-member quasi-judicial regulatory agency. Each member is appointed by the governor, and confirmed by the state senate for six-year terms. The commission regulates the rates and services of public utilities operating in the state which includes both privately-owned and municipally-owned electric utilities, natural gas distribution utilities, water and combined water-sewer utilities. With the exception of major construction projects, the commission does not regulate electric cooperatives. Also under commission jurisdiction are intrastate common and contract motor carriers and railroad operations.

The commission has the responsibility to set utility rates including the determination of a utility's revenue requirement and the structure of rates. Recently, the commission has been implementing peak-load pricing as the basis for designing electric utility rates. Under this principle, rates are set on the basis of the costs customers incur by using electricity at times of peak demands.

Under a recently enacted law, electric utilities and cooperatives every two years must submit to the commission ten-year advance plans covering major construction projects. The commission must then approve, modify or disapprove the plans.

Electric utilities and cooperatives must also receive commission certification to construct specific major facilities included within the advance plans.

In addition to these responsibilities, the commission must approve issuance of securities, certify depreciation rates used by utilities, establish uniform systems of accounts, approve affiliated transaction contracts and conduct audits and inspections of utilities.

The Department of Industry, Labor, and Human Relations (DIHLR) has many programs with energy implications. None is more visible or influences energy conservation more directly than the department's responsibilities for the administration and enforcement of state building codes. In January 1975, DIHLR promulgated building codes which, in addition to traditional public health, safety, and welfare considerations, included energy use standards for all new buildings. This standard was based on extensive technical review, which involved key faculty at the University of Wisconsin; the Wisconsin Energy Model had been used in the analyses related to standard setting. In June 1975, these rules were "sidetracked" by a legislative committee, which was under attack from housing industry interests and from masons, who contended that the energy conservation standard would cause them to lose their jobs.*

The Office of Emergency Energy Assistance (OEEA) was created to deal with fuel hardships which arose during the Arab oil embargo in late 1973.† The office is empowered by federal regulations to order the delivery of fuels to individuals and fuel dealers who are unable to meet their energy needs. The fuels delivered are withdrawn from the fuel set-aside for the state, a theoretical inventory of the various types of petroleum fuels held by those private petroleum firms bringing fuels into the State.‡ The office has certain other powers, under either state or federal law, including the power to obtain information on use and inventories of fuels. This information is then compiled for use in preventing or alleviating shortages which occur because of imperfections in the market mechanism as controlled by federal regulations. The energy office serves as advisor to the state legislature and the governor on energy matters and has worked on developing legislation which bears on energy use within the state. The energy office has also reacted to legislation proposed by others within the state and has used energy modeling to determine the effects of various legislative proposals. The energy office reacts to various actions proposed, or already in place, by other state and federal agencies and seeks to protect the interest of the citizens of the state, as affected by the actions of the other agencies. The energy office seeks to minimize the negative effects of any occurrence in the energy area upon the businesses, citizens, and workers within the state. It attempts, through public speeches, press releases and other attention-getting devices, to give the general public and businessmen the facts about the energy situation and what they can do to improve it.

The University of Wisconsin (UW) has the tripartite educational mission of research, teaching, and public service. Although best known for energy systems modeling activities, university energy researchers are involved in a wide range of

* A new Wisconsin code went into effect in July 1978. See note at the end of section II.C. in Appendix C.
† In late 1976, OEEA was combined with the State Planning Office into a single "Office of State Planning and Energy."
‡ The products are allocated to the states by the Federal Energy Administration based on historical use before the Arab oil embargo. This was done so all states would share equally in any hardships.

studies – from basic solar energy research to techniques for monitoring the environmental impacts of power plant siting. Students are trained in interdisciplinary approaches for dealing with environmental and energy problems and later hold key agency positions within state government; state governmental problems have furnished worthwhile applied research areas for many students. The University Cooperative Extension Service has taken research and demonstrations results and brought them into the public forum through several public informational efforts. In short, there is a critical symbiosis between the university system and state government – a partnership that extends back through several decades. This cooperative spirit, pioneered in agriculture, but readily transferred to environmental and energy concerns, has been aptly named "the Wisconsin idea."

The Department of Administration (DOA) functions as the governor's agency within the state bureaucracy. The department is charged with preparation of the executive budget, which in recent years has become a major piece of policy legislation. DOA also houses the state's Federal/State Coordination Office and the Bureau of Facilities Management. The latter oversees all state buildings, and can initiate such procedures as life cycle costing in the planning of all state facilities. DOA also includes the State Planning Office, which is the state's comprehensive planning agency. This office is largely involved with physical, environmental, and economic planning.

The State Planning Office's programs are divided into three broad areas: state development policy planning; land use planning; and planning coordination (see Figure B.7). It has primary responsibilities in the areas of economic development, planning and coordination, land use planning, and coastal zone management, as well as in the process-oriented "planning coordination" area. In meeting its comprehensive planning and coordination responsibilities, the State Planning Office functions in several ways: (a) as a coordinator, liaison, or critical reviewer in working with interagency or intergovernmental groups or individual agencies; (b) as program developer and manager of new multifunctional, intergovernmental programs such as coastal zone management planning or state economic development planning; (c) as a policy analysis and research unit; (d) as a public involvement/ educational agent; and (e) as a provider of executive office services including legislative development and review, special projects or analysis, and limited budget issue involvement. As noted in Figure B.7, many of the planning office program areas and functions relate closely to energy and environmental concerns. One activity warrants special mention; close work between the university's Energy Systems and Policy Research Group and Planning Office staff has led to an analysis of the costs of alternative physical development patterns in terms of money, land consumption, and energy costs. The Wisconsin scenarios, described in Chapter 6, reflect some of the energy impacts described by this analysis.

One other aspect of Wisconsin's institutional setting as it pertains to energy and environment deserves special consideration. In 1972, Wisconsin passed the Wisconsin Environmental Policy Act (WEPA). The act, which is patterned after the National Environmental Policy Act of 1969 (NEPA), establishes a state policy to encourage harmony between human activity and the environment, promotes efforts to reduce damage to the environment, and stimulates understanding of important ecological systems. The act mandates a thorough analysis of environmental impact before any major state action is authorized. Agencies must consider alternative technologies and economic consequences of state-initiated projects; private actions regulated by state government are subject to the same procedures. The underlying premise of WEPA is that substantive policy decisions can be improved and a better balance

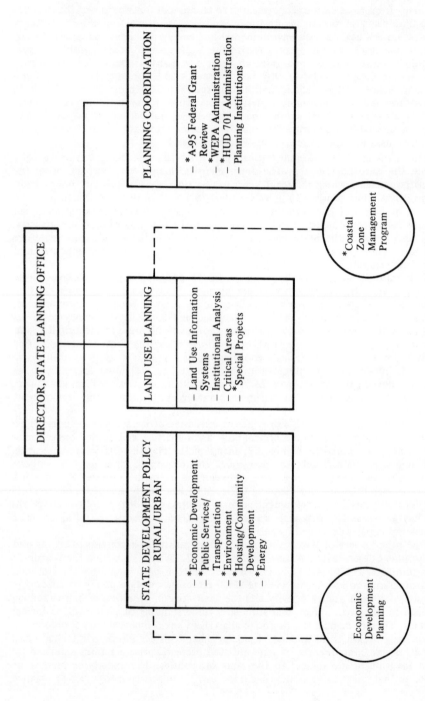

FIGURE B.7 Diagram of the State Planning Office programs in Wisconsin. An asterisk indicates energy-related functions.

will emerge between environmental and economic objectives if a broad range of environmental impacts, alternatives to the proposed action, and public comment are examined well before the final decisions are made.

Although the environmental impact statements and other documents are not binding on state governmental decision-making, WEPA (and NEPA) have had a far-reaching effect. Because of WEPA, environmental (including energy) considerations are now routinely a part of governmental decision-making, and the process is more accessible than ever before to citizens. Major energy related decisions — construction of a Great Lakes oil shipment terminal, construction of electric generating facilities and transmission lines, regulatory action related to utility rate changes, railroad line abandonments — have been subject to and delayed, modified, and even halted based on environmental questions raised by the Wisconsin Environmental Policy Act process. In fact, the environmental impact statement, and the associated review process, have become pervasive and extremely useful planning tools in energy decision making.

C Selected Management Practices

I. AIR QUALITY MANAGEMENT

Loretta Hervey and *Robin Dennis – IIASA*

I.A. INTRODUCTION

Air pollution is currently causing discomfort and disease in all industrialized nations, East and West. They have responded to this problem through a variety of economic, technical, and institutional approaches. The IIASA three-region study provided an opportunity to examine how three countries with highly diverse governmental and economic institutions have approached an environmental problem which is common to each. The previous sections of this chapter described this diversity. At one end of the scale is the United States, with decentralization of power, a diffuse decision-making structure, and a philosophy of free enterprise. In stark contrast is the GDR, with centralized decision-making, nationalized industry, and a tradition of comprehensive planning. France may be typified by a mixture of these elements – a long history of centralized government and nationalization of some energy enterprises.

   This section provides a cross-national comparison of management in the three countries. Emphasis is on the national rather than regional level. During the course of the IIASA study, IIASA scientists analyzed parallel legal documents dealing with environmental protection in the three regions. They also obtained empirical values of pollution concentrations in the cities of each study area. This material provided a basis for a cross-national comparison of such factors as government roles in supervising industry, the chain of authority in the implementation of pollution legislation, pollution standards, and sanctions against polluters. An attempt was also made to assess each country's progress in executing its legislation, through examination of current concentrations of pollutants in the ambient air.

   In the first part of this section, the evolution of pollution legislation is traced in France, the United States, and the GDR, with special attention given to emerging patterns of federal-regional responsibility in the environmental sphere. In the following part, the current structure of governmental bureaucracies which have been set up to implement environmental legislation are examined in each study area. Next, attention is focused upon the limits now in effect for pollutant concentrations in the ambient air* and for emissions† in France, the GDR, and the United States; here conceptual and definitional problems in comparisons of pollution "standards" are emphasized. Strategies for obtaining compliance to legislation, such as financial penalties, are summarized in the fourth section. Finally, environmental legislation is considered in the light of existing levels of pollution in the cities of each region. This section is based for the most part upon information provided in legal texts and not upon empirical studies.

I.B. HISTORICAL DIFFERENCES IN POLLUTION CONTROL LEGISLATION

I.B.1. France

Stationary Sources. Of the three countries under scrutiny, France has had most experience with direct government supervision of polluting industries. As early as 1810 Napoleon decreed that plants that emit offensive odors could not be built without permission. Under the 1917 "Law of Classed Establishments" the requirement for authorization was extended to dangerous as well as offensive plants.‡ The final group of emittors to be brought under government control were combustion installations: in 1948 these units were ordered to conform to construction, installation, and output norms, and further to submit to periodic control visits. In 1964 they were included for the first time in the list of "Classed Establishments."§

The 1960s were marked by legal efforts to standardize pollution control measures and to extend government prerogatives. A general 1961 law ordered responsible officials to determine permissible levels of particulate, toxic, malodorous, and radioactive emissions. In 1963, uniform monetary fines were imposed on plants which failed to conform to emission restrictions, and departmental prefects were authorized to take emergency action against polluters in case of danger to public health. During this decade, prefects also acquired the power to create "zones of special protection" with stringent emission standards in heavily polluted metropolitan areas.¶

Recent pollution legislation in France has been mainly directed toward specific industries. For instance, in 1966 emission norms and other technical instructions were issued for the operation of thermal power plants. The following year formulas were published for calculating minimum chimney heights in new combustion installations; subsequently, emission limits for cement factories, iron-ore smelters, urban incinerators, cast-iron foundries, and steel works have appeared.**

French authorities have also attempted to decrease emissions more directly by limiting the sulfur content of fuels. A 1967 decree specified that the sulfur content of heavy fuel oil Number 1 and light fuel oil could not exceed 2 percent, while that of heavy fuel oil Number 2 was limited to 4 percent. In 1968 the sulfur content of

---

* *Ambient air pollution concentrations* are defined as quantities (mass/unit volume or parts per million by volume) in the ambient air.
† *Emissions* are defined as quantities (weight or volume) of given pollutants discharged at their source, e.g. plant chimneys.
‡ Jarrault, P., La Législation Française Relative à Prévention de la Pollution par les Sources Fixes (Centre Interprofessionel Technique d'Etudes de la Pollution Atmosphérique (CITEPA) Les Editions Européennes, "Thermique et Industrie," undated), p. 5.
§ *Ibid.*, pp. 7, 25–30.
¶ *Ibid.*, pp. 2–28.
** *Ibid.*, pp. 12–20.

domestic fuel oil was restricted to .7 percent, with progressive decreases to .3 percent forseen for the 1970s.*

Motor Vehicles. Legislation aimed at cutting down emissions from motor vehicles first appeared in the early 1960s in France. In 1963 a test of the opacity of smoke emissions was ordered for all new motor vehicles. The following year it was determined that the total quantity of unburned hydrocarbons could not exceed .15 percent of the fuel consumed during vehicle operation. Finally, a 1970 decree aligned French legislation with Regulation 15 of the Geneva Accord of 1958, as well as with the 1970 Directives of the Council of Ministers of the European Community.†

Ambient Air. The concept of "ambient air quality standards" has not been developed in French legislation.‡ The government has preferred to control pollution directly at the level of the emitting plant, rather than by setting general air quality standards and then giving plants or local authorities responsibility for ensuring that they are met. This seems to accord with France's traditionally highly centralized government and its history of government initiative in policing industrial emissions.

I.B.2.   The United States

The history of environmental legislation in the United States attests to the federal government's very gradual assumption of responsibility for pollution control. In the 1955 Air Pollution Control Act a federal role was seen only in the funding of local anti-pollution programs and research. The 1963 Clean Air Act gave the Secretary of Health, Education, and Welfare (HEW) the authority to involve dangerous polluters in a conference — public hearing — court suit procedure; but this process proved so time-consuming that it only underscored the inability of the federal government to take action against polluters.§ Only after the passage of the 1967 Air Quality Act was the Secretary of HEW empowered to go directly to court to force a stop to dangerously high levels of pollution.

Ambient Air. The Air Quality Act also marked the federal government's first attempt to set nationwide air quality norms. The provisions of the act reveal the indirect tactics which legislators found it necessary to employ at this early stage: HEW was required to publish "air quality criteria" for dangerous pollutants; the states were then to develop "air quality standards" designed to meet the federal criteria, to produce plans for implementing and enforcing the standards, and, finally, to gain federal approval for these measures. If a state proved lax, HEW was permitted to intervene. However, not one state implementation plan was approved between 1967 and 1970, and HEW could not force compliance to nonexistent plans.¶

The failure of the 1967 act led U.S. legislators to restate its provisions in a much more detailed and stringent manner in the 1970 Clean Air Act Amendments. The pollution criteria of the earlier law (which had functioned simply as guidelines for the states' own standards) were replaced by national air quality standards, which

---

* *Ibid.*, p. 32. Here the percentages of sulfur refer to the weight of the fuels, not the volume.

† Benarie, M., "Air Pollution Legislation and Governmental Controls of Air Quality in France" (Vert-le-Petit: Institut National de la Recherche Chimique Appliquée, 1975), Table 3.

‡ The first step taken in this direction occurred in the early 1970s when ambient air "reference values" for SO_2 and particulate matter were promulgated for use in calculating required chimney heights.

§ William D. Hurley, *Environmental Legislation* (Springfield, Illinois: Charles C Thomas Press, 1971), pp. 34–41.

¶ *Ibid.*, pp. 43–50.

the states were required to adopt without modification. The pattern of interaction between federal and state governments which had characterized the 1967 act was carried over into the new law, for the states were ordered to develop plans for attaining and maintaining the national standards, and to submit them to the new Environmental Protection Agency (EPA) for approval. However, the amendments specified more exactly the content of the states' plans: they were to include land-use and transportation schemes, emergency plans for high-pollution occurrences, and outlines for statewide pollution surveillance systems. The states were to secure federal approval for their plans by May 31, 1975, but extensions have since been granted until the 1980s.*

Stationary Sources. The U.S. federal government has taken the initiative in controlling pollution from stationary sources much more slowly than its French counterpart. Until recently, U.S. legislators have preferred the more indirect approach of focusing their attention on ambient air quality and leaving point-source emission control to local authorities. This policy seems to reflect the country's overarching institutional structure: separation of federal and local power and government reluctance to interfere with private industry.

However, U.S. lawmakers did call for several federal emission standards for stationary sources in the 1970 amendments. Here the EPA was instructed to publish standards for rare but dangerous pollutants not likely to be covered by state implementation plans. In addition, the EPA was given the task of developing performance standards, including emission standards, for certain industrial plants. In the early 1970s standards were issued for such plants as new or reconstructed steam generators, sulfuric and nitric acid plants, cement plants, and iron and steel mills.†

Motor Vehicles. Perhaps because the issue of federal versus state jurisdiction is not as contested for mobile sources of pollution, the federal government has taken a direct approach toward curbing motor vehicle exhaust. When the need to regulate automobiles was recognized in the early 1960s, lawmakers skipped the stage of drafting guidelines ("criteria"); instead, in a 1965 act they directed the Secretary of HEW to set national emission standards for new foreign and domestic vehicles. By 1970, CO emissions from new cars were to be 71 percent lower than those from 1963 models, and hydrocarbon exhaust was similarly to be reduced by 82 percent. In the 1970 Clean Air Act Amendments, legislators took the radical step of calling for a nearly emission-free car engine within 6 years (later extended to 8).‡

I.B.3. The German Democratic Republic

Ambient Air. Because the GDR was founded in 1949, its legislators have had little time and many basic organizational problems to resolve, so environmental issues

---

* U.S. Environmental Protection Agency, "A Progress Report: December 1970–June 1972" (Washington, D.C., November, 1972), pp. 1–2. Also, U.S. Environmental Protection Agency, "Progress in the Prevention and Control of Air Pollution in 1974" (Washington, D.C., 1975), pp. 61–69. See as well, Gladwin Hill, "Air Pollution Drive Lags, But Some Gains are Made." *The New York Times*, May 31, 1975, pp. 1, 15.

† U.S. Environmental Protection Agency, "A Progress Report: December 1970–June 1972," pp. 1–2. Also, U.S. Environmental Protection Agency, "Progress in the Prevention and Control of Air Pollution in 1974," pp. 33–35, 41–52.

‡ Hurley, *Environmental Legislation*, pp. 51–55. Also, James Naughton, "President Signs Bill to Cut Auto Fumes 90 percent by 1977." *The New York Times*, January 1, 1971, pp, 1, 11. See as well, U.S. Environmental Protection Agency, "Progress in the Prevention and Control of Air Pollution in 1974," pp. 5–12, 53–60.

had to wait for attention. The first attempt to regulate air pollution in the GDR was in a 1968 regulation, in which "threshold values" — levels of pollution above which damage to human health is believed to occur — were defined for ambient concentrations of 48 substances. Public officials were directed to consider these values when issuing siting permits, planning new investments, and reconstructing existing plants.*

The philosophy underlying the GDR's approach to environmental protection was first clearly expressed in the 1970 "Landeskulturgesetz." Environmental problems were incorporated into the planning process which characterizes GDR policy-making in general. As the law states, "the requirements of a socialist society are to develop productivity in a planned manner, so as to lead to an increase in the utility and productivity of natural resources and guarantee the maintenance and beautification of the natural environment."† The conviction that economic and conservationist goals can be coordinated through planning is the hallmark of GDR environmental legislation.

Stationary Sources. Underlying the GDR's plans is the assumption that industry and government can work together to control pollution. At the level of the national government, both ambient air quality and emission norms have been developed; 1973 legal directives set threshold values for ambient air concentrations of 113 pollutants, and provided as well formulas based on ambient air pollution levels and chimney heights for calculating permissible emissions. It is foreseen that industry officials will use these prescriptions to ensure that emissions from plants do not cause ambient air quality norms to be violated.‡

Despite this delegation of responsibility, the central government bodies retain ultimate leverage over emitting plants. For instance, the chairman of the National Council of Ministers (*Vorsitzende des Ministerrates*) has the power to restrict industrial operations, or to order a change in fuels during dangerous occurrences of pollution. Punitive measures have also been spelled out for disciplining plants with chronically excessive emission levels. §

Motor Vehicles. The GDR's emphasis on cooperation between government and industry is also found in measures to control emissions from motor vehicles. A 1974 directive gave the federal Department of Exhaust Gas Inspection (Abgasprüfstelle der DDR) the task of setting emission threshold values for internal combustion engines and developing techniques for testing motor vehicles. At the same time the directive called for the creation of "Exhaust Gas Deputies" (Abgasbeauftragte) in all plants connected with the importing, producing, or repairing of motor vehicles. Their task is to assure self-policing in plants by checking whether motor vehicles meet threshold emission values.

By 1974, norms had also been set for permissible idling time in moving traffic, carbon monoxide (CO) emissions (by weight of vehicle), and lead content of fuels.¶

---

* *Gesetzblatt der DDR*, Part II, No. 80, July 25, 1968, "Anordnung zur Begrenzung und Ermittlung von Luftverunreinigungen (Immissionen)." pp. 640–642.

† *Gesetzblatt der DDR*, Part I, No. 12, May 28, 1970, "Gesetz über die planmässige Gestaltung der Sozialistischen Landeskultur in der Deutschen Demokratischen Republik – Landeskulturgesetz," p. 67.

‡ *Gesetzblatt der DDR*, Part I, No. 18, April 24, 1973, "Fünfte Durchführungsbestimmung zum Landeskulturgesetz – Reinhaltung der Luft." pp. 157–162.

§ *Ibid*.

¶ *Gesetzblatt der DDR*, Part I, No. 37, August 6, 1974, "Zweite Durchführungsbestimmung zur Fünften Durchführungsverordnung zum Landeskulturgesetz – Begrenzung, Überwachung, und Verminderung der Emissionen von Verbrennungsmotoren," pp. 353–356.

This overview of the evolution of environmental legislation in France, the United States, and the GDR has revealed contrasting styles of problem-solving. Governmental philosophy about reconciling economic and ecologic goals seems to be most clearly articulated in the legislation of the GDR. There the emphasis is on the planning of investments so as to avoid unhealthy concentrations of pollutants. The centralized decision-making system of the GDR has permitted the parallel development of both emission and ambient air quality norms at the national level, and the maintenance of these norms is assumed to be a cooperative venture of government and industry.

In France, the highly centralized government has laid most emphasis on the direct policing of industry by means of emission restrictions, rather than on the intermediate step of supervising ambient air quality.

In the United States, in contrast, the responsibility of the federal government has been confined to the setting of air quality standards (and emission standards for several types of stationary sources), while state authorities are charged with working out implementation plans for meeting the standards and policing industry. The division of power among national, state, and local authorities, as well as the restriction of government interference in private industry, has thus produced a more complex and diffuse approach toward pollution control than is found in the GDR and France.

I.C.   IMPLEMENTATION OF LEGISLATION

Just as the approaches toward the setting of pollution norms in France, the GDR, and the United States seem to reflect the general institutional structure of each country, the chain of authority set up to implement environmental legislation follows a similar pattern.

For instance, the centralized management and planning characteristic of the GDR government as a whole is reproduced in agencies for environmental protection. At the national level, the "Council of Ministers" (*Ministerrat*) has responsibility for policymaking, planning, and central management of pollution control activities. The federal "Ministry of Health" (*Ministerium für Gesundheitswesen*) has been given the task of setting ambient air threshold values and developing a nationwide pollution monitoring system. Concomitantly, the "Ministries of Machine and Vehicle Construction and Transportation" (*Ministerium für Allgemeinen Maschinen-, Landmaschinen-, und Fahrzeugbau* and *Ministerium für Verkehrswesen*) must set emission threshold values for internal combustion engines. Finally, the Ministry for Environmental Protection and Water Management" (*Ministerium für Umweltschutz und Wasserwirtschaft*) is responsible for assuring the coordination of all pollution-abatement measures.

At the local level in the GDR, the distribution of tasks between "district councils" (*Räte der Bezirke*) and polluters accords with the national policy of cooperation between government and industry. Thus, emission threshold values for individual plants are set by the councils with the help of the plants themselves. If a plant finds it impossible to meet these limits, it must work with its local council to develop plans for lowering emissions. Representatives of government and industry also collaborate in planning "accommodation" measures to decrease the harmful effects of unavoidable pollution, and "compensation" measures in case of injuries to workers or damage to their living conditions.*

* *Gesetzblatt der DDR*, "Füenfte Durchführungsverordnung zum Landeskulturgesetz – Reinhaltung der Luft," pp. 157–160.

As in the GDR, the strong central government of France has stressed the central coordination of pollution control activities. Since 1973, the "Directorate for the Prevention of Pollution and Nuisances" (*la Direction de la Prevention des Pollutions et des Nuisances*), within the "Ministry for the Protection of Nature and the Environment" (*Ministère de la Protection de la Nature et de l'Environnement*), has been responsible for preparing a national program for combatting pollution. The "minister of the environment" (*ministre de l'environnement*) is in charge of a corps of "environmental inspectors" and "regional environmental delegates" (*inspecteurs generaux de l'environnement* and *délégués regionaux à l'environnement*); he has as well ultimate responsibility for all environmental legislation, and must take action during episodes of exceptionally high pollution. Several other ministers at the national level are concerned with pollution problems, the "minister for industrial and scientific development" (*ministre du développement industriel et scientifique*), the "minister of public health" (*ministre de la santé publique et de la securité sociale*), and the "minister of the interior" (*ministre de l'interieur*).[*]

As far as actual regulation of noisome industries is concerned, the French government uses the following clearly articulated procedures. Before a potentially dangerous plant may begin operations, it must receive authorization from the "Bureau of Classed Establishments" (*Conseil Supérieur des Etablissements Classés*), a service under the jurisdiction of both the "Bureau of Mines" (*Service des Mines*) and the departmental prefect. If the plant is permitted to open, it must conform to precise technical prerequisites set forth as conditions of authorization. These include specification of fuels to be used, permissible emission rates, and monitoring procedures. The instructions result either from application of legal directives, which have been worked out by representatives of the industrial branches and the government, or (if no such directives exist for a particular type of plant) from the deliberations of the "Bureau of Classed Establishments." After granting an authorization, the inspectorate has the further responsibility of making periodic control visits, to assure that the technical prescriptions are being followed.[†]

In the United States the chain of authority in environmental affairs is based upon the traditional division of power between the national and state governments. This has led to complicated federal-state interactions, in which states must win federal approval for their pollution-control programs. On the federal level the EPA is responsible for funding and coordinating research on environmental problems, for trying to introduce conformity into pollution-abatement schemes across the country, for giving financial support to local programs, and for establishing ambient air quality standards and some emission standards. The administrator of the EPA also has recently acquired the authority to bring willful violators of pollution laws to court, and to order investigations of plants suspected of having illegally high emissions.[‡]

Wisconsin may be used to illustrate the role of state governments in pollution control in the United States. In response to the requirements of the 1967 Air Quality Act, the Wisconsin Department of Natural Resources (DNR) was given the task of establishing a comprehensive air pollution abatement program for the state. In 1970 it assumed responsibility for developing the "air quality implementation plan" called for by the Clean Air Act Amendments. This plan had to provide for

---

[*] Jarrault, La Législation Française, pp. 45–46.
[†] *Ibid.*, pp. 9–20. See also Benarie, "Air Pollution Legislation and Governmental Controls of Air Quality in France," p. 2.
[‡] Hurley, *Environmental Legislation*, pp. 34–50.

industrial emission standards strict enough to assure compliance with federal ambient air standards, as well as emergency plans for pollution crises, a statewide pollution surveillance system, and inspection of emitting plants. When the EPA rejected all state implementation plans in 1973,* the Southeastern Wisconsin Regional Planning Commission (SEWRPC) stepped in to work with the DNR. The two agencies are currently cooperating in developing a Regional Air Quality Maintenance Plan, which is based on an evaluation of SEWRPC's 1985 Land Use Plan and transportation projections. The Wisconsin Public Service Commission is yet another state agency involved in pollution control; it polices electric utilities by requiring them to submit every 2 years a 10-year plan for new construction. Before building is commenced, the commission must also carry out an environmental impact analysis.† Thus, in the United States, responsibility is not only distributed between federal and state government, it is further spread among a multitude of state agencies.

I.D. AMBIENT AIR QUALITY STANDARDS

Before making cross-national comparisons, it is important to consider that the concept of a standard may not be exactly equivalent in France, the GDR, and the United States. In fact, the word *standard* is only found in U.S. legislation; here a *primary ambient air standard* is defined as the "maximum level of a pollutant which should be permitted to occur in order to protect human life," and a *secondary ambient air standard* is "the maximum level of the pollutant which should be permitted to occur in order to protect animal and plant life and property from damage, and thereby protect the public welfare from any known or anticipated adverse effects of an air pollutant."‡ In the GDR, the term *ambient air "threshold value"* is used in place of *standard*. This term is defined as "the maximum concentration of a pollutant, which according to medical knowledge does not have a harmful effect on the human organism."§ Its denotation is thus quite similar to that of the U.S. primary ambient air standard. The term *reference value* is used in French legislation to indicate desirable limits for pollution concentrations in the ambient air. The sphere of applicability of such "reference values" is narrower than that of U.S. standards and GDR threshold values, for they are used mainly in calculating permissible chimney heights.¶

International differences may also be seen in the time periods for which a norm or standard applies. For instance, the U.S. air quality standard for carbon monoxide (CO) is given in the form of an 8-h average, while the corresponding GDR threshold value is a 24-h average. Though these may be converted to a common time unit, the original units might reflect different theories about the duration of pollution which is likely to affect health.

The current limits for concentrations of selected pollutants in the ambient air of the United States, the GDR, and France are presented in Table C.1. The figures

---

* The rejections resulted from the states' failure to consider the problem of maintaining clean air standards, as population and motor vehicles increase.
† Section III in Appendix D describes energy/environment models in Wisconsin.
‡ Southeastern Wisconsin Regional Planning Commission, "Regional Air Quality Maintenance," p. 11.
§ *Gesetzblatt der DDR*, "Fünfte Durchführungsverordnung zum Landeskulturgesetz – Reinhaltung der Luft," p. 157.
¶ Jarrault, La Législation Française, p. 15. Also M. Benaire *et al.*, "Etude de la Pollution Atmosphérique de la Ville de Strasbourg du 1er Juin 1971 au 30 Juin 1972," (Vert-le-Petit: Institut National de la Recherche Chimique Appliquée, October 24, 1972), pp. 11–12.

TABLE C.1   Highest Concentrations of Pollutants Permitted in the Ambient Air of France, The United States, and the GDR ($\mu g/m^3$)

	France (24-h av)	United States	GDR(24-h av)
CO		10,000 (8-h av)[a]	1,000
		40,000 (1-h av)	
SO_2	250	365 (24-h av)[a]	150
NO_2		100 (annual av)	40
HC		160 (3-h av)[a]	
Particulates	150	260 (24-h av)[a]	
		75 (annual av)	
Dust			150
Soot			50

SOURCE: Benarie, M. "Air Pollution Legislation and Governmental Controls of Air Quality in France." Table I. *Gesetzblatt der DDR*, Part I, No. 18, 24 April 1973, "Erste Durchführungs-verordnung zum Landeskulturgesetz — Reinhaltung der Luft." pp. 164—166. Code of Federal Regulations 40, part 50. Washington, D.C., July 1976.
[a] Concentration not to be exceeded more than once per year.

TABLE C.2   U.S. Emission Performance Standards for Fossil-Fuel-Fired Steam Generation Units with Heat Input of More than 250 Million Btu per Hour

Pollutant	Fuel	Maximum Emission per 10^6 Btu Heat Input (kg/2-h av)
SO_2	Liquid	.36
	Solid	.54
Particulates	All	.04
NO_2	Gaseous	.09
	Liquid	.13
	Solid	.31

SOURCE: Dunham, J.T., C. Rampacek, and T.A. Henri. "High-Sulfur Coal for Generating Electricity." *Science* 184 (4134): 346—351, Apr. 19, 1974. In 1979, these standards were being reviewed.

given for the United States are primary ambient air standards; secondary standards are either the same or more restrictive than the primary standards.

When considering these figures, it is tempting to ask which country has the strictest norms for air quality. It would appear that the GDR "threshold value" for SO_2, $150\,\mu g/m^3$, is more rigorous than the French "reference value" of $250\,\mu g/m^3$, and the U.S. "standard" of $365\,\mu g/m^3$. (All are 24-h averages). However, it is difficult to judge whether one country's limits are uniformly more rigorous than those of another, because comparable norms would not be found for each of the pollutants under study.

I.E.   EMISSION STANDARDS AND NORMS

France, the GDR, and the United States also show differences in their approaches toward limiting emissions from stationary sources. A fundamental question is whether emission standards are set at the national level for all plants of a given type, or whether permissible emission levels are determined for each plant individually, on the basis of such factors as the existing level of pollution.

In the United States, the national emission standards that have recently been issued for new stationary power plants, certain types of chemical factories, and incinerators are applied uniformly to plants of a given type. An example of emission standards currently in effect in the United States may be found in Table C.2. In the GDR, in contrast, permissible emission levels are set on an individual basis. For this purpose, formulas have been issued for calculating permissible emissions at given stack heights and pollution conditions. In France, emission regulations are similarly tailored to plants individually. Technical instructions, including emission limits, are worked out by the "Inspectorate of Classed Establishments" for each new plant which receives authorization to begin operations. For some facilities, such as thermal power plants, cement works, iron and steel mills, and incinerators, maximum admissible pollution concentrations have been standardized in legal directives; but as Benarie has explained, "they are matched by the Inspectors to each individual plant (e.g., by way of dispersion and stack height calculations)."[*] Specific formulas for calculating required stack heights under given meteorological conditions and existing pollution levels have also been issued by French lawmakers. The following formula is one of the standard formulas used in France for calculating necessary stack heights for a given level of emissions from new combustion facilities:[†]

$$h = \sqrt{\frac{Aq}{C_m}} \sqrt[3]{\frac{1}{R\Delta T}}$$

where

h = stack height in meters
A = 340 for SO_2, 680 for particulate matter.
q = pollutant emission rate in kilograms per hour.
ΔT = temperature difference between the emitted gas and the ambient air (annual average of area) in $^\circ$C.
R = gas rejection rate in cubic meters per hour.
C_m = air quality reference values (.25 mg/m^3 for SO_2, .15 mg/m^3 for particulate matter, minus the annual average SO_2 or particulate matter concentration).

A 1973 GDR legal text provides a table of values for "effective" increases in stack heights, discriminated according to the amount of gas emitted, the speed with which the gas is discharged, and its temperature. A second table indicates permissible emissions of SO_2 on the basis of "effective" chimney heights and the existing level of pollution. These values have been generated from a dispersion model.

In the GDR, emission limits for other pollutants are calculated according to the equation[‡]

$$e_z = S \cdot MIK_k$$

where

e_z = the permissible emission of a given gaseous pollutant in kilograms per hour.

[*] Benarie, "Air Pollution Legislation," p. 2.
[†] Benarie, "Air Pollution Legislation," p. 3.
[‡] *Gesetzblatt der DDR*, "Erste Durchführungsbestimmung zur Fünften Durchführungsverordnung zum Landeskulturgesetz – Reinhaltung der Luft" pp. 166–171.

TABLE C.3   French Motor Vehicle Emission Standards. (Allowable emissions during a 13-minute standardized test.)

Legal Weight of the Vehicle (kg)	CO (g)	Hydrocarbons (g)
Below 750	120	10.4
750–850	131	10.9
850–1,020	140	11.3
1,020–1,250	161	12.2
1,250–1,470	182	13.1
1,470–1,700	203	14.0
1,700–1,930	223	14.8
1,930–2,150	244	15.7
Above 2,150	264	16.6

SOURCE: Benarie, M. "Air Pollution Legislation and Government Controls of Air Quality in France." Table 3.

S = the "multiplication factor" for other gaseous pollutants.

MIK_k = short-time interval, ambient air concentration threshold value of a particular pollutant.

The "multiplication factor" is based upon the emission limits for SO_2 (which in turn depends upon the general level of pollution existing in a given area, as well as "effective" chimney heights).

These different approaches suggest an underlying divergence in the concept of emission limits. In the GDR and France, the relationship between emissions and ambient air quality has been worked out precisely: permissible levels of emissions vary with existing ambient air concentrations. If changes in the ambient air quality occur, for instance, because of the introduction of new industry, then emission limits can be modified. In contrast, the emission standards being developed in the United States are less flexible; it is just assumed that if industry complies with the standards, ambient air quality will be protected. Thus, while U.S. emission standards seem to be considered fixed quantities, France's maximum admissible concentrations and GDR emission threshold values are more adaptable; they may be revised to accord with new environmental conditions or even economic goals.

A more uniform approach has been taken toward limiting emissions from motor vehicles in the 3 countries under study. French motor vehicle emission norms comply with the stipulations of the Geneva Agreement of March 20, 1958; the quantity of pollutants collected in a 13-minute standardized test may not exceed the values presented in Table C.3. Nearly the same emission limits for carbon monoxide (CO) were to be used in production controls in the GDR in 1975. It was planned, however, that beginning in 1976 the norms for each weight of vehicle would become more stringent.*

In the United States, emission norms for light-weight passenger vehicles are expressed per vehicle mile rather than as the cumulative result of a testing period. According to the 1977 amendments to the Clean Air Act, CO emissions are to be limited to 3.4 g per vehicle mile. NO_x exhaust is to be cut to 0.1 g per vehicle

* *Gesetzblatt der DDR*. "Zweite Durchführungsbestimmung zur Fünften Durchführungsverodnung zum Landeskulturgesetz," p. 355.

mile. Automobile manufacturers have managed to obtain a number of deferments for meetings these standards, however. The latest is until 1981.[*]

I.F.   ENFORCEMENT STRATEGIES

The international differences noted in previous sections may also be seen in the area of enforcement. The types of sanctions applied to plants which disregard environmental legislation seem again to reflect the general institutional structures of the countries under study and the relations between government and industry which these engender.

For instance, the interest of the French government in controlling pollution in the plants is expressed in the relatively high financial penalties currently in effect for exceeding emission limits and hampering control checks. If a plant operator refuses an inspection, he may be imprisoned for up to 3 months and fined from 400 to 20,000 F ($80 to $4,000). Unsatisfactory findings during an initial inspection can lead to a fine of 400 to 2,000 F ($80 to $400), as well as an injunction to stop operations. An additional penalty of 100,000 F ($20,000) and 2 to 6 months in prison can be imposed on an operator who ignores such an order. The effectiveness of these control actions is suggested by the government claim that the percentage of plants found not to comply with emission regulations dropped from 20 in 1963 to 7 in 1969.[†] However, harder data on the frequency with which the fines are applied would be needed, in order to evaluate the stringency of French control strategies.

In contrast, the small fines levied against recalcitrant polluters in the GDR indicate that financial penalties are not an important part of this country's air pollution control strategy. Plants which do not adhere to pollution regulations during everyday operations or pollution emergencies could be required to pay 10 to 300 M ($5 to $150). Numerous infractions in an attempt to gain unfair economic advantage can result in a fine of 1,000 M ($500). "Dust and Exhaust Money" can also be exacted from an emitting plant, based upon the length of time that emission norms are exceeded and the pollutants involved. The imposition of this fine is meant to be more constructive than punitive, however, for it is thought to supply an economic stimulus for the installation of antipollution devices. GDR control strategies seem in general to focus more on planning future decreases in emissions, rather than on rigorously punishing current offenders.[‡]

In the United States, the complicated division of responsibility for pollution control between federal, state, and local government seems to have hindered the enforcement of environmental legislation in the past. The 1963 Clean Air Act empowered the administrator of the EPA to initiate an "abatement conference — court suit" procedure to stop health-endangering pollution, but this has proved inordinately time-consuming. (The procedure involves not only the EPA and the delinquent industry, but also state, regional, and local environmental agencies, a public hearings board, and judicial officials). The fact that the conference-hearing–court suit process was used only 10 times in 7 years attests to its impracticality.[§] Only since the 1970 Clean Air Act Amendments have federal and state

[*] *Environmental Quality: The Eighth Annual Report of the Council on Environmental Quality.* Washington, D.C., Dec., 1977, p. 22.
[†] Jarrault, La Législation Française, pp. 23, 28.
[‡] *Gesetzblatt der DDR.* "Fünfte Durchführungsverordnung zum Landeskulturgesetz – Reinhaltung der Luft," pp. 161–162.
[§] Hurley, *Environmental Legislation*, pp. 34–50, 58–59.

environmental agencies had the authority to make investigations of emitting plants and to initiate criminal proceedings. Willful violations can be punished with a $25,000 fine per day and a year's imprisonment. While such sanctions have rarely been applied, state and federal authorities seem to have been eager to take advantage of their right to investigate emitting plants. In the last 6 months of 1974, for instance, the EPA carried out 2,517 investigations with 234 enforcement procedures, and states made 81,160 investigations and 7,205 enforcement actions.*

I.G. EMPIRICAL FINDINGS

France, the GDR, and the United States are currently in the process of extending their networks of monitoring stations in order to collect more reliable and representative measurements of pollution concentrations.

In 1972 the French government developed a 5-year plan for expanding its network of monitoring devices to include all densely populated or highly industrialized areas, as well as for standardizing measurement procedures. The plan includes tying authorization of "Classed Establishments" to participation in monitoring activities. At the present time, available data are restricted to measurements of SO_2 and particulate matter concentrations in 18 French cities.[†]

In the GDR, environmental officials are also in the midst of developing and publishing standardized measurement procedures. In addition, plans have been drawn up for establishing ambient air concentration "registers" in populated areas, so that statistical data on background concentrations can be recorded. Currently, dust and SO_2 concentrations are being measured in 19 cities and towns of the GDR.[‡]

Until the late 1960s monitoring equipment was in operation in only 6 cities in Wisconsin, a typical midwestern state in the United States. When the Department of Natural Resources obtained authority to develop a statewide pollution control program in 1967, it immediately began to extend monitoring activities. There are currently stations in 29 cities, including 10 continuous monitoring sites. Particulate matter and SO_2 are the pollutants most often measured, but a small number of stations also monitor oxidants, hydrocarbons, COH, and CO. A centralized laboratory was opened in 1973 in order to facilitate quality control of analysis procedures.[§]

International comparisons of pollution concentrations must be undertaken very

---

* Hill, "Air Pollution Drive Lags," *Times* pp. 1, 15.
† P. Jarrault, La Législation Française, p. 33; J. Syrota, "Les Données du Problème de la Pollution Atmosphérique," *Pollution Atmosphérique,* No. Special (July 1972) pp. 43–44; Centre Interprofessionel Technique d'Etudes de la Pollution Atmosphérique (CITEPA), "Statistiques françaises de la Pollution due à la Combustion," Study No. 40.; M. Benarie, "Etudes de la Pollution Atmosphérique de Mulhouse, Strasbourg, Rouen, et Vaudreine," (Vert-le-Petit: Institut National de la Recherche Chimique Appliquée, 1967–1973).
‡ Manfred Zier, "Einige Ergebnisse von Schwebestaubmessungen in unterschiedlich verstaubten Gebieten der DDR," In *Erfassung und Auswirkung von Luftverunreinigungen*, from the series, Technik und Umweltschutz (Leipzig: VEB Deutscher Verlag für Grundstoffindustrie, 1972), pp. 65–80; *Gesetzblatt der DDR.* "Erste Durchführungsverordnung zum Landeskulturgesetz," p. 162; Gerhard Mueller, "Das oekonomische Experiment zur Reinhaltung der Luft im Bezirk Halle," In *Technologie der Abwasserreinigung und Emissionskontrolle der Luft*, from the Series, Technik und Umweltschutz (Leipzig: VEB Deutscher Verlag für Grundstoffindustrie, 1973), pp. 111–129.
§ State of Wisconsin, Department of Natural Resources, "1973 Air Quality Data Report."

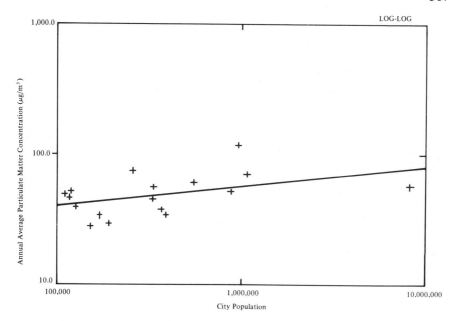

FIGURE C.1   Particulate matter concentrations (annual average) vs. city population for French cities (1967–1973).

cautiously, even if cities of similar size are considered. The mix of industries may differ between cities, and measurement techniques have not been standardized. Because of such uncontrolled factors, only tentative conclusions can be drawn from Figures C.1, C.2 and C.3.

It must first be noted that there is a marked positive relationship between annual average particulate matter concentrations and city size in each of the 3 countries under study. If particular points are taken from the graphs and compared, it appears that the GDR has the highest particulate matter concentration for a given city size, followed by France and Wisconsin. For instance, the city of Plauen in the GDR (population of 80,871) recorded an annual average particulate matter concentration of $70 \mu g/m^3$ in 1970, while St. Etienne in France (metropolitan population of 110,897) registered an annual average particulate matter concentration of $61 \mu g/m^3$ in 1972, and Beloit, Wisconsin (metropolitan population of 81,880) reported an annual average particulate matter concentration of $28 \mu g/m^3$ in 1973. The findings may be misleading, however, because of the need to compare readings from different years and from cities with different types of industry.

It may be fairer to assess the success of air pollution control efforts by looking at changes over time in each country. Of the 17 French cities for which pollution concentrations could be obtained, 9 showed a consistent decrease in particulate matter, and 8 in SO_2, during the past decade. Readings in the remaining cities either stayed constant or showed wide fluctuations over time. A French observer has attributed the general improvement in France to a decrease in the sulfur content of

368

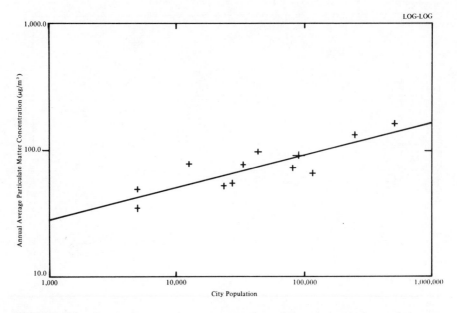

FIGURE C.2   Particulate matter concentrations (annual average) vs. city population for GDR cities (1965–1969).

fuel, to new regulations requiring taller stacks in emitting plants, and to the creation of zones of special protection.*

In GDR cities, pollution control efforts during the latter part of the 1960s seem to have been successful in holding pollution concentrations steady. None of the cities for which readings were available showed a decrease in pollution by 1970, but unfortunately, measurement results could not be obtained for subsequent years.

A survey of ambient air particulate matter concentrations in Wisconsin revealed a consistent decrease at each measurement station between 1971 and 1973. The EPA reported a 27-percent reduction in national levels of sulfur dioxide between 1970 and 1976, but less than half of the 313 air quality control areas in the United States are currently meeting Federal particulate standards.[†]

I.H.   CONCLUSION

The question of how three countries with very different political structures have approached the same functional problem of controlling pollution is complex. This comparative analysis of environmental legislation has suggested that the institutional structure of each country has exerted an idiosyncratic influence on each component of strategies for combatting pollution. In France, a highly centralized government

---

* M. Detrie, "Etude de l'Evolution de la Pollution due à la Combustion en France 1972–73–74."·Pollution Atmosphérique, No. 66, (April–June 1975), pp. 89–92.
[†] "The Delay in Meeting U.S. Clean Air Goals, *The New York Times*, Jan. 6, 1978, p. 18.

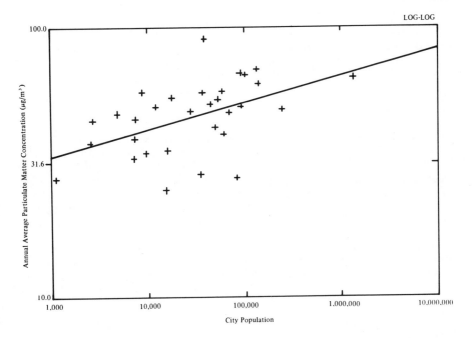

FIGURE C.3   Particulate matter concentrations (annual average) vs. city population for Wisconsin cities (1973).

can be shown from a long history of government initiative in the policing of industry, the centralized administration of pollution control activities, and the seemingly severe penalties for exceeding emission norms. The diffusion of power in the United States perhaps underlies the gradual involvement of the federal government in the area of pollution control, the delegation of responsibility for setting air quality standards to the federal government and for controlling emissions to state and local governments, the complicated procedure whereby federal approval must be gained for state pollution programs, and finally, the difficulty in implementing effective enforcement measures. The centralized decision-making and emphasis on cooperation characteristic of the GDR may be seen in its comprehensive planning of measures for decreasing pollution, the collaboration between government and industry representatives in setting emission norms, and the self-policing of plants.

Whether the strategies of one country are more effective than those of another in combating pollution cannot be determined at the present time. Final evaluation of pollution legislation will have to await the full implementation of all the laws currently "on the books." Most of the legislation in the three areas is so new that target dates for compliance have not yet been reached, or have been subject to deferments. For instance, technical instructions for combustion installations issued in 1975 in France called for the installation of pollution monitoring devices by 1978. The managers of plants built before 1976 were also given until 1978 to comply with emission norms.* For GDR briquette plants, 1976 was given as a deadline for meeting emission threshold values published in 1973.† In the United States, 16 states have won deferments until 1977 for the implementation of federally-approved abatement programs, and many power plants and steel mills are seeking deferments until the late 1980s for meeting emission standards.‡

II. ENERGY-RELATED BUILDING PRACTICES

One energy-related area that has come under closer scrutiny recently in each of the three regions, is standard-setting for energy use in buildings. Each region has developed minimum performance standards or recommendations for several types of structures. The standards are generally becoming more comprehensive and more strict as energy prices continue to climb and energy conservation measures become more desirable. Minimum performance standards for buildings help prevent needless energy wastage and encourage consideration of energy efficiency in building design.

The next three sections briefly describe the energy building codes and practices in the GDR, France, and Wisconsin. A comparison of particular standards in the regions is given in the final section.

II.A. THE GERMAN DEMOCRATIC REPUBLIC

Alfred Wischnat — Institut für Energetik

Energy alternatives in construction have been attracting more and more attention in recent years in the GDR as in other countries. Due to the growing trend towards lightweight buildings, consideration of thermal insulation in construction is surpassing static structural work in importance. The significance of thermal insulation in construction does not just result from the need to preserve existing buildings but above all from the intention to serve the people who use them. And, no less important, thermal insulation in construction is also a question of economy, especially where buildings are heated.

In the GDR, the National Standard TGL (Technische Güte- und Lieferbedingungen) 10 686, Sheets 1–6, dealing with "constructional-physical protective measures/thermal insulation" must be applied to all problems concerning thermal

---

* *Journal Officiel de la République Française*, "Equipment et exploitation des installations thermiques en vue de reduire la pollution atmosphérique d'économiser l'energie." (July 31, 1975), pp. 7778–7781.
† Guenter Deysing, "Die Entwicklung der Volkswirtschaft im Bezirk Cottbus und die sich daraus ergebenden Aufgaben für die sozialistische Landeskultur." In *Luftverunreinigungen in bestimmter Gebiete und Technologische Verfahren zur Emissionsverminderung* in the Series, Technik und Umweltschutz (Leipzig: VEB Deutscher Verlag für Grundstoffindustrie, 1974), p. 15.
‡ Hill, "Air Pollution Drive Lags," *Times*, pp. 1, 15. Also, U.S. Environmental Protection Agency, "Progress in the Prevention and Control of Air Pollution in 1974," pp. 41–52.

insulation in construction. In recent years this standard has been supplemented and extended. As a result of this revision the new standard TGL 28 707, Sheets 1–10, dealing with "constructional thermal insulation" was binding in the GDR as of January 1, 1976. The principles governing this standard will be explained in this section.

Principal Requirements for Thermal Insulation in Construction. To protect against any moisture penetration, thermal insulation, along with heating, ventilating, and air conditioning systems, will have to meet the following fundamental requirements

- minimum hygienic conditions for rooms permanently used by people
- functional efficiency of the building
- preservation of buildings by prevention of any penetration of moisture and reduction of temperature-dependent stress in structural elements
- minimum expenditure on heating, ventilating, and air conditioning

Maximum efficiency must be the guiding principle when these requirements are met.

As an essential prerequisite for meeting these demands, the functional unity of a building and the technical equipment installed has to be ensured in view of the climate of the area of the site. For that reason the standard explicitly requires the design engineer in charge of heating, ventilating, and air conditioning installations to be drawn into planning and architectural activities at a very early date.

Thermal Resistivity of Structural Elements. Before special problems of thermal resistivity can be dealt with in detail, some standard specifications concerning the climate in the GDR need to be explained. The territory of the GDR has been divided into 3 regions of thermal resistivity. These regions have been defined on the basis of critical winter temperatures (outdoor air temperature established for the coldest 5-day period from 1901 to 1950). Winter temperatures calculated for regions 1, 2, and 3 were $-15°C$, $-20°C$, and $-25°C$. With regard to wind and rainfall, a site is characterized by the wind–rainfall index (WNI), expressed by the relation

$$WNI = \frac{Nv}{a}$$

where

N = mean annual rainfall in millimeters from 1901 to 1950
v = mean annual wind velocity in meters per second from 1961 to 1970
a = 1,000 mm · m/sec

The wind–rainfall indices in the 4 wind–rainfall regions specified for the GDR are less than 2.0; 2.0 to 2.6; 2.6 to 4.0; and greater than 4.0.

Calculation of the thermal resistivity required of any structural element is to be based on the consideration that inside wall temperatures must reliably meet constructional and hygienic requirements with regard to indoor temperatures. The site of the building has to be classified according to the relevant thermal-resistivity region and the wind-rainfall index taken into account. Building preservation proceeds from the need to prevent any generation of dew water. The dew-point temperature of the indoor air determines the minimum thermal resistivity to be established. The standard specifies admissible maximum values, which are mandatory, for the temperature difference between indoor temperature t_i and that of the inside surface of the structural element, Θ_i. Admissible maximum temperature differences for inhabited rooms with an indoor temperature of $20°C$ and a relative humidity of 60 percent, for example, are for

- outside walls $6.5°K$
- outside walls of corner rooms $4.5°K$
- partition walls in flats (with heating systems that can be controlled or shut off individually) $6.5°K$
- roofing $3.5°K$

An additional safety margin, which for example amounts to $-1.5°K$ in the case of outside walls, has to be considered for inhabited rooms subject to hygienic regulations. The minimum insulation values are calculated according to the equation

$$R = R_0 - (R_i + R_e)$$

where

R_i = the heat transfer resistance of the inside surface
R_e = the heat transfer resistance of the outside surface
R_0 is obtained from the relation

$$R_0 = R_i \frac{t_i - t_e}{t_i - \Theta_i}$$

t_e = the temperature to be used in calculations for the thermal-resistivity region involved.

The units of R are square meters — degrees Kelvin per Watt ($m^2 \cdot °K/W$).

If R_e is assumed to be constant for all buildings in direct contact with outdoor air in winter ($0.04 \, m^2 \cdot °K/W$, or, in terms of α, the heat transfer coefficient, $\alpha_e = 25 \, W/m^2 \cdot °K$), R_i will be between 0.07 and $0.17 \, m^2 \cdot °K/W$ (or, in terms of α, $\alpha_i = 6$ to $14 \, W/m^2 \cdot °K$), depending on the kind of ventilation (gravity or forced-draught).

The standard gives all parameters needed to establish minimum thermal resistivity for any particular application. For easier handling in everyday use, the standard directly specifies the minimum thermal resistivity values for the most important structural elements related to the thermal-resisitivity regions, e.g. for the outside walls of inhabited rooms ($t_i = 20°C$; relative humidity = 60 percent):

- in thermal-resistivity region 1 — $0.50 \, m^2 \cdot °K/W$
- in thermal-resistivity region 2 — $0.60 \, m^2 \cdot °K/W$
- in thermal-resistivity region 3 — $0.70 \, m^2 \cdot °K/W$

The standard not only recommends reference values for thermal resistivity; because of unsteady temperature influences in summer conditions it also specifies minimum values for the heat capacity of exterior structural elements. The criterion applied is the temperature amplitude attenuation, which is defined as the quotient of the daily outdoor air temperature amplitude and the reduced temperature amplitude for the inside surface of the structural element. A temperature amplitude attenuation of 10 is, for example, required for outside walls with an arbitrary share of glass elements and without direct exposure to the sun.

Economical Thermal Insulation. The requirements and reference values discussed so far are mandatory for the designing of buildings in the GDR. In addition, the standard contains recommendations which should be used to assess thermal insulation efficiency of structural elements in heated buildings. It is assumed that the expenditure on installation and operation of a heating system depends on the expenditure on thermal insulation. (The heating requirements of buildings needed for heating system design, are calculated in the GDR according to National Standard TGL 112-0319,* dealing with heat requirements of buildings.) There is an obvious need to design both building and heating system so that total expenditure is kept at a minimum. The expenditure index G serves as the criterion for efficiency calculation.

$$G = J_B f_B + j_B + J_H f_H + j_H$$

where

J = investment costs in Marks per square meter (M/m^2).
f = capital charge factor in inverse years $(1/yr)$.
j = operating expenses in Marks per square meter per year $(M/m^2/yr)$.
index B = structural element.
index H = heating system.
The units of G are Marks per square meter per year $(M/m^2/yr)$.

Optimum thermal resistance, i.e. optimum insulating layer thickness of any structural element involved, can be established on the basis of G. In cases where the optimum resistance is lower than the minimum values prescribed by the standard, the minimum values of the standard must be applied.

Summary. Thermal insulation in construction, especially the thermal resistivity of structural elements, has attracted much attention in the GDR. National Standard TGL 28 706, dealing with constructional thermal insulation, which was binding as of January 1, 1976, represents up-to-date national and international knowledge and experience in this field. Requirements and reference values will not only contribute to ensuring and maintaining functional efficiency of buildings but will above all serve the people who use them. Joint consideration of building standards and expenditures with the aim of reaching an optimum balance is an essential factor in reducing the demands made on the resources of any national economy. It is especially this point that future activities in the GDR will be concerned with in dealing with thermal insulation in construction.

II.B.   FRANCE

Bertrand Chateau – Institut Economique et Juridique de l'Energie (IEJE)

France has to face very different climate conditions from north to south and from east to west. There is a hot, Mediterranean climate in the south; a wet oceanic climate in the middle west and north; and a continental climate in the east and in the mountains. Therefore, 3 climate areas (A, B, and C) are distinguished in the building standards as shown in Table C.4. The degree-days and "basic minimum

---

* This standard is being revised.

TABLE C.4 Climate Designations of the French Departments According to Legislation for Low-Rent Housing

Department	Over 500 m	200–500 m	Under 200 m
Ain	A	A	B
Aisne		A	A
Allier	A	B	B
Alpes(-de-Haute Provence)	A	B	B
Alpes (Hautes)	A	A	
Alpes-Maritimes	A	B	C
Ardeche	A	B	B
Ardennes	A	A	A
Ariege	A	B	
Aube	A	A	A
Aude	A	B	C
Aveyron	A	B	
Belfort (Territoire de)	A	A	
Bouches-du-Rhone	A	B	C
Calvados		B	B
Cantal	A	A	
Charente		B	B
Charente-Maritime			C
Cher		B	B
Correze	A	B	B
Corse	A	B	C
Cote-d'Or	A	A	A
Cotes-du-Nord		B	B
Creuse	A	B	
Dordogne		B	B
Doubs	A	A	A
Drome	A	B	B
Essonne		B	B
Eure		B	B

Department	Over 500 m	200–500 m	Under 200 m
Lot	A	B	B
Lot-et-Garonne		B	B
Lozere	A	B	
Maine-et-Loire			B
Manche		B	B
Marne		A	A
Marne (Haute)		A	A
Mayenne		B	B
Meurthe-et-Moselle	A	A	A
Meuse		A	A
Morbihan		B	B
Moselle	A	A	A
Nievre	A	B	B
Nord			B
Oise	B	B	B
Orne	B	B	B
Paris (Ville-de-)			B
Pas-de-Calais			B
Puy-de-Dome	A	A	C
Pyrenees (Atlantiques)	A	B	B
Pyrenees (Hautes)	A	B	C
Pyrenees (Orientales)	A	B	C
Rhin (Bas)	A	A	A
Rhin (Haut)	A	A	A
Rhone	A	B	B
Saone (Haute)	A	A	A
Saone-et-Loire	A	B	B
Sarthe		B	B
Savoie	A	A	B
Savoie (Haute)	A	A	

Département			
Gard	A	B	B
Garonne (Haute)	A	B	B
Gers		B	B
Gironde			C
Hauts-de-Seine	A		B
Herault	A	B	C
Ille-et-Vilaine			B
Indre		B	B
Indre-et-Loire		B	B
Isere	A	B	B
Jura	A	A	
Landes			C
Loire		B	B
Loire (Haute)	A	A	
Loire-Atlantique	A		
Loiret			C
Loir-et-Cher			B

Département			
Seine-Saint-Denis			B
Seine-Maritime		B	B
Seine-et-Marne			B
Sevres (Deux)			B
Somme		B	B
Tarn	A		B
Tarn-et-Garonne		B	B
Val-de-Marne			B
Val-d'Oise			B
Var	A		B
Vaucluse	A	B	C
Vendee		C	C
Vienne		B	C
Vienne (Haute)	A	B	B
Vosges	A	A	
Yonne		B	B
Yvelines		B	B

SOURCE: Association technique des industries du gaz en France, "Chauffage au gaz des locaux d'habitation et service d'eau chaude associée." Collection des techniques gazières. Ed. Société du journal des usines à gaz, 1975.

376

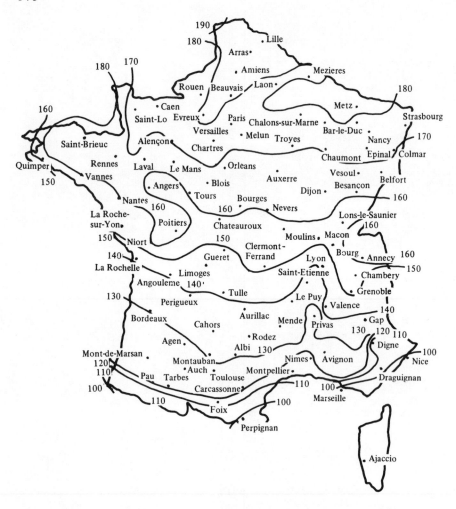

FIGURE C.4   Length of the heating season for all parts of France.

external temperature" also differ widely among regions in France. The degree-days for 83 meteorological points aggregated into 14 groups are given in Table C.5 and the "basic minimum external temperature" for all the departments are listed in Table C.6.

The lowest number of Celsius degree-days observed in France is 1,300 and the highest is 3,300; the lowest basic temperature is $-14°C$ and the highest $-2°C$. In most parts of France (area B) 2,450 degree-days are considered to be a reasonable average value.

The length of the heating season for each part of France is drawn on the map

TABLE C.5   Degree-days for 83 Meteorological Points

	Altitude (m)	October			Nov.	Dec.	Jan.	Feb.	Mar.	April			May		Total from Oct. 1 to May 20
		1–10	11–20	21–31						1–10	11–20	21–30	1–10	11–20	
Group I															
Dunkerque	9	51	65	87	321	422	434	387	375	102	92	82	73	64	2555
Boulogne-sur-Mer	73	49	63	85	315	425	431	387	369	102	92	82	73	64	2537
Abbeville	57	57	71	94	342	446	453	396	357	100	89	78	67	57	2707
Lille	55	60	74	98	357	465	463	407	369	101	90	79	68	57	2693
Saint-Quentin	98	60	75	100	266	477	481	413	366	101	89	77	65	54	2724
Group II															
Reims	94	59	74	87	363	474	484	407	357	96	84	72	60	48	2665
Romilly	77	59	73	85	354	471	474	404	350	94	82	70	58	46	2620
Auxerre	207	53	68	94	348	462	465	399	325	86	75	64	52	41	2532
Chateau-Chinon	598	62	77	98	369	505	515	452	372	102	92	82	71	61	2858
Langres	464	65	81	100	696	530	543	460	384	103	91	79	67	55	2954
Saint-Dizier	139	41	75	90	343	530	545	448	405	103	75	53	60	57	2825
Group III															
Metz	189	62	78	104	384	518	518	441	378	97	84	71	58	45	2838
Nancy	203	65	80	105	381	508	518	438	381	100	87	74	63	49	2854
Strasbourg	151	60	77	104	387	524	527	441	372	93	90	67	54	41	2827
Mulhouse	267	59	75	101	378	521	533	446	475	98	85	72	59	46	2948
Group IV															
Belfort	422	62	79	107	296	533	549	460	378	101	88	75	62	49	2939
Luxeuil	272	64	80	107	390	521	536	452	394	106	93	80	67	54	2944
Besancon	311	55	71	97	366	502	505	424	353	95	82	69	57	44	2719
Dijon	220	53	70	97	369	499	508	415	341	89	77	65	52	40	2675
Mont-Saint-Vincent	603	65	80	106	384	524	533	457	372	102	92	82	71	61	2935
Macon	216	51	67	93	354	487	493	407	325	89	77	65	52	40	2600
Amberieu	253	50	66	91	348	493	499	413	341	89	77	65	53	41	2626
Lyon	196	44	60	85	333	474	484	399	322	84	72	60	47	35	2499
Group V															
Grenoble (Eybens)	223	47	64	90	348	502	505	413	329	89	76	63	50	38	2614
Challes-les-Eaux	291	52	70	98	378	524	533	441	363	98	80	68	55	43	2797
Bourg-Saint-Maurice	865	62	81	111	417	533	595	485	409	105	93	81	68	56	3096
Lus-la-Croix-Haute	1037	81	96	123	426	580	586	513	468	127	115	103	91	80	3339
Embrun	870	52	71	100	387	539	533	443	369	99	87	75	63	52	2870
Group VI															
Millau	409	37	43	77	309	434	443	373	325	87	76	65	53	42	2374
Gourdon	205	32	48	71	288	412	412	340	270	72	62	52	42	31	2132
Le Puy-en-Velay	714	62	77	103	375	511	521	391	353	103	96	84	72	61	2905
Saint-Etienne-Boutheon	399	52	68	93	351	471	487	393	353	96	85	74	62	51	2636
Clermont-Ferrand	329	48	53	87	333	455	462	393	332	89	78	67	56	46	2509
Vichy	430	46	62	86	333	456	465	393	332	89	78	67	56	45	2509
Limoges	282	53	67	89	327	450	446	385	338	93	83	73	63	53	2520

TABLE C.5 – Continued

	Altitude (m)	October 1–10	11–20	21–31	Nov.	Dec.	Jan.	Feb.	Mar.	April 1–10	11–20	21–30	May 1–10	11–20	Total from Oct. 1 to May 20
Group VII															
Chateauroux	160	45	60	84	324	437	443	376	319	85	74	63	52	41	2403
Bourges	157	47	62	86	330	449	449	382	325	87	76	65	53	42	2453
Nevers	176	55	69	93	342	459	434	393	341	94	82	70	58	46	2536
Romorantin	80	59	65	90	345	443	440	373	329	88	77	66	56	46	2467
Tours	96	31	50	77	324	431	428	365	316	85	74	63	52	42	2338
Orleans-Bricy	125	52	67	91	342	456	456	387	338	91	80	69	57	46	2532
Group VIII															
Chartres	155	54	69	94	351	459	459	393	347	94	83	72	61	50	2586
Paris-Orly	89	52	66	91	345	453	353	387	335	88	77	66	54	43	2510
Paris-Montsouris	78	48	63	87	333	440	440	376	319	84	72	60	48	36	2406
Paris-Le-Bourget	52	50	65	89	336	443	446	382	332	88	76	64	52	41	2464
Beauvais	101	60	74	98	360	462	468	404	366	100	89	78	66	55	2680
Group IX															
Rouen	68	55	70	94	343	443	449	387	347	98	86	75	64	53	2569
Cap-de-la-Heve	101	45	59	81	306	397	406	365	338	98	87	76	66	56	2380
Caen	66	53	66	87	318	412	415	365	344	100	89	78	67	57	2451
Alencon	140	60	74	98	354	446	453	387	347	99	98	77	66	56	2605
Cherbourg-Chant	8	41	52	69	255	339	350	323	316	91	83	75	67	58	2118
Group X															
Dinard	65	44	57	78	291	375	381	337	322	94	84	74	65	55	2257
Ile de Brehat	25	35	46	64	243	319	335	309	304	90	82	74	66	58	2025
Ile d'Ouessant	27	39	47	61	219	285	307	281	282	85	78	71	65	58	1878
Brest-Guipavas	98	36	50	71	276	353	357	329	310	95	87	79	72	65	2180
Lorient (Lann-Bihoue)	42	46	57	75	270	372	363	329	307	87	78	69	60	50	2163
Rostrenen	262	54	65	84	300	403	403	362	357	101	92	83	75	66	2445
Rennes	35	46	60	82	306	397	397	345	313	89	79	69	59	50	2292
Group XI															
Le Mans	52	50	64	87	324	434	428	371	332	90	79	68	56	45	2428
Angers	54	46	60	72	312	419	409	354	313	86	75	64	54	44	2308
Nantes	26	40	54	75	291	397	391	343	298	82	72	62	52	42	2199
Ile d'Yeu-Saint-Sauveur	32	22	39	56	324	326	332	301	279	77	67	57	48	38	1877
La Rochelle	7	31	45	67	273	378	332	329	285	79	68	57	46	35	2025
Poitiers	118	45	60	83	318	425	425	365	316	87	76	65	54	44	2363
Cognac[a]	30	31	53	57	265	411	442	327	301	77	65	45	41	42	2157
Angouleme[b]	83	42	46	64	288	419	366	374	335	98	76	47	50	58	2263
Group XII															
Bordeaux	47	29	44	66	276	384	378	320	270	74	64	54	44	34	2037
Cazaux	24	26	40	61	255	357	357	309	263	70	61	52	43	33	1927
	61	28	44	67	282	397	403	326	273	72	62		41	31	2078

					172	231	293	284	229	66	58	40	42	34	1610
Pau	189	31	45	65	270	381	381	320	270	75	65	57	48	33	2048
Saint-Girons	411	30	47	71	297	423	428	351	295	85	75	65	55	45	2222
Toulouse-Blagnac	151	23	40	63	276	400	403	331	273	74	63	52	41	31	2070
Group XIII															
Carcassonne	123	19	35	57	252	369	384	315	263	69	58	47	37	25	1930
Perpignan	43	20	16	44	183	291	310	247	208	49	39	29	19	9	1464
Montpellier	5	17	31	50	222	353	372	303	257	66	55	44	33	22	1825
Nimes	52	15	28	49	234	357	369	298	242	60	49	38	27	16	1782
Group XIV															
Montelimar	73	28	44	67	282	415	425	343	276	72	60	48	36	25	2121
Orange	53	21	37	60	264	391	397	323	260	66	54	42	30	19	1964
Marignane	3	16	26	47	225	350	372	306	248	64	52	40	8	16	1790
Toulon	28	23	11	28	159	260	283	245	211	55	45	34	23	13	1356
Saint-Raphael	2	20	20	37	183	295	322	270	236	62	51	40	29	18	1583
Nice	5	21	12	30	171	279	301	250	220	58	47	36	25	15	1465
Bastia	10	22	12	29	165	273	295	247	229	63	52	41	30	20	1478
Ajaccio (Campo del Oro)	4	21	15	33	171	273	293	255	236	66	56	46	35	25	1531

a Town added 1961–62 — averages of 4 yr (1960–64) are given as reference.
b Town added 1961–62 — averages of 3 yr (1961–64) are given as reference.

TABLE C.6 Average Minimum Outside Temperatures of French Departments

	Temp. (°C)		Temp. (°C)		Temp. (°C)		Temp. (°C)
Ain	−8	Dordogne	−5	Loiret	−7	Haute-Saone	−10
Aisne	−7	Doubs	−10	Lot	−6	Saone-et-Loire	−8
Allier	−8	Drome	−6	Lot-et-Garonne	−5	Sarthe	−7
Alpes (Basses)	−9	Eure	−7	Lozere	−6	Savoie	−10
Alpes (Hautes)	−9	Eure-et-Loir	−7	Maine-et-Loire	−7	Haute-Savoie	−12
Alpes-Maritimes		Finistere	−4	Manche	−4	Seine[a]	−7
Inland	−9	Gard	−5	Marne	−10	Seine-Maritime	−7
Coast	−2	Haute-Garonne	−5	Haute-Marne	−10	Seine-et-Marne	−7
Ardeche	−6	Gers	−5	Mayenne	−7	Seine-et-Oise[a]	−7
Ardennes	−11	Gironde		Meurthe-et-Moselle	−11	Deux-Sevres	−7
Ariege	−5	Inland	−5	Meuse	−11	Somme	−9
Aube	−10	Coast	−4	Morbihan	−4	Tarn	−5
Aude	−5	Herault	−5	Moselle	−11	Tarn-et-Garonne	−5
Aveyron	−6	Ille-et-Vilaine	−5	Nievre	−7	Var	
Bouches-du-Rhone	−5	Indre	−7	Nord	−9	Inland	−5
Calvados	−5	Indre-et-Loire	−7	Oise	−7	Coast	−2
Cantal	−8	Isere	−10	Orne	−7	Vaucluse	−6
Charente	−5	Jura	−10	Pas-de-Calais	−9	Vendee	
Charente-Maritime		Landes		Puy-de-Dome	−8	Inland	−5
Inland	−5	Inland	−5	Pyrenees-Atlantiques		Coast	−4
Coast	−4	Coast	−4	Inland	−5	Vienne	−7
Cher	−7	Loir-et-Cher	−7	Coast	−4	Haute-Vienne	−8
Correze	−6	Loire	−8	Hautes-Pyrenees	−5	Vosges	−11
Corse	−8	Haute-Loire	−8	Pyrenees-Orientales	−4	Yonne	−8
Cote-d'Or	−4	Loire-Atlantique		Bas-Rhin	−14		
Cotes-du-Nord	−2	Inland	−5	Haut-Rhin	−14		
Creuse	−8	Coast	−4	Rhone	−8		

SOURCE: Association technique des industries du gaz en France "Chauffage au gaz des locaux d'habitation et service d'eau chaude associée," Collection des techniques gazières. Ed. Société du journal des usines à gaz, 1975.
[a] In 1968, Seine and Seine-et-Oise were divided into seven departments: Essonne, Hauts-de-Seine, Seine-St.-Denis, Val-de-Marne, Val-d'Oise, Ville-de-Paris, and Yvelines.

TABLE C.7 Summary of Insulation Recommendations for Winter Nonelectric Heating made by Centre Scientifique et Technique du Batiment[a]

Winter	Insulation Coefficient G (kcal/m³ · h · °C)						
	Apartments				Individual Houses		
	Current Housing	Corner Housing	1st Floor or Upper Floor Housing	1st Floor or Upper Floor Housing/Corner	Single Unit House	Duplex or Housing at End of Row	Row Housing at End of Row
Climate zone A	0.95	1.2	1.3	1.55	1.9	1.7	1.5
	(0.7)	(0.8)	(0.9)	(1)	(1.1)	(1)	(0.9)
Climate zone B	1.1	1.35	1.6	1.8	2.2	2.0	1.8
	(0.75)	(0.85)	(1)	(1.1)	(1.25)	(1.15)	(1.05)
Climate zone C	1.2	1.5	1.75	2.0	2.4	2.2	2.0
	(0.8)	(0.9)	(1.1)	(1.2)	(1.4)	(1.3)	(1.2)

TABLE C.7 – Continued

Coefficient k of Opaque Partitions (kcal/m²·h·°C)

Winter	Roof	Floor in Individual Attic		Outside Walls of Apt.	Corner Apts.	Individual Walls	Individual Walls Against Garage	In Open Area	On Foundation Enclosure, Non/Weakly Ventilated	On Foundation Enclosure, Poorly Ventilated	On Foundation Enclosure, Well Aired	On the Ground	On Individual Cellar
Climate zone A	0.8	0.9	> 600 kg/m²	1.5	1.5	1.5							
			451–600	1.4	1.4	1.4							
			351–450	1.3	1.3	1.3	1.5	0.7	Insulation on Periphery	1.5	1.0	Insulation on Periphery	1.0
			251–350	1.2	1.2	1.2							
			151–250	1.1	1.1	1.1							
			< 150	1.0	1.0	1.0							
Climate zone B	1.0	1.2	> 600 kg/m²	1.7	1.5	1.5							
			451–600	1.6	1.4	1.4							
			351–450	1.5	1.3	1.3	1.6	0.8	Insulation on Periphery	2.0	1.2	Insulation on Periphery	1.2
			251–350	1.4	1.2	1.2							
			151–250	1.2	1.1	1.1							
			< 150	1.0	1.0	1.0							
Climate zone C	1.2	1.5	< 600 kg/m²	1.9	1.7	1.7							
			451–600	1.8	1.6	1.6							
			351–450	1.7	1.5	1.5	1.7	0.9		1.4	1.4		1.4
			251–350	1.5	1.4	1.4							
			151–250	1.3	1.2	1.2							
			< 150	1.0	1.0	1.0							

SOURCE: Association technique des industries du gaz en France, "Chauffage au gaz des locaux d'habitation et service d'eau chaude associée." Collection des techniques gazières. Ed. Société du journal des usines à gaz, 1975.
a The numbers in parentheses correspond to the extreme values of electric heating.

TABLE C.8   Energy Use in Residential Buildings (1972)

	Per Unit Volume	Per Unit Floor Area
Fuel consumption	112×10^6 cal/m^3	280×10^6 cal/m^2
Electricity consumption	9.2 kWh/m^3	23 kWh/m^2
Total energy consumption	140 kWh/m^3	350 kWh/m^2

shown in Figure C.4. The length of the heating season varies from 190 days in the north to 100 days in the south.

Criteria for Current Building Practices. Until the decree of April 10, 1974, concerning insulation standards, there was no uniformity in building practices. The only guidelines are those of the CSTB (*Centre Scientifique et Technique du Batiment*) for low-rent buildings (Table C.7). Typical insulation of the different kinds of buildings can be represented by the following ranges of the parameter G with the unit kilocalories per cubic meter per hour per degree Celsius (kcal/m^3/h/$^\circ$C):

- small building, concrete, very cheap, bad insulation $G = 1.7–2.5$
- small single-family house, traditional, 90 m^2 (e.g. in
Paris suburb) $G = 1.4–2.2$
- average traditional buildings (before 1940)   house $G = 1.3–2.1$
          apartment $G = 1.1–1.7$
- very big buildings $G = 0.9–1.4$

The average volume of the house or the apartments depends on the age of the buildings:

- buildings before 1949   house $V = 180$ m^3
          apartment $V = 150$ m^3
- 1949–1961   house $V = 190$ m^3
          apartment $V = 170$ m^3
- 1961–1970   house $V = 205$ m^3
          apartment $V = 185$ m^3
- 1970–1975   house $V = 250$ m^3
          apartment $V = 190$ m^3

Actual Energy Uses. In 1972, the total volume of all the heated residential buildings was 2.88×10^9 m^3; the energy consumption for heating, cooking, and air conditioning was 322.8 Gth* of fuel and 14.6 TWh; the electricity consumption of lighting, mechanical use, etc., was 120 TWh. The actual energy use in the residential buildings for the year 1972 can be seen in Table C.8.

Total consumption by use is approximately:

- heating   285 kWh/m^2
- cooking   20 kWh/m^2
- hot water   35 kWh/m^2
- specific electricity uses (lighting and machinery)   10 kWh/m^2

Building Codes. It would be too long and too difficult to present a complete history of building code development. Two recent decrees seem to be important.

* 1 Gth = 10^{15} cal.

TABLE C.9   The Seven Classes of Housing Defined by the 1974 Building Decree

	Type[a]	Value of Ratio[b] k	Habitable Space
I	Independent	Indifferent	$V < 150\ m^3$
II	Independent	Indifferent	$V \geqslant 150\ m^3$
	Nonindependent	$k > 1.75$	$V < 150\ m^3$
III	Independent	Indifferent	$V \geqslant 300\ m^3$
	Nonindependent	$k > 1.75$	$V \geqslant 150\ m^3$
IV	Nonindependent	$1.25 < k \leqslant 1.75$	Indifferent
V	Nonindependent	$0.75 < k \leqslant 1.25$	Indifferent
VI	Nonindependent	$0.25 \leqslant k \leqslant 0.75$	Indifferent
VII	Nonindependent	$k \leqslant 0.25$	Indifferent

[a] A room is independent if (1) it is not connected to any other dwelling, (2) the connected dwelling is not heated, or (3) the connected dwelling is partitioned into rooms of less than $15\ m^2$.
[b] k is the ratio of the surface of the horizontal partitions, the sloping horizontal parts touching the outside walls, the floor of the ventilation enclosure, or a nonheated room, to the habitable surface.

- Decree 69-596 of June 14, 1969, which gave the general rules for the construction of buildings for housing
- Decree 74-306 of April 10, 1974, which modified the prior decree with regard to heating.

The purpose of the first decree is to make uniform the standards of construction in order to guarantee the quality of the buildings for the users of those buildings. The purpose of the second decree was to save energy in buildings (it was during the oil shortage). Apart from these decrees there is a code made by the CSTB which is fundamental from the architect's point of view but which is not a law.

The decree of April 10, 1974, was made by the government (the prime minister) in order to minimize energy expenditures. It called for a constant temperature of $18°C$ in residential buildings. It deals with two kinds of measures: one concerned with insulation standards, and another concerned with the regulation of heating systems.

This decree distinguishes 7 kinds of residential buildings (Table C.9), 3 climate areas, and 2 steps in the practical application of the decree. For each kind of building, each climate area and each step, it gives a minimum-allowable insulation standard G, which is in units of kilocalories per cubic meter per hour per degree Celsius ($kcal/m^3/h/°C$). See Table C.10.

Expected Effects of Decrees. The effects of this decree on the energy consumption will appear increasingly in the next years. The energy consumption for heating will be reduced by 40 or 50 percent for the residential buildings constructed after July 1, 1975. In the year 1985, between one-fourth and one-third of the residential buildings will have been built with the new standards. Therefore, the energy consumption in 1985 will be about 10 to 15 percent lower than the consumption that could be expected without insulation standards. In 2000, 50 to 60 percent of the residential buildings will be built with the new standards, and energy consumption for heating will be 25 to 30 percent lower than the expected consumption without standards.

In France, the most important impact on the economy is the reduction of imports of oil and natural gas and thereby the reduction of "the payment in

TABLE C.10 Minimum Permissible Insulation Standards by Housing Class as Set by the 1974 Building Decree (value of G in Kcal/m³ · h · °C)

| | Date Application Made for Permission to Build | | | | | |
| Housing Class | May 1, 1974 | | | July 1, 1975 | | |
	Climate Zone A	Climate Zone B	Climate Zone C	Climate Zone A	Climate Zone B	Climate Zone C
I	1.98	2.28	2.49	1.38	1.50	1.72
II	1.85	2.15	2.37	1.25	1.38	1.63
III	1.72	1.98	2.19	1.12	1.25	1.50
IV	1.55	1.75	1.98	1.03	1.16	1.38
V	1.38	1.59	1.75	0.95	1.03	1.25
VI	1.20	1.42	1.55	0.82	0.90	1.08
VII	1.08	1.25	1.38	0.73	0.82	0.95

dollars." In the year 1985, 5 to 7 Mtep* will be saved each year, which represents about \$400–\$600 million†, and in 2000, 15 to 20 Mtep will be saved each year.

Another effect of the decrees that is also very important is the decrease of air pollution of SO_2, NO_x, and CO. Burning one Mtep of heating oil gives about 14,000 metric tons of SO_2 in France; each Mtep of fuel, gas, or oil burned in a furnace gives 2,600 metric tons of NO_x (assumed to be NO_2) and 5,800 metric tons of CO.

II.C. WISCONSIN

J. Mitchell – University of Wisconsin – Madison

The designs and construction techniques used in buildings in Wisconsin have evolved in response to many factors. These include the functions for which the building is intended, the budget available to the builder, the style of the architectural firm selected, and the construction materials and labor force available. It has only been recently that energy requirements for space heating and air conditioning have assumed some importance in the design of buildings. The energy used for these purposes results from the interaction between building design and the regional weather patterns.

Wisconsin has a climate with a relatively long cold winter and a relatively short, mild summer. The heating season is approximately 180 days (6 months) long, with monthly average winter temperature of about $20°F$ ($-7°C$). The design winter temperature in southern Wisconsin is $-10°F$ ($-23°C$), and is the average air temperature that is exceeded less than 22 h each year. Wisconsin has approximately 4,500 Celsius heating degree-days,‡ which is the sum (over the days in the heating season) of the number of degrees that the air temperature is less than $18°C$ ($65°F$). This value is a measure of the heating requirements for buildings in different regions. In summer, the design temperature is $33°C$ ($92°F$). Cooling conditions, in which the air temperature is about $26°C$ ($80°F$) occur for 500 h (20 days) during the average summer.

Prior to the recent concern over energy, buildings were designed to meet the objectives described above. Heating and cooling system requirements were usually determined after the design was firm, and equipment selection was then made. The space conditioning requirements were determined following the established engineering procedures described in the handbook of the American Society of Heating, Refrigerating, and Air Conditioning Engineers (ASHRAE).

Buildings in Wisconsin reflect this lack of concern over energy use. It is difficult to accurately ascertain their total energy use, since design calculations are only for the "worst" case operating conditions, and also may not reflect changes in building operation or control.

In order to provide some information on energy use in buildings, we have conducted a survey of commercial buildings in Madison, Wisconsin. These data, in addition to the building characteristics and function, consist of the monthly utility records for the natural gas and electricity consumed over the last 4 yr. The buildings range in gross floor area from 1,000 to 50,000 ft^2 (100 to 5,000 m^2) and in height

---

* Megatons of petroleum equivalent (Mtep) $\cong 11 \times 10^{15}$ cal.
† If there is no electric heating during this period of time.
‡ Fahrenheit heating degree-days can be obtained by multiplying Celsius degree-days by 9/5.

from 1 to 8 stories. The types included are hospitals, schools, office buildings, retail buildings, hotels, and food stores. Natural gas is used almost exclusively in these buildings for space and water heating, and electrical use is predominantly for lighting, air conditioning, and office equipment.

The results of this survey are summarized in Table C.11. These results show that building function is the major determinant of use. There is no influence of building size on energy use. The energy use for space and water heating varies by about a factor of 3 over all buildings, while electrical use varies up to a factor of 80. The average total energy use for space and water heating is about 3 times that for electricity. The dollar costs associated with the average energy uses are about $0.3 and $0.4/ft^2/yr for natural gas and electricity. These low energy costs indicate the difficulty of motivating conservation measures solely by economic considerations.

Wisconsin Energy Code for Commercial and Industrial Buildings. Since 1914, the state of Wisconsin has had a building code that specifies construction requirements for most commercial and industrial buildings. The provisions of this code are enforced by the Department of Industry, Labor, and Human Relations (DILHR). Enforcement is achieved by approval of the building plans by DILHR prior to construction of the building. Until 1974, the code was primarily concerned with requirements for structural integrity, safety, and health in individual buildings. It was not concerned with energy measures for the state as a whole.

In December 1973, a committee of experts was appointed from the public at large to develop an energy conservation code which would become law upon approval by the legislature after public hearings, and upon adoption by DILHR commissioners. The Energy Conservation Committee first developed a set of emergency rules which were permanently adopted in June 1974. These rules lowered the inside design temperatures and the design ventilation requirements per person, and allowed ventilation rates to be based on the actual occupancy of a building rather than its maximum capacity. A second set of rules developed by the committee became law in January 1975. These rules raised the winter outdoor design temperatures in the state, specified maximum infiltration rates, and specified the maximum heat loss through the building's exterior surface. This latter provision was quite controversial, and was finally suspended in June 1975. The suspended rule underwent review by another appointed committee, and the maximum heat-loss rule became part of the Wisconsin Administrative Code as of December 1976.

The main effect of the majority of the provisions of the code is to allow architects and engineers to lower energy uses where feasible. As such, these provisions do not apply to all buildings, and may not apply even to a portion of a building. Thermostat turndowns and ventilation reductions are applicable to existing buildings, while the design specifications apply only to new buildings. The resulting energy use changes are difficult to determine; however, it is felt that there will be measurable savings.

The thermal performance specification sets an allowable maximum energy loss through the building exterior surface. This maximum allowable heat flow through the envelope area (walls, windows, doors, and roof) is specified to be 13 Btu/h-ft$_e^2$ (130 kJ/h-m^2).* The nature of this rule allows an estimate of energy savings both for specific buildings and for the state as a whole. The energy changes depend on resulting changes in building construction techniques and on the continued pattern of construction of commercial buildings. Both of these effects are difficult to assess.

The result of a selected survey of building plans made early in 1974 is shown in

---

* ft$_e^2$ = the number of square feet of envelope.

TABLE C.11 Energy Use in Buildings in Madison, Wisconsin

Space and Water Heating (10^5 Btu/ft$^2 \cdot$ yr = 10^4 kJ/m$^2 \cdot$ yr)	Number of Buildings	Building Type
3–4	2	Hospitals
2–3	1	Hotel
1.5–2	4	College, hotels
1–1.5	8	Offices, retail stores, schools
0.75–1	7	Offices, retail stores, schools
0.5–0.75	1	Medical clinic
Average = 1.5×10^5 Btu/ft^2/yr		

Electrical Use (kWh/ft$^2 \cdot$ yr)	Number of Buildings	Building Type
80–90	1	Food store
30–40	2	Office
20–30	4	Offices, retail stores
15–20	7	Hospital, offices, retail stores
10–15	4	Hospital, offices, retail stores
5–10	8	Office, school, retail stores
3–5	2	School
1–3	3	Church, school
Average = 15.5 kWh/ft^2/yr		

388

TABLE C.12   Designed Space Heating Energy Use in Commercial Buildings in Wisconsin

Envelope Heat Loss (Btu/h · ft_e^2)	Number of Buildings (1974)	Number of Buildings (1975)
20–30	10	} 79
15–20	4	
13–15	7	19
10–13	7	59
5–10	1	34

Average envelope loss in 1974: 17 Btu/h · ft_e^2; in 1975: 15.2 Btu/h · ft_e^2.

Table C.12. This survey showed that buildings are currently designed for an envelope heat loss of about 17 Btu/h-ft^2. A larger survey made in the summer of 1975 after the rule had been suspended is also shown in Table C.12. This shows an average envelope heat loss of 15.2 Btu/h-ft^2. Clearly, there has been increasing concern over energy use, mainly through awareness of energy price and availability. The rule, if in force, would have served to change the design of about one-half of all buildings constructed. The remainder would have met the design requirements without enforcement.

Energy projections for the state were made to evaluate the effect of the code. In the absence of the code, it was estimated that buildings would have an average envelope heat loss of 16 Btu/h-ft$_e^2$, while with the code the value would be 13 Btu/h-ft$_e^2$. For both cases it was assumed that floor area would increase in proportion to the projected population increase. The energy savings in the year 2000 resulting from the code are estimated to be approximately 0.7×10^{12} Btu/yr, or about 4 percent of the expected total heat loss through the walls. This is approximately 0.4 percent of the energy use in the commercial sector. In terms of energy, this represents a saving of approximately 7 million ft^3 of natural gas, enough to heat roughly 2,000 homes in the year 2000. Thus, while the savings are a small percentage of the total energy use, the effect on given users may be significant.

Evaluation of the direct economic impact of the thermal performance specification was controversial. It was recognized that additional costs would be involved in constructing buildings, and that these might be on the order of 3–5 percent of the total building cost. Even though the cost of the added insulation could be recovered in a few years, it forced a significant increase in first cost, which, in the current economic situation, is seen to be a deterrent to construction.

Secondary economic effects were anticipated by the glass and masonry industries. The performance specifications discourage installation of glass over large areas, and lead to increases in the cost of masonry walls by requiring added insulation. The specific economic impacts are difficult to evaluate, but in view of the current construction industry slowdown, any adverse effects were felt to be intolerable.

Summary. The construction techniques used in Wisconsin buildings have evolved with time in response to energy price and availability. The engineering and architectural professions have recognized these increased costs, and have, in general, designed buildings accordingly. Energy codes serve as a ceiling for those building owners who can afford to disregard energy prices. The savings in energy use through building codes is a small proportion of the total energy use. However, energy savings may still have a significant effect on those users who would otherwise be unable to obtain fuels. The scope of energy codes, the political processes required for their implementation, and the economic considerations all serve to make codes a controversial mechanism for energy conservation.*

II.D.   SUMMARY AND COMPARISON

The three preceding sections demonstrate the increasing concern for energy efficient building practices in each of the three regions. Standards or recommendations concerning energy losses from various types of buildings exist in each region. These standards typically represent minimum performance as determined by the standard-setters; the standards are not determined from minimization of total costs, including factors such as fuel, insulation, and interest costs.

Close examination of the three preceding sections reveals that comparisons of the standards of the regions is difficult because the bases for standard-setting in the three regions are different. For example:

- GDR — standards set for the minimum thermal resistivity for several types of surfaces (e.g. outside walls, outside walls of corner rooms, and roofs) for three climate zones.
- France — standards set for maximum heat loss per unit time, temperature difference, and volume for several types of residential buildings for three climate zones.
- Wisconsin — standards set for maximum heat loss per unit time and area (excluding infiltration and ventilation) through total building envelopes (walls, windows, doors, and roof).

In spite of these basic differences between the regions in philosophy of standard-setting, an attempt was made to compare the standards for the outside walls of buildings. As shown in row 1 of Table C.13, each of the regions is divided into several climate zones. It is noteworthy that the ranges in minimum design temperatures (row 2 of Table C.13) and the ranges in heating degree-days (row 3) used in the regions have little overlap; that is, Wisconsin has the coldest climate with minimum design temperatures of -23 to $-32°C$, the GDR is next coldest with -15 to $-25°C$, and France is the warmest with -2 to $-14°C$. These temperature and degree-day data indicate that, if energy costs, insulation costs, and other costs were the same in all regions, larger expenditures would be justified for energy conservation in Wisconsin than for a similar building in the GDR or France. However, energy prices, material costs, and other economic factors are not the same in all three regions. Therefore, the economic optimum for insulation would be different for similar buildings in each of the regions even if the climates were identical. Such economic differences can be expected to affect standard-setting although the standards are not intended to be economic optima.

* Following considerable additional discussions, a new Wisconsin code defining energy standards for all new public and commercial buildings (including residential buildings with more than two units) took effect in July 1978. It specifies maximum allowable heat flow through the envelope area according to the number of stories, e.g. 12 Btu/h/ft² for 1- or 2-story buildings; 13 Btu/h/ft² for 3-or 4-story buildings, and still larger values for higher buildings. This code also institutes, for the first time in Wisconsin, energy equipment design performance standards, e.g., combustion efficiencies. In the residential sector, a new code was put into effect in December 1978 for construction of new 1- and 2-family dwellings; it includes thermal transmittance standards. See J.S. Buehring, "Energy Conservation and Fuel Strategies in the Residential and Commercial/Service Sectors," in W.K. Foell (ed.), *Proceedings of the 1978 Conference on Alternative Energy Futures for Wisconsin* (Madison: University of Wisconsin — Madison, 1978).

TABLE C.13 Selected Data For Energy Standards or Design Recommendations For Buildings

	GDR	France	Wisconsin
1. Number of temperature zones used for building codes	3	3	4
2. Range in minimum design temperatures used over those zones	°C − 15 to − 25 °F + 5 to − 13	− 2 to − 14 + 28 to + 7	− 23 to − 32 − 10 to − 25
3. Range in heating degree days	°C Not Available °F	1,300 to 3,300 2,300 to 5,900	3,900 to 5,100 7,000 to 9,200
4. Description of conditions for the standard	Outside walls of inhabited rooms with temperature of 20°C and relative humidity of 60 percent; includes ventilating	Outside wall of apartment with nonelectric heating in low-rent buildings[a]	Current Standard Heat loss (excluding infiltration and ventilation) through total building envelope (walls, windows, doors, and roof). Indoor temp. of 19.4°C. Applies to commercial buildings and apartment buildings with 4 or more units. ASHRAE Standard 90-75 (not currently used but may be modified for use in Wisconsin) Minimum thermal performance for new buildings. Indoor temp. of 22°C. Applies to outside walls under Wisconsin climate conditions.

391

TABLE C.13 – Continued

	GDR	France	Wisconsin			
			Standard for maximum heat loss: 41 W/m² (13 Btu/h · ft²)	Standard for maximum conductance (W/m² · °K):		
				Detached one- or two-family units	Other residential buildings 3 stories or less	All other buildings over 3 stories
5. Published standard or recommendation converted to common units.	Standard for minimum resistivity 0.50 m² · °K/W for warmest zone 0.70 m² · °K/W for coldest zone	Recommendation for maximum conductance related to wall characteristics: 1.2–2.2 W/m² · °K for warmest zone 1.2–1.7 W/m² · °K for coldest zone[a]				
			warmest zone	1.1	1.5	1.8
			coldest zone	0.97	1.2	1.6
6. Rough estimates of allowable heat loss for outside wall of two-story apartment building (W/m² · °K)						
warmest zone	2.0	1.2–2.2[a]	1.3[b]		1.5	
coldest zone	1.4	1.2–1.7[a]	1.1[b]		1.2	

SOURCES: (1) The three previous sections, prepared by engineers from each of the regions, and (2) American Society of Heating, Refrigerating, and Air Conditioning Engineers (ASHRAE) Standard 90-75.

NOTE: To convert W/m² · °K to Btu/h · ft² · °F, multiply by 0.176.

[a] The maximum allowable heat loss per unit time, temperature difference, and volume was reduced by 30 to 40 percent on July 1, 1975. The standards used in this table were obtained from the Rhone-Alpes section and correspond to the May 1974 insulation standards. Thus, the values shown here for France are higher than current values.

[b] To estimate the maximum heat loss for an apartment building outer wall meeting the Wisconsin standard, the following assumptions were used: indoor temperature of 67°F, two-story apartment building, story height of 10 ft, four apartments per building, 900 ft² per apartment, and roof conductance (Btu/h · ft² · °F) of 0.04 in the coldest zone and 0.05 in the warmest zone.

392

A description of the conditions for the standards for outside walls of buildings are listed in row 4 of Table C.13. The actual standards or recommendations are listed in row 5. Two different standards are listed under the Wisconsin column. The first is the current standard being used by the Department of Industry, Labor, and Human Relations. The second is the standard recommended by the American Society of Heating, Refrigerating, and Air Conditioning Engineers (ASHRAE). The ASHRAE standards or a modified set of standards similar in structure to them may be used in Wisconsin in the future.

Out of the many possibilities for comparison between the regions, the allowable heat loss through an outside wall of a two-storey building was arbitrarily selected in row 6. The assumptions and qualifications listed in the table should be carefully noted. Since there are so many differences in assumptions and techniques, the similarity of the overall results exhibited in row 6 is surprising. In each of the regions, less heat loss is allowed (more insulation is required) in the colder zone than in the warmer zone. The allowable heat losses appear to have some relationship to the climate data. These standards can be expected to change from time to time, as energy costs continue to climb and closer scrutiny is given to energy practices in construction. As indicated in a footnote to Table C.13, the French standards have already become more strict than those shown in the table.

III.   ENERGY-RELATED PRICING PRACTICES

The following sections on energy prices and pricing policy in France, the German Democratic Republic, and the United States, reveal many differences in institutions, policy goals, and political constraints. Despite these obvious differences, what are revealing are the common themes that develop in each of the next three sections.

The most notable is that in each region, price levels were found to be at inappropriate levels, with the common realization that prices needed to be adjusted on a continuing basis to meet the needs of the changing resource, economic, social, and political situation. Another common theme was the recognition of the high capital costs involved in supplying energy and the need to guarantee the fiscal soundness of the energy supply sector, whether private or public, so that it can compete in the financial markets. A related theme was the commonly recognized principle of marginal or incremental cost pricing which was seen as a necessary condition to achieve economic efficiency. In each of the countries, however, this principle was qualified in application by the reality of numerous constraints and trade-offs. Finally, each region is shown to be highly sensitive to and influenced by changes in the international energy markets.

Any comparison of pricing in the three countries also requires recognition of the differences in the three regions. In both France and the GDR, the regulatory authorities are national and centralized. The United States has both national and state regulatory control. In addition, different regulatory bodies have responsibility for the various energy types. It is perhaps this characteristic combined with the private ownership of the energy supply industry in the United States which has led to the split between principle and policy. In the GDR and France, the principles and policy are more closely related although clearly not the same for the two regions.

In the GDR, the consumer is protected by fixed prices in energy and industry bears the brunt of the price increases. France exhibits the opposite tendency — the competitive position of industry is protected with lower energy prices than for the domestic sector. In the United States, a clear pattern emerges only in the form of the consistency with which various interests jockey for position. To reiterate a previous point, however, none of these pricing arrangements were found to be satisfactory and in each nation, change in prices and pricing policy is continuing.

III.A. THE GERMAN DEMOCRATIC REPUBLIC

L. Jordan – Institut für Energetik

In the German Democratic Republic, price control is operated and supervised by the designated public authorities. These authorities have to enforce and supervise the application of the principles of state-controlled price policy, which has been defined and decided by the government under the direction of the Socialist Unity Party (SED), the leading political party. Central controlling power has been delegated to a Price Board headed by a minister, who is directly responsible to the Council of Ministers for the implementation of the state-controlled price policy.

One of the most important principles which is never ignored by the party executives and the government is the stability of consumer goods retail prices and of charges for services to the population. The Council of Ministers has decided on a policy published in the Official Gazette of the GDR, committing all public authorities and economic executive bodies within their fields of activities to invariable observance of this socioeconomic principle. Supervision is conducted by the public authorities themselves with price supervising committees set up by the Supervisory Bureaus attached to the public authorities at all levels.

Other general principles of the price policy pursued in the GDR concern

- Serious consideration and efficient planning of necessary price variances
- Centralized decision-making concerning steps to alter prices on the basis of cost calculation, in terms of the productive sector of the national economy and in terms of the consequences for the consumer (central price concept)
- Close approximation of prices to the estimated value of the socially necessary expenditure of labor for products and services
- Economic stimulation applied to supplying and consuming enterprises, with the aim of encouraging objectives of national economic importance (e.g., establishing a predefined energy demand structure or efficient use of energy), with the price acting as an economic incentive
- The binding character of any newly-fixed price for all producers and consumers of products and services

The price policy pursued after World War II and also after the GDR was set up in 1949 is based on the principle of maintaining the prices (frozen prices) that were valid in 1944 and after, and exceptions have been made only in individual cases where alterations were reasonable (but not in the energy supply industry). At the end of the 1950s and early in the 1960s, economic and organizational developments in the GDR made it necessary to evaluate the material asset, i.e. capital goods and current funds, and the results of material production in new terms. The gap between cost and prices has become so wide in the past 15 to 20 yr that the prices obtained for primary industry products has in many cases not even covered costs. This experience at last led to the preparation and step-by-step execution of an industrial price reform (IPR) for the national economy of the GDR. The first stage of the IPR, which already included the energy supply industry, started April 1, 1964. It resulted in an increase in energy prices of, on the average, 60 to 80 percent. Thus, the objective of IPR, to establish the principle of economic efficiency (recovering of costs and generation of profits) in individual enterprises and corporations, was achieved.

The very name of the IPR indicates that only the prices to industrial producers were altered. Prices of consumer goods to be paid by the public remained constant. In this way the socio-economic principle of price control was defined and consistently applied in close cooperation with the other general principles stated above.

In the course of further economic progress in the GDR, there has been increasing awareness that the financial means required to renew and indefinitely extend the productive fund, i.e. capital goods and current funds, would in the future have to be provided by the enterprises and corporations themselves; responsibility would rest with the individual management. This arrangement, which is still fully valid, was defined as the principle of self-generation of the financial means needed for extended production. It increases the scope of individual responsibility born by the directors of enterprises and corporations, and economic executive bodies for organizing and financing the reproduction process as far as the departments they head are concerned. In the energy supply industry, this problem is of particular importance for price fixing in view of the very high funding requirements involved in energy production or generation and supply.

Any enforcement of the principle stated above, concerning self-generation of the financial means needed for extended reproduction, requires, however, that the share of profits contained in the price has to be calculated in consideration of the productive funds already advanced. For the energy supply industry this arrangement actually results in relatively low fund-related profitability rates as compared with the average calculated for all other industries within the national economy. The profitability rates related to cost-pricing, however, are substantially above the national economic average. This situation is due to the ratio of fund expenditure to cost-price, which in turn can be related to the high funding requirements that mark the energy supply industry.

On the basis of the knowledge discussed above, energy supply prices were calculated in the years from 1968 to 1970 for the 1971−75 five-year plan period. These energy supply prices were calculated and fixed according to the general principles governing state-controlled price policy and price setting, previously explained, with the following additional guidelines relating to energy supply price policy:

● Very close approximation of energy supply prices to the socially necessary expenditure of labor for energy supplies

● Approximate calculation of the socially necessary expenditure of labor from the average cost in the industry and the previously centrally fixed average fund profitability rate, as related to the entire national economy

● Consideration of necessary cost-price deviation in view of actual conditions in the 1971−75 five-year plan period (e.g., relative price for fuel oil and city gas)

● Avoidance of subsequent price alternations in the energy-intensive industries within the national economy in the 1971−75 five-year plan period

● Prevention of any price rises affecting the population, religious communities, and other consumers; reduced price increases for agricultural enterprises (increase up to the industrial price level planned for December 31, 1970, according to IPR)

● Freezing the new energy supply prices for the first time ever, for a period of at least 5 yr (up to December 31, 1975).

The energy supply prices worked out according to these guidelines were declared binding for the 1971–75 five-year plan period by the Council of Ministers. Changes in the price levels of energy were associated with some changes in rate schedules. This did not result, however, in any breakthrough with respect to the required simplification of the rate system (above all for electric energy) which has been sought for years. The prices and rate schedules were substantially altered in proportion to the price level that had developed for the energy supply involved. Supply types were maintained with the only changes concerned with the relation between price levels of various substitutable energy supplies.

On the basis of price analyses drawn up for the years 1972 and 1973 and of investigation into the effectiveness of the energy prices, which are taken from 1975 for the 1976–1980 period, an "energy supply price concept for the 1976–1980 period" was worked out. The expenditue and price calculations carried through led to further substantial alteration in energy supply prices beginning January 1, 1976. These price alterations were approved in March 1975 by the GDR Council of Ministers.

When the new energy prices were calculated, the following special principles were applied to energy supply price determination:

● The socially necessary expenditure of labor for the supply of energy, calculated for the year 1985 with the aid of the reproduction model of the GDR energy supply industry, served as the basis or starting point for all price calculations.

● In addition, the development trends of foreign trade expenditure for the import of energy in the next 10 yr were taken into account.

● Necessary value-price deviations, which result from the application of the particular energy form and from the ratio of value to utility (e.g. in the case of city gas) should be considered.

● No price alterations should affect the population, religious communities, agriculture (to some extent), and other consumers specified in the price regulations.

● There should be payment of product-related subsidies out of the public budget for energy suppliers who supply consumers allowed to pay low prices and for energy suppliers whose industrial sales price has been specified so that it is below the socially necessary expenditure of labor (e.g. in case of brown coal and coke).

● Calculated energy prices should for the first time be oriented towards long-term applicability, i.e., over a period of about 10 yr.

This energy price alteration has been connected with a rearrangement of price lists and rate structure. These prices and rate structures are expected to be more intelligible and easier to apply.

III.B.   FRANCE

Daniel Blain – Délégation Générale à l'Energie, Ministère de l'Industrie

In France, the production, transportation, and distribution of gas, electricity, and coal are primarily supplied by public firms. In addition, the state also possesses regulatory control of the petroleum industry. Within this general context, the prices of energy can be considered as being administered; their determination is subject to economic fluctuations, financial factors, and international constraints. The past development of energy prices allows us to discern a number of principles which are applied in the setting of energy prices.

Principles for Setting Energy Prices

In an economy operating at the optimum, the prices of goods are equal to marginal costs. From a dynamic perspective, one must consider the marginal costs of medium-range development. Under marginal cost pricing, whatever the market situation, monopoly or more or less perfect competition, the choice of firms and consumers are properly directed and waste is avoided. For more than a decade, this principle has served as a guideline for the general orientation of energy price setting. For example, during the years from 1960 to 1970, energy prices decreased, in constant prices, due to the decrease in the price of imported energy and increases in productivity. Moreover, the structure of prices for a given energy commodity for different uses is similar to the structure of the development costs. The best example of this is price setting for residential, service, and industrial uses of electricity.

The problem of administering prices is made more complex when constraints or economic objectives are taken into account. These constraints lead to modification of the structure and the level of some prices. Thus the policies of regulation may lead, during periods of increasing inflation, to postponement of certain price increases. The goal of ensuring the competitive position of French industry justifies the desire to adjust energy prices for large industrial consumers to the price level found in other countries. Finally, the consideration of external costs such as those relating to employment, the environment, or security of supply, may justify the price difference found between the production level and the consumer level; these differences are effected by means of taxes or subsidies.

Administrative Procedures Employed for Setting Energy Prices

The firms in the energy sector are placed under the dual guardianship of the Ministry of Economy and Finances which officially publishes energy prices — the tariffs for public gas and electricity utilities, and the maximum price (scale price) for coal and petroleum industries. From the level of prices previously set, firms can request a rate change for reasons such as variations in the price of imported energy, increases in production costs related to the increase of the general level of prices and salaries, or due to difficulties in financing new investments. The firm's request is examined by the public authorities who establish new prices taking into account the particular situation of the firm and the general economic climate. The price adjustments are established by agreement between the firms and the regulating authorities. The final decision results in a compromise between the general principle of marginal cost and the realities of economic fluctuations or permanent constraints. Thus, during a period of inflation the increase of administered prices tends to lag behind that of the general level of prices and results in a later recovery of costs.

Increase of Energy Prices Since the End of 1973

At the end of 1973, the price of crude petroleum tripled from 90 F/ton to 270 F/ton.* This increase justified an increase in the price of refined petroleum

* A franc is approximately equal to 20 cents.

products of 198 F/ton. The price setting of petroleum products is complex because they are linked products obtained by refining. For a given crude petroleum price, the price of each product will be within a broad range which is determined by the technical costs of conversion by cracking. When considering these costs on a short-term basis, these technical costs do not play a role because new conversion facilities cannot be rapidly added.

The increases in price decided upon at the end of 1973 and at the beginning of 1974 were determined by the global energy prices and policy, and by international constraints. During such periods of inflation and instability in foreign trade, it seemed desirable to minimize the financial pressure on industry in order to preserve competition, and instead to put the larger price increase on fuels purchased for private (household) use. Thus there was a rise of 125 F/ton for residual fuel oil, 160 F/ton for gas and oil, and 400 F/ton for motor fuels. Such a price increase structure was made possible by the fact that the other European countries adopted a similar policy. In fact, significant price divergences between various countries would have resulted in grave perturbations in the exchange of refined products.

The rise in petroleum product prices had two consequences: on the one hand they perceptibly increased the production costs for large users, and in particular for central power stations, and on the other hand they created distortions in the combustion fuel market and encouraged the consumer to switch to gas or coal since the prices of these two fuels had not changed. This orientation was certainly desirable for medium-range planning but could not be immediately realized for lack of availability of gas and coal.

The setting of energy prices at the beginning of 1974 took into account the technical and economic constraints peculiar to the energy sector and also general economic constraints, particularly the inflation problem. Thus the first electricity, gas and coal price increases were lower than they theoretically could have been. The increases in electricity prices were below the increase in production costs and the rate increases were larger for the residential sector than for the industrial sector. Similarly, the increases in price of industrial and residential gas were below those for residual fuel oil and residential fuel oil.

During the latter part of 1974 and 1975, new increases in energy prices were instituted which made the prices for diverse energy commodities more consistent. It should be noted that at the time of new increases in the price of raw petroleum, there was an increase in the price of heavy and residential fuel but not of motor fuels. Similarly, new increases in the price of electricity and gas caused the industrial rates rather than the residential ones to increase.

With the rate of inflation remaining rather high, the increases in energy prices are decided upon with great caution, especially because the public is particularly sensitive to any increases. However, the increase in imported petroleum prices which appears permanent has led the government to adopt a new energy supply strategy based on energy conservation, the development of nuclear energy, the increase in natural gas consumption, and petroleum research in France.

This strategy requires an important investment effort which creates financial problems for the energy companies. Price levels should be sufficient to provide access under favorable conditions to national and international financial markets. It is through the conciliation of the various constraints and medium-range development objectives and through price increases from time to time that the decision-makers will be able to adapt the energy market to the situation created by rapid price increases of petroleum.

III.C.   THE UNITED STATES

Charles Cicchetti – Wisconsin Office of Emergency Energy Assistance

There are many characteristics one may assign to the manner in which energy prices are established in the United States. But two of them are decidedly inappropriate; they are neither established in a freely competitive manner, nor, in a consistent one. In addition, the explosion in world oil prices in 1973 greatly changed the energy pricing practices in the United States. The manner in which energy prices are established and affected by government policy in the U.S. will be discussed. There will be a discussion of pre-embargo oil prices, current oil price policy, natural gas pricing, electricity pricing, other primary energy sources, and current prospects for change.*

Pre-Embargo Oil Pricing

Despite the fact that some of the staunchest advocates of free enterprise capital economics in the United States are members of the oil industry, that sector is the most protected and favorably regulated major industry. Many people in the world have discovered the meaning of the words *oil cartel* since 1973. However, consumers in the United States have always had to confront the realities of a cartel for oil. The form of this cartel has often changed, but its effects of controlling prices and quantities has been quite real. The current OPEC-dominated (Organization of Petroleum Exporting Countries) cartel is different, due to its foreign origin, but the concepts of restricting supply to keep prices high and competition slight are normal for the U.S. oil industry.

The history of the U.S. oil cartel can be outlined as follows.

● John D. Rockefeller gained control of a large part of the refinery capacity in the United States, but was forced to break up his empire by the U.S. government.

● The governments of producing states in the early part of this century enacted conservation laws. Each state set production levels that controlled supply and helped keep the prices of crude oil, taxes to the state treasury, and oil producers' profits high.

● When the economic depression of the early 1930s hit the U.S. economy, demand for crude oil dropped sharply. Producing states and oil companies started to drop their oil prices to compete for this reduced demand. President Franklin D. Roosevelt developed and promoted legislation that formed an Interstate Oil Compact Commission. This act required the producing states to coordinate their production restrictions, and made it illegal for any state to sell oil that exceeded the agreed-upon amount. The federal government of the United States established, acting with the state governments, the quantity of oil that would be produced in the United States.

● After World War II the United States was no longer self-sufficient in crude oil production. The vast reserves in the Middle East provided an alternative source of

---

* This paper, presented at the initial workshop (November 1975) of the research project, placed considerable emphasis on policies and debates current at that time. Many of these policies and conditions have changed since then. However, the editor and research team members feel that this paper nevertheless provides one important perspective on energy-related pricing practices at a crucial time, and therefore chose to leave this paper in its original form.

reserves at very low cost. In order to protect domestic oil producers, a voluntary import quota program was established by President Eisenhower in the early 1950s. When the voluntary program failed, President Dwight D. Eisenhower established a mandatory oil import quota program which he claimed was for national security purposes. This program also established that imports be set at a fixed percentage of domestic production, and once again supply was controlled by the federal government of the United States. Since domestic production was fixed by state and federal government, and the basis for imports was the level of domestic production, this meant that the entire supply of crude oil to the United States was controlled and prices kept high.

● From the late 1950s until the spring of 1973 import quotas and domestic production were fixed by the United States in order to keep out cheap foreign imports and to keep the U.S. domestic oil producers protected from that source of competition. This meant that the United States paid twice as much for crude oil consumption as it would have paid had imports been allowed to freely enter the United States. It also meant, as some critics of the program have indicated, that the national energy policy of the United States was "to drain America first."

By the end of 1971 and early 1972 it was clear that domestic oil production in the United States was leveling off. At the same time, demand for petroleum products continued to increase at a brisk pace. This put pressure on President Richard Nixon to increase the oil imports that were allowed to enter the United States. He did this on a temporary emergency basis. This meant that the U.S. oil industry was encouraged to lobby for favorable legislation in Washington D.C. rather than search for oil in the oil production regions of the United States. It also meant that U.S. refinery capacity was built outside of the United States because of the enormous capital investment and the uncertainty about continued imports of crude oil caused by their temporary nature.

● During this same period the oil petroleum exporting countries were showing an ability to increase the posted price that was used for the purposes of calculating tax responsibilities of the major oil companies that were producing in the OPEC nations. During this period the amount of tax that was being paid per barrel was permitted to be credited against the U.S. corporate income tax obligations of these same companies for the United States portion of their business. This meant that multinational oil companies were willing partners in the OPEC price increases prior to the embargo. The taxes could be paid out of U.S. tax obligations, and, at the same time price increases attributed to posted price increases were permitted to be passed on to consumers in the United States.

● By the spring of 1973, President Nixon, under pressure from major oil companies who were unable to get sufficient crude oil for their refineries to meet the demands of their customers, ended the Mandatory Oil Import Quota Program. This meant that for the first time large quantities of nonquantity-controlled products and crude oil would be permitted to flow into the U.S. economy. At that point, the U.S. price of crude oil was about $4.25 per barrel, while the imported price of that same crude oil was only about $2.00 to $2.50 per barrel.

The 1973 Oil Embargo and Current Oil Pricing in the United States

Just prior to the announcement of the OPEC embargo in 1973, a slight decrease in the cost of crude oil in the United States was perceived. But, before consumers could gain the benefit, war broke out in the Middle East. Along with that war came the political and economic realization of the strength that the producing countries possessed with respect to world oil pricing. The price of foreign oil increased by more than 500 percent in less than 6 months. In addition, the quantity of oil that was available for consumers was curtailed.

In the United States it was initially believed that the embargo would matter very little because only a small part of the U.S. imports, which were then less than 30 percent of daily consumption, were coming from OPEC nations that were involved in the embargo of 1973. A miscalculation had been made, however, for the oil refineries that were built outside of the United States to meet the U.S. needs during the latter part of the mandatory Oil Import Quota Program were cut off from supplies and therefore could not supply the U.S. market. This increased the size of the U.S. shortage far beyond what had been expected. In addition, domestic oil prices were allowed to increase a minimum of 25 percent over the pre-embargo level. This fact, plus a decision which allowed any new U.S. oil production to be priced at the OPEC level, resulted in enormous profit increases for U.S. oil companies.

During the shortage the United States formed the Federal Energy Administration. A two-tier pricing system of crude oil was established in the United States. It also established an allocation system in order to have all the states share the petroleum shortage equitably. This was done for petroleum products as well as for crude oil. Although the embargo has ended and the petroleum shortage is less important because a slight surplus of petroleum products exists in the United States today, programs established in 1973 to deal with the shortage have still been retained. Two of these programs are being debated continuously by the executive and legislative branches of government. Both affect the pricing of crude oil, and therefore, the pricing of petroleum products.

- The crude oil allocation program requires some refineries in the United States that have supplies of low-priced, $5.25 per barrel, oil to share this oil with other refineries who have to import crude oil or purchase new domestic oil at prices of more than $13.00 per barrel. Under this program, a refinery is sometimes forced to give up the cheaper oil to a competitor and then to repurchase crude oil at more than $13.00 a barrel to replace the cheaper oil that it was forced to sell.

- The crude oil entitlement program reinforces the crude oil allocation program. Under this program, oil companies, which after the allocation of crude oil among refineries, find that they are importing or using more domestic new oil at a higher price than the average refineries in the United States, are entitled to receive a payment of approximately $7.00 per barrel from those oil companies that have refineries that use a greater proportion than the national average of low-priced old domestic oil.

Both programs, during the current period of relative oil surplus, result in economic incentives that encourage a greater importation of foreign oil and a reduction in the production of "old" domestic oil. (One check on the system is that if a U.S. oil company begins production of domestic oil, it is allowed to convert one barrel of old oil for each barrel of new oil produced and thus receive a price of $13.00 per barrel instead of $5.25 per barrel. This incentive is not sufficient to stop the growth in oil imports to the United States.)

In the 2 years since the oil embargo, U.S. oil consumption has been reduced about 6 percent. However, imports, which were about 26 percent in 1973, are around 40 percent of U.S. needs today. This means that the economic incentives encourage oil companies to import oil rather than produce domestic oil, which is in violation of the objective to make the United States independent of foreign sources of oil. While there is widespread support to reduce imports of foreign oil in the United States, President Ford has been unable to convince the Congress that the 2 programs which are encouraging greater imports should be ended.

The way President Ford proposed to end these programs was to make all domestic oil companies winners, and this is the reason for the conflict. He would do this by letting all U.S. prices rise to the price level set by the OPEC nations. Under such a plan, the higher profits dispersed among U.S. oil companies would have been large enough that the companies would have all gained. The opposition to the President has come from the Congress, which opposes such a dramatic price increase, claiming that it would encourage greater inflation and threaten the economic recovery that has just begun to be observed in the United States. President Ford and the Congress are at a stalemate, and as a result, there are rising prices and greater dependence upon foreign oil. Neither side appears to be gaining from this standoff. It is hoped that enough political forces can be brought together to end incentive programs that encourage greater imports and at the same time to establish a single U.S. price, which will not have an adverse effect upon the economic recovery that is underway.

Natural Gas Pricing in the United States

The development of natural gas pricing regulation in the United States was quite different from the policy of regulating oil prices in the United States. First, the price of natural gas paid by consumers is regulated at the state level. Consumption is regulated by Public Service Commissions in most of the fifty states. Each commission determines the cost of supplying natural gas to customers by distribution utilities and the cost is marked up to provide a return to the owners of the utilities. This is the basis for charging consumers of natural gas for the volume taken.

Distribution companies purchase natural gas from interstate pipelines. The owners of the pipelines buy the gas from producers of the natural gas, who sometimes own the pipelines themselves. The pipelines are in turn regulated on a cost-of-service basis, similar to the utilities that distribute the gas, by the Federal Power Commission. For the past 15 years the Federal Power Commission has regulated the price that pipeline owners can pay for the gas they purchase from the producers of the natural gas. The regulatory powers of the Federal Power Commission are not uniform nationwide, however. They are not in the business of regulating the price of natural gas that is consumed in the state in which it has been produced. For many years this price in the intrastate market was below the price of natural gas sold in more distant interstate markets. In the last few years, however, the price difference has reversed. This means that gas in a producing state might be sold in that state for as much as $2.00/1,000 \text{ ft}^3$, while that same gas, if sold thousands of miles away, might only be purchased for resale at about $.50/1,000 \text{ ft}^3$. This two-tier pricing has, over time, led to a situation where gas is available for intrastate demands but is no longer available to meet a growing interstate market. The most serious energy problem in the United States today is that the natural gas that had been assigned to the interstate market is presently being curtailed, as contracts to supply this gas are routinely abandoned by the pipeline owners with the approval of the Federal Power Commission.

Policy that would eliminate the two-tier pricing system is in order but there is national debate in the United States over how and at what level this new price should be set. President Ford is more inclined to set all gas prices at close to $2.00/1,000 \text{ ft}^3$, thus making all gas companies, and all gas producing states, winners.

The Congress, on the other hand, is more concerned with the effect on inflation and consumers of total deregulation and seems more inclined to set a price closer to the current interstate price of $.50/1,000 ft^3. It is hoped that rational thinking will again take hold, but it is doubtful that this will happen until the problem surrounding the natural gas shortage become more obvious to the voters of the United States. In addition to that general concern, a second concern is that natural gas policy reform will take place in a crisis situation and rational thinking will be difficult, if not possible under such circumstances.[*]

Electricity Pricing

Electricity price regulation in the United States is primarily a function of state regulatory commissions. These are the same commissions that regulate the price of natural gas in the consuming states. The Federal Power Commission plays a role in regulating the price that one electricity-producing utility can charge another when electricity is exchanged by those utilities. Most electric utilities in the United States are investor-owned utilities. State regulation of electricity pricing follows the same procedures as natural gas price regulation at the state level. The basic approach is to estimate the cost of producing electricity and then an adjustment is made to recover a fair return for the investors who own the utility. This procedure establishes the level of revenue that can be collected by the utility from its customers.

Most gas and electric utilities in the United States have practiced some form of volume discount pricing to encourage greater energy use for several decades. In the last few years this practice of volume discount pricing has come under serious challenge by consumer intervenors in regulatory proceedings. In recent times, the price of electricity and natural gas has increased due to inflation, higher capital costs, and higher operating costs related to the oil embargo of 1973. Load management and time-of-day pricing of electricity are both being considered in the United States and Wisconsin is taking a leading role.

Not all electric utilities in the United States are investor-owned. Some are owned by the cities in which the electricity and natural gas is distributed. Some are owned by cooperatives in the rural portions of the United States. Many of these do not generate their own electricity but purchase it directly from federal generating authorities. Often such public production and distribution of electricity is more heavily located in those portions of the United States in which hydroelectric power is a significant part of the electricity supply.

Coal and Uranium

Both coal and uranium are not directly regulated from a price standpoint in the United States. However, both are primarily used to produce electricity which is directly regulated at the consumer level. In addition, the price of both coal and uranium moves in concert with the price of oil and natural gas. This has meant that the effects of the Arab oil embargo of 1973 on coal and uranium prices in the United States have been quite dramatic.

---

[*] The Natural Gas Policy Act, which became law in November 1978, greatly changes U.S. gas pricing policy. It extends federal price control to the interstate market for the first time. It will also allow steady rises in the price ceiling for natural gas. New natural gas will be decontrolled in 1985. – ED.

Postscript

The United States is the most energy intensive society in the world. After reviewing in a critical way the weaknesses of American energy pricing policy this fact might surprise some. Upon further reflection, it might be concluded that the weakness of American energy pricing policy may be a partial cause of the greater energy intensiveness of the American society. American policymakers must try to learn how societies in which energy has been far more scarce, have developed sensible, comprehensive rational energy pricing policies. Efforts are being made to learn from the experiences of other countries. It is hoped that other countries, which look with envy at the high level of U.S. per capita income, will not try to imitate these foolish pricing practices, only to see the United States institute different and more rational practices.

D Models for Management of Energy/Environment Systems

INTRODUCTION*

A model is always a simplified representation of reality which reflects the status and the interest of the modeler (or of the person in charge of the modeling). Thus, one finds purely cognitive (descriptive) models, meant to improve one's knowledge of reality (physical, social, cultural), as well as decision (prescriptive) models which help a person or an institution make the best possible decision. Even in the same sphere of decision-making, the final decision varies according to the status, the functions, the temporal horizon, and point of view of the decision maker.

In dealing with energy matters, for example, one usually distinguishes between (1) the corporate models which help in choosing a sales strategy or a long-term investment strategy in a given market (coal, oil, natural gas, electricity), and (2) the public planning models of a governmental authority which identify the difficulties that could arise if the firm's strategies prove incompatible with the plans of the government.

From one nation to another (the United States, the German Democratic Republic, France), the structure of economic decision making (in other words, the totality of relations which connect centers of power) varies. One state may limit itself to indirect monitoring of the activity of firms, whereas another state actually determines the objectives to which the firms must adapt their programs. In this case, the scope of interaction between firms and the state can correspond to the boundaries of the studied region; in another case it can greatly exceed these boundaries.

These few considerations imply that no evaluation of a model can be made (except an evaluation of its internal coherence) without referring to the *objectives* and the *resources* of the authority in charge of the model. With reference to a given region (the state of Wisconsin, the GDR, or Rhone-Alpes), the relevancy of a decision model increases as a function of the self-governing capability of the region.

The IIASA comparative study provided an opportunity to appraise and compare

---

* The Introduction is taken in part from Martin and Finon.[20]

energy system models in three regions with greatly different socioeconomic characteristics and institutional structures. This comparison was valuable to each region not only in assessing its potential use of models from other regions, but as an indication of how models are tied to the policy objectives and characteristics of a region. Although each region employs a large variety of models, only the major *system-wide* descriptive and planning models were appraised. Sectoral and operations models were excluded as were site-specific models for locating and designing energy facilities. A review article is available in which a great number of energy models are cataloged and summarized, including additional models in the three countries.[2]

The following section presents descriptions and appraisals of the system models. Each of the three collaborating institutions described its own set of energy/environment models; and each appraised the models of the other two groups from the perspective of its own system and methodological requirements for planning and policy analysis. For example, the Wisconsin group identified the types of information it desires and examined whether the French models treat these areas adequately. It must be emphasized that the groups had limited descriptions of the models that they appraised. The appraisals are not detailed and there was no opportunity for misunderstandings and inaccurate interpretations to be corrected. Nevertheless, the participants felt that the procedure was a valuable one and contributed to finding new directions for each of the collaborating research groups.

I. THE GERMAN DEMOCRATIC REPUBLIC

I.A. DESCRIPTION OF THE MODELS

Peter Hedrich — Institut für Energetik

The energy sector of each country is one of the national economic subsystems which have a direct and considerable influence on the growth rate of the national economy and the increase of the national income. Therefore, it is a permanent objective to continually provide a rational basis for the provision of society with a demand-determined supply of energy. A tool for the proper achievement of this goal is the application of mathematical/economic models for optimization of the energy sector with consideration of national economic constraints. It is in the interest of society to include the largest possible system in the optimization models. According to the current level of our understanding, that kind of objective can be achieved only with mathematical/economic model systems which consider all essential economic, technological, and technical parameters, and to a limited degree, also political/economic influences.

I.A.1. Previous Developments in the Application of Mathematical/Economic Models for Long-Term Planning

In the GDR, mathematical/economic models for mid- and long-term planning have been applied with success in the energy sector for many years. From this experience, it has been recognized that the optimization of economically important subprocesses can actually only be achieved through the minimization of costs in the entire national economy. However, in the use of mathematical/economic models, only limited possibilities exist to characterize the total national economy in the necessary depth and quality. Therefore, an energy sector submodel was developed, taking into account the crucial national economic constraints. The energy sector was not built up as an administrative/technical unit. It includes all essential processes of energy supply and conversion, energy transport, and the industrial and nonindustrial energy uses, as well as the total import and export of energy over a long time period.

In the initial stage of the application of the models it was not possible to include the energy sector comprehensively in one model. Splitting energy use into industrial and nonindustrial processes could not be achieved. Included in a central model, however, in one relatively complete aggregation (but sufficient for central national planning and decisions) were all essential facilities of primary petroleum processing, heat and electrical energy production, coal mining and coal processing, the production of city gas and the preparation of natural gas, as well as the importing of solid, liquid, and gaseous fuels. As an economic objective function, the minimization of social costs was used. The model brought together the following aspects:

- The development of demand as a function of time
- The sequence of investments
- The time-dependent occurrences of investment and plant expenses
- The variable load-factor of the plants in successive periods of time
- The economic necessity for prematurely closing down existing plants
- The change in the technical/economic indices as a function of time
- The development of technology in successive time periods and the constant modernization of equipment according to the latest technological innovations
- The economic/dynamic view of the selection of plants considering the mutual influence of plants available at different time periods; i.e., the influence of earlier plants on those built at a later time, and vice versa
- An appropriately concise presentation and grouping of the primary energy production and energy conversion plants as well as the primary energy resources of the country
- The interdependency between the plants of the energy sector
- Necessary economic restrictions

The time period considered extended 15 years from the end of the current 5-year plan and was divided into multi-year sections of unequal length. As soon as this model had been found reliable in practice, models for the individual branches of the energy sector (e.g., coal mining, the gas sector, the electricity and heat sectors, and primary natural oil processing), were developed according to the same principle. A separate model was built to optimize that part of the energy demand in which a substitution of fuels is possible and which is important enough for an optimization. These models were used independently of each other for optimization of single branches. Although the results of the submodels gave deeper insights into the structure of the single branches, it was not possible to combine them in order to obtain balanced results representing the optimal solution for the energy sector as a whole. Therefore, a system of models was developed for linking the already existing models, thus making them a tool for analyzing the whole energy sector.

I.A.2. Construction and Application of the Central Mathematical/Economic Model System of the Energy Sector

For the construction of a model system, it is assumed that the combination of the advantages of all the branch models leads to a super model, which in practice cannot be managed. A method which would allow coordination of the submodels of the branches is therefore searched for. A central coupling model system is being developed that, in its entirety as well as inside each single model, complies with the same demands as the central model of the energy sector. The basic assumption for the harmony of these single results is the uniformity of all submodels with respect to the type of model used, to the objective criterion including its concrete form of application, to the time period under consideration and its subdivision, as well as to the structure of the nomenclatures. In addition to this, it was decided to give increasing importance to the regional aspect. With this goal in mind, the construction of models of the complex regional energy supply for regional units of the country is necessitated. In these models all quantities that can be influenced on a regional basis are optimized. Results for subregions had to be obtained as soon as possible, with the personnel and experience available.

Therefore the construction of the model system was planned to be done in two stages. The first stage contains (1) the modification of the individual branch models and the energy demand optimization model in such a way that they could be coupled, and (2) the creation of an appropriate coupling algorithm and the testing of this model system in the practical planning activity. In the second stage it is planned to elaborate step by step, complex regional models for political units of the country and selected cities and areas of industrial agglomeration, and seek to prove this by check calculations for selected cases. It was agreed that the step-wise designing of the single regional models already begins during the construction of the first stage and should be continued after completion. Currently, the primary stage appears in the first phase of its practical application, whereas for the second stage, a large part of the regional models still has to be worked out.

The first stage of the central model system consists of four main parts (Figure D.1). They are:

1. The central optimization model, which contains the entire energy sector in aggregated form

2. The demand optimization model, which encompasses the substitution and optimization part of the energy demand

3. The optimization part of the energy sector subsystems, energy production, and energy conversion

4. The coordination model for the direct coupling of the production optimization models of the various subsystems of the energy sector and of the demand optimization model, taking into consideration essential restrictions with respect to the total energy sector

The following strategy is used: In the first step, the energy demand of all economic sectors is calculated with the help of the demand optimization model and other research methods. The results of these calculations are produced in such a way that they can be, without contradiction, immediately introduced into the central optimization model as an essential part of the model. On this basis, the optimal energy supply and plant structure is determined by means of the central optimization model. Both models, when considered as a unit, represent an extended central optimization model. It is possible to reverse the order so that the central

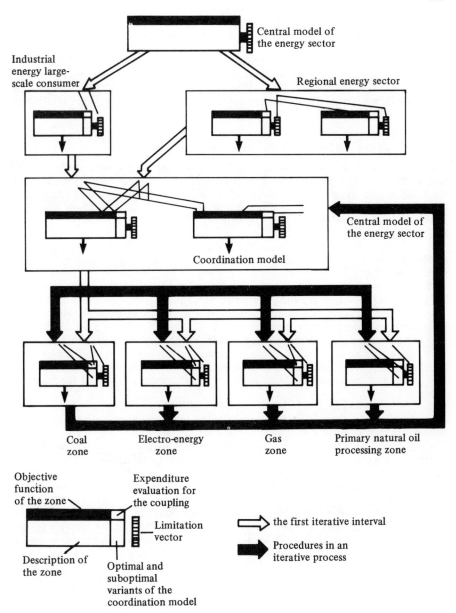

Central model of
the energy sector

Industrial
energy large-
scale consumer

Regional energy sector

Central model of
the energy sector

Coordination model

Coal
zone

Electro-energy
zone

Gas
zone

Primary natural oil
processing zone

Objective
function
of the zone

Expenditure
evaluation for
the coupling

Limitation
vector

Description of
the zone

Optimal and
suboptimal
variants of the
coordination model

the first iterative interval

Procedures in an
iterative process

FIGURE D.1   A schematic diagram of the central mathematical/economic model
system of the GDR energy sector.

optimization model is first evaluated in order to define realistic constraints for the demand optimization model. In this connection, one cannot say that the first step is the most important.

The first suggestions for the planning of the individual subsystems of the energy sector are deduced from the results of the optimization, and they are presented in the form of indices; each individual subsystem can then start with the optimization within the given limits. The results of these independent optimization calculations then flow into the central coordination model.

I.A.3. Coupling Algorithm for the Coordination of Submodels

Because of the large amount of labor and time that must be spent for the coordination of the submodels, it is necessary to carry out all formal calculation work for the balancing of the individual results and the selection of the optimal structure for the energy sector with the help of a suitable algorithm. Such a coupling algorithm must fulfill the following five basic conditions:

1. It must consistently represent the relevant conditions of the planning system in use and the general interdependency of all energy-producing and energy-consuming sectors.
2. It must be highly practical; in other words, the costs of labor and calculation time must remain within reasonable limits.
3. All variants appearing as intermediate or final solutions must, in principle, be technically and economically feasible.
4. The coupling algorithm must allow a variable application of the single models. This means it must be possible to use each single model either independently or as an integrated part of the model system, without further adjustments.
5. The coupling algorithm must allow for the active cooperation of the planning experts.

A series of "decomposition processes" for the solution of large systems is known from the theory of linear optimization. Their mathematical validity has been proved. Their practical use (applicability), however, is small, particularly with regard to the above five basic conditions. For this reason, a coupling algorithm for the practical control of the model system of the energy sector has been developed in the GDR. As previously noted, a preliminary balancing resulted from using the central optimization model to get data for the energy supply capacities. In this context, all necessary restrictions on the economy must be considered, e.g., import facilities, investing capacities, and the labor market. Considering these limits, possible ranges of energy use are determined both for the regions and for large industrial consumers, and the costs for providing the amount of energy desired are calculated. These structures serve as limits for the application of regional models within the energy sector and for a demand model of the large industrial consumers, and simultaneously prevent the appearance of unrealistic energy demand structures, either in the regions, or from the large consumers.

Using these models, primary optimized energy demand structures and primary energy supply input concepts are obtained within the established bounds. These structures, however, still need to be checked with the sectors of energy extraction. For this purpose the calculated energy demand structures are inserted into the central optimization model:

$$Z = \sum_{j,k,t} c_{jkt} x_{jkt} + \sum_{i,t} c_{it} i_{it} + \sum_{\mu} Z_{\mu}^{B} p_{\mu} + \sum_{\kappa,\tau} Z_{\kappa\tau}^{B} p_{\kappa\tau} \to \text{Min}$$

$$\sum_{j,k} a_{ijkt} x_{jkt} + i_{it} + \sum_{\mu} b_{it\mu} p_{\mu} + \sum_{\kappa,\tau} b_{it\kappa\tau} p_{\kappa\tau} \geqslant \hat{b}_{it}$$

$$x_{jkt} \qquad \qquad \lessgtr X_{jkt}$$

$$i_{it} \qquad \qquad \lessgtr I_{it}$$

$$\sum_{\mu} p_{\mu} \qquad = 1$$

$$\sum_{\kappa,\tau} p_{\kappa\tau} \qquad = 1 \ (\text{for each } \tau)$$

where

Z = value of the objective function (total cost).

c_{jkt} = specific social costs of the energy conversion plant j of the sub-system k in a year t.

c_{it} = specific social costs for the import of energy in a year t.

a_{ijkt} = specific coefficient of either the extraction or the input of the energy form i in the plant j of the subsystem k in a year t.

x_{jkt} = quantity processed in the energy conversion plant j of the subsystem k in a year t.

i_{it} = amount of energy supply i imported in a year t.

Z_{μ}^{B} and $Z_{\kappa\tau}^{B}$ = total social costs of the variant μ, which was calculated in the demand optimization model for the large industrial consumers, and of the variant κ, which was obtained in the model of the region τ, respectively.

$b_{it\mu}$ and $b_{it\kappa\tau}$ = demand for energy form i in a year t for the variant μ (large industrial consumers) and the variant κ of the region τ, respectively.

$\hat{b}_{it}$ = energy demand which is not optimized.

$p_{\mu}, p_{\kappa\tau}$ = weight factors $(0 \leqslant p \leqslant 1)$.

x_{jkt} and I_{it} = limitation for the capacity of the conversion plants and the energy import, respectively.

To avoid double counting in handling both energy production and energy conversion and use at the same time, a given variant of energy demand must be associated only with the costs resulting from the direct use of the various energy forms. When costs for the energy production are used in the calculations, they must be eliminated from the total cost of the variants.

The calculations of this model provide an initial balanced and optimized energy supply and plant structure. However, since the central optimization model works with highly aggregated indices, it has to be checked with the various sectors of energy supply represented by detailed models. These models contain reference data deduced from the central model for the amount of energy to be produced by a given sector as well as for the costs associated with the energy input. In addition to this it is necessary to calculate for each sector some other variants of energy supply that take into account the given economic restrictions, i.e. upper and lower bounds of capacities that can or have to be used are centrally determined. Within these limits, however, full freedom of choice is given. In this manner, several variants of energy supply structures are created so that coordination with the energy demand structures of the fuel consumers is needed. For that purpose another central model is applied. As opposed to the models which have been described earlier, it consists of vectors describing the output and input of the various forms of energy in the individual sectors. The model, called the "*coordination model*," has the following form:

$$Z = \sum_{\mu} Z_{\mu}^B p_{\mu} + \sum_{k,\lambda} Z_{k\lambda}^E \rho_{k\lambda} + \sum_{\kappa,\tau} Z_{\kappa\tau}^B p_{\kappa\tau} + \sum_{i,t} c_{it} i_{it} \rightarrow \text{Min}$$

$$\sum_{\mu} b_{it\mu} p_{\mu} + \sum_{k,\lambda} f_{ikt\lambda} \rho_{k\lambda} + \sum_{\kappa,\tau} b_{it\kappa\tau} p_{\kappa\tau} + i_{it} \geqslant \hat{b}_{it}$$

$$\sum_{\mu} q_{st\mu} p_{\mu} + \sum_{k,\lambda} q_{kst\lambda} \rho_{k\lambda} + \sum_{\kappa,\tau} q_{st\kappa\tau} p_{\kappa\tau} \lessgtr Q_{st}$$

$$\sum_{\mu} p_{\mu} = 1$$

$$\sum_{\lambda} \rho_{k\lambda} \leqslant 1 \text{ (for every } k)$$

$$\sum_{\kappa} p_{\kappa\tau} = 1 \text{ (for every } \tau)$$

$$i_{it} \lessgtr I_{it}$$

where

$Z_{\mu}^B, Z_{\kappa\tau}^B, Z_{k\lambda}^E$ = total social costs for the variants calculated in the optimization models of the subsystems k ($Z_{k\lambda}^E$), of the regions τ ($Z_{\kappa\tau}^B$), and in the demand optimization model for large-scale industrial consumers (Z_{μ}^B) respectively.

$b_{it\mu}; b_{it\kappa\tau}$ = demand for supply of energy form i in a year t for the variants calculated in the demand optimization model.

$f_{ikt\lambda}$ = variant λ of either the output or the input of the energy form i in a year t through the subsystem k.

$q_{st\mu}, q_{skt\lambda}, q_{st\kappa\tau}$ = extent to which our individual subsystem or region is restricted by the restraint s in year t with respect to the total energy sector or the economy as a whole.

Q_{st} = limit for the restrictions.

p, ρ = weight factors ($0 \leqslant p, \rho \leqslant 1$),

c_{it} = specific social costs for the import of energy.

i_{it} = energy import.

In order to avoid double counting, those cost elements that are accounted for in other sectors have to be eliminated from the cost factor associated with a variant of a given sector. For each sector, the solution of this vector model is balanced and optimized with respect to the total energy sector. The optimal variant may be a vector already calculated by our individual branch model or a combination of two or more of them. If such a "mixed variant" occurs, its technical and economic feasibility must be checked by planning experts.

Because of the high level of aggregation in the coordination model, a renewed application of the submodels of the sectors may be necessary in order to get a more concrete and precise idea of the optimal variant of the central model. Complete submodels are used for this purpose. In order to avoid double calculations, one just has to remove the cost factors for the use of energy provided by other sectors. The limits for an individual model are composed of all variants of energy production and use which already have been calculated for the sector represented by the model. Here the optimal variants determined by the coordination model are also included. Contrary to the conventional practice of linear optimization models, these vectors are incorporated into the decision part of the optimization model. Factors that express the importance of a given variant for the optimum of the entire energy sector are estimated and used to weight the variables. The optimal variant obtained in the coordination process is the most effective with respect to the entire system, when subjected to the conditions that must hold at this stage of the calculations. Therefore, it takes the value zero in the submodels. The use of the other variants results in a deviation from the optimum. The value assigned to a suboptimal variant in the submodels therefore is its deviation from the optimal variant. The "reduced costs" which are obtained by the linear optimization as a dual solution, can be applied as values of the deviation.

$$Z_k = \sum_{j,l,t} c_{jklt} x_{jklt} + 0 \cdot \psi_k^* + \sum_{\lambda} r_{k\lambda} \psi_{k\lambda} \to \text{Min}$$

$$\sum_{j,t} a_{iklt} x_{jklt} + f_{ikt}^* \psi_k^* + \sum_{\lambda} f_{iklt} \psi_{k\lambda} \geqslant 0$$

$$x_{jklt} \qquad\qquad \lesseqqgtr X_{jklt}$$

$$\psi_k^* + \sum_{\lambda} \psi_{k\lambda} = 1$$

where

c_{jklt} = specific social costs of the energy conversion plant l of the plant category j, of the subsystem k in a year t.

a_{ijklt} = specific coefficient of the outputs or the input of the energy form i in a year t of a certain plant and of category j in a subsystem k.

X_{jklt} = quantity processed by the plant l in a year t.

$f_{ikt}^*, f_{ikt\lambda}$ = supply and demand of the energy source i in a year t by the subsystem k; * denotes the optimal variant of the coordination model; λ denotes the suboptimal variable of the coordination model, $f_{ikt}^* \in f_{ikt\lambda}$.

$r_{k\lambda}$ = "reduced costs" of the coordination model for the variant λ of the subsystem k.

$\psi_k^*, \psi_{k\lambda}$ = weight factors.

This technique allows the selection of that structure of a sector which is more effective than the optimal structure chosen by the central model. This is indeed the case when the cost decrease in a specific sector compensates for the cost increase with respect to the entire system that arises from the application of a suboptimal variant.

A second advantage of this technique is that in cases where the optimal variant has been identified by the central model and cannot be realized technologically or economically in its formally calculated structure, there are always alternatives available, along with an indication of their excess economic costs relative to the cost of the optimal variant.

If in one or more individual sectors the process of optimization results in an improved structure of the output of and the demand for energy, the process of iterative approximation has to be combined with a renewed application of the coordination model. The optimal structure of the entire system is found when the results of the optimization for the individual branches are in agreement with the result of the coordination model. The process may be stopped when the deviation between the structure of the entire system and the structures of the individual branches is below a given tolerance parameter.

In practical applications, the number of iterative steps is low. In the calculations performed so far, the number of iterations was between 3 and 4. The fast convergence is due to the structure of the algorithm as well as to the careful balancing before the application of the model system.

I.A.4. *Application and Problems of the Model System*

The description of the parts of the model system developed so far, and of the yet incomplete areas, have demonstrated that a stepwise procedure has to be followed, not only in developing such tools for preparing decisions, but also in their application. This is important from several viewpoints. No given tool used in the process of planning can automatically be generalized to make a practical algorithm, even if it is highly practical and flexible in itself. This sounds contradictory, but it is certainly true with respect to the application of the models. It takes several years of practical experience for those who run the models as well as for those who have to interpret the results, i.e. the decision makers in the government and the authorities leading the individual branches, to find the right way of dealing with mathematical/economic calculation procedures of this kind. And even this statement is valid only if the right, applicable level of aggregation has been found. The main problem is the correct interpretation of the results of the models. One must be able to extract from the results the essential features of the real world, taking into consideration the various aggregations that have been made to obtain the results and to use them for finding the right decision.

The application of models and model systems should by no means be understood in such a way that, with the help of these modern tools, final plans can be produced by computers. Only by creative processing of the results by experts, can plans and other decision fundamentals be elaborated. These are, however, in every aspect superior to plans calculated in the conventional way, due to the higher degree of balance and optimality as well as to the governing role of the "objective function" which guarantees that subjective elements are eliminated in the planning process. Quite often, teams of scientists or operations research groups are commissioned not only for the construction and application of the models, but also for the definition of the objective function and the interpretation of the results. This is only for the first steps. Efficient decision making is only accomplished when there is close cooperation between decision makers and modelers, and when there is a mutual understanding of the necessarily different ways of viewing the given problems. By merging the two viewpoints the new quality is created which is necessary in getting away from either the complete rejection or the glorification of the new technique; and ways can then be found for its effective use.

The fact that a model system is available does not necessarily mean that one should refrain from the use of its submodels. On the contrary, an effective use of a model is only achieved when it is adapted for the solving of specific problems. Depending on the type of problem and its complexity, either the entire system, a subsystem, or an earlier version may be appropriate in finding a solution. Too much use of a model prevents, rather than promotes, successful utilization, since the optimization itself has to be done in an optimal way. Although the human role seems to be decreasing with increasing rationalisation of work preparation and calculation stage of the evaluation process (which can only be done with use of a computer), still, the creative capacity of humans increases through the possibility of people–machine–people dialogue. This is the case if people understand and shape this process such that they analyze, evaluate, and give directions at various intermediate stages, in other words, in a creative controlling manner. This is possible, but only when one has extensive experience. The simple and efficient coupling algorithm that has been developed in the GDR is especially suitable for this purpose. It provides a tool for controlling collaboration of all branches of the energy sector, which is based on the principle of democratic centralism, and for utilizing extensively the advantages of such collaboration. Previous experience shows that the coupling algorithm is suitable for coupling systems with quite different structures, if the models are adjusted in a consistent manner. From a mathematical–methodological point of view, we believe that it is possible to incorporate the energy sectors of several countries into one model system. The main difficulty in doing this lies in the fact that the economic conditions differ significantly in the individual countries. With the progress of economic integration of socialist countries, increasingly favorable conditions for such coupling will appear inside the Council for Mutual Economic Assistance (CMEA). There is still enough time available for the construction and use of such a hierarchial model system, since the availability of optimization models for the energy sector in the interested countries is a necessary condition. In future work on balancing and optimizing the energy sector, the problem of differing economic conditions should not be overlooked.

I.B. APPRAISAL OF THE GDR MODELS BY RHONE-ALPES

Dominique Finon and *Jean-Marie Martin — Institut Economique et Juridique de l'Energie (IEJE)*

The German Democratic Republic has a socialist economy with centralized planning. The models have, on these grounds, an explicit role in helping to determine the objectives of different branches of production and the standards of household consumption, within the framework of constraints imposed by political factors. Programming tools which permit the optimization of a function under constraints appear to be used; they especially formalize the energy system — one of the areas appropriate for the application of such tools. The future of the economy in a country like the GDR may certainly be more easily controlled and thus is more predictable than the future of market economies, for the parameters for the operation of the entire economy are in the hands of a single decision-making body. The normative approaches correspond explicitly to the objective function of the planning and political bodies; for this reason these approaches have a relevance that is lacking in the market economies. The absence of a market also makes the utilization of planning necessary. Therefore the use of formalized methods of linear programming is of considerable help.

It is thus no coincidence that a great number of optimization models exist in the GDR. They have been applied to the energy sphere both at the level of the sector as a whole and at the level of its component parts; one may find models for the oil, gas, coal, and electricity branches. For electricity there is also a model for the siting of nuclear equipment and a model for the short-term management of electric power plants. For coal there is a simulation model pertaining to the rail transport of lignite and so forth. In the realm of consumption there are two models: an optimization model of energy substitutions for major energy consumers in the industrial branch; and a regional optimization model for the providing of energy to the residential and service sectors by means of hot water for heating.

At a higher level one finds an optimization model for the sector as a whole, as well as a model for centralized coordination. The models developed at the Institut für Energetik in Leipzig (consumption and global models) are interrelated in such a manner that their results are consistent.[1] It is not certain, however, whether the research on branch models conducted at other institutions (Berlin, Vetschan, Schwedt, and so on) has been coordinated with the work at Leipzig, i.e. whether the structure and results of the more specific models are consistent with those of the more general models. It is certain, a priori, that the linear programming utilized in all the models assures a certain unity and homogeneity of conception, especially since most have the same objective function (minimization of costs discounted over a long period of time). But different methods of decentralized planning, inspired by methods of decomposition in linear programming (Dantzig-Wolfes's algorithm of decomposition, for example) also exist. They have been used already (in Hungary, for example), and permit one to ensure that programs situated at different levels of decision-making are consistent (for example, the Kornai-Liptak method).

Available reports and descriptions do not specify the exact relations between different institutions and ministries; they also do not specify the exact role of these models in the development of energy plans in the GDR. It would be interesting to know if the models are operational and sufficiently viable to assist planners at the present time in determining the future objectives of energy production, as well as the evolution of production plants and the consumption of energy. More particularly, it would be interesting to have some precise data on the ease of using the models, on the complexity of the information systems utilized, and on their sensitivity to the modification of parameters.

In any case, the GDR seems to have one of the most extensive experiences with energy modeling in the world, at least with optimization models. This type of experience is perhaps not generalizable to countries with market economies, at least not to those in which national planning is undeveloped (the United States, and the FRG, for example). However, it is possible to imagine the use of models in France, Italy, or England, where planning methods (seeking to minimize the costs to the society as a whole) are inspired by neoclassical theory. It is true that major difficulties impede the use of such models in energy sectors in which most enterprises are private — their opposition to all planning is absolute. At the very most, they confront government objectives that conflict with their own, and eventually get them modified so all the objectives are in harmony. France provides us with proof of this, for there the outcome of a plan has become more and more removed from objectives defined five years earlier — in proportion to the increasing power of the international oil oligarchy.

Thus, from an institutional point of view, public agencies may have difficulties in using such models. A further consideration is that the use of several of the models leads to problems of data collection, which should not be underestimated. In particular, the optimization model for substitutions of different forms of energy developed by the Institut für Energetik* would necessitate a survey of all production plants in the sectors under consideration, in order to enumerate existing equipment and to determine the method of utilizing energy. Such a survey also necessitates very precise information to which it is difficult to obtain access.

This type of model may be utilized in market economies, however, to determine the structure of production and consumption of energy which would be most efficient for the society. This does not signify that the market and state regulation would permit the attainment of ideal results. Moreover, the models may be utilized for more forecasting purposes, by using the coherence of the normative approach to explore possible energy futures. In particular, this type of model may aid in studying the future of new technological processes or new sources of energy (hydrogen, solar energy, geothermal energy, the heat pump) in order to guide investment in research and development.[†]

It is interesting to see the very great similarity between the ENERGIE model of the Institut Economique et Juridique de l'Energie (IEJE) and the models of the Leipzig Institute,[‡] although the former is less perfectly formalized than the latter. The philosophies of the two studies are identical at the level of the analytical approach to the production and consumption systems and at the level of the modeling technique used (linear programming, minimization of cost discounted over a long period, and so on).

It should be made clear that all possibilities for this type of tool have not been used in the GDR; indeed, such models permit the consideration of environmental impacts, and possibly the associated damages, in the form of social costs or of constraints on the limitation of environmental disturbances. (Only the model which deals with the siting of nuclear power plants in the GDR considers this aspect). This might be explained by the fact that concern for the preservation of the environment seems to be, for the present, less frequently expressed in socialist countries than in market economies. In regard to other political objectives, one assumes quotas on the import of fuel produced by the Council for Mutual Economic Assistance (CMEA) and other countries, as well as production goals of other economic sectors which determine energy demand (goals based on the general plan). This method of taking into account political objectives of governments in energy matters may not be directly applied to market economies because of institutional differences.

In conclusion, from a formal point of view the GDR models may be utilized in

---

* Study cited in J.P. Charpentier, p. 61.[2]

† This prospective type of model necessitates a time horizon of 25–30 years. It is difficult to transpose this distant horizon to socialist economics, for there the majority of exogenous parameters depend on public decision-making bodies, which impose their own 15-year horizon. The less rigid market economies have greater uncertainty associated with them that permits more flexibility in the choice of a time horizon.

‡ This may be explained by the fact that the GDR models are (or should be) inserted more or less directly into the planning process.

western economies without much adaptation, if the needed data exist. If they are utilized for planning purposes, they cannot help but raise certain problems between private firms and public agencies. Their main use could be in exploring futures because they give much coherence to energy planning. On the other hand it would be interesting to analyze the reasons why so few methods other than optimization are utilized in the GDR.

I.C. APPRAISAL OF THE GDR MODELS BY WISCONSIN

Wesley K. Foell – Energy Research Center, University of Wisconsin – Madison; and James Pappas – University of Wisconsin – Madison

It is important to note that the GDR efforts can be described as primarily aimed at long-term planning activities with emphasis on the energy/economy (as opposed to the energy/environment) relationship. As such, they combine demand projections, technological development estimations, and investment planning in a system that allows for analysis of alternative growth strategies. Although it would appear that there are energy-related environmental modeling activities going on in various institutions and planning organizations in the GDR (including the Leipzig Institut für Energetik), these models have not been integrated into the central energy planning models of the GDR. Consequently it is quite difficult to determine the manner in which environmental consequences and strategies enter the modeling and planning process.

The complexity of the energy/economic modeling requirements is demonstrated by the size of the GDR modeling activity and the need to use a decomposition routine for solution. Although this presents no insurmountable computational barrier in Wisconsin, it does create a somewhat more complex modeling problem in a system where centralized planning activities are the exception rather than the rule. This stems from the fact that with decentralized decision making, even if an optimal (whatever that is) plan could be structured, it would be difficult to accomplish implementation. Further, it would probably be nearly impossible to achieve the participant–model–participant–model interchange necessary to solve such a large model in a society where decision-making responsibility is fragmented to the extent it is in Wisconsin. Also, it is difficult to conceive of a univariate objective function similar to the cost minimization objective employed by the GDR which would be appropriate for such a model applied to the Wisconsin socioeconomic system. Given the mobility of many major sectors of the Wisconsin economy and the fact that Wisconsin's systems are a subset of the broader energy/environment system of the United States, a considerably more complex objective function would undoubtedly be required in an optimization routine similar to that utilized in the GDR. It would also appear difficult to construct objective functions which would include in a comprehensive manner the environmental considerations which strongly influence Wisconsin energy planning through the process of public hearings and procedures.

However, in spite of these limitations, the GDR activities provide substantial benefits for energy/environment modeling in Wisconsin. This stems from the high degree of integration involved in the modeling activities. The GDR has advanced far in examining and modeling the significant interrelationships between the various sectors of an economy. This integrated analysis provides a clearer picture of the trade-offs across the total energy sector and, hence, a more complete and accurate statement of the alternatives available to the decision makers.

The GDR experiences in these areas as reflected by their modeling approach provide much needed insights for the modeling activities of Wisconsin. The need for integration is strong, irrespective of whether one can employ an optimization procedure for systemwide decision making or must limit the modeling activities to analyzing the impacts of the behavior of various participants in the system. Also, even if a centralized modeling activity such as that employed by the GDR cannot be used as the primary decision tool, it does provide a means for both analyzing the degree of efficiency associated with projected activity patterns of participants in a socioeconomic system and for assisting in the development of policies aimed at providing signals for those participants which will lead to activities which are consistent with maximization of social welfare.

In addition to the very broad issue of the transference of the GDR modeling methodologies, it is possible to examine specific aspects of those models and activities as they relate to the question of adaption to the requirements of a Wisconsin energy/environment modeling system. In the area of demand analysis, it is difficult to visualize how the GDR system of developing a plan for future economic activity could be adapted to a market-oriented system such as exists in Wisconsin. Not only does such planning fail to account for the basis of consumption decisions in a market economy, but more importantly, its deterministic structure also introduces a serious inability to analyze the sensitivity of policy decisions to the stochastic realities of the system. This shortcoming, while serious in a planned economy, would be very deleterious for planning in a market economy where variation from the expected is the rule, and analysis of the impact of such variation on policy alternatives often provides the basis for selection of one course of action over others.

The shortcomings of the GDR demand projection techniques notwithstanding, their efforts in this area related to conversion of final product demands to energy requirements through the use of technical process coefficients appear to hold interesting possibilities for use in energy demand projection efforts in Wisconsin. That is, once a set of final demands for Wisconsin's industry has been estimated, the GDR activities in developing process energy-intensity coefficients should prove useful for converting those demands to energy requirements. This conversion is extremely important in a state like Wisconsin where energy requirements will undoubtedly play an increasingly important role in determining the future structure of the industrial sector.

Another area where the GDR activities might prove useful for energy modeling in Wisconsin is in utility investment planning. Both the individual electric utilities and the Public Service Commission in Wisconsin need an integrated planning approach in order to optimize the additions of new generating, transmission, and distribution facilities. The linking of industry with the entire energy sector in the GDR model provides a means of approaching this integation. If in addition it proved feasible to include regional environmental constraints explicitly in that type of model, the approach would be of considerable interest to Wisconsin energy modelers and planners.

II. FRANCE

II.A. DESCRIPTION OF THE MODELS

Jean-Marie Martin and *Dominique Finon – Institut Economique et Juridique de l'Energie (IEJE)*

As has been stressed in section II of Appendix B, economic and, in particular, energy activities in the Rhone-Alpes region do not constitute a self-contained economic system, since the institutional and economic structure of France is very centralized. Moreover, there are no energy models adapted particularly to the Rhone-Alpes region. The majority of the models which do exist represent French activities in a centralized manner. Therefore, national rather than regional models will be the focus of this section.

II.A.1. Models of Decision Making

The majority of these models are very specific and are relevant to operational research or the simple administration of enterprises.

The Oil Branch Models[2]   At the branch level, various oil companies have elaborated:[3]

• models which optimize the administration and the operation of a refinery, taking into account its technical characteristics, the quality of oil supplied to the refinery, and the production program imposed by company headquarters, and also taking into account the company's market in the area of the refinery. In order to do this, the variable expenses (the buying of crude oil, utilities, and various products) are minimized as given objectives of production; the specific characteristics of products are also taken into account, with the assistance of programming techniques.
• models of transport and distribution which minimize the transport expenses, as well as models of the availability of different oil products taking into account the siting of refineries, of departmental storage places, and of main areas of consumption. These models are most often regional and also use programming or variational algorithms.

Much more general and global models exist, which attempt to optimize the strategy of oil companies by planning their investments in exploration, refining, and distribution, and by optimizing their strategy of acquiring markets (fuels, light products, and so on). Again, it is necessary to remember that half of the French oil market is controlled by multinational firms whose investment policy depends on the strategy of all the other multinational firms. Strategic models do not exist at the national level in these branches.

The Gas Branch Models   Except for the models that optimize the management of a gas pipeline, taking into account the possible growth of different regional markets and the availability of gas (national resources, import contracts), and the models for the management of reservoirs with underground storage in order to handle peak demand, few models for gas have been developed in France by Gas de France.

However it should be mentioned that different methodologies have been utilized in place of formal models, either to analyze the competitiveness of gas, or to help in choosing investments.

To analyze competitiveness, the markets for gas have been studied case by case by considering the different domains where it is usable and/or used;* one determines an equivalent price for gas from the price of a competing fuel, taking into account the profit of utilization, costs of equipment, and costs to gas users. To help in the choice of investment, Gas de France studies the profit of investment projects; with the help of a criterion, it determines from a multitude of profitable operations (in other words, those for which the rate of profit is more than the rate imposed by public power) those which produce the best forecasted financial result.[4] It is in effect necessary to cut down on less profitable projects because investment credits granted by public authorities are limited.

The Electricity Branch Models   This branch has been an object of particular attention on the part of the modelers: the first linear programming models used in France were developed in 1954 by Electricité de France (EDF) for the purpose of choosing electrical investments. Since this time, the company's researchers are making progress in utilizing new computational techniques (nonlinear programming, dynamic programming, the theory of optimal control, and so on). We would like to point out that very specific models exist such as those for optimizing the nuclear fuel cycles,[5,6] for optimizing the network of electricity transport, and for maximizing the reliability of this network.[7] But it is appropriate to dwell upon more general models, in particular on models for demand forecasting and for choosing between electricity investments.

The models for forecasting electricity demand used by EDF are relatively simple and based upon extrapolation of past trends, using statistical relations of the simple or multiple regression type.[8] These relations (generally logarithmic) are used to calculate the quantities of electrical energy at the global level (or at the level of highly aggregated sectors such as the residential, service, or industrial sector) at time t:†

$$\log C_t = a + b \cdot t$$

or the models relate quantities of electrical energy to economic activities as represented by an operational economic index of the gross national product (Product National Brut or PNB) or industrial value added (Valeur Ajoutée Industrielle or VAI):

$$\log C_t = a + b \log PIB_t.$$

Forecasters at EDF have concluded that these models provide the best results and that all efforts to associate electricity consumption with other variables (such as the relative price of capital, of labor, or of fuels as compared with electricity in industry, or such as income and/or the number of households in the residential and commercial sector) prove to be unsatisfactory.[9] It is necessary to point out that this econometric approach assumes that the consumption of electricity is inelastic with respect to price, and that the market for electricity has developed in a relatively autonomous manner in a specific domain. The new commercial strategy of EDF and the great increase in the price of petroleum products, however, makes compartmentalization of markets impossible for different types of energy and makes these

---

* Some specific domains are tubular boilers, different types of drying, and the baking of clay.
† Aggregation may be according to low and high voltage consumption.

methods more subject to criticism. At the present time it is necessary to supplement econometric forecasts with the commercial objectives of a firm; further the forecasts must be supplemented by various scenarios for the future. One could never completely discard methods of extrapolation, but beyond a horizon of five years, such projections should be used with much caution.

In addition, a short- to medium-term forecasting model of the daily load curve is used to define the output power according to the hour, the day, the week, and the month, by extrapolating various coefficients which characterize important parameters.[10]

Let us now consider the models for the choice of electricity investments. An extensive bibliography exists on this subject.[11,12,13] These models minimize in the long run (1975–2000) the actualized costs of electricity production over a long period of time, in accordance with given production objectives. These objectives are determined by projections of total electricity demand that are worked out (1) with the aid of the econometric models discussed above, and (2) by a representation of this demand by means of weekly load curves. The different types of equipment for electricity production, incuding hydroelectric equipment, are explicitly taken into account and are characterized both by their capacity and by the services they are supposed to render (in other words, their functioning during the different hours of the load curve, taking into account their availability). The risks associated with hydropower and hourly electricity consumption are taken into account with the help of probabilities established from past samples; these permit one to take into consideration possible failures of the production system.

The actual model* uses the theory of optimal control. The objective function of minimization is a function of cost composed of three terms (investment, operating cost, and cost of failure†). The control variables are the quantities of equipment to be installed year by year, and the constraints express an obligation to satisfy future demand as well as the forced (or limited) development of certain types of equipment. The algorithm has two parts: first, the control variables are determined and then the optimal management for equipment of given power is defined. The program allows one to obtain an optimal equipment plan at the national level, the duration of the economic life of equipment, the probability of failure, the marginal costs of production of a kilowatt-hour (according to the hour, day, and month) and values in use. The marginal costs which have thus been determined serve to establish electricity tariffs. In order to do this, one adds to them the marginal costs of transport and distribution calculated elsewhere and a "toll" which permits the EDF to attain a budget equilibrium and even to possess an appreciable self-financing capacity.[15,16] The values of use determined by the model aid in the comparison of individual hydroelectric projects with reference equipment (for conventional thermal or nuclear energy) serving the same purpose in order to study their profitability.‡

These models of investment choices are particularly complex because the system of French electricity production is a mixed hydropower–conventional thermal (or nuclear) energy system.§ This necessitates a rather detailed representation of the management of hydropower equipment (water flows, locks, reservoirs, pumps)

---

* Called the "new national model of investment."[14]
† The cost of power failure is a nonlinear function increasing in relation to the duration and the amplitude of the power failure.
‡ This decentralized procedure is called the "Blue Note."[17]
§ The models use nonlinear programming.

during different hours of the year, taking into account the daily, weekly, or seasonal carry-overs which are available. In the model now in use, a submodel simulates the management of the electrical capacity in such a manner that the diagram of the weekly (or monthly) load of the conventional thermal capacity is as flat as possible. It is necessary to stress that among the evolving models of investment choices only the model "Investments 85" constructed in 1965 was disaggregated into five regions; the Rhone-Alpes region, together with the Mediterranean–Cote d'Azur region, constituted the southwest region of this model. The southwest region was linked with other regions by variables describing interregional exchanges. The objective was not to specify transport equipment, but rather to try to outline a preliminary scheme for the localization of production equipment, taking into consideration the location of hydropower resources and consumers.

It is necessary to point out that these investment models only deal with private costs and, in no case social costs such as the degradation of the environment arising from atmospheric or water pollution, or from land use. In other words, not a single environmental constraint has explicitly been taken into account. From a practical point of view, for example, these models have never explicitly integrated the choice of siting for electricity installations since almost all the models have not been modified for individual regions.* In France, where there are only a few rivers whose flow is sufficient to safely support the installation of numerous sources of thermal pollution, the problem of cooling prevails over transport expenditures when choosing the siting of central thermal installations.

Consideration of environmental impacts, however, has not been excluded from the concerns of EDF. These include harmful effects of radioactivity, noise, and oscillations of electrical or radioelectric origin, and other harmful effects causing changes in the air, water, and ground. Ecological problems have been evaluated with reference to a group of factors from fields as varied as physics, medicine, biology, or psychology. Some of the elements are purely qualitative or subjective and have been taken into account because of judgments or explicit or implicit choices made by alert citizens who are presumed to express the attitudes and the aspirations of the community. The evaluation of the relative importance of ecological problems posed by different production installations has been calculated using a single unit by means of "ecological points." Seven types of ecological problems have been catalogued for reference plants, e.g. 600 MW units in conventional thermal plants. Then, for a given type of ecological problem, the present value of impacts brought about by different techniques has been calculated. Finally using a comparison between the different types of impacts with the help of a preference function,[†] the total value of impacts of different installations has been calculated in terms of "ecological points." Consequently, one can evaluate the ecological gain of each action undertaken to reduce harmful effects to the environment. With this technique, one can also obtain an implicit evaluation in monetary terms of an "ecological point," an evaluation which will, however, remain more or less inexact. There is no room to dwell further upon this approach to environmental problems which, in fact, is not directly related to the EDF's models of investment choices.

At the sectoral level, no comprehensive decision model exists which is designed

---

* The regionalization included in the model "Investments 85" was not fine enough to permit this problem to be taken into consideration.
† This function of preference expresses the level of concern attached to each category of harmful effects and is based on subjective considerations (acceptable levels of change in the natural environment, quality of the atmosphere, and so forth).

to influence the decisions of public authorities or of organs close to those. This applies, too, to the regional energy system. Previously, a method of energy planning did exist and it was used within the framework of the IV French Plan (1961–65) and V French Plan (1966–70). The method included an informal model which permitted one to determine how France could be supplied with energy at the lowest cost, taking into account the objective of having a reliable supply. But this method was abandoned in 1970 at the time of the conception of the V Plan, for the public authorities no longer had command over the energy system.

There is also a simulation model for the financing of the energy sector which permits one to forecast from 1970 to 1985 (or 1990) the medium- and long-term consequences of changes in energy policy (tariffs, taxes, investments, regulation)* for the financing, employment, and annual investment needs, and the budgets of enterprises in the energy sector.

The Cognitive Models   Very few efforts have been made in France to study the French energy system with the help of models in order to better understand the system and to explore its future effectiveness. One may take note, for example, of the scenario method; it permits one to reduce the complexity of the system studied through the selection of the most important factors, and to trace different scenarios for the development of nuclear energy up to the year 2000.

At the Institut Economique et Juridique de l'Energie (IEJE) Grenoble, an optimization model for the energy sector has been developed without any ties to the public authorities.[18,19] It does not, in other words, serve directly to help the sectoral decision makers. Its goal is to test the reaction of the French energy system to modification of its political and economic environment in, for example, the

- Price of oil
- Cost of nuclear facilities
- Development of certain technologies
- Policy of preserving the environment
- Policy of making the supply of energy secure or of limiting oil dependency

The model uses linear programming to reduce all the quantified costs of investment and utilization to satisfy energy demand; at the same time the model considers utilization expenses over the period 1975–2020. The activities in the energy sphere are approached in a centralized manner; France is considered as a whole.

The system is described by means of a network in which the nodes represent economic operations (extraction, import, processing, transformation, transport, consumption) defined as all energy-related activities in the French territory. It integrates the consumption of energy with possibilities for choosing between the different forms of end-use energy. In its current version, only SO_2 emissions have been taken into consideration from among all negative influences on the environment, but the method of formalization could easily be extended to other types of environmental impact.

The model chooses between the different processes for producing different types of energy on the basis of minimizing the cost while satisfying demand and conforming to various political constraints (limitation of dependence on oil, possible acceleration of the nuclear program, limitation of the levels of emissions, and so on). The variables of the model are, in other words, the flows through the pathways of

* FINER's model constructed by D. Blain at the Ministry of Economics and Finances, No. 1972.

the figure during different years (variables of exploitation) and the equipment capacities to be created in the future (equipment variables). The different parts of the model are then composed of a subsystem of consumption and a subsystem of production.

The Subsystem of Consumption   Demand is partly endogenous to the model. In addition to the sector's own consumption, the consumption to be satisfied is disaggregated into three groups of consumers (industry, transport, domestic furnaces), nine types of final energy (coke, coal, gas, electricity, motor fuels for the transport systems, napthalene for chemistry, domestic fuel oil, fuel oil with a high sulfur content, and heavy fuel oil with a low sulfur content). One also distiguishes between two types of use, substitutable use and unsubstitutable use. Substitutable use is characteristic of heating where there is competition between different forms of energy. One considers various domains in which the characteristics of the competition between types of energies are different (use of steam and ovens in industry, heating of individual homes, and collective heating in the residential sector).

Suppose c is a group of consumers and

$$\phi = \text{a form of final energy.}$$

$x^1(\phi, c) = $ the flows of this form ϕ directed towards unsubstitutable use.

$x^{11}(\phi, c) = $ flows directed towards thermal use.

$r(\phi, c) = $ the profit from utilizing ϕ in the equipment of the consumer.

$D(\phi, c) = $ the specific energy needs of the consumer.

$U_c = $ the consumers' need for useful thermal energy.

$T(\phi, c) = $ the initial capacity of the energy-using equipment of the consumer for thermal purposes.

$X(\phi, c) = $ the capacity created between the starting date and the date under consideration.

Constraints on satisfying the energy demand are:

specific needs: $x^1(\phi, c) > D(\phi, c)$ for all ϕ

substitutable needs: $\sum_{\phi} r(\phi, c) \cdot x^{11}(\phi, c) \geqslant U_c$

capacity constraints: $x^{11}(\phi, c) \leqslant T(\phi, c) + X(\phi, c)$

The objective function of this subsystem is a part of the objective function of the total system and includes the cost of the equipment utilized and the expense of purchasing energy. We should stress the fact that the model integrates possibilities of choice between energy types at the level of final consumption, parallel to the concentrated decisions of the energy production system. The representation of substitution between energy types has nothing to do with price elasticities of consumption, the use of which is critical in every long-term model.

The Subsystem of Production   The model connects different subsystems of production (coal, gas, electricity, and oil). One can show with the network the interdependencies between operations and the ways of managing the equipment installations, e.g. the contribution of electrical equipment to the various hourly positions of the load curve, taking into consideration the different types of crude oil and different degrees of distillation. In the new version used at the present time, the model integrates low enthalpy geothermal and solar energy for the heating of buildings and the recovery of the heat from power plants.

Optimization permits choices to be made among

- Energy forms in the different competing domains
- Processes having different capital requirements
- Types of energy to be imported and types of energy which should be locally produced
- Various degrees of pollution production and the consumption process*

It is thus possible for the years 1975–2020 to obtain calculations of (taking into account the values of the different parameters):

- The balance of primary energy
- The national or disaggregated balance of final energy consumption
- The supply of equipment for production and consumption
- The activity of the various plants
- The increase of investments necessary for the adaptation of the energy capacity
- The needs for currency necessary for import of fuels
- The total expenses from year to year (whether realized or not)
- The emission of pollutants considered in the model

This type of model, which by no means replaces the decision makers, would permit an analysis of the rigidity of the energy structure, the competition between energy types in the various domains where competition exists, and possibly their margin of operation. This is the ideal tool for obtaining some idea of the future of an energy type or new technology (for instance, solar energy, geothermal energy, hydrogen, or recovery of heat from power plants) 15–25 years from now.[†] In the

---

* The limitation of emissions is developed at the national level in France. Such a procedure may seem unreasonable especially if only a single impact is considered. However, at the national level, one can fix thresholds of emissions or of waste materials which may not be exceeded, and which would be defined in such a way that the harmful effects observed by individuals would be at an acceptable level in the most polluted geographical sectors. See on this subject, D. Finon, "Evaluation of the Costs of an Environment Protection Policy on the French Energy System" in *Energy and Environment* (Paris: Organization for Economic Cooperation and Development (OECD), 1974, pp. 239–273).

† Others have a much more normative concept of this type of tool and would like to use it to calculate the optimal distribution of the various energies and to deduce optimal prices and tariffs (with the help of dual variables) which allow the guiding of the consumers' choice in the best way for the society. We prefer to give a more exploratory function to this type of tool.

The model in its new version is actually used in a very pragmatic manner in the energy sector of nine countries of the European Economic Community (EEC), with the help of a network general enough to be applied to each. The goal is to calculate at the same time the annual needs for investments and currency until 1985 and to trace various energy futures up to 2000–2020, taking into account the values of the parameters. One foresees the further study of the compatibility of the local optimum with the national optimum of the nine sectors that are integrated.

future the model will be reviewed to study specifically these new energies and techniques; it will also be improved at the level of the consumers by a disaggregation that is more driven by the type of use and other factors.*

This type of model can be (and will be even more so in an improved version) a good instrument for analyzing the three fundamental elements of the energy policy:

- the energy economy
- the development of national resources
- the choice of the sources of import

with the aid of various criteria: the lowest cost for the community (taking into account the financing problems), the least economic dependency on other countries, the reliability of supplies, and finally, the limit of ecological consequences.†

In summary, no specific models exist in the Rhone-Alpes region, but there are models covering all the French activities in one branch or one sector. This is mainly due to the institutional and economic centralization of France.

Among the existing models, the most numerous are decision models covering one branch and, for a particular branch, those using well-specified methods. They utilize, in general, optimization techniques. At the national sector level, the only formalized model that exists is without a real tie with the centers of public or private decision making.

II.B.   APPRAISAL OF THE FRENCH MODELS BY THE GDR

Peter Hedrich and *Dietmar Ufer — Institut für Energetik*

France is a country that is setting the pace on the international level in the field of mathematical/economic model application for the optimization of long-range planning of large-scale energy systems. The activities performed by Electricité de France in this field provide good examples.

It can be said that the trend of activities by the "base," i.e. in the individual branches of the energy industry, has followed EDF's lead, and resulted in advances on problems of the development of the structure of systems and energy suppliers, economy and financing, and to some extent of environmental control. Significant arrangements with the consumers have also been established.‡ A model or model system covering the overall energy industry of the country was not developed for planning purposes by France because of the existing social conditions, and the diverging interests of the individual enterprises and monopolistic groups on both the national and international level. Even the individual branches, such as those of

---

* In connection with the research developed at the Institut Economique et Juridique de l'Energie by B. Chateau and B. Lapillonne on a prospective basis (by systems analysis of the energy demand in the year 2000), this demand was studied from an analytical point of view in the consumer's sector, taking into account present and future technologies.

† The reduction of the foreign dependency, by the development of national resources and the energy economy has strong limits resulting from the criterion of cost minimization.

‡ The great variety of models for the operational control are not dealt with here.

428

electric power generation, do not apply nationwide models due to the fact that there was no undertaking of a completely monopolistic character.*

The awareness of these circumstances apparently gave rise to the objective of developing a model system of the energy industries all over the country, a system that permits long-range forecasting of strategic character in

- Application of energy supplies and their selection
- Scientific and technological development and required research and development assignments
- Environmental protection and ecology
- Safeguarding of the energy supply
- Potentials and limits of energy imports

With perfect knowledge of the interdependence of production, conversion, and consumption, the energy application processes could be applied with discrimination in the industrial and nonindustrial activities, and in households. Thus, a key step was taken. If the results obtained from these models are to serve for immediate decision making, it is absolutely necessary to take the obvious measures in the field of economic planning and to see to the situation regarding ownership, both of which have been neglected. The model in its existing form is appropriate to study the effects on the modified strategic elements and the environment, in the sense of business gaming. We are in strong agreement with the fundamental French attitude that statements of importance about regions can be made only incidentally to general consideration about the energy industry.

II.B.1.   Model Characteristics

The model serves for planning the structural variables of the energy system in the entire country; it does not carry out technological calculations. It also forecasts the determining quantities of demand and, within the framework of energy technology and national economy, the most convenient technological processes for the energy forms that can be interchanged. Thus, the limits of the system are fixed in response to the actual requirements. The model system is capable of making suggestions for strategic statements about the exploitation of national energy resources, about the most convenient structure and operation mode of the energy conversion equipment, and about the import of energy supplies. The modeled groups of statements are assessed under the present conditions for the activities within the next 5 to 10 years. They appear to satisfy the principal needs with the exception of the analysis of

---

* The development in the GDR took place in the reverse direction. In the first half of the 1960s the theoretical bases were being worked out. The starting base was the overall model of the energy industry with its sectors of coal, gas, electric power, oil, and public district heating, as well as imports and exports. In 1967 the National Planning Board adopted this model for application in long-range national planning; the model was also adopted by the Ministry for Coal and Energy. There was a step-by-step development of:

- Submodels in the relevant branches and sectors of energy consumption and supply
- An adequate coupling algorithm
- Regional models for the decisions appropriate to the Bezirks.

These models were adopted into the planning practice. The setting up of regional models will be finished in the near future.

environmental impacts and the possible gaining in importance of the regions. Significant extensions of the model could be achieved, however, if the problems about uncertainty of the input information could be solved.*

The main arrangement of the overall model, submodels of subsystems including the energy application activities, and regional models, matches in its fundamental setup the overall conception tried out during the previous 5 years in the GDR. The substance of the economic criterion, namely, minimum cost for the overall system, is the only adequate criterion in the economic realm; however, its consequences were not elucidated in detail.

The time span through the year 2020 has within it a period that can be accurately modeled. From our point of view and practice, however, we must call into question the application of a conclusive and deterministic model for such a long time span. For such computations, the farthest horizon should be the year 1995, or 2000 at most. This in particular applies to the reliability of the economic input, and the case of multivariant computations. Complex optimization could be omitted for the period from 2000 to 2020. The complexity calculations, however, must still be considered significant for the period 2000–2020. This point is discussed further in section III.B. with respect to the Wisconsin model.

The main characteristics of the French models include real temporal complexity of periods of several years, bringing of the initial condition up to date, grouping of variables according to capacity and employment to capacity, and prevention of multiple assessment. Dealing with the plants available at the start of the period under review, and utilization of mean values for the transport expenditure and environment factors are relatively effective and suitable, from our experience. Certain doubts, at least theoretical ones, arise with regard to the cost trends over the periods of several years. Concentration of investment cost on one item is not advisable in our opinion. The exponential simulation of operating cost can be traced back to the experience gained with monosystems in which such cost can be fully applied. The direct complexity in the matrix block, however, requires linear increase as far as the proportionality between the forms of energy is concerned. Nonproportional economic trends should be represented by their direct causes.

The model could be improved by taking depreciation into consideration. The provision for the comparison of the plants existing at the end of the period under review appeared to be lacking. The constraints applied and the political–economic formulations of questions regarding the resource restrictions and utilization of national resources, appear to match the GDR experiences. The data structures — both inputs and outputs — satisfy the requirements, but some problems arise when making provision for and interpreting the output data. From the standpoint of economic calculation and importance to the energy system, it requires utilization of all accessible national and possibly international scientific capabilities. The model apparently utilizes standard programs for the analysis of results, i.e. sensitivity analyses. Of special interest would have been a description of the programs for efficient command of such models in the preparatory and analysis phases.

We wish to emphasize once again our opinion that any overestimating of the models should be avoided. They must be considered only an aid in making decisions.

In spite of the differences in detail, when approaching the problem in accordance with the method applied, the French model has many similarities to the overall energy models used for years in the GDR. Accordingly, the two tools used offer the potential of a real exchange of experience fostered by IIASA. However, we would

* Significant work was and is being done in this field in the Soviet Union.

like to underline once again the doubts mentioned above with regard to the barriers and limits of such a procedure with respect to the socio-economic facts. The overall method of solution and its use within the limits of the Common Market, in our opinion, only give way to mere academic reflections if they are not used in national economic decision making.

The bibliography quoted in the French publications used in drafting this analysis,[18, 19, 20] show that the research groups at the University of Grenoble were not fully aware of the level reached in socialist countries. The sources, including those concerning the GDR, are outdated and in no way report fully the level reached. In particular, the publications by the Soviet Union and the GDR, including work by other socialist countries that have applied similar methods, would certainly have been a rich source of knowledge and suggestions.

II.C. APPRAISAL OF THE FRENCH MODELS BY WISCONSIN

Wesley K. Foell – Energy Research Center, University of Wisconsin – Madison; and *James Pappas – University of Wisconsin – Madison*

Although there is considerable centralization in energy planning in France, the private sector plays a significant role and, hence, the energy modeling activities there are somewhat more directly akin to those in Wisconsin than in the GDR. From the French activities it seems that there are several areas in which Wisconsin can benefit from transference of methodologies. The broadest of these is the programming model developed at the Institut Economique et Juridique de l'Energie in Grenoble (IEJE). This procedure holds promise for analyzing not only alternative state energy policies but perhaps more importantly the impact of various proposed national energy policies on the state. Its integrative structure would allow its use for evaluating the energy/environment impact of alternative development futures for Wisconsin and the optimization of the total energy system, subject to constraints on availability of particular primary energy fuels. Thus, it could be a potentially important tool for analyzing the future structure of Wisconsin's energy industries. In this area, such an approach could provide important inputs to both private sector decision makers and state policy planners.

One of the severe limitations in applying the above model to regional problems in Wisconsin is linked to the manner in which environmental constraints are imposed in the model. As the model now stands, environmental constraints are expressed in the form of total emissions of SO_2 or other pollutants. In practice in Wisconsin, the constraints on energy system development that arise through environmental considerations take the form of a multiplicity of impact factors, far more complex than can be expressed through emissions alone. To use an optimization model of the above type to include environmental considerations in a significant way would require modification of the constraints and perhaps the statement of the objective function. However, after pointing out this difficulty, it does not seem at all unreasonable to consider the possibility of moving in the direction of these extensions of the French energy model, that is, building into it the description and consideration of more detailed regional environmental constraints and costs. The creation of such a tool would have considerable benefit for Wisconsin energy modelers.

Given the history of a long and extensive effort in modeling of the French electric energy system, it is perhaps not surprising that this area provides some of the greatest potential for model transference. Although the French use of trend projection methods of long-run electricity demand estimation suffer serious shortcomings in times of major structural changes in energy supply/consumption patterns, the work on short-run demand analysis is exceedingly important for load management purposes. Given not only increasing total demand but also an even more rapid growth in peak demand due to summer cooling requirements, improving the load characteristics of demand is one of the major problems facing the Wisconsin electric utility system. This can be accomplished only by means of analysis of that load composition. The French have progressed far in this analysis, not only in modeling the load characteristics of electricity demand, but also in costing the supply of electricity over the load structure. This costing makes possible further French contribution in the area of electricity pricing. Here the French have proved to be leaders in experimenting with various price strategies aimed at improving the system efficiency through load adjustment.

Although the French investment model for the electricity industry is sound and would be useful as an alternative to the corporate planning models currently employed in Wisconsin, its lack of specific environmental analysis means that substantial modification would be necessary. Nonetheless, its potential for systemwide analysis is substantial, and it might prove a useful methodology for use by the Wisconsin Public Service Commission to evaluate the cost impacts of alternative link requirements between the various electric utility companies serving areas of Wisconsin. As in the GDR, experiences with the greater integration of the French electric system provide a potential for improving on the efficiency of future capacity expansion in the Wisconsin electric utility industry.

Finally there are the oil and gas models of France. Both models hold limited promise for transference to Wisconsin due to the very limited nature of activities of these industries in Wisconsin. There are no oil or gas reserves in the state and only one refinery. Further, distribution of natural gas is not expanding due to projected supply shortfalls in the future. Hence, only the models of transport and distribution of petroleum products appear to have direct applicability for Wisconsin modeling activities.

III. WISCONSIN

III.A. DESCRIPTION OF THE MODEL

James Pappas – University of Wisconsin – Madison

Energy system modeling in Wisconsin is comprised of a variety of efforts in both the public and private sectors, aimed at an analysis of problems associated with energy supply, demand, and environmental impact. The fragmentation of these efforts is extreme, with many parallel modeling activities being carried on simultaneously.

The nature of both Wisconsin's energy system and the modeling activities associated with that system developed largely from the social, economic, environmental, and political structure of the state.[21,22] Wisconsin is richly endowed with both natural and human resources. It does not, however, have any significant energy resources. Historically, agriculture, resource extraction and processing, and tourism or recreational activities have played major roles in the state's economy. An intensive, broad-based industrial sector has developed in the southeastern portion of the state and it is here that the vast majority of the state's populace now reside.

Wisconsin's energy system evolved in response to the energy requirements generated by this pattern of economic growth and development. This evolution occurred largely through the interaction of suppliers and consumers in a private market setting with virtually no integrated planning and relatively limited direct government intervention. This historical pattern of a limited government role in Wisconsin's energy system development stems from many factors. The virtual lack of energy resources in the state, however, is undoubtedly a major factor, particularly when coupled with a national policy aimed at making energy readily available in the private sector markets at relatively low prices. In short, the energy sector has historically been neither a major component of Wisconsin's gross state product nor a major constraint on the state's economic development. It has not, therefore, been an area of major concern to the state government.

Because of the primary reliance on private sector development of the Wisconsin energy system, and the relatively limited government concern related to this sector, the resultant disaggregation in energy analysis and planning makes it impossible to describe a unique, well-integrated energy modeling system for the state. Instead, one finds a variety of parallel modeling activities being carried on not only by the suppliers (and major consumers) of various energy resources in the private sector, but also by numerous state agencies. There has been a recent realization of the importance of energy to the state's economic well being on the part of the state's political leaders. Because of this disaggregation, the various modeling approaches being used in both the private and public sectors will be outlined, as well as the institutional mechanisms through which linkages occur.

While energy modeling in Wisconsin encompasses the entire range of activities associated with analyzing the state's energy system — from long-range forecasting and planning to operational management — most individual efforts are rather narrow in scope. That is, they focus on either a specific energy source, or on a particular energy policy problem. An exception to this generalization is the work of the Energy Systems and Policy Research Group (ESPRG) at the University of Wisconsin. This multidisciplinary research activity has resulted in the development of a computerized dynamic simulation model of Wisconsin's energy system. The WISconsin Regional Energy Model (WISE) combines an engineering and economic approach to model the state's energy system within a multidimensional framework that describes energy demand, conversion, transport, and uses explicitly accounting for technological, economic, and environmental interactions. It consists of a collection of submodels that combine in simple mathematical terms data and information about energy flows in Wisconsin to describe or simulate the energy system and its relationship to other characteristics of the state, e.g. demographic, economic, and environmental. A simulation structure was chosen for several reasons. First, simulation is a convenient method of integrating the variety of analytical techniques likely to be employed in a multidisciplinary effort of this type. Second, a simulation structure provides a great deal of flexibility in both the modeling process and application of the model to systems analysis. For example, it enables one to modify selected components of the system without the necessity of reworking the entire model, and to focus attention on specific areas of the energy system as well as on the system as a whole. Finally, the simulation structure lends itself to the scenario generating approach that is extremely useful in the analysis of major policy issues and alternatives. That is, simulation facilitates the application of the model to questions of the "what if" type.

Rather than dwell on the specific structure of the WISE model (which is examined in detail in other ESPRG publications*), and also in Chapter 3 of this volume, we shall limit our discussion to an overview of its capabilities and use. The WISE model is designed primarily for intermediate to long-range planning analysis. The typical horizon employed is the year 2000. Among other applications, WISE has been used to: (1) forecast energy demands by energy source and user classification, (2) estimate the additions required to the electricity generating, transmission, and distribution facilities in the state and evaluate the financing requirements, total system costs, and environmental impacts of alternative generating systems (i.e. nuclear versus fossil fueled) designed to meet the additional requirements, (3) examine environmental impacts associated with alternative future energy use patterns, and (4) analyze the role that conservation can play in determining the state's energy future. From these applications, it should be apparent that the WISE model is capable of both forecasting energy/environment futures for the state and analyzing the impacts of alternative policy decisions relating to both public and private sector activities in the energy area.

It is important to note that the development and actual employment of the WISE model rests almost exclusively with the ESPRG at the University of Wisconsin, a research team not formally or institutionally linked to Wisconsin's energy system planning and operational decision making. Lacking a direct tie to the decision-making bodies in the state, the use of the WISE model for input into energy policy analysis has rested on its ability to provide timely and easily comprehended responses to important energy policy issues as they arise. This response capability has been designed into the WISE model through the use of the simulation structure and an interactive control language which provides users with convenient access to both the models and data systems, and allows for intervention in simulated energy futures in order to test both the consequences of policy changes and the sensitivity of these futures to various assumptions employed in the analysis. It is further enhanced by the formal and informal working relationships that have been established by the ESPRG with several administrative and regulatory departments of the state of Wisconsin. The result is that while the ESPRG cannot be considered to be among the energy system policymaking bodies in Wisconsin, it does play an important role as a provider of technical expertise in policy analysis and, as will become clear from the material which follows, it has had a significant effect on the development of an analytical approach to policy analysis within several of the Wisconsin state agencies which have major decision-making responsibility in the energy/environment areas.

The description of other energy modeling activities in the state will be on the basis of model types and use. Because of the virtual inseparability of energy use and economic activity, virtually all modeling activities incorporate a general economic forecast for the state. These forecasts are prepared in both the public and private

---

* A detailed survey of the structure and use of the WISE model and a comprehensive list of publications describing it are contained in W.K. Foell, J.W. Mitchell, and J.L. Pappas, The WISconsin Regional Energy Model: A Systems Approach to Regional Energy Analysis, Institute for Environmental Studies Report No. 56 (Madison: University of Wisconsin – Madison, Sept. 1975).

sectors using a variety of methodologies, ranging from simple trend projections to complex econometric and input/output models. Within the state agencies, independent forecasts are prepared by the Department of Industry and Labor and Human Relations, the Department of Revenue, and by faculty at the University of Wisconsin. Although these forecasts are prepared for a variety of different uses and are not often reconciled, there is a high correlation between the various projections. This undoubtedly stems in large part from the fact that Wisconsin's economy is inextricably tied to the entire U.S. economy and all state forecasts are inherently based on the same projections of national economic activity levels.

Population size and characteristics provide another basic input into all energy modeling activities. In Wisconsin, this factor is modeled in detail by the Office of the State Demographer. This model considers age, sex, and county, and includes considerations of migration, fertility, and mortality. Detailed population projections are provided to the twenty-first century. Energy demand forecasts in Wisconsin (other than those prepared by the ESPRG) have typically been on a single energy source basis. Until very recently, virtually all of this work was done in the private sector and on a firm by firm basis. Thus, for example, individual electric utilities could be expected to project demand by major user categories within their respective service areas. Typically these projections entailed extrapolation of historical trends adjusted for any major structural change in user composition which the utility was aware of (e.g. the planned expansion of a major industrial customer or the location of a major new industrial facility in the firm's service area). Such projections were used as input for investment planning and seldom extended beyond a five-to-seven–year period. Ten-year projections were in the *very* long run and went well beyond the relevant planning period. These simple demand models served quite well over an extended period due to the regularity which characterized the development and growth of not only electricity but also the entire energy system in Wisconsin until the beginning of this decade.

As a result of the disruptions which have characterized the entire energy system since 1970, the electric utilities are no longer able to rely on historical trends for planning purposes. This has been accentuated by a necessary lengthening of the planning horizon for individual firms, brought about in part by the longer construction period associated with the use of nuclear technology and in part by the more active role in the planning process taken by government agencies and representatives of special interest groups in the public (e.g. environmentalists and conservationists). This change in demand forecasting requirements was both sudden and substantial, catching many electric utilities generally unprepared to respond adequately in the development of needed forecasting methodologies. It led to a contract between the major electric utilities in Wisconsin and the Stanford Research Institute, a large private consulting firm, for an in-depth analysis and forecast of energy demands in Wisconsin through the year 2000.[23]

The nature of demand modeling in the other energy industries closely parallels that in the electric utility sector. Gas utilities and suppliers of coal, fuel oil, and gasoline have all tended to use historical data on customer use, population and income growth, and market penetration to develop projections of future demand. For many cases, the state of Wisconsin is not the relevant market area and, hence, no "Wisconsin" projection is forthcoming. This is particularly true for the coal and petroleum sectors where the primary suppliers tend to operate in a national or international market and for whom the Wisconsin market is an extremely small part, so small, in fact, that it is often treated as some fixed percentage of the national market — usually around two percent. In the case of those natural gas transmission and distribution companies whose primary market area is Wisconsin, their lack of direct ties to the production of natural gas, coupled with a situation where the demand for their product far exceeds any foreseeable supply, limits the benefits from detailed demand analysis and forecasting. Such modeling has therefore had limited development.

Recently the state has moved into the arena of energy demand forecasting on several fronts. These activities began when the Public Service Commission (PSC) aggregated the forecasts of individual electric utilities to develop a clearer picture of the projected generation, transmission, and distribution system in the state. They have relied to this point on the projections provided by the utilities and by ESPRG at the university,[24,28] while working on the development of an "in house" capability for demand estimation.

The other state agency currently involved in energy demand analysis and projection is the Office of Emergency Energy Assistance (OEEA). This newly formed agency is charged with responsibility for assisting in the allocation of energy resources when the market mechanism fails because of a major imbalance between supply and demand (i.e. when price is not allowed to play its role) and to assist in the development of an energy policy for the state. The OEEA is involved primarily with short-term energy issues and thus has not developed the capability for intermediate to long-range energy forecasting but relies instead on the ESPRG work and other externally generated projections in those instances where required. It has, however, developed an extensive set of computerized energy consumption data bases and retrieval software for analyzing that data. These data include a monthly allocation of all petroleum projects coming into the state, which shows for every distributor of petroleum products where he obtains his supplies and to whom the products are sold. These data are used to keep track of the origin of Wisconsin's petroleum supplies and to analyze the short-run impacts of a disruption in that supply. Similar data are collected for both coal and natural gas flows in Wisconsin. An additional data file listing the primary fuel requirements, alternative fuel capabilities including storage and switching time, and daily use rates has been prepared for all low-priority natural gas customers in the state. These data are being used by the OEEA to analyze the impacts of a natural gas curtailment and the alternative allocation schemes that have been proposed for the remaining gas.

Investment planning activities in Wisconsin closely parallel those in the demand area. The vast majority of such efforts are carried on by the individual firms operating in the state. A variety of corporate planning models are utilized in these efforts. These models typically project the time pattern of finance requirements based on forecasts of future system capacity needs and estimates of the technologically available means of satisfying those needs. These corporate planning models are usually detailed engineering/economic models of either a simulation or mathematical programming nature. Where a linear programming approach is used, constrained cost minimization over the planning horizon is the typical objective. Although the electricity generating capacity submodel (GENCAP) in WISE is somewhat less detailed than most corporate planning models, it is representative of the simulation structure employed.

Probably the only energy firms where corporate planning models explicitly model in detail a Wisconsin component are the electric and natural gas utilities serving the state. Electric utilities, for example, use extensive models to convert projected consumer demand into capacity requirements using load curve analysis. These forecasts of capacity requirements are in turn used to analyze the economic impacts of alternative generation and distribution systems and from this, detailed projections of capital investment and financing requirements are obtained. These models have typically employed a five- to seven-year planning horizon in the past but recent events have lengthened it to ten to twelve years.

Although the major coal and petroleum suppliers all utilize such corporate planning models, in most cases the Wisconsin component is small relative to their total activities — involving perhaps no investment where sales are channeled through independent distributors — and, hence, is either combined with surrounding states for a regional analysis or not disaggregated at all from the national model. In those situations where a Wisconsin component is analyzed it invariably relates to distribution facilities which typically are relatively low-cost components with short planning horizons and, hence, are not major components in the model.

The only state agency that carries on any investment planning analysis in the energy system is the PSC and its effort is limited primarily to the electricity industry. The PSC approach is essentially equivalent to a corporate planning model in which system costing is the primary objective. The model structure is similar to GENCAP but with more detail concerning load flows by user class. It is used to evaluate the investment plans of individual electric utilities and for analysis of alternative rate structures. This effort has been done on a company by company basis and only recently has work begun on a systemwide effort patterned after the work of ESPRG.

A final area where energy-related modeling is taking place in Wisconsin relates to environmental impact. Here the effort is more completely integrated into state planning activities due to the need to ensure compliance with both state and national environmental standards. In this effort the Department of Natural Resources (DNR) has responsibility for both developing standards to ensure compliance with the codes and for monitoring emissions in the state. In this effort, they are working closely with several other state agencies as well as developing their own models for some specific analysis. They are for example working closely with the PSC in the development of impact statements for future electric utility generating plants and transmission systems. Here the methodology is similar to that employed in the ESPRG Environmental Impact Model but with greater emphasis on its specific relationships. Similar work is being carried on by the utility firms in the state as part of the licensing for new plants.

DNR is also working on broader models of air and water quality. One of these efforts involves monitoring by DNR of primary fuel use by each of the major energy-using facilities in the state. Emission data are then constructed from the fuel use survey and a physical diffusion model develops ambient concentration levels for various pollutants. These data then provide the basis for establishing pollution abatement requirements for the facilities.

The above methodology is also being employed for long-range environmental quality analysis and planning for southeastern Wisconsin, the most heavily industrialized and populated section of the state.[25] Here an economic planning model provides specific industrial and transportation energy use projections through the year 2000. These fuel-use figures are converted to emissions factors which are then combined with projections of area sources of pollution (e.g. residential housing and commercial areas) to develop estimates of air quality. A scenario-generating capability allows the impact of alternative development plans and pollution abatement standards to be analyzed.

To summarize, energy/environmental planning in Wisconsin is highly fragmented and, hence, there is relatively little centralized effort in this area. Even in the case of the energy utilities (i.e., electric and natural gas distributors) where the state has long played a major role in regulating activities, the individual firms are the primary decision makers and as such have historically done virtually all of the planning. Recently the PSC and DNR have taken a more active role in these planning activities due primarily to (1) mandates laid down in both Federal and state environmental protection legislation,[26,27] (2) concerns about the risks inherent in nuclear generation of electricity, and (3) major structural changes in the energy supply/demand relationship which indicate a long-term supply shortfall unless significant modifications in energy use patterns are forthcoming. Other state agencies (particularly OEEA and the Department of Planning) are also moving rapidly to develop the data systems and modeling techniques necessary to introduce energy relationships into state policy analysis more explicitly. The efforts are being assisted by the work of ESPRG and other research groups at the University of Wisconsin.

III.B.   APPRAISAL OF THE WISCONSIN MODEL BY THE GDR

Peter Hedrich and *Dietmar Ufer* − *Institut für Energetik*

In the state of Wisconsin there has been a great number of initiatives taken to assess future trends in the energy industry and their consequences for other spheres of economic and social activities. The majority of these initiatives concern investigations by private enterprises engaged, for example, in supplying electricity, which need the resulting data and other evidence to pursue a policy that results in maximum profits. A policy stressing maximum profits leads to one-sided development directed only towards fields that are of interest to the enterprise concerned. Other aspects, e.g. supplies to the state or even the United States as a whole, and energy suppliers other than those involved in the specific business transactions, scarcely attract due attention in these circumstances. Since, in addition, public institutions are interested in energy demand developments, energy supplies, and the relevant problems of environmental protection, there may be uncoordinated parallel work.

The initiative taken by the Energy System and Policy Research Group (ESPRG) of the University of Wisconsin, which is making efforts to systematize all the Wisconsin activities in this field, therefore marks great progress. A comprehensive system of models is intended to serve investigations into the energy supply industry and environmental protection, not from the point of view taken by just one enterprise or any other isolated group of interested parties, but within the scope of the entire state. It must be regarded as a good development that the research group plans to cooperate with the public authorities and present calculations that are of practical significance. The confinements of these efforts become apparent, however, if it is or would be necessary to apply the knowledge gained against the resistance put up by certain groups representing vested interests (such as energy supply enterprises, landlords, and the automobile industry). The power of public authorities to influence private enterprises can safely be regarded as quite limited. Much valuable knowledge that might be of use to people can therefore not be put into effect.

The model is therefore not suited for immediate preparations of decisions to be taken by the energy supply industry or at government level but is rather intended to serve studies dealing with the consequences for the energy supply industry and the environment of various economic, technological, demographic, and other developments and strategies. This situation is apparent from the fact that the results of investigations using the model are not expressed in quantities that are clearly specified in terms of place and time, but mainly represent variants, trends and statements of the "if−then" type.

It is also necessary to state that the work done by the University of Wisconsin is concerned only with overcoming the uncoordinated state of energy supply planning in one state. There has not been any attempt made so far to work out a system dealing with the planning of energy supplies and environment protection covering the whole of the United States on the basis of the same principles. It is also not apparent that a territorial energy supply strategy is to or can be established for the United States with the aid of the Wisconsin model.

The contrast with energy supply planning in the GDR results from the different arrangements of production in the GDR and the United States. As a part of socialist economy, the GDR energy supply industry is under central management. Planning proceeds in the interests of society as a whole, with the planning process being organized in the way of a pyramid, reaching from the industrial plants with their staff up to the Ministry of Coal and Energy Supplies and top-level government (reflecting the principle of democratic centralism). All industries, and indeed the entire social progress, are subject to planning in socialist society, without consideration whether one branch or another may or may not temporally attract special attention for reasons of overall trade policy or current events (remember the so-called oil crisis!). The results of scientific work done to develop the energy supply industry are taken into account when the GDR National Economic Plan is being drawn up. That plan, which is actually worked out with the cooperation of the working people in the factories and fields is in the end given legal status. Its specifications are put into effect at all public authority and industrial management levels.

The Wisconsin model serves to forecast developments over a period of up to 30 years. In calculating the inputs, it primarily uses trend computing. It may be possible to extend the period covered by a forecast by one or two decades. In any case, it has to be considered, however, that in reality the developing processes usually do not proceed in a continuous mode but may include discontinuities at one time or other. The model takes this condition into consideration by defining and computing qualitatively different model approaches (scenarios).

In the GDR, pure trend computing is used in a limited way only (in minor subsectors for tally calculations) in the course of planning activities covering two or three decades. The methods applied in the Wisconsin model are of interest to us, however, for forecasts reaching beyond the year 2000.

The Wisconsin model is a variant (descriptive) model. It is not intended for or capable of optimization. In view of the widely varying conditions of ownership characterizing the energy supply industry in Wisconsin, this limitation is realistic and theoretically correct. Any optimizing criterion agreeing with the interest of the entire population of the state would not be recognized by the private enterprises, which are driven by their urge for maximum profits.

The model system worked out by the University of Wisconsin does not comprise energy supply and environmental protection but, rather, the entire economy including substantial spheres of social developments. This arrangement is necessary because additional data concerning, for example, developments in industry, agriculture, and other branches outside the actual energy supply industry, are not made available by other institutions. In the end, therefore, the Wisconsin model covers all economic activities in the state in terms of developments to be expected, in order to be able to provide statements concerning the energy supply industry and environmental protection. If other branches of the economy, for example agriculture or transportation, were to start such investigations, this situation might lead to ineffective repetition of work.

In contrast to Wisconsin conditions, energy supply planning in the GDR is part of national economic planning as a whole. The inputs needed for energy supply planning from other industries (concerning, for example, the production of cement or rolled steel) are calculated by these industries in the course of their own planning. The feedback from energy supply planning to the other industries operates within the entire national economic planning process.

For determining the ultimate energy demands, the Wisconsin model uses almost exclusively (above all for industrial activities) economic quantities to characterize volume and growth of production. This procedure is handicapped because certain structural alterations, which may be significant for the energy supply industry, are not recognized and therefore not considered. A disaggregation of the industry into 20 branches cannot make up for this deficiency.

The method of useful energy supply planning by consideration of energy-intensive products and their specific energy consumption indices, which in the GDR has been practiced for a long time, permits changes in national economic structure to be taken into account in energy supply planning. Planning with genuine natural physical indices is, in addition, well suited to cover any interdependencies in industry and other fields. Interdependence schemes based on economic quantities only, as prepared in Wisconsin, can in contrast be expected to provide much less accurate evidence.

Available information on the Wisconsin model does not show how the interaction between the substitutable energy supplies in the various branches of the energy supply industry is taken into account and planned. Planned energy supply substitution according to a defined or still-to-be defined strategy is not at all foreseen for the industrial consumption of energy. As a result, there is an impression that every individual energy supplier is dealt with in a more or less isolated manner within the model system, with the electricity supply industry clearly enjoying a prominent position. The latter situation is probably due to the power stations being the only major energy conversion plants in Wisconsin.

From the point of view of the GDR, it appears as a drawback that the Wisconsin model does not provide for the computing of comprehensive energy supply balances, balances dealing with individual energy supply according to available resources and the uses that are made of these supplies, and comprehensive primary energy balances.

The structure of the Wisconsin model and the way in which the submodels are coordinated are very efficient. Similarly to the central model system applied to the GDR energy supply industry, the arrangements allow calculations with the submodels as well as calculations involving the coordinated model as a whole. Output of results, in some cases with graphs, is quite suitable for nonexpert staff.

The Wisconsin model comprises submodels investigating the consequences on the environment of activities by the energy supply industry. These investigations are very valuable since they may be the starting point for activities to limit, or avoid damage to the environment by all branches of the energy supply industry. Coordination, in terms of a model, of activities by the energy supply industry and environmental control, which has not been practiced yet in the GDR, offers great possibilities to investigate the interaction between the two.

The Wisconsin model has been worked out in social conditions that differ from those in the GDR, and the objective is therefore different, too. The procedures and methods applied are, however, of interest for the GDR. Their application seems to be suitable for cases that do not permit application of optimizing models that are in use in the GDR. Even with such distant planning horizons, however, a more or less comprehensive energy supplier balance, with consideration of the interdependencies of the suppliers, should be worked out. The procedures applied for environmental control planning and its coordination with energy supply planning are also of interest to the GDR for planning periods covering 10 to 20 years and appear to be applicable in their present form.*

III.C.   APPRAISAL OF THE WISCONSIN MODEL BY RHONE-ALPES

Dominique Finon – Institut Economique et Juridique de l'Energie (IEJE)

This analysis will only take into consideration the WISE model of the University of Wisconsin because few specific details are available about other models.[†] The WISE model has been developed in a very pragmatic way, with the intention to provide clarification to decision makers and even to provide the public with a better understanding of the consequences of different energy choices in terms of environmental impacts. The model permits a very disaggregated presentation of energy production and consumption activities, because its developers have a detailed understanding of various consumption and production processes; the method permits one to calculate quite precisely the different undesirable effects resulting from each type of activity. This type of model is not meant to be a tool for planning, but rather a tool for forecasting energy consumption, the evolution of production, and environmental consequences – taking into account many possible starting points. Optimization methods simulate one energy policy, e.g. to seek the least social cost under the constraints of limiting dependence on oil or reducing harmful effects. The method utilized in the WISE models, however, permits one to test many different policies. It is, for example, possible to measure the impact of an energy conservation policy that imposes insulation standards for housing or that improves the load factor in cars; these parameters are exogenous to the WISE model since the standard of optimal insulation may have been an outcome of an optimization model.

The WISE model appears to be a neutral model representing the energy system of Wisconsin, defined in terms of the totality of the activities associated with the production and consumption of energy. It would be applicable to all energy systems in the world, considered from this point of view, except that it has been conceived for a system which is strongly dependent on the outside world for its supply of primary fuels. The application of this model, in this sense, should pose more problems for the GDR than for the Rhone-Alpes region (or for France) to the degree that the essential energy needs in the GDR are satisfied by locally-mined coal.

The logic of the approach under discussion necessitates a very elaborate disaggregation of various subsystems in order to arrive at the fundamental determinants of demand. For example, at the level of space heating in the residential and service sectors, it requires information about the climate, insulation, outside surface area of housing, type of housing, the number of housing units, and so on. Thus, one of the difficulties in applying this type of model lies in obtaining the tremendous amount of data needed for the assignment of values to the parameters, as well as in

---

* The review of the Wisconsin energy model was based on: W.K. Foell, The Wisconsin Energy Model: A Tool for Regional Energy Policy Analysis, Institute for Environmental Studies Report No. 35 (Madison, University of Wisconsin – Madison, Nov. 1974); and J.L. Pappas, "Draft Outline for the Description of the Energy System Modeling Activities in Wisconsin," (unpublished).
† As described in Chapter 6, it appears that these models are almost identical to the branch models utilized in France by Electricité de France (EDF) as well as by the oil companies.

defining the values of the coefficient in relationships between two variables. For instance, in the industrial subsystem it is necessary to know the coefficient of energy intensity corresponding to energy consumption per unit of value added.

It is difficult to avoid certain inconsistencies when using such disaggregated methods. Thus, to return to the industrial subsystem, it is necessary to extrapolate from the available data in order to obtain the coefficients of energy intensity for future consumption of energy; this presupposes that the techniques will remain fixed over long periods of time. Moreover, it is necessary to know the economic activities of different branches during the next 20 or 30 years and this requires a certain level of estimation. This is perhaps easier in the case of end-use energy in the domestic, service, and transportation sectors. The data must be evaluated rather arbitrarily, and much is dependent on the subjectivity of the modeler and his experience in the field of modeling.

Moreover, since it is not possible to formalize everything with the same finesse, certain areas are less well formalized than others; this produces distortions in the accuracy of the results and increases the error in the findings obtained by aggregation of the partial results. Thus the representation of freight transport in the state of Wisconsin would appear very crude, in view of the precision of the representation of the urban and intraurban passenger transport. In the same manner, in the industrial and domestic sector, the possibility of replacing fuels by electricity through the substitution of heating methods or industrial processes has been neglected.* It is sometimes more interesting to remain at a certain level of aggregation of economic phenomena when this permits one to obtain information more easily or when this permits one to profit from errors' canceling each other in the different components of an aggregate.†

In any case, the simulation technique under discussion here is very useful, in view of the flexibility it has in permitting one to construct a global model, domain by domain, to modify or improve a given point in the representation, and to develop more precisely the formalization of certain other points. Moreover, it is ideal for coupling with the scenario method, which permits a consistent definition of parameters.

In conclusion, one may perhaps criticize a certain unevenness in the exactness of representation of the various parts of the model, the necessity to control a large number of parameters, and to investigate an enormous mass of data. The model remains an extremely pragmatic tool directly useful in aiding the decision makers to measure the consequences of their present and future choices; moreover, its careful design permits much flexibility.

The model, however, is better conceived to study the environmental impacts and the regulations concerning pollution rather than to study the development of the overall energy system. It is nonspecific and can be easily applied to all energy systems which present the same conditions of fuel dependency as the state of Wisconsin. However, this nonspecificity is connected with a concept of systems as a group of activities without a purpose and without capacity for self-reproduction (in which the total would be the sum of the parts). It is perhaps here that one sees the methodological limits of this approach in providing long-term forecasts; a system

---

* It is possible that from the point of view of environmental impacts, certain simplifications of representation may be justified. But they cannot be justified if, at the same time, one seeks a precise forecast of the consumption of energy.
† For example, the evolution of the consumption of electricity in households is a logistic curve corresponding to the penetration of the various secondary domestic appliances.

442

has its own dynamics and its own logic which must be brought to light in order to model it and to try to represent its modes of evolving. The WISE model assumes a system without its own internal dynamics, for it presents a multitude of exogenous parameters whose level is more or less arbitrarily determined. Here, more is at stake than a theoretical and abstract observation, for this important external factor could be a cause for questioning the significance of the model's results.

REFERENCES

1. Institut für Energetik – Leipzig. "The Model System for Long Term Planning of the Energy Sector in the GDR." Translated by A.C. Foell (IIASA), 1975.
2. Charpentier, J.P. A Review of Energy Models: No. 2 July 1975. Report No. RR-75-35. International Institute for Applied Systems Analysis, Laxenburg, Austria, Oct. 1975.
3. Maurin, H. *Programmation Linéaire Appliquée.* Technip. Paris, 1967.
4. Toromanoff, M. "Le Choix des investissements au Gaz de France." *Revue Française de l'Energie* 260, Feb. 1974.
5. Charpentier, J.P., G. Naudet, and A. Paillot. *Simulation Model of the Nuclear Fuel Cycle.* Commissariat a l'Energie Atomique, France, 1973.
6. Model SEPTEN, Service des Etudes Nucléaires, Direction de l'équipement de l'EDF France, 1972.
7. Dodu, J.C. *Probability Model for the Study of the Security of Supply from a Transport Network.* Electricité de France, 1973.
8. Finon, D. "Forecasting the Consumption of Energy and Electricity: The Methods Used in France," In C.J. Cicchetti and W.K. Foell (eds.) *Energy Systems Forecasting, Planning and Pricing; Proceedings of A French-American Conference.* University of Wisconsin – Madison, Feb. 1975.
9. Pioger, Y. "Forecasting Power Consumption and Models for Constructing Load Curves," In C.J. Cicchetti and W.K. Foell (eds.) *Energy Systems Forecasting, Planning and Pricing; Proceedings of a French-American Conference.* University of Wisconsin – Madison, Feb. 1975.
10. Pioger, Y. "Forecasting Power Consumption and Models for Constructing Load Curves." In C.J. Cicchetti and W.K. Foell (eds.) *Energy Systems Forecasting, Planning and Pricing; Proceedings of a French-American Conference.* University of Wisconsin – Madison, Feb. 1975.
11. Masse, P. and R. Gibrat. "Application of Linear Programming to Investments in the Electric Power Industry." *Management Science* 3, 1957.
12. Bessiere, F. "Methods of Choosing Production Equipment at Electricité de France." *European Economic Review*, winter 1969.
13. Bessiere, F. *Energy Systems Forecasting, Planning and Pricing; Proceedings of a French-American Conference.* C.J. Cicchetti and W.K. Foell (eds.). University of Wisconsin – Madison. Feb. 1975.
14. Levi, D. and D. Saumon. *Description of the New National Model of Investment.* Internal Memo of the Electricité de France (EDF), May 1973.
15. Stasi, P. "The Rational Use of Electricity: The Contribution of Tariffing," in *Symposium on the Rationalization of the Consumption of Electrical Energy*, Varsovie, 1962.
16. Berthomieu, C. "Theory and Practice of Electricity Pricing in France." in C.J. Cicchetti and W.K. Foell (eds.) *Energy Systems Forecasting, Planning, and Pricing; Proceedings of a French-American Conference*, University of Wisconsin – Madison, Feb. 1975.
17. Boiteux, M., and F. Bessiere. "The Use of Aggregate and Marginal Methods in Choosing Investments," in J.R. Nelson, *Optimal Investment Decisions.* Prentice-Hall, Englewood Cliffs, New Jersey, 1962.
18. Finon, D. "The Energy Model – Optimization of the French Energy Sector Through a Global Approach." Dissertation, Grenoble, Mar. 1975.

19.   Finon, D. "Optimization Models for the French Energy Sector." *Energy Policy* 2 (2): 136–151, June 1974.

20.   Martin, Jean-Marie, and D. Finon. Institutions et models energetiques en Rhône-Alpes. Institut Economique et Juridique de l'Energie, Grenoble, Sept. 1975. (This paper is section II.A. of this appendix.)

21.   *The State of Wisconsin Blue Book 1973.* Wisconsin Legislative Reference Bureau, Madison, 1973.

22.   Bowman, J.D., R.W. Colley, C.P. Erwin, M.E. Hanson, M.T. Kwast, J.W. Mitchell, and J.L. Pappas. Survey of Energy Use in Wisconsin. Institute for Environmental Studies Report No. 65, University of Wisconsin – Madison, Mar. 1976.

23.   Stanford Research Institute Energy Study for the Wisconsin Utilities. Internal Document, Wisconsin Electric Power Company.

24.   Buehring, W.A., W.K. Foell, P.H. Hunter, D.A. Jacobson, P.D. Kishline, J.L. Pappas, and D.B. Shaver. Alternative Future Electricity Generation Requirements for the State of Wisconsin, Energy Systems and Policy Research Report No. 4. University of Wisconsin – Madison, Oct. 1974.

25.   Regional Air Quality Maintenance Planning Program Prospectus. Southeastern Wisconsin Regional Planning Commission, Waukesha, Wisconsin, 1974.

26.   National Environment Policy Act of 1969. Public Law 91 – 190, 42 U.S.C. 4331.

27.   Wisconsin Environmental Policy Act, Chapter 274 of the Law of 1971 for the State of Wisconsin, 1971 Assembly Bill 875, Apr. 28, 1972.

28.   Buehring, W.A., J.S. Buehring, R.L. Dennis, W.K. Foell, and M.E. Hanson. Assessment of Alternative Energy/Environment Futures in Wisconsin. Institute for Environmental Studies Report No. 81, University of Wisconsin – Madison, July 1977.

E Evaluation and Choice of Energy/Environment Alternatives

William Buehring and *Ralph Keeney* – *IIASA*
Wesley K. Foell – *Energy Research Center,*
University of Wisconsin – *Madison*

I. INTRODUCTION

Chapters 4, 5, and 6 have provided alternative pictures of energy and environmental futures in the German Democratic Republic, Rhone-Alpes, and Wisconsin. The scenario-writing process through which these futures were studied is purely *descriptive* in nature, that is, it only provides a description of some of the characteristics of the system as it moves through a series of states. However, the process does not tell us *what path* to take from one state to another, given a particular *objective* or *goal* which we wish to achieve in the system. It does not provide a formal approach to the *evaluation of alternatives*. What path should be followed if, for example, conventional costs for energy facilities are to be minimized? If environmental impact is to be minimized? If subregional economic equity is to be preserved? We denote procedures for choosing such paths, i.e. alternatives, as *prescriptive* techniques. Some of the system models described in Appendix D could be classified as prescriptive in nature. For example the ENERGIE model originating in Grenoble could be used to choose energy supply strategies which would lead to minimum discounted energy system costs (including capital and operating costs).

No formal objectives or objective functions have been defined for the scenarios – other than the statement of an overall policy rationale or framework within which the evolution of the system could be described. Furthermore, the scenario descriptions in Chapters 4, 5, and 6 provide little guidance for embedding the energy/environment information into a *decision process*.

This chapter describes one of the approaches used by the IIASA research group in the evaluation of energy/environment alternatives. It uses the framework of multiattribute decision analysis. As will be seen from the following sections, the approach was chosen in part because of the belief that it also contributed greatly to the *communication* process, another essential ingredient of energy/environment management. The approach is not presented here as a solution to the evaluation problem. The lack of an appropriate formal approach for incorporating uncertainty into policy evaluation and for dealing explicitly with the unknown remains a critical issue for resource system analysts and managers.

444

II. THE DIFFICULTIES OF ENERGY/ENVIRONMENT MANAGEMENT

In the context of this book, the energy/environment system of a region includes its socioeconomic, technological, and ecological characteristics. The difficulties of managing this system can in part be explained by the following characteristics.

The Interdependencies of Economic, Technological, and Ecological Characteristics of a Region. These interdependencies are not only extremely difficult to quantify, but they imply that conflicting objectives need to be considered within the management process. A well-known example is the current controversy about whether high rates of economic growth are compatible with a high-quality environment. Another example on a regional level is whether specific environmental protection measures are compatible with local economic growth and maintenance of jobs.

Difficulties in Identifying Costs and Benefits and in Associating Them with Specific Societal Groups. Accounting in a quantitative way for impacts on air quality, aesthetics, and resource supply is very difficult, especially over time. In addition, the costs and the benefits are not always bestowed upon individuals or groups in an equitable manner.

Uncertainties – Changes Over Time. There are uncertainties about the benefits and costs of any particular management policy. Even if there exists a good understanding of the system interdependencies today, they may change drastically over time in a manner that we do not understand or may not even expect. Some of the environmental effects have very long-term delays making them difficult to estimate with present information.

Difficulties in Communicating This Complex Material. Even if the above information is precisely known, it is difficult to communicate to individuals and institutions that must make decisions on the management problem or implement strategies. The problem of communicating quantitative and technical information to people who are not specialists is even more difficult. As the complexity of our technologically oriented society increases, this problem is increasing in importance.

Multiple Decision Makers Within Overlapping Institutional Frameworks, e.g. Multiple Levels of Government. Because the energy/environment system cuts across so many parts of society, institutional structures that have evolved are complex. This results in a multiplicity, and sometimes unidentified array, of policymakers who are deeply involved in the management problem.

There has been considerable interest in formal methodologies to cope with the above problems and to combine environmental impacts into a single figure of merit for evaluation of alternative courses of action.[1,2,3,4] Others have suggested utility assessments for risk analysis[5] and for evaluation of alternative power plant sites.[6,7,8] This chapter suggests and illustrates multiattribute decision analysis as an appropriate approach for formally addressing some of the above complexities in managing energy/environment systems. The approach is introduced in the next section; the remainder of the chapter is devoted primarily to illustrating the approach for examining alternative electricity supply strategies in the state of Wisconsin.

III. MULTIATTRIBUTE DECISION ANALYSIS

As described in Chapters 4–7, a simulation model has been used to examine the environmental consequences of the alternative energy scenarios for the German

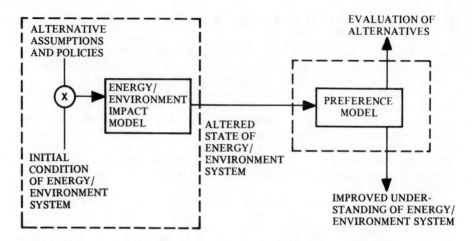

FIGURE E.1.   Relationship between the impact model and the preference model.

Democratic Republic, Rhone-Alpes, and Wisconsin. The environmental impact models* used for that purpose are meant to be as objective as possible, i.e., an attempt was made to minimize subjective or value-judgment content. However, in a strict sense this was not possible since no model can be more than a reflection of the model-builder's view of a simplified image of reality. It is hoped that the model provides the best description that he can produce.

Because of the earlier-mentioned complexity of energy/environment systems, it is extremely difficult to utilize this model *directly* for evaluating specific policies. With this in mind, we suggest that it may be useful to introduce a preference model into the process. The use of a preference model, coupled with the impact model, can provide a convenient framework to *help* a decision maker evaluate alternatives in terms of the degree to which each of a set of objectives is met.

The relationship between the energy/environment "Impact Model" and the "Preference Model" is illustrated in Figure E.1. The outputs of the Impact Model are impact levels of the attributes, i.e., the degree to which an attribute alters the state of the system. For instance, the policy of introducing nuclear power facilities may result in a certain level of radioactive waste, of power generated, of water used, of land occupied, and of death. The impact model might give point estimates of such levels or present the information in a probabilistic fashion. Then the decision maker is supposed to consider the possible states and select a policy from the alternatives.

To effectively process all the information in one's mind is a very difficult task. From the characteristics of the problem outlined in the last section, three of the major complexities leading to this difficulty are:

● The uncertainties about the impact of any alternative, especially considering the time frame involved

---

* The models are summarized in Chapter 3 of this volume. More detailed descriptions can be found in the references listed there.

- The multiple objective nature of the problem and the necessity to make value tradeoffs between various levels of attributes
- The differences between the preference structures of the individual members of the decision-making unit and the lack of systematic procedures for articulating and resolving these differences

Two general approaches for addressing these issues are an informal qualitative one and a formal quantitative one.* In the former approach, one processes the pros and cons of each alternative in his own mind and discusses his thinking with other concerned members of the decision-making body. Eventually a decision will result from agreement or compromise. The formal approach attempts to quantify each decision-maker's preference structure and couple this with the implications of the impact model. The individual preference models allow one to explore the areas of agreement and disagreement between decision makers. The process itself is important in addressing the third complexity mentioned above. The formal approach will be the focus of the following pages.

The result of quantifying one's preferences is a model of these preferences called a utility function. When multiple objectives are involved, a measure of effectiveness, or attribute, is needed to indicate the degree to which each objective is met. Hence we have the terminology, multiattribute utility function. This multiattribute utility function is nothing more than an objective function (to be maximized) with one special property: in cases involving uncertainty, the expected utility calculated for an alternative is an appropriate measure of the desirablity of that alternative. Thus, if one accepts a set of reasonable axioms postulated by von Neumann and Morgenstern,[10] one should choose the alternative leading to the highest expected utility.

For discussion purposes, it is convenient to divide decision analysis into four steps: structuring the problem, identifying the impacts, quantifying the preferences, and evaluating the alternatives. The next four sections of this chapter respectively cover these steps.

IV. THE PROBLEM: THE CHOICE OF ALTERNATIVE ELECTRICITY SUPPLY STRATEGIES

Each of the three regions provides a wealth of examples of the complexity of this management problem. One problem that arises in all three regions and which is becoming increasingly important and visible for a broad spectrum of decision makers and the public is the evaluation of alternative electricity supply strategies.

In Wisconsin, much of the discussion of this question has focused on the relative advantages and disadvantages of nuclear and coal electricity-supply systems; the environmental impacts of the two systems have been the major topics. More recently, the question of the desirability of continued growth of electricity supply has been brought into the discussion. In the eyes of a significant fraction of the Wisconsin community, the societal choice of levels of energy use is a major component of environmental management. It is one of the most complex aspects of the problem.[11]

In Rhone-Alpes, the question is of a similar nature although the specific

---

* Whether a group chooses the formal or informal process is itself a decision. Some of the advantages and disadvantages of each of these approaches are suggested by Keeney and Raiffa.[9]

TABLE E.1   Six Alternative Policies for Wisconsin Electrical Generation from 1970 to 2000

Policy 1	• Electrical generation increases at average annual growth rate of 4.7%. • Almost all new plants fueled with coal. • SO_2 emissions controlled by using stack gas removal systems and low-sulfur coal. • 99% particulate control.
Policy 2	• Electrical generation – same as Policy 1. • Almost all new plants are fueled with coal. • No SO_2 stack gas removal systems and same amount of low-sulfur coal as Policy 1. • 89% particulate control.
Policy 3	• Electrical generation – same as Policy 1. • Almost all new plants use nuclear fuel. • Emission controls for SO_2 and particulates – same as Policy 1.
Policy 4	• Electrical generation – same as Policy 1. • After 1975, all coal is low-sulfur from distant mines in western states. • 50% of new plants after 1982 use coal and 50% use nuclear fuel. • After 1975, all coal and uranium is obtained from surface mines. • Emission controls for SO_2 and particulates – same as Policy 1.
Policy 5	• Electrical generation increases at an average annual growth rate of 2.8%. • Almost all new plants are fueled with coal. • Emission controls for SO_2 and particulates – same as Policy 1.
Policy 6	• Electrical generation – same as Policy 5. • Almost all new plants use nuclear fuel. • Emission controls for SO_2 and particulates – same as Policy 1.

alternative strategies differ slightly in form from those in Wisconsin. Furthermore, the choices are generally made at the national level. The current strategy favored by the government is the increasing penetration of electricity use in the energy market, with a major fraction of the electricity supplied by nuclear power. The current plan of Electricité de France is to have in the Rhone-Alpes area an installed capacity of approximately 6,000 MWe by 1980, and possible continued expansion thereafter. However, an energy study by the Institut Économique et Juridique de l'Energie in Grenoble provided a vivid picture of an alternative plan that involved significant energy conservation and increased emphasis on nonelectrical forms of energy.[12] Although the discussion and analysis of environmental impacts of alternative systems were initially not as intensive as those in Wisconsin, they are now receiving increased attention in both public and government circles.

In the GDR, the electricity generation technology has been almost exclusively based upon lignite fuel. Although the economic and environmental tradeoffs have been considered in the selection of energy strategies, the available options seem to have been relatively narrow in scope. However, when viewed farther into the future, for example, over the next 50 years, there appears to be a range of alternatives available. As in the other two regions, altering the nature and magnitude of energy demand would seem possible by influencing the economic infrastructure. Similarly, over time it appears feasible for the GDR to choose from a spectrum of supply technologies, including electricity (via nuclear energy) or a range of nonelectrical strategies, for example, district heating.

It is therefore possible to discuss a similar subset of electricity supply strategies within each of the three regions. Because more extensive environmental analysis had been performed for Wisconsin, it has been chosen as a case to illustrate the application of decision analysis to evaluate alternatives. However as will be discussed at the end of this chapter, the approach appears to be appropriate for application in the other regions as well.

IV.A. THE ALTERNATIVES FOR ELECTRICITY SUPPLY IN WISCONSIN

The policies which we will examine for electricity supply in Wisconsin will be defined by two decision variables:

- The fuels used to supply the electricity
- The degree of conservation of electricity, i.e. the limiting of demand

More specifically, the six policies evaluated are briefly described in Table E.1. The average annual growth rates of approximately five and three percent were selected from several alternative electricity generation scenarios presented in a previous publication.[11] The other characteristics of the policies in Table E.1 have been arbitrarily selected simply as illustrations. These policies by no means completely span the alternatives facing Wisconsin. For example, one issue not addressed in these six policies is the impact of alternative power plant cooling systems.

IV.B. THE OBJECTIVES AND ATTRIBUTES

In our analysis, we will focus on aspects such as the environment, human health and safety, and nuclear safeguards, rather than economic considerations. The latter have received considerably more attention historically, and we feel the features of decision analysis are better illustrated with the former.

After considerable discussion with individuals in policymaking roles in Wisconsin, a set of objectives for examining alternatives was outlined.[13] The process of specifying objectives requires some value judgments — deciding which objectives are important enough to include. For each of these, an attribute is specified to indicate the degree to which that objective is met. This resulted in the 11 attributes in Table E2. The units and ranges of possible impacts for the 6 alternatives evaluated are included in the table. These attributes are an aggregation of the numerous impact categories provided by the impact model described in the next section. Since the selection of attributes also depends on preferences and value judgment, another set of attributes may be more appropriate for a particular individual. For example, some people may feel that since occupational risks are presumably taken voluntarily, occupational fatalities should be considered separately from public fatalities. The first attribute in Table E.2 is the sum of all quantified health and accident fatalities, both occupational and public. In the overall process, there should be an iterative interaction between the utility assessment and the specification of the aggregated attributes.

TABLE E.2 Attributes for Initial Application of Multiattribute Decision Analysis to the Wisconsin Electrical Energy System

	Measure	Worst value	Best value
$X_1 \equiv$ total quantified fatalities	deaths	700	100
$X_2 \equiv$ permanent land use	acres	2,000	1
$X_3 \equiv$ temporary land use	acres	200,000	10,000
$X_4 \equiv$ water evaporated	10^{12} gal	1.5	0.5
$X_5 \equiv$ SO_2 pollution	10^6 tons	80	5
$X_6 \equiv$ particulate pollution	10^6 tons	10	0.2
$X_7 \equiv$ thermal energy needed	10^{12} kWh(t)	6	3
$X_8 \equiv$ radioactive waste	metric tons	200	1
$X_9 \equiv$ nuclear safeguards	tons of plutonium produced	50	1
$X_{10} \equiv$ health effects of chronic air pollution exposure	tons of lead	2,000	1
$X_{11} \equiv$ electricity generated	10^{12} kWh(e)	0.5	3

450

V. THE ELECTRICITY IMPACT MODEL

The generalized framework of the composite environmental impact model in Figure E.1 is elaborated upon in Figure E.2. The assumptions that specify a policy, namely a specified regional electricity demand and supply mix over a period of time, are provided as input to the Electricity Impact Model (EIM),[13,14] which was summarized in section IV.D.3. of Chapter 3. As described there, the primary input to the EIM is a set of assumptions about (1) quantity and sources of electrical generation as a function of time,* and (2) important parameters (e.g., technological relationships, accident rates), possibly time-dependent, that affect impacts. The primary output is an array of "quantified" environmental impacts associated with the power generating facilities as well as the supporting fuel industries. These systemwide impacts, which are aggregated into the 11 attributes $X_1, X_2, \ldots, X_{11}$, occur as a direct result of the electricity generation; a significant portion of the impacts may be imposed outside the region where the electricity is generated. For example, uranium is mined in the western part of the United States to fuel nuclear reactors located in Wisconsin.

It is difficult to display in a general fashion the ways in which electricity use results in impacts, but Figure E.3 shows the pathways for a large number of effects. Pathway 1 includes impacts such as air pollution from coal-fired plants, radioactive releases from the nuclear reactor, chemical releases from the power plant, and waste heat. The direct effects of electrical generation shown as Pathway 2 are effects at the power plant such as land and water use. Pathway 3 accounts for occupational health risk, such as uranium miners' exposure to radiation. Pollution from nuclear fuel reprocessing plants is represented by Pathway 4. Occupational accident risk at the power plant itself is shown as Pathway 5. Pathway 6 represents the usual economic costs and the unquantified impacts associated with electrical generation. To compare future alternatives, the decision maker must combine these quantified impacts with the unquantified impacts, conventional costs, and other factors that affect his decision process.

The calculation of quantified impacts from a particular energy system in a particular year is based upon impact factors that relate impacts to a unit of electricity generation for a reference plant in the specified year. The impact factor can be varied as a function of time to simulate changes in technology or regulation. There are numerous impact factors associated with each energy system in the EIM; an example is cases of black lung disability from underground bituminous coal mining per kWh of generation from coal plants.

Since all impacts cannot be quantified, the output of the EIM cannot be considered a complete set of impact information. Environmental impacts can be divided into quantified impacts (those included in the EIM) and unquantified impacts, i.e., all other environmental concerns not included in the EIM. Some impacts are unquantified because: (1) they have just been recognized as potentially important and therefore have not been investigated; (2) they are not even recognized as impacts; or (3) quantification is based almost entirely on value judgment. However, merely specifying and defining the impacts to be calculated requires some value judgments. Two examples of recognized unquantified impacts that are not included in the EIM are: the potential long-term global climatic effects of continued CO_2 release from fossil fuel combustion[15] and the potential long-term risks

---

* This information can be provided by other models, such as other submodels of the WISconsin Regional Energy Model.

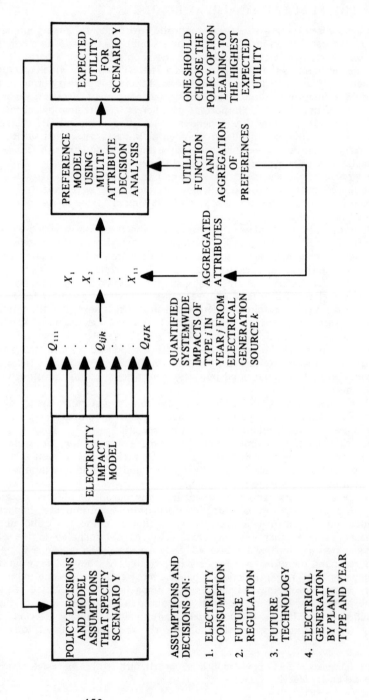

FIGURE E.2   Composite environmental impact model.

452

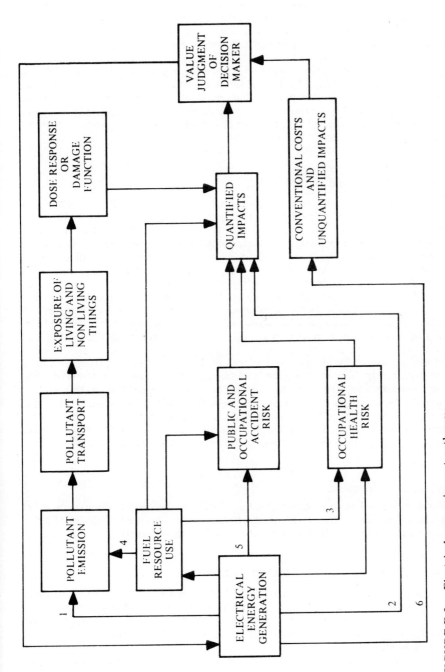

FIGURE E.3   Electrical energy impact pathways.

453

454

associated with radioactive waste.[16,17] Such potential impacts are difficult to quantify in conventional terms, but concerns over such recognized unquantified impacts can be included in multiattribute decision analysis by defining an appropriate proxy attribute. For instance, the amount of CO_2 released could be a proxy variable for its long-term climatic effects.

Since there is uncertainty associated with each impact factor in the EIM, the levels of impacts determined by the model could be expressed in terms of a probability distribution. With the present EIM, most of the impacts estimated do not have explicit probability distributions associated with them because, in general, the available data do not warrant the increased effort required to incorporate probability distributions in the model.

VI. THE PREFERENCE MODEL

Once all of the impacts of each alternative are specified as clearly as possible, it is still a very difficult task to identify the best policy. This is primarily due to the complexities of the problem outlined in section II. In this section, we introduce multiattribute utility as an approach for addressing these complexities in a systematic and rational manner. First, we will briefly review multiattribute utility theory, next suggest a procedure to render it operational, and finally discuss its implementation in conjunction with our electricity supply strategy problem.

Let us introduce some terminology in the context of our problem. We will define x_i to be a specific level of attribute X_i. For example, since X_1 is measured in number of deaths, then $x_1 = 230$ means a consequence of 230 deaths. The problem is to find a utility function $u(x) = u(x_1, \ldots, x_{11})$ over the 11 attributes $X_1, \ldots, X_{11}$.

If we have assessed u, we can say x is preferred to x' if $u(x)$ is greater than $u(x')$. More importantly, if any of the quantified impacts were expressed in terms of probability distributions, the decision analysis framework presented in this section would still be useful. In such a case, the probability distributions and utility functions would be integrated to provide expected utility. If the total impact of an alternative was quantified by probability density function $p(x)$ over consequences $x \equiv (x_1, \ldots, x_{11})$, then the expected utility $E(u)$ for that alternative is given by

$$E(u) = \int u(x)p(x)\,dx$$

integrated over all possible consequences. The ability to handle preferences under uncertainty is one of the strengths of utility theory. This quantification of probabilities and utilities greatly facilitates the use of sensitivity analyses.

VI.A. MULTIATTRIBUTE UTILITY THEORY

The main results of multiattribute utility theory concern representation theorems stating conditions under which a utility function can be expressed in a specific simple functional form. If such a form is appropriate for an analysis, it is then generally much easier to proceed with the assessments necessary to specify the utility function.

The basic notions used in deriving representation theorems are the concepts of preferential independence and utility independence. Let us state these concepts in terms of our problem and then state the representation theorem used in structuring preferences in the next section.

● *Preferential Independence*: The pair $\{X_1, X_2\}$ is preferentially independent of $\{X_3, \ldots, X_{11}\}$ if one's preference order for x_1, x_2 combinations in $(x_1, \ldots, x_{11})$, given $x_3, \ldots, x_{11}$ are held fixed, does not depend on the levels at which they are fixed.

This assumption is equivalent to saying the value tradeoffs between fatalities and permanent land use levels do not depend on radioactive waste, energy generated, and so on. It implies for instance, that the indifference curves over X_1 and X_2 levels do not depend on $X_3, \ldots, X_{11}$.

● *Utility Independence*: Attribute X_1 is utility independent of $\{X_2, \ldots, X_{11}\}$ if one's preference order for lotteries* on X_1, with $x_2, \ldots, x_{11}$ held fixed, does not depend on the levels at which it is fixed.

This assumption is equivalent to saying that decisions concerning alternatives which have different impacts on fatalities only (and which have the same impacts in terms of SO_2 pollution, radioactive waste, energy generated, and so on) can be made by considering these impacts on fatalities only and that these decisions will be the same regardless of the fixed levels of SO_2 pollution, radioactive waste, energy generated, and so on.

Using such independence notions, a multiattribute utility function can be split into parts. The following is an illustration of one such decomposition.

● *Theorem*: Given $\{X_1, \ldots, X_{11}\}$, if $\{X_1, X_i\}$, $i = 2, \ldots, 11$, is preferentially independent of the other attributes and if X_1 is utility independent of $\{X_2, \ldots, X_{11}\}$, then either

$$u(x_1, \ldots, x_{11}) = \sum_{i=1}^{11} k_i u_i(x_i), \text{ if } \sum k_i = 1 \qquad (1)$$

or

$$1 + ku(x_1, \ldots, x_{11}) = \prod_{i=1}^{11} [1 + kk_i u_i(x_i)], \text{ if } \sum k_i \neq 1 \qquad (2)$$

where u and u_i, $i = 1, \ldots, 11$, are utility functions scaled from 0 to 1, the k_i are scaling constants with $0 < k_i < 1$, and $k > -1$ is the nonzero solution to $1 + k = \prod_{i=1}^{11} (1 + kk_i)$ if (2) holds.

Equation (1) is the additive utility function and (2) is the multiplicative utility function. More details about these, including suggestions for assessment, are found in Keeney and Raiffa.[18] The important point is that provided the appropriate assumptions hold, the 11 attribute utility function can be assessed by assessing 11 one-attribute utility functions, u_i, plus 11 scaling constants, k_i. Such a decomposition makes assessment of u a much simpler task.

* A lottery is defined by indicating all possible consequences which may occur and their associated probabilities. Lotteries on X_1 are lotteries involving uncertainties about the level of X_1 only.

VI.B.   ASSESSING A UTILITY FUNCTION

The actual assessment process requires personal interaction with the decision maker, since his utility function is (and should be) a formalization of his subjective preferences. The utility function allows us to combine, in a logically consistent manner, the contribution of fatalities, SO_2 pollution, radioactive waste, electrical energy generated, and so on, into one index of desirability (namely, utility) for each possible state $(x_1, \ldots, x_{11})$. To capture the decision-maker's preferences requires that he explicitly address two types of issues:

1. The relative desirability of different degrees of achievement of a particular objective.
2. The relative desirability of some specified achievement of one objective versus another specified degree of achievement of a second objective

Addressing the first issue allows us to determine the u_i's in Eqs. (1) and (2), whereas information about the second issue is needed to specify the k_i's. Let us illustrate the types of questions used to obtain a utility function.

A question illustrating the first issue might be presented to the decision maker as follows:

"Suppose you must choose between two alternatives. It seems to you that their impacts in terms of all the attributes except energy generated are about the same. Alternative A, which is the status quo option, has very little uncertainty and will result in 1.5×10^{12} kWh(e) over the next 30 years. On the other hand, alternative B is innovative and has a large degree of uncertainty. Best estimates and experiments indicate that with alternative B, there is about a 50-50 chance of 1.1 or 2.1×10^{12} kWh(e) in the same period. If you have complete responsibility for the decision, which alternative would you choose?"

It is easy to see that B leads to an average of 1.6×10^{12} kWh(e), but because of the risks involved, the sure 1.5 may be preferred. A question addressing the second issue is as follows:

"Two competing policies C and D will result in identical consequences in terms of all attributes except fatalities and electricity generated. Policy C will give you 2.0×10^{12} kWh(e) but result in 500 fatalities over the next 30 years. Policy D leads to only 1.4×10^{12} kWh(e) but the associated deaths are 250. If the responsibility is yours, which of the two policies would you select?"

Collectively, responses to questions like those above directly address the uncertainty and multiple objective complexities raised earlier in this paper. One would naturally expect that if different individuals of a decision making unit went through such a line of questioning, they would respond differently. This would result in different utility functions. By examining these utility functions, it may be possible to get a clear indication of the substance and degree of disagreement. This is a first step toward resolving the differences.

VI.C. ASSESSMENTS

Utility assessments were completed for all 11 attributes for 2 individuals familiar with Wisconsin energy planning.* In section VIII, we also will briefly describe some related results involving the assessment of the preferences of some policy makers. Here we only briefly review some of the details of the assessment. A thorough review of one assessment is found in Keeney.[19]

The assessment procedure was divided into five steps:

1. Familiarizing the "decision maker" with the concepts of utility theory
2. Verifying preferential independence and utility independence assumptions
3. Assessing single-attribute utility functions
4. Assessing the scaling constants
5. Checking for consistency

The familiarization process is basically an explanation for the person whose preferences are being assessed by the person doing the assessing. The purpose is to agree on terminology and motivate the interest in the problem.

The preferential independence conditions were verified by examining indifference curves in 2 dimensions (i.e., with 2 attributes allowed to vary) with all other attribute levels fixed. The basic question was whether these indifference curves depended on the fixed levels of the other attributes. For all pairs we checked − 10 pairs for each individual − there were no dependencies; this indicates each pair of attributes was preferentially independent of the other nine.

Similarly, by assessing a utility function for 1 attribute conditioned on the other 10 being held at fixed levels, one can examine the dependency on those fixed levels. Again we found no dependencies; therefore, each attribute was utility independent of the others. This implied the utility function, in each of the two cases, would necessarily be of the form of Eq. (1) or Eq. (2).

To be consistent with either Eq. (1) or Eq. (2), the utility function u_i over attribute X_i is set equal to 0 at the least desirable level of X_i in the range. The shape of the function is determined by asking questions of type 1 discussed in the previous section. The results for Individuals A and B are given in Figure E.4 for 6 of the attributes. The shapes of the curves indicate that for tons of plutonium and electricity generation, Individual B preferred the midpoint of the range to a lottery that resulted in a 50-percent chance of the least desirable level and a 50-percent chance of the most desirable level. Individual A had different preferences for plutonium levels; he preferred the "best−worst" lottery over a certain 25.5 tons of plutonium.

Individual A felt that the most preferred level of electrical generation was approximately 1.5×10^{12} kWh(e) and that the least desirable level in the range was 0.5×10^{12} kWh(e). Therefore, his utility function for that attribute reaches 1.0 at 1.5×10^{12} kWh(e) and is less than 1.0 at the highest value of electricity generation. Several of the utility functions, including those in Figure E.4 for fatalities, were linear; in that case the individual was indifferent between the midpoint and a 50-50 lottery involving the extreme levels of the attribute.

Questioning on the utility function shape for the plutonium attribute revealed why the 2 individuals had such different preferences for that attribute. Individual

---

* These individuals frequently were consulted by persons having responsibilities for evaluating and selecting energy policy in Wisconsin; they had no direct decision responsibilities. Thus, the assessments here are meant to be illustrative; the results were not to be directly used in prescribing policy.

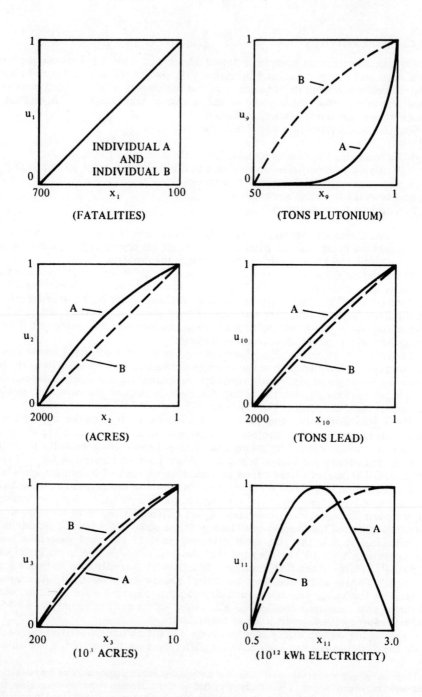

FIGURE E.4   Selected single-attribute utility functions for two individuals.

458

TABLE E.3   Utility Function Scaling Constants

	Individual A	Individual B
$X_1 \equiv$ total quantified fatalities	0.354	0.267
$X_2 \equiv$ permanent land use	.004	.018
$X_3 \equiv$ temporary land use	.033	.021
$X_4 \equiv$ water evaporated	.083	.016
$X_5 \equiv$ SO$_2$ pollution	.008	.060
$X_6 \equiv$ particulate pollution	.008	.008
$X_7 \equiv$ thermal energy needed	.017	.011
$X_8 \equiv$ radioactive waste	.132	.057
$X_9 \equiv$ nuclear safeguards	.177	.152
$X_{10} \equiv$ health effects of chronic air pollution exposure	.118	.339
$X_{11} \equiv$ electricity generated	.066	.051
Sum	1.0	1.0

A felt that once plutonium production is greater than a certain minimal level, the opportunity for undesirable events, such as theft, diversion, and terrorist attacks, will certainly exist because of increased problems of accountability, storage, and transportation. Furthermore, he felt that if plutonium production were very large, the likelihood of these undesirable events would only slightly increase. Therefore, Individual A had the "risk-prone" utility function shape for plutonium; he was willing to accept a 50-percent chance of the highest level (50 tons in this case) of plutonium production in order to obtain a 50-percent chance for the lowest level (1 ton), rather than taking a certain 25.5 (the average of 50 and 1) tons of production. On the other hand, Individual B felt that, over the indicated range, each additional ton of plutonium is more likely to result in these undesirable effects. Stated another way, he felt that the problems associated with accountability, storage, and transportation for 50 tons of plutonium were more than twice as difficult than for 25 tons of plutonium. Therefore his utility declines at an increasing rate for each additional ton of plutonium produced.

The scaling constants for the utility functions are shown in Table E.3. For both individuals, the sum of the k_i's is one, indicating the additive utility function (1) is appropriate. The values of the k_i depend strongly on the ranges of the attributes shown in Table E.2. If the range of one of the attributes were changed, *all* k_i would change. Comparison of the k_i's for an individual indicates the relative importance of each attribute for the specified ranges.

Both utility functions were subjected to internal consistency checks. When inconsistencies were identified, their respective implications were discussed with the appropriate individual, and he was asked to reconcile these by changing some of his assessments leading to the inconsistency. To help choose which assessments to change, we presented data indicating different manners in which the assessments could be altered to achieve consistency. Each of the preference assessments utilized here — which should be considered preliminary assessments — required approximately 1 day of assessment time. Such an effort often leads to important insights and an improved understanding of the problem. It also identifies gaps in knowledge (e.g. the health impact of lead emissions) relevant to preference assessments. To investigate these gaps may require significant efforts by researchers (e.g., the medical profession). With such information available, it would be possible to responsibly

TABLE E.4 Attribute Levels and Expected Utilities for Six Electrical Energy Policies in Wisconsin from 1970 to 2000

	Reference case[a]	Policy 1	Policy 2	Policy 3	Policy 4	Policy 5	Policy 6
$X_1 \equiv$ fatalities (deaths)	100	380	380	240	680	280	210
$X_2 \equiv$ permanent land use (acres)	1	420	420	1,100	770	380	730
$X_3 \equiv$ temporary land use (acres)	10,000	140,000	137,000	85,000	43,000	99,000	71,000
$X_4 \equiv$ water evaporated (10^{12} gal)	0.5	0.72	0.71	0.84	0.79	0.55	0.61
$X_5 \equiv$ SO_2 pollution (10^6 tons)	5.0	12	23	8.0	8.6	9.5	7.4
$X_6 \equiv$ particulate pollution (10^6 tons)	0.2	0.69	6.2	0.40	0.56	0.51	0.37
$X_7 \equiv$ energy needed (10^{12} kWh(t))	3.0	4.9	4.9	5.2	5.3	3.8	3.9
$X_8 \equiv$ radioactive waste (metric tons fission products)	1.0	61	61	160	110	54	105
$X_9 \equiv$ nuclear safeguards (tons fissile plutonium)	1.0	11	11	30	21	10	19
$X_{10} \equiv$ chronic health effects (tons lead emitted)	1.0	124	1,110	71	100	92	66
$X_{11} \equiv$ electricity generated							
(10^{12} kWh(e) nuclear)		0.36	0.36	0.99	0.68	0.33	0.64
(10^{12} kWh(e) coal)		1.37	1.37	0.74	1.05	0.99	0.68
(10^{12} kWh(e) coal + nuclear)	3.0	1.73	1.73	1.73	1.73	1.32	1.32
Expected Utilities							
Individual A	0.938	0.620	0.569	0.589	0.383	0.711	0.680
Individual B	1.0	0.789	0.624	0.785	0.631	0.846	0.849

[a] Attributes set at extreme values.

460

assess the utility function of a key "energy decision maker" with 1 to 3 days of his time.

VII. APPLICATION OF UTILITY FUNCTIONS TO EXAMINE POLICIES

The scaling factors in Table E.3 and the $u_i(x_i)$ completely specify the multiattribute utility function, $u(x_1, \ldots, x_{11})$. These two preliminary utility functions were used to evaluate expected utilities associated with the several energy policies (see Table E.1) concerning electrical generation in Wisconsin over the period 1970 through 2000. The impacts of each policy, characterized by levels of the attributes,* and the expected utilities for both individuals are listed in Table E.4. The reference case in the first column is listed simply for orientation. This case uses the "most desirable levels," that is, the lowest impacts and highest electrical generation, and results in an expected utility of 1.0 for Individual B. Since Individual A preferred a lower level of electricity generation to the maximum 3.0 (Figure E.4), his expected utility was not 1.0 for the reference case.

The implications of the remaining 6 policies in Table E.4 are output from the EIM. The attribute levels shown are the cumulative effects of electrical generation from 1970 through 2000; no time-discounting or measurement of preferences that depend on the timing of the impacts have been used in this illustrative application. The basic differences between the policies have been highlighted in Table E.1. The first four policies have identical electrical generation with different supply mixes and pollution control, while the last two policies have lower electrical generation with different supply mixes.

If it is assumed that the individuals expressed their true preferences and that they behave in a logically consistent manner, the expected utilities can be used to indicate their overall preferences. Under these conditions, Table E.4 shows that both individuals should prefer the low electricity policies over the first four policies. This is primarily because increasing electrical generation, without changing the supply mix, results in higher levels of impacts. The decrease in utility associated with higher levels of impacts must be more than offset by increased utility associated with the increased level of electrical generation if cases with higher electrical generation are to have higher expected utilities. For these particular policies, Individual A has approximately the same utility for the lower level of electrical generation as for the higher level (Figure E.4) and therefore has no increase in utility to balance the decrease associated with increased levels of impacts. Individual B does have some increase in utility associated with the increased level of electrical generation but for these policies the increase was not sufficient to compensate for the decrease in utility associated with increased levels of impacts.

No strong preferences are evident for policy 1 over policy 3 or for policy 5 over policy 6. Thus, if the purpose of the assessment were to indicate whether a mostly coal or mostly nuclear energy future is preferred by the decision maker, further analysis would be necessary. If these techniques were applied to a real policy study,

---

* Of course, the impacts of energy policies are not known with the certainty indicated in the table. With more effort, the present deterministic EIM could be used as a basis for a probabilistic simulation model to characterize policies by probability distributions over levels of the attributes. One would combine these probability distributions with the utility functions to calculate expected utilities for evaluating the policies.

TABLE E.5   Ranges of the Four Attributes Used in Utility Assessments

	Units	Range
$X_1 \equiv$ Total quantified fatalities	Deaths	100–700
$X_2 \equiv SO_2$ pollution	10^6 tons	5–80
$X_3 \equiv$ Radioactive waste	Metric tons	0–200
$X_4 \equiv$ Electricity generated	10^{12} kWh(e)	0.5–3.0

the attribute list would be expanded to include other impacts and to include conventional costs.

The utilities in Table E.4 can also be directly used if uncertainty is incorporated into the models. For example, if Individual A had a choice between an alternative 1: Impacts of policy 3 for sure, and an alternative 2: A 50-percent chance of the impacts of policy 4 and a 50-percent chance of the impacts of policy 5, he should prefer alternative 1, since his expected utility for this is 0.589 and for alternative 2 it is only $0.5(0.383 + 0.711) = 0.547$. This expected utility feature is one of the main reasons for using multiattribute utility for analyzing problems where uncertainties are important. In this example, the uncertainties could be associated with the levels of impacts or the ability to carry out the policies.

VIII.   INITIAL UTILITY ASSESSMENTS OF POLICYMAKERS IN THE THREE REGIONS

The detailed utility assessments discussed in section VI of this chapter quantified the preferences of energy/environment specialists from Wisconsin, but not actual policymakers. Those assessments are in themselves important — both the process and the results — but they do not indicate whether policymakers would be willing to investigate the usefulness of multiattribute utility to help them examine some very complex questions. To examine this question, preliminary utility assessments were completed for 5 individuals from the GDR, Rhone-Alpes, and Wisconsin. The group included a mixture of policymakers and energy/environment specialists. The resulting utility functions were used to evaluate a subset of the alternative electricity supply policies discussed in the previous section (Table E.1).

To further simplify the task (because of time limitations) only 4 of the 11 attributes in Table 2 were used. The 4 attributes and their ranges are given in Table E.5. Collectively these 4 attributes covered a variety of value-tradeoff issues embodied in the energy planning and evaluation processes. The non-Wisconsin individuals were made aware of current trends in Wisconsin electricity use so that they could understand the ranges of that attribute. The preliminary assessments presented here required 2 to 3 hours from each of the individuals whose utility function was measured.

The scaling constants for the resulting utility functions are shown in Table E.6. Three of the individuals' overall utility functions turned out to be multiplicative and the other two additive. Total quantified fatalities had either the largest or second largest k_i in all 5 cases. Electricity generation ranked first in importance for the only individual who did not have k_1 larger than the other k_i.

These 5 preliminary utility functions were used to evaluate expected utilities associated with several policies for electrical generation in Wisconsin over the period 1970 through 2000. The levels of the 4 attributes and the expected utilities

TABLE E.6 Utility Function Scaling Constants for Five Individuals

	Fatalities (k_1)	SO_2 (k_2)	Radioactive Waste (k_3)	Electricity Generated (k_4)	Multiplicative Scaling Constant (k) (Eq. 2)
A	0.30	0.05	0.015	0.030	13.8
B	0.60	0.016	0.14	0.10	0.8
C	0.33	0.275	0.0	0.55	$-$ 0.4
D	0.65	0.02	0.24	0.09	a
E	0.61	0.14	0.14	0.11	a

[a] These individuals had additive utility functions (Eq. 1).

TABLE E.7 Expected Utilities for Five Individuals for Four Policies

	Reference Case: Attributes at Extreme Levels	Policy 1: Mostly Coal, Good Pollution Control	Policy 2: Mostly Nuclear Energy	Policy 3: Low-Sulfur Coal from Distant Mines and Some Nuclear Energy	Policy 4: Mostly Coal with Less Electricity
Total quantified fatalities	100	380	240	680	280
SO$_2$ pollution (10^6 tons)	5.0	12	8.0	8.6	9.5
Radioactive waste (metric tons)	0.0	61	160	110	54
Electricity generated (10^{12} kWh(e))	3.0	1.7	1.7	1.7	1.3
Expected utility for individual A	1.00	0.53	0.66	0.14	0.65
B	1.00	0.56	0.63	0.14	0.65
C	1.00	0.76	0.83	0.64	0.41
D	0.92	0.62	0.66	0.24	0.73
E	1.00	0.65	0.72	0.31	0.74

for each of the individuals are listed in Table E.7. The reference case — attributes at extreme levels — is listed simply for orientation; it uses the "most desirable levels," that is, the lowest impacts and highest electrical generation, and results in an expected utility of 1.0.

The implications of the remaining 4 policies in Table E.7 are output from the EIM. Policy 1 has most of the generation at coal-fired plants with relatively good pollution control. Nuclear power contributed only about 20 percent of the cumulative generation from 1970 through 2000. Policy 2 has the same electricity generation as policy 1, and nearly 60 percent is from nuclear sources. Policy 3 has about 40 percent of the generation from nuclear sources and the remainder from coal-fired plants that use low-sulfur coal obtained from surface mines that are more than 2,000 kilometers from the power plants. Policy 4 has about 25 percent less electrical generation, and coal-fired plants produce about 75 percent of the total generation.

Table E.7 shows that all 5 individuals should prefer one or more of the other policies to policy 3. This is primarily the result of the large number of fatalities expected for policy 3 and the relatively high scaling factor each of the individuals place on fatalities (Table E.6).

Individual C indicated a strong preference to achieve a certain level of electrical generation, and therefore he had higher expected utilities from policies 1, 2, and 3 than from policy 4, which had a lower level of electricity generation. Individuals A, B, and E would view policy 2 (higher generation mainly from nuclear sources) and policy 4 (lower generation and less nuclear power penetration) almost the same.

It is clear that if this technique were applied to a detailed policy over a longer time of study, considerably more analysis would be necessary and the attribute list would be expanded to include other impacts and conventional costs. However, this experience with individuals from the 3 regions indicated that at least some policy-makers were willing to think hard about their preferences and quantify them in a manner that could aid the analysis of policy choices that they faced.

IX. BENEFITS OF THE ASSESSMENT PROCESS

In the previous two sections it was shown how a utility function can assist one in evaluating policy. The *process* of assessing the utility function has many benefits in itself. The process can be a substantial aid in identifying important issues and sensitizing individuals to them, generating and evaluating alternatives, isolating and resolving conflicts of judgment and preference between members of the decision-making team, communication between several decision makers, and, in this particular application, identifying improvements needed in the impact model.

IX.A. COMMUNICATION

The assessment of preferences forces individuals to be more precise in deciding why they feel certain levels of attributes are important. Clearly policymakers must face such issues regularly. However, because of the complexities that cloud their choices, the value trade-offs involved are sometimes a bit hazy. The assessment formalization helps to make the trade-offs more explicit. With a better understanding of one's own values, it should be much easier to communicate them to others. The communication then serves as a catalyst to identify parts of the problem which were previously overlooked. As an example, the initial reaction to a trade-off involving human fatalities and other impacts is often discomfort, as one must effectively place a value on human life (or a reduction in someone's lifetime). The viewpoint eventually reached is that such tradeoffs are practical questions that must be addressed for rational decisions.

IX.B. IDENTIFYING IMPORTANT ISSUES

When one assesses preferences, it is often the case that the respondent says something like "I can't answer that definitely, because it depends on . . . ." This sometimes indicates important structural relationships not in the model. For instance, a decision maker may say that trade-offs between fatalities and energy generated depends on who is dying, how, and when. If this is important in making the decision, then obviously the decision maker should have the information when the decision is made. In trying to informally analyze the entire problem, such issues are sometimes overlooked.

As mentioned earlier, some people feel that occupational risks are partially compensated by salary premiums and therefore occupational health and safety should be considered separately from health and safety of the general public, who expose themselves to the risks involuntarily. In addition, some people feel that an illness that disables or gradually leads to death is worse than a fatality caused by an accident. The timing of the impacts must also be addressed. Radiation health impacts may not appear for many years after the exposure due to the electrical generation, while uranium mining fatalities occur some years before the generation occurs. The generation itself may be taking place over a period of years. Thus, in the limit, one can imagine separate impact categories for occupational health impact in time period 1, occupational accident impact in time period 1, public health impact in time period 1, and so forth. The process of aggregating or disaggregating these impact categories is part of the preference assessment.

IX.C. ISOLATING AND RESOLVING CONFLICT

Roughly speaking, the scaling factors in Eqs. (1) and (2) in section VI.A. designated by k_i indicate the importance of the respective attributes of the possible concerns. If these are different for different individuals, it may be possible to go behind the answers and get at the reasons for the differences. For example, one might find that an individual who originally assessed a rather large k_5 (associated with SO_2 pollution) relative to k_1 (associated with fatalities) had knowledge about very large detrimental impacts of SO_2 of which other individuals were not aware. Upon reflection, some individuals may then change their preferences to reduce the conflict.

The assessment process, a period of reflection, and discussions with other people resulted in some changes in scaling factors and single-attribute utility functions for at least one of the individuals involved in this study.[19] The statements concerning one's preferences that are required during assessment are sometimes difficult to provide, especially when one must associate for the first time some unquantified effects with a proxy variable. After such an experience, individuals may be more likely to discuss their judgments about particular attributes which they have weighted differently from other individuals.

IX.D. IMPROVEMENTS IN IMPACT MODELS

All of the above three advantages of the formalism of preference models have desirable effects for the development of the impact model. It helps to focus on what impacts should be modeled, on structural relationships and interdependencies to indicate how to model these impacts, and on data necessary for a responsible modeling effort. The modelers are made aware of additional areas of concern and what proxy variables are appropriate for impacts that are difficult to quantify in conventional terms.

IX.E. GENERATING ALTERNATIVES

Because of different preferences, we may find that a particular "best" overall alternative is rated very good for most of the members of the decision group, but rather low for a few. From detailed examination, it might be clear that the difference is caused by attribute X_3, for example. Then by focusing thought on alternatives which might improve attribute X_3, the group may find an alternative much better for those who disliked the original alternative and only slightly worse for those who liked it. Conceivably, one might even find a new alternative better for everyone. Because of the complexity in the problem, it is sometimes possible to generate such "dominant" alternatives.

X. POTENTIAL IMPLEMENTATION OF THE METHODOLOGY

This chapter has described a methodology for using decision analysis in conjunction with environmental impact analysis of energy systems. In addition to the methodology presented, an example was presented for the evaluation of several energy/environment policies in the state of Wisconsin. It was shown how a utility function can assist one in evaluating alternative policies, and that, in addition, the *process* of assessing the utility function also has many benefits in itself. This section suggests some possible mechanisms and benefits of applications of this methodology in the three regions studied in the IIASA research program.

Because each of the three regions has a very different set of energy/environment models as well as greatly differing institutional structures for decision- and policy-making, the use of decision analysis would differ in each case. It might be more applicable to policy issues in a given region than in others. However, in view of the many person-years of scientific effort that have been devoted to constructing energy/environment models in each of the countries, it does not seem at all unreasonable to consider devoting a modest amount of time to the construction of preference models for use with impact models. A relatively small amount of effort may have a significant effect. Some alternative approaches to the application of the methodology are outlined below for each of the three regions.

X.A. WISCONSIN

Energy/environment decision and policymakers in Wisconsin operate within a relatively decentralized structure, that is, the decision making is diffuse (see Appendix B, section III). As a consequence, the information and technical expertise is also distributed broadly throughout a number of agencies and offices. The methodology described in this chapter could be used to conduct formal assessments of decision- and policymakers at various levels of government to provide them with a better understanding of the trade-offs between the many complex issues. Clearly, in this case the method would not be used to provide a recipe for overall formal decision making but rather as a tool to improve communication, clarify some of the more complex issues, help generate alternatives, and to help individual decision-making units in the system.

A second use of the methodology would be the assessment of the scientific and technical staff of Wisconsin energy and environment commissions to aid them in structuring their research priorities. One of the major objectives of this application is the identification of gaps in knowledge and in methodology. In Wisconsin, the approach might be of value to the Public Service Commission, the Department of Natural Resources, the Department of Transportation, the State Planning Office, and perhaps others.

A less conventional and as yet untested use of this methodology would be as a means of interaction with public interest groups for the purpose of clarifying their understanding of and positions on energy/environment issues. For example, in Wisconsin the Environmental Defense Fund, the Sierra Club, and the League of Women Voters might be appropriate clients for this method. It would help not only to clarify the issues and perhaps raise the level of the discussions, but it might also help these public interest groups to arrive at their positions on a specific issue. Clearly, this use is not without its problems; it is understandable that a user of such an approach must be convinced that it will provide him with additional information with which to make his decisions and with which he can better achieve his objectives.

X.B.   RHONE-ALPES

Each of the applications for Wisconsin is also of potential use in the Rhone-Alpes, but because the region is far less self-governing than Wisconsin the applications of the methodology would be different. Use of the methodology as an aid in laying out research priorities might be appropriate for helping French national agencies to understand the regional aspects of their policies and to establish their research priorities related to regional questions. Electricité de France is planning a major expansion of nuclear power for the Rhone-Alpes region. The use of an impact model in conjunction with a preference model could help to clarify the issues as perceived by local groups in that region. From another perspective, we found interest on the part of local agencies in using this approach as a discussion tool. During the IIASA workshop, Management of Energy/Environment Systems, in November 1975, various local French participants expressed interest in further experimentation with the method.

X.C.   THE GERMAN DEMOCRATIC REPUBLIC

Each of the above approaches could also be applied in one way or another in the GDR. However, because there is much greater use of formal government planning in the GDR, less emphasis would probably be given to its use in interaction with local and public groups. It seems admirably suited for use in efforts to obtain appropriate objective functions for formal optimization models in the energy and environment sectors. One major problem associated with the use of formal optimization procedures is defining suitable objective functions and constraints. Clearly, these objective functions and constraints should take into account a multitude of costs, benefits, system attributes, and the like; decision analysis could help considerably to determine the ways in which these should be combined within a formal optimization procedure. Research is currently underway at IIASA and the University of Wisconsin to develop a formalism for incorporating decision analysis into formal optimization procedures for energy/environment system planning.

XI. FINAL COMMENTS

The above suggestions are only indicative of possible uses of decision analysis as a tool for embedding impact models into an institutional framework for policy design and analysis. Such an approach would require in each of the three regions the development of some knowledge of decision analysis and utility theory. Admittedly, the use of the technique is as much an art as a science. However, the same could be said about building an impact model from an infinite array of possible environmental impacts.

In ending this discussion, we must add the obvious caveat. Even though a preference model combined with an impact model can be used to evaluate alternatives, the answers and implications for action are all conditional on the model's being a complete representation of the real world. This is clearly never the case. The composite model can serve as an aid to decision makers but it cannot and should not replace them or their judgment in making decisions.

REFERENCES

1. Leopold, L.B., F.E. Clark, B.B. Henshaw, and J.R. Bassley. "A Procedure for Evaluating Environmental Impact." U.S. Geological Survey Circular 645, 1971.

2. Inhaber, H. "Environmental Quality: Outline for a National Index for Canada." *Science* 186: 798–805, 1974.

3. Bender, M., and S.B. Ahmed. "Index of the Composite Environment (ICE): A Basis for Evaluating Environmental Effects of Electric Power Generating Plants in Response to NEPA." Oak Ridge National Laboratory, ORNL-TM-4492, 1974.

4. Morrison, D.L., R.H. Males, R.M. Duke, V.L. Sharp, and R.L. Ritzman. "Environmental Benefit-Cost Analysis for Power Generation." *Proc Am Power Conf* 34: 238–254, 1972.

5. Papp, R., P.E. McGrath, L.D. Maxim and F.X. Cook, Jr. "A New Concept in Risk Analysis for Nuclear Facilities." *Nucl. News* 17 (14): 62–65, Nov. 1974.

6. Keeney, R.L. and Keshavan Nair. Evaluating Potential Nuclear Power Plant Sites in the Pacific Northwest Using Decision Analysis. Report No. PP-76-1, International Institute for Applied Systems Analaysis, Laxenburg, Austria, 1976.

7. Keeney, R.L., and G.A. Robilliard. Assessing and Evaluating Environmental Impacts at Proposed Nuclear Power Plant Sites. Report No. PP-76-3, International Institute for Applied Systems Analysis, Laxenburg, Austria, 1976.

8. Burnham, J.B. "A Technique for Environmental Decision Making Using Quantified Social and Aesthetic Values." Pacific Northwest Laboratories, Richland, Washington, PNWL-1787, 1974.

9. Keeney, R.L., and H. Raiffa. "Critique of Formal Analysis in Public Decision Making," In A.W. Drake, R.L. Keeney, P.M. Morse (eds) *Analysis of Public Systems*. MIT Press, Cambridge, Massachusetts, 1972.

10. von Neumann, J., and O. Morgenstern. *Theory of Games and Economic Behavior*. 2nd Ed., Princeton University Press, Princeton, New Jersey, 1947.

11. Buehring, W.A., W.K. Foell, P.H. Hunter, D.A. Jacobson, P.D. Kishline, J.A. Pappas, and D.B. Shaver. Alternative Future Electricity Generation Requirements for the State of Wisconsin. Institute for Environmental Studies Report No. 26, University of Wisconsin – Madison, 1974.

12. Institut Economique et Juridique de l'Energie, Grenoble. *Alternatives Au Nucléaire*. Presses Universitaires de Grenoble, 1975.

13. Buehring, W.A. "A Model of Environmental Impacts from Electrical Generation in Wisconsin." Ph.D. dissertation, Dept. of Nuclear Engineering, University of Wisconsin – Madison, 1975.

14.   Buehring, W.A., and W.K. Foell. Environmental Impact of Electrical Generation: A System-wide Approach, Report No. RR-76-13, International Institute for Applied Systems Analysis, Laxenburg, Austria, 1976.

15.   Broecker, W.S., "Climatic Change: Are we on the Brink of a Pronounced Global Warming?" *Science* 189 (4201): 460–463, Aug. 8, 1975.

16.   U.S. Atomic Energy Commission. "High Level Radioactive Waste Management Alternatives." WASH-1297, May 1974.

17.   Avenhaus, R., W. Häfele, and P.E. McGrath. Considerations on the Large Scale Deployment of the Nuclear Fuel Cycle. Report No. RR-75-36, International Institute for Applied Systems Analysis, Laxenburg, Austria, 1975.

18.   Keeney, R.L., and H. Raiffa. *Decisions with Multiple Objectives,* Wiley, New York, 1976.

19.   Keeney, R.L. Energy Policy and Value Tradeoffs. Report No. RM-75-76, International Institute for Applied Systems Analysis, Laxenburg, Austria, 1976.

Author Index

Subject Index

An *n* following a page number indicates a footnote; a *t* indicates a table. Page numbers in italic type indicate figures.

486

and housing type, in Wisconsin,
207, *208*
residential, in Bezirk-X Base Case,
80, *81*
in France, 133t, 135−136
regional comparison of, all
scenarios, 235
in Wisconsin, 166, 191
service sector, in Bezirk-X Base
Case, 80, *81*
regional comparison of, all
scenarios, 238−239, 238t
in Rhone-Alpes Base Case, 131
in Rhone-Alpes scenarios, 144
from solar energy, 48
Stack heights. *See also* Emission standards; Pollution control
in Wisconsin Base Case, 189
Stadtgas, 48, 83t
State Planning Office (Wisconsin),
351, *352*
Strip mining, of lignite, in Bezirk-X
Base Case, 83
Substitution optimization model
(GDR), 342
Sulfur content, of oil, in France,
355−356
Sulfur dioxide emissions. *See also*
Environmental impacts;
Pollutant emissions
in Bezirk-X Base Case, 90−93, *90,*
91, 92, 93
in GDR, 71
and human health, in Bezirk-X Base
Case, 93−96, *94*, 95t
regional comparison of, 263−265,
264, 265, 264t
in Rhone-Alpes scenarios, *152,* 154,
160
in Wisconsin Base Case, 182, 182t,
188−189, *189, 190*
in Wisconsin scenarios, 203, *203,*
212
Synthetic fuels, 48. *See also* Energy
sources
in Wisconsin Base Case, 181, 184,
190
in Wisconsin scenarios, 174, 175

Technological assumptions, for Rhone-
Alpes Base Case, 128−136
for Rhone-Alpes scenarios,
144−146, 144t, 145t

for residential sector, in Rhone-
Alpes Base Case, 134−136
for service sector, in Rhone-Alpes
Base Case, 131−133
Thermal discharges. *See* Waste heat
disposal
Transportation, in Bezirk-X Base Case,
83t
in Bezirk-X scenarios, 112
in France, 120
in GDR, 280−282
and pollutant emissions, 55
responsibility for, in Wisconsin,
348−349
in Rhone-Alpes, 300−303
in scenario writing, 23
in Wisconsin, 166
in Wisconsin scenarios, 174
Transportation energy consumption,
in Bezirk-X Base Case, 85−87,
86, 96−97
in Bezirk-X scenarios, *101*
regional comparison of, 231−234,
231
in Rhone-Alpes Base Case, 128, *130*
in Rhone-Alpes scenarios, 145−146
in Wisconsin Base Case, 176−177
in Wisconsin scenarios, 194, 215
Transportation model, *41*

Unemployment, in France, 117
United States, energy pricing in,
399−404
University of Wisconsin, 350−351
Uranium consumption, in Wisconsin
scenarios, 212−213
Uranium mining, in Rhone-Alpes Base
Case, 142, 143, 143t
Uranium pricing, in U.S., 403
Urbanization, in GDR, 15t, 280t
in IIASA Regional Energy/
Environment Study, 2
modeling of, 39
and personal transportation energy
use, in Wisconsin scenarios,
213, 214
in Rhone-Alpes, 15t
in Rhone-Alpes Base Case, 127
in Rhone-Alpes scenarios, 123
in scenario writing, 22−23
in Wisconsin, 15t, 170t, 171
in Wisconsin scenarios, 192, 194,
215

Appetite for Death

By the same author

A Deepe Coffyn
A Tasty Way to Die
Hotel Morgue
Recipe for Death
Death and the Epicure
Death at the Table
To Kill the Past
Death à la Provençale
Diet for Death
Canaletto and the Case of Westminster Bridge

Janet Laurence

Appetite for Death

MACMILLAN

First published 1998 by Macmillan
an imprint of Macmillan Publishers Ltd
25 Eccleston Place, London SW1W 9NF
and Basingstoke

Associated companies throughout the world

ISBN 0 333 74049 1

1 3 5 7 9 8 6 4 2

A CIP catalogue record for this book is available from
the British Library.

Typeset by Intype London Ltd
Printed and bound in Great Britain by
Mackays of Chatham plc, Chatham, Kent

To Ben,
who inspired Rory,
and Alfie,
who appeared halfway through the writing

Acknowledgements

Many thanks to the following who provided much necessary information: Michelle Berriedale-Johnson, for details on running a specialist food production company and also on food intolerances; Richard Anderson of Puddings and Pies, for showing me round his food company and sharing his experiences; Dr Christina Scott-Moncrieff and Dr Yvonne Greenish for medical details. Any errors in this book are mine, not theirs.

Heartfelt thanks also to Tessa Warburg, Shelley Bovey, Maggie Makepeace, Brigid McConville and Lizzie Pewsey (The Group) for invaluable advice, understanding and support.

Finally, as always, my deepest thanks to my long-suffering husband, Keith, who puts up with scratch meals, untidy house and monosyllabic wife until the current opus is finished.

Chapter One

Darina Lisle raised a silver spoon loaded with mashed fish finger and potato. A pair of eyes so blue they made sapphires look overrated gazed into hers, their concentration absolute. Then the food vanished into an eager mouth, a look of bliss came over the small face and a fat fist banged down in ecstasy. It caught the edge of the plastic bowl with its prettily patterned rim and the contents shot out, splattering the kitchen wall and the tray of the high chair.

The blue eyes grew round in wonder and a gurgle of appreciative noises were almost intelligible as two chubby fingers dabbled experimentally in the splodges then picked up a fragment of fish and carefully conveyed it to their owner's mouth.

'What a greedy guts,' said Jemima Ealham. She was sitting comfortably in a cushioned kitchen chair nursing a glass of white wine and made no attempt to help.

'I'd call him a keen trencherman,' laughed Darina, rescuing bits of food from the tray of the high chair. 'Rory is the sort of man I like to cook for.' Some of the depression that had crept over her during the last few weeks, like fog infiltrating a sunny stretch of water, dampening all sparkle and muffling thought, lifted.

'Don't worry about that,' Jemima said idly as Darina

1

went over to the sink for a cloth. 'Mrs Starr will be in soon, she can clear up.'

'Haven't changed your habits since school, I see. Still get everyone else to do your dirty work.' It was said with a lightness that removed any possible sting from the words and Jemima didn't appear to take offence. She was a tall girl, not as tall as Darina, but well over medium height; thin rather than slim, with a restless energy that kept her shifting in her chair, reaching for the plate of cheese straws, pouring more wine, fiddling with the buttons on the jacket of her shocking-pink tailored suit, worn, it seemed, without any form of blouse underneath. The sharp knees revealed by the short skirt made her oddly vulnerable, an impression heightened by the short brown hair and too big nose that dominated an elfish face. Large blue eyes reflected emotions that changed too rapidly to be identified.

'Never do anything you can get someone else to do for you is one of Dad's maxims, and look where it's got him.' Jemima grinned at Darina.

Darina finished the wiping up and returned to feeding the small child. 'If you're still hungry when you've finished that, I'll grill you another fish finger,' she told Rory, for once abandoning her long held principle of not cooking in other people's houses unless she was paid for it. Feeding people was Darina's business. Before she'd turned into a writer and television demonstrator, she'd been a caterer, but babies were a novelty. She intended them to stay that way, at least for the immediate future, but it was impossible not to succumb to the charm of his big, wondering eyes.

'I've seen fillet of beef attacked with less gusto,' Darina commented as Rory cleaned off the spoon with

2

enthusiasm. 'Perhaps it's time you offered him something more challenging than fish fingers?'

'Don't you start! Dad's trying to get his latest girlfriend to start a line of gourmet baby foods, says kids like Rory need educating.'

'Really? Sounds great. What sort of line is she in?'

Jemima lost her animation. 'Val Douglas? Not sure exactly, she has this company that's something to do with foods for people who can't eat certain things. She and Dad are pretty chummy at the moment. And, well, you know Dad, always thinks he knows best for other people.'

What Darina remembered best about Basil Ealham were his absences. Jemima's father had rarely made an appearance at their school. Once, however, he'd landed on the hockey pitch in a helicopter, leaving Jemima covered with glory and for once not having to explain that her father was far too important running his business empire to attend founder's or sports' day. More recently, on the rare occasions she glanced at the financial pages, she'd seen his name mentioned in take-overs, always on the winning side.

'Did you say Val Douglas? I've met her. She used to write cookery articles for one of the women's magazines but I haven't seen her around at press do's or the Guild of Food Writers for some time.'

Jemima appeared uninterested in this piece of information. 'Well, Dad thinks the time's ripe to launch a gourmet baby food and that Val should do it.'

'Is she going to?'

Jemima gave a hoarse little laugh. 'If she wants to keep in Dad's good books, she will. They fight enough as it is.'

3

'Fight?' Darina found it hard to imagine the controlled and pleasant Val Douglas fighting with anyone. 'What about?'

'Oh, I don't know, whether streamlining production would affect quality, that sort of thing, Val gets quite heated.'

Darina could remember Val sounding off about commercial production methods that reduced the best of ingredients to anonymity.

'At the moment,' Jemima continued, 'they're on about what privileged babies need for their daily diet. I can't see why they bother. Why not fish fingers? After all, they've got protein and everything, haven't they?'

'Nutritionally, they're excellent,' Darina agreed. 'But they're not much of a culinary experience. Why not challenge a baby's taste buds? Stimulate their palates? After all, early habits shape the rest of our lives.'

'I suppose your mother was a marvellous cook,' Jemima said idly.

Darina laughed. 'Ma hates cooking! But a gastronomic cousin used to stay with us and he was always experimenting in the kitchen. I grew up waiting for the next meal.'

'And now you're taking over from Delia Smith.' Jemima sounded genuinely impressed.

Darina gave a derisive snort. 'Wish I was! You see before you a struggling food writer. I lost my regular column recently and still haven't found another.'

'But you're on television! I saw one of the programmes, what was it, a year ago?'

'Over a year, and nothing since,' Darina said gloomily, feeling more and more depressed. 'I haven't even got a book commission at the moment. Since I got married, nothing seems to have gone right.' She hadn't meant to say that, somehow it had slipped out.

Jemima sat up a little, a wicked light in her eyes. 'Darina the great optimist in the dumps? I don't believe it. Mind you, I've never thought marriage had much going for it. Love 'em and leave 'em, that's my motto.' Her air of bravado suggested otherwise.

'I'd hate to leave William,' Darina said simply.

'How long have you been married?'

'Eighteen months.' It had been a cold March day, blustery, the wind had whipped her veil across her face as they stood outside the church for the wedding photographs. Finally the photographer had asked for a volunteer to stand behind her and hold the fine tulle in place. With Darina's height, it hadn't been difficult to find a girlfriend who would be swallowed up and not intrude in the family grouping.

'Practically still a bride! You wait!'

'You haven't had a go yourself?'

'Far too canny,' Jemima said positively.

Darina laid down the spoon and wiped excess food off Rory's mouth with the side of her finger. He gave her an enormous grin that lit up his face like northern lights on a winter's night, uttered another mouthful of almost intelligible phrases and picked up the spoon.

Again the load of depression shifted from Darina as she smiled at him and reached for the implement.

He screamed with outrage and waved the spoon possessively. It caught her eye and the momentary maternal impulse vanished. 'Ouch! Don't do that!'

'He hates giving anything up,' Jemima said laconically, sipping her wine. 'Just like his grandfather. He's going to be such a handful.'

'Can you really feed yourself?' Darina asked Rory. He gave her another big grin, said, 'Da,' dug the spoon clumsily into the bowl and raised some food to his mouth. With an enormous effort he managed to eat most of it.

'I can see why you're all dotty about him.'

'I'm not dotty about him,' Jemima declared. 'I find it quite easy to resist the charms of nappy-changing, screams in the middle of the night, toys scattered everywhere and Rory relentless in the pursuit of what he wants. As I said, he reminds me too much of Dad.' Then she spoilt the impact of this by popping a kiss on the baby's head as she brought a glass of wine over to Darina.

'Isn't he like your sister at all?' Darina asked as she watched, fascinated, the baby's struggles to eat his lunch. Such determination, such greed!

Jemima shrugged her narrow shoulders. 'Can you see any resemblance?'

'I never really knew Sophie,' Darina said apologetically. 'She was so much younger than us, ten years, wasn't it? I only met her when she was a little girl, that time I went on holiday with you all.' From some deep recess of memory she dragged out a picture of a small child hugging an enormous teddy bear that had taken up much too much room on the journey out to Italy, sucking her thumb and surveying her big sister's friend with large brown eyes. 'When did she die?'

'When Rory was born.' Jemima circled her glass of wine on the table.

'How dreadful! Why? I thought childbirth was pretty safe these days.'

'I wasn't there at the time but Dad said it was toxaemia.'

'It sounds as though she didn't have proper care,' Darina suggested doubtfully. It was difficult to imagine a child of the well-heeled Ealham family not being given the best of medical attention under any circumstances, let alone a pregnancy.

Jemima sighed. 'She'd run away from home. Just dropped out of sight. We didn't know where she was or what she was doing until the hospital called Dad and said she'd had a child and was dying.'

Darina tried to imagine losing sight of a sister like that and failed. 'How dreadful! Your father must have been out of his mind with worry!'

Jemima was silent.

'Why did she leave home?'

Jemima shrugged again. 'I don't know. I was living in town when she left, running my fashion boutique.' She looked at Darina. 'Since Mother died, I haven't spent much time at home. I tried to keep in touch with Sophie, I really did, but it was difficult.'

Rory banged at the table with his spoon and shouted for attention. His plate was empty.

'Shall I do another fish finger or is there pudding?'

Jemima caught her underlip with her upper teeth as she thought. She looked like a hamster dressed by Dolce e Gabbana. 'What did Maeve say he was to have afterwards?' she addressed the air. 'Oh, I know, one of those fruit fromage things and I think she said grapes or a clementine.' She gave a flashing grin, 'That's it, she had the cheek to tell me they had to be peeled! The girl seems to think I'm an idiot. The fridge is over there,' she added, smiling charmingly.

Darina stayed where she was and after a moment Jemima gave her another grin that suggested anything was worth a try, and went and fetched her nephew's dessert.

At school Jemima had been the leader, issuing orders, expecting them to be obeyed. Darina had been one of the few girls who hadn't done her bidding. They'd made friends on a school trip to Paris. Jemima, at thirteen, had met a young man and slipped away from a visit to some Russian folk dancing to meet him for dinner in a fashionable restaurant. It had been Darina who'd covered up when Jemima's absence had been noted. Large, conscientious and law abiding, if Darina said someone was there who wasn't, authority believed her. Receiving Jemima's thanks, Darina had said bluntly that she was an idiot but she wouldn't mind hearing what they'd had to eat. A somewhat spiky friendship had flourished from that point, Jemima seemingly charmed by someone who didn't jump to do her bidding, Darina fascinated by her irreverent approach to life.

Rory's arms waved happily as Darina spooned raspberry fromage frais into his rosebud mouth and watched him concentrate on the new taste. 'Maeve's his nanny?'

' "Nanny" is going a bit far for an Irish girl whose only qualifications, as far as I can find out, are the bringing up of umpteen brothers and sisters. Still, Rory likes her and I don't know how we'd manage if she left.' She topped up her glass of wine. 'Dad seems to think she's a good thing as well,' she added in a colourless voice.

There was silence for a while. When, Darina wondered, would this child realize that he was motherless? What would it mean to him? He wouldn't lack for the material things of life. The kitchen looked as if it had come straight out of a glossy designer magazine but there was no friendly clutter of utensils and odd impedimenta on any of the granite worksurfaces; no board stuffed with messages, shopping lists and postcards, everything was pristine and soulless. Did Rory have a nursery with fantasy painted walls and a rocking horse? Were there toys scattered around or was everything there as well ordered as here? Was this Maeve girl mother as far as he was concerned? It certainly didn't seem as though Jemima was making much of an effort to take her sister's place. 'My rescuer,' she'd greeted Darina as she'd opened the door of Blackboys, the Ealham mansion, half an hour earlier, the boy clutching at her legs. 'It's time for Rory's lunch and I'm useless with him.' Then she'd kissed Darina warmly and taken them all through to the kitchen.

Jemima's call had come out of the blue. They hadn't met since they'd left school and how she'd got hold of Darina's number was a puzzle. Despite the gap of so many years, Jemima had sounded really delighted to have made contact with her again. So much so that Darina had found herself accepting an invitation to lunch, 'to discuss,' Jemima had said, 'a small matter I need help with'.

Darina had put down the phone wondering, in an amused way, what it could be; Jemima had been well known for taking advantage of friends at school. Then she'd chided herself. Hadn't Jemima given her that Italian holiday when she was fifteen? There were many schoolgirls in their house who'd have helped Jemima with homework, lent her clothes or done any number of favours to have gone with her to the lush villa in the

Tuscan hills equipped with swimming pool and daily maid. But she'd asked Darina, whose Latin and maths were worse than her own and whose clothes wouldn't fit even if Jemima had liked their style.

As Darina offered Rory the last spoon of fromage frais, there was the insistent beep of a mobile phone.

Jemima snatched up the instrument from the table. 'Dominic, hi!' she said eagerly. 'Great to hear you, how are things?' Holding the phone, she rose and walked over to the other side of the kitchen.

Darina tried to concentrate on Rory but it was impossible to turn her ears off. 'No, sorry, Dom, Dad's back tonight and I want to be here. No, look, I've said I'm sorry,' she pleaded. 'It's, like, really difficult. He'll want to talk about the negotiations and everything. It's not often I get him without Val around.' Pause. 'Of course I'll miss you.' Her voice was soft. 'Can't wait to see you. Tomorrow then? I'll ring you.' Jemima clicked her phone shut and came back to the table without comment.

'So,' said Darina, scraping out the pot for still greedy Rory, 'what's this matter you need help with?' Please let it not be cooking, she prayed to herself. The days were gone when she was grateful for any sort of catering that came her way.

Jemima looked across at Darina, her gaze open and direct. 'I want you to find out who Rory's father is.'

'You don't know?' Darina was astonished.

Jemima shook her head. 'By the time Dad reached hospital, Sophie was in a coma; she never regained consciousness.'

'But someone must know,' Darina protested. 'What about her friends?'

'She didn't tell anyone,' Jemima said with a note of finality.

'Hasn't your father tried to find out?' Darina couldn't imagine the mighty Basil Ealham not motivating an army of private detectives into discovering who was responsible for his daughter's pregnancy.

Jemima looked exasperated. 'He says it doesn't matter, that Rory is Rory. He's besotted with him.' She made it sound a dangerous perversion.

'But you think it's important?' Darina separated out several clementine segments and handed one to the child, who took and examined it closely before placing it in his mouth with a grunt of approval. She put several more segments on the tray in front of him. He obviously liked having control over his food.

'Don't you?' Jemima sounded amazed at the question.

'Well, yes, but why have you waited so long?' Darina considered the child now picking up the next piece of fruit with a fat finger and thumb. 'I mean, Rory's what, fifteen months old?'

Jemima thought for a moment. 'Seventeen months.'

'Shouldn't you have tried to find out who his father was when he was born?'

'Yah, well, we didn't,' Jemima said stubbornly.

'And no one contacted you?'

Jemima shook her head. 'As I said, we don't know anything about where she was living, what she was doing, or who her friends were.'

There was something very odd here. 'I'm not a private detective,' Darina said repressively, not at all certain she wanted anything to do with this curious task. 'I wouldn't know where to start.'

11

'Nonsense, you've solved any number of crimes if half of what I hear is true. It was when I met Esther Symes and she told me how well you'd been doing that I got the idea.'

So that was who must have given Jemima her number. 'You know how Esther always loves to exaggerate everything. Remember when we were in the fourth form and she told us her uncle was President of the USA?'

Jemima gurgled with laughter. 'Weren't we all impressed? Until we found out he was really just president of some American corporation.' She looked closely at Darina. 'Are you saying you haven't solved any murders?'

'Well, not exactly,' Darina prevaricated. 'But it was just luck, a matter of being in the right place at the right time.'

'You always were a modest soul. But you can't deny that you're married to a policeman, a detective inspector no less. He can tell you exactly how to go about things.'

'Actually, he's just been promoted, he's Detective Chief Inspector William Pigram now, with the Thames Valley Police. That's why we've moved up from Somerset.'

'I want to hear more about him,' Jemima commanded. 'Esther says he's dreamy.'

Darina smiled. 'I didn't think tall, dark and handsome men were in fashion these days.'

'Ooh, he sounds delicious! A sort of Mr Darcy?'

'Well, yes,' Darina acknowledged, thinking that William wrestled with difficult emotions just as hard as Jane Austen's hero.

'Oh, heaven! I get so bored with wimps. That's all I

seem to meet these days, wimps or macho men bent on proving they don't need women.' Darina wondered which Dominic was. But a macho man would surely have insisted on Jemima going out with him that evening. 'I bet you can twist William round your little finger and get him to help you in any way you want.'

'He's working his way into his new job. It's an important move and I wouldn't want to bother him with this sort of thing,' Darina said repressively, knowing all too well that giving her advice on how to investigate anything was the last thing William would do.

'Come on, if you're not writing books or doing television programmes, surely you can spare a little time to do some sleuthing?' Jemima looked pleadingly at Darina. 'It would mean so much to me. And I'll pay you, of course.'

Which was more than anybody else had done! But, 'I don't do it for money,' Darina said.

'Well, you ought to. Come on, please, it's so important.' Her eyes were luminous, her body tense.

When Jemima let down her defences, she was difficult to resist. And it was true, Darina didn't have any deadlines at the moment. But trying to fight for a regular place in the media market was time consuming and there was William to consider. The last thing he needed at the moment was her irritating him by invading his work space.

But surely investigating Rory's fatherhood wouldn't count as police work? After all, it wasn't as though any crime had been committed. There was something here though that Darina didn't understand. 'Just why are you so keen, Jemima? If your father's happy not to know, why aren't you?'

Jemima ran a hand through her short fair hair and looked exasperated, as though the answer should have been perfectly plain. 'Heavens, Darina, you know what a time I and my brothers had growing up, don't you think Rory ought to be saved from all that?' Jemima's expression was fierce. 'If only I'd realized how completely Dad was going to take him over, I'd have come back sooner. He's ruined my life, I'm not going to have the same thing happen to Rory. If you think food's important for a child, how much more so are proper parents!'

'He might be someone totally unsuitable.'

'Or someone who'd give him a decent upbringing and not insist on the importance of possessions and status,' Jemima insisted.

How well would Jemima manage without the money that bought her expensive clothes and provided this luxurious home? Darina wondered, then went after a different angle. 'Don't you have any idea who Rory's father is?'

Jemima shook her head. 'Apparently she didn't have any boyfriends, or girlfriends come to that. Sophie, well, Sophie found people a bit threatening.'

Jemima had never been particularly perspicacious and Darina realized Sophie must have lacked social skills to a high degree for her sister to have noticed this much.

'Dad says Rory was several weeks premature, you can't imagine how tiny he was when I first saw him,' Jemima looked at the sturdy infant banging the highchair tray and her gaze softened for a moment before she switched her attention back to Darina. 'Sophie had been missing for seven and a half months when Rory

14

was born. So if he was six weeks' premature, it must have been someone she met after she disappeared from my brother and sister-in-law's, mustn't it?'

Darina didn't see that it necessarily followed but decided not to pursue it for the moment.

'But if you don't know where Sophie was living or what she was doing when she became pregnant, how can anyone even start an investigation?'

Relief bloomed on Jemima's face. 'I knew you'd do it! And I know exactly where you can begin, with my brother.'

Rory banged imperiously on his tray.

'What does he want now?' asked Darina. 'More food?'

Jemima rose and found a baby's mug. 'Orange juice to finish off the feast.'

Rory grabbed the mug with both hands and started sucking. How simple life was at that age!

'Which brother?' Darina asked. There had been two on that Italian holiday: Job, an introverted under-graduate who had made a point of avoiding any contact with the rest of his family and Jasper, a ten-year-old boy who'd kept them in fits of laughter.

'My dearly beloved elder brother, Job,' Jemima said wryly. 'When Sophie left here she went to him and Nicola. Did you know he'd married?'

Darina shook her head. 'I haven't heard anything of you or your family for years. There's a limit to the number of Christmas cards you send without getting one back,' she added severely.

Jemima gave a shamefaced smile. 'Well, I was sort of involved with other things. Everything's so exciting when you first leave school,' she added as though that explained matters. 'When I bumped into Esther the other day, it was the first time I'd seen any of our lot since we all left.'

'What's Job doing these days? Did he do anything with his writing? I remember he was always scribbling in a notebook.' Which he'd taken enormous pains to make sure nobody could read. Jasper had managed to get hold of it one day. Darina could see him now, dancing around the swimming pool, holding it up in the air, evading a vengeful Job, for once jerked out of his moody melancholy. Both brothers and the notebook had ended up in the water. Jasper had had the grace to apologize and offered to try and rescue the soggy pages but Job had stalked off, blind with rage, and it had been days before he'd brought himself to speak to any of them.

'He edits the city pages of a weekly magazine.'

'But surely if Job knew anything, he'd have told your father?'

'He hates Dad, he's always trying to do him down in his column. He says he has no idea where she went but I'm sure he knows something.'

'Why don't you ask him?' It all seemed odder and odder to Darina.

Jemima sighed. 'We've never really got on and ever since I started to work for Dad, Job won't have anything more to do with me. It's as though I've gone over to the enemy.'

'You're working for your father? I thought you hated him?'

'That was when I was growing up. I can hold my own now and I thought it was time I worked myself into the firm. So I suggested he took me on as an assistant.' Jemima refilled her glass. 'By the time he retires, I'll be able to take over the company.'

The thought of Jemima, who had always had trouble concentrating on anything longer than it took a flea to jump the width of a bed, at the head of an international organization was, if not exactly laughable, difficult to take seriously. Had she changed in the last twelve years or was she kidding herself?

'Anyway, all you have to do is tell Job Dad doesn't want Rory's parentage investigated and he'll spill all.' Jemima took a piece of paper out of her pocket and handed it to Darina. 'I've written down his details for you.'

So, she'd been all prepared, maybe she had changed!

Darina quickly scanned the details. Job and Nicola Ealham lived in Battersea, just over the river from her house in Chelsea. Quite convenient, as Jemima must realize. Without quite knowing why, she folded up the slip of paper and put it carefully in her handbag. 'I'll think about it,' she said. 'I'm not going to promise anything.'

'Just talk to Job,' Jemima urged. She leaned forward. 'It's important, Darina, really important.'

Somewhere a door slammed and a distant voice shouted, 'Jemima? Where the hell are you?'

'Dad! He's not supposed to be back until this evening!'

Heavy footsteps could be heard approaching the kitchen door.

Jemima stretched a hand across the table to Darina and squeezed her wrist painfully hard. 'Don't breathe a word, promise?'

Darina nodded. Once she and Jemima had sworn eternal friendship and never to rat on the other.

The kitchen door was flung open and Basil Ealham

17

stood there. 'How's my boy?' he shouted. Rory dropped his piece of fruit and flung his arms in the air, his face beaming as he shouted delightedly at his grandfather.

Jemima's face as she watched her father scoop up the little boy was impossible to read.

Chapter Two

Basil Ealham lifted a delighted Rory up high.

'He's only just had his lunch,' Darina warned.

'Hmm, perhaps you're right.' The strong hands lowered Rory and Basil sat himself down on one of the kitchen chairs with the child on his knee. Rory reached for the last of the cheese straws. Jemima whipped the plate away.

'Spoil sport,' said her father.

Deprived of his titbit, Rory turned his attention to the glasses that were in his grandfather's top pocket, plucking them out and opening a sidepiece. 'This is Darina Lisle, Dad,' said Jemima, waving a negligent hand towards her guest. 'You remember she came to Italy with us that time?'

Darina found herself being assessed by a pair of eyes as blue as Rory's but a great deal keener. 'You had to return to England after a couple of days on business,' she murmured. 'I'd be surprised if you remember me.'

'Not at all,' Basil said crisply. 'You produced a great meal for us the first night, tagliatelle with prosciutto, tomato and basil, and a marvellous salad. I was most impressed.'

So was Darina with his feat of memory. She'd forgotten all about that arrival. The plane had been late,

Mrs Ealham had drunk whisky throughout the flight and gone to bed as soon as they reached their destination. Everyone else had been hungry and the villa, set high up in the Tuscan hills, seemed miles from any habitation but on the table had been a collection of food supplied for their arrival.

Rory tried to put the glasses on. They fell to the floor.

'Hey!' objected Basil. 'None of that, now.' He rescued the spectacles and returned them to his pocket. Rory's face puckered.

Jemima scooped the baby up. 'Time for your rest,' she said.

'Just a minute, young lady,' Basil said sharply. 'Why aren't you at the office?'

'I'm looking after Rory. It's Maeve's day off, remember?'

'So where's Mrs Starr?'

'She had to go to the dentist,' Jemima said smoothly.

Darina remembered that tone from their schooldays. She wondered what Jemima had told Mrs Starr to stop her coming in that morning.

'So I rang Darina and suggested we had lunch here rather than in town.'

'What about Jasper, couldn't he have looked after him?'

'In town, said he had to see his agent.'

'Jasper's making a name for himself as a novelist,' Basil said to Darina. 'Too experimental for me but apparently he's well thought of,' he continued expressionlessly. Then he turned back to his daughter. 'Presumably everything's up to date in the office?'

'Of course, Dad, you know you can rely on me!' Jemima said in injured tones. 'Have you had anything to eat? I can lay an extra place, there's plenty of lobster salad.'

'No thanks, I was fed on the plane.'

'What happened to this morning's meeting?'

'The Italians wouldn't play ball last night so I walked out on them.' Delight filled his face. 'They must be mad as all hell. They were sure I'd compromise.'

'More fool them.' Jemima hoisted Rory on to her hip. 'They'll regret not being more co-operative.'

'You better believe it!' Basil said ominously. 'I thought I'd call in and see Rory before the office. I couldn't believe it when I saw your car outside.'

Jemima tightened her hold on the child. 'Entertain Darina for me whilst I put Rory down, will you?' Her tone was imperious enough for Basil Ealham himself.

His right eyebrow raised itself fractionally. Then, 'I'll be delighted,' he said and gave Darina a grin astonishingly like his daughter's. 'Let's go somewhere more comfortable, shall we?'

Darina allowed herself to be led into a vast drawing room furnished with deeply cushioned sofas and chairs, their pale upholstery set off by the deep polish of antique occasional tables.

'What will you have to drink?' Basil opened a door in the corner of the room and Darina caught a glimpse of a well stocked bar.

'Thanks, but Jemima gave me some wine.' Darina held up the glass she'd brought with her. 'And I'm driving so this will do me fine.'

'Good girl! Tonic water with a dash of Angostura Bitters is my tipple.' He emerged with a large glass of pink liquid and took a seat on the opposite sofa.

Basil Ealham was every bit as impressive a figure as

Darina remembered. A shade under six foot, he had a powerful body downplayed by the cut of his well tailored suit. His fine head was held slightly in advance of the rest of him, his beak-like nose, so unfortunately inherited by Jemima, carved the air as though to cut a path for his figure to follow. There was about him the same restless energy that inhabited his daughter and Darina wouldn't be at all surprised if it wasn't in Rory's genes as well.

Basil leaned forward, his legs slightly apart, his whole attention focused on her. 'Nice to see you again. I always thought you'd turn out to be a stunner.' He managed to make that sound both sincere and unhackneyed. His eyes were admiring but kept a slight distance. 'What are you doing with yourself these days? No, don't tell me.' He surveyed her even more closely and Darina felt like a mouse being inspected by a python with lunch on its mind. 'I'm sure you must have put that cookery talent to good use but I don't see you as just a cook. I know, you run your own catering company.'

'I'm impressed,' Darina said calmly, wondering if this was a genuine guess or whether he knew something about her. 'I did at one time. These days, though, I earn my living writing about food rather than cooking it. Oh, and I do the odd television spot – demonstrating,' she couldn't resist adding.

'Now it's my turn to be impressed,' Basil said jovially, not relaxing the intensity of his gaze for a moment. 'I shall have to tell my friend Val I've met you, I'm sure she'll recognize your name.'

Which suggested that he hadn't. Well, no reason why an industrialist should know a humble cookery writer.

Still, Darina's depression intensified. 'Jemima mentioned Val Douglas's name. I know her slightly, we used
to meet at press receptions but I haven't seen her
around for some time.'

'She concentrates on manufacturing food these days.
Is doing extremely well. I've been helping her, with
procedures, management, that sort of thing.' He didn't
even try to sound modest.

Darina remembered Val very well. In her own way
she was as commanding a figure as Basil, tall and attractive but Darina would have expected Basil Ealham to go
for someone less brisk, more sensual. Then she chided
herself. She'd only seen Val in business mode, perhaps
socially she softened and opened herself up, like an
aubergine melting into sweet flavoursomeness under
the influence of heat. She restrained an involuntary
gurgle of laughter at the ridiculous image and concentrated on what Basil was saying.

'Val saw the potential of the market supplying
people with food intolerances and went for it. She's even
in supermarkets these days. Really impressive! But it's
small stuff, she needs to get more commercial and introduce a new line that can command more sales. Gourmet
baby food, I've told her, that's what she needs to work
on. It's a market worth one hundred and twenty million
pounds, even one per cent of that is ten times more than
she's making at the moment and with her talents she
could easily grab much more.' He smiled at her. 'When
she's got her range together, you must come and sample
it, we'll be planning a big press launch.'

'I'd be very interested.'

'Talking of Val, would you mind if I gave her a quick
call?' Darina had to admire the way he actually waited

for her demur before plucking a mobile phone out of an inside pocket.

'Val?' Basil leant back into the corner of the sofa, his gaze fixed somewhere on the ceiling. 'I'm back. Yes, got in this morning, tried to ring you on my way from the airport but you weren't at your desk.' Slight pause while Basil listened to whatever explanation Val had for not being glued to the end of a telephone waiting for a call he might just make. 'OK. Now, look, come over this evening and we'll go through those projections you've been working on.' Another pause.

Darina rose and walked over to the french windows. The garden blazed with autumnal colours. Well ordered herbaceous beds surrounded smooth green lawn with a small, ornamental fountain in the centre. Beyond, she could glimpse the edge of a swimming pool.

'Well, I can see you weren't expecting me back so soon. All right, then, we'll just have dinner tonight and go over the figures tomorrow evening as originally planned.' There was an edge to Basil's voice. Unused to people not being ready with whatever he wanted when he wanted it, obviously. But Val was holding her own, thought Darina with some amusement as it became clear that she had other plans for this evening.

Not for long, though.

'Cancel,' Basil said calmly. 'I want you here.' There was no mistaking the note of possessiveness in his voice. 'Shall I send a car? No? Well, I'll expect you by eight.' More protests from the other end of the phone. 'No,' he said with a slight edge to his voice, 'it'll just be you and me. You know Jasper never eats with us and Jemima is going out.' Darina remembered Dominic, now Jemima would be able to see him after all – but at the cost of the

quiet evening with her father she had looked forward to.
'You know,' Basil's voice changed, 'I've missed you. Can't
wait for this evening, bye.' There was the sharp click of a
mobile's cover being snapped back into place. 'Sorry
about that.'

Darina returned to her seat as Basil slipped his
phone back inside his jacket.

'Now, where were we?' he asked complacently.
Darina decided he was as pleased to have been able to
demonstrate his power to her as he had to Val.

Basil relaxed back and said with a new, boyish
charm, 'I'm so glad Jemima is looking up some of her
old friends. She needs some outside contacts. I think
sometimes she's too involved with the family.'

This was not a side of Jemima that Darina recognized. At school, she had always had masses of friends,
she'd spread her favours as liberally as strawberry jam
on clotted cream scones. Her quick wits, irreverent attitude and attractive appearance had made her an icon.

Perhaps, though, she'd never actually made a real
friend. Since school Darina had occasionally seen her
name in gossip columns, linked to a wide variety of
young men, all rich or famous.

'She says she's enjoying working with you,' she
murmured.

'Ah, yes, my right-hand girl! Well, it keeps her out of
trouble and, who knows, she may be of use one of these
days.'

Darina didn't like the dismissive way he said that.
'She's always been very enterprising,' she said firmly,
'and she's really interested in your business.'

'Yes.' Basil drew the word out as though Jemima's

attitude was somehow suspect. The old sensation of being girls together against authority filled Darina.

'We all voted Jemima girl most likely to succeed in any field she chose,' she said, her manner openly provocative.

'She's always known how to put herself over,' Jemima's father agreed with a silky smoothness. 'It's a valuable asset – as long as it's backed by genuine commitment.'

All at once Darina lost the impulse to fight Jemima's corner. They weren't schoolgirls any longer and what, after all, did she know of Jemima's doings since they'd thrown away their panama hats?

'Isn't your grandson great?'

Basil's face lit up, rather like Rory's had when she fed him. 'Little monster,' he said fondly, one hand negligently playing with the edge of a cushion. 'Chip off the old block! I can see him running the empire when I finally decide to retire.'

How old was Basil? wondered Darina. He looked around fifty but the evidence suggested he was nearer sixty, after all, Jemina's elder brother must now be about thirty-five. But Darina had read somewhere that Basil Ealham had never been to university, he'd clawed his way up from humble beginnings, so he might have married early. Even so, he must be at least fifty-five. Did he really see himself controlling his empire until his grandson was ready to take over? Was that what was worrying Jemima? Nothing to do with her father dominating Rory's life as he grew older?

Darina was by no means sure she wanted to accept Jemima's commission but she thought she might as well take advantage of a Basil relaxed and complacent after

26

his little victory over Val. 'I was sorry to hear about poor Sophie. It must have been devastating. To have been worried for so long and then to have your worst fears confirmed like that . . !' Darina let the end of the sentence die away as Basil's face darkened, literally. Blood suffused his face and his eyes sparked dangerously.

'What has Jemima been saying?' His voice was harsh.

The change in him was more than disconcerting, Darina found herself repelled by his sudden animosity. 'I was interested in Rory,' she said stiffly, trying not to feel she had to justify herself. 'Sophie was such a little girl when I last saw her. It was hard to realize she'd grown up, let alone given birth to such a big boy.' Basil's eyes closed as if he couldn't bear the memory. 'Her death must have been dreadful,' she added gently.

He opened pain-filled eyes. 'I've never felt so helpless in my life,' he said simply. 'Here I was, able to command anything money could buy and there was nothing I could do to save her life. She looked just so small, so shrunken.' He sounded exhausted. 'I couldn't believe it, nobody dies of childbirth these days. The doctors said it was pre-eclampsia, and that if she'd only had proper attention earlier, it could all have been brought under control, she needn't have died at all. God knows where or how she'd been living.' As though he couldn't bear to sit still any longer he got up and went over to a table loaded with photographs in silver frames. He picked one up and held it out to Darina. 'That was Sophie before she left home.'

It was a posed, studio shot, the sort that would once have graced the front page of *Country Life*. The girl who wore a single string of pearls and matching stud earrings

27

looked about seventeen. Brown hair was held back with a velvet alice band from a shy, trusting face with brown eyes full of sweet innocence. Darina was struck by how much she resembled her mother.

'I'm sorry, I probably shouldn't ask you this but I can't help wondering, why did she leave home?'

She'd feared a return of his antagonism. Instead, Basil shrugged his big shoulders in a helpless gesture. 'If only I knew! You can't imagine how many times I've asked myself that question. You know what youngsters are, so mixed up they hardly know themselves why they do things.' It was hard to tell whether he was being genuine or not.

'And you don't know who Rory's father is?'

The blood flooded back into Basil's face. 'Jemima told you that, too, did she?'

Darina said nothing.

'If I could get my hands on the man who abandoned her like that, I'd lynch him,' Basil ground out.

Why hadn't he tried to find out who the man was? If he had been that vengeful, surely he would have employed every aid his money could enlist? Then it suddenly occurred to Darina that perhaps he had tried – and failed. Perhaps he didn't want to admit there was something else his money couldn't buy. In which case, what chance had she got?

'So Rory will grow up not knowing who his father is,' Darina persisted.

'Won't hurt him,' Basil insisted, taking the photograph back. 'Better that than to have the burden of a useless failure hanging round your neck as you grow up.'

'That's what you think the man must have been, a useless failure?'

Basil's eyes narrowed. 'You're very interested,' he said in a voice that was suddenly cold.

This wasn't a man it was safe to cross, Darina decided. 'Having met Rory, I can't help but be interested.'

Once again his grandson proved the key to softening Basil Ealham's attitude.

'Look,' he said as he put the photograph back on the table, 'aren't we all bowed down with the weight of our parents? What about yours? Hasn't your father affected your approach to life? What was he? Ah, I remember, a doctor.'

What a memory the man had.

'So, he will have imposed standards of caring on you, and of duty. Without his influence, you might have turned out very differently.'

Darina didn't want to consider the influences that had shaped her. 'And are you going to mastermind Rory's upbringing?'

'You bet I am! A great deal better than the sort of chap that loves and leaves without a second thought.'

Was that how it had been? Darina remembered the sweet, trusting face of Sophie Ealham. Sweet faces sometimes hid complex characters with less attractive attributes. Basil wouldn't be the first father to have blinded himself to the truth where a daughter was concerned. Darina found herself being drawn into the mystery of Rory's birth as question after question occurred to her. It was like being presented with an unexpected set of ingredients and wondering how to assemble a satisfactory dish.

'Jemima's taking a long time to settle Rory,' she commented.

Jemima entered. 'Rory's down at last,' she said, running a hand through her hair as though the task of settling him down had been exhausting. 'Shall we eat?'

Chapter Three

After lunch Jemima saw Darina off with regret. She'd brought back so many good memories.

Sometimes Jemima thought that school days really had been the happiest of her life. Her mother had been alive, life seemed to be under a certain control – there'd been hope things would get better. Then school had finished and soon afterwards Jemima had come home after a long session shopping in the new car that had been her eighteenth birthday present. Her mother hadn't been able to come with her, a bad headache, she'd said. So Jemima had carried in glossy bags filled with terrific clothes and dashed upstairs to show them off, hoping the headache was better.

Jemima had entered that bedroom an eager adolescent and emerged an embittered adult. She'd known immediately she'd seen the still figure, it hadn't been necessary to read the note propped up against the empty pill bottle. For a little while she'd sat on the bed, held the cold hand and remembered her mother's last words. 'It won't be nearly as much fun without you, Mum,' Jemima had said. And Julie Ealham had sighed, 'I hope life will always be fun for you, darling.' And Jemima had flounced out of the room, angry because

31

her mother seemed to have given up on life when there was just so much there for her if only she'd take it.

But Jemima, her two brothers and her sister hadn't been enough for Julie Ealham. Not enough to compensate for their father and his behaviour.

Jemima had looked at the cold, rigid face and felt something inside her shrivel up, like a sea anemone curling in its fronds. Then she'd rung Basil and the doctor and the house where Sophie had been sent that morning. Having done what had seemed necessary, she'd methodically hung up the new clothes.

As Jemima drove her Mercedes coupé fast along the narrow roads, she was deeply conscious of her father sitting in his office like an over-active spider in the centre of a pulsating web. She'd told Darina she wanted to take over the company when Basil retired. What a laugh. Jemima Ealham in charge of a multi-million corporation!

Why hadn't she told her old friend the truth? That her boutique had gone bust because Basil had refused further funds, that she couldn't find anyone to give her an interesting job and the only sort of flat she could afford on the salary she could command was too poky and too far out of the centre of things to be considered for a moment. Everyone she'd known at school seemed to have gone on to interesting careers or had got married to upwardly mobile men. Why was she, the girl they'd voted most likely to succeed, the only failure?

Then she thought of what she'd asked Darina to do and for a moment fought panic. What had she started? Could Darina discover the truth? Esther had said how clever she was. 'The thing is, sweetie, she never gives up, just keeps going at it until she's got an answer. It's nothing to do with fingerprints and all that, I think it's because she works out the human factor.' And Jemima had had this sudden impulse.

Now she wondered if the truth mightn't be something best not discovered. Perhaps it wouldn't mean a better upbringing for Rory than hers. And what would her father do? The thought of a Basil threatened with Rory's removal from his control was suddenly so terrifying, Jemima almost called Darina there and then to cancel the investigation. Then she pushed the thought away as the complex mix of emotions that had decided her to ring her old friend returned in full force. Her father had to learn other people had rights as well.

Clinging to that thought, Jemima parked her car behind Ealham House, an aggressive looking red-brick building that had won some award for progressive architecture, and walked inside with quick steps. If you looked purposeful, people thought you were someone important.

Rosie Cringle looked up as she entered the office. 'Mr Ealham wants you in his office. He said as soon as you got back.' Jemima's secretary was a mouselike but immensely efficient girl.

Jemima gave an unconscious tug to the bottom of her jacket, picked up the file that was sitting ready on her desk, tapped on the communicating door between her and the Chairman and Managing Director's office and entered without waiting for a response.

Basil was on the telephone. He waved her to a chair in front of his enormous, bare desk. Behind him she could see he already had up the latest production figures for the most troublesome company in the conglomerate. 'Right, you do that,' Basil said unemotionally into the telephone. 'Just remember your job depends on it and there are no second chances,' he added pleasantly before putting the receiver down. 'Ah, Jemima. Good lunch, was it? Nice girl that. Now, here are the notes I made in the plane coming back. Get them printed out.' He handed her a floppy disc. 'You'll note several action points for you, don't hang around on them. When's that meeting I asked you to arrange?'

'Tomorrow at ten,' Jemima said smoothly, rather pleased with herself. Basil had wanted her to get hold of an elusive industrialist with a deep distrust of the Ealham corporation. It had taken a good deal of persistence first to track him down and then to persuade him it would be a mistake not at least to meet.

'Good work,' said Basil absently. Coming from him this was high praise and Jemima felt a fizz of achievement.

'And those projections I asked for?'

She handed over the file, blessing Rosie for pressuring her to complete it the previous day. It made her feel efficient. This job was proving a success. Producing projections was boring but she loved sitting in on meetings, watching her father run rings around captains of industry as he produced ideas that sounded off the wall then made you see were just a revolutionary way of dealing with a problem that had defeated everyone else. Sometimes the ideas were so simple you knew they couldn't work – until he insisted you tried, when they did. She was really looking forward to hearing him talk about what had happened in Milan this evening. She'd got one or two ideas of her own that she wanted to tell him about.

'You've only got half the figures here,' Basil said,

throwing the projections on the desk. 'What's wrong with you, your mind on that wimp Dominic?' He sounded bored rather than irritated and Jemima suddenly saw a similar looking document already on the desk.

'By the way, Val's coming over this evening. I take it you've got plans?' Basil swung round to his computer screen and Jemima knew their time together was over.

'Yah,' she said quickly. 'Dominic's taking me out.'

Basil grunted, his attention already given to the figures he was playing with.

That evening Jemima drove up to London with Oasis blaring out of the car stereo. She sang along at the top of her voice, refusing to think of anything but the frustratingly heavy traffic. She had to get there early because otherwise Dominic might decide to go out for a drink and there was no way she was going to chase him round the various watering holes he could choose from.

Parking for Dominic's flat was always a problem if you didn't have a resident's permit. Jemima left her car perched on a corner, picked up her long-handled Prada bag and swung it over her shoulder. Her stiletto heels clicked decisively as her legs flashed along in tight, wetlook trousers. She had the key to Dominic's flat all ready in her pocket. As she let herself in she called out, 'Surprise!' And it was.

Had she been an idiot or had she actually wanted to catch him in the act? Jemima only knew she didn't feel taken aback as she walked into the bedroom and found the two of them at it like ferrets up a trouser leg.

The girl had seen her first. Her startled eyes locked

35

on to Jemima's furious ones then her green enamelled nails dug into Dominic's back so that he arched away from her, cried out, then collapsed, his sweat-licked skin gleaming in the low light.

Jemima marched out of the bedroom and helped herself to a large whisky from the collection of drinks Dominic kept on the glass and chrome side table. She'd helped him furnish this flat, had chosen the silver and white decor. 'Too thirties, angel, but it suits the architecture,' she'd said, giggling, as they drank champagne to celebrate the decorators' departure.

'So now you know,' Dominic said, coming up behind her, tieing the sash of his kimono. He poured himself an equally large glass of The Macallan. His breathing had returned to normal, his dark hair was slicked back, his tone conversational. 'Sorry you had to find out this way. You should have told me you'd changed your mind about this evening.'

Jemima shrugged and moved away; he needed a shower.

He sat down in one of the square armchairs. The kimono opened itself revealing his smooth knees and hairy legs. 'Like a bear,' she'd used to say, running her fingers gently over the dark fuzz, feeling its softness send sensual little messages along her nerve ends.

'Who is she?' Jemima leant against the chrome shelving unit that ran along one wall.

'No one you know.' Half Dominic's whisky had gone but he seemed totally calm, even bored. How could she ever have found this well bred but pompous fool entertaining?

The ache that ever since her mother's death had

never been far away filled her gut. Why did the people she loved disappear?

'She's a sweet little girl,' Dominic added idly.

'Sweet . . . little . . . girl,' Jemima repeated through her teeth. Suddenly she lifted the heavy cut glass tumbler and threw it hard and accurately across the room.

Dominic ducked and the tumbler smashed against the wall, shattering the glass of the modern etching that had been her house-warming present.

'You bastard,' she screamed and flung herself at him, her nails just managing to draw blood before, with surprising strength, he grabbed her wrists and forced her to the ground. She fought back, rage, humiliation and a host of less identifiable emotions giving her a power she hadn't known she possessed. It wasn't enough, though, and at the end she collapsed into a heap on the carpet, sobbing as though her heart would break.

Dominic helped himself to more whisky. 'Don't pretend you really care,' he said, breathing fast. 'The only person who matters to you is you. Oh, and your father,' he added.

'I hate my father!' Jemima flung at him, with a hiccuping catch to her voice.

'So you always say. You never lose an opportunity to lay into him yet you take his money. You're spoilt, immature and self-centred,' he continued dispassionately, 'and it's time you got a grip. You're a good lay but there's more to life than sex.'

The effrontery of it made her breathless. When she thought of how he'd begged her to make love. The way he'd whimpered under her caresses.

She got herself to her feet and found her bag. 'You'll

be lucky if she gives you half as good a time,' she told him coldly. 'You don't deserve someone like me.'

His eyes narrowed unappealingly. 'Any man who deserves you needs to be removed from society.'

She laughed unsteadily. 'Have fun with your bimbo, I don't suppose she knows any better than you, poor cow.'

Halfway down the corridor, she heard him calling her. 'Leave the key, you bitch.'

She flung it at him, her aim so bad the metal pinged off the wall and lay shining on the carpet as she swayed out of the block.

Her car had been clamped. It had only been there half an hour and it had been clamped!

Well, might as well make the fine worthwhile. Jemima walked to a local pub where she was reasonably certain of finding someone she knew.

Much, much later, escorted by a beefy twenty-something who'd been touchingly grateful for her sudden appearance in his life, she paid her outrageous fine. 'There you go,' the young bull said, after the clamp had been removed, and opened her car door. She got in, he slammed it and stood back.

Then she realized he hadn't asked for her phone number. After all the expertise she'd lavished on him, he hadn't even wanted to see her again.

She gunned the engine. Chaps like him were ten a penny, she could have as many as she wanted – any time. She roared away, not even looking in the rear view mirror as she left him behind.

After their excessive activity, she felt completely sober but she drove home with unaccustomed carefulness. While she drove she wallowed in self-pity. A cruel fate was against her. If only she'd been able to spend the evening with her father, everything would have been all right. She wouldn't have known about Dominic's two-timing, nor been treated as a one-night stand by that callow sod.

By the time she reached Blackboys it was the early hours of the morning and Jemima had decided that the person to blame for everything that was wrong with her life was Val Douglas.

Chapter Four

Darina had gone home from Blackboys to several hours of housework, the pristine standard of the Ealham household having made her horribly conscious of her shortcomings in this area. As usual her husband, Detective Chief Inspector William Pigram, was late. So it was nearly nine o'clock before she cooked them both a stir-fried dish of chicken and fine shreds of vegetables zested with fresh ginger and lemon grass. Minimum cooking, maximum flavour, she'd thought.

'I'm sorry, I'm not very hungry,' William said, laying down his fork. 'I was so starving in the office, I got myself some sandwiches.'

Darina sighed and pushed the remains of her meal away. 'My lunch was very filling,' she said.

William picked up both plates and dumped the remains in the bin. 'How did your reunion with your old friend go? Lots of giggles over the doings of the lower fourth?'

'Darling, those leftovers could have done lunch tomorrow!' Darina protested. Then thought how unlike William to sound sour. She looked carefully at her husband. Little of Mr Darcy about him today, unless you counted the gloomy lines of his clean cut face. Very unheroic were the dark smudges under his grey eyes while the puffiness around them and the network of minute red lines on the whites themselves were positively worrying. As was the depth of the vertical crease between his brows. And the way he placed hands either side of his forehead and squeezed, as though trying to relieve a headache.

Then Darina was shocked to notice several strands of silver in the curly darkness of his hair.

Ever since William had been promoted to take charge of the CID of a small police force in the Thames valley, it had been a case of hallo and goodbye. Hallo late each evening, if, that is, Darina wasn't already asleep when he returned home, goodbye in the early morning when William often left the house before Darina was up. Their relationship these days seemed full of tension. When was the last time they'd had a relaxed evening together, or had friends round, or even made love?

'Any chance of us enjoying a quiet weekend?' she asked as he started filling the kettle for coffee. 'We could go for a walk somewhere. You look as though you could do with some fresh air and exercise.'

'Tell me about it! But it's no go. I'm buried in paperwork and this evening Roger rang. He's appropriating Terry Pitman, my inspector, and another officer for what looks like several days. Division are mounting an operation to clear up the gang of high-class burglars that's been stripping all our patches.' He put the kettle down with an angry thump.

'No! But that's good news, isn't it?'

'Good news that hardened criminals are to be removed from our patch and life made safe for valuable antiques. Bad news that while it's all going on my lot will be too thin on the ground to check the nefarious activities of less hardened criminals; every little weed will grow into a bloody great thistle.' William sat and knocked back the rest of his whisky.

'How long is this going to go on?' she asked, trying to sound sympathetic and understanding and hearing it come out irritable instead. She reached out and placed her hand against his cheek, hoping touch would get through to him. 'Unremitting work is no good for anyone. You need to take a break.'

William managed a brief smile, kissed her hand, then sank back against the banquette. 'I need to get on top of things first,' he sighed.

'Bloody Roger,' Darina said savagely. Superintendent Marks was no friend of hers, she found it difficult to understand why William was such close friends with the over-large, overbearing and charmless – as far as she was concerned – officer.

It had been Roger who'd persuaded William that moving to a home counties' constabulary would be good for his career pattern. The promotion to chief inspector had been welcome but this unrelenting pressure was not. 'Superintendent Marks,' she continued through her teeth, 'is using you to save his skin. These staff shortages are threatening the success of his division and he knows he can bully you into working twice as hard as anyone else.'

'We're all suffering,' William said quietly. 'Roger has promised me a new sergeant and that should make life easier.'

'As long as he isn't anything like Detective Inspector Terry Pitman,' Darina said caustically.

'Terry's a good officer,' William protested. 'And he

expected to be promoted into my position, it's no wonder he slightly resents my presence.'

'Slightly!' Darina hooted. 'If thought transference worked, you'd be in some rat-infested hole in the outer Hebrides by now. Face it, darling, as far as Terry's concerned, you're a networking country toff who can't tell a local villain from a Victorian lamp-post and he's just waiting for you to make the mistake that will see you back in Somerset.'

'Thanks for the vote of confidence,' William said quietly and leant back, closing his eyes.

'Darling, don't be like that. I'm just saying that's what Terry thinks. I know and you know that you thoroughly deserve your promotion, that you're one of the brightest detectives in the entire country.'

'Perhaps you'll suggest, then, how I get that over to Terry Pitman?' He kept his eyes closed.

The kettle boiled. Darina rose, rubbing her forehead where depression threatened to turn into a raging headache. She had to tiptoe round William in velvet slippers these days.

Perhaps she had been wrong to persuade him they should live in Chelsea rather than renting somewhere close to his new station.

But when they'd gone to look at the house he'd found, it had seemed so small and, well, *mean*, compared to the spaciousness of the house between the Thames and the King's Road that she'd inherited from her cousin. 'Would it really be so difficult to commute?' she'd asked, pushing vainly at the patio window that should have opened on to a minute, overgrown lawn. The terrace outside her Chelsea drawing room wasn't any larger but it was surrounded with mature old-fashioned roses, wisteria climbed the mellow brick and small shrubs provided an ever varying pattern of greens and golds that constantly refreshed the eye.

The size of the main bedroom in the house for rent was no larger than the boxroom at the top of the Chelsea house. 'Wouldn't you like to be at the centre of everything?' she'd asked, running a finger over the back of a mock leather settee and looking at the dirt. 'On the doorstep of theatres and exhibitions, not to mention restaurants?' William liked his food. What she hadn't said was that she felt it would kill any creative instinct she had if she was forced to live in this graceless, poky house. Not because of its size, their cottage in Somerset hadn't been any larger, but because it had no character, was a mere collection of boxes that would close oppressively round her, leeching out her spirit.

William hadn't put up any arguments and she'd thought he'd been relieved to settle into the space of her Chelsea home, now vacant after a long let to tenants who had paid a pittance and left its previous elegance looking worn and down at heel. Now, though, she realized that commuting nearly an hour to and from Weybridge each day was yet another pressure on him.

'Anyway,' said William, opening his eyes, 'it'll please Terry he's going to be part of Operation Chippendale.'

'Operation Chippendale!' Darina hooted.

William gave her a tired grin. 'Some sort of *double entendre*, you think?'

'I think Roger fancies his muscles! Heaven protect me from the vanity of macho policemen.' Darina poured hot water on to coffee grounds then set cheese and fruit on the table. On her way home that afternoon, she'd visited an excellent delicatessen and bought some of the

Vignotte William loved for its creamy yet firm texture, plus a piece of the traditional farmhouse Cheddar that was so difficult to find. She added a selection of the savoury biscuits she'd prepared for a piece she was working on. Not that it had a home yet, she was still trying to interest editors in an article on superior accessories for simple meals. But who had the time today to prepare such delicious titbits?

She brought the cafetière to the table, pushed down the plunger then tried to amuse William with a description of the Ealham household. 'You must meet Jemima, one day when you're not so busy,' she finished. 'She's a real character.'

He roused himself, cut a large piece of the Vignotte and transferred it to his plate with three of the home-made biscuits. 'I like the sound of Rory better.' William looked at Darina. 'Isn't it time we started our own family, darling?'

She bit back a flip remark about chance being a fine thing and fought panic. 'You know we decided it would be better to wait a bit. Until you're settled and my career's on a steadier path. When at the moment would you have time to see a child, let alone play with him, or her?'

William started to slip slivers of cheese into his mouth, biting neat little bits out of a biscuit between each piece. 'This pace isn't continuing for ever,' there was a hint of steel in his voice. 'This is just a bad patch, a few weeks and I should be through the worst. But what about you?'

'Me?'

'When do you think you will have your career on track?'

She looked down at the steam gently rising from her cup of coffee, wisping around as though starring in some television commercial. Hopelessness filled her. 'You know how difficult it is, how much competition there is.'

'So why don't you give it a break and start a family instead? After all, it's not as though we're that desperate for money.' At least he hadn't said the loss of the money she was earning at the moment wasn't going to make a whole lot of difference to their lifestyle.

'You don't understand, I've got something of a name at the moment, if I don't try and capitalize on that now, I'll never make it.' Darina looked with pleading eyes at her husband.

'No, I don't understand,' he said roughly, as though patience was something he no longer had the energy for. 'There's more to it than you wanting to write about food or do some television programmes. Why don't you tell me, why don't you say it – you just don't want children!'

'That's not true,' Darina burst out, then stopped, wondering. Was she fooling herself? Trying to put off the decision until her biological clock said, now you don't have to worry because it's too late? But she was only in her early thirties, that time was far off. And these days you could have children even if you were past the menopause. Her mother's voice saying it was against nature sang in her head. Her mother who was so sure of her opinions on everything, who agreed with William that she should be getting on with starting a family, and who had needed quite a different daughter from the one she'd got. 'Darling, this isn't the time for discussions of this sort, we're both too tired,' she prevaricated.

'Jemima made a suggestion today,' she continued,

determined to deflect him from what was beginning to seem like an obsession. If she gave him the opportunity to be dismissive about the idea of her searching for Rory's father, surely that would make him better tempered? For that she was prepared to sacrifice her dignity.

'Do you know, I don't think I want to hear about Jemima,' he said, rising. 'I can hardly keep my eyes open.' He finished off his cup of coffee, cut a thick finger of Cheddar and left the room.

Darina felt first lost, then angry. She'd been left with all the clearing up and William was turning into someone she wasn't sure how to deal with. What had happened to the delightful husband she'd married?

As she wrapped the remains of the cheese with exasperated efficiency, the thought came that for someone who wasn't hungry enough to eat what had been a delicious stir fry, William had consumed an amazing amount of cheese. Then she dismissed it. Tomorrow she was going to give Job Ealham a ring.

Next morning Darina rang the number Jemima had given her. Job answered the phone, his voice edgy and impatient. In the background she could hear children arguing.

'I'm sorry if this is an inconvenient time, my name's Darina Lisle. Jemima suggested I rang, it's to do with your nephew, Rory.'

'Rory?' Anxiety replaced intemperance. 'Nothing's wrong, is there?'

'No, not at all,' Darina soothed, wondering how to approach what had initially seemed a relatively simple matter. She decided to go for plain truth without a garnish. 'Jemima wants me to find out who his father is.'

'For God's sake!' Impatience was back. 'How on earth does she think you're going to do that? None of us knows a thing.'

'Apparently your father is dead against the idea.' Darina followed Jemima's scenario. 'He won't co-operate in any way. I agree with you,' she added quickly. 'The chances of picking up any leads at this stage are remote but if I could have a few words with you? I'm only just across the river, I could come straight over.'

There was silence from the other end of the tele-phone. Then Job said, but not to her, 'Dinosaurs didn't eat their cereals, that's why they're extinct.' Muffled screeches suggested his children weren't going to buy that but it had amused them. 'If you're that keen, you'd better come over,' he said in a resigned tone. 'Jemima can be remorseless in pursuing her crazy ideas. I shan't be able to give you long, though,' he added curtly, 'I have to leave for my office soon.'

'No, that's fine, I'll be with you in about twenty minutes,' Darina said hastily.

She grabbed the bag she'd prepared the night before, picked up her car keys, gave one last glance to the A-Z and set off for the Albert Bridge. As she passed almost static queues of cars and lorries trying to get into central London, she was heartily glad she was going against the traffic.

Job Ealham lived in a tangle of streets around the back of Clapham Junction. Darina found the address without much trouble, more difficult was somewhere to park. She had to walk a little way back to the house, past rows of small, Victorian cottages, no doubt originally destined for labourers, now a mixture of well painted, gentrified dwellings and untidy buildings in need of a face lift. Job's was one of the latter, its tiny front garden decorated with weeds and a leggy climbing rose, the front door's paintwork peeling, the windows dusty and smeared. Darina moved a battered scooter and pressed the bell. She failed to hear it ring so banged a knocker that would require painstaking polishing to restore its brass finish.

The man who opened the door was as lanky and dour looking as she remembered. Even the jeans could have been the ones he'd worn on the Italian holiday. But instead of a dark T-shirt, he sported a faded blue formal shirt, neatly buttoned and worn with a thin, bright red tie. He'd filled out a bit but his eyes were just as wary. Then they suddenly lightened and a brief smile lit his face. 'Yes, it *is* the girl who cooked us those great meals at that god-awful villa. I knew your name rang bells.'

Darina was used to having both a name and an appearance that people remembered. A height a shade under six foot, a frame that was always fighting fat and long blonde hair meant you could never hide in a crowd. But every now and then it had its advantages. She gave him a big grin. 'Nice to see you again, Job. I'd have sworn nothing about that holiday made enough of an impression for you to have remembered anyone there beside yourself.'

His mouth lengthened derisively. 'No doubt I deserved that. Come in and tell me what you've been up to since then.'

The door opened directly into a living area that had obviously once been two rooms. Toys littered the floor. The furniture looked battered and a sofa and chairs had the worst of their drawbacks hidden underneath Indian throws that had needed a better aim, the material was scrunched untidily around the lumps and sags.

'Do you want a coffee?' Job asked as Darina let herself down gingerly into one of the armchairs and felt a spring give.

'No, thanks, I've just had breakfast.'

'Wish I had. You don't mind if I eat as we talk do you? It's more than I can manage when I'm monitoring the children.' He threw himself in a highly dangerous manner into another rickety armchair and picked up a plate loaded with two thick pieces of attractive-looking bread generously spread with butter and marmalade.

'Please, carry on. That bread looks wonderful, do you get it locally?' Darina rootled around in her leather shoulder bag thinking she'd be prepared to drive across the bridge regularly if there was a baker here supplying real loaves.

Job stopped eating and grinned at her. 'Nicola makes it. In between organizing a local play group, bringing up the kids and running a home-based computer business. She's a fanatic on good eating, makes the muesli, buys organic meat and vegetables, the lot.'

'My word!' Darina marvelled. 'It sounds as though you got yourself a bargain in the wife department.' The whole set-up here couldn't have been farther from the Ealham mansion less than thirty miles away in the Thames valley. Only the computer business suggested these Ealhams had even a nodding acquaintance with commercialism.

Job gave her a lopsided smile as he picked up his mug of coffee from a table any self-respecting junk shop wouldn't give floor room to. 'Nicola says I'm her mission, the reason she was born. She says she's never met anyone with less natural born talent for living.' He looked down into his coffee and his smile faded. 'That was before she met Sophie.' He glanced at his watch and spoke briskly. 'It's Nicola's turn to take the kids to school today. Someone's supposed to be coming to look at the washing machine so I said I'd be here until she got back. I'd say you've got about twenty-five minutes. Which should be more than enough time to convince you I know nothing new about Sophie that'll be of any use in finding out where she went to from here.'

Darina at last located her notebook and brought it out with a pencil.

'Good lord, you are being serious! But you're wasting your time.' He picked up the second piece of bread. 'What's got into Jemima anyway?' All at once he looked very like his father.

'I think she's worried about his grandfather's influence on Rory. She says if only we can locate his father, Rory will have a better chance at life than you all had.'

'Ah!'

'You sound as though you don't agree.'

Job shifted in his chair. 'I yield to no one in my contempt for my father.' His voice was bitter. 'He's a bully and he tried to force his twisted values on us. I escaped as soon as I could. Jemima, well, Jemima is more ambivalent.' His tone grew detached. 'She believes she hates him but she crawled back to him when her business failed.'

Darina thought of Jemima's clothes and of Black-boys, Basil Ealham's luxurious house. No doubt the new job carried a powerful car with it as well. She remembered how Jemima would describe the delights of her holidays when term started. Delights that had always involved considerable expense. 'She mentioned something about a fashion boutique.'

'Yeah,' Job's lip curled distastefully. 'Jemima persuaded the father she despises to invest in a shop she said she'd make the success of London.'

'I'd say she had quite an eye for fashion.'

'No doubt about that. But no talent for hard work. Running your own business takes hard graft. Jemima only knows how to enjoy herself. It wasn't much more than a year before the enterprise went bust.' He thought for a moment while Darina silently acknowledged that what he'd said was probably true.

'My own bet is that Jemima thinks if she can find out who Rory's father is, he'll make trouble with Dad. Either he'll demand money or Rory. Whichever it is, Dad'll hate it.'

'Your father says he'd like to get his hands on whoever it is.'

'He's not the only one,' Job was suddenly grim.

Was that why Sophie had disappeared, because she knew her family wouldn't accept whoever it was she'd fallen for? It sounded a good reason but why, in that case, hadn't Rory's father come forward when Sophie collapsed? How could he let her disappear without contacting the police or the hospitals?

'You think it's a good idea to try and find him, then?'

Job shrugged his shoulders, 'I don't think you're going to get anywhere,' he said, his voice losing its sudden force.

'You think it doesn't matter if Rory is brought up by his grandfather? Is it what Sophie would have wanted?' Darina found herself intrigued by Job's mixture of passion and detachment. He sounded as though it had been a considerable struggle to come to any sort of terms with his upbringing, yet he could still be dismissive about how Rory was to be raised.

Job finished his last bit of bread and marmalade and brushed crumbs off his fingers. 'Look, Sophie and Jasper are different from Jemima and me. After Mum died they could see Dad as the all powerful giver of good things, they didn't have to endure the fighting or Mum's misery. Sophie adored him and I think, yes, that she would be very happy to know he was looking after her son.' He sounded controlled, almost academic, as if his brother and sister's lives had little to do with him.

'And Jasper seems content to live with his father,' Darina commented, now totally intrigued by these new insights into life with Basil. 'I gather he's writing a novel.'

'So he says,' again that little curl of the lip. Darina remembered the notebook that Jasper had stolen from his big brother and Job's desperate struggle to get it back.

'It must be great for him to have you to come to for advice,' she said, deliberately disingenuous.

'Jasper knows better than that!' The curl became more pronounced. 'My business is reporting the financial scene; I'm not a creative writer, I discovered that a long time ago.'

Darina wondered how much agony it had caused him.

'Anyway, what's your part in all this?' Job asked.

What indeed? 'I'm married to a detective,' she said cautiously. 'I've been involved in the odd case so Jemima asked if I could help.' It was more or less the truth. 'Why don't we start by you telling me exactly when Sophie came here to stay and why,' she suggested, fixing him with a frank stare.

Job's face re-acquired its earlier shuttered expression. For a few moments there, he'd opened up and talked like a normal human being. Now it was as though the wary, suspicious undergraduate she'd met all those years ago, who'd acted as though he was living under some sort of totalitarian regime, was back.

Was he going to change his mind about talking to her? 'I promise none of what you say will get back to your father, at least not through me,' she added hastily.

He gave a great sigh and some of the suspicion left his face. 'Can't do any harm, I suppose, certainly not as far as poor Sophie is concerned. All right, then. I'll have to think, though, we're going back aways here.'

Darina watched as he stared at the ceiling.

Then he looked at her. 'OK. Sophie came to us about two and a half years ago.'

'How old was she?'

'Oh, eighteen and a bit? Yes. She left school after two years of having a go at GCSEs, without any success, which didn't please Dad. She just wasn't academic. So Dad sent her to Switzerland, to some finishing school where she was miserable. Then a friend of his suggested she brought Sophie out; you know, cocktail parties, Ascot, Henley, all that, so she could meet lots of young people. Dad even gave a ball for her and his friend's daughter.'

This sounded more promising. Surely Sophie could have met all sorts of young men during her season. 'Who was this friend of your father's?'

'No idea! My father knows any number of socially

adept women, half of whom want to share his bed, the other half rather more.' His voice was caustic. Darina scribbled a reminder to herself to ask Jemima.

'So Sophie came out?' she prompted Job.

'Right.'

'And then?' she asked as he showed no signs of continuing.

'I don't know!' he said in exasperation. 'Jemima's no doubt told you I severed all connection with my father when our mother died.'

'But your sisters and Jasper?'

He gazed out of the back window that gave on to a tiny patio area with a rabbit hutch and a paddling pool covered with dead leaves. 'From time to time one or other of them comes and visits'.

'But you don't make much of an effort to keep in touch?' Darina tried to sound neutral but she found it difficult to understand someone who could ignore family ties so completely. An only child herself, she had longed for a brother who would explain things to her, escort her to parties and introduce her to his friends, and a sister to share clothes and giggle with.

In Italy she and Jemima had giggled together. They'd giggled about the boy who had hung around the walls of the villa, waiting for a sight of them. They'd giggled about Job and his scribbling. They'd giggled about the maid who cleaned the place and washed and ironed their clothes, handling them as though they were studded with diamonds. Once they'd seen her holding up Jemima's striped culottes and gazing at her reflection with awe. For a time Darina had felt she'd almost had a sister. Really, so when she'd suggested at the end of the holiday that Jemima give the maid the culottes Jemima had actually agreed. Afterwards she'd said that the girl's reaction had been well worth the loss of one of her favourite garments.

Job shrugged his thin shoulders. 'The only one who rang regularly and came often was Sophie. So it wasn't really a surprise when she turned up one evening with a small holdall and asked if she could stay.'

'You knew she was unhappy at home?'

'How could she be anything else?' He sounded surprised and his dark eyes sparked at her. 'She had nothing to do. She'd hated all the partying bit, said she couldn't talk to the girls, they were all too snobbish.'

'Didn't she meet any young men she liked?'

'Please! Sophie didn't have party chat and she didn't know how to flirt. She wasn't intelligent enough to distance herself from the world my father thought she should belong to, so she floundered. Worse, she was drowning. By the time she came here she was a nervous wreck.'

'And your father hadn't noticed this?' Darina thought of Basil's bright blue eyes that shone such a searchlight into people. Could he really have failed to see what was happening to his younger daughter?

'Father only notices what he wants to. And Sophie didn't want him to see her unhappy. But when he started suggesting she became his hostess, ran the house, all that sort of thing, she couldn't deal with it.'

'So she came to you.' Darina made it a statement.

Job nodded. 'I was her big brother,' he said bitterly. 'She thought I could make life safe for her. Instead, I must have made it worse.'

Chapter Five

William stood at the window of his office looking down into the police parking lot and waiting for Detective Inspector Terry Pitman to answer his summons. A child was kicking a football. He looked about five, dressed in a too large T-shirt and dirty jeans.

The ball was kicked inexpertly against a wall between two cars emblazoned with police markings. Not the dignified blue and white Avon and Somerset shield and chequered band William had grown so fond of over the past few years; these were more strident.

'You'd have him pick up that ball and run with it, wouldn't you?' Terry Pitman's voice suddenly sneered behind him. 'Tell him to forget Wembley and aim for Twickers,' the last word was given a savagely affected twist. He was short and thin with sharp eyes an unusual shade of light hazel and mid-brown hair slicked back in a way that emphasized both the thinness of his nose and his face's curious lack of contours.

No doubt the man would have resented anyone who had been given the job he obviously thought should have been his but a public school and Oxford educated superior living in Chelsea had seemed to rouse an additional bitterness.

'Close the door and sit down,' William said curtly,

turning and leaning against the windowsill. That way the light fell on the sergeant. 'I had Superintendent Marks on the phone last night,' he started.

'Ah, yes, your mate,' Terry murmured with another little sneer as he subsided on to the chair opposite William's desk.

Would Terry Pitman have gained the promotion he so desperately sought and believed should have been his if his man-management skills had been greater? 'You and DC Hare are to join the super's team for Operation Chippendale. You will both report to Divisional Head-quarters this afternoon to be briefed,' William said.

Terry's sneer vanished. 'That's great,' he said with a rush of unaffected enthusiasm. 'I'll tell Chris.'

'No, don't move,' William said, his voice steely. 'You're a bloody good detective, inspector, but you're not going to get any further in the force unless you change your attitude.' He heard himself with despair. Why couldn't he manage a telling off in the bluff, all boys together way Roger had? 'There's no reason why you should like me,' any more than there was any reason he should like Terry. But, under different circumstances, he thought that he could. Terry had an eagerness, a rat-like determination to get through to the truth of whatever lay behind a particular case, that he approved of. 'But you're lumbered with me as your superior officer. If you can't treat me as such, then get out. Do I make myself clear?'

Terry's face was wiped of all expression; he sat rigidly in his chair. 'Sir!'

With relief, William realized there was no hint of insolence in the way the word was barked out.

'By the time Operation Chippendale is over, I shall

expect you to have recognized that we are all on the same side.' William held his gaze for a long moment and watched Terry, much his own age, struggle to control his feelings. 'That's it, inspector,' he said cheerfully. 'We go forward from here. Oh, one more thing,' he added as Terry rose with the sort of alacrity that suggested springs had been released. 'Go down and check on what that boy's doing in the car park. He's too young to be on his own, even on police premises.'

'I'll get DC Hare to suss it out, sir.' Terry moved rapidly towards the door.

'No, inspector, I told you to do it yourself,' William said pleasantly.

For a split second the other man hesitated. Then, 'Right, guv,' he said smartly and left the office.

William turned to look at the car park, just in time to see a girl emerge from the door below and screech something at the child. The boy picked up his ball and ran towards her, tripped over a loose shoelace and fell. Roars of pain rose.

The girl picked up the boy and cuddled him, the strident ticking off that rose up to William a complete contrast to her body language.

Then Terry Pitman joined the scene. William couldn't make out what he said but she visibly bristled as she held the child to her.

Pitman picked up the ball and handed it back to the mother with a dismissive air. The child leant against her, thumb stuck in mouth, surveying the officer with a resentful stare.

William sighed. Was that a problem teenager in the making? An opportunity to create a sense of trust in the police had been lost. He should have taken a tougher line with Terry Pitman from the moment he realized how the sergeant was reacting to his arrival. He should have realized a conciliatory approach would be taken as a sign of weakness. Was he losing his grip? If only he could get on top of the work on his desk, perhaps he'd manage to beat his constant tiredness and rediscover a sense of vitality. He pulled a bunch of reports towards him and made a mental note to have a word with the desk sergeant to see if anyone had been aware of the child playing alone in the car park.

Later that morning William returned to the station from interviewing the proprietress of a high-class dress shop over a series of thefts. She was convinced a member of her staff was tipping someone off when new stock came in. Normally a detective sergeant and a constable would have conducted the interview but with the loss of two of his staff to Operation Chippendale and the remainder already covering incidents, William had gone himself. It was the sort of job he got too little of these days. Interacting with the public, eliciting details and instigating inquiries he had always found an enjoyable challenge.

The only drawback was the resultant paperwork. On the way back to the station gnawing hunger gripped him. Lunchtime was some way off yet. He bought a couple of chocolate-covered snacks, to hell with conscience and a healthy diet. Appetite had to be fed.

He pushed through the station's swing doors. As he made his way across the entrance hall towards the stairs leading to the CID quarters, he was subconsciously aware of a pleasing and familiar scent that cut through the institutional aroma of dust, disinfectant and silicone polish.

'Sir!' called the desk sergeant, 'there's someone waiting to see you.'

Only then did he identify the scent as Darina's favourite. What on earth had brought her here? he wondered.

A neat, petite figure dressed in a dark brown skirt and jacket that had a certain dash stood up.

He went forward. 'DCI Pigram,' he said helpfully.

The girl raised one eyebrow and gave him an amused smile that managed to suggest intimacy. There was something familiar about her and William trawled his capacious memory. 'I'm probably the last person you expected to see here,' she said with a distinct Somerset burr.

Good heavens! Turn that cap of russet curls into a mid-brown pageboy and a face from the past came into focus. 'Of course, it's Detective Constable Pat James!' William was aware that the ostentatious way the desk sergeant was scanning his incident book masked a deep interest in this unexpected visitor. 'How splendid to see you again. Come upstairs and fill me in on what's been happening to you.' He led the way, relief at being able to postpone the paperwork fighting with despair at losing precious time. But overweighing all that was pleasure. He and Pat had worked well together at one time, her unobtrusive efficiency had helped smooth the path of more than one investigation.

'I understand you're married now,' Pat James said as she followed him up the concrete staircase. 'My congratulations. Darina, wasn't it?'

He nodded. 'We finally made it to the altar about

eighteen months ago. And how about you?' he asked, opening the door into his office.

She shook her head. 'Haven't found anyone I want to settle down with yet.'

'I'm sure you will soon,' he said heartily. 'It's good to see you again, how long ago was it we worked together, three years?'

'Three and a half,' she dimpled at him, settling down in the chair so recently vacated by Terry Pitman. 'And it's Sergeant James now.' She said it with an air of expectancy.

'Congratulations,' he said heartily. 'It's no surprise, though, I knew you'd make it. Tell me what you've been doing since we last met.'

While she told him about her transfer from the Somerset to the Wiltshire Police three and a half years ago, he studied her unobtrusively.

It was no wonder it had taken a moment to recognize her. Pat James had always had an air of composure but now there was a new confidence about her. Her clothes had a chic they'd lacked before, she'd learned how to use make-up and this plus the new hairstyle gave her previous rather ordinary looks immediate impact. In fact, she was now something of a knockout.

'Are you up here on a case or having some time off?' he asked as she finished an account of her sergeant's exam.

Pat gave him a demure smile. 'I've been seconded to you by Superintendent Marks, William.'

He stared at her, as thrown by her use of his full name, hardly ever employed by his colleagues on the force, as by what she had said.

'You mean he hasn't told you?' For the first time

Pat James looked disconcerted. 'Well, I know I'm not supposed to be starting until Monday but he said he was going to let you know.'

'Did he!' William said grimly. He reached for the phone just as it rang.

'Bill? Roger here. Your chaps have just arrived, many thanks. Now, in return, I've arranged an additional sergeant for you. Maybe only temporary but it should help your immediate workload. Nice little piece of goods, name of Pat James, says you were once a team in Somerset. She worked for me when I was in Wiltshire and she's just made sergeant. Know you would have preferred a man but she should be all right, bright enough. She'll be along first thing Monday. Well, say thank you!'

'Ah, yes, thanks, I'm sure she'll work out fine.'

'We must have a pint sometime soon,' Roger added perfunctorily then rang off.

William controlled the urge to slam the receiver down. Why couldn't the man have let him know earlier? 'Well,' he said, sitting back. 'Welcome to the station. I must warn you we were stretched before two of the chaps went off to join Operation Chippendale, now we're elastic that's about to ping.'

She laughed dutifully.

'It was good of you to come straight round, I'm afraid you can't meet what's left of CID until Monday, everyone's out at the moment. But I'll take you downstairs and introduce you to some of the uniformed lot.'

'Could you fill in a bit of the background to this manor? The super said life would be very different from the sticks.'

'Of course.' William sank back into his seat, aware of

how unsettled she made him feel. What was it about her? Her new look or the way she seemed to think they enjoyed a special relationship? Then he told himself not to be ridiculous. They were old colleagues, of course she presumed they would enjoy some sort of friendship. 'We're understaffed with a backlog of cases that could keep you here twenty-four hours a day if you let it.' William refrained from telling Pat that his predecessor had been a sick man who'd been allowed to remain in his position too long.

'Sounds as though there'll be lots for me to do,' Pat said brightly.

William laughed. 'Sergeant, you have no idea how much!' He wondered how she was going to get on with Terry Pitman. The CID room at the moment only had one other woman, a very junior detective constable who came from a high rise in north London and was used to fighting her corner.

'First, there's the obvious, this is a suburban rather than a rural area,' he started but got no further before the phone rang again.

It took a little time for William to get all the details. Then he studied his notes for a few moments, thought about his empty CID room and looked across at Pat. 'How'd you like to start your new job? There's been a fire in a food factory on our patch. Arson is suspected and there's a body.'

Pat rose with alacrity. 'Right, guv, I'm ready, note-book and all.' There was a satisfied smile on her mouth as she picked up her handbag.

*

Eat Well Foods was situated on a trading estate a couple of miles from the police station.

There was a map of the various firms occupying the estate but Eat Well Foods was clearly signalled by fire engines, police cars, a crowd of watchers and a line of blue and white tape sealing off the scene.

The windows of the factory had exploded in the heat of the fire and soot marks licked their way up the outside walls. Pools of water were everywhere and as William drew up, he could smell the fumes. They reminded him of the time his mother's deep-fry pan had spontaneously combusted but with an added bitterness and acridity and a terrible top note of out-of-control barbecue. This was an odour that sank into your consciousness. It was noticeable that every window of every other building in the vicinity was shut.

'Euough,' said Pat James in disgust.

Inside the scene of crime tape stood a group of people: three or four firemen, several uniformed police, a burly man in an anorak and dark trousers, a tall, slim woman in a trench coat and a man in a well cut suit, his fair hair swept back from an attractively open face.

William flashed his warrant card at the officer guarding the taped-off area. 'CID,' he said. 'Where's the fire chief?'

'Over there, sir.' The officer waved at the little group.

Followed by Pat, who carefully picked her way through the puddles with what looked like a new pair of shoes, William approached the burly man in the anorak. 'DCI Pigram, sir,' he introduced himself. 'Chief Shorrocks?'

'Right, Chief Inspector,' he acknowledged. 'Glad you could come so promptly.' He drew William a little apart.

'The fire was reported around four o'clock this morning. It was under control by six but the premises couldn't be properly inspected until a short while ago; the heat, you understand.'

William looked at small tendrils of steam still rising from the inside of the building and could appreciate the difficulty.

'This is Officer Melville,' the chief waved forward one of the firemen. 'It was he who called me in.'

'Can you tell me what you found, officer?' William asked.

The fireman's craggy face was smudged, his eyes reddened and tired. He took off his helmet and ran a hand round the back of his neck. 'It's a one-storey building, as you can see, and the roof held. Both the offices and the factory, though it's more like a huge kitchen than a factory if you ask me, were badly damaged. The body was in the corridor between the two areas.'

Overcome by the fumes? Or was there a more sinister reason for his death? It was unlikely William would be able to determine much from the body, fire would have obliterated all obvious clues. It would be down to forensics and the pathologist to detect the cause of death. Reluctantly, though, he faced the fact that he would have to inspect the charred corpse.

'Any idea who it could be?' Pat asked.

'We gather there was a night security man,' the fire chief interpolated.

'And you suspect arson?' William offered.

The fireman nodded. 'There was broken window glass inside one of the offices, suggesting a break-in. The office was obviously where the conflagration started. I'd say an accelerant was used and it smelt like petrol. Scorch marks up the walls together with the intensity of the fire suggest it was thrown around pretty liberally but your forensic boys will make sure.'

'There's a Scenes of Crime team on their way. Who reported the fire?'

'Someone passing the estate rang in.'

'Did you get a name and address?'

Melville nodded. 'It's all on tape but I reckon it was a kosher call, not one of those pyromaniacs who set the thing off then call the brigade and hang around to watch the fun.'

William looked back at the ruined factory. 'Who's the owner?'

'Place is rented by a Mrs Douglas, that's her, over there.'

'Right, we'll have a word. Thanks, Officer Melville, we'll need a full statement from you.'

The fireman nodded, seemingly resigned to the formalities. 'Any time, sir.'

William went over to the woman. 'I understand you're the proprietor of Eat Well Foods, Mrs Douglas?'

She nodded. Her eyes were shocked, huge and dark. In any other circumstances she would have been beautiful, now strain had hardened the lines of her classically shaped face and the creamy skin had an unnatural pallor. The short, glossy dark hair was dishevelled and she wore no make-up.

'I gather you had a night security officer patrolling your factory?'

Her eyes closed briefly. 'Gerry Aherne,' was all she said.

'When was the last time you saw him?'

'Yesterday evening, as I left, about seven thirty.' It seemed an impossibility but her face grew even paler and her eyes larger.

'Where does he live?'

She pointed to one side of the factory. 'There's a small apartment at the back.'

William looked at a fireman. He shook his head. 'No sign of anyone there, sir,' he said.

'Mrs Douglas, is there anyone you can think of who could have a grievance against you?'

She looked at him, her dark eyes dilated – with fear? Shock? Bewilderment? 'Are you saying the fire wasn't an accident, that someone did this deliberately?' She hunched her shoulders and folded her arms across herself in a gesture of denial.

'I'm afraid it looks as though the fire was started deliberately,' William said expressionlessly, watching her carefully.

The crossed arms tightened and she shook her head vehemently. 'There isn't anyone, I mean, I can't think anyone would do such a thing.'

Her companion placed an arm around her shoulders. 'Do you have to question her now?' he asked William. 'She's in shock, she should be home, in bed.' His voice was angry but also uncertain.

William looked at him politely, 'And you are, sir?'

'Paul Robins,' the man said, his spurt of anger subsiding. 'Public Relations consultant to Eat Well Foods.'

Val Douglas moved away from his arm. 'Paul, I know you're trying to help, but there are things to see to.' She glanced at the crowd on the other side of the blue and white tape. 'I've got to tell them to go home,' she said with a sigh.

68

'It's the staff,' Paul explained to William. 'They all turned up for work as usual. Well, they would, wouldn't they? I'll talk to them,' he said to the woman.

'No, it's my job.' She advanced towards the crowd. 'Look, I'm sorry, but, as you can see, we won't be able to do any work today. Why don't you all go home and I'll let you know when production can start again.' She scanned their faces.

There must be about thirty there, William reckoned, mainly women. Their expressions were excited, apprehensive, frightened even. He couldn't see any that looked knowing or unsurprised.

Mrs Douglas squared her shoulders, a natural authority begining to emerge. 'Look, Eat Well Foods is going to remain in business. I'll find other premises until we can rebuild here.'

'It had better be near,' someone shouted out.

She nodded. 'Of course, trust me.' At that moment, William thought, even he might have.

A short, sturdy girl rather better dressed than the others came forward. 'What about the records? Have they survived?'

Mrs Douglas saw immediately what she was getting at. 'Thanks, Shaz, I'm not being allowed to check on anything at the moment.' She looked back at the ruined premises. 'But I shouldn't think so.'

'Then I'll make a note of everyone's address and telephone number,' the girl said. She pulled out a small notebook and the others clustered around her.

'The perfect secretary,' Mrs Douglas said and the girl gave her a gratified smile. 'Stay behind when you've finished, Shaz, and I'll see if I can put two thoughts together on where we go from here. And we'll have to tell our regular customers we can't fulfil any orders today.'

'Pretty much in control, isn't she?' murmured Pat to William.

He nodded. It was an impressive performance. Val Douglas had courage, was a woman who wouldn't let go easily. He wondered what the finances of Eat Well Foods were like.

'I appreciate you have a lot to deal with, Mrs Douglas,' he said as she rejoined Paul Robins. 'But we shall need to talk to you.'

She eyed him. 'Talk to me?'

'We need to know about the company, about your nightwatchman and how the fire could have started.'

The slightest of flushes stained the pale cheekbones. 'I can't help you there, I'm afraid. I wish I could.'

'Look,' Paul Robins said aggressively, 'this is a devastating experience for Val, for Mrs Douglas. You suggesting she might have had something to do with the fire is ridiculous.'

'I'm not,' William said mildly.

'Oh, well, that's all right then.' Paul stuck his hands in his pockets and kicked at some loose rubble on the ground.

'Paul, I think we need to draft a statement we can give the press,' Val Douglas said. She sounded as though her stock of energy was exhausted. 'If we don't tell them something, all those reporters who were here earlier are going to print I don't know what. You should call a conference.'

'Of course,' he said eagerly. 'Look, if you won't go home, come to my office.' He put his hand on her back as though to guide her away from the ruined factory.

'Would you mind giving me details of where your office is, please, sir?' Pat asked.

Paul Robins dug out a card and handed it to her. She gave it a glance then handed it to William. Robins Associates it read, with an address in a nearby town.

Just then a Rolls Royce glided up and stopped beside William's old Bentley. Two thoroughbreds but one was at the end of its life and the other had hardly commenced its career. Out stepped a man tailored and groomed to a fine finish. Piercing eyes swept the scene.

'Basil!' Val Douglas breathed with what seemed enormous relief. 'Thanks for coming back.'

He strode possessively over to her, holding up and stepping underneath the blue and white tape as though it was fairground decoration.

'Sir!' expostulated the uniformed constable.

William quietened him with a wave of his hand.

'I've finished my meeting and cleared my diary. Now we can sort you out,' the newcomer said. He put his arm around her shoulders, where Paul Robins's had so lately been, and would have swept her away but William stepped forward.

'If I could have details of where I can contact Mrs Douglas?' he asked amiably.

Cold blue eyes looked into his and he had the impression they weren't pleased to find they were on a level with his own. A man used to dominating others with his size. 'And who are you?'

'Chief Inspector Pigram, sir, CID. I'm investigating the fire.'

'Are you, by God! I would have thought that would be a matter for the fire department.'

'They've found a body, Basil,' Val said and her voice

trembled. Now this man had appeared, it seemed reaction was setting in. 'It looks as though it's our night-watchman's.'

'Good God!' he said sharply. 'In that case, I understand.' He, too, reached into an inside pocket but his cards were carried in a silver case. He detached and handed one over. 'You can contact Mrs Douglas through my office.' The full name was Basil Ealham, Chairman and Managing Director of Ealham Industries with another local address.

'Will you be taking Mrs Douglas there, sir?' Pat asked.

Basil looked down at her. 'I've said you can contact her through my office,' he repeated with a touch of pomposity.

'Thank you, sir,' William said quietly. There was no point in antagonizing the man unnecessarily; William thought he'd be very surprised if obstacles were placed in the way of an interview with Val Douglas. When the investigation started to uncover sensitive material, if it did, that was the point when Ealham would try to take control.

'But, the press statement?' Paul Robins said helplessly as he watched his client being taken over.

'We'll ring later,' Basil Ealham said curtly.

Paul Robins looked pleadingly at Val but William doubted she even realized he was still there.

It was only as the car purred away that William remembered that his wife's old school friend, the one she'd lunched with yesterday, apparently in some style and not far from the address he'd just been given, was called Ealham. Why hadn't he paid more attention to what she'd said?

Chapter Six

Nicola Ealham took her two children to the school gate and gave them a gentle push in the direction of the classrooms. 'See you at four o'clock,' she called as they gathered speed, melting into the flow of children. Kinsey looked back over her shoulder and waved, the fat pigtails with their blue butterfly bows bouncing on her eight-year-old shoulders, but seven-year-old Arthur was too busy punching the arm of his best friend to be concerned with saying goodbye.

Nicola grinned to herself as she turned to walk back home. There wasn't much wrong with her little world. As long as the washing-machine man came and didn't extract Danegeld for fixing the darned thing. But she'd just got paid for that programming job she'd done for a local estate agents and she could probably cope with the damage.

Anyway, she wasn't going to worry. A warm September sun was shining and back home Nicola had plans for making a batch of oat bread and trying out a new recipe for soya pancakes which she planned to serve with maple syrup for supper. If they were a success, she'd make some more and stuff them with organic mushrooms for a meal over the weekend. Nicola believed what you fed people was important, especially children. After all you didn't expect a Rolls Royce to run on poor petrol, did you?

She let herself into the house. 'I'm back,' she called cheerfully then realized that Job was sitting in the living room talking to a very tall, blonde girl.

'Hi, darling.' Job smiled up at her. 'Meet Darina Lisle. She went to school with Jemima and she's trying to find out who Rory's father is.'

'Good heavens, lost cause that.' Poor little Sophie, every time Nicola thought about her she felt sad. Nobody had been able to help her, not Job, not herself. 'Why now? I thought your father wasn't going to bother. Mind you, I always did think that was odd, his not wanting to know, I mean.' She sat down on a large bean bag and gazed with open curiosity at the girl, who smiled back with easy friendliness.

'It's Jemima,' said Darina. 'She's the one who's so concerned.' She hesitated a moment then added, 'Something to do with balancing the effect Rory's grandfather will have on his upbringing, I think.'

'I quite understand,' said Nicola cheerfully. Basil represented so much that she was anti – possessions, ostentation and disregard for other people, particularly people who depended on you like your wife and children. 'We've been worried about that ourselves. My suggestion he lived with us was as popular as raw steak to a vegetarian.'

'I've got to go,' Job said, unwinding his long body. 'Why don't you talk to Darina, darling, after all, you saw much more of Sophie than I.'

Nicola caught Darina's hopeful look and decided that, after all, oat bread could wait for another half hour or so. 'The man hasn't turned up for the washing machine?' she asked, looking up for Job's parting kiss.

'Yup, he's in the kitchen.'

'Why on earth didn't you say!' Nicola was up in an instant. On the kitchen table, in between dirty cereal bowls and half-drunk mugs of milk (trust Job not to insist the kids finished them), were oily lumps of machinery. Carefully inspecting one of them was a spotty youth, his overalls looking as though they'd never seen the inside of one of the machines he spent most of his life communing with.

'Well?' she demanded.

'Wouldn't have a coffee going, would you, miss? My old lady wouldn't get up this morning.'

Nicola put the kettle on. 'Right, now tell me about my machine.'

Ten minutes later, blinded by his combination of engineering expertise and inability to communicate it to her, she'd agreed to the replacement of a highly expensive part on the understanding he'd have the machine working by the end of the day. Carrying two fresh cups of coffee, she returned to the living room.

'I sometimes think I should take evening classes on the maintenance of kitchen machinery.' Nicola handed over one of the coffees and sank down on the bean bag again.

'I'm useless. Can just about fix a plug – and William's not much better. We reckon it's cheaper in the long run to give DIY jobs to a professional first time around.'

Nicola inspected the girl more closely. About five years younger than herself, she reckoned, and someone she felt an immediate liking for. Nicola usually made up her mind instantly about people. When she'd met Job, they'd both been reaching for the same Thurber book in the university library. She'd looked at his reserved face and lanky body, added a liking for surrealistic humour and decided. She'd suggested they went and had tea in a nearby café. He'd hesitated, looking agonized, and she could see he was torn between wanting to accept her invitation and dreading it would develop into a relationship he couldn't sustain. 'One exchange of a library book is what I'm talking about, not a commitment for life,' she'd said, grinning at him, knowing that her freckles, short ginger hair and the impertinent tilt to her nose would be immensely reassuring. It had almost reconciled her to the fact her looks were so unprepossessing.

The girl sitting opposite her was no classic beauty either, too big boned. But she had an openness about her, a warmth in the eyes that were neither grey nor quite hazel, that was more attractive than model-girl looks. 'I can't imagine how you and Jemima became friends,' Nicola said suddenly. Jemima was one of the few people she had never been able to make up her mind about. Sometimes she despised the way she snatched at what she wanted out of life, other times she liked her zest and thought with a bit of hard work they could have a good relationship. But Jemima regarded her with the wariness of a cat assessing hostile territory and hid behind a finishing-school drawl until Nicola could have shaken her.

'Not much alike, are we?' Darina sounded amused. 'Perhaps that's why we got on. Jemima was always so much fun. She did and said the most dreadful things but made you laugh.' She fell silent for a moment then

76

added, 'Yesterday was the first time we'd met since school.'

'Good heavens, that must be, what, thirteen years ago? But, then, Jemima doesn't really know much about friendship. Lives in a little world of her own. Her father has a lot to answer for.'

'Job says she's dependent on him.'

'He buggered up all his children's lives.' Nicola spoke with quiet passion.

Darina leaned forward. 'Tell me about it.'

Nicola was more than happy. It was a long time since she'd had an opportunity to exorcize some of the anger she felt against Basil Ealham. 'To start with he turned their mother into an alcoholic.'

'Ah!' A small sigh that said a lot. 'When Jemima and I were about fifteen, I spent a holiday with the Ealhams in Italy and afterwards I wondered. Jemima would never talk about it though. Did Job?'

'Yeah. I'd guessed actually. I reckoned there had to be major damage in his background, he was so withdrawn and he'd never talk about his family. I didn't even realize he had a brother and two sisters until he suggested we got married. I told him I wouldn't begin to think about it until I'd met his relations. I had to get him to confront his problems somehow!'

'I often wondered why Job came on that holiday. After all, he was at university, most undergraduates I've known would die rather than go abroad with their family. Not that Basil stayed more than a few days with us. Business, we were told.'

'Always business,' Nicola agreed. She crossed her legs yoga style on the bean bag. 'Job probably went because he adored his mother. I wish I'd met her, she died just before we got together – I only found that out later, too. When I think of all Job bottled up . . .' For a moment Nicola felt the suffocation that came whenever she confronted how badly damaged Job had been. She took several deep breaths and reminded herself how successful she'd been in coaxing him into something approaching the sort of normal human being who could ask for help.

'You're the first person I've met I can talk to about Job's mother. What was she like?'

Darina thought for a moment. 'Very unpretentious. Almost aggressively so. I admired a skirt she had on once, it was long, pleated, in navy, just the sort of thing that would look good with my hips,' she glanced wryly at herself. 'She told me it came from Marks and Spencer's and made it sound as though she'd gone somewhere forbidden and that it was some sort of victory. Jemima was always telling her she should get some decent clothes and that their house needed redecorating.' Darina gave a short laugh. 'She thought the villa we were staying in was marvellous. Apparently it belonged to some business friend of her father's and it was full of the most beautiful furniture, a lot of it modern, very expensive I should think.'

'Jemima likes expensive things,' Nicola murmured. 'Did you visit Blackboys while her mother was alive?'

Darina nodded. 'Several times. My mother said it looked as though it had been furnished by a second-rate department store with no expense spared. Everything colour co-ordinated with no taste.' She laughed again, 'She'd love it now.'

'I hate it,' Nicola said repressively. 'Talk about preten-

78

tious! Come on, tell me more about Julie. Did she seem happy?'

'Heavens, no. I used to wonder why she stayed with her husband. He'd make awful, snide remarks to her and she'd just sit there and say nothing. The night after we arrived we heard them shouting at each other. I remember Sophie coming into our bedroom, crying. Then Basil left and Sophie was even more upset. Jasper didn't like it either.' She smiled at Nicola. 'Jasper was such a clown. That second night he walked on his hands all the way down the table in the middle of the meal, glasses and plates everywhere, with Basil shouting at him to stop being such a fool. He didn't disturb a thing, then leaped off like an acrobat and said with an enormous grin, "For my next trick, walking on water!" And Basil just creased. Jasper was over the moon. After his father left, he was really depressed for several days. Jemima and Job were relieved.'

'What about their mother?'

'She was certainly less tense but she drank as much if not more.'

'How did she manage the cooking? Or was there a cook laid on?'

'No, I did most of the cooking.' Darina's face suddenly lit up. 'I loved it, all those marvellous vegetables and I'd brought Elizabeth David's *Italian Cooking* with me. I think that's when I decided food was going to be my life.'

'I wonder what the Ealhams thought of it all! According to Job, his mother was a terrible cook. She and his father both came from very poor backgrounds and her idea of a really good meal never progressed beyond steak and chips.'

'They should never have married,' Darina said sadly.

'Old story, he got her in the family way, then felt he had to marry her.'

'Well, something to be said for him, then.'

'Thought he'd make sure of his home comforts so he could concentrate on making his fortune,' Nicola said caustically. 'The women came later. That's when Julie's drinking started, apparently. Then everything was downhill.'

'Why didn't she leave him, has Job told you that?'

Nicola thought about the way Job used to close up like a hedgehog rolling itself into a ball, all prickles, and the long, slow process of getting him to open up and unburden himself. 'He thinks she really loved his father and couldn't bear the thought of life without him. More interesting is why he didn't leave her. My theory is that he liked playing around and didn't want to commit himself to anyone else. After all, he's never married again. Julie was one of life's victims. She ended up taking an overdose of sleeping tablets. Job has never forgiven his father.'

'That's why he won't have anything to do with him?'

Nicola nodded. 'Wouldn't even invite him to the wedding. Not that I think it worried Basil, he'd made it clear he didn't think I was up to much; no background, no connections, no money.'

Darina shook her head. 'What an arrogant bastard.'

'In spades,' Nicola said levelly.

'Jemima says that since she started working for Basil, Job won't speak to her.'

Nicola pulled at her short, ginger hair with both hands. 'Aaargh! He can be such an idiot! He's lost one sister and now he's doing all he can to lose the other.'

'Tell me about Sophie.'

Nicola leant back against the bookshelves. 'I think she was her mother all over again. Frailty thy name is Sophie, was what I always thought.'

'Job says he doesn't know why she left you, do you?' Darina's gaze was very level and Nicola thought how difficult it would be to hide something from those eyes.

Nicola looked down at the freckles on the backs of her hands. Freckles like brown sugar, Sophie had said. They'd been sitting at the kitchen table. It had been a lovely May day with the sun shining and they'd been enjoying the wild cherry tea Sophie liked so much, not really talking, just appreciating the warmth and the feeling that conversation wasn't necessary. Sophie had run her finger over Nicola's hand, then put her mouth down and licked it. 'You taste sweet,' she'd said. 'Like sugar.'

Nicola had grinned at her. 'You better not eat me, you know sugar isn't good for you.'

Nicola dragged her mind back to the present. 'Sophie was so hungry for love. But I think she was afraid of it, too. Her mother died when she was eight and she'd grown up with a series of housekeepers and a father who was hardly ever there but demanded everything from her when he was. He wanted too much. He wanted her to be intelligent and bright and ambitious.'

'Like Jemima,' murmured Darina.

'Yeah, like Jemima.' Nicola said sourly. 'But Basil was always on at Jemima, too; about her men, her clothes, her failure to stick at anything. Basil always wants to make people into his idea of what they should be. It wound Sophie into knots. She was in a terrible state when she arrived here, bursting into tears at nothing at all, you had to handle her as though she was made of incredibly short pastry.'

Darina smiled at the metaphor.

'But being with Kinsey and Arthur, our children, was just what she needed. She loved them and they adored her. They couldn't believe it when she went off like that.' Nicola paused then added, 'Neither could I.'

'Not so trusting, after all, then?' Darina said gently.

Nicola shook her head sadly. 'I'd thought we were friends. I really thought she'd be able to tell me anything.'

'Can you tell me exactly what happened?'

Nicola had been over the events of that week so often she was able to rattle them off without thinking. The routine had become familiar over the couple of months Sophie had been with them. Sophie had taken the children to school and collected them as usual. Nicola had taken her turn in running the play group on the Tuesday and the Thursday mornings while Sophie did some housework. On the Tuesday afternoon they'd cooked together because Martin Price was coming to supper.

'Who is Martin?' Darina interrupted. 'A boyfriend of Sophie's?'

Nicola laughed. 'Heavens, no. Martin was at university with Job. He runs a financial company in the city now. He married about the same time we did and he and his wife, Eleanor, are great friends.'

'But Eleanor didn't come to supper that night?'

'No,' Nicola said more slowly, thinking about that for the first time. 'Eleanor was in Cornwall, looking after her mother, I think she'd broken her arm. Eleanor had rung me before she left and I promised her we'd look

82

after Martin. He came round for supper several times. He was sweet with Sophie, didn't make her feel an idiot, you know?' She thought about that for a moment. 'Anyway, Martin came to supper that night. And the next night he took her out to the cinema.' She felt the quality of Darina's attention alter. 'But there was nothing like that about it,' she protested. 'He was just being friendly.' She looked down at her hands, lying between her crossed legs. 'Perhaps I should tell you a little more about Martin. He was very upset at that time. His son, Charlie, had been killed in a traffic accident and he thought Eleanor blamed him for his death. Martin's the type who always feels guilty, whatever happens. Whatever the truth, he was really worried Eleanor wasn't going to come back to him from her mother's.' Nicola looked at Darina and added quickly, 'But she did and they're fine now. So you see that there couldn't have been anything between Martin and Sophie. He took her out to give Job and me an evening to ourselves. However much you like someone, you need a little time out every now and then.'

Darina made a note, it was impossible for Nicola to tell what she was thinking. 'So that brings us to Thursday, what happened then?'

Nicola realized she'd stopped talking, caught up in remembering that last week. Nothing was what had happened then. Nothing out of the ordinary, anyway. Except, 'She did seem a bit quiet,' Nicola said. 'But she was never exactly noisy. Sometimes you hardly noticed she was there.' She could see Sophie now, sitting in the corner of that ratty old sofa as relaxed as a cat.

'I've never known anyone who seemed so happy doing nothing. Not reading, not sewing, not listening to

music, not watching the television, just doing absolutely
nothing at all. And all over that weekend she seemed to
be getting quieter and quieter. The only time I heard her
laugh was when she played with the children. Martin
came round for Sunday lunch and he managed to raise a
smile or two from her but apart from that, it was like
living with someone who was turning into a ghost.'
Nicola gave a small shiver, she wasn't normally that
imaginative.

'Did you ask if anything was worrying her?'

Nicola screwed up her face. 'It was difficult with
Sophie. If she thought you were getting at her, she dissolved into floods of tears. Sure, I asked her if everything
was all right and she said it was. After she disappeared, I
asked Martin if anything had happened the night they'd
gone to the cinema but he said nothing, she'd been
sweet and he couldn't think of anything strange.'

'She left, when?'

'Monday. I had to go out on a job. Mostly I work
from home, I've got a work station in our bedroom. But
Monday I had to visit a small company down the high
street. When I got back at lunchtime, Sophie had gone.
Packed a small bag, left us a note – and vanished.'

Nicola felt tears pricking at the back of her eyes.
She'd never manage to get over the way Sophie had
disappeared or the tragedy of her death. She went to a
desk in the corner of the room, found a piece of paper
and handed it to Darina. 'You'd better see it, I suppose.'

As Darina unfolded the note, Nicola could see again
the large, unformed letters that said, 'Thanks for everything. I've got to go now. See you soon, lots of love,
Soph.'

'And she never contacted you?'

Nicola shook her head, trying to swallow the lump in her throat. After all this time, she should be able to handle the fact of Sophie's disappearance better.

'Did she have any money?'

'That's one of the first things we thought of. She'd drawn thirty pounds out from her bank account a few days before and, as far as we could find out, that was all she had.'

'She didn't draw any more?'

'No, nor use her credit cards. It was as though she realized they could give away where she was.' Nicola didn't add that when Basil had first found that out, they'd all thought it meant Sophie was dead. The news of her actual death had been doubly tragic. She'd been alive for all that time and they hadn't known.

'It's Job's theory that Sophie ran away not from us but from Basil.'

'What does he mean? Was Basil threatening to take her home? Presumably he knew she was staying with you?'

'Oh, yes. But after she arrived here, Job went over to Blackboys, it was one of the few times he's been there since his mother died, and told Basil that if he didn't leave Sophie alone, she'd have a nervous breakdown. Eventually his father agreed that he wouldn't contact her for at least three months. I think Job said the words Basil used were, "I'll let the girl get herself together." But she used to ring him up every weekend, tell him what she'd been doing, ask him how he was, all that sort of thing.'

'It didn't worry her to talk to him?'

'No, really, she adored him. It was just too much for her being with him, trying to fulfil his demands.'

'Did Sophie talk to her father that last weekend?'

Nicola thought for a moment. 'No,' she said at last. 'I remember now, he was abroad. She tried to get him at some hotel but he wasn't there. She left a message for him to ring her but he didn't.'

'Was she upset at that?'

'Didn't seem to be. But, as I said, she was so quiet, it was difficult to know what she was thinking. Just like a ghost.' It was an image that kept coming back to Nicola, like a haunting.

'So after you left her in the house on the Monday morning, you never saw or heard from her again.' It was a statement and all Nicola had to do was nod.

Darina frowned and looked at her notes. 'Can you give me your friend Martin's address and telephone number?' she asked finally.

'But he doesn't know anything,' Nicola protested. 'After she disappeared, we really grilled him. We thought if anybody knew where she'd gone, it'd be him. After all, he was the only person outside the family she'd seen while she was here. Oh, just a minute, there was someone else. He worked for a friend of Basil's, she was in food. I remember Sophie telling me she produced dishes for people with food intolerances and I thought it sounded really interesting.'

'Val Douglas,' Darina contributed.

'I've got it, Paul Robins, that was the name.'

Darina wrote it down. 'You met him?'

'Yup, he just rang the doorbell one afternoon not long after Sophie arrived. Said he was in the area, knew she was staying with us and thought he'd drop in. Quite attractive, if you like that rather smooth, nothing under the surface type.'

'Was Sophie pleased to see him?'

Nicola tried to think back. She couldn't believe that she had so completely forgotten all about this visit. 'It was difficult to tell with Sophie, she talked to everyone as though they were the most important person in the world.'

'Captivating,' was Darina's comment.

'Yes, it was,' Nicola acknowledged. She supposed she would always miss Sophie.

'But you didn't see this Paul Robins again?'

Nicola shook her head.

'He couldn't have called round when you weren't here?'

'Well, yes, I suppose so,' Nicola acknowledged. 'But Sophie would have told me. I'm sure it was just that one time.'

What was this investigation going to drag up? Nicola hoped it wasn't going to upset Job. 'Look,' she said to Darina, 'I'm sure it's a good idea to try and find out who Rory's father is and I'll give you Martin's details if you think it'll help, but please don't talk again to my husband.'

'The Ealhams aren't an easy family to be involved with, are they?' Darina said.

Chapter Seven

Darina left Job and Nicola's house wondering about Sophie.

Had she been as lacking in intelligence as Nicola seemed to suggest? She certainly seemed incapable of surviving on her own. Someone who had lived all her life surrounded by love in a completely protected environment. Yet she'd disappeared and managed to live nearly eight months without contact with anyone she'd known up until then. How?

When she'd disappeared, the Ealhams had contacted the police but, because Sophie was over eighteen, there'd been little they could do. However, a sympathetic officer had unofficially checked with social services and then told them that Sophie had not applied for any benefits. At that point, the family had feared she must be dead.

Darina had gathered a few more details from Jemima. Basil had disappeared to his office before they'd had lunch, brusquely instructing Jemima to follow as soon as Mrs Starr appeared.

Over lobster salad Jemima had told Darina about the boutique she'd been running in London at the time of Sophie's death, and the man she'd been involved with. 'One of those real shits who give less than nothing but take everything and do it with so much charm and style, you'd be happy to go on giving to them until hallelujah day.' Her face had had an unfamiliar, yearning expression. 'He had those dark eyes that seem to look right down to your fanny, and what a body! Some Sundays we'd never get out of the sack. Mondays I could hardly crawl to the shop. Oh, it was wonderful!' She'd glowed as she talked.

'What happened?'

'What always happens to my men, he found something else.' Not somebody, Darina noticed. 'In Titus's case it was rafting down the Colorado River. He said it was no place for a girl and it would only be for three weeks. That was fifteen months ago. I hear the Colorado River is drying up so maybe I'll see him again one of these days.'

'You haven't had a boyfriend since?' Darina was sceptical.

'Good heavens, darling, what do you take me for, a nun?' Jemima placed a bowl of fruit and a cheese platter on the table. 'There was Mike, he was a journalist, always dashing off on some story or other. Never had any money. "Waiting for my expenses, sweetie," was his excuse every time the bill came round. I gave him the boot when I met James.' She cut into a golden peach. 'James was a financial consultant, fearfully rich. He took me to all the best places, and was almost as good in bed as Titus.'

'So what went wrong with him?'

'His mother! Practising to be the mother-in-law from hell. James adored her and she was always round at our place. Mummy dear had nothing else to do but involve herself in our activities. Just when I couldn't stand it any more, I met Dominic. That was about six months ago.'

'And what's he like?' a bemused Darina asked, thinking that Jemima had always seemed to need men. On the Italian holiday, it hadn't been long before she'd made contact with Claudio, the youngster who'd hung around the villa. After that, there was rarely a day she hadn't gone off with him somewhere. Once Claudio had produced a friend and they'd made up a foursome but all the boys had been interested in was removing the small amount of clothes the girls were wearing. Jemima hadn't seemed to mind but Darina had. 'Honestly,' she'd told her friend afterwards, 'you want to watch it. It's not that I'm a prude but haven't these lads heard about chatting a girl up?'

'Oh, you!' had been Jemima's only comment. Next time she'd suggested they make a foursome, Darina had said she preferred to enjoy the pool at the villa. She'd wondered that Jemima's mother hadn't protested at her daughter's behaviour but Mrs Ealham spent every day sitting beside a long drink that rapidly grew shorter until it was replenished. Her only comment ever seemed to be to tell Sophie to keep her sunhat on. It had been Darina who applied the suntan lotion to the little body and Jasper who kept her amused. Job had been as elusive as Jemima.

'Dominic? Raaather tasty!' Jemima drawled. 'Unfortunately he's in television. What with his hours and the way Dad's such a bear if I take time off, I don't see nearly enough of him. Anyway, compared with Titus, he's not so great.' For a fleeting instant her mouth drooped.

'I'm not surprised you didn't have any spare time to

look for a missing sister.' Darina said crisply. 'I'm just amazed you manage to combine your social life with working for your father.'

Jemima suddenly looked vulnerable. 'Don't say things like that, please! Nobody really understands; I need men, it's like a sort of hunger. It's not just sex, though that's part of it, I need to have someone I can connect with, you know? Someone who cares. But that doesn't mean I can't work as well. And I did care about Sophie, really I did.' She sat holding half a peach, ripe juices slowly dripping on to her plate. 'It was just that there was too big an age gap between us. It was me and Job, and her and Jasper.' She gazed at Darina, her mobile face despondent. 'As I told you, she wasn't the brightest of kids. Dad never seemed to realize it but holding a conversation with her was like trying to talk to someone who didn't know what time of day it was. She had no idea of the sort of life I led and wasn't interested in hearing about it. But her small brain didn't seem to matter to Dad.' She put the piece of peach down on her plate and sat looking at it as though a scorpion might crawl out.

She was jealous of her sister, Darina suddenly realized. All those years Basil hadn't turned up at school, had abandoned her on holiday, she'd been desperate for his attention. Instead, he seemed to have given it to her baby sister. 'Perhaps he was trying to make up for the fact she didn't have a mother,' she suggested.

'Guilt, more like,' Jemima said bitterly. 'How Mum put up with him all those years, I'll never know. Marriage, huh! Who needs it!'

Darina had no wish to explore that argument. 'But

didn't you say he'd backed your boutique? And now he's given you a job you seem to enjoy.'

'Only so he can demonstrate his power,' Jemima said bitterly. 'He's never given any of us any real independence. Jasper gets an allowance so he can write but it's not enough for him to have his own place.'

Darina thought that Jasper was lucky not to have to combine his writing with a daytime job.

'And my salary isn't anywhere near enough for me to live on my own any more. The trouble is, we're too used to this sort of lifestyle.' Jemima gave an all-encompassing glance to the beautifully furnished room, the silver and crystal on the table, the perfectly ripe fruit and cheese. 'But I can't bear it if Rory has to go through what we did, all the bullying, the shouting and Dad never being there when he's needed.' There was a note of genuine desperation in her voice.

Darina had been working herself up to say that she couldn't take on what seemed to her a hopeless task but she found herself unexpectedly moved. 'Tell me more about this hospital business,' she suggested. 'Did someone take her there, or did she go by ambulance? Either way, there must have been a name or a record of some address?'

Jemima shook her head. 'If only it had been that simple! Apparently she collapsed in the street and a shopkeeper sent for an ambulance.'

'And how did the hospital know who to call? Did she tell them?'

'No, I think she was in a coma when she arrived. Dad said they'd found her driving licence with this address and got the telephone number from directory enquiries.'

'Driving licence? In her handbag?'

Jemima nodded.

'Wasn't there anything else in there that would help to trace her?'

'Look, I've told you, there was no way we could find out where she'd been living.'

'Exactly where did she collapse?'

Jemima grinned suddenly. 'I knew I was right to ask you for help, you don't let up on the questions.'

'What did you expect? That I'd conjure information out of nowhere? So, where did the ambulance pick her up? I can't imagine your father didn't ask.'

'Oh, yeah! He interrogated everyone he could get hold of. She was in the Portobello Road when she collapsed. And it's no use asking me what she was doing there.'

'Did she have a shopping bag with her?'

'There was a sort of string bag in her coat pocket.'

Had she been just about to start shopping when she collapsed? 'And what time of the day was it?'

'One p.m.'

'Lunchtime,' said Darina thoughtfully. 'What else do you know?'

'Well,' Jemima put both her elbows on the table and fiddled with a ring while she talked. 'As you can imagine, Dad went into the whole thing pretty thoroughly. Apparently the ambulance men said that by the time they got to her, Sophie had just come round. Someone had put a folded coat under her head and was holding her hand. She told the ambulance man that her head ached and it felt as if someone had hit her. He asked the crowd if anyone had seen anything but various people said she'd just collapsed. The paramedic couldn't find anything wrong except that her hands, legs and feet were all terribly swollen. Sophie said she felt awful and he decided to take her to the hospital. On the way Sophie was sick and by the time they arrived she was in a coma.' Jemima ducked her head and ran her thumb along her forehead. 'I hate thinking of her like that, all on her own.' She seemed genuinely moved. If she had been jealous of Sophie's hold on their father, it didn't seem to have affected her love for her sister.

'And she didn't tell them anything about herself?' asked Darina gently.

Jemima shook her head. 'As I said, they found this address on her driving licence. Mrs Starr gave them Dad's office number. He said their first diagnosis was that Sophie had had a stroke.'

'A stroke?' A nineteen-year-old? Darina couldn't believe it.

'I know,' Jemima said sadly. 'But apparently it's not unknown. It wasn't until she was examined that they realized she was pregnant.'

'Good heavens!'

'She didn't look it, you see. She was wearing a loose dress and the baby was so small. Then they realized she was suffering from pre-eclampsia, that's a form of toxaemia,' she added kindly. 'That was when they brought in an obstetrics team, who said the baby was in difficulties and they performed a caesarean. Result, one minute little Rory but Sophie never regained consciousness. Apparently it was an aneurysm in the brain, a weakness in a blood vessel which burst.'

Darina could think of nothing useful to say.

'They also said she was half starved,' Jemima added after a moment.

'Half starved?' Darina repeated in astonishment

'Well, malnourished was what Dad actually said.'

'And how long after Sophie disappeared was that?'

'Eight months.'

'So she could have been pregnant when she left. Perhaps that was why she went!'

Jemima bent to eat the rest of her peach, the juice dripping down her chin. 'Dad says Rory was about six weeks premature. He was tiny at birth. So Dad says it's impossible to find out who Sophie had been sleeping with because it had to be someone she'd met after she left Job and Nicola and we know nothing about where she went.'

And that had been all Jemima could tell her.

It wasn't a lot to go on. There were, though, a couple of leads Darina could follow up.

Once back in her house, after talking to Job and Nicola, Darina firmly put the problem of Sophie to one side. If Rory's parentage had waited seventeen months, a few more hours or even days were not going to make much difference. It was three weeks since Darina had delivered her last cookery article and so far she'd drawn a blank on the next commission. Oh for the days when she had had a regular column and the only worry was what she was going to put in it!

Darina drew out her file of notes. She flicked through several ideas: Ten ten-minute pasta sauces; seven variations on a basic bread dough; a Scandinavian buffet for thirty; summer picnics. None of them excited her and what on earth was the use of ideas for summer picnics in September? Especially for magazines that would be thinking of their Christmas issues.

Christmas! Of course! She'd given no thought to the great eat-in, when magazine after magazine would be producing supplements to guide the desperate cook over a holiday season that seemed to grow longer every year. Christmas was almost back to the time when the festivities had lasted twelve days.

Darina brightened. A series of recipes for the Twelve Days of Christmas? Bringing in festive dishes from all round the world plus some of the history of Christmas eating. It was probably too late to interest a magazine but maybe one of the broadsheet newspapers?

Her imagination fired at last, Darina switched on her computer and started making notes, consulting books from her extensive library.

Deep in the mysteries of Christmas porridge, mince pies made with rump steak, a rotting fish dish from Sweden and any number of variations on ham, Darina lost track of time. In the afternoon she went off to Westminster library for more research and spent the evening working on recipe ideas. William rang to say something had come up and he'd be late. 'Is it something exciting?' she asked. But he'd already gone and he was so late she was asleep by the time he arrived home.

When she awoke, it was to an empty bed and the sound of the front door closing.

Knowing by now that William would tell her what he was involved with in his own good time, Darina went back to her article idea and sent it off to someone who she thought might be a receptive editor.

The phone was ringing as she came back from the post.

'Have you found out anything yet?' It was Jemima.

'Heavens, give me a chance!'

96

'But have you been in touch with Job?'

'Yes, I went and talked to him and Nicola yesterday morning.'

'And?'

'And not very much,' Darina said repressively. 'But do you know someone called Paul Robins? I think he works for Val Douglas.'

'Paul? Of course I know him. He's a bit of a creep, does Val's PR. Where does he come in?'

'Apparently he visited Sophie while she was staying with Job and Nicola.'

'Paul did? No one told me that!'

'Do you have his phone number?'

'I can get it. In fact, Val appears to be staying with us at the moment. Her factory burned down the night before last.'

'Good heavens! What happened, dodgy electrics or overdone cakes?'

'Police seem to think it's arson,' said Jemima carelessly. 'They're coming to interview her this afternoon and Dad's doing the big protector bit, insists she can't be on her own.'

'Doesn't she have family? I seem to remember at least a couple of children.'

'They're both grown up, flown the nest,' Jemima said blithely. 'I don't think Dad would have got involved with her else. Can you come over tomorrow? It's Saturday and no work! You can see a bit more of Rory and bring me up to date with what you've found out. We haven't discussed what your services cost yet, either.'

Darina was about to say Jemima needn't worry about that when she thought, no, sod it, doing this investigating was taking up valuable time, it should be paid for. 'OK, I'll see you tomorrow morning.'

Darina investigated the fridge for lunch, finally found some cold pasta with pesto lurking at the back, decided the flavour was worth the slightly dried edges and took it out into the garden with her notes on Sophie.

The timing of Rory's birth seemed to her critical. According to what Jemima had said, he must have been conceived soon after Sophie left Job and Nicola's.

Darina looked at the two names she'd ringed in her notebook. One of them must know more than he'd told so far. In fact, Paul Robins hadn't told anything to date. Well, he would have to wait until Jemima produced his telephone number. But Nicola had given her Martin Price's office number. Why not his home number? Did that suggest she knew, even if only subconsciously, that Martin had become involved with Sophie in some way.

Darina looked at her watch. Just after two. No one had long business lunches these days. She reached for the telephone and was put through by an efficient sounding switchboard girl.

'Martin Price,' said a composed voice.

Darina introduced herself then, 'Nicola Ealham has given me your name,' she began.

'Yes,' the voice said in a comforting way, as though she had established her right to contact.

'I'm looking into the last months of Sophie Ealham's life.' Darina paused as she heard a distinct intake of breath. 'Nicola said you had been to the cinema with Sophie a few days before she left their house and I wondered if you would be willing to talk to me about that evening.'

After the slightest of hesitations Martin Price said,

'As Nicola must have told you, I don't know anything about what happened to Sophie.'

The disadvantage of talking to someone on the telephone was that you couldn't see the other person's face, particularly their eyes. The advantage was that you concentrated entirely on their voice and voices could give away as much as eyes, sometimes more. The comfortable confidence of Martin's voice had vanished.

'So I gather, but I need to talk to someone other than the family, you see.'

He refused to be disarmed. 'It was so long ago, I don't think it would be any use.'

'It's amazing what comes back when you start to talk about it,' Darina said persuasively. 'I know it's a long shot but, well, it's like laying ghosts.' The word had come from Nicola's description of Sophie and it seemed as though it rang bells with Martin Price as well for the faintest of sighs came down the line.

'I suppose if you feel it would help, I can't refuse.'

'That's very generous of you, Mr Price. Could I come to your office or would you prefer me to visit you at your home?'

'No, no!' he said quickly. 'My office would be best. Have you a time in mind?'

'In about an hour?' Darina suggested.

There was a pause. Martin Price was obviously weighing up various pros and cons. 'I'm rather busy this afternoon. Look,' he said with sudden purpose, 'why don't we meet for a drink somewhere?'

He wanted neutral ground, wasn't keen on her invading his territory. Darina grew more and more interested. 'Great, where do you suggest?'

'Why not the Savoy? I could be there,' he paused and

Darina imagined him looking at first his watch and then his desk, 'say six o'clock?'

'Fine,' she said swiftly, before he could change his mind. 'In the Grill Bar?'

'Right!' he said heartily. 'How will I know you?'

'Tall, big and blonde,' she said.

He responded admirably. 'I can't wait! See you then.'

Darina recognized him as soon as she entered the busy bar. Not by his solitary state but by his expression. This was a worried man. His eyes glanced round the bar and one hand tapped at the arm of the chair restlessly, the other held what looked like a gin and tonic which he sipped at nervously.

She went up to him. 'Martin Price?'

He started and spilt some drink as he scrambled to his feet. 'Darina Lisle?'

'It's very nice of you to meet me like this.' She smiled at him, sat down, took a very small notebook out of her bag and placed it on her knee.

Martin Price eyed it as though it might contain semtex.

She gave him another of her reassuring smiles. 'I have such a dreadful memory but if it worries you, I'll put it away.'

'No, not at all,' he said quickly and managed to attract the attention of a waiter. 'What will you have to drink?'

'A dry white wine would be lovely.'

He had a distinct look of a bloodhound, with a creased face and deep pouches under eyes that were a washed-out blue half hidden by tortoiseshell framed glasses. He looked about medium height with narrow shoulders and was dressed in a well cut suit.

The waiter vanished and Martin made a visible effort to appear helpful and unconcerned. 'Now, let's see what I can tell you. I'm afraid it isn't much. Poor Sophie, I was really very upset, first when I heard she'd disappeared and then, of course, to learn that she was dead.' He took off his glasses, whipped out a handkerchief and rubbed them hard while blinking rapidly.

'It must have been a great shock,' Darina said gently. 'And you really had no idea she was planning to leave her brother and sister-in-law?'

He replaced his glasses, pushed the handkerchief back in his pocket and shook his head decisively. 'None at all. As I told Job and Nicola at the time, I was as shocked as they.'

'And you know of no reason why she should want to leave them?'

Again that positive shake of his head. 'I only wish I did, as I told them at the time.' It was like a stuck record that could only keep repeating one phrase.

Her glass of white wine arrived and Darina raised it to him. 'Thank you for this,' she said.

He blinked nervously at her.

She put down the glass. 'Now, can you remember what the film was you went to see?'

His face lightened, obviously they were on safer ground here. 'Certainly. It was *Sleepless in Seattle*. Sophie hadn't seen it and it was showing in some sort of rerun season near where the Ealhams live.'

'Where do you live?' Darina asked artlessly.

'Just off Ladbroke Grove,' he said automatically.

The noise of the bar faded into the background.

101

Ladbroke Grove was only a few streets away from the Portobello Road, which was where Sophie had collapsed. Had no one made this connection before? But Jemima perhaps didn't know the Prices and maybe Job and Nicola didn't know where the ambulance had picked up Sophie.

'I believe your wife was away at the time?' Darina said, writing the name of the film in her little notebook. She didn't need to make a note of where he lived.

'That's right.' The worried look was back. 'Eleanor had to go to Cornwall, to look after her mother,' he added quickly.

'Nice for Sophie to have someone to take her out,' Darina continued easily. 'Nicola said she didn't seem to have any boyfriends.'

'No.' Martin fiddled with his glass. 'She said she found men difficult to talk to.'

'But she didn't find you difficult?' Darina suggested.

He turned an intense gaze on to her. 'She said she could relax with me, I didn't frighten her.'

'Frighten?' Darina repeated the word with a delicate emphasis. 'Had she had bad experiences then?'

'I don't know, she wouldn't say.' Martin leaned forward and spoke earnestly. 'You have to understand, Sophie was someone very, well, fragile. If she wasn't happy with a subject, you didn't talk about it. She was,' he paused as though searching for the right words, 'she was like a wild anemone, blow on her too hard and she'd sink to the ground.' He smiled self-deprecatingly. 'I'm not usually poetic but that was the effect Sophie had on you.'

Once again Darina thought back to the little five-year-old girl in Italy. Even then she'd been shy and sensitive. If anyone came to the villa, she melted away or clung to her mother. Julie Ealham's death must have been a devastating blow to her.

'She was a sweet little girl,' Darina said.

No wonder, then, that she'd clung to her father. Darina looked at Martin and decided to ask him a question that had been forcing itself upon her. 'Was Sophie, well, slightly retarded, mentally, I mean?' Then wished she hadn't as Martin's eyes bulged and his face grew red.

'Retarded? Of course not! She was absolutely normal. Look, who have you been talking to?' He sounded very angry and people looked round them.

'It was just an idea,' Darina said hastily. 'Her family have been so insistent she wasn't very intelligent.'

Some of Martin's anger faded and he looked sad. 'I know her father was upset she didn't pass any of her exams but I thought Nicola and Job valued her other qualities.'

'It was just me picking up the wrong message,' Darina insisted. She tried to move the conversation where she needed it to go. 'Tell me more about that last night,' she suggested. 'You picked her up from the Ealhams?' Witnesses had to be taken step by step through events, William had told her once. If possible, they should be led to relive each minute. Only that way would the telling little details come out.

Martin shook his head. 'No, I didn't think I had time to pick her up so we met at the cinema.'

'What sort of night was it? The weather, I mean. Was it hot, cool, rainy?'

Gradually, amidst the busy, bustling, noisy bar and after a stumbling start, Darina got Martin to go back to the evening he'd taken Sophie to see *Sleepless in Seattle*.

Just as the memories started to come more fluently, a large party came into the bar.

Darina finished her wine and said, 'Look, it's mayhem in here. Why don't we go outside? It's a lovely evening.'

He had no fault to find with this suggestion, called for the bill and gave the waiter a note. 'Keep the change,' he said, slipping his hand underneath Darina's elbow to steer her out of the bar. He was shorter than she was, perhaps five foot nine, but he managed to give her the impression she was being protected. It was a good feeling.

As they walked towards the River Entrance, Darina thought how reassuring Sophie must have found Martin.

Once outside, they wandered into the small garden that ran between the hotel and the embankment. The sun was still shining and the air was soft but with a hint of autumn. They found an empty bench and sat down.

'So,' said Darina. 'Sophie turned up on time, seemed pleased to see you, asked for popcorn to eat during the film, then afterwards you went to a restaurant.' That bald account left out the impression he had given of a mature man flattered and grateful to have the opportunity of taking out a young, very pretty and very innocent girl, one who seemed younger than her nineteen years. He'd been on his own for three weeks by then, aching with the loss of his son, worried that his wife wasn't going to return to him. Had he been susceptible to the charms of those large brown eyes gazing trustingly into his?

Martin seemed relieved to have the evening reduced to such mundane phrases. 'Yes, that's how it was. As I've said, there wasn't any suggestion she was thinking of disappearing.'

'Did she say anything about the film?' Darina asked, flicking the collar of her jacket up; the evening was cooling now, a light breeze stirring the yellowing leaves that had gathered at the edges of the path.

Martin gazed over to where a young man and a girl were standing close together, his arms around her waist, pulling her towards him. They seemed oblivious of anyone else's existence. It was an intensely private moment and Darina looked away but Martin didn't.

'Did she say anything about the film?' Darina repeated patiently.

Martin dragged his attention back. 'The film? Let me see.' He put clasped hands between his knees, looked down at his well polished shoes and gave every appearance of thinking hard. 'She said it was so strange, two people falling in love without ever having met each other.'

'And what did you say?' Darina prompted.

'What?' He turned towards her and she could see he'd been far, far away somewhere. 'Oh, I said something about sometimes it only took a moment to fall in love and it was very natural to recognize a soul mate through letters.'

'What did she say to that?'

She had Martin's full attention now. 'You know, I'd forgotten all about this bit. Strange how things can come back to you, like finding them at the back of a forgotten cupboard. She said but how if you'd made a mistake and they weren't a soul mate after all?'

'Did that mean she'd had a failed relationship?'

'Maybe,' Martin sounded doubtful. 'But Nicola said she hadn't had any boyfriends.' Was this a man who accepted everything he was told?

'While I was talking to Nicola, she remembered someone called Paul Robins had called on Sophie. Did Sophie mention the name to you?'

Martin shook his head. 'No, she never mentioned any men, apart from her brothers and her father, of course.'

'How did you think she got on with her father?'

Martin studied his fingers, weaving them in and out of each other. 'I sensed that their relationship was complicated.'

'How do you mean?'

'She told me once she loved him but she'd had to leave home because she needed control of her life.' Well, that didn't sound the comment of someone mentally challenged.

'You mean her father was pressuring her in some way?'

He shrugged his shoulders and didn't say anything.

'You saw her for lunch on the Sunday. Did she seem any different from usual?'

He thought carefully. 'She never said much when there were other people around, even her family, but I did think she was even quieter than usual that day.'

That agreed with what Nicola had said. Had something happened between the Wednesday night and the Sunday? If so, Martin didn't know. Darina changed direction. 'Do you have any idea where she could have gone?'

A vigorous shake of his head. 'Do you think I wouldn't have told Job and Nicola if I had?'

'And, later, you didn't see her around the Portobello Road?'

She'd caught him unprepared. For a fleeting second something flickered behind his eyes. 'No, of course not,' he said.

And she knew he was lying.

Chapter Eight

Pat James managed the unfamiliar police car with skill and efficiency. She'd carefully worked out the route before they set off so that DCI William Pigram could concentrate on his thoughts rather than telling her where to go.

As they moved smoothly through the undistinguished streets, Pat decided that this weekend she'd take out her own little Ford Escort and familiarize herself with the area. She'd already found somewhere to live. That was something she'd got sorted out before calling at the station.

The small flat she'd found was on top of a greengrocer's. It was supposed to be furnished and it did have a bed, two armchairs and a much too large mock-leather settee. A couple of badly made occasional tables, a hanging cupboard with a door you could hardly open the wood had warped so much, an equally badly made chest of drawers, and that was about it. But it was reasonably clean, had a kitchenette and tiny bathroom and was five minutes' walk from the police station. She'd handed over one month's rent in advance and promised herself she'd look to find somewhere to buy as soon as she knew the new job wouldn't be temporary.

Her new job! Excitement fizzed in her and her foot

automatically pressed on the accelerator. She forced herself to slow down. This assignment was going to be different from Somerset and Wiltshire! Not perhaps inner city stuff yet but more exciting than rural crime. And she was working with William Pigram again.

She had, Pat cheerfully acknowledged to herself, lost her heart to the tall detective the first time they'd worked together. She'd begun to think men like him didn't exist. Acne, haircuts from hell, slouched shoulders, beer bellies, she'd met them all. Arrogant attitudes from macho marvels or wimps who needed nannying, there seemed little in between.

Until she'd partnered William Pigram in a murder inquiry in Somerset. The tall detective had been a revelation to Pat James. Always courteous, always willing to explain anything that puzzled her, the only fault she had had to find with him had been his invariably gentlemanly attitude. Refreshing at first and then frustrating. Finally, she had met Darina Lisle and gradually recognized that the tall, blonde cook had captured the detective's heart and she herself couldn't hope to aspire to more than colleague status.

That was when she had organized a transfer to Wiltshire and tried to forget William in working for promotion and a move to something more exciting. But when Superintendent Roger Marks had called her along to his new division and casually held out the prospect of working with the newly promoted Chief Inspector Pigram, she'd known instantly that she had to find out if he was as exciting as she remembered. 'It's not promotion,' the super had said. 'But the station's desperate for another sergeant and I remembered how keen you were to get closer to the action.' His small eyes had glinted at her out of his large face.

She hadn't realized the superintendent had even noticed her when she'd worked under him in the Wiltshire force. Total chauvinist, she'd marked him as. One of those officers who felt women were all right in their place and their place was not commanding men. Sergeant status was acceptable, inspector maybe, but anything higher than that and you were flying in the face of nature.

Now she was actually in the same car with William. Already she'd been working with him for over twenty-four hours. How fortunate she'd decided to call into the station after she'd fixed up her accommodation.

The road Pat was driving down was a nondescript assembly of high-street multiples interspersed with antique shops and up-market fashion boutiques. They passed a library and then the town hall. There was no sense of a unifying style, no local identity. Pat thought back to the grey-stoned country towns she had worked in before and felt a twinge of nostaglia, quickly forgotten. William still appeared lost in his thoughts.

He'd seemed really glad to see her. Had he noticed her new hairstyle, though? And the way she'd sharpened up her image?

Pat sneaked a sideways look at her companion as they waited at traffic lights. For a second when he'd turned to her in the station, she'd been, well, not exactly disappointed, but it was as though he'd lost a little of his gloss. Perhaps it was because he looked so tired. He was puffy round the eyes and his sparkle had gone. But he was just as handsome as ever, still a rival for Cary Grant or Greg Peck. There was a dark fleck in his grey eyes that was totally mesmerizing – once you forgot about the puffiness. He'd always made the other men he worked with look ordinary. Whoever saw a policeman in a three-piece suit today? Or with such shiny shoes? But that was typical of the attention he gave to detail. If Pat had learned one thing above all else, it was that patient investigation and the amassing of tiny details led to successful crime busting. Leave inspired hunches to crime novels!

As the lights changed and traffic began to move again, she couldn't resist asking him, 'Do you think Mrs Douglas set fire to her own factory, guv?'

'Suggesting I theorize ahead of data, sergeant?' The voice was reproving but the glance he gave her was teasing.

Pat felt her heart turn over and she grasped the wheel more tightly.

'The only thing I'm certain of at present,' he continued, 'is that that fire was started deliberately and that we have a corpse.'

'So we're dealing with murder!'

'Well, he may have been overcome by fumes but the preliminary report says there's a dent in his head that doesn't look accidental.'

Pat couldn't help feeling excited. The early stages when you knew nothing about the victim or anybody else concerned with the case, were, in her opinion, the most interesting.

'We're not going to Mr Ealham's office?' The question had been occupying her mind ever since William had tossed an address on to her desk and told her to organize a car for them both. She slowed the car then swung across a convenient gap in the traffic and turned right.

'No, apparently Mrs Douglas is at Mr Ealham's private residence.'

'Very protective, isn't he? I wonder if he's banned that PR chap who was so keen to get together with her.' Much as she liked her independence, Pat thought she wouldn't mind having someone being so protective of her every once in a while. 'You said he was an industrialist?'

'His corporation is up there in the top-twenty biggest companies in the UK.'

'Good heavens! No wonder he acted as though he owned everything in sight,' Pat said, impressed. 'Including Mrs Douglas.'

'Quite!' William's voice was dry.

'And we're going to interview her on his territory?'

'Initially, yes. I'd have preferred to see her at her own home but talking to her at Ealham's house will certainly prove interesting.'

'Right!' said Pat.

'As to her possible involvement, I have a completely open mind,' William said. 'We turn left here,' he suddenly added.

'Ooops, sorry,' Pat apologized as she swung the car into a quiet lane. They had left the built-up area behind and were in lush farmland, inhabited by neat cows, well-tended buildings, scenic hedges and trees. It was all subtly different from the agricultural country Pat was used to. The difference, she thought suddenly, was quite simple – money.

Money was even more evident on their arrival at Basil Ealham's residence. The gravel drive that swept up to the mellow frontage looked as though it had been freshly raked, the lawns as though they had just been mown, the flowers arranged in their beds that morning. There was no crack in the paintwork, no flaw in stone or tile, it could all have fitted into some upmarket TV miniseries without the property department having to spend a penny.

The door was opened by a middle-aged woman dressed in a white blouse and dark skirt. Not a uniform but pretty close.

'I'll see if Mrs Douglas is available,' she said pleasantly. 'Will you wait in here?' She ushered them into a library, its shelves filled with books, its furniture leather, a bowl of attractively arranged flowers on the corner of a large, well polished desk. It all smelt like the interior of a very expensive car with just a hint of old books. Pat ran an envious finger over the desk's surface. All of a sudden she hated the thought of the flat she'd just rented. What sort of a home was William and Darina's, she wondered? He was inspecting their surroundings with interest but nothing in his attention suggested they were unfamiliar, indeed, he looked supremely at ease as he noted titles on one of the shelves, assessed the porcelain figures on the mantelpiece, murmured, 'Chelsea', then went and stood at the window, looking out at the garden.

That was the moment when Pat decided that she was going to make every effort to attract her superior officer. Something was wrong with him and she suspected it had to be his marriage. After all, he was obviously doing well in his career, he'd just been promoted. Pat remembered one of her mother's maxims, 'If you want something, go for it.' Well, her mum had achieved her own hairdressing salon, was doing very nicely, thank you. All because she hadn't let anything stand in her way. Her father had left when Pat was four. She remembered nothing of him.

Pat's self-reliance had done her well so far, no reason why it shouldn't take her all the way.

She sat herself in the corner of one of the pair of leather sofas and pulled out her notebook. The minutes lengthened. 'She did know we were coming?'

William half turned, 'Oh, yes, she knew. It's all part of the game.'

'Game?'

'Making us wait. It's telling us who's in charge here.'

'Not us, you mean?'

'Quite.'

'So how do we win?'

'By not allowing ourselves to be moved in any way.' He went and sat down in one of the deep, leather arm-chairs and contemplated the toes of his highly polished shoes.

From somewhere beyond the library door came a wail of despair that turned into loud crying.

William's head came up, then he relaxed back into the chair again.

The crying in the depths of the house died down. Silence again.

Finally, the panelled mahogany door swung open. There stood a small child, dressed in a bright blue T-shirt, socks and a pair of lace-up shoes. Thick fair hair flopped untidily over a wide forehead. Eyes the same colour as the shirt surveyed Pat and the small mouth chewed on a chubby finger. After a moment the finger was taken out of the mouth and pointed at her. 'Da!' said the child then turned his attention to William, gave him a beaming smile and, with a burst of unintelligible chatter, set off across the carpet towards him. 'Duh!' he said and tapped imperiously on his knee. 'Duh?'

William bent down to him. 'Duh, to you too!'

The baby chuckled happily, waving his bare legs about as he was hauled up to sit on William's lap, reaching out with his hands to grab at the gold chain running across the dark waistcoat.

Pat watched William settle him on his knee and take out a gold watch, click open the cover, press the top knob and hold it swinging while a pretty chime echoed round the room.

The child gazed at it in round-eyed wonderment, then grabbed it. William let go of the chain and allowed him to turn the watch around in his hands, inspecting it with the grave air of a master clockmaker, holding it to his ear then looking up at William in enquiry.

William pressed the top knob again and the child stared in fascination as the repeater chimed out four o'clock once more. Pat thought how at ease William seemed with the child, how relaxed his expression as he looked at the small figure, so intent on the new toy. She knew few men who took so easily to babies, particularly when they had none of their own. The awful thought came to her that perhaps Darina was pregnant.

'There you are, Rory!' said an exasperated voice. Unnoticed, Val Douglas had entered the room.

Despite her frustration with the child, she looked considerably better than she had the previous day. The short hair was newly washed and grey eyeshadow, black mascara and a coral lipstick brought the fine features to life. She wore a short jersey skirt, knitted silk top and an animal print overshirt, all in tones of gold and cream. Heavy gold chains round the neck and on her wrist could have been the real thing and an aura of some expensive perfume wafted across the room with her.

'You little scamp,' Val said, picking Rory up off William's lap. 'You know you're not supposed to be in here. I'm so sorry,' she said to William. 'I hope we haven't had an accident. He slipped off while I was changing his nappy, heaven knows what's happened to Maeve.'

'No, he's fine,' William said, rising and running a finger down the back of the child's head. 'Is he yours?'

Val laughed, looking all at once much younger. 'No, Rory's Basil's grandson. I'm sorry I've kept you waiting, things are in a bit of a state today. Let me find Maeve, then I'm all yours.'

But before Val Douglas could reach the door, it flew open and a girl erupted into the room.

'Is it that my father's dead?' she demanded, grabbing at Val's arm and staring into her face.

Black curly hair sprang round her head, her skin was creamy pale and she had widely spaced dark eyes.

Val took a step back. 'Maeve, what are you talking about?'

'My father! Basil says he died last night in your damn factory!'

Pat sat up and William's long figure stiffened to attention.

Val sat down suddenly on the coffee table with her burden. 'My God, Maeve! You mean Gerry was your father?'

'You know he was!'

'I knew nothing of the sort,' Val stated positively.

'Sure you did! It was Basil that recommended him!' The girl flipped a hand across her face, as though to brush away irrelevancies. 'But that doesn't matter. I want to know, is he really dead?'

116

At the sound of the hysteria in her voice, Rory buried his head in Val's neck and gave a cry. 'Hush,' she soothed him and her hand caressed his back.

William rose. 'The body found in Eat Well Foods has yet to be identified but I'm afraid that everything seems to suggest that it is that of Gerry Aherne.'

The girl gave a great cry and Pat recognized it as being the same one that they'd heard coming from the back of the house earlier. She clutched her arms across her chest, flung back her head and cried, 'No, no!'

William came and took the child. Val rose and went to draw the distressed girl to her.

Rory started crying, leaning forward and stretching his arms out to the weeping girl.

Basil Ealham appeared in the doorway. 'I couldn't stop her,' he said to Val. 'I'm sorry I exposed you to this.'

'Did you know Gerry Aherne was her father?' Val demanded, trying to soothe Maeve, patting her back as though she was Rory. They were much of a height and the gesture looked awkward.

The big man shrugged his shoulders then glanced towards William and Pat. 'This is something we can discuss later. I suppose you'd better answer the police questions now, they won't be satisfied until they've got your story. Will you?' he demanded.

Pat admired the way William managed to look official even while holding a crying child.

'It would greatly help us if Mrs Douglas could answer some questions,' he said quietly.

'I'll take him,' Basil ground out and snatched the boy from the detective. 'Come on, now, Maeve,' he said curtly to the crying girl. 'There's nothing can be done and Rory needs his nappy.'

Pat found Basil Ealham chilling both in the way he dominated everyone else in his vicinity and his total lack of sympathy for the weeping girl. The only touch of humanity he seemed to have was in the way he held young Rory. This large man, immaculately dressed in a well tailored pale grey suit, blue shirt and silk tie, competently hefted the child and managed to seem perfectly natural. 'Maeve,' he repeated, his tone now exasperated.

Maeve swallowed hard and took Rory from Basil's arms. 'You're a bastard, you know that?' she spat at the large man. Then, in a voice creamy with love and concern, 'Come on, darling, let's get your nappy on and make you comfy.' Basil watched her walk across to the door without emotion.

'Excuse me,' William called after the girl. 'Would you mind if we talked to you about your father?'

The girl looked over her shoulder at him, the top half of her body leaning back to balance the weight of the boy. 'Ask him, he's supremo around here,' she said, jerking her head towards Basil, once again spiteful. 'I work for him, it's his time.' She swept out with Rory.

'Now,' said Basil. 'If we all sit down, we can get on. I'm sure it won't take long.' Stay more than ten minutes and I'll have you chucked out was the subtext. He sat down at one end of a large sofa and spread his arm along its back.

Val remained standing. 'I'm sorry, Basil, I'd rather do this on my own.'

He looked up at her, his expression politely questioning, his attitude implacable.

'If I need your support, I'll call you,' Val went on, still standing. She seemed to have grown in stature. 'I'm sure it's only a matter of routine.' It was a cue for him to leave gracefully.

'Routine,' Basil repeated, looking at William. 'Nothing more?'

'Not at the moment, sir,' William said.

It was easy to see Basil Ealham didn't like it, equally that there wasn't much he could do about it. 'If you're sure, darling,' he said and rose from the sofa.

'Quite sure,' Val said firmly. It was obvious that this was a relationship based on equality.

'I'll be in the study, then, I have work to do.' The big man left the room with smooth economy.

Pat wondered just how many rooms this house had. There must be a lounge and a dining room, this was obviously a library and now a study had been mentioned. No doubt somewhere there was a nursery. Was there a morning room also? An afternoon room? How many different living areas were needed by the rich? Did they change their surroundings as often as their clothes?

Chapter Nine

William waved towards one of the chairs. 'Would you like to sit down?' he asked courteously and watched while Val Douglas gracefully lowered herself into its comfortable embrace.

For once he forgot his constant sense of tiredness as a surge of adrenalin energized him.

He sat opposite Val Douglas. He had no notebook. Pat would record the interview details for the record, he himself would have almost total recall of everything that was said. 'Can you start by telling me something about your business?' His tone was carefully designed to be encouraging without establishing sympathy.

Val smoothed down her skirt, thinking, then looked calmly at him. 'I started Eat Well Foods about seven years ago. I discovered my two daughters were suffering from an intolerance to certain ingredients, dairy foods, chocolate and wheat were the main ones. Being a trained cook, I had little difficulty in adapting recipes to cut out what they couldn't eat but it was time consuming and I found there was very little I could buy off the shelves. No biscuits, no baked products, almost no breakfast foods that didn't have either wheat or added sugar. And the number of products that contained whey was mind-boggling. I was also a cookery writer in those days and discovered that there were an increasing number of people who suffered in the same way as my daughters and almost nobody was producing food they could eat. I saw a niche market that offered potential.'

She spoke dispassionately and fluently. This was a story she had told before and the shock she had displayed at the factory had been absorbed.

'I started production in my own kitchen. I was lucky in that it was large and I could enlist help from my neighbours. I sold first to local health-food shops and a few delicatessens. But sales mounted steadily and I soon saw that I would need proper premises. Also the regulations regarding the manufacture of food were becoming more onerous. So I prepared a business plan and approached my local bank. Three banks later I found a manager prepared to back my belief that this was a business with a future.'

For the first time Val Douglas met William's gaze and he was startled by the depths of commitment she displayed.

'That was when you first rented the factory?'

A glint of amusement sparked in her eyes. 'No, first we started production somewhere much smaller. But we soon outgrew that and I went back and said I needed more money for somewhere bigger with more staff. I'd just got a trial order from my first supermarket and I was sure the future was just round the corner. We found our current premises two years ago.'

This was a remarkably determined woman. William reckoned he'd heard only part of the story, the successful part. Skated over were the hiccups and obstacles that had been placed in her way. 'And now?'

The amusement vanished, replaced by a look akin to

despair. 'We supply a health-food chain, three supermarkets and a number of local outlets with a range of items, some of them baked, some ready prepared meals, plus non-dairy ice creams. If we can't find somewhere to continue production, the company will go to the wall.'

'How's the search going?' William asked.

'I'm confident that by the end of the weekend we shall be able to restart production.' She glanced at her watch. 'I am expecting a call in about twenty minutes.'

It was a warning that she had put a limit on the amount of time she was prepared to give them.

'Tell me about your nightwatchman, Gerry Aherne,' William invited.

Again, she hesitated, then spoke more slowly. 'About six months ago we had a minor break-in one night. The police said it was probably youths who were after petty cash. We don't keep much money on the premises but what there was went. Also a transistor radio my secretary kept by her desk. Some damage was done, presumably in a search for something more valuable, but nothing serious.'

'Did you have an alarm system?' asked Pat.

'Oh, yes,' Val sounded bitter. 'And it was activated. But by the time the police responded, the culprits had gone. The investigation got nowhere and I became very worried about the potential for sabotage. There are some weird people out there today prepared to hold food companies to ransom over the possibility of providing the public with poisoned food. I spoke to one or two people and decided that we needed someone permanently on the premises.'

'Would Mr Ealham have been one of the people you spoke to?' William asked.

She nodded. 'Basil's wide business experience makes him a valuable adviser.'

'And did Mr Ealham provide you with Mr Aherne as a nightwatchman?'

A small frown creased the broad forehead. 'No. I advertised and Gerry Aherne was one of the few who applied. He wasn't ideal, I suspected he was more than fond of alcohol, but the others were even less promising. I know I wasn't offering a fortune but with so many unemployed today, you'd have thought a regular job would have been reasonably attractive.'

'A flat went with the job?' William continued.

'Not at the beginning. I thought Gerry should have somewhere to sit and make himself a cup of coffee and offered him the choice of two surplus rooms. He said he had nowhere to live and could he take both. It meant putting in a shower and buying a bed but the cost was minimal and I could see advantages to having him constantly on the premises.'

'You weren't afraid he'd make himself too comfortable?'

She gave him a sharp look. 'Fall asleep, you mean? Yes, at first I was. I took to calling in at odd hours, just to check. I never once found him anything but alert. Twice he was patrolling the factory as I let myself in.'

'Did anyone know you were checking on him?'

There was a wealth of comprehension in her glance. 'On a couple of occasions Mr Ealham knew, other times no one did.'

'Presumably Mr Aherne produced references?'

'He did and I took them up. Nothing was out of order or suspicious in any way.'

'Can you remember who gave the references?'

'No, but they'll be on his file. Oh, I forgot,' she brought a hand up to her mouth.

'Destroyed by the fire?'

She nodded, distressed. 'Oh, so many records will have gone. Recipes, tests, procedures.'

'You didn't keep any records outside the factory? On your own personal computer, for instance?'

Relief suddenly dawned on her face. 'How stupid of me! Yes, most of the recipes I worked out at home. Some were refined at the factory but I'll have the basic information.'

Was she a very good actress or had she genuinely forgotten?

Distress quickly replaced the relief. 'But nothing will bring back Gerry. And I'd far rather have him alive than a record of my recipes.'

'You liked the man?'

'Chief Inspector, I'd not want any man killed in that way,' she chided him gently, 'but, yes, Gerry was a very likeable man. As I said, I suspected he might be too fond of a drop of whisky but he was immensely amiable, everyone got on with him. He helped the company in many ways. After the factory opened at eight o'clock, he'd go to bed but he hardly ever slept beyond two o'clock in the afternoon. Then he'd be available for odd jobs and errands.'

'And you didn't know he was the father of one of Mr Ealham's employees?'

'Maeve? No, I had no idea.' Her eyes were limpidly clear. 'Her name isn't Aherne, it's O'Connor.'

'She said Mr Ealham got him the job.'

'That's not true. As I said, it was advertised.'

'At what time did the factory close the night before last?' William asked.

'Five thirty, as usual. That is to say, all the staff left then. I stayed until just after seven.'

'What is the routine? I mean,' he added as she looked puzzled, 'does the last person lock up or do you inform Mr Aherne and leave him to secure the premises?'

'Oh, I see what you mean. We do, did,' she caught her breath slightly, 'both. That is, tell Gerry the premises were clear and lock up the office side.'

'And how many people have keys to the premises?'

'There's myself, my secretary, Sharon Moore, and Ron Farthing, he's the accountant.'

'Three people, that's all?'

'Well, Gerry had keys of course.' She thought for a moment, nibbling on her first finger, the brownish red of her nail varnish matched her lipstick. 'Oh, and Paul, my PR consultant. He had a key as well.' Her gaze didn't quite meet William's.

'And where did you spend the night before last?' William asked expressionlessly.

'Why should you want to know that? You don't think I could have set fire to my own factory, do you? That would be ridiculous!'

'It's just routine,' he assured her blandly.

Her gaze fell again. 'Well, it's no secret, I was here.'

'With Basil Ealham?'

'Yes, with Basil,' she agreed, her self-possession back in place. 'He will confirm it. His daughter, Jemima, was out all evening but Jasper, his younger son, came in before we went to bed.'

'Who informed you of the factory fire?'

'The police rang me on my mobile phone. The

number's recorded at the station.' Her eyes closed for a moment.

'You went straight to the factory?'

'Yes.'

'What time was this?'

She thought for a moment. 'About five o'clock in the morning.'

'Did you go alone?'

She shook her head. 'No, Basil went with me but he couldn't stay, he had a breakfast meeting. There was nothing he could do in any case. There was nothing any of us could do except watch my business go up in flames,' she added bitterly.

'Did you wonder about Mr Aherne?'

She bowed her head. 'Yes,' she whispered. 'I asked the firemen if he was safe but nobody knew anything. I just hoped that somehow he'd escaped or that he hadn't been in the factory when the fire had started.'

That made her sound either a cock-eyed optimist, disingenuous, or that she had some reason for believing, despite what she'd said earlier, that Gerry Aherne wasn't always the most reliable of nightwatchmen.

'Mrs Douglas, do you know if your nightwatchman had any enemies?'

Her eyes grew larger. 'As I said, he was well liked and, no, I can't think anyone would have had a grudge against him.'

'Or against you?' That suggestion was also a shock.

'No!' she said instantly. Then a slight wariness appeared, her eyes flickered away from his, her hand gripped at the arm of the chair. 'I suppose if you are averagely ambitious, you make the odd enemy along the way but I can't think of anyone who would have burned down my factory.'

'No ex-staff who might bear a grudge? Or even one presently working for you?'

'We are an excellent team,' she said stiffly. 'No one has had to be dismissed. If anyone's left, it's been for personal reasons.'

'We'll need a list of names and addresses,' Pat said.

'Talk to my secretary. She's working in one of Basil's offices, I think he gave you the details?' She rose. 'Now I'm sorry, Chief Inspector, but I do have calls to make. Have you got all the information you need?'

'For the moment,' said William, rising also. Now that the interview had drawn to a close, he was conscious once again of how tired he felt. He squared his shoulders and tried to inject energy into his voice. 'We shall need an official statement at some stage and we will need to talk to your staff. One more thing, do you know where I can find Miss O'Connor?'

'The nursery is on the second floor,' she said and held out her hand. 'I'll do anything I can to help discover who did this dreadful thing.'

'Thank you, Mrs Douglas,' William said as he shook her hand.

She held his for a moment and inspected him closely. 'You look as though you could use some rest,' she said with a concern that left him almost breathless.

'We're used to long hours in the police,' he said woodenly.

'Of course,' she said. 'I'm at your disposal.' She withdrew her hand and left the room.

'At our disposal as long as we don't interfere with her business,' Pat said, a little sourly William thought.

'Shall we try and find the nanny?' he suggested.

The wide staircase took them up past the first landing decorated with highly polished chests, one of which held another elaborate arrangement of flowers, a second a superb bronze head. The walls held a collection of nineteenth-century watercolours. The staircase to the second floor was narrower.

'Servant's and children's quarters,' murmured Pat as they reached the second-floor landing, decorated with nothing more than a set of rose prints mounted on green with gilt frames.

It was refreshing to have Pat James back with him, William reflected. There was none of the lethal tension between them that Terry Pitman generated and seemed to pass on to the other members of the CID. With Pat, William could concentrate on doing the job and not watching his back. He must remember to ring Roger Marks and thank him properly for arranging her arrival.

It wasn't difficult to sort out the nursery door from the several that led off the small landing, it was named with a porcelain rocking horse. William knocked and they went in.

Maeve O'Connor was sitting on the floor with Rory, now with nappy and dark blue shorts on his bottom, building bricks. Rory looked up the moment the door opened. 'Dah!' he said excitedly, clambered up and ran across the room towards William. 'Dah!' he repeated, holding out his arms.

William was only too willing to pick him up. 'Wheigh-hey,' he said, swinging him up high. 'You're a very friendly fellow, aren't you, young Rory?'

'That he is,' agreed Maeve O'Connor, sitting with her legs tucked beneath her. No nanny's uniform for her, she wore jeans that clung tightly to her nicely rounded bottom, and a pink T-shirt that sported a large red elephant. Small breasts stood to attention.

William placed Rory carefully back on the floor, crouched down and, ignoring his shout of protest, picked up a blue brick and placed it on top of three already there. 'Can you put another on top?'

Rory chuckled and with enormous care added a red one.

'Good boy,' said William admiringly.

Rory took a big swipe, knocked the pile over and burst into delighted laughter.

'Oh, it's the destructive creature you are,' Maeve said indulgently and started another pile. Her eyes were pink round the edges and there was a suspicion of a tremble in her voice.

'Miss O'Connor, I'm sorry to trouble you, but I need to speak to you about your father.'

'You do, do you?' she said and her voice was hard. 'And what is it I can tell you?'

'Can we sit over here?' William went to a table with chairs standing beside a low sash window with safety bars.

'Sure, if that's what you want. You build yourself a castle now, Rory,' she told the boy. After a moment's hesitation, he picked up a brick and started using it to bang another.

Pat came and sat down at the table also with her notebook and pencil.

Maeve sat half turned away, her gaze on the boy on the floor.

'Gerry Aherne was your father?' asked William.

'Yes,' she said flatly.

'Your names are not the same? You are called O'Connor?'

'He never married my mother,' she said in the same flat tone. 'None of them did. They'd get her in the family way and then leave.'

'How many children does she have?' asked Pat with what seemed genuine curiosity.

Maeve flashed her long dark eyes. 'Ten, not that it's any of your business.'

'All by different fathers?'

William wondered if Pat realized how horrified she sounded.

Maeve shrugged. 'There's two or three of them have the same.'

'And did Gerry Aherne sire any more apart from you?' William asked.

She shook her head. 'There's only me from him.' Her eyes watered and she brought her arm across her nose in a rough gesture.

'How well did you know him?' he asked gently.

'He'd drop by every once in a while, to see how we did, me mam and me. He'd bring me a gift or two. Not often, usually he'd be up to his neck in something,' she said fiercely. 'Me mam said he was nothing but trouble and she'd never have married him.'

'Did he come here?' William glanced around the room.

'Once or twice.' She placed her arms on the table, laced her fingers together and looked out into the garden. A long way below the window, a half moon of a rose bed could be seen and the flash of a river through trees at the end of a lawn. In repose you could appreciate the fine bone structure of her face, the deliciously straight nose and the curve of her generous mouth. Even without make-up and her hair looking as though she'd cut it with nail scissors, she was extremely attractive.

'Did you tell him about the nightwatchman job?' William asked her.

Her expression closed in on itself. 'I didn't know about no nightwatchman job.'

'But your father was out of work when he called?'

'As usual,' she agreed harshly.

'So how did he get to know about the position at Eat Well Foods?' he persisted.

She looked back at the child, now carefully and precisely placing one brick on top of another and remained silent.

'Did you mention your father to Mr Ealham, was it he who told you about the job?' William persisted.

'He told me about no job,' she said stubbornly.

'But you did tell Mr Ealham your father needed employment.' It was more statement than question.

She picked at a hangnail on her forefinger. It came away leaving a small, livid scar. She lifted the finger to her mouth and sucked at the wound.

'When did your father tell you he'd found a job?'

She shrugged her thin shoulders, still sucking at the finger. 'Two weeks later he comes here and says he's taking me out for a meal,' she said. Then she leaned towards William. 'Well, he'd never taken me out for a meal in his life before! I asked him who he'd robbed and he told me not to be cheeky to me da.' Suddenly her face crumpled and tears started. 'That's when he said he had a job. It didn't mean nothing to me when he said where he worked. I didn't know it were Mrs Douglas's firm.

Stuck-up cow!' she added, her voice virulent. 'Thinks she's got Basil where she wants. Little does she know!' She went and got a tissue from a side table on which were various nursery items.

'Know what?' Pat shot in with.

Maeve wiped her eyes. 'Know what?' she repeated.

'What does Mrs Douglas not know?' Pat asked carefully.

The red-rimmed eyes were cold. 'How should I know?' Maeve said curtly. She went and sat again on the floor with Rory. 'Clever boy! Now, can you manage one more?' She gave another block to the boy. He staggered to his feet and placed it carefully on top of the swaying tower. Then crowed with delight, clapping his hands together as the bricks tumbled on to the floor. 'Grrrr, what a little monster you are,' she said happily, pulling him to her in a quick embrace.

'Where were you the night before last?' William asked.

She looked across at him. 'Why, here, of course.'

'You sleep on this floor?'

'Rory's room's next to this and mine's next to his. We've got our own bathroom,' she said proudly.

William summoned a mental picture of the landing with its doors. That left two unaccounted for. 'What are the other rooms up here used for?'

'One's a boxroom, the other Jasper uses for his writing, when he's not playing with the boy!'

'But at night-time you and Rory are up here on your own?'

She gave them a sly look. 'You could say that, yeah.'

'Did your father make any friends after he moved here?'

She shook her head. 'He never told me he knew anyone.'

'Did he make friends easily?' Pat asked.

'Oh, aye, down at the pub, you know. He'd talk to anyone that one.' Tears once again threatened. Rory looked up from his bricks, staggered to his feet, came over, put his arms around her and pushed his face into the curve of her neck. 'Oh, it's the lovely boy you are,' she said, holding him tightly.

'Would you know if your father went to a dentist, either here or in Ireland?' William asked.

Her face dissolved into laughter. 'Da? Dentist? Sure and they take money, don't they? If he had a tooth that ached, he took it out with a string and a door. He didn't have more than half o' them left.' Well, that gave them something to go on in the difficult process of identifying the burnt corpse.

'Have you a photograph of your father?' William asked.

'And what you'd be wanting a picture for? He's dead, isn't he?' she said belligerently. Then she shifted Rory more comfortably in her arms and seemed to relent. 'Didn't I take a snap that first time he came? Thought I might never have another chance and, well, he was me da.'

'Would you lend it to us?'

She weighed that one up for a moment. How swiftly she could change moods. 'You'd promise me I'd get it back?'

William nodded. 'We'll take a copy,' he said.

She left the room, still holding the boy.

It only took a couple of minutes before she was back, holding some snaps.

Maeve sat at the table and allowed Rory to help her spread out the prints. 'See, that's you,' she told him. William leaned over a whole series of shots of Rory playing in the garden: Rory alone, Rory with an attractive young man, Rory with Basil. The boy picked up that one and waved it at William. 'Dah!' he said excitedly. 'Dah!' He brought it to his mouth and kissed it.

'Here it is,' said Maeve, picking out a snap of a smiling man. She held it for a long moment. 'What a bugger he was. Me mam'll be sorry.' She handed it over slowly.

It was a good shot, half length and full face. Gerry Aherne looked fifty-something, a big man with a crumpled face, large ears and a lopsided smile. A face small children and dogs would trust. An open-necked shirt revealed a creased neck and a suspicion of a hairy chest. A pair of sunglasses hung from a breast pocket by one of their sidepieces.

'You'll have it back in a few days,' William assured her and gave it to Pat, who placed it carefully in her bag. 'Thank you, Miss O'Connor. As soon as we're satisfied we've been able to identify the dead man, I'll be in touch.'

Apprehension crossed her face. She clutched at Rory. 'You'll not be asking me to see him?'

'No,' William reassured her quickly. 'I'm afraid that sort of identification isn't possible.' As comprehension came, she buried her face in Rory's small shoulder. But only for a moment.

'I'll wait for your call, then,' she said with quaint dignity. 'And I'll not call me mam until you're sure.'

'I'm afraid we shall have to take a formal statement

134

from you at some stage. Detective Sergeant James here will be in touch.'

Maeve nodded her head gravely.

'Don't bother to see us out, we can find our way downstairs,' William said, ignoring the fact that she showed no sign of wanting to show them the way. He had an overwhelming desire to caress Rory's fair head, told himself not to be so stupid, and strode out of the room.

As they started down the stairs, he wondered whether to beard Basil Ealham in his study that afternoon or wait until more of the background had been filled in. Surprise might give an advantage but the man must realize he would be questioned at some time and, on balance, William thought more information could give him an important edge.

But as they started down the last flight of stairs Basil Ealham came up towards them, his face dark with controlled fury. 'You should have asked my permission before interviewing one of my staff,' he said.

William halted. It was symptomatic of the industrialist's ire that he had failed to realize he'd given William the advantage of being able to tower over him. 'I didn't want to disturb you over a matter of routine,' William said easily, looking down at the angry man. 'After all, you knew I wanted to talk to Miss O'Connor. I gather you told her father about the nightwatchman job with Eat Well Foods.'

He watched the man take a deep breath and control his temper. 'Maeve O'Connor is one of my staff, I take an interest in her welfare, which included that of her father,' he said stiffly.

'Exactly,' said William pleasantly. 'We'll need a statement from you, sir, but it can wait for the moment.'

With well concealed delight he saw he had surprised the other man. 'I'll be in touch,' he said. 'Come, sergeant, it's time we talked again with the fire service.'

Basil Ealham stood back to let them pass down the stairs and William didn't like the expression on his face. It was that of a man who had been bested and didn't intend to let it happen again.

Chapter Ten

'You've been at Blackboys?' Darina said, astonished. It was ten o'clock at night and William had come in half an hour earlier, looking exhausted. She'd heated up some soup then sat at the kitchen table, drinking coffee and watching him eat both the soup and half a loaf of bread plus a large hunk of cheese. He hadn't wanted the chop she'd offered him, said he wasn't that hungry!

'Then it must be you who was interviewing Val Douglas!' She couldn't control her dismay.

He looked up at her sharply. 'You mean you know her as well?'

'As well?' She didn't like the tone of his voice.

'As well as the Ealhams.'

What mischievous fortune had decreed William's first major case in his new job should involve people she knew? 'I don't know Val that well,' she said carefully. 'I used to run into her at press shows and things. Jemima told me about her.'

'And Jemima is Basil Ealham's daughter?'

'His elder daughter.'

'How many children does he have?' William sat back, his hand round the stem of his wine glass. His eyes looked at her clinically and she felt excluded from his mind.

'Four. Two boys and two girls,' she said slowly. 'The eldest, Job, is married and living in Battersea. Jemima, the one I was at school with, is next. She works for her father and lives at home. Jasper's about twenty-four and apparently he lives at home as well. Sophie was the youngest but she died giving birth to a son about eighteen months ago.'

'Ah, yes, that must be young Rory.' For a moment his expression lightened.

'You met him?'

'Couldn't seem to get away from him,' he said ruefully.

Darina did not want to get on to the subject of Sophie's son. For a number of reasons. This was a really wretched coincidence. If William knew what Jemima had asked her to do, he'd explode and tell her she couldn't possibly get mixed up in his case. And he might well have a point. 'Tell me about this fire and the dead man.' She poured more wine into his glass and pushed the cheese a little closer.

Whether it was the mention of young Rory or the effect of the wine was impossible to tell but William seemed to loosen up a little.

'So the Ealhams only come into it because Val is having a thing with Basil?' Darina suggested with relief when he'd finished his account. It might be a wretched coincidence but it needn't mean their paths crossing if she decided to continue looking into Rory's parentage.

William cut a bit more off the piece of mature Cheddar that had already been hacked almost to nothing. 'I'm not so sure about that.'

'But you said Val had advertised the job and didn't

know this nightwatchman chap was the nanny's father. Isn't it just coincidence?'

'I don't trust that sort of coincidence. And, anyway, Maeve O'Connor, the nanny, more or less said she'd told Basil Ealham her father was looking for a job.'

'Ah!'

'Did you meet Maeve when you had lunch with, what was her name, Jemima, the other day?'

Darina poured herself a glass of the wine. 'It was her day off, Jemima was looking after Rory.'

'Did you meet Basil?'

'The great industrialist? Yes!'

'What did you think of him?' It was almost like the old days, when William had been happy to discuss case details with her.

'A bully,' she said cheerfully. 'I wouldn't care to work for him.'

'Mmmn,' William sounded as though he agreed with her. 'What do you think about him as a man?'

'Sexually, you mean? Well, he can be very charming when he wants and that kind of power can be a terrific turn-on.'

'But not to you?' William smiled at her and Darina felt something melt deep inside her solar plexus.

'No,' she said softly. 'Not to me.' She cherished the little moment between them. Then added, 'I like my men thoughtful and with give and take.'

He stretched out a hand. 'I haven't been giving you too much recently, have I?'

'With a new job, you've had enough to cope with and I don't think I was exactly helpful suggesting we lived here.' She gave a glance round the kitchen that arranged itself around them with well loved style and comfort.

'If only it was nearer the station,' he said but he sounded resigned.

'Do you want to find somewhere more convenient for the job?' Darina felt she had to ask.

'Not at the moment, no,' he said. The wine bottle was empty. He got up and fetched another.

'Do you suspect Basil of having an affair with the nanny as well as Val Douglas?'

'Not much escapes you, does it?'

'You think he found her father a job because he was sorry for her? It doesn't really sound like Basil.'

'No, it doesn't, does it?'

'You think he had his own reasons for engineering the man into Eat Well Foods? Has he put money into it?'

'It's a distinct possibility. Another factor is that Paul Robins, Mrs Douglas's PR consultant, appears to have a strongly possessive streak about her himself.'

'So you think Basil might have put him in there to spy on them?'

'Another possibility.' William licked his finger and picked up some cheese crumbs.

Darina's mind was busy. Where did Sophie fit in with Paul Robins? Had he been interested in her? If so, what about Val Douglas? She wanted to discuss this with William but she feared to disturb the rapport that had sprung up between them.

'How did Val Douglas strike you?' she asked instead.

'Surprisingly warm and sympathetic.'

'Why surprising?' Darina asked curiously.

'Oh, you know, successful business woman, involved with Basil Ealham, I expected her to be rather hard.'

'Stereotyping, William?' she teased him.

'I hope not! Her warmth, in fact, makes her more

impressive. She appears highly organized, motivated and ambitious. And to be closely involved with Basil Ealham.'

'You're beginning to make her sound calculating as well,' Darina said slowly.

'Arson is often used as a way for failing businesses to recoup losses.'

'So you think Val might have set light to the factory herself? Knocking out her watchman in the process?' She made it sound a ridiculous proposition.

'At this stage, as you well know, we can't afford to ignore any theory. I should perhaps say that Pat agrees with you that it's highly unlikely.'

'Pat?'

'I forgot to tell you. You remember Pat James?'

Yes, Darina did indeed. A small, quiet girl who'd obviously fallen for William in a big way. Obvious to Darina, anyway.

'She's been promoted to sergeant and seconded to my lot. What with Terry Pitman and DC Hare being commandeered for Operation Chippendale, she's a godsend.'

'What a good thing,' Darina said colourlessly.

'Isn't it!' William seemed more lively now. 'Such a relief to have someone around who's a pleasure to work with.'

Darina rose. 'What do you say to a reasonably early night for once? We could take the rest of the bottle up with us?' she suggested, lifting the rather good Cabernet Sauvignon that William had opened.

An unmistakable gleam came into his eyes and for a blissful moment she thought they were on their way. Then he sighed deeply. 'I'm sorry, darling, I really do need to go over some notes. Tell you what, you go up and I'll join you as soon as possible.' He took the bottle from her, refilled his glass and gave it back.

'In that case, I'll probably be asleep before you can drag yourself away.' But William had left, gone to his briefcase and his precious notes.

Clutching glass and bottle, Darina went upstairs deciding two things. First, that there was no way she was going to give up the hunt for Rory's father, not while she had a promising lead to follow, and second, that she was not going to tell William.

Darina never knew what time William came to bed. She woke at six thirty and found him in the hall, about to leave without any breakfast, complaining of a bad headache.

She gave him two aspirin, saying, 'Food is the best cure for a hangover.'

'Hangover? What the hell do you mean by hangover? I only had a couple of glasses of wine, for God's sake.' William gave her a quick kiss on the cheek, grabbed his briefcase and then banged the front door behind him.

No breakfast, and probably just sandwiches for lunch, if that. William wasn't eating properly! Torn between worry and exasperation that he couldn't be more sensible, Darina turned her investigative talents to the fridge. She must find a quick to cook dish that she could set before him whatever time he got home that night.

The fridge yielded only half a packet of old fashioned cured bacon and the end of the Cheddar. But in the freezer she found some large Dublin Bay prawns.

William loved those! She put them in the fridge to defrost slowly then made a gently flavoured mayonnaise to accompany them with *arachide* oil from France, French mustard, wine vinegar, some grated lemon zest and a dash of extra virgin olive oil. What next?

William loved almost anything with pasta. Thanking heaven for Italy, Darina found she had some penne, short, quill shaped pasta. She would buy a few really fresh courgettes, dice them small, fry them with the bacon in more of the olive oil, add chopped basil and chives from the garden, then serve with grated Cheddar and a salad. The whole meal would be ready in the time it took William to relax with a drink.

Darina liked knowing her day's menu was organized, it left her mind free to concentrate on other things, like answering the telephone.

'Darling, it's your mother. You sound as though you've been on the go for hours and it's only eight o'clock. You'll never get pregnant racketing around the way you do.'

'How are you, Ma?'

'Fine, darling. My arthritis is giving a lot of trouble and I think I'm going to have to see someone about my left eye, I'm sure there's a cataract there. But it's nothing. I just thought I'd give you a ring and check you hadn't departed for foreign parts.'

'I'm sorry, I was going to call you this evening,' Darina said feebly, feeling thoroughly put in the wrong.

'Darling, you know mornings are much the best time to catch me. Now, how are you both?'

Darina tried to pull herself together. Why did her mother always manage to wrong foot her? Diminutive, charming, an attractive sixty-something, Lady Stocks always made Darina feel too-large, clumsy and socially inept. She tried to convey how hard William was working and the difficulties she was having without sounding as though she was complaining.

'Need a break, both of you,' came the brisk response.

'Would that we could but William's got to get to grips with his new job.'

'And you need to re-establish yourself,' Darina's mother suddenly sounded sympathetic. 'I know, I'll come up and stay with you and we can do lots of lovely things together. How about towards the end of next week? I could clear my diary for at least five or six days.'

Darina felt her heart sink. 'That sounds lovely, Ma, but can I get back to you on it?'

'I'm not going to let you put me off,' Ann Stocks said blithely.

'Of course not,' Darina said hastily, 'I just want to be free to enjoy your visit.'

'Give me a ring on Monday, darling, I shall need to get my social life sorted out, you know.'

Darina spent a few more minutes emphasizing how pleased she would be to see her mother, replaced the receiver, sank back against her kitchen dresser and tried to recover.

After a few minutes she set out for Blackboys.

It was another golden autumn day and Jemima was sitting on a wide terrace. A white painted wrought-iron table at her elbow held coffee and croissants. She was wearing lime-green shorts with a white T-shirt appliquéd with toning green diamonds and a khaki waistcoat with many pockets and military type buttons that looked too large for her. In a chair on the other side of the table sat a young man.

'Darina,' he called as she appeared on the terrace. 'Terrific to see you again.'

Jemima waved a lazy hand. 'Come and have some coffee.'

Darina walked across. 'I'm surprised you remember me,' she said to Jasper.

'He doesn't,' his sister said. 'But he likes to make people feel welcome.'

Jasper pushed his sunglasses up on to his forehead. 'I do so remember Darina. How could I forget such a golden goddess?'

'You were, what, ten years old last time you saw her?' Jemima said sceptically.

'Nearly eleven!' he said amiably.

'Well, I certainly remember you,' Darina told him affectionately. 'Though you've grown a lot since then.'

He was almost as big as his father with longish, sun-bleached hair, a deep tan and Basil's piercing blue eyes. He was reading a copy of a well reviewed recent novel that was remarkable for its avant garde use of language. Darina found it hard to equate this hunk of male machismo with her remembrance of a small, lithe boy full of fun.

'Are you enjoying that?' she asked, sitting down. 'I gather you're a novelist yourself.'

Jasper closed the book, tapped the cover and wrinkled his nose. 'Pretentious is what I'd call it. Yes, the chap knows how to write, some of the imagery is startling, but the premises are contentious and insufficiently developed, the storyline thin to the point of non-existence, the characterization pathetically inadequate.'

He flipped the glasses back down his nose and gave Darina another of his sunny smiles.

She wondered what he meant by premises. 'Have you had any books published?'

Jemima gave a hoot of laughter. 'Jasper published! That'll be the day.'

'My agent says it will only be a matter of time before the publishing world recognizes my worth,' he told her imperturbably.

'In your dreams, bro,' she jeered affectionately at him. 'The day you're top of the bestsellers will be the day I'm Madonna.'

'The work goes forward,' Jasper said calmly but the fingers tapping on the book increased their tempo. 'My agent is pleased with progress and won't Job be as jealous as hell when my novel is published.' He removed his glasses and gave Darina a smile that would have done credit to a cat who'd swallowed a pint of cream. Then he suddenly focused on Jemima. 'Borrowing Dad's clothes? He'll be mad as hell. *Obsession* is just not his taste, too obvious! Anyway, the too-large look isn't you.'

'Arbiter of fashion now, is it?' Jemima didn't sound at all concerned. 'The sun isn't as warm as one thinks and, anyway, I've seen you in it before now.'

Jasper looked as though he was going to argue further and Darina said quickly, 'I remember you reading to Sophie in Italy, Roald Dahl I think it was, *Charlie and the Chocolate Factory*? You acted out all the parts and she couldn't wait for more.'

Jemima felt the coffee pot. 'This is cold, I'll get some more.'

Jasper rubbed a finger over the cover of his book. 'Sophie,' he said quietly.

'Jemima told me what happened, I was so sorry.'

Jasper tried to flash her a smile. 'Yeah!'

'I'm sorry, I didn't mean to upset you.'

He waved a hand as though to say it didn't matter. 'We had fun that holiday, didn't we?' he said after a moment. 'Sometimes I think it was the last time our family did. Mum got weirder and weirder after that, it drove Dad bananas.' He looked across at her, his eyes hidden behind the dark glasses. 'Everyone blames Dad, you know, but Mum was no plaster saint.'

Darina thought it best to say nothing.

Jasper gazed over to the Gothic pool house. 'I saw her once in there with the gardener,' he said.

Darina stared at him. 'How old were you?'

'About five I think. I thought he was hurting her! Mum made me promise not to tell anyone. She said it was a game grown-ups played.'

Darina was shocked. 'Did you ever tell anyone?'

'Dad, years later. He said we all had our appetites and not to worry about it. He didn't seem to care but he must have done, surely?'

Darina eyed Jasper carefully. 'Your parents stayed together.'

'I suppose you could call it that.' He gave her a sudden grin. 'I didn't fall apart then and I'm not going to fall apart now, just because you bring back a few dodgy memories.'

She couldn't see his eyes behind the dark glasses. 'How did Sophie manage growing up without a mother?' she asked.

He removed the glasses and looked at her, his expression frank and open. 'As far as Sophie and I were

147

concerned, Dad was mum as well. Job and Jemima, they were OK, they'd grown up. People say Dad hasn't time for anything but business but they're wrong. He always made time for us. He was gutted when Sophie disappeared like that.' Tiny pause. 'I was too.'

'You must have visited her at your brother's, didn't she say anything about her plans? Weren't there friends she could go to?'

'I never knew she was planning to do a bunk!' He sounded injured. 'I mean, it had been us two against the world for so long and then she was that secretive!' The wide blue eyes looked bewildered. 'I just couldn't believe it!' He replaced his glasses. 'At least we've got Rory.'

'I'm afraid we have,' Jemima said. She arrived holding the boy with one hand and the coffee pot in the other.

Jasper leapt up. 'Hey, careful, you could spill it on him.' He put the pot on the table.

Rory clasped him round the knees and laughed up at him.

'Oh, the divine innocence of youth,' said Jasper and raised his nephew. 'What has heaven's rascal been up to this morning?'

'You can be nanny,' Jemima said dryly. 'Maeve's got to go out. Apparently that poor man that got killed in the fire was wearing a ring and they think if she can identify it, they can be sure it was her father.'

'Has our mighty force insufficient minions to send one here with the item?' Jasper held Rory up high and wiggled him while the boy screeched with delight. 'I told Dad Maeve should have time off, after all, she's lost her father, poor bugger,' he added in a return to his prosaic style.

'She hardly knew him,' Jemima said, pouring out more coffee.

'Sometimes,' Jasper said with a touch of despair, 'I think you have stone where your heart should be. The idea of a father can be creative, reassuring. The absence of even the idea can be as catastrophic as losing someone one knows and loves.'

'You weren't exactly devastated when Mother died,' Jemima said waspishly.

'But then she wasn't an idea,' Jasper said dismissively. 'But back to Maeve. Does Dad know she's gone out? You know what he's like about her leaving Rory.'

'He and Val left just before the police called Maeve.' She passed a coffee over to Darina. 'Val was going spare, marching up and down the hall, looking at her watch every two seconds. Finally she shouted up that if he wasn't ready, she would go without him.' She gave a little giggle.

'Good, I like a woman with sufficient chutzpah not to relinquish her independence,' said Jasper, lowering Rory to the ground. The boy screamed with disappointment, holding up his arms for another go. 'I can see him interfering more and more over this factory business and she'll not be able to take it. It won't be long before Dad's little idyll has reached journey's end.'

'I wouldn't bet on it. She was hanging on his every word last night. I reckon that fire and then being interviewed by the police destroyed any desire for independence. You know, Jaz, this one's lasted longer than I ever remember any of Dad's fancies.'

'Sweet sis, how ephemera do distress you. Our lord

and master reserves his heart for his family. Everyone else only borrows it for a blink of time.'

'Get lost, Jaz,' Jemima said in a bored voice. 'I can't stand it when you talk what you think is novelese.'

'What you mean is you want space for girl chat with Darina,' Jasper said in a normal voice. 'Come on, Rory, we'll go and feed the ducks.' He gave him a croissant. 'Hold that until we get to the river.' The boy clutched it in both hands and set off in his determined, waddling walk, across the sweep of lawn towards the willow trees that hung over the water.

'Does he really have an agent?' Darina asked in a low voice as she watched the two figures slowly move away.

'Lord knows! He disappears up to London at regular intervals but I doubt any agent would want to see an author as struggling as he is,' Jemima sighed. 'But you never know with Jaz. He really can write. He won some sort of competition while he was at school and got a tremendous fuss made of him. Dad was really delighted. He bought him a laptop complete with printer.'

'Does he do anything besides write?'

Jemima gave an elegant little shrug of her narrow shoulders. 'Smokes pot and snorts the odd line of coke every now and then. But I'll say this for him, he's a bit of a poseur but he really does seem to work at his writing.'

Darina watched Jasper leaning down to talk to the boy, the tiny figure looking up at him. All at once Rory stumbled and dropped the croissant. Jasper prevented him from falling, then picked up the bread and handed it back.

'I've got Paul Robins's office number for you.' Jemima produced a piece of paper. 'Now, what else have you found out?'

Darina told her about Martin Price. 'He knows something, I'm sure of it. Look, your sister collapsed in Portobello Road, right?'

Jemima nodded.

'And Martin lives just round the corner. The odds are that at some stage he ran into her, it's like a village there.'

'If he won't tell you, how are you going to find out?' Jemima asked curiously.

'I'll think of something,' said Darina with more confidence than she felt.

Jemima looked sad. 'Dad thinks she shacked up with someone. Typical of his mind,' she added with sudden venom.

'You sound as though you despise him,' Darina said, remembering Job's comment on Jemima's ambivalent attitude to her father.

'I'll never forget what he did to Mum.' Jemima looked away. 'It was all his fault, the way he put her down the whole time, his women, the fact that he was never there for her. I tell you, if Val Douglas really does move in, she's an idiot.'

Jemima didn't seem to know that, according to Jasper, Julie Ealham had sought consolation and found it at least once.

'Why do you work for your father then?'

Darina was shocked by Jemima's look of distress. 'Because I want the sort of power he's got and because I don't know what the hell else I can do.'

'Power needs to be grabbed,' Darina said slowly. 'And then held on to.'

'Oh, I'm ready to grab,' Jemima said fiercely. 'You don't know how ready!'

Could she retain that determination? Jemima's

schoolgirl enthusiasms had had a way of evaporating but maybe she had changed. 'Look,' Darina said, putting down the empty cup. 'I'm prepared to look into where Sophie went. I think she might very well have taken a job. If she'd been shacked up with a sugar daddy, wouldn't he have made enquiries after her collapse? Contacted the police, or something? Just as Job and Nicola did after she disappeared from them? I mean, he must have known she was pregnant.'

'Oh, Darina, of course! Why didn't I think of that? Why didn't Dad?'

Yes, indeed! Was Basil Ealham the sort of man who wasn't surprised if a woman walked out on him and never followed up on her? Darina began to feel sorry for Val Douglas.

'But it could take me a little time, time when I ought to be writing articles and book proposals.'

'I said I'd pay you,' Jemima said eagerly. 'Come on, tell me how much you need and I'll write you a cheque now for a week of your time in advance.'

She really did seem determined! 'I've worked out what I think would be fair.' Darina fished in her bag and brought out a slip of paper which she laid before Jemima.

Jemima merely glanced at the figures. 'That's fine,' she said. 'I'll go and get my cheque book.'

'I need a couple of other things. Do you know who it was who suggested Sophie came out?'

'Oh, that was the Honourable Cynthia Beauchamp. She had a real thing for Dad at one time. The relationship didn't last any longer than the season. But I think she was very kind to Sophie.'

'Would she talk to me, do you think?'

'Don't see why not. I never knew her well, though. Too society for me. Anyway, I'll give you her telephone number and you can try.'

'And I need a good photograph of Sophie, full face.'

'You're going to get somewhere with this, aren't you?' Jemima said in an odd voice.

'That's what you want, isn't it?'

'Of course it is!' Jemima jumped up energetically. 'Come with me, we'll look in the photo album, then I'll write that cheque and find you the Hon. Cynth's details.' She started towards the house. 'I think you've done wonders already, I really didn't think you could get this far – I mean this quickly.'

In the library Jemima dragged out a collection of photograph albums from one of the bookcases and started looking through them. 'How about this one?' She pointed to a shot of Sophie kneeling beside a labrador, smiling up at whoever was taking the photograph. With her brown hair fluffed appealingly around her face, she looked as cuddly as the dog. And you would have recognized her anywhere.

'Perfect.'

Jemima peeled open the protective, transparent covering, levered off the snap and looked at it regretfully. 'I'd like it back when you've finished with it.'

'Of course. I'll see if I can get it copied, then you can have it back immediately.' Darina put the photograph inside the cover of her notebook.

'Here's Cynthia Beauchamp's number.' Jemima opened an address book on the desk. She scribbled it down and handed the piece of paper to Darina. 'OK, that's that organized. Now come up to my room and I'll find my cheque book.'

She led the way up the graceful stairs. 'This is my room. My God!' she said, standing stock still. 'Someone's been in here!'

At first Darina couldn't see anything to suggest an unauthorized visitor.

Jemima's large bedroom had a white muslin hung four-poster bed, a small sofa and two button chairs upholstered in rose-spattered polished chintz, and several side tables bearing books, an untidy pile of letters and other trivia. A sophisticated looking media centre including a television set stood between a tallboy that looked as though it belonged in a museum and an equally attractive secretaire, its writing flap down and one of the small drawers open.

Jemima rushed across the room. 'This was shut!'

'Are you sure?'

'I always keep it closed.'

'Could your Mrs Starr have needed to open it? Or Jasper?'

'Don't be silly,' Jemima snapped. 'Jasper knows my room's private, just as his is. And Mrs Starr doesn't do housework on the weekends.' She looked in the small drawer, gasped and started pulling out the others, searching increasingly frantically. 'They're not here!' she cried. 'They've gone!'

'What are gone?'

'My pearls! Dad gave them to me for my twenty-first birthday, they're worth a fortune!'

Darina came over to the secretaire. Jemima appeared to use the drawers as a jewellery chest. Rings, earrings, bracelets, chains and brooches flashed expensively at her. Any thief would surely have taken those as well. 'Are you sure you didn't put them somewhere else?'

'I couldn't have done!' Jemima cried, then dashed across the room. Darina followed her into a dressing room. More drawers were opened. Undies fluttered out to lie on the floor like large silk butterflies, tights were strewn here and there; sweaters were pulled off shelves, hangers loaded with designer clothes were rattled along rails. Then she moved into a connecting bathroom and searched in a wall cabinet.

Darina followed behind, checking odd corners that might have been missed.

Finally Jemima turned, her face white. 'I told you, they've gone. Someone's taken them!'

Chapter Eleven

Maeve O'Connor entered the police station with her heart fluttering uncontrollably. Officials of any kind were not good news, but police! They could fine you, lock you away, maybe even extradite you back to Ireland.

Of one thing Maeve was absolutely certain, and that was she wasn't going back to Ireland. Back to her mam's? With the screaming kids, the one bathroom with the toilet that was always getting bunged up, the terrible kitchen where the stove never worked properly? To the life with never enough to eat, never new clothes, and her mother always with a new man, always dreaming that this was the love some gypsy had promised her when she was sixteen? No, she'd got away from all that and she wasn't going back, especially with her father dead and never to come bustling in in his noisy way with a present for her and a kiss for her mam.

Maeve couldn't say she'd known her father, half a dozen appearances while she'd been growing up had not been enough for knowing. But he'd been an excitement in her life, like knowing the lottery might bring up your numbers. And when he got the job only twenty miles away from Blackboys, she'd begun to think that they might, after all, have a relationship. All that had now gone up in smoke.

Maeve clutched her bag and looked at the heavy double doors of the police station. What was waiting for her on the other side? They'd said something about a ring on the phone and that they wanted her to make a proper statement. Hadn't what she'd told that policeman been enough? Oh, but that could just be a clever ruse to get her down here. If only Basil had been at home when the call had come. She could have told him and he'd have sorted it.

Through her worry and distress, the thought of Basil was like a rock. No, more like a soft overcoat, made from that fine stuff, not cashmere, alpaca. She'd gone down to the kitchen late at night once, searching for something to snack on before going to bed. He'd opened the front door just as she went back through the hall. She was supposed to take the back stairs but they were no fun. No soft carpet, no shining brass rods that Mrs Starr got Betty in to polish every week, no nice pictures to look at as she climbed up to her lovely room with its own bathroom. An avocado suite, with a toilet that never failed to flush, she still got a thrill every time she entered the room. Anyway, Basil had caught her there in the front hall.

She'd given him a big smile, this huge man who had total power over her, and hoped he wasn't going to chew her up.

'Lovely Maeve,' he'd said as soon as he saw her. 'Come here, lovely Maeve.'

She'd put her plate of cold steak and kidney pie from the previous day on the hall table. She'd been wondering how long before he made a move. Maeve knew all about men, not from personal experience but from watching her mam; Maeve had backhanded the little runts who wanted playtime with her. There was no way she was going to end up like her mother. When she gave up the goods, it was going to be for someone who could offer her something.

Her first job in England had been with a couple who were both doctors. Busy life they led, hardly ever at home. Two lovely little kids, too. Maeve had really enjoyed being with them, the boy had reminded her of her favourite brother when he was that age, full of life and fun. The doctors hadn't given no trouble either, except the mother had all these ideas about how Maeve ought to behave with them, not smacking them, letting them 'create their own environment', whatever that meant. Maeve had listened, nodded and said, 'Yes Emily,' because they'd told her to use their Christian names, then had gone right back to her own methods. Which were to make sure the kids knew what was right and what was wrong.

Anyway, she'd been happy working for the doctors, even though their house was a mess and the car they gave her to drive was pretty beat up. Only they'd got jobs in America and said they couldn't take her. The kids had cried and Maeve had cried too. But she'd been given some really nice references and the agency had sent her for an interview to Blackboys.

There'd been a Norland Nanny there too. They'd both sat in the hall, a hall so palatial Maeve had rubbed her shoes on the mat for nearly five minutes before she dared to step on to the marble floor. Maeve had looked at the other girl's uniform and thought, no point in my staying, not in this place, not when there's a proper professional in for it.

The Norland Nanny had been first and she'd given Maeve a satisfied smile as she left. So she reckoned her interview was only a matter of courtesy. She'd been given Rory to hold. 'He's a year old. His previous nanny only likes babies. On their first birthday, she leaves,' the big man she hardly dared look at told her.

She'd reckoned he told her that so she shouldn't think this was a place people didn't like to stay. Rory patted her cheek and looked at her with gorgeous blue peepers and it had been love at first sight. Then Maeve had looked at the man behind the desk and recognized the same eyes, only full of age and experience. Like an electric shock it had been and from the way he'd looked at her, she'd known he felt something too. Afterwards she couldn't remember what he'd asked or what she'd replied. She only knew she'd got the job.

She'd wondered when he would make his first move. He was nothing like her mother's men. They could never wait for what they wanted.

The waiting stopped that night he came, smelling of whisky, through the front door in a soft, warm, golden coat. He'd pulled her into his arms as though he'd done it a thousand times and for Maeve it was exactly as she'd imagined. Except she'd never realized how soft a coat could be. He'd laughed when she'd said that and told her it was alpaca.

That was how she always thought of him, making her feel soft and warm like pulling on a coat of alpaca. But lately more and more often there'd been Val Douglas. It had been weeks since he'd come up to her bedroom. Maeve was afraid that the other woman was

159

going to move in permanently. Where would she be then?

After the two police had spoken to her yesterday, Maeve realized she knew something that might be important. Something that Basil might be interested in keeping quiet. If he realized what she knew. However, Maeve wasn't going to tell the police. At least, not yet. Not even though it might have had something to do with the fire that had killed her father. For she hoped like anything that it didn't and, after all, Da was gone and she was still here. She didn't want to lose any of her privileges at Blackboys.

Maeve looked again at the big double doors of the police station. If she didn't go in, there'd be a call to ask where she was. Basil would demand to know why she hadn't gone and he wouldn't be like an alpaca overcoat any more.

Maeve was afraid of Basil's temper. It hadn't been turned on her yet but he could bawl out Jemima like nobody's business. Maeve never minded that, sometimes Jemima treated her like a nasty leftover that had been forgotten at the back of the fridge. But when Basil got to sounding off at Jasper for going out instead of working at his writing, Maeve couldn't help but feel sorry for the lad. She and Jasper enjoyed laughs together, playing with Rory when Jasper said he needed a break from creativity, which seemed to be more and more often. Only Rory seemed immune from Basil's temper. He could do what he liked with his grandfather.

Maeve decided anything was better than having to face an angry Basil. After all, why should she be afraid of the police? Maybe the ring they were going to show her wasn't her father's and maybe he wasn't dead after all.

Maeve had no such real hope but dreams were better than fears, weren't they? She took a deep breath and went through the double doors.

It was a severe disappointment to find that she wasn't going to be interviewed by the nice tall policeman who'd talked to her in the nursery but by the girl who'd been with him and a rat-faced man with a nasty gleam in his eye. 'I'm DI Pitman and I believe you've already met DS James,' he said brusquely. Then he explained something about recording the interview and announced who was in the room, as if she didn't already know.

Maeve's nervousness increased. 'If you'll just show me the ring, I'll be identifying it and then I can go.'

The inspector handed over a small plastic envelope, his fingers disdainful. 'You told us on the telephone you'd know if it was your father's or not. For the benefit of the tape,' he added, 'I am handing over police exhibit A.'

Maeve took the envelope as though it might suddenly turn into a jumping bean. Gold shone dully through the transparent plastic. 'I thought it'd be like, sort of melted and dark,' she said.

'He fell with his arm below him,' Sergeant James said quietly. 'So it was protected by his body.'

Maeve didn't want to think about any of the implications of that. She opened the envelope and took out the ring.

She'd only told the detectives half the truth yesterday. Even if her father had wanted to marry her mother, it would have been impossible. He'd married someone else years earlier. 'I was only a slip of a lad,' he'd told her once. 'And when she fell in the family way,

161

it seemed the decent thing to do.' Not when Maeve had been conceived, though. Then he hadn't even tried to hang around. She'd asked where her half-brother or sister was. 'Ah, isn't that the thing! Three days after we were married, she lost the babby.' It seemed he'd left his wife after that. Had she only pretended to be pregnant? Whatever, the marriage had been a fact and he'd continued wearing the ring.

She turned the circle of gold, looking at the scratches on its wide surface, and remembered her father's thick finger.

'Well?' demanded the inspector impatiently.

Slowly Maeve tilted the gold band. Yes, there, inscribed inside, were the inititials G M A I F and a date. Gerry Matthew Aherne and Isabel Fitt.

She'd known it would be so, known her father must be the man who'd perished in the factory fire but even so she wasn't prepared. She sat quite still and tried to accept that he would never breeze into her life again.

'Well?' the inspector repeated. Now there was a man with no understanding.

'It's his,' Maeve said expressionlessly.

'Just so that there'll be no doubt, Miss O'Connor, you are saying that this ring belonged to your father, Gerry Aherne?'

She nodded.

'For the tape, please,' the inspector insisted, crossly.

'Yes, it's my father's can I go now please?' Maeve jerked it out all in one phrase.

'We need to ask you a few questions first, Maeve, and then get you to sign a statement detailing what you told DCI Pigram yesterday.' Sergeant James gave her a smile that Maeve tried to find reassuring. But the policewoman's attitude had altered. The previous day she'd seemed relaxed, now she appeared anxious and harassed. Was it any wonder, when she had to work alongside this toe-rag?

'Did your father have any savings?' the inspector ground out.

Maeve couldn't help smiling. 'My father, savings? You have to be joking, he didn't know what it was not to spend whatever he had to hand.' Oh, he could be generous all right. She fingered the gold cross and chain he'd given her with his first pay packet. Once he'd given her mother a fine rosary. And he'd always brought a bottle of something whenever he came.

'How do you know that?' Pitman leaned forward aggressively. 'I thought you hadn't seen him often.'

'I knew how he was with money,' Maeve said pugnaciously. This inspector was just how she expected the police to be, suspicious and trying to make her say things she didn't want to. Given half a chance, he'd plant something on her. What was a poor Irish girl to do?

'So you say. What if I told you your father had a considerable sum of money?'

'I'd say you were a liar,' Maeve riposted, hardly pausing to think about what he'd said.

'Maeve,' the policewoman interjected her soft voice. 'Maeve, we found a bank statement in your father's room. It showed he had over fifteen hundred pounds.'

'My father? A bank account?' Maeve was bewildered. 'He never told me he had a bank account.'

'See,' jeered the man. 'You didn't know everything about him and money after all.'

'Do you know where he could have got this money from?' Sergeant James asked, her manner pleasant.

'Well, he had a job, didn't he?' Maeve jerked out. 'He'd been there several weeks, he could have saved it, couldn't he?'

'The man you say never saved anything?' Again that jeering tone.

The policewoman shifted in her chair. 'I'm afraid we've checked into how much your father was being paid and there's no possibility he could have saved that much.'

'He won it on horses, then,' Maeve shot back.

For a moment she thought they'd accept that. For a moment even she did, though gambling was one of the few faults her father didn't indulge in. 'I never have the luck,' he'd told her once when she'd shown him her lottery ticket. 'Horses, cards, the dice, even the lottery. I've tried them all and nary a penny have I won. I gave it all up years ago. I'd rather drink my money away, or spend it on a pretty woman, like my girl here,' he'd pulled at a curl of her dark hair, 'or her mother.' Or some other woman, she'd thought without rancour, because that was how men were.

'So your father was a gambler?' the inspector asked her, narrowing his eyes as though that way he could see the truth more clearly.

She nodded, not at all sure why she was lying but certain her father needed his reputation protected. For how would he have come by such a sum unless dishonestly?

A uniformed policeman entered the small room and whispered something in the inspector's ear. He rose and followed the officer out.

It seemed to Maeve that the policewoman felt as easier for his absence as she did herself. She leant back in her chair and looked at the girl. 'You were fond of your father, weren't you?'

Maeve felt tears pricking at the back of her eyes and nodded. Then remembered the tape. 'Yes, I was,' she said strongly.

'And he was obviously fond of you.'

Maeve pulled at a loose thread in her jeans and didn't feel the tape needed anything from her in response.

'And you did him a great favour by telling Mr Ealham he needed a job.'

Tears started to fall. 'And if I hadn't, he'd still be alive today,' Maeve wailed suddenly. The truth of that hit her with terrifying force. You tried to do good and look what happened!

Sergeant James passed a tissue over. 'Life plays some rotten tricks sometimes,' she said. Then added, 'I can understand wanting to protect your father but isn't it more important that we catch whoever killed him?' Maeve dabbed at her eyes and said nothing. 'If he was involved in something, something that was earning him large sums of money outside his nightwatchman's pay, we need to know. Then maybe we can work out why he was hit on the head and who did it.'

Reluctantly Maeve saw the force of this.

'So, I'll ask again, was your father a gambler?'

Maeve hesitated. The sergeant waited patiently.

'No,' Maeve finally whispered.

'Your father never gambled?'

'No,' she said more strongly. 'He never had the luck, you see.'

'What about drugs?'

Drugs! Maeve thought about the little stash of

marijuana hidden in her room. 'He liked a drop of drink, that I know, but nothing about drugs!'

'You don't think he could have been selling them?'

'A dealer you mean?' Maeve began to feel frightened. 'I know nothing about any of that,' she repeated stubbornly.

'Can you suggest, then, where the money could have come from?'

Maeve shook her head, remembered the tape and said, 'No I can't.'

'You have no idea at all?'

'No, none.' She felt exhausted by the strain of trying to work out what it was they wanted.

The inspector came back into the room, sliding round the edge of the door, and there was something in his eyes Maeve didn't like at all.

'We have to take you back to Blackboys,' he said. 'Something's come up.'

Both Maeve and the sergeant looked at him and Maeve knew that whatever had come up, it wasn't going to do her any good at all.

Chapter Twelve

The Eat Well Foods case had everyone in CID at the Thames Valley police station working at full stretch. Earlier that day William had held his morning briefing meeting.

He'd introduced Pat James. The other female officer, DC Rose Armstrong, a quiet girl with short brown hair and a large mole on her prominent cheekbone, had shaken her hand enthusiastically. 'They're a bunch of sods but not bad ones,' she'd said with a cheeky look at the males.

'In your dreams, love,' said one while the others hooted sardonically.

William held up his hand for quiet. Behind him was the start of an incident board. A map of the area had the factory marked, there were photos of the dead man, of the scene of devastation around him, of the factory front. 'The house to house by uniformed branch has yielded nothing,' he had said as they settled to listen with close attention. For the first time he felt they were all with him, working as a team. He blessed Operation Chippendale. Perhaps by the time Terry Pitman returned, this new spirit would be strong enough to withstand his subversive effect. 'Nobody saw anything, nobody heard anything. Forensics are still sifting through evidence. At the moment all they can offer us is that the fire was started deliberately and that the accelerant used was petrol.'

On the board the nightwatchman's name had a question mark beside it. 'However a few useful leads have come up,' William continued, the quality of the room's attention giving him renewed confidence. 'We've found bank statements belonging to the dead man and have spoken to the bank manager. Over the last six weeks, Gerry Aherne deposited between two and four hundred pounds in cash every Thursday or Friday. The account was opened the day after he started work at Eat Well Foods with a payment of two hundred pounds. However, the firm's accountant has confirmed that on Aherne's first day he gave him a wage advance of twenty-five pounds. Either Aherne was not expecting the larger sum or he was trying to give the impression he had no resources.' He paused.

'Any indication where the money came from, guv?' asked one of the younger constables, his quiet face enlivened by keen eyes.

William shook his head. 'I've instigated inquiries with the Irish authorities to see if they know anything of Aherne. Armstrong, I want you to follow up with them.' Rose looked pleased.

'Do you think this is an IRA job?' someone called out.

'There's nothing to suggest they could be involved. More likely is that it's something to do with the Eat Well Foods company. I want every one of the employees contacted, a list of names and addresses is available over there.' He indicated a pile of computer printouts that

Pat had produced after she'd extracted the list from Val Douglas's secretary the previous evening. 'I want to know everything they can tell us about the company, its products and its employees, including the night-watchman. He'd only been there for six weeks but he lived on the premises and must have had contact with at least some of them during the day.

'Look for any suggestion the company is in financial trouble or that any of the present or former employees has a grudge against the management or against the dead man. Lennon,' he looked at Peter Lennon, a long serving detective sergeant in his late thirties. 'You're in charge of the employee side.' The sergeant nodded.

'Keene, you take the accountant and go through the company's financial records. I don't suppose you've got a fine enough comb in your bag for this case so you'll have to make do with your initiative.' There was a general snigger at this but John Keene, a balding constable in his late twenties, looked resigned to being a target for hair-challenged jokes.

'Next, the dead man had a ring on his finger which has happily escaped damage by fire. There are initials on the inside and there's just a possibility Aherne's daughter may be able to identify it. Pat, you've already met her, arrange to see her again, show her the ring and take her statement at the same time. At the local police station this time, I want her off her territory. Let's see who can partner you.' As he ignored Pat's look of disappointment that clearly signalled she had expected to work with him again, the door opened and his two missing officers entered to a chorus of derision.

'That was a quick cop!' 'Nicked 'em with a nice

169

Georgian chest, did you?' 'How are the six packs?' 'Show us a leg, Terry!'

Terry Pitman scowled. Dressed in his usual jeans and leather jacket, he looked as though he needed a good night's sleep and his stubble was more than designer.

'Quiet, chaps,' ordered William. 'Do I gather you had a successful time, inspector?'

Chris Hare, the burly youngster who'd accompanied Terry, couldn't hold back. 'It was fantastic, guv. There must have been forty of us, all over the shop. Only thing was, us two didn't get a look at the villains.'

Terry silenced him with a look that said if he uttered another word he'd have his entrails for breakfast. 'The ringleaders have been rounded up and the super has expressed satisfaction over a successful operation,' he grated out.

'Didn't nick 'em yourself, though, Tel,' someone sang out mischievously.

'We all know not everyone on a major exercise actually gets the satisfaction of fingering the villains' collars,' said William repressively. 'I'm sure you have valuable experiences you can share with us all in due course. In the meantime, glad to see you back, you've rejoined us at an interesting time.'

'Yeah,' said Terry. 'We heard.'

Which probably explained the five o'clock shadow and Chris Hare's rumpled look. They must have come straight over from being stood down. Well, he could do with the increased manpower now at his disposal. William thought rapidly. 'Sergeant James, meet DI Terry Pitman and DC Chris Hare. This is Pat James, boys, courtesy of the super. We worked together once in Somerset and I can recommend her tenacity and acumen.'

Chris Hare grinned at Pat in a friendly way. Terry Pitman looked as though she was first cousin to a mangel-wurzel.

'Hare, you work with Keene; if tales of your darts prowess are anything to go by, you know how to add up.' Chris Hare was in fact something of a financial whizz kid. He and Keene had recently uncovered a major fraud by a local solicitor and were a good team. 'Inspector, you take the sergeant here and interview Gerry Aherne's daughter. Sergeant, bring him up to speed on the case.'

'But, guv,' Terry started.

William looked at him. 'Yes, inspector?' he said frostily.

'Nothing, guv,' the other man muttered and gave Pat a brief nod.

'Glad to meet you, inspector,' she said with careful formality.

'Right, that's all organized then. I shall concentrate on Basil Ealham's possible involvement. When big industrialists turn up in connection with arson, no matter how remotely, my nose starts twitching. OK, everyone, meet back here at six o'clock.'

There was general movement.

William gathered together some papers and watched Terry Pitman and Pat James approach each other with the wariness of a pair of alley cats. As he went out of the door, he heard Terry say, 'Well, what are you standing about for? I'm not about to become your nanny.'

'Nor I yours,' Pat riposted swiftly. 'I take it you'll liaise with the local station re interviewing Maeve

O'Connor and I'll organize a car. You can call me Avis, I try harder.'

She'd hold her own, William decided.

Much later that morning, William drove over to Black-boys to meet Basil Ealham. 'Should be able to make it by noon,' the man had said curtly.

The first thing he saw was a police car in the drive then two more, unmarked cars. One was a CID pool car and the other he knew intimately. His heart sank.

A uniformed constable opened the door to him. William showed his warrant card. 'What's up?'

'Your officers have just arrived,' the man said stolidly. 'They're upstairs, on the second floor.'

The nursery floor. 'Nothing wrong with the boy?' William asked anxiously.

'The boy?'

'Never mind.' William took the stairs with controlled speed, reached the second floor and found not the nursery door open but one further on. It led into a generous sized bedroom that seemed full of people.

The room was furnished simply but with a certain style: polished pine bed with matching bedside cabinet and dressing table, and a built-in wardrobe that had its doors open. In front of it, Pat James and Terry Pitman confronted a distraught Maeve O'Connor. Another uniformed officer waited by the bed. Standing by the window, tapping at the glass with an impatient, scarlet painted finger was an unfamiliar girl of thirty-something, and seated in a small armchair in the background, looking profoundly uncomfortable, was Darina.

'Morning,' William said cheerfully. 'DCI Pigram.' He

showed his warrant card and ignored his wife. 'Perhaps you'd like to tell me what's going on, inspector.'

'Yes sir,' Terry said smartly. 'Miss Ealham,' he indicated the girl standing by the window, 'rang the local police to report some missing jewellery. PC Carter,' he nodded towards the uniformed officer, 'arrived with PC Potts, who is currently downstairs. Miss Ealham apparently suggested they search the room of her nephew's nanny.' Maeve O'Connor gave a small moan and brought the back of her hand up to her mouth. Large eyes deeply distressed looked into William's. 'This they did and then phoned the station where James and I were interviewing O'Connor. We brought her here a few moments before you arrived, sir.'

Which didn't explain why his wife was sitting in the corner looking as though she wished she was somewhere else. William looked across at her, and raised an enquiring eyebrow.

'I was visiting Jemima when she found her pearls were missing,' she said, looking wretchedly uncomfortable.

William decided further details could wait. 'And have these pearls been found?'

The uniformed officer came forward and opened the top of a small set of wardrobe drawers. 'This is exactly how it was when we searched, sir.' He picked up a pair of white pants.

'Hey, those are my things!' Maeve shouted. Terry Pitman took hold of her arm as she tried to grab the pants from the constable. 'You've no right to mess with my things.'

She was pulled back and they could all see that nestling amongst a jumble of underwear was a purse of soft

173

grey suede with gold lettering. The constable took it up and shook out a double strand of pearls. Lying across his large, tanned hand, the carefully graded nacreous beads shone with creamy brilliance. Everyone gazed at their iridescent, pink, gold and silver lights with hints of blue and green. The constable upended the pouch and out popped two larger pearls, a perfect colour match, mounted on gold posts.

Maeve's face was chalk white. 'I never,' she whispered. 'I know nothing, nothing!' She swung round to confront Jemima Ealham. 'You put them there! You've never liked me and now you want to be rid of me. It's not enough I lose my father, I have to lose my job as well!'

'It wasn't I who found my pearls in your drawers,' Jemima said in a bored voice.

'But it was you who put them there,' repeated Maeve obdurately, her eyes flickering wildly.

'That's nonsense,' Jemima said dismissively. 'I have nothing against you.'

Cool as she appeared, William could see that the scarlet-painted nails tapped a betraying tattoo on her upper thigh.

'Sure and you haven't liked me from the first day I came here.'

'I've nothing against you,' Jemima repeated impatiently. 'I'm just happy to get my jewellery back.' She held out her hand for the pearls.

The constable returned the string and the earrings to their suede home. 'I'm sorry, miss, but these are evidence.'

'Evidence?' she looked at him as though she couldn't quite understand.

'In the case against O'Connor.'

William thought how the dropping of any courtesy title seemed to strip a person of all their dignity.

'Maeve O'Connor,' said Terry, 'I arrest you . . .'

'Oh, for heaven's sake,' said Jemima, disgusted. 'I don't want her arrested! I've got my pearls back, that's all I was worried about.'

'Then why call us out?' Pat asked.

'If I'd just come charging up here, I should think she would have had something to complain about,' Jemima sounded self-righteous. 'But Darina can confirm I never came near her room after I found the pearls were missing. And that my secretaire was disturbed.'

Attention focused on Darina.

'When we entered Jemima's bedroom, the secretaire was open,' she said, speaking calmly. She looked straight at William. 'She said that she had left it closed and that someone had been in her room. She looked through the drawers and said her pearls were missing. After we'd searched her room, dressing area and bathroom, she called the police.'

It was a neatly succinct account.

'Thank you,' William said in a level tone. Then to Jemima, 'You are sure you do not wish to press charges?'

She shook her head. 'I told you.'

'Then I think we can leave the matter. Thank you, constable.'

The uniformed officer gave him a nod and, looking disappointed, left the room.

'Have you finished interviewing Miss O'Connor?' William asked his inspector and sergeant.

'Yes,' said Terry.

'No,' said Pat.

'Well, which is it?' he asked impatiently. 'Sergeant?' There was a note of appeal in his voice he was unaware of.

Pat smiled at him. 'Actually, we'd more or less finished, guv, except for the statement. But we can contact her later for that.' Her style was soothing and he smiled at her.

'Not here, you can't,' said Jemima. Everybody looked at her. 'You can't expect her to go on working for us, not after what's happened.'

If Maeve's look had been a knife, it would have killed. 'You bitch,' she said.

William wondered what the truth of the matter was. He thought it unlikely the girl had taken the pearls. It would have been a singularly stupid action and he didn't think she was that unintelligent. Nevertheless, 'If you leave here, Miss O'Connor, will you please let my officers know where you will be?'

'I don't know that I'm leaving yet,' she told him bravely. 'It's Mr Ealham who employs me, not Jemima.'

'Well, we'll need to know,' he repeated. 'Inspector, if you have finished with Miss O'Connor for the moment, you and the sergeant can return to the station and take over from Marks.'

Terry Pitman and Pat James nodded and left the room.

Which left the three girls and William.

Jemima shrugged. 'Come on, Darina, let's leave here.'

Darina looked at her husband. 'I don't need you,' he said. 'But won't you introduce me to your friend?'

She looked a little happier. 'Jemima, meet my husband, William.'

'Well, well,' Jemima said. 'Mr Darcy at last?'

'I'm sorry?'

'A private joke,' she told him, her blue eyes sparkling. It was as if she had forgotten the business with the pearls. 'I'm delighted to meet you.' She put a soft hand in his. 'Darina, you didn't tell me the half! William, come and have a drink with us.'

'I have a date with your father,' he said. Despite his reservations over her part in this affair, he could feel the power of her attraction. It was a subtle magnetism, a mixture of her good looks, the warmth of her smile, the neat curves of her body and the total attention she gave him, as though he was the person she was most interested to talk to in the entire world.

'Ah, well, another time.' She gave him another of those special smiles then left the room.

'You can fill me in on all this later,' William said in a low voice to Darina as she followed her friend.

Maeve slowly slid down on to the bed and sat clutching her hands, her head bent, the picture of misery.

'Was it your father's ring?' William asked her gently.

She nodded hopelessly.

'I'm sorry.'

'What can I do?' She looked up at him in appeal.

'Tell Mr Ealham the truth,' he told her. 'Whatever it is.'

As he came down the stairs, he saw Jemima talking to her father in the hall. She must have button-holed him the moment he came in the door. Darina was nowhere to be seen.

'So you see, she's got to go,' he heard Jemima say as he reached the hall.

Basil Ealham glanced towards the detective. 'We'll talk about this later,' he told his daughter curtly. 'Right, inspector, let's get this over with.'

William followed Basil into the library.

Basil waved William to a chair, then sat opposite him with an expression of patient enquiry on his face.

'I'd like to know your exact connection with Eat Well Foods,' William said.

Basil raised an eyebrow but said smoothly, 'I am investigating acquiring the company.'

'So at the moment you have no financial connection with it?'

The very briefest of pauses. 'No, I haven't.' Basil crossed one leg over the other and contemplated his beautifully polished and no doubt custom made shoe.

William wondered just how much money he had loaned Val Douglas and exactly what the arrangement had been. He took time to make a note in his little book. The other man sat quite still and William could feel the ferociousness of his concentration, he was like a predator who is suddenly aware something dangerous was coming through the undergrowth.

'Can I take you back to the night the fire broke out in the Eat Well Foods factory,' he said, aware of every nuance of the industrialist's body language.

Basil shifted the angle of his leg and waited.

'Mrs Douglas came over and spent the evening with you?'

Basil nodded, his eyes never leaving the detective's face.

'You talked about, what?'

'I can't see that it's any of your business,' the words were studiedly casual, 'but there's no reason why I

178

shouldn't tell you.' Retaining his right to choose what he disclosed, William decided. 'We chatted about our respective children's activities. I told her about the nego-tiations I'd been involved with in Italy. We then ate a meal my housekeeper had prepared and talked about plans for a new range for Eat Well Foods.'

'And your possible involvement?' enquired William pleasantly.

'Yes.' The clipped word was the first slight sign of impatience. 'I'm interested in the company for its potential rather than its current performance.' Basil straightened himself slightly in the chair.

'And does your housekeeper live in?'

The hard blue eyes were startled by this seeming change of direction. 'Mrs Starr?'

'You said she'd prepared a meal for you. Does she live in the house?' William repeated patiently.

'Ah, I see what you mean. No, she comes in each day, except Sundays. She also has every other Saturday off. Today, for instance, she isn't here.' For the first time Basil removed his gaze from William's and scrutinized his well manicured nails. 'Which makes this business of the nanny and Jemima's pearls devilish awkward.'

'Right,' William acknowledged easily then refused to be deflected. 'So the night before last she would have left at what time?'

Basil dropped his hand and looked at William again, 'Oh, about seven, I suppose. We looked after ourselves. I don't like staff hanging around when it's not necessary.'

'And was either of your children home?'

Basil shook his head. 'Jemima had a date, God knows what time she came home, and Jasper took himself off somewhere. I like my privacy when I'm entertaining. We heard him come in about eleven.'

'You didn't see him?'

'We were already in bed.' It was said blandly.

'So you were together from the time Mrs Douglas arrived here until, when?'

'Until we were woken by her telephone ringing at some god-awful hour sometime before dawn.'

'Four fifty-two precisely,' said William, reading from a page of his notebook.

'If you say so. I was in no fit state to check the time.'

'Oh?'

'I'd taken a sleeping pill. I'd had two very tough days and I needed a good night's sleep. Val took one as well,' Basil added. 'Neither of us wished to be disturbed.'

'But you were.'

'God knows how long that bloody phone rang before I heard it.'

'You answered?'

'I did and then had the devil's own job to wake Val, she was right under.'

Was she? Or had it been a carefully calculated simulation of deep sleep? Wittingly or not, what Basil had said meant that either of them could have faked taking a sleeping pill and slipped out of bed without the other realizing. Or both of them could be in on it. But, in that case, why say they'd taken sleeping pills? Surely if they'd conspired together, they'd want to alibi each other?

Of course, both of them could be innocent. 'What happened then?'

'I drove Val to the factory. Hell of a mess it was! I

stayed as long as I could then had to go to the office and reorganize my day.'

Stopping off at the house to change, thought William; he couldn't possibly have dressed so carefully at five o'clock in the morning. 'And then returned just before noon,' he stated, again making a show of consulting his notebook.

Basil looked bored.

William made another note, snapped the book shut and stood up. 'Well, thank you, sir.'

'Finished, have you?' Basil appeared surprised the interview was over so soon.

'For the moment.' William let the qualification hang in the air. 'I'll let you know if we need to speak to you again.'

Basil said nothing but he did not look happy.

Chapter Thirteen

When Jemima had been telling her father what had happened with her pearls, Darina had murmured an excuse and slipped past into the garden, intending to find Jasper and Rory.

What was going to happen to Rory now? Another nanny, another surrogate mother? What effect was this going to have on him?

Darina had tried to persuade Jemima not to bring in the police. If she was convinced the nanny had stolen her pearls, why not wait for her to come home then ask Maeve if she could search her room with her present? No, Jemima insisted that unless the police were called in, the nanny would not believe the pearls hadn't been planted on her.

Darina remembered Maeve's distress and astonishment at the discovery of the pearls. Was the girl a talented actress or had she really not known they were there?

Calling in the police didn't mean the wretched things couldn't have been placed in Maeve's room earlier, before Darina had been taken upstairs by Jemima to discover the open secretaire.

Then Darina wondered at herself for being so suspicious. Was Jemima really capable of such behaviour?

Darina remembered how scathing she'd been about Maeve O'Connor's qualifications and the bitter comment on how her father had seemed to enjoy the nanny's company as much as Rory did. But could she have actually gone to such lengths to get rid of her?

There was no sign of Jasper and Rory in the garden but on the terrace, clearing up abandoned breakfast things, was someone Darina recognized.

Val Douglas looked up and frowned at her. 'Don't I know you?' she enquired in a peremptory manner.

'Darina Lisle, we used to meet at the foodie press do's.'

'Of course!' Val's face relaxed. 'How could I forget, only I didn't expect to see you here. Nor you me, I expect.'

'Well, actually, Jemima told me you and her father were friends.'

'Ah, you're a friend of Jemima's!' A hint of wariness in the voice and eyes.

'We were at school together. I haven't seen her for years,' Darina said casually. 'We ran into each other the other day and it's been great catching up.'

'Where's Jemima now?' Val asked, brushing croissant crumbs off the table.

Darina explained.

'Oh, my goodness!' Val sat down. Her eyes looked strained. 'What on earth is Basil going to do now? And he's got the police coming to interview him as well, what a mess!' She looked up at Darina. 'Has Jemima told you about the fire at my factory?'

Darina joined her at the table. 'Well, actually, William Pigram, the chief inspector who wants to talk to Basil, is my husband.'

'Good lord!' Val said. 'How strange, you being married to a policeman, but I don't know why, after all, it's a job like any other.'

'Not quite like any other,' Darina said in a heartfelt way.

'No, I suppose not,' Val said slowly. She looked at the loaded tray. 'I was going to take this in and start making some lunch. Mrs Starr is off today. Would you like to come and have a cup of coffee in the kitchen? I've love to catch up on your doings since we last met.'

'Love to,' said Darina with alacrity. 'I'd like to hear about Eat Well Foods.' She picked up the cafetière and the dish that had held the croissants.

In the kitchen Darina started stacking dirty china into the dishwasher while Val put the kettle on then bustled about assembling ingredients on the scrubbed pine table.

'Have you found somewhere else to carry on production?' Darina asked.

Val placed dried mushrooms in a pyrex glass jug. 'I think we might have, actually. All due to Basil. He's found somewhere with excess capacity that is happy to take on our production as an emergency measure. We met their managing director this morning.' The kettle boiled and Val poured some water over her mushrooms then checked her collection of rice, onion, fresh mushrooms and cheese.

'What about your staff?' Darina put the last mug on the top rack and shut the machine.

'Ah, you've hit upon the snag. They won't use any of our employees, they're trying to keep theirs in business. I can't afford to pay mine for doing nothing but if I don't, they won't be there when we get our premises up and running again. It looks as though it's going to take several weeks at the very least.' She sounded enormously frustrated. 'The other thing is, the production methods of this company are much more mechanized than ours. I've always worked on the "made by hand" principle, it's the only way you can get quality. Basil says it's time-consuming and expensive and I need to look towards expansion and that means using more machines, not people.' She ran a hand through her short hair. 'He's going to be badgering me to use this fire to change all my methods.'

'Why don't I make the coffee?' Darina suggested, filling the kettle again and putting it on.

'Thanks. I must go and find some white wine,' she said abruptly and left the room.

By the time Val returned, carrying a bottle, Darina had the coffee ready. 'Is it risotto for lunch?' she asked, looking at the ingredients assembled on the table.

Val nodded. 'With all the hassle going on with the factory, I thought we needed the contentment factor of carbohydrates and they're much better not mixed with protein.' She looked sweetly serious as she said this. She opened the wine, poured some into a saucepan and put it on the stove to heat.

Though not a follower, Darina was well aware of the theory behind the various combining diets. But, 'Contentment factor?' she asked.

'Carbohydrates raise the spirits, make you happy,' Val said. 'I don't know why it's such a dirty word with so many people.' She started rapidly slicing the mushrooms, the knife flashing with the speed of her attack. 'And a couple of days on rice and lentils does wonders for purging the body of toxins.'

185

Darina made a mental note to try this one day – but not yet. She pushed the plunger down on the cafetière and poured out a couple of mugs. 'Won't you have to give your staff redundancy if you have to let them go? Couldn't that be as expensive as continuing to pay them even if they aren't working?'

Val shrugged. 'It shouldn't be much, the company hasn't been going long enough. I just hope our insurance will cover the cost. Thanks for this,' she raised the mug of coffee, then started on the last of the mushrooms.

'You should have got Basil to check it out,' Darina said. 'I bet he's a whizz on comparative costs and benefits. Shall I do the onions?'

'Would you? I only wish I'd known Basil when I was getting going,' Val sighed. Then said, 'Except we would probably have argued so much about production methods we would never have got together.'

'How did you meet?' Darina found a sharp knife, rapidly removed the onions' outer skin then cut them in half through the root.

'Oh, some local charity function we were both involved in. It was deadly boring and we couldn't wait to escape. Basil took me to dinner at a wonderful restaurant not far from here and after that, well, one thing led to another.'

Darina could see that with Basil it would. If he was interested, he'd be remorseless in pursuit. But Val didn't sound as though she'd put up much resistance. Had it been a nasty shock to realize how different their approaches to her business were? Darina made horizontal and vertical cuts through the onion halves, keeping the roots intact, then sliced down, releasing neat little fragments.

Val finished neatly slicing the mushrooms and poured olive oil into a large pan. Darina remembered concise and well written articles under the Douglas by-line in a number of different publications. 'Was it a wrench to give up writing when your food company got going?' she asked curiously.

Val picked up the chopping board and scraped the onion into her heated oil. 'Do you know,' she said, stirring, 'it was a relief? I'm not creative with words, only food. The recipes were all right, it was the articles that were so difficult.'

'They didn't read that way. Why did you keep at it, if that was the case?' Darina washed the knife and swabbed down the board.

'It was the cooking I really enjoyed and, I don't know, I think I had a mission, to bring healthy cooking to people who needed it.' Val stirred the onions, her movements jerky, as though from an inner turmoil. 'And I needed the money. When my husband and I divorced I got the house and support for the girls. But I knew that would end when they left home. I had to build a career.' She sounded harassed, as though the worry had attacked her nerves, leaving them as susceptible to strain as a tender plant was to frost.

'So you started the food company as a better bet than journalism?'

'Do you want to rinse that rice for me?' Val pointed her wooden spatula at the bowl of rice she'd measured out earlier.

Darina found a sieve and poured the rice in.

'Thanks. No, it wasn't quite like that.' She rubbed a hand over her eyes. 'As I explained to your husband the other day, I saw a market niche.'

Darina rinsed the rice under the tap. 'How did you find out your daughters couldn't cope with certain foods?' she asked curiously.

'They had terrible eczema,' Val said promptly, still stirring the onion. 'The doctors said they'd grow out of it and gave me a cream for them. It wasn't very satisfactory and I hated the thought of them being regularly anointed with cortisones. Then a friend suggested I take them to a homoeopathic doctor and she diagnosed food intolerances. After I removed wheat, dairy foods and chocolate from their diet, the change was dramatic. Not only did the eczema clear up but they just felt generally so much better.' Val added the rice to the now transparent onion and stirred some more. 'Do you want to see if those porcini are soft yet?'

Darina investigated the dried mushrooms. They had reconstituted themselves in a startlingly successful way, their hard chips swollen and softened into thick slices of ceps. She fished them out on to a board. 'Do you want them chopped?'

'Just slice them roughly, please.' Val found a fine sieve and strained the mushroom juices into the hot wine.

'And now your daughters are grown up?'

For a moment Val's strained face relaxed. 'Kate's in Australia and Sally's at university.' She looked at the rice mixture for a moment, then added without expression, 'They keep hoping I'll get together again with their father.'

'What's he like?'

'Digby? Army,' Val said succinctly as though that explained everything. She added some hot liquid to her pan and started stirring again but slowly this time. 'Very charming, very correct, very rigid thinker. Expected me to be there in the background, doing all the right things so he could rise to the top. Was even quite proud when I got articles accepted, as long as the writing of them didn't interfere with what was going on in his life.'

'Sounds a bit like Basil,' Darina said, smiling.

'Heavens, no! Nothing like Basil! Basil is . . .' the spoon stopped stirring.

'Happy to have you run your company as long as you do it his way?' offered Darina.

Val stood with an expression of bewilderment on her face. 'He makes me feel wonderful! All he has to do is put a hand on my arm and I turn to jelly.' She gave an involuntary shiver and started attacking the rice again.

Something about the way she'd said it made Darina feel uncomfortable. She changed the subject. 'Jemima said you might be starting a line of baby foods, would that be for children who are food intolerant? Are there many of those?'

Val shrugged as she added more hot wine, 'I'm not sure of the figures. Certainly wheat and dairy products cause problems for some. But the baby-food idea was Basil's. He suggested there was a need for what you might call gourmet dishes for the just weaned. But we're having arguments about them, too. I say they mustn't have any preservatives or colouring agents in them. Basil says that means distribution will be too expensive. We must spend half of our time together arguing.' She pushed back her hair again in an impatient gesture then added, 'He seems very involved with his grandson.'

'Yes,' Darina agreed. 'Rory does seem to be a very appealing child.'

'Oh, yes,' Val said instantly. 'I love him to bits.' It sounded a little perfunctory.

'Would baby food fit into Eat Well Foods?'

'If it's done my way. There's a fantastic market out there and I'm certainly going to need something to improve the balance sheet after this fire.' She added all the sliced mushrooms to her pan, fresh and dried. 'It couldn't have come at a worse time. I've got to go abroad next Thursday, to attend an international conference on food intolerances and allergies. I'm presenting a paper on the problems of providing ready prepared food for sufferers. I'd thought of cancelling but it means so much in terms of prestige, I really can't afford not to go.' The tension was back. Did prestige matter so much to her? Or was it the other pressures – the trouble with her company and Basil?

Val stopped stirring for a minute and turned to Darina. 'Look, would you be interested in working up some recipes we could test for a gourmet baby-food line? I was a regular reader of your newspaper column and I think we have much the same approach to food. No concessions on flavour but simplicity of style. Say if you're too busy. It would be on a proper commercial basis, of course,' she added perfunctorily.

Too busy? Darina almost laughed. 'I think I could manage to give it some time,' she said carefully. 'We'd need to discuss exactly what sort of foods you are thinking of, costings, and all that.'

'Of course,' Val said impatiently. 'But you'll do it?'

'I'll certainly give it some thought.' The idea of developing food for babies definitely interested her. Put those tiny taste buds on the right road and you might be able to develop a lifelong interest in food. Public schools had a lot to answer for. Shepherd's pie, bubble and squeak, baked beans, jam roly-poly, the list of dire dishes they'd programmed generations of young men into defining as their life's diet went on and on. What William really liked to eat at the end of a hard day was not one of her concoctions, delicious though he always said they were, but what she called nursery food. Maybe if he'd been gastronomically challenged when a baby, he'd be more adventurous.

'But what about production? Are you going to have to move over to more mechanization, as Basil suggests, or can you continue your way?'

Val added more hot liquid to her risotto and continued her vigorous stirring. For a moment she said nothing. Then, 'He's asked me to marry him.'

A number of possible responses ran through Darina's mind. 'That's quite a step,' she managed at last.

Val's short bark of laughter had a touch of hysteria. 'Isn't it! Well, I'm glad you didn't go all sentimental.'

'Sentimental isn't a word I associate with Basil Ealham,' Darina said wryly. 'He's a very, well, exciting man?' She made it a question.

Val wiped sweat from her forehead with the back of her hand. 'That's it!' she said with a note of doubtful triumph. 'Exciting. He gathers you up and it's as though you're travelling on a fast, powerful train, rushing along but with perfect control, not a moment's worry.' More liquid, more stirring. 'Rushing along, never stopping, never being allowed to make your own decisions, saved from yourself, saved from the world!' She sounded as though she was about to lose control. 'Big, brave Basil, the weak and feeble woman's friend,' she said, her voice high and unsteady.

The kitchen door opened and Rory trotted in followed by Jasper.

'Dah, dah, duh,' Rory said, waving his starfish hands in the air as he made for Val.

She turned from the stove. 'Rory I can do without you.'

He laughed and grabbed one of her legs.

'Let me go!' she shouted at him. 'Get out of the kitchen!'

Rory burst into noisy tears.

Jasper came and snatched him up, his face set and angry. 'Bitch,' he said with quiet venom. 'There, there, Rory. Nasty woman didn't mean it and we don't want to be in here anyway. We'll go and find your pushcar, shall we?' He didn't look at either Val or Darina as he carried the boy out.

'Oh, God!' said Val hopelessly as the door closed behind them. 'Now he'll tell Basil!'

Chapter Fourteen

By the time Darina had soothed Val and laid the table for the Ealham lunch, then refused an invitation to join them, William had left Blackboys.

He returned home at half past eleven that evening looking exhausted and saying he'd eaten and all he wanted was a large whisky. But he took the biscuit tin up with the drink and sat in bed watching a late-night movie on the television and showering crumbs around until the biscuits were finished.

'Do you have to go in tomorrow?' Darina asked without much hope they'd have a day together.

'Not unless something unexpected comes up.'

'Thank heavens!' she said gratefully. 'We can have a nice quiet day.'

They started well with breakfast in bed. William brought up a tray with coffee and marmalade-laden toast.

'Oh, this is bliss,' Darina said, lying back on the pillows. Then noticed William scratching at his leg as he sat on the bed beside her. 'What's wrong?'

'Nothing,' he said abruptly, stopping the scratching and reaching for his coffee.

'How did your interview with Basil go?'

He sighed with frustration, 'I suppose there's a

normal human being inside there somewhere but over the years he's built up so many defences, constructed so many public faces, I think it would take Freud to uncover it.'

'So you didn't learn anything useful?'

William reached down absentmindedly to scratch his leg again, realized what he was doing and stopped. 'Look,' he said aggressively. 'I don't want to discuss the case, all right? It's bad enough you being so closely involved with the Ealhams, and I don't really understand how that's happened when you say you only met Jemima the other day after a gap of donkey's years, well, as I say, that's bad enough without you trying to wheedle police business out of me.'

Darina nearly spilt her coffee! 'William! You know I hate invading your territory. And you always used to like discussing your cases.' In fact he'd said it was a help, that he found her intuitive approach could sometimes succeed where basic slogging away at details had failed.

William said nothing, merely sat solidly on the bed and pressed his lips together as though to prevent further hasty words escaping. And he was back to scratching his leg again.

'Let me look at that,' said Darina, putting down her coffee.

Reluctantly he pulled up his pyjama trouser leg and revealed a nasty patch of angry looking flesh. 'What is it?' she asked.

'Nothing, I get it from time to time. If it hasn't disappeared by tomorrow, I'll go and get some ointment from the doctor. It's years since I had anything like it,' he added crossly. 'It was always around when I was a child. The doctor would give me some ointment; he said I'd grow out of it and I did. Until now. Now tell me what you've arranged with your mother.'

'She wants to come up on Thursday but I'm going to try and put her off until next Monday at the earliest, I've got so much to sort out. And it would be nice if you had some time to spend with us. Do you think you'll have cracked this case by then?' she asked hesitantly.

'I damn well hope so! We've got enough people working on it,' he said and for a moment she thought he'd start telling her how it was going. Instead, he went and had a shower, leaving Darina staring after him and remembering the way he'd smiled at Pat James in the nanny's bedroom. She seemed to have the knack of saying the right thing to him!

Though William wouldn't discuss the case with Darina, he seemed to spend a great deal of Sunday thinking about it. Even when they went for a walk along the river, he lapsed into silence. After a little she gave up trying to stimulate lively conversation and left him to his thoughts, concentrating her own on ideas for baby foods. Which wasn't something she wanted to discuss with William. He would only see it as a useful crack in her determination to put off having children that he could use to persuade her now was the time to start a family.

So it wasn't the happiest of Sundays and on Monday for once Darina was happy to see William leave the house early.

Particularly when she had a call from a magazine editor expressing interest in one of her ideas. If, that is, she could produce the finished article by Wednesday.

Darina forgot about tracking down Sophie or working on recipes for gourmet baby food.

It was wonderful to have something positive to work on. Soon she was lost, concentrating on the screen of her computer, trying to capture the spirit of the publication that wanted the article. Aimed at the busy cook without much money, all its recipes had to be short and expressed very simply.

Gradually Darina forgot how unsatisfactory the weekend had been.

After she'd finished her first draft, she rang her mother.

Ann Stocks was not best pleased. 'But, darling, I've rearranged my entire diary so I could come to you on Thursday and stay a week. I haven't seen you since you moved to London and precious little for too long before then.'

Darina felt guilt creeping up on her like dry rot.

'You've no need to think I'll be a nuisance. I have masses of London friends who'll be only too delighted to see me.'

'Don't be like that, of course you're never a nuisance. I just want to have the time to enjoy your visit. I've found a couple of exhibitions you'd like and there's a new restaurant I want your opinion on, I thought we could lunch there.'

'Now, darling, you know I can't tell veal from pork,' Ann Stocks said happily.

'But you can always tell what sort of clientele they're aiming at and exactly who's eating there,' Darina said wickedly, knowing her mother's penchant for style. 'But if you come this week, I'll still be punishing the clock. Make it Monday?'

As she put down the phone on a reconciled Ann Stocks, Darina wondered for the first time whether it was her prickly relationship with her mother that meant she was so reluctant to bear children herself. She would really hate not to have a close relationship with them but what did she know about how to achieve it? 'They fuck you up, your mum and dad,' Philip Larkin had so memorably written. She didn't want to fuck up any child of hers.

That reminded her of little Rory and the problem of who his father was. After the scene in the kitchen with Val, Darina thought this could be another reason why Jemima was so keen to discover his parentage.

But first she had to finish her article on a Valentine's Day meal for two.

Uninterrupted by any husband arriving home until well after ten o'clock, Darina was able to work at reducing the number of words in her recipe method while increasing the clarity of her instructions, then on creating three hundred words on the art of using food to demonstrate love.

When William eventually came in, she offered him her lover's meal: smoked salmon pasta with a sauce of smoked-salmon ribbons and cream with basil leaves, a salad of tender green leaves with a mustard and honey dressing, followed by a small heart-shaped meringue and chocolate gateau.

An almost unintelligible grunt said William wasn't hungry. Then he found some cheese in the fridge, cut off a chunk and took it up with a glass of whisky to bed.

Darina insisted on checking the rash and found it had spread further. In the middle of the night she woke to find William frantically scratching a bleeding leg and complaining of a raging headache.

She found some soothing ointment, gave him a

couple of aspirin and then lay awake worrying about him.

Tuesday she finished the article, e-mailed it through to the magazine in the late afternoon, then prepared an invoice. All very satisfying.

Then she wondered about the empty state of her fridge. Was there any point in preparing yet another meal that was going to be flung back in her face? (She'd eaten the smoked salmon pasta for lunch, hardly tasting the food as she worked on her article.) William's constantly tired face came to mind. How much of his bad temper these days was because he was struggling to cope with the new job? She cursed the fire at Eat Well Foods. It had brought nothing but trouble to them as well as to Val Douglas.

Then she wondered about what might be going on between her husband and his new sergeant and told herself not to be silly.

But she couldn't stop thinking about William. Finally she picked up the phone and tracked down Val at the Ealham headquarters, had a discussion with her about what exactly she needed in the baby-food line, then raised another matter.

After a most helpful conversation, Darina went out and posted her invoice then continued on to the shops and bought some chicken breasts. These she stuffed with prosciutto and mango slices. Perhaps this would hit the spot with William.

He got back before ten and wolfed down the food. 'Didn't have time for any sandwiches today,' he told her, sopping up the last of the wine sauce she'd served with the chicken.

Darina was not going to offer her head for another chewing off. She said nothing.

William grinned shamefacedly at her. 'I can tell you that we seem to be making no progress very rapidly.'

'No progress at all?' she asked, cheering up.

'Well, we're working our way through all the staff at Eat Well Foods, taking statements about the company and, especially, the nightwatchman. So far nothing of interest. But Gerry Aherne appears to have a whole list of minor offences on record in the Irish Republic and it's becoming a bit of a mystery as to how Eat Well Foods took him on as a reliable nightwatchman.'

'Forged references?' suggested Darina.

'More than likely,' agreed William, helping himself to a sliver of cheese and a couple of the Prince of Wales Duchy biscuits. 'Unfortunately, most of the records seem to have disappeared in the fire and we can't check.' He bit into one of the biscuits and gave her a level look. 'I'm also looking into Basil Ealham and his relationship with Val Douglas.'

He seemed to expect her to say something but Darina couldn't think of a comment that wouldn't be taken the wrong way. 'Have you unearthed anything interesting?' she asked at last.

'Only that the man is confoundedly successful, everything he touches seems to turn to gold.'

'Val had better look out then,' Darina said with a gurgle of laughter. 'Too bad if she turned into a statue, even if one worth a large fortune.'

William's expression didn't lighten. 'Yes, Mrs Douglas does seem to be fairly heavily entangled with your friend Ealham.'

'He's not my friend,' Darina protested. 'Jemima's my friend.'

'And he's just her father,' William said sardonically, helping himself to the meringue dessert Darina had once more produced.

His attitude was so different from what it had been on Sunday that Darina almost told him about the search for Rory's father. Then decided she couldn't risk it. Instead she told him about Val asking her for ideas for gourmet baby food. 'She's very keen everything should be as home-made as possible. No preservatives or colourings. All as pure and fresh as if it had been made by a caring parent.'

'Hmm, sounds as though you're getting even more closely involved in this business,' William said a little grimly.

'Does it worry you? Do you want me to cancel?' Darina asked, wondering how she'd react if he said yes.

He said without hesitation, 'No, of course not. I can't see that your talking to Val Douglas about baby food should interfere with our investigation. But, a friendly word of caution, don't get yourself too involved.'

'Ah, you mean Eat Well Foods is in financial trouble?'

'It looks like it. Not only because of the fire, they seem to have had serious cash flow problems for some time. The accountant said they're looking for someone either to take the company over or to provide a major investment of capital.'

'Enter Basil Ealham,' murmured Darina.

'Ealham admitted that he was investigating acquiring the company.'

'Val Douglas appears to be in two minds about it,' Darina contributed.

'Oh?' William looked interested. 'Why? I would have thought it was the answer to her prayers.'

'She doesn't approve of Basil's ideas on the production of convenience foods.'

'Really?' William digested this. 'Anything else you can contribute?'

'Uh huh? You saying that maybe my friendship with the Ealhams could be of use after all?'

'I deserved that, I don't know what gets into me these days, darling, you know I always value your opinions.'

'Do I? Well, Val did tell me quite a lot that was interesting but nothing to do with the case. She and I think your leg rash might have something to do with a food intolerance.'

'What nonsense!' William protested. 'I told you, it's a recurrence of the eczema I used to have as a child. I got the local doc to prescribe me some cream today and it feels better already.'

'But where does the eczema come from? That's the real question. Val says her daughters had bad cases as children and changing their diet cured it.'

'But my eczema disappeared as I grew up,' William said, looking profoundly unconvinced.

'Apparently food intolerances often go that way. They cause trouble when you're small, then your immune system learns to cope but only up to a point. Later on, particularly if you are under stress, the system gets overloaded and you start having trouble again.' Darina went and picked up a piece of paper from the dresser. 'Val gave me the name of a homoeopathic doctor. Why not go and see him? It can't do any harm and it might help.'

William glanced at the paper, 'What on earth will this chap do?'

'Diagnose what foods may be giving you trouble, then we can work out a diet that excludes them.'

William's face was a study. 'One of those cranky regimes that stops you eating everything you like, I know! No, thank you.'

'But what if it made you feel less tired?' Darina suggested hopefully.

William looked again at the piece of paper then stuffed it in his pocket. 'I can't see it'll do any good and with all I've got on at the moment I won't have time.'

Wednesday morning Darina collected the copies she'd ordered of the snapshot of Sophie Jemima had given her. Then found her A-Z of London and took the tube up to Ladbroke Grove. The station sat almost beneath the arterial A40 motorway into central London. To the north was North Kensington, a scruffily residential area served by two busy shopping streets, Ladbroke Grove itself and the Portobello Road, which turned into an open-air market every weekend. To the south was the more prestigious village of Notting Hill, which boasted gracious crescents of porticoed houses and a shopping area offering everything from cookery books to Indian artefacts, including a wide selection of restaurants and dress shops.

Darina had checked Martin Price's address in the telephone book. It didn't take long before she stood outside a well cared for stucco building that suggested money and class. There was no sign of anyone moving inside and after a few moments she walked back under the A40 and found Portobello Road.

Was she pinning too much on the fact that Sophie had collapsed here? Perhaps she'd been visiting, there were a number of specialist shops in the area. But Darina didn't think so. Nothing she'd heard about Sophie suggested a girl who shopped far afield. Much, much more likely was that this was where she'd found somewhere to live.

Had someone taken pity on her and offered her accommodation? Had she really not needed money?

Or had she looked for a job?

The more she thought about Sophie's dilemma, the more convinced Darina was that she must have found a job. But what sort? Martin had been adamant Sophie wasn't retarded but the fact remained she had absolutely no qualifications. She was used to looking after children but would any parent take a girl off the street, without references and only a small bag of clothes? It was surely most unlikely.

One of these small shops or a restaurant, though, might very well be prepared to offer work to a well-spoken and obviously well-bred girl like Sophie, particularly if they didn't have to worry about National Insurance, tax and all the other tedious official bits that went with hiring permanent staff.

Darina looked around her. North Kensington seemed a better bet than the smarter Notting Hill.

Unconsciously, she squared her shoulders, prepared herself for a long slog and walked into the newsagent by the tube station.

It was the first of many calls. The routine was always the same. Darina produced the photograph of Sophie, explained she was trying to trace her and asked if she'd been seen or worked in the shop some eighteen months to two years ago.

The sheer variety of shopkeepers and restaurateurs were what kept Darina going: Cockneys, Liverpudlians, Greeks, Italians, Asians, West Indians; this small area was an ethnic stew pot. Often it was hard to make herself understood and equally often she found it hard to understand what was said to her. Darina decided Ladbroke Grove made Chelsea seem hopelessly rarefied.

As she worked her way along the street, Darina wondered again why Basil hadn't hired someone to do this after Sophie died. Hadn't it occurred to him that this must be where she'd been living, could have been working?

Perhaps it really hadn't mattered to him. Perhaps he really meant it when he said he didn't care who Rory's father was.

Or perhaps he had instigated inquiries which had led nowhere. In which case, what was the point of her continuing?

Lunchtime approached and Darina abandoned her search to attend a launch party for a new line of frozen pizzas. At least she'd get some good conversation there, it was always fun meeting other food writers. Her morning's activities had left her profoundly depressed.

After a lively session tasting frozen pizzas and receiving a report that put forward evidence that they tasted better than fresh pizzas (but not those prepared at home, murmured someone), Darina made her way back to Chelsea thinking about the frustrations of the morning. Maybe she was doing this the wrong way round. She'd talked to Martin Price but what of Cynthia

Beauchamp, who'd sponsored Sophie's season? And there was Paul Robins, the Eat Well Foods' PR man. She hadn't talked to either of them yet.

When she got in, Darina rang Cynthia's number. A blasé society voice warmed after Sophie's name was mentioned and the Hon. Cynthia Beauchamp said she would be at home the following morning at eleven o'clock. 'I can't think what I can tell you, though,' she drawled.

No doubt it would be another dead end.

Chapter Fifteen

Jemima pushed several files together on her desk and watched her secretary put on her coat.

'Mind you get that report finished,' Rosie Cringle said. 'Mr Ealham will be wanting it in the morning.'

Jemima stared at her coldly.

Rosie's neat little nose suddenly glowed, she was upset at the implied snub. Then her usual enthusiasm drained out of her face, she shrugged and picked up her bag. 'I've done what I can, now it's up to you, I'm off to see the dentist, you probably don't remember I had an appointment.'

Jemima said nothing, merely watched her leave with only the slightest of flounces, closing the door carefully when no doubt she wanted to slam it. God rot all such efficient, conscientious girls.

She lifted the top file and looked at the one underneath it. Then she shuffled all of them together again, shoved them to one side of the desk and leant back in her chair, gazing out of the window at the car park. Heavens but she was bored! What had ever made her think she could work her way to the top of the pile here when her father got someone else to duplicate all her efforts? He couldn't even rely on her to do the simplest report! All she was doing was drawing a salary just about sufficient to keep her in designer clothes. Was there any point in staying?

But she knew if only her father could bring himself to trust her, she could enjoy working here. Anyway, with her qualifications, what else could she do? Dad had suggested she train as a buyer for a big chain but fashion wasn't nearly as interesting as big business.

She bit on a finger and thought.

It was only gradually she became aware of voices coming through from her father's office. She heard first his tones and then the voice of Val Douglas. She couldn't hear what they were saying but they were plainly arguing. Quietly Jemima rose, found the glass she kept on the side cupboard and went over to the connecting door.

Putting the glass against the wood, she listened.

They were having quite a time of it. Basil was insisting he knew best about production methods, Val was fighting him every inch of the way. Jemima smiled to herself as she took in just how independent the woman could be. So someone dared to stand up to him!

The telephone on her desk rang and she had to abandon her eavesdropping.

It was reception. 'There's a Mr Dominic Masters asking for you,' the bored voice said.

Dominic? Jemima felt a sudden thrill. She hadn't expected this. She almost told the girl to send him up to her floor, then realized that she didn't want to run the danger of her father overhearing them the way she'd been able to listen in on him and Val. 'Tell him to wait in the boardroom, I'll be right down,' she said, put down the phone, looked at the glass she was still holding, then went across and held it once more against the wood.

Silence.

No, not quite. They'd stopped arguing but they were still in there and the few sounds she could pick up were graphic.

Silently she put down the glass on the top of a filing cabinet then, very, very gently, she pulled the door slightly ajar.

Her father was kissing Val, his mouth working possessively on hers. Val was giving tiny, gasping moans, her hands plucking and pulling ecstatically at his jacket.

As Jemima watched, Basil finished the kiss, gazed triumphantly at the closed eyes of the woman he was so tightly clasping, then wrenched open her silk shirt and swooped on her naked breast, sucking the nipple with passionate intensity. Val's hand moved to the back of his head, pressing it against her and arching her back, as though desperate for his caress. But Jemima saw her open her eyes and a curiously detached expression come over her face.

Softly Jemima closed the door and leant against it for a moment. Then remembered that Dominic was waiting for her.

He was studying the larger-than-lifesize portrait of her father when she entered the boardroom, his hands in his pocket, his moody face patently uninterested in Basil's thrusting countenance.

'Hello, Dominic,' Jemima said, closing the door behind her.

He turned and smiled at her. A slightly uncertain smile. 'Jemima, hi! I was passing this place and I thought it was time we met again.' He made as if to move towards her but then thought better of it and remained where he was, one hand on the back of one of the red leather chairs. 'I've missed you.' His voice was low and compelling.

Jemima looked at him. His shoulders were squared, his head held high, as though daring her to question his presence.

Was she supposed to melt at the very idea he could still want her? She was interested to discover that he failed to move her in any way. 'Am I supposed to forget what happened the other night?' she enquired interestedly.

He flushed slightly. 'Come on, you know that was nothing. A diversion, that's all.'

'Diversion? Well, well.' She walked round the table and stood opposite him, the length of polished wood between them. 'Is that what you call it?'

Dominic took an eager step forward, realized he couldn't reach her, gave a quick glance to assess the distance round the table then decided to stay where he was. 'You know I adore you.' He spoke with calculated sincerity.

'That's why you haven't rung or contacted me before this?' Jemima strolled to the top of the table and took her father's chair, lolling back and looking at him, enjoying his discomfiture.

He gestured deprecatingly with his hand. 'I, well, I thought it better to give you a little time to get over what happened.'

'I didn't notice any flowers arriving with your apologies,' she continued blandly.

He moved up to where she was sitting and drew out the chair next to hers, seating himself and leaning forward so that he could take her hand. 'You can't make me feel any worse than I do already.'

Jemima allowed her hand to remain in his. Then realized that his palm was sheened with sweat. She looked at him more carefully. 'Is that so, Dominic?'

More confidently he kissed the tips of her fingers, a move that once had begun a series of increasingly passionate touchings that had reduced her to a quivering mass of expectancy.

Jemima touched his eyebrow lightly, took in the earnest gaze of his eyes. 'Tell, me, Dominic, how's business these days?'

He drew back, disconcerted, but still held on to her hand. 'Business?'

'I remember we once discussed whether my father might be able to help if you needed an extra guarantor for your bank loan.'

'Uh, well, yes, we did, didn't we?'

'So, how's business?' She caressed the side of his thumb with hers and gazed at his face.

He shifted slightly in the chair and glanced down at their entwined hands. 'Well, now you mention it, an extra guarantor wouldn't come amiss actually.'

God, he must think her stupid! Or was it that he was desperate? Jemima looked at him through half-closed eyes. What would he promise her to get her support?

She settled more comfortably into the chair, took his hand to her mouth and gently bit the tip of one of his fingers. Power surged through her. What an aphrodisiac it was! She could have had him on the boardroom table right then and there. Upstairs her father and Val, downstairs she and Dominic?

She bit harder on his finger.

With a quick intake of breath he pulled his hand away. 'That hurt!' he said indignantly.

'Did it?' Jemima enquired sweetly. She felt wonderful. So this was how it was to know you could save someone and have them grateful for ever or condemn them to financial disaster. No wonder her father loved it all. 'Dominic, thank you.'

'Uh?' he stared at her, puzzled and definitely unsettled. 'You mean, you'll speak to him? Get your father on my side?' He gained confidence as he spoke.

Jemima gave a contemptuous flick to his nose. 'You really are the pits, you know?' she said conversationally.

His expression became totally blank.

'How you had the gall to turn up here today I'll never know.' She rose sinuously from the chair. 'I think you know your way out.'

'You mean, you won't speak to him?' He sounded dismayed and as though he could hardly believe it.

'You're even stupider than I thought, Dominic. You should have realized any hope of my father's financial support disappeared when you two-timed me.' Ice laced her voice but inside Jemima was warm and glowing.

'You bitch,' he said bitterly, rising. 'You're just like him. It's not enough to do a chap down, you've got to rub his nose in it.' He advanced towards her, his face contorted with rage. She took an involuntary step back. 'I'll get you for this, see if I don't.'

For a moment she thought he was going to hit her but then he thrust his hands into his pockets and, still breathing heavily, turned and walked out of the room.

He must really be in trouble, she realized. The thought thrilled her, he deserved everything that was coming to him. She refused to worry about his threat, Dominic was all wind and no force. She stretched her hands above her head and felt power run through her.

By the time she walked out to the lift, he'd left the building.

She entered her office and found the door into her father's standing open.

'Come in, Jemima,' called Basil as she stood in the doorway.

He was seated behind his desk, with Val perched on it, her hand in his. 'We've got news for you, Val and I are engaged.'

Jemima looked at them both carefully. Val was smiling graciously, her shirt neatly buttoned, and her father exuded satisfaction.

'Congratulations,' Jemima said without expression.

Basil didn't seem to notice her lack of warmth. 'We're going to have a celebration dinner,' he said exultantly. 'You, us, Jasper and Val's daughter.'

'How nice,' Jemima said politely. 'Have you told Jasper?'

'Just rung him. He's delighted.'

How had he managed to convince Basil of that? Jemima wondered wryly. Or had Basil brought him to realize that his allowance and living space depended on acceptance of Val? Life would no doubt change for both her and Jasper.

Jemima went over to Val and gave her a cool kiss. 'I hope you'll be very, very happy,' she told her. Then flung her arms round her father. 'And you, Dad.'

He hugged her, almost crushing the breath out of her body. 'See you back at the house,' he said as he released her. 'Come on, darling, let's go.' He grabbed Val's hand and pulled her, laughing, off the desk. 'Oh, and Jemima, that new nanny is hopeless. You're going to have to help look after Rory until I get back from my trip.'

Jemima watched them go, then went back to her own office. The information about Rory's nanny had failed to get through to her. Entirely occupying Jemima's mind was the knowledge that Val wasn't at all in love with her father but was marrying him neverthless. Somehow this information was valuable.

Wondering how best to make use of it, she switched off her computer and picked up her bag. Then, just as she was leaving the office, her mobile phone rang.

Chapter Sixteen

Pat James listened to William conducting the late afternoon briefing session with a feeling of deep frustration.

The frustration was twofold. Despite everyone's efforts, this investigation seemed to be getting nowhere and despite her best endeavours, Pat was not getting far in re-establishing her relationship with the DCI. Oh, he seemed to be grateful to have her expertise all right but, after that first, heady day spent together, she hadn't seen any more of him than any other member of his team.

'Let's just run through what evidence we've managed to unearth about the actual fire,' William said. 'Forensics have confirmed that the accelerant used was petrol, leadfree. Any results on inquiries to local petrol stations on anyone filling a petrol can?'

'No, guv,' said Rose. 'But it would be quite easy to fill the car and then a can without the attendant noticing. Or to use a station in some other area.' Her face was earnest, her mid-brown hair beginning to fall out of the bun she'd lately taken to wearing it in to keep it off her collar.

'How about if it had been waiting around to be used in a lawn mower?' suggested someone else.

'Mine uses leaded,' Chris said dolefully. 'I have to keep special cans.'

'Fires are the very devil,' William continued. 'They destroy so many clues. The post-mortem has, as we know, established that Gerry Aherne was hit on the back of the head with the proverbial blunt instrument but forensics have found no trace of a possible weapon.'

'How about a rolling pin?' Pat suggested suddenly. 'If it was a food factory, there could have been one lying around and it might have burned in the fire.'

'Good thinking, sergeant,' William rewarded Pat with a quick smile. 'As soon as we've finished here, get on to forensics and see if they can identify a possible rolling pin amongst the debris. And check with that secretary to see whether it's likely one could have been lying around in the office. After all, it's not something you use for filing.'

Pat glowed and made a note in her book.

'Nor are there any footprints,' William continued. 'Forensics say the clothes the arsonist was wearing could be contaminated with both petrol and smoke but until we have a suspect we can't examine his garments.'

'What about the Douglas woman?' someone asked.

'Not enough evidence to ask for a search warrant and I can't see Ealham allowing us to turn over either his lover's wardrobe or his own.

'Now, turning to the location of the business park, the house-to-house inquiries have unearthed someone in this street here,' William turned to the map on the incident board and pointed to a residential road running alongside the industrial park, 'who might have heard the arsonist leaving. A Mike Jones was sleeping on his sister's sofa in her front room, he'd been thrown out by his girlfriend.' There was a snigger from some of the men. Pat sighed at their juvenile approach.

William continued unperturbed. 'Mike got up around one o'clock to have a pee and heard a car coming out of the park. His sister's house isn't far from the entrance and he says it sounded like someone going very fast, then changing gear to go round a corner, skidding, then roaring off down the road. He says he remembers it because it was such an expensive sound, like a BMW or a Mercedes.'

'Audi?' suggested someone.

'Roller?' came from someone else.

'Porsche?'

'Quite,' said William. 'The timing fits in with the fire service's estimate of when the fire was started.'

'What about the chap who reported the fire?' Rose asked.

'Youngster coming home from a late date and his story checks out. Now how are we doing with the reports from the Eat Well Foods staff? Peter?'

'Just finishing, guv,' Peter Lennon said with quiet satisfaction.

'Good work,' said William. 'OK, everyone, we'll have a look at what they can tell us tomorrow. And I want an investigation into Basil Ealham's background.'

'If he's proposing to invest money in the company, would he set fire to its premises?' Terry Pitman asked, sounding sceptical.

'He would if he wanted to clear it of bad debts,' Pat shot in and thought she saw William give her a grateful look, but it was so fleeting she could easily have been mistaken.

'Ealham's a self-made man, comes from a deprived background. We need to look at any contacts he's kept up from those times.'

'Someone shady he could have used to set fire to the place?' Chris Hare suggested.

William nodded. 'And anything else that could have a bearing on this case. Terry, I want you to take charge of that aspect.' Terry Pitman looked far from pleased but said nothing.

'OK, troops, for today, that's it.'

There was a general exodus.

But Pat stayed behind to catch up on the latest reports.

An hour later William came into the incident room. 'Good heavens,' he said. 'You still at it?'

'Nearly finished, guv.'

He lingered by her side, making her very conscious of his presence. She wondered if he was going to suggest they went for a drink together, now that there were none of the others around to see him ask her. Keeping her eyes on the report she was reading, she willed him to do so.

'See you tomorrow then,' he said abruptly. 'Don't work too hard.'

Pat watched his tall figure leave disconsolately. There was something wrong with him, she knew it. Was it this case or his marriage?

She worked on, hoping against hope that William would return and suggest that drink.

Instead Terry Pitman suddenly appeared in the incident room. 'Sucking up to the boss, are we? Showing how hard we can work?' he said in his snide way, coming up behind her.

She shut down the computer she'd been working on and swung round in the chair. 'What's your problem?' she shot at him.

'I don't have a problem, if there is one, it's yours,' he said calmly, leaning against the edge of a table, watching her.

'I know your sort, you believe a woman's place is in the kitchen or working a keyboard. And you always feel everybody else gets a better chance at the top than you,' she added. This was a shot in the dark, stimulated by the resentment of William he so clearly displayed. 'You can't accept that just maybe someone is more intelligent and harder working than you.'

He flushed, the betraying colour surging into his cheeks. 'Quite the little psychologist, aren't you?' he sneered. 'Always think you have the answer to everything.'

She looked at him, leaning against the desk, muscles tensed, and reckoned he was longing for a scrap, dying to work out his frustrations on her. 'So what brings you back? Wanting to suck up to the boss?' she riposted.

'Just needed to pick up one or two things,' he thrust his hands into his trouser pockets and continued staring at her with challenge in his eyes. 'If you ask me, it's going to be a waste of time, going after this Ealham chap,' he said abruptly. 'It's a really long shot.'

Instantly Pat felt resentment at his questioning of William's handling of the case. 'Where would you look instead?' she asked in a way that made it plain what she thought about the matter.

'Quite the loyal little lieutenant, aren't we?' he said softly. 'But how closely are we looking at Val Douglas, eh? If being in bed together doesn't mean Basil Ealham is out of the frame, couldn't the same apply to her? After all, it's equal opportunity these days, isn't it?'

What a prickly, unpleasant person he was! The last

thing Pat wanted was to spend any more time in the same room as him but she was damned if she was going to creep away leaving him in possession of the office. She also knew that if she was going to get anywhere in this job, she had to learn to work with this man. 'Maeve O'Connor rang in with her new address,' she told him.

Terry said nothing but she thought some of his tenseness relaxed just a little.

'She's gone into the local youth hostel and is trying to find another job. Not going to be easy without references from the Ealhams.' She tossed the notebook back on to the desk.

'She's lucky to get away with not being prosecuted,' he said neutrally.

'Do you think she really did steal those pearls?'

'Do you?' he turned the question.

Unfair, Pat thought, she'd asked first, but, again, she restrained herself. 'She had everything to lose. A good job in luxurious surroundings, not to mention a cosy relationship with the master of the house.'

'That was never mentioned!' Terry's hands came out of his pockets.

'You haven't read the transcript of my report properly,' Pat said calmly.

He looked at her blankly.

'The bit that says when the guv asked her if she and the boy were alone on the nursery floor at night-time, she answered, "You could say that, yeah."'

'And you interpret that as meaning she was having an affair with Basil Ealham?' His scorn was patent.

'Don't you?'

'Isn't there a son? I'd have thought he'd be the one.'

Pat smoothed her skirt along her thighs. 'Not when

you add it to her comment that Val Douglas was a stuck-up cow who thought she had Basil Ealham where she wanted.'

He pounced quickly. 'That isn't in the report.'

'It isn't?' Pat was startled. She was sure it had all gone in. And William had checked it. 'Let's see.'

It took a little time to find the right report and Terry didn't help. He remained where he was as Pat finally unearthed and quickly scanned it. 'You're right,' she said in disgust.

'Keep up the good work.' He patted her on the shoulder in a maddeningly condescending way and sauntered out of the CID room.

Furiously Pat started to amend the report. Anger seethed through her. Not only had Terry not told her what he thought about the nanny, he'd found her out in a slip. Unacknowledged even to herself was the fact that William had checked her report and not noticed the omission.

Keen to get on top of the remaining staff statements, Pat stayed late that night and was in early the next morning.

They were a turgid lot, full of irrelevant data. The only interesting thing about them was the way that, together, they built up a picture of a happy company and if the company was on the financial skids, rumour hadn't yet started amongst the staff.

She'd reached the last but one as Terry walked in.

'Spent the night here, did you?' he asked and for once his tone was almost friendly.

She didn't notice. Her attention was entirely focused on the statement she was reading. 'Have you seen this?'

she asked excitedly, not caring that it was Terry she was showing it to instead of William.

He took the report and she watched him read it, a smile of anticipation on her face.

'When did this come in?' he asked.

'Must have been last night, it was waiting with several others to be entered this morning.'

'I think we should follow it up now,' Terry said. 'Come on.'

Pat didn't question his decision or feel they should wait for William's arrival. She grabbed her jacket and followed him.

Heidi Walker lived in a council house several miles from the Eat Well Foods factory.

'Basil Ealham's office isn't far away,' Pat said as she drove them over.

For a moment Terry was silent, then he said, 'Perhaps the guv could be right about Ealham's involvement in this case.'

Pat felt it must have taken something for him to say this. 'I wonder how reliable a witness Heidi Walker is?' she offered.

'We shall see,' he said and she felt that some sort of truce had been signed between them.

They parked behind an A-registered Ford Escort that looked in astonishingly good condition for its age. The little garden was neat, the windows sparkling and the door freshly painted in a smart navy blue. The brass fittings shone with that brightness that only comes from regular cleaning. 'Bought from the council?' murmured Pat.

The woman who opened the door was large, like a cottage loaf, with a comfortable bosom, big hips and a generous head of fair hair, done up in a loose but neat heap on the top of her head. Her kind, placid face looked polite enquiry at the two detectives.

'DI Pitman and DS James,' said Terry, flashing his warrant card. Pat showed hers as well. 'We want to talk to you about your statement on Eat Well Foods.'

'Ach, so, it's the fire,' Heidi said with a strong continental accent. 'Come in, I put coffee on, yes?'

'That would be great,' Pat said, reminded that she hadn't had any breakfast.

Heidi showed them into a neat front room and took herself off to the kitchen.

'Need your caffeine fix, sergeant?' asked Terry, peering at photographs on the mantelpiece. But, again, the sneering note was, for the moment, absent from his voice.

'Jump starts me into the day,' Pat said cheerfully, admiring a drawn-threadwork cloth on the coffee table that stood in front of a well upholstered three-piece suite. It only took a few minutes before Heidi was back with a jug of what smelt like real coffee and a plate of small pastries that could only have been home-made. 'Now I don't go to factory, I have time to bake,' she said, putting the tray on the coffee table and giving them a big smile as she poured out the strong, black liquid.

Pat took an almond slice and bit into it, releasing a shower of pastry crumbs. It was the most delicious thing she had ever tasted, with a real almond flavour and fresh raspberry jam. Terry was already reaching for another.

Heidi beamed at them. 'Is good, yes? At home I am pastry chef.' She handed each of them a minute square of linen which unfolded into a small napkin, also edged in drawn-thread work.

'Where is home?' Pat asked.

'Austria, near Zell-am-See. Is big lake, not far from mountains. I meet my James when he on holiday there. I come here twenty years ago. I like it here but miss mountains. When you grow up with them, hard to forget, no?'

The coffee was as good as the almond slices. Pat drank hers with deep appreciation. 'I'm sure,' she said. 'Now, you've given a statement to the police about your work with Eat Well Foods.'

'Is something wrong?' For the first time a frown appeared on Heidi's face. 'I say something wrong?'

'No, Mrs Walker,' Terry leaned forward, his hand hovering over the pastries. 'We just want to clarify one or two things.' As though not realizing what he was doing, he transferred another almond slice to his plate.

'My English is not good,' she said cheerfully.

'Your English is as good as your baking,' Pat assured her, which brought another beaming smile to the woman's face. 'It's about the time you saw the night-watchman, Gerry Aherne, in a café when you were shopping. Can you go through it again?'

'Tell you again?' Heidi said, her cheerfulness undiminished.

'Just so we are in the picture,' Terry said.

'OK, no problem. I was in town, I leave early that day, look for special present for my husband, is birthday soon, you know? And there is craft market with café. I think perhaps I find piece of glass my husband like.' Heidi glanced over at a small table that carried a collection of modern glass paperweights. 'He collect,' she said.

'But nothing good there. I just go when I see sitting at table in café Gerry.'

'How well did you know Mr Aherne?' Pat asked. 'I understand he hadn't been working at the factory long.'

Heidi nodded vigorously. 'We both join company at same time, is connection, yes? He very friendly. Walk round factory in afternoon, talk workers. I know he live tiny apartment in back. I bring him once cake; sachertorte, but my recipe.' She grinned at them, 'My husband, he say sachertorte to die for.'

'So you got on well with Gerry Aherne,' Terry said.

'Yes, I like talk, hear him explain Ireland. Beautiful place he say. Perhaps James and I visit.'

'So when you saw the nightwatchman in this café, you thought you'd join him?' suggested Pat.

Heidi's light blue eyes widened and she leaned forward, confidentially. 'I think, yes. But then I see he with other man. Other man have back to me, he talking to Gerry, stabbing finger at him.' She poked her own finger towards Pat in an aggressive way. 'Then Gerry grab his hand,' she brought her hand down with a jerk on to the coffee table, making the tray rattle. 'Gerry very, very,' she searched for the right word.

Pat longed to prompt her but knew that would be fatal. In the other chair she could feel Terry equally intent on the woman.

'Gerry very powerful,' Heidi said at last. 'Dominant? Is right? Is correct?'

'Could be,' Pat assured her. 'So Gerry didn't see you?' The report hadn't covered this point.

'But, yes!' said Heidi instantly. 'He see me. I think I look too much at them. He see me and he shake head.'

She demonstrated, gazing at Pat and making the tiniest possible movement of her head.

'So the other man at the table with him didn't see?' asked Terry.

'So, yes!' agreed Heidi. 'I know Gerry not like him to know I there. So I go,' she added with an air of finality.

'You didn't tell the police who interviewed you this,' Terry said. 'All you told them was you saw Mr Aherne and another man in the café and they appeared to be arguing.'

Heidi shrugged. 'Not always I understand what people ask,' she said. 'And sometimes people not understand what I say.'

Terry glanced at Pat and she knew they were both thinking that the police officer who'd questioned Heidi Walker needed to brush up his interviewing techniques.

'And did you mention this occasion to Mr Aherne afterwards?' asked Pat.

'Yes, of course! Very strange, mysterious, I think. So, next day, I take biscuits to Gerry after work finish and I ask.'

'And how did he react?' asked Terry. 'I mean,' he said as she looked blankly at him, 'was Mr Aherne annoyed or angry?'

'Angry? Why angry? It happen, I there.'

'So, he wasn't angry,' Pat soothed her. 'What did he say?'

'He say sorry not talk with me yesterday. Big business, he say, and do so!' Heidi laid her right forefinger against the side of her nose and looked knowing.

'Business,' repeated Terry. 'You're sure he said business?'

'Sure I sure.' Heidi looked injured.

'Did he say anything else?' Pat asked.

Heidi shook her head.

'You saw Gerry Aherne and this man last Tuesday, that's right?' Terry asked.

Heidi nodded.

'On the Wednesday afternoon you spoke to Mr Aherne and he told you it had been big business.'

Again Heidi nodded.

'And the Wednesday night the factory caught fire,' he said, more to himself than anybody else.

Heidi looked frightened. 'You think man in café start fire?'

Terry didn't answer. 'You recognized the man you saw in the café?'

'No,' said Heidi unexpectedly.

'But you said—' Pat interposed.

Terry held up his hand, stopping her. 'Tell us what you said to the police.'

Heidi looked flustered for the first time. 'They say do I know who Gerry saw at café. I say yes.'

'Then you did know,' Terry said, exasperated.

'No, not then. Police, they ask me, what he look like. So I tell, tall, fair hair. And they say, do I know who he is. And I say, yes, I do not know name but I see him with Mrs Douglas Thursday morning, after fire.' That was where the statement had ended.

Pat again saw Basil Ealham arriving in his Rolls Royce as all the women were giving their names and addresses to Val Douglas's secretary. Saw the large man put his arm around her shoulder, his fair hair gleaming in the chilly morning sun.

'Basil Ealham,' she breathed to Heidi.

Heidi looked back at her in surprise. 'No, not Mr Ealham.'

Pat and Terry stared at her in astonishment. The answer had seemed so obvious to both of them.

'Mr Ealham, I know,' Heidi said agitatedly. 'Mrs Douglas bring him round factory, he talk with us. This man I not see in office. But he there Thursday morning.'

'Paul Robins,' said Pat suddenly. 'Of course, the PR man!'

Why on earth, she wondered, could that smooth looking chap have needed to meet the nightwatchman in a tucked away café? The natural habitat for both would surely have been a bar or pub. And had Paul Robins tried to threaten Gerry Aherne?

Chapter Seventeen

The Hon. Mrs Cynthia Beauchamp lived in a four-storey terrace mansion just off Eaton Square. The door was opened by a maid and Darina taken up to a first-floor drawing room.

'How nice to meet you,' her hostess said, coming forward.

Darina judged the Hon. Cynthia Beauchamp to be in her forties. She was lithe figured and blonde haired, with a face that looked as though it just might have had an extremely skilful lift, the golden skin was so nicely taut and the area round the bright blue eyes so unlined.

'It's very good of you to see me,' Darina murmured. Then decided that a bit of name dropping wouldn't come amiss here. 'You're almost neighbours with my husband's uncle and aunt, Lord and Lady Doubleday.' She left the sentence hanging.

Cynthia's face lightened. 'Oh, dear Geoffrey and Honor, we know them well! So, you're related?'

'William's father is Geoffrey's brother.'

'His uncle! Well, isn't that nice!' Darina was waved to a chair. The drawing room had an interior designer's touch without being oppressively over decorated. 'I feel I know you already. Now,' the blue eyes looked at her thoughtfully, 'your husband is the policeman, yes?'

'Yes,' Darina agreed.

'Recently promoted, I believe.' So Cynthia Beauchamp not only knew the Doubledays well, she actually listened to what other people told her. Darina's expectations of this visit rose a little. 'You must be very proud.'

Darina agreed she was.

'And no wonder, then, that you have taken to investigation as well. Are you a private detective?' The blue eyes were inquisitive.

'No, not at all,' Darina said quickly. 'Only I have been involved in several cases and Jemima has asked me if I could help in trying to find Rory's father.'

'Ah, yes, Rory's father. Well, before we get down to that, can I offer you some coffee?' A tray was all ready, the coffee in a smart vacuum flask, the cream and sugar in silver containers, the cups and saucers fine porcelain.

'Now,' Cynthia said, handing a cup of coffee to Darina. 'How can I help? I was just devastated when little Sophie disappeared,' she continued without a pause. 'And then when she died, well,' she spread out her hands in a helpless gesture. 'And Basil was just broken by it all.' Cynthia sat down and ran a hand through her blonde curls. She'd shed any hint of artifice and looked genuinely moved.

'I understand it was you who suggested it would be a good idea for Sophie to have a season?'

Cynthia drank some of her coffee. 'I'd met her several times at Basil's house and she was such a sweet girl but lost, no idea what to do. She wasn't a modern miss, she needed a husband and a family to devote herself to. And I had such a ball when I came out,' she added with a faint smile.

Yes, Darina could see this confident woman as an

equally confident but fresh young girl conquering the young men she met as much by her personality as her looks. She wondered what had happened to her husband.

'Of course, it was long past the days when one was presented to the Queen but, even so, there were all these parties and my father gave a wonderful ball at Manston, our country seat.'

'And did you meet your husband then?'

'Oh, Charlie! Yes.' Again that little smile of reminiscence. 'Mummy was so pleased! Even then she could see he was going all the way. Background, breeding and a terrific sense of the money markets.'

'So it worked out well?' Darina probed.

Cynthia's frank eyes met hers. 'For the first twenty years, yes. Then he got careless and I found out what was going on. Women I might have managed to ignore; after all, a man needs his little pleasures and one can't expect to keep the flame alight for ever, can one? But when I found out there were boys, well,' a small toss of the head tried to dismiss the knowledge, 'that was too much.' Cynthia put down her drink and lit a cigarette. 'I mean, there were the children to consider. Anyway, I came out of it all right, kept the house,' her gaze encompassed the elegant room, 'and an income to go with it. But, well, it's lonely.' Again that frank gaze met Darina's. 'Still, one has one's friends.'

'And you met Basil Ealham?'

'As you say, I met Basil Ealham.' A sardonic note entered Cynthia's voice.

It must have seemed meant. The lonely, attractive socialite and Basil, ever ambitious, ever magnetic, ever one to need lovely ladies. And with the vulnerable, shy, motherless Sophie.

'What sort of arrangement did you come to over Sophie?'

A trace of hauteur entered the bright blue eyes. 'Arrangement?'

'I'm sorry,' Darina stumbled, aware of her error, 'I mean, did she come and stay with you here?'

'Ah, I see what you mean.' The touch of frost melted away. 'Yes, for part of the time. My own daughter, Tiggy, was her age and I took them around together.'

Darina saw immediately what a convenient arrangement this must have been for the Hon. Cynthia Beauchamp. Basil would surely have contributed handsomely to expenses.

'You must have got to know Sophie well.'

'Indeed I did. Such a loving little girl. She and Tiggy got on so well together.'

This was the first Darina had heard of Sophie having a close friend her own age. 'Didn't Tiggy have any idea where Sophie might have gone after she left her brother's?'

'Oh, she was so upset. Do you want to talk to her yourself? She's upstairs.'

It sounded as though Tiggy hadn't found a husband during her season.

Darina said she would find that very helpful and Cynthia rang a bell then despatched the maid to bring down her daughter.

When Tiggy arrived, it was with a tiny baby with a puckered mouth giving forth weak, plaintive cries.

'My first grandson,' Cynthia said reverently. 'George, five weeks old!'

Darina dutifully admired him while thinking she preferred babies a little older, like Rory.

'He's hungry,' Tiggy announced. 'I'll feed him while we talk.'

Tiggy was a big girl with her mother's open manner, lots of naturally fair hair worn loose and a cheerful face. She sat down in a corner of the sofa, unbuttoned the big blue shirt she was wearing over jeans, revealing heavy breasts in a nursing bra, and soon had the baby contentedly sucking, watching his determined feeding with an expression of such tenderness Darina suddenly felt a pang of real envy.

'We're talking about Sophie Ealham,' Cynthia said.

Tiggy looked up immediately. 'Oh, poor Sophie! When I think how she never saw her baby, I can't bear it.'

'Jemima wants to find out who his father is,' Darina told her.

Tiggy made a small face. 'Jemima, eh! Pity she didn't care a bit more while Sophie was alive.'

Darina looked expectantly at her, 'You mean Sophie didn't feel she could confide in her?'

'Sophie couldn't confide in any of her family,' Tiggy said roundly, hitching little George up closer to her breast. A tiny hand waved briefly before he settled again. 'Her eldest brother, Job, lived in some rarefied world of his own, Jemima was too involved in her own activities and as for Jasper!'

'What about him? I thought he was very close to her.'

'Did you never wonder why all their names start with J except for Sophie's?' asked Tiggy.

'No,' said Darina, wondering now why it had never

occurred to her. Cynthia said nothing but her eyes watched her daughter.

'Apparently Jasper told her one day that his father wasn't hers!'

Darina remembered the story about the gardener and the pool house. Had Julie Ealham become pregnant and had Basil then accepted Sophie as his own? 'Poor Sophie,' Darina said.

'Poor Basil,' Cynthia said roundly. 'I knew,' she told her daughter. 'Basil told me. He said his wife had had a very brief affair with someone totally unsuitable and had confessed all to him and, "thrown herself on his mercy", I seem to remember was the phrase used.' Her mouth looked as though she'd sucked on a lemon. 'Basil said he'd felt he had to forgive her and assume total responsibility for Sophie.' She fiddled with a gold bracelet for a moment then added, 'He said it wasn't difficult, she was such a lovely child.'

No doubt it had suited Basil to have something over his wife and remaining married to her meant he could enjoy other women without having to make any commitment, thought Darina cynically. No doubt Jasper had put two and two together as he grew up.

'Sophie said to me that she wouldn't believe it at first and that she really went for Jasper. But apparently he told her it was quite easy to prove, it just needed a blood test and asked her if she'd like to have one done.'

'What a bastard,' murmured Cynthia.

'Well, that convinced her but she didn't feel she could trust Jasper after that,' said Tiggy.

'How dreadful,' Darina said. 'They were both so fond of each other. I spent a holiday with the Ealhams in Italy once and Jasper was the one who looked after Sophie, she was only about five at the time.'

'I think she adored him,' Tiggy agreed. 'But he made her feel she wasn't part of the family and she couldn't take that.'

'Oh, poor Sophie,' said Cynthia, visibly distressed. 'Basil really loved her. In fact,' she glanced down at her drink, her eyes hooded, 'well, I felt quite jealous at times.' She gave a self-deprecating laugh and lifted her cup.

'Did you see her after she moved to her elder brother's?' Darina asked Tiggy.

She shook her head. 'Afraid not. My father was working in New York on a special assignment and after the dance that Sophie and I shared, I went out there. That's where I met Angus and after that, well, everything else went out the window.'

'Angus is Tiggy's husband,' Cynthia explained, a trifle unnecessarily. 'He's in futures. Works terribly hard.'

'Never home before eight or nine o'clock,' said Tiggy gloomily. 'George is going to grow up with a stranger for a father. We live in Clapham and it takes ages for Angus to get home so Mummy thought we might like to stay with her while I got used to having George. At least Angus gets here before I've fallen asleep.'

'My husband's always late home as well,' Darina commiserated with her. 'Everyone seems to work so hard these days. But, back to Sophie,' she said hastily.

'Oh, yah, Sophie. Well, as I said, I went off to America and by the time I came back, Sophie had, well, disappeared.'

'Do you know of any friends she could have gone to or got help from?'

Tiggy shook her head. 'Like I told Mummy at the time, Soph was hopeless making friends. She never chattered like the rest of us, just was, you know? Either sat or stood so quietly half the time you forgot she was there.'

'But you became friends with her?'

'Oh, yah. Well, she was staying here, wasn't she? And she had a good eye for fashion,' Tiggy said with sudden enthusiasm. 'We'd go shopping for clothes and she always knew what was going to suit me.' She looked down at the open sides of the blue shirt. 'Can't wait to get out of this sort of thing but it's no use dressing up at the moment, the milk leaks out or George is sick on me. Anyway, I can't fit into anything good. Come on lad,' she gave the baby a little shake, 'don't go to sleep on the job. He takes for ever,' she said to Darina. 'I have to keep reminding him what he's supposed to be doing. At nighttime we both go to sleep together,' she giggled.

'So you have no idea where she could have gone to?' Darina was beginnning to despair of keeping the conversation on target.

Tiggy looked regretful. 'I'm sorry, I really can't think. I told Mummy and Basil when I got back that, as far as I knew, Sophie didn't have any other friends. Come on, little one,' she caressed George's minute nose with one finger. His creased face creased some more and he began sucking again.

'Have you met Rory?' Darina asked Cynthia.

She nodded. 'Once. By the time he was born, Basil and I had parted.' She looked down at her hands, lying in her expensively clad lap, then smiled. 'I couldn't take his possessiveness any longer.'

'Mummy! You told me you found out he was seeing someone else,' protested Tiggy.

Cynthia looked daggers but rallied. 'There was that, too. One does like to have a monopoly on one's man. Anyway, he did ring me and ask if I'd like to see Sophie's child and of course I went. I thought Rory seemed a dear little boy. Have some more coffee.'

Darina handed over her cup, little George went on quietly sucking and his mother and grandmother gazed at him in mutual adoration. 'Can I just get Sophie's movements straight in my mind,' she said. 'She stayed here until the season ended, that would have been August?'

'Not exactly,' Cynthia said. 'We had a dance in early July and then Sophie went back to her father. Before that she divided her time between us and Blackboys. It depended on whether there were parties and balls in London to go to. For Ascot and Henley, Tiggy and I would drive down to Blackboys and pick up Sophie. Basil usually arranged a driver. Once or twice we spent the night there.'

'I never really liked that,' Tiggy said suddenly.

'Didn't you, sweet?' her mother said in astonishment. 'Why?'

'I couldn't stand Basil.' Tiggy sounded uncomfortable.

'You never said.'

'No, well, there wasn't much point. You were dotty over him.'

'I was not "dotty over him",' Cynthia protested roundly.

'Yes you were. Sliced bread wasn't in it. Actually, that was one of the reasons I went to the States. Of course I wanted to see Daddy but I really couldn't bear the sight of you and Basil together.'

'Sweetie!' Cynthia gazed at her daughter in amazement.

'I was never so relieved as when I came back and found that you weren't together any more. Except I was upset about Sophie. If it hadn't been for that, it would all have been perfect,' she added sorrowfully.

'Why didn't you like Basil?' Darina asked as her mother seemed silenced.

'Oh, I don't know. I was so young,' Tiggy said with all the maturity of her new-found motherhood. She couldn't be more than about twenty-two. 'I didn't like the way he looked at me,' she said after a moment's thought. 'What was it you called certain young men you didn't like me going around with?' she asked her mother. 'NTS?'

'NST,' her mother said, reviving. 'Not Safe in Taxis.'

'Well, he had that sort of look.'

'Good heavens,' Cynthia said faintly.

'And his hand would linger on my shoulder. And when I danced with him at our ball, he held me much too tight. It was, well, it was really embarrassing.'

'Sweetie, you should have told me.' Tiggy looked at her mother and after a moment Cynthia added, 'Well, I see your problem. But I'm really sorry, darling. What a shit the man was. Thank heavens I never married him.'

'You wouldn't have, would you?' Tiggy was appalled.

'Perhaps not,' Cynthia agreed but there was a lingering trace of regret in her voice. Darina reckoned it had been a near thing. Perhaps if Sophie hadn't disappeared, who knew?

There wasn't anything more Cynthia or Tiggy could tell Darina that was of any use but she stayed a little longer, finishing her drink and admiring the tiny

George. Then she took her leave, thanking them both sincerely for all they'd told her.

Cynthia showed Darina out herself. 'I do hope you manage to find Rory's father,' she said. 'I told Basil at the time he should do everything in his power to find out who he was. But I don't think he took my advice, perhaps because of who Sophie's father had been. I mean, he may have thought blood had spoken and the truth would be more of a burden to Rory than ignorance.'

As Darina walked back along the King's Road to her house, she thought that this offered a more reasonable explanation for Basil doing nothing about Rory's father than anything else she could think of. It didn't make her task any easier, though.

Her next move must be to talk to Paul Robins.

Darina looked at her watch. If the traffic wasn't too bad, she should be able to arrive at his office just before lunch, which might mean she could persuade him to have something to eat with her. It was always easier to get people to talk over food.

Chapter Eighteen

Paul Robins didn't start Thursday in a temper but he certainly ended it in one. What his secretary called 'one of his paddies'.

When, early in the morning, he actually managed to get hold of Val he really thought that this might be his day. 'At last,' he said jovially.

'Sorry, Paul,' she said, sounding remote, almost as though she was attending to something else while talking to him, 'I have been busy.'

Oh, yes, sure. Busy with Basil!

'There really has been a lot to see to,' she went on, sounding tired.

Instantly, he'd felt compassion. She'd been hit hard by the fire and its aftermath. He remembered the shadows under her eyes that awful morning. Had he really not seen her since then? 'You should let me take more of the burden,' he told her tenderly. 'Come out to lunch. I'll bring a draft press release on your new arrangements.'

'Paul, that's sweet of you but I really haven't time. Fax it to me.'

'We need to talk,' he began to get upset. 'Discuss what else is needed to reassure all your customers. Public relations is more than press releases, you know.'

'We've got things well in hand, Paul. Shaz is sending out a letter to all our major accounts. Thank heavens for a freelance accountant, he had all their details.'

'But,' he pressed her, 'what about your end buyers? They aren't going to get a letter.'

'Paul, I haven't time for this, you know I'm off to that conference this evening.'

Ah, yes, the conference! To think that it had been his idea. Good for her image, he'd said. Underline her authority in the field of food intolerances and make useful contacts. The first thing he'd said after the fire was that she mustn't think of cancelling her paper. Now it was an excuse not to see him. Val had no right to treat him this way. 'I'll drive you to the airport,' he offered.

'That's kind of you, Paul, but Basil's going to take me.'

Burning jealousy filled Paul's breast. 'He seems to monopolize all of your time these days,' he said resentfully. He knew exactly what the situation was, at least he thought he did, but the amount of time she spent with that big bag of wind still got to him. He wondered that she'd even bothered to ring him from the scene of the fire. If Basil had been able to stay with her, she probably wouldn't have.

'Oh, Paul, don't go all hurt pride on me,' Val snapped. 'You don't seem to understand what I'm up against.'

Once he would have melted and apologized for upsetting her. 'Of course I do,' he snapped back. 'And you're not the only person to have business troubles. Keeping a PR company going over the last few years hasn't been easy.'

'Paul, I've got to go now,' she sounded very tired. 'Fax me that release.' The line went dead.

For some time he just sat there, staring at the phone

and trying to get to grips with the various emotions that seethed within him like molten iron in a crucible, red hot and very dangerous.

He got Rachel, his secretary, to fax the draft release through to Val, then he attacked paper work with furious energy.

Halfway through the morning Rachel buzzed through. 'The police are here and want to speak to you,' she said, all excited.

Oh God, he thought, another weary trawl through his connections with Eat Well Foods and where he was on Wednesday night last week. How many people could produce evidence they were in bed at four o'clock in the morning if they hadn't got a partner and wouldn't it be suspicious if they could?

'Send them in,' he said.

Instead of the two uniformed constables who'd interviewed him before, it was a man and a woman in plain clothes. After a moment, Paul recognized the girl as having been with the chief inspector at the factory on the morning of the fire.

'DI Pitman and WDS James,' said the man and Paul's depression deepened. He'd met men with that sneering look in their eyes before.

'All these initials,' he said in a jolly tone, just to show he wasn't in the least fazed by their appearance. 'What do they mean?'

'Detective Inspector and Woman Detective Sergeant,' the girl said helpfully as they put away their warrant cards.

'An inspector and a sergeant, aren't I the lucky one!' Watch it, he said to himself, you're coming on much too strong. 'How about a cup of coffee? We offer nice biscuits with it.'

'No, thank you,' said the sergeant. 'We've just had some.'

Paul told his secretary not to put calls through. Then he waved his visitors towards his sitting area, a wide, curving white leather sofa behind a round glass table and a couple of white leather armchairs.

The two detectives edged round the table and lowered themselves on to the squishy leather with care. He took one of the chairs. 'How can I help you?'

'We'd like to hear about your relationship with the nightwatchman, Gerry Aherne,' the inspector said abruptly.

Somehow Paul had known that was what they were there for.

'Aherne? We exchanged the odd word once when I called at the Eat Well Foods office one evening, that's hardly a relationship,' he said judiciously. 'It was a shock to hear of his death,' he added, for once sounding sincere.

'We understand you met him in a café near here a couple of days before he died,' Pat James said in her quiet way.

How the hell did they know that? The only people who ever went into that craft market were tourists, that was why he'd chosen it. How it kept going, he didn't know, there never seemed to be many customers.

'Oh, of course. I came across him in town and it seemed only right to offer him a cup of coffee.' He dismissed the occasion as hardly worthy of attention.

'Surely a drink would have been more acceptable?'

said Inspector Pitman, his eyes firmly fixed on Paul's face.

'I dare say but coffee was what I offered,' Paul said sharply.

'And what did you discuss?' the girl asked.

'I really can't remember. Nothing of moment. Probably the weather,' Paul said helpfully.

'Our witness says you were arguing,' Pitman challenged him.

Who in the name of everything unholy could it have been? How much did they see? Paul felt sweat breaking out on his forehead. He went and opened a window, letting in the noise of the high-street traffic. 'Never know what the weather's going to do at the moment,' he said cheerfully. 'Let me know if you can't cope with the racket.' The two officers looked at him as though they usually worked in the middle of the M1.

'We'll manage,' said the girl, Sergeant James. 'What were you arguing with Aherne about?'

'Threatening him, the witness said,' added Pitman, his eyes boring into Paul's.

'Threatening? Oh, that's an exaggeration,' Paul said, too quickly.

'Really?' Pitman raised an eyebrow. 'Perhaps you'd like to give us the unexaggerated version.'

Paul found his hands playing with the heavy perspex cigarette box that stood on the glass table. He took out a cigarette and fished in his pocket for the gold Dunhill lighter Val had given him. Then offered the box to the police. Neither admitted to smoking.

'Well, let's see how anybody could think I was threatening that poor man,' he said easily, drawing nicotine laden smoke into his lungs. 'What were we talking

243

about?' He paused, his brain working overtime. 'We started with how he was getting on with the company. I mean, nightwatchman, it's not the greatest of jobs.' He sounded indulgently compassionate. There was no reaction from either of the officers. 'Anyway, I was asking Gerry how he was getting on with the job and, yes,' he said as though light had suddenly dawned, which in a way it had, 'that's when your witness, whoever it is,' and he'd give a good deal to know who, 'must have seen us. Because I was trying to impress upon him the importance of security and I may well have overdone it.' He could see himself now, so angry he could hardly speak, spitting out words across the table, jabbing his finger in Aherne's face. But if the police knew what he'd said, they'd hardly be trying to get it out of him, would they?

He gave a little laugh and hoped his nervousness wasn't coming through. 'Perhaps if you didn't know what I was saying, it might have looked a little threatening. But, of course, Aherne knew it wasn't.'

Pat flicked a few pages back in her notebook. 'Our witness spoke with Mr Aherne the following day and asked him what it had been about.'

Who the hell could it have been? Aherne knew hardly anyone apart from the workers at Eat Well Foods and his damn daughter. Was it her? Well, Aherne wouldn't have told the truth, no matter who it had been. 'And what did he say?'

'Apparently he said it had been ''big business'',' Pat flicked the pages back again.

So that was it? Paul relaxed a little. 'Well, I suppose to him it might well have been. I mean, he'd been out of work for a long time, hadn't he?'

'According to the Irish police, Gerry Aherne has served a term for blackmail,' said the inspector.

Paul's heart almost stopped. 'Blackmail?' It came out as a squeak. 'Get a life, officer. What could Gerry Aherne possibly have to blackmail *me* about?'

'It's an interesting question,' agreed Pitman, continuing to hold Paul with his intense stare. 'Why don't you tell us.'

Paul stubbed out his cigarette and made a play of lighting another. 'Gerry Aherne could have nothing over me.'

'He was blackmailing someone,' Pat James said, her voice soft but positive. 'Regular amounts of cash have been paid into his bank account. Large amounts.'

'Well, they weren't from me, I can tell you that.' Paul was on sure ground here. 'I wish I knew where to get large amounts of cash from! You can check my accounts and my bank statement any time.'

'So maybe you decided to kill the man instead,' Pitman said with quiet menace.

Paul took another drag on his cigarette. 'No,' he said positively. 'I did not kill Gerry Aherne and I did not start that fire. For God's sake,' he added passionately, 'that's the last thing I'd do! Eat Well Foods are my main client. Not only that, I've got money invested in the firm.'

'Have you indeed?' Both police officers looked at him with interest. 'There's no trace of your investment in the company.'

At first all Paul felt was confusion. 'It was a personal arrangement between Mrs Douglas and myself.'

'You mean you made her a loan?' suggested the little sergeant.

'Covered by shares in the company.' A slow anger

245

began to burn in him. Of course there must be a record of his investment. He remembered Val's lovely face lit by such gratitude it had taken his breath away. He'd enjoyed doing something for someone he loved. Done it with a recklessness and generosity that had made him feel like a god with the power to change lives. 'My father died and left me some money just as Val, Mrs Douglas, was trying to set up her company. I was going to handle the public relations and I had, I have, complete confidence in her.'

'How much was your investment?' asked the sergeant.

They'd stopped being polite, he noticed automatically. No 'sirs' now.

'One hundred thousand pounds.' He could hear despair in his voice. How could he have been so unbusinesslike not to insist on a share certificate? He'd written out a cheque and the money had disappeared from his account into Val's. How easy it had been for her! She'd told him he now owned thirty-three per cent of the company and he'd believed her.

'Have you ever been paid a dividend?' Sergeant James asked.

'Well, it's a new company, any money that's been made has been ploughed back, invested in expansion, you know? It made more sense for my consultancy to be paid a generous fee.' That was how Val had put it. And it really had seemed sensible.

'You probably signed a private agreement,' Sergeant James suggested in a kind way.

'Oh, yes, I did,' he said eagerly. How could he have forgotten the official looking piece of paper she'd produced, laughing at such formality between them. He hadn't bothered to read it, just scribbled his signature before removing her clothes, very slowly, garment by garment.

For a moment Paul felt relief. He shouldn't have doubted for a moment. But the burning sensation wouldn't go away.

'I'd like to go back to your meeting in the cafe,' the inspector said smoothly.

For the next thirty minutes he took Paul through his account of this again and again. Looking for discrepancies, of course. Paul had to concentrate very hard, which enabled him to convert his anger over the share situation they'd revealed into adrenalin that took him through the ordeal.

He didn't know if the officers had got what they came for but they looked as though they had plenty to think about as they left his office.

He shut the door behind them, lit another cigarette and tried to get Val on the telephone. Unavailable, he was told. He left a message for her to ring but there was no one who was so good at making herself unavailable when she wanted as Val.

Was she with Basil? The thought was acid in his stomach. Why the hell had he gone along with her on her involvement with the man? All right, if Ealham acquired the company, they would both be sitting pretty financially speaking. But what made Val think she had to offer herself as well as her company? Did she enjoy keeping the two of them on her little string? And how much longer could she keep Basil from knowing about their relationship?

Paul stubbed out his cigarette and immediately lit another one as he wondered whether Val was now just playing him along rather than Basil. She couldn't dump him, he'd ask for his money back and she couldn't afford repayment, he knew that. Why couldn't she reel Basil in? If only Val would stop arguing with him over the way the business was to be run, she could have sold him the company long before this, Paul was sure of it.

Nobody knew better than he how rational she could make any proposition sound, however dodgy it might prove to cool analysis. There was the time she'd had that idea for providing special meals for food intolerant passengers on British Airways. By the time she'd finished working on him, he'd been convinced all he had to do was knock on BA's door. Until he'd tried it.

He still squirmed as he remembered how quickly he'd been seen off by the airline.

Round and round went the thoughts whilst he smoked cigarette after cigarette.

He made one more attempt to get hold of Val. He left another message almost choking with anger. Just wait until he got hold of her! Then he remembered she was off that evening to the conference and that Basil was taking her to the airport.

No, Paul decided. Basil wasn't. He would.

Having made this decision he began to feel a little better. He checked the time, a quarter to one. He wasn't in any mood for lunch but a drink would be welcome. He started towards his drink cabinet just as Rachel buzzed through and said there was a Darina Lisle in reception wondering if she could have a word with him.

For a moment the name meant nothing, then he remembered Val telling him about the talented cook she'd asked to work on baby-food recipes for the range she wanted to launch. That bloody Basil wanted to launch!

'Tell her to come in,' he said. She probably wanted to discuss public relations possibilities for the new line. He remembered seeing her once on television. She'd come over very well and maybe he could persuade her to hire him for a personal publicity campaign. Paul rose, smoothed his hair into place and adjusted the set of his jacket.

She was a stunning girl, he thought as she came in, even better looking in the flesh than on the small screen. Blonde hair had always been one of his weaknesses. Val had been blonde when he first met her. When she'd gone back to her natural dark brown, saying the upkeep was more than she could afford, he'd told her it was a great mistake. It was soon after that she'd met Basil, who apparently preferred brunettes.

'Mr Robins, this is very kind of you.' Darina held out her hand to him.

It was a warm, dry hand that made him aware just how sweaty his was. 'I understand you are doing great things with baby food,' he said in an effort to get their meeting off to a comfortable start.

She looked a little startled. 'Oh, yes, of course,' she said. 'Val will have told you. I hope I can produce some good ideas.'

'I'm sure you will. Won't you sit down?' he asked her courteously.

'Thanks, but I wondered if I could offer you lunch,' she produced a most attractive smile.

Paul was taken aback, he was usually the one who offered a meal. Always because he wanted something.

What did she want? 'Lunch is a delightful idea,' he murmured. 'Do you have somewhere in mind?'

She shook her head. 'I was hoping you could suggest a place.'

'Why not? After all, this is my territory. Come with me.' He led the way out. 'Be back later,' he told Rachel on the way out.

'There's a very nice place just on the edge of town, by the river,' he said, opening the door to the car park. 'Do you mind if I drive you there?'

She appeared delighted by the suggestion and he enjoyed helping her into the low slung Porsche that was his pride and joy.

He didn't bother with small talk and she seemed content to sit quietly as he wove skilfully through the traffic until they reached a well-preserved beamed and thatched building that sat tranquilly by the river.

It was another Indian summer day and Darina enthusiastically endorsed his suggestion they sit outside.

'The food has something of a reputation,' he assured her as menus were brought and he ordered a whisky for himself and a mineral water for her.

'I'm driving,' she explained. Well, so was he but one whisky wasn't going to harm.

'Looks great,' she said, her eyes skimming the dishes on offer. 'What will you have?'

Which reminded him with a start that it was her lunch. What was this all about?

They both chose fresh scallops with grilled red peppers to start, followed by steak for him and a leek tart for her. 'And to drink?' she asked.

'Uh, I think just a glass of the house red,' he said. He

could always have another whisky back in the office if he needed it.

The garden sloped down to the river. A couple of dinghies lay on the grass in a far corner. 'I love the sound of water lapping banks, don't you?' said Darina while they waited for their food.

He nodded. 'My home is on the river, not far from here.' He'd had to pay a premium for the location but it had been worth it. With the way property was rising at the moment, it was going to prove an excellent invest-ment. Suddenly he couldn't wait for her to orchestrate their discussion. 'This is delightful, but I'm sure you haven't asked me out so we can look at moving water.'

Darina fixed him with an open gaze and said, 'I've been asked by Jemima Ealham to look into where her sister, Sophie, spent the last few months of her life. I've spoken to Nicola and Job Ealham and apparently you visited her while she was staying with them.'

Paul was so astonished that for a moment he couldn't speak. A range of emotions ran through him ending with a wave of nostalgia. He could see Sophie now, her small, trusting face with those marvellous brown eyes, hear the slightly breathy way she had of speaking that made him feel so strong and powerful. 'Yes,' he said slowly, 'I did.'

'Did you know her well?'

'I met Sophie when her father came to see Eat Well Foods. Basil Ealham had met Val at some function or other and thought her business sounded interesting.' Paul pushed away the memory of Val's excitement, how she'd impressed upon him that this man could be important to the company.

'And Sophie came too?' Darina asked and he realized he'd stopped speaking.

'I took her round the factory.' He smiled reminiscently. 'She seemed very interested, said it was just like their kitchen at home only multiplied. And she really enjoyed the sampling session at the end.'

'Did she like cooking?'

Paul shrugged. 'Never knew. Given her background, I thought it highly unlikely she knew one end of a rolling pin from the other.' He grinned at Darina, who smiled back at him.

'So you got on well together.'

'Famously.' What Paul didn't say was that the way Sophie had hung on his words had done his soul good. Particularly as he'd disliked her father on sight and he was quite sure the great Basil wouldn't approve of any relationship between the two of them. 'I took her out for a drink after that and to a couple of gigs I thought she'd enjoy. She liked up-beat music, you know?' Again, Paul failed to mention what a refreshing change taking a young, innocent girl around had been from the heady sophistication of a liaison with an older woman.

'Did she mention any friends?'

Paul thought briefly. 'Nah, I don't think she had any. Just a minute, there was one, Wiggy, was it? Some such silly name.'

'Tiggy Beauchamp was the girl she came out with.'

'Of course! Though I don't think Sophie was too impressed with her season.' He had a quick mental picture of Sophie in a skimpy, very short dress, putting her heart and soul into dancing with him at a disco, then flopping down with a Coke and saying, 'I haven't had so

252

much fun since, well, since I don't know when.' Her brightness had faded as she spoke.

'Did she let you know she was moving to her brother's?'

'Look, what is this?' he protested. 'You're sounding just like the police.'

'Oh, I'm sorry,' Darina looked distressed. 'I just want to find out all I can about Sophie.'

He capitulated, he could never resist women when they looked at him like that. 'Well, yes, she did.'

'So, she considered you a friend,' Darina said, her gaze sharp. 'Did she tell you why she was leaving home?'

Paul shook his head. He was suddenly conscious he hadn't asked Sophie many questions. She had been such a restful little thing and had always been so interested in him. The idea she'd thought him a friend was unbearably poignant. 'She said something about helping her brother with his family. It seemed, well, rather natural.' He looked at Darina then burst out with, 'Her father was hardly a sympathetic man!'

'Did Sophie tell you that?'

'No,' he admitted. 'But she seemed very much in awe of him. It was always, "my father wouldn't like this," or "my father always says."'

'Did she tell you she was thinking of leaving her brother's?'

'No,' he said positively. 'It was a shock to hear she'd disappeared.'

'How did you hear?'

'Val told me. She and Basil were seeing something of each other.' He swallowed as he remembered his chagrin at the time. He had a swift vision of Val in his bed, gloriously relaxed, running a finger down his spine and telling him, her voice all sultry, how Basil's precious younger daughter seemed to have disappeared. 'The poor man's distraught,' she'd said. 'I think he needs comforting so don't expect to see too much of me for a bit.' He could date the decline of his relationship with Val from that point.

'Did you ever think you might be Rory's father?'

Paul's mind reeled. 'Hey,' he said urgently. 'Don't go getting the idea that just because I took the girl out for a drink or two we made it to bed!'

'You're saying you never made love to Sophie Ealham?'

'Damn right I am!'

Chapter Nineteen

Back at Paul's office, Darina got out of the Porsche as elegantly as she could and said goodbye.

She started to walk back to her car, thinking about what she'd learned that morning.

Sophie had been a sweet girl who hadn't been too bright in the brain department but not backward. Darina was now certain of this. Cynthia Beauchamp would never have brought her out if she had been. Given maturity and confidence, Darina was sure she would have grown into the sort of person everyone wanted as a friend, sympathetic and intuitive, who would always spare the time to listen.

She'd obviously had more of a relationship with Paul Robins than anybody else had realized. Had it gone further than Paul claimed?

Martin, too, had obviously been attracted to Sophie. Darina thought she must have been the kind of girl who made any man feel better about himself, more attractive, more intelligent, and maybe nicer.

Everyone was hungry for approbation, everyone needed to feel better about themselves. Darina left the question of Sophie for a moment and asked herself if she was making William feel good about himself? And if not, was there a gap there for someone else to fill? A certain WDS perhaps? Darina had no very clear idea of how a police station operated but she was sure there'd be plenty of opportunity for a small, curvy, intelligent female sergeant to stroke her boss's ego.

Darina reached her car and told herself that jealousy was demeaning, degrading and had a nasty tendency to make things worse. Her job was to make sure William wanted to come home each night.

Then she sat in the driving seat and forced herself back to considering the mystery of Sophie's disappearance.

There were really several mysteries here. First, what had caused Sophie to leave Blackboys and go and live with Job and his family. Job seemed to think it was because Basil was pressuring her to act as hostess for him. But Tiggy had suggested she was upset at finding out he wasn't actually her father.

Was it true? Just because Jasper believed it was didn't prove anything.

It did make sense, though.

Quite apart from the detail of her name, Sophie had inherited nothing of Basil's blazing personality. Each of the other children had a cutting edge, even Jasper, that Sophie seemed to have lacked. Then there had been her mother's deep unhappiness. Darina had seen that herself. The fact that she hadn't left Basil did suggest he'd had some sort of hold on her.

The second mystery was why Sophie had left what seemed to have been a happy haven with Job and Nicola. Could either Paul or Martin have had anything to do with her disappearance? Darina could imagine the effect a passionate pass, for instance, could have on a sensitive girl but surely a word to Nicola or Job could have sorted things out and made sure she wasn't troubled again? No, it sounded much more as though Sophie had felt threatened. What by? Rape?

The word had come from nowhere and now reverberated in Darina's mind. Had Sophie been so sensitive she hadn't felt she could turn to her relations after such a violation? Perhaps she'd thought she mightn't be believed. Especially if it had been a family friend that had been responsible.

But Darina found it difficult to imagine the gentle Martin capable of rape. Paul, though, whilst on the surface coming over as someone rather weak, might just be the sort of man who, when insulted or cornered, could wind himself up into the sort of rage that precipitated rape.

But while Martin had been very tense during their talk in the embankment gardens, Paul had appeared relaxed. Darina was almost certain that Martin knew something he hadn't told her and that Paul had been completely open, about Sophie at any rate.

How strange both conversations should have taken place by the same river. But so much narrower and more attractive flowing by the restaurant than its dirty, if stately, progress through London.

Lastly there was the mystery of who Rory's father was. Poor Sophie, the result of one unfortunate affair giving birth as the result of another. For surely, whatever had happened it must have been unfortunate.

Jemima had stated that Rory was six weeks premature. Which meant that he had to have been conceived after Sophie left Job and Nicola. But what if he'd been only four week's premature, or even less? That would make it possible Sophie was already pregnant when she left Battersea and that Paul, for instance, could be Rory's father.

Rory had blond hair and blue eyes. Sophie's eyes and hair had both been brown. Paul had fair hair and blue eyes, less intense in colour than Rory's but perhaps the boy's would fade as he grew older. Paul was tall and Sophie had been short. What about Rory? You could tell from the length of a child's foot how tall he was likely to end up. Darina wished she had noticed the boy's feet. She looked at her watch. Nearly half past two. Could she call at Blackboys and check? It was so near. But if Jemima was at the office and a strange nanny was in charge, would Darina be allowed to see Rory and his gorgeous grin?

Forgetting that she didn't want anything to do with small children and refusing to acknowledge that a look at Rory's feet wasn't going to prove a thing, Darina let in the clutch and set off.

As she left the town behind, Darina could see autumn had well and truly arrived. Red hips and haws jewelled the hedgerows and the newly ploughed fields resembled dark brown corduroy. The late sun would soon be gone.

When she reached Blackboys, it was Jemima who opened the door. 'Oh, it's you!' she said, sounding both surprised and pleased. 'Thank God! Everything's total chaos here. The new nanny's just left, Dad's off on a business trip, Mrs Starr says it's not her job to look after Rory and you can't trust Jasper. Rory's furious because his lunch is late and I'm going out of my mind.'

She led the way through to the kitchen. Her feet were bare and she was wearing expensive looking designer jeans with a T-shirt.

Rory was in his high chair, banging the tray with a spoon and screaming, tears squeezing themselves out of screwed-up eyes, his cheeks flushed with temper.

At the other end of the table stood a stolid looking Mrs Starr, ignoring Rory as she fussed about making a cake, her lips firmly pressed together, an obstinate expression on her face. But her eyes were watchful.

'Oh, heavens,' groaned a harassed Jemima. 'Leave him for one minute and he thinks the world's come to an end.'

'Gah!' shrieked Rory, waving the spoon. 'Gah, gah, gah, raaaham!'

'OK, OK, OK!' Jemima went to the fridge and got out a small strawberry fromage frais. On a discarded plate Darina could see the remains of a fish finger. No gourmet baby foods in this house!

'Mrs Starr, are you sure you couldn't, just for a few days?' pleaded Jemima, sitting down beside the high chair and starting to push pink goo with astonishing efficiency down a now silent child who reached forward like a starving fledgling.

'Couldn't take the responsibility, miss,' Mrs Starr said firmly, carefully folding flour into a fruit-cake mixture.

'Well, do you think you could make us some coffee?' Jemima said, sounding at the end of her tether.

'Soon as I've got this in the oven, miss.' Mrs Starr gave the cake mixture a few more turns and reached for the prepared cake tin.

'I'll do it,' said Darina and filled the kettle.

Mrs Starr evened out the mixture, wrapped the tin with several layers of newspaper, secured them with string, placed the tin in a roasting pan lined with more paper, popped several layers of tin foil over the top and carefully placed the shrouded mixture into the oven. Then she got out two cups and saucers and started preparing the coffee tray, her lips firmly pressed together.

'Right, that's it,' announced Jemima as Rory gulped down the last of his dessert. 'It's rest time for you, my lad.' She hauled him up out of his high chair. 'Come upstairs with us,' she said to Darina. 'Take the coffee into the library, Mrs Starr, we'll have it there.'

Rory's room on the second floor was out of some fantasy child's kingdom. Murals from nursery rhymes decorated all the walls, there were silver stars on a blue ceiling, his cot was full of soft toys and a mobile of planes, space craft and shooting stars idly circled above.

When Rory realized he was being put into his cot, he howled, large tears sparkling on cheeks red with rage. Jemima tried to lay him down. He fought back and stood, screaming, clutching the top rail of the cot.

'You know you're tired,' Jemima told him coldly. 'What you need is a good sleep. Come on,' she said to Darina. 'As soon as we leave, he'll settle down.'

But Rory's outrage followed them down the stairs. In the library a tray of coffee stood on a low table. 'Heavens, I need this!' Jemima poured out the cups and handed one to Darina, then flopped into a chair. 'Christ, I must look a mess,' she muttered, pushing her short hair back from her face. 'This thing's got ketchup on it!' she pulled the T-shirt away from her chest in disgust, then levered herself swiftly up and walked with quick, jerky strides across to the window. 'I don't know what to do,' she said, sounding near to tears.

'Tell me about it,' Darina invited.

Jemima half sat on the narrow windowsill, her

hands gripping the wood, the knuckles white. 'I was nearly killed today,' she announced.

'What do you mean?' Darina couldn't be too alarmed, it was typical of the dramatic statements Jemima liked to make.

'I was crossing the road with Rory in his push chair and a car shot out of nowhere and nearly mowed us down!'

'Good heavens! Weren't you watching?'

'Of course I was! It was deliberate I tell you.' Jemima was near to tears. 'Dad says I've got to look after Rory while he's away, that we can't get another nanny until he gets back. I know what it is, he doesn't trust me to get the right girl. It's too much, Darina!'

'He trusts you to look after him,' Darina pointed out.

But Jemima wasn't listening. 'I'm not a nanny and I can't look after that boy night and day. And now this! I tell you, someone's after me.'

'It sounds like an accident,' Darina said comfortingly.

Jemima turned back to the window and started tapping it with her nail, staring at the leaves blowing down from the trees. 'I can't stay here and look after Rory, I've got to go, I've got to!' she repeated desperately. Then she swung round again, her face suddenly illuminated. 'Darina, this is your opportunity! Val told us yesterday that you're working on baby-food recipes for her. You take Rory and test your ideas. It's perfect!'

Oh, no, it wasn't! 'I don't know anything about babies,' Darina protested, listening to the screams that still floated down from upstairs. 'And what on earth would your father say?'

'Oh, he'd think it was a great idea! Anyway, he's all

excited about marrying Val. You know they announced their engagement last night?'

'Really?' Darina was startled, she hadn't thought Val would succumb to the lure of financial security. Then she told herself not to be cynical, after all, Val herself had said how attracted she was to Basil.

Jemima nodded. 'You better believe it. We had a family dinner here last night, champagne and the works. Val's daughter, Sally, came, all giggles and sucking up to Dad. He was thrilled, all over her as well as Val,' she said in disgust.

'Wasn't Val pretty pleased as well?'

'Oh, you know her, cool and contained. What Dad sees in her beats me.'

Darina remembered the hysterical woman in the kitchen. 'Jasper could tell you different,' she said.

'What do you mean? Jasper didn't say anything last night.'

So, he'd kept quiet about Val's loss of control. Darina warmed towards him. 'Well, why not get Val to look after Rory? After all, she'll have to after they get married, won't she?'

Jemima waved an impatient hand. 'She's going abroad tonight. Some conference or other.' She came back and flung herself into the chair again, her face pale and tense. 'Darina, you've got to. I'm frightened. Someone's after me. Leaving Rory with me means he's in danger too.'

Darina had never seen Jemima in such a state. There was a febrile excitement about her and her whole body was tense with some suppressed emotion. Was she really frightened for her life? Darina couldn't believe the traffic incident had been anything more than a near accident, after all, who could wish her dead? But Jemima didn't operate by the laws of logic.

Jemima leaned forward, hugging her upper arms, 'Please say you'll take Rory, Darina, please! Each for the other and never to rat, remember?'

Just suppose for a moment that the car had nearly run Jemima and Rory down deliberately. Just suppose that Darina's enquiries had frightened someone into trying to remove Jemima. Could she ever forgive herself if a second attack was successful? And Jemima did have a point about using Rory as a guinea pig for her baby-food ideas. A faint frisson of excitement ran through her as she thought of having the child all to herself. 'How long would it be for?' she asked cautiously.

'Oh, darling, that's wonderful, I knew I could count on you.' Jemima was instantly ecstatic, over the moon in her relief. 'Come upstairs and I'll get his things together, the sooner you take him over the better. He can sleep in the car.'

'Hang on a minute,' Darina protested. 'You do realize I won't be able to do any more poking around into where Sophie went and who could be his father while I have him with me, don't you?'

'Oh, you can still do that,' Jemima said airily. 'He plays perfectly happily by himself while you're on the phone and if you want to go out, you can take him with you.'

She made it all sound so simple!

'You'll have to tell me exactly what Rory's daily regime is, when he eats, when he has rests and goes to bed, when he should be taken out, all that.' Darina had only the dimmest idea of what an eighteen-month-old baby's life should be.

'Sure, Maeve wrote everything down for the next nanny and I made sure that stupid cow didn't take the instructions with her.'

It obviously took someone of character to remain in the Ealham employ for any length of time and Darina's respect for both Maeve and Mrs Starr increased.

Wondering if she was being a complete idiot, Darina followed Jemima up to the nursery, where Rory's screams had died down to a steady grizzle.

All Jemima seemed to think was necessary for her to take with the child was a packet of disposable nappies, some baby wipes and a change of clothes.

Darina had other ideas. 'How long before you get back from wherever it is you're going?'

'Only a few days. And if I'm not back by then, Dad will be.'

'Two days, that's my limit. After that you'd better have some other arrangement in place. Right, now I'll need far more clothes than that, and what about his cot? And his favourite toys? And that list Maeve made out?'

'Surely he can sleep in a bed?' Jemima argued. 'He's quite a big boy now.'

'Exactly,' Darina said grimly. 'If he's not in a cot, he'll be everywhere, I can't possibly leave his door closed. And what about a buggy? I can't carry him everywhere.'

'Big strong girl like you,' Jemima grumbled. But Darina refused to be deflected and finally Jemima agreed.

'What about a playpen?' Darina asked as Rory followed them down the stairs, negotiating the treads with confident agility. No longer forced to rest, he seemed to have recovered his temper and the angelic smile shone out.

'Oh, he doesn't like a playpen and Maeve said he was really too old for one.'

Darina sighed.

It took a good half hour to get everything together Darina felt she needed to take with her. Finally she and Jemima loaded everything into the back of the large Volvo station-wagon that was more used to coping with quantities of food than baby impedimenta.

'You'll need his car seat.' Jemima shot off round the house and came back carrying a padded plastic shell. She showed Darina how to fix it on the seat of her Volvo and together they strapped Rory in. 'One more thing.' Jemima was off again, back into the house.

Darina and Rory were left looking at each other. Rory had a most peculiar expression on his face. Darina, panicking, felt he was summing up the situation.

Jemima returned. 'If he gets very grizzly, try him with some of these.' She dropped several little boxes of raisins into Darina's hand. 'He loves them.'

Fruits of the sun, she thought, just the thing, concentrated sweetness and vitamins. 'You'd better tell me where you're going.'

Jemima shook her head. 'I don't even know myself. Look, you've got my mobile number and I've got yours so we can keep in touch. I promise you it will be all right. And you'll enjoy looking after Rory, he's a poppet.'

'If that's the case, why aren't you taking him with you?' Darina shot back.

'Darling, look what a performance it is.' Jemima gave a meaningful glance at the loaded back of the car. Now that it had all been organized, she seemed to have forgotten that she was frightened.

'Don't let anyone know you've got him,' Jemima said suddenly.

'I thought it was yourself you were frightened for. Who on earth do you think would try to harm him?' Darina didn't like this at all.

'I don't know, darling. But Dad's got pots of money, someone could be trying to kidnap him.' It was the first thing she'd said that made any sense.

Jemima reached up and hugged Darina. 'You're the greatest, really you are. I won't forget this.' Then she stuck her head through the open window and gave her nephew a kiss. 'Bye, Rory, be a good boy now. Gotta go,' she said and vanished.

Darina got into the car and looked at Rory. 'It's you and me now, kiddo. Whadya think?'

His eyelids drooped and a moment later he was asleep.

Thank the Lord, Darina thought and drove home very carefully.

Chapter Twenty

'And so you're convinced that Gerry Aherne was trying to blackmail Paul Robins?' William said. He'd returned in the mid-afternoon from a meeting with Superintendent Roger Marks to find Terry Pitman and Pat James waiting to tell him the results of the interviews they'd carried out that morning.

'Right, guv,' agreed Terry.

'And what's your opinion, sergeant?' William turned to Pat. She was looking particularly attractive that day, in a cinnamon coloured two-piece of some sort with a bright coral coloured scarf at her neck. It was peculiarly soothing the way he knew he could turn to her and not get a spiky response.

Still, since this case had come along, the team had at last begun working together, forgetting to feel aggrieved at being asked to pull their finger out.

'Yes, I think Aherne probably was,' Pat said quietly.

That was a surprise, somehow William hadn't expected Pat to back her colleague. In fact he was amazed they were still speaking to each other.

'I don't think, though, that Robins clocked him one,' Pat continued and gave Terry the sort of glance that said they'd disagreed strongly on this.

'Honestly, guv,' said Terry quickly, 'the bloke's got

all the motivation. First off, Aherne's threatening the existence of the firm. One word to Ealham his girlfriend has an arrangement with Robins and he takes his money elsewhere. Second off, if that happens, he loses not only his girlfriend but his money as well. His PR company will be looking pretty sick too; by his own admission Eat Well Foods is his major client!'

'All that could be said to go for the Douglas woman as well,' Pat said quietly. She looked at William. 'Ealham told you they both took sleeping pills. How far is it from Blackboys to the industrial estate? At that time of night, twenty minutes, no more. Allowing time to slosh around some petrol and strike a match, say an hour round journey. Neither of them can alibi the other.'

'The story Robins tells of investing money in her firm without shares or any formal acknowledgement certainly puts her into a rather different light,' William said slowly, remembering the charming woman they had interviewed. He would not have thought her capable of such devious behaviour. 'But we only have Robins's word that he did, indeed, invest his money in the firm.'

'If he was lying, he's a fantastic actor, guv,' said Terry.

Pat nodded as though she agreed with this. 'But if he isn't, and I doubt it myself, what a cool lady Douglas is. Talk about butter, ice cream would remain frozen in her mouth.'

William could only agree with her. 'Right,' he said. 'Terry, look into the bank accounts of both Robins and Douglas. See if you can match any outgoings with the monies that have been paid into Aherne's account. And see if you can find any trace of the money Robins claims he invested with Eat Well Foods. I can't see any justification at the moment for looking into Ealham's accounts, we'll encounter considerable opposition and I have no doubt that his cash drawings could easily hide any payments to Aherne. But we have a classic triangle here: Douglas, Ealham and Robins. Any of them could have an excellent reason for silencing a blackmailer. Sergeant, you and I will visit Douglas again.' He looked at his watch, half past four. 'She's off to some international conference tonight or tomorrow. Ring her now and say we need to speak to her immediately. Call her mobile number.'

Pat went off to phone, returning in a few minutes. 'She's at her flat, guv, packing for her trip. She says she could see us now if it's really urgent. Very helpful she sounded.'

Val Douglas would, William thought. That lady had managed to get where she was today by giving the impression of sweet co-operation. Inside, he was beginning to suspect, she was hard as tungsten.

There were one or two other details he had to attend to before they could leave, though, and by the time he and Pat set off, it was nearly five o'clock.

'How are you getting along with Terry?' he asked as Pat drove them to Val Douglas's flat.

'We're speaking,' Pat said without expression.

'He's a good detective,' William said, 'but tact is not one of his strong points.'

'Tact? He acts like a giant hedgehog determined to push people out of his path, all spikes and shove,' Pat said bitterly. 'He's the type who believes women are only good for two things and I'm not going to spell them out.'

'Most of it's due to his background,' William said after

a brief pause for thought. He didn't approve of revealing personal facts about officers but in this case he was certain it was the right thing to do. 'What I'm going to tell you is in confidence, I don't want it spread around the station.'

'Right, guv,' Pat said eagerly.

'Terry's mother abandoned him and his two younger brothers when he was six years old. His father took to drink, couldn't keep things together and the two younger boys ended up in care. Terry remained with the father. I believe there were a couple of failed relationships with other women but basically he was brought up without a mother by an alcoholic.'

Pat was silent for several minutes. 'It explains a lot,' she said finally. 'Thanks for telling me, guv. I shan't let it get around.'

He thought he could rely on her.

Then she said, 'By the way, guv, I missed a detail in my report on our interview with the nanny.'

William listened to her in dismay as she revealed the slip. How could he have failed to spot it? He'd always prided himself on his memory. Almost as bad was the fact that Pat revealed Terry Pitman was aware he'd missed something.

He spent the rest of the journey fuming in silence.

'This is it, guv.' Pat pulled up outside a respectable looking but by no means luxurious block of flats. Built in the thirties, William decided. The expanse of lawn around the block was more generous than would have been allowed in modern times but it needed cutting and weeds were growing out of the low wall running alongside the pavement.

According to the list in the foyer, Val Douglas lived on the top floor. A creaky lift took them up.

As they came out, they could hear two voices raised in argument, one male, one female. Then a front door opened and a very angry Basil Ealham emerged. 'You're a bitch, you know that? I'm not going to accept this!' Then he saw William. 'My God, what do you want now?' he shot at him, strode over to the lift and pressed the button. The doors opened immediately, he entered, the doors closed and he was gone.

Left standing in the doorway was Val Douglas, her hair mussed and lipstick smeared. She looked very upset as she stared at William. 'I'd forgotten you were coming,' she said abruptly. 'You'd better come in. I warn you, I haven't got long.' She went back inside the flat.

William suddenly became aware that the door of the next flat was slightly ajar. As he looked, a bright eye met his. Then the door slowly closed with a slight click.

He followed Pat through a small hall and into Val Douglas's living room.

This was square, without distinguishing features and furnished with more taste than cash. It looked as though redecoration had been needed for so long its owner had given up even thinking about it.

Val waved the two police officers towards a small sofa and a button back chair. She took the only armchair. She didn't offer them refreshment but sat biting her lip.

'A lover's tiff?' William offered.

Her eyes looked as though she'd been crying. 'None of your business.'

'If it affects the Eat Well Foods company I'm afraid it probably is,' he said calmly.

'My God, you want your pound of flesh, don't you?'

she said and sighed. 'I suppose everyone will know soon enough. I've broken off my engagement to Basil.'

'We didn't know you were engaged,' Pat said quietly.

She switched her gaze to the sergeant. 'Oh, yes, it happened yesterday. We had an official dinner last night. All the family, well, not quite all. My daughter Sally came,' her voice softened for an instant. 'She was really pleased I'd, as she puts it, found happiness. My other daughter is in Australia. Then we had Jemima and Jasper. Basil rang Job and Nicola but they declined the invitation. However, he said they sent their good wishes.' Her voice now was sardonic, almost sarcastic. 'We managed without them. Dom Perignon, Beluga Caviar, fillet of venison (so much more recherché than beef, my dear), and soufflé Rothschild with real gold leaf. It was quite a meal.'

She made it sound as though the trappings had been more important than the reason for the celebration. Had she wanted a quiet evening à deux with her fiancé? Had the family not proved as welcoming to the news as she'd hoped? The change in her voice as she'd mentioned Basil's children had been almost dramatic.

William had spoken to each of them and each had confirmed that Val had spent the night of the fire at Blackboys. Jemima had come over as intelligent, not particularly in favour of her father's liaison, as she'd termed it, but acknowledging she had little say in the matter. She'd said her father and Val had been in bed by the time she herself had returned around one thirty in the morning.

Jasper had been equally frank and told them he was merely living at home until he could afford to set up his own establishment. 'This rather spoils you for the starving artist in a garret syndrome,' he'd said, encompassing the comforts of Blackboys with a wave of his hand. 'But as soon as my first substantial advance comes through, I'll be off. The old man can do what he likes.' Then he'd added, 'So, to answer your question, I was out until about eleven thirty Wednesday evening. No one was around when I got back. I went to bed and knew nothing more until morning.' It had all been said with an insouciance that suggested nothing his father did really mattered to him. So neither Jemima nor Jasper had actually seen Val but there was no good reason to doubt she and Basil hadn't been in bed as they claimed and were there when the call about the fire had come through.

'So you had a family celebration last night,' Pat said to Val. 'What went wrong today?'

'Oh, that was nothing,' she said with a fine attempt at lightness. 'By the time I get back on Monday, it'll all have blown over.'

William cleared his throat. 'Paul Robins has stated he invested one hundred thousand pounds in your company. Is that true?'

He'd expected her to deny all knowledge. Instead she slowly nodded. 'Yes, when I was first organizing the factory.'

'But we haven't found his name in the list of shareholders,' said Pat sharply.

'I used a nominee name,' Val said easily.

Pat leafed back through her book and read out a list of some six names. The last was Kate Douglas Ltd.

Val nodded. 'That's my elder daughter. Her shares and Paul's were invested together as a company. It was a tax move suggested by the accountant I had at the time.' Her gaze was limpid, full of candour.

Pat looked again at her notebook. 'The list of shareholder names for Kate Douglas Ltd does not contain that of Paul Robins,' she told Val.

Val looked fleetingly disturbed. 'It doesn't? I know Paul signed the right documents. Oh, dear, it's so long ago, at least three years. You'll have to ask my accountant about it, he handled all the ins and outs. He always has such good ideas for saving tax – within the law of course,' she added, sending them a glance from under her eyelids that William could only call coy.

'Perhaps you'll give me his name?' Pat raised her pencil.

Val went over to the desk and let down the front. Behind all looked neatly arranged, documents in the little niches, some papers on the base. She picked up an address book and leafed through it, then looked at William with wide eyes. 'I'm sorry, I've just remembered, he moved and I had his new address in the office. It's probably gone in the fire. That damned fire!'

'Just give us his name, I'm sure we can track him down,' he said steadily.

'Piers Maurice,' she said quickly. 'And Shaz, my secretary, knows where he is, she can give you the details tomorrow.'

What was the woman doing? Trying to cover up a devious plot to embezzle Robins's money, or revealing herself as someone who had little idea of accountancy? Whichever, it was interesting and suggested that Paul Robins had been speaking the truth.

'I'd like to return to the night of the fire in Eat Well

Foods,' William said. 'You say you spent both the evening and the night with Basil Ealham?'

She nodded. 'As I told you, I arrived at Blackboys about eight o'clock. Originally I had other plans. But Basil returned from abroad early and I cancelled them after he rang me at lunchtime.' She picked at the crease of her smart jeans. 'We had a quiet supper together, talked about plans for a new baby-food line for my company then went to bed about midnight.' She looked up at William. 'And that was it until my mobile rang at about five o'clock in the morning.'

'You slept in a double bed?' he asked.

She nodded again.

'Did you take a sleeping pill?'

Her eyes were suddenly alert, as if she saw where the questions were leading. 'Yes, I was very tired.'

'The phone woke you?'

'No, Basil did.'

'Then he's a fairly light sleeper?' William suggested.

A momentary hesitation before she nodded.

'But that night he says he took a sleeping pill as well.'

She shrugged. 'If that's what he says, then he did. Perhaps his aren't as strong as mine.'

'So if Mr Ealham left the bed while you were sleeping, you wouldn't be aware of the fact?' It was almost a statement.

'No,' she whispered, her eyes huge. 'Are you suggesting Basil set fire to my factory?' She plucked nervously again at her jeans.

'We're just investigating possibilities,' William told her.

'Well, even if I was sleeping deeply, I'm sure I would have known if he'd left the house!' She said it with an air of bravado.

The confidence with which she'd faced his questioning a week earlier seemed to have vanished. Because she'd had a row with Basil? And just which one of them had broken off the engagement?

'How long are you going to be away?' asked William abruptly.

'Away?' she repeated as though not quite understanding what he was saying. 'Oh, of course, the conference! I'll be back on Monday. I have to get ready,' she said abruptly. 'I have a taxi coming to take me to the airport.'

'You weren't expecting Mr Ealham to take you?' William asked, surprised.

'No, his plane leaves from Heathrow, mine from Gatwick.'

'We'd like to know where you can be contacted,' he said.

'Of course.' She went to the desk again. 'This has got all the details.' She handed William a leaflet promoting an international conference on food intolerances. 'I just hope you can find who was responsible for poor Gerry's death before I return.' Her voice was clipped, her mind obviously now on catching her plane.

Was he wise, letting her leave the country like this? But William knew he'd already decided that there was little risk. She would come back all right.

'What did you think, sergeant?' he asked as Pat drove them back to the station.

'That was a very different woman from the one we saw before.'

'Which one do you think broke the engagement and do you think they'll be getting together again?'

'Oh, it was her!' Pat was positive. 'He wouldn't have been nearly so angry if he'd called it off. He was a man who'd been thwarted and he didn't like it one bit. As to whether it will all be on again, that was a very angry man we saw. But she no doubt knows him better than we do.'

'That's true,' said William. 'But I'd say it'll be some time before he calms down.'

At the station, he left Pat writing up her notes and said he'd see her tomorrow. He knew she'd hoped he'd ask her out for a drink but he was exhausted. All he wanted was to get home and have Darina provide him with one of her delicious little meals, a glass of wine and an early night.

The hall seemed remarkably cluttered as he opened the front door. Before he could work out why, he heard a child crying. A very angry child. The noise came from the spare room next to his and Darina's. 'What the hell?' he said, taking the stairs two at a time.

The bed had been pushed aside and a cot faced the doorway.

A small child stood grasping the cot rail and crying noisily. The moment he realized he had an audience he raised the pitch of his voice, creasing his hot, flushed face into a mask of thwarted passion. The noise echoed round William's brain, preventing thought.

'Oh, darling, you're back!' said Darina from behind him.

'What on earth's going on?'

'I'm babysitting Rory for a couple of days. I can't get him to settle at all, I thought this might help!' She held up a cassette player. 'I haven't got any nursery rhymes but maybe this will do the trick!' She plugged the little machine in, set it near the cot and pressed a button. Mendelssohn's *Hebrides Overture* filled the room.

Rory continued to howl.

'I can't stand this,' William said abruptly. He picked the child up.

Rory stopped crying but his body shook as he continued to take deep, hiccuping breaths. He leant his head against William's chest. William sat down on the bed and held him gently.

'Is that a good idea?' Darina asked anxiously. 'Won't he just start crying again when you put him down?'

'We can't have him screaming away like that. Let's take him downstairs.'

'I don't really know what's best,' Darina said, sounding most unlike her normally decided self. 'I thought first he wasn't ready to go down, he slept in the car coming back. So I took him out and played with him. Twice. But each time I put him back, the screaming started again. I thought maybe if I left him he'd go off. But it just got worse. I don't think he's ever left Blackboys before.'

'Poor boy,' William said, liking the feel of the child in his arms. Rory had quietened right down now and was gazing fascinated at the cassette player. 'Let's go and have something to eat, shall we?' He rose and carried the boy downstairs.

The table in the kitchen was laid for two. 'Can you get us some wine? I daren't put him down,' he said as he settled himself in his usual place with the boy on his lap.

But Rory insisted on being lowered to the ground, then went straight for a cardboard box beside the fridge that appeared to contain a variety of toys. He pulled out several cars, a bag of building blocks and a bright yellow plastic telephone.

'He doesn't seem to be sleepy at all,' William remarked, watching as Rory made the telephone ring, again and again. 'What on earth are you doing babysitting?' he added after a moment. 'I thought you didn't like children.'

Darina poured out two glasses of wine then put on a pan of water and brought some prepared runner beans out of the fridge. 'I never said I didn't like children,' she protested, pushing her long hair back behind her ears. 'I just said I didn't want them yet. And every minute Rory's here, confirms that. He takes over totally.'

William watched Rory abandon the telephone, pick up a large motor car and bring it to him, knocking it hard on his knees.

'He wants you to wind it up,' Darina explained, heating a sauce on the stove. 'He's used to having every wish immediately gratified.'

'OK, lad, here you go.' William wound the key, set the car on the floor and watched it zoom off towards the kitchen door. Rory scampered after it, clapping his hands with glee.

It took four goes of that before Darina was able to place plates of hot ham with an orange sauce and the runner beans on the table.

'No, darling,' said Darina to Rory as he banged his car against William's knee again. 'You play with your bricks.' She started building a tower with the blocks, then left it to sit down and have her supper.

Rory proceeded to make clear that he wanted his car wound up again.

Somehow they managed to eat their supper and keep Rory amused.

William found the whole story of why Darina had brought the boy home quite odd. 'But Basil Ealham can afford to employ any number of nannies,' he said when she'd finished. 'So why doesn't he?'

'He's off on a business trip somewhere, doesn't know Jemima's gone away.' Darina sounded as doubtful as he was over the situation.

'That's another thing. Why on earth should she think someone's out to get her? Come on, darling, there's something here you're not telling me.'

He then listened with increasing incredulity as she told him how Jemima had hired her to find out who Rory's father was. Darina was mixed up in his murder case and she hadn't told him anything about it. William felt all his tiredness and frustration with their lack of progress build up in his chest like steam in an engine.

'So, instead of devoting yourself to your career, which is the reason you've given me for not starting a family, you're following futile leads in a way that threatens an official murder investigation,' he said coldly.

Rory looked up from the edifice he was building on the floor and started to cry. Darina picked him up and sat him on her lap, where he grizzled and fidgeted. 'I knew you'd object, that's why I didn't tell you.' She removed a long hank of cream coloured hair from Rory's little fist. 'I couldn't see that it had anything to do with your case. And you wouldn't discuss anything with me.' Darina sounded as angry as William felt. 'Ever since you started this job you've come home late, tired and ill-tempered. Why on earth shouldn't I try and find out something about Sophie's life before she died? It can't have anything to do with the fire in Val Douglas's factory, even if Paul Robins was involved with her.'

The name struck through the fog which was growing around William's anger and threatened to break his control.

'What do you mean? Are you saying Paul Robins was involved with Sophie Ealham?'

'Only that he took her out,' Darina said in a low voice as she reached down for one of Rory's toys to try to distract him. 'They met when Basil took her along on his first visit to Eat Well Foods.'

'You found this out and never told me?' William couldn't believe it.

'I haven't had a chance. I only spoke to him today.'

Rory looked from one to other of them and started crying again.

'Doesn't he ever sleep?' William asked furiously.

Chapter Twenty-One

Darina was wakened by the alarm. Her arm groped for the button and for a moment she lay there in the silence and wondered why it should feel so blessed.

Then she remembered. They'd gone to bed not speaking to each other. No sooner had Darina managed to drift off than Rory had started up.

'Oh, for Christ's sake,' William had said.

Darina had lain still and hoped Rory would go back to sleep. William had drawn the duvet over his ears.

After a few minutes Darina had slipped out of bed and gone through to Rory. He was sitting up in his cot, his face flushed and tear streaked, smelling. She got him up and changed him, wrinkling her nose as she removed the dirty nappy and wiped his bottom. 'Poor boy,' she said as his crying died down to the odd snivel. 'You must have been so uncomfortable.' She re-poppered his sleeping suit and picked him up. He felt warm and alive and his blue eyes looked back at her with interest. 'Time for beddy-bies,' she said and laid him in the cot again bracing herself for more cries. For a moment he looked unblinkingly up at her, then his eyelids dropped and he was asleep.

Darina stood there for several minutes looking at the long lashes that brushed perfect skin, the little hands closing and unclosing themselves like pale sea anemones beside his small, beautifully formed ears. Life starts with such simple demands, she thought: love, food, sleep and cleanliness equal happiness. Then, suddenly, it's all complicated. What happens?

Look at her, she thought miserably. Her life was in a complete mess and her relationship with William rapidly deteriorating. Soon they wouldn't be speaking to each other and she had this terrible feeling little Pat James was consoling him down at the station. Her food writing was getting nowhere and ideas were drying up. This investigation into Rory's parentage was annoying William and getting nowhere. Every time she thought she might have something, it slipped through her fingers. She was finding it more and more difficult to concentrate on getting behind what facts she had because she was worrying about her life and William's, not Sophie's. At the moment if the answer to the question of who Rory's father was burst in front of her three times lifesize, she doubted she could recognize it.

Wearily she went back to bed, to find William scratching his leg in his sleep. She gently took his hand away, found the tube of cream on his bedside table and carefully rubbed a little into the red and angry patch on the hairy flesh. Then lay down and closed her eyes.

It had seemed no more than minutes before Rory woke her again. This time William flung back the bedclothes and stomped off to the spare room. A few minutes later the crying had stopped and he was back. 'I put on the music, he seems to like that,' he said, slipping back into bed – and starting to scratch his leg again.

'Darling, do go and see that homoeopathic doctor, please?'

She could feel him stiffen beside her. 'How the hell do you think with a murder investigation on, I can find time to go and see a quack,' he ground out.

'It might help you, really!'

He turned away from her, humped up under the duvet and said nothing. But he had stopped scratching.

The next time Rory started, Darina was awake and next door in an instant and this time she took him back to bed with her. Now here he was, his little body lying between herself and William, still asleep.

'It seems very quiet, Rory not awake yet?' William groaned beside her.

'Look,' she said and showed him the baby.

William looked. 'You little monster,' he said. 'So that's what disturbed nights are all about.'

'He didn't seem to disturb you very much,' Darina said.

'No,' he admitted. 'After I turned on his music that time I never heard a thing. Tired, I suppose. Just shows . . .' His voice trailed off.

'Shows what?'

'How sometimes you don't know whether someone's in the bed with you or not,' he said without further explanation.

Rory woke just as William was leaving the house.

Darina was amazed at how long it took her to get a small child up, changed and fed. By the end of the process, coming on top of her disturbed night, she felt like a piece of linen after a day in the tropics, crumpled, flagging and not fit for use.

She consulted the piece of paper, written in a large,

unformed hand, that detailed Rory's regime. At some stage in the morning, it said, Rory would need a rest. So would she! Useless to imagine she could do any work.

It was another fine early autumn day.

The question was, should she abandon the search for Rory's father in the face of William's opposition.

No, she couldn't see how it could cut across his investigation into the food factory fire.

Darina went and found a jacket for Rory, fastened him into his car seat, put the baby buggy in the boot and set off for Ladbroke Grove. As she'd hoped, he had a sleep on the way there. She found somewhere to park, worked out how to open the buggy, then unfastened his seat belt. He opened his eyes and gave her his best grin, waving his arms and talking excitedly in his own special language.

Darina fastened him into the buggy and set off.

It was amazing how having a baby along made everything both so much easier and took so much more time.

Everyone wanted to talk to Rory. And he played up to his audience like a pro, smiling, clapping his hands and wanting to stroke dogs. Shopkeepers, assistants, restaurateurs, they all loved him. Which meant they wanted to give him a sweet, or a biscuit, anything. Darina had to work at persuading them to look at Sophie's photograph. She slipped the offerings into her pocket, 'for later', dreading a return of his tantrums of the previous evening.

But he seemed to have settled down. Nothing disturbed his temper. Half-way through the morning he even fell asleep again, his head on one side, his arms flopping as she manoeuvred the buggy up and down pavements and steps, into and out of shops.

Darina had no more luck that morning than she'd had before. No one she spoke to could remember seeing Sophie. She began to feel sorry for police who had to conduct house-to-house inquiries and longed for someone, anyone, to say they recognized the girl in the photograph. Was this exercise going to be a complete waste of time?

Lunchtime neared.

There wasn't much more of this part of Ladbroke Grove to cover. Darina found herself outside a small restaurant that offered reasonably priced French food, made a quick decision and entered.

'Do you mind babies?' she asked the young girl who came forward.

'*Mais, non!*' she said. 'He is so beautiful.' Nobody else was in the restaurant yet and the girl fussed over settling Rory into a high chair she produced from the back. Darina wondered just how many restaurants there were in London that would welcome a child so whole-heartedly.

She looked at the menu. Lamb and herb sausages, she was assured, were made in house, and served with julienne of courgette and carrot. Darina reckoned Rory could eat all that and ordered an adult- and a child-sized portion.

The sausages were delicious. Darina cut one into tiny pieces with the courgette and carrot and Rory ate his with gusto. Then she considered dessert. All the experts said it wasn't good to give small children food with a high sugar content. Which meant a chocolate terrine with a coffee crème anglaise had to be turned down. Likewise the raspberry sorbet. But they did have some fresh strawberries. Darina ordered a portion and mashed up a little with cream for Rory, which went down well. Darina ate the rest of the strawberries herself without cream. Babies might need fat, she definitely didn't.

As they ate, she talked to Rory. 'The seasoning of the sausage is really excellent,' she told him. 'Can you tell exactly what's in there?' He looked back at her with wide eyes and she was sure he shook his head. 'Not sure I can,' she said delightedly. 'But I think there's definitely some onion and parsley, a little fresh coriander and just a hint of tarragon. Ah, I see you agree with me.' Rory chuckled at her and opened his mouth for more.

Altogether Darina found she was enjoying herself hugely. While they ate, the restaurant filled up around them and Rory drew interested looks. No Prada bag or Gucci belt would have drawn such attention.

When the waitress brought her bill, Darina showed her the snapshot of Sophie.

'I'm sorry, I work here only short time. I ask for you.' She disappeared out to the back.

'He come soon,' she told Darina a few minutes later.

'Soon' proved an optimistic forecast. Normally she wouldn't have minded waiting but keeping Rory amused proved more and more difficult as he got bored with being in the high chair. She tried letting him get down and wander about but a couple of businessmen were far from amused when he pulled at one of their trousered legs. She rescued him with many apologies, took Rory back to the table, sat him on her lap and offered him the cruets to play with. Then let him go through her handbag. Just as the entire contents had been placed on the table and she was thinking she'd have to give up, a middle-aged man in a checked shirt and jeans came to the table. A large hand placed the snapshot on the table in front of Darina. 'This girl not work here,' he said and his accent was also French, 'but maybe I see her. Why you want to know?'

So used was Darina to receiving a negative response to her enquiries, for a moment she failed to take in what he'd said. Then it sank in.

'This is her son,' she said eagerly as the man ruffled Rory's hair. 'She was called Sophie. Unfortunately, she died giving birth and I'm trying to find out where she was living and working before that. It was some-where round here,' she added.

The man ran a thick finger down Rory's cheek. 'Beautiful boy.'

'She ate in here, did she?'

'Maybe.' He picked up the snapshot again and studied it, glancing at Rory as though to detect a likeness.

Something was holding him back from telling her more.

'Was she with anyone?'

'Yes,' he said, almost reluctantly.

'A man?'

No hesitation now. 'Of course.' His look said for a girl as lovely as Sophie not to have been with a man would have been against nature.

'Young, middle-aged, old?'

The Frenchman gave her a self-deprecating smile, 'I say he not old, he about my age.' He twinkled at her. Then it was as though he'd come to a decision. 'He often in here. Sometimes with wife. But two, three times with this girl.' He tapped the snapshot.

'Do you know his name?'

Again the hesitation. 'No, mademoiselle, no, I do not.'

That was nonsense, of course he knew the man's name. But if he was a regular customer, the restaurateur probably wouldn't want to tell her.

She decided to try her luck. 'Monsieur Price will be very glad you are so discreet,' she said.

He was very still for the briefest of moments. Then, 'Mademoiselle, I do not say it is Monsieur Price.'

'No, I understand,' she assured him with a big smile. 'Come, Rory, we've got to go. The meal was delicious,' she added, setting the boy on the floor.

The *patron* came and helped her sort out the levers of the buggy. In no time Rory was settled back in his seat and Darina was on her way.

Back in her car, Darina got out her mobile and rang Martin Price. 'I've got to see you again,' she told him without ceremony.

'There's nothing more I can tell you,' he protested.

'I think there is. I've just had lunch at *La Bonne Auberge* just off Ladbroke Grove.'

There was a long silence. Then a tired voice said, 'All right, where do you want to meet?'

'The embankment gardens where we walked.' She looked at her watch. 'In three quarters of an hour.'

'I've got a meeting,' he said.

'Cancel,' she said shortly. 'It can't wait. Of course, I could always call on your wife,' she added as he started to protest.

She felt a heel but what else was she to do? She

couldn't possibly meet him after work, who'd look after Rory? By then he'd be needing to be bathed and have his supper. And she needed to wrap up this investigation so she could get out of William's hair.

Martin Price made up his mind. 'All right, but make it in an hour,' he said.

'OK,' she agreed and rang off before he could think of any more conditions.

It wasn't difficult to find a free parking meter on the embankment.

Rory had fallen asleep during the drive from Ladbroke Grove, the motion of the car seemed to be a great soporific, and he hardly woke as Darina manoeuvred him out of his seat and into the buggy. Strapped into place, he surveyed the world through half-closed eyes as she pushed him along the pavement towards the gardens. She was getting quite used now to avoiding hazards such as shopping baskets and briefcases, all liable to knock the side of the buggy or attract Rory's curious attention.

By the time they reached the gardens, Rory was awake and looking around him with interest. 'Dog!' he said suddenly. Darina was sure it was 'dog' and not his favourite 'da'. He pointed to a perky little szchitzu with a pink bow holding up the long hair on its head, the rest of its coat cut short for summer wear.

Darina got Rory out of the buggy and held him by the hand as he set off towards the little dog. Its owner appeared to be a well-dressed middle-aged woman. 'Come on, Puzzle,' she said, yanking on a long lead, as Rory lurched towards the dog with happy cries.

'Can he say hello?' asked Darina.

After a moment's pause, the woman smiled and

stopped, allowing Rory to pat the small animal, who frisked enchantingly and tried to lick his face. Rory, backed away with excited squeals, then came forward again, his hands outstretched.

Suddenly someone shouted out, 'Hey, isn't that your buggy?'

Darina turned, to see a couple of teenagers in jeans, baggy T-shirts and shaved heads moving off with Rory's chariot.

'Stop!' she cried. 'That's mine!' Then she scooped up Rory and dashed after them.

The two boys gathered speed, heading for the exit next to the Savoy Hotel. Normally fast, Darina found herself hampered by having to carry Rory. She made up for her lack of speed by shouting at the top of her voice, 'Stop! Thief!' in a time-honoured manner. Heads turned as she charged past but nobody seemed willing to help. In her arms Rory started to cry. She clutched him tighter and tried to run faster.

Then, just as she thought they'd get away, a burly man coming in the opposite direction grabbed at the buggy. 'Not yours,' he said and wrenched it away, holding it in front of him like a combined shield and weapon.

For a moment the youngsters hesitated, assessing the possibilities.

He hefted the buggy challengingly, his shoulders broad under his bright blue anorak, his bony face threatening. 'Don't mix with us, mister,' one cried and they darted off.

'Oh, thank you,' Darina gasped. 'I only took my eye off it for a moment. I never realized . . !' She collapsed on to a bench with Rory and tried to soothe him.

'Can't afford to take your eye off anything these days,' the man grunted. 'All right, are you?'

'Yes, thanks,' she said, then saw Martin approaching. 'Here's my friend!'

The man looked at Martin with an uncertain expression. And Darina had to admit that with his creased face, narrow shoulders and grey suit he looked the sort of ineffectual man who'd be useless in a crisis. 'OK, if you're sure you're all right, I'll be off,' her rescuer said and left, walking with firm steps, hands in pockets.

Martin hadn't noticed anything. 'Sorry I'm late,' he said, sounding as out of breath as she was. 'Damn phone wouldn't stop ringing.'

'Not to worry,' she said and set a wriggling Rory on the ground. She felt she knew how Jemima had got into such a state. What if those youngsters had wanted to snatch Rory instead of just his buggy?

Martin sat himself down with a small sigh and watched the boy set off in the direction of some pigeons. They fluttered off and settled again a little way away. Rory followed. Darina went and grabbed his hand. The buggy incident had thoroughly unsettled her. 'You'll never catch them,' she said as she led him back to the bench. She sat down, took a ball from her bag and threw it very gently towards him. 'I need one of those retractable dog leads,' she told Martin.

He looked at the fair-haired boy. 'Is he yours?' he asked.

Rory pounced on the ball with delight and staggered forward with it to Darina. 'Can't you guess who he is?' she said.

Martin took the ball from her and Rory fixed his big blue eyes on him and moved away, excitedly clapping his hands together, waiting for him to throw it. But Martin just sat looking at the child. 'Sophie's,' he said and it wasn't a question. 'Sophie's son.'

'Yes,' said Darina.

Rory ran forward and grabbed at the ball, chattering away. Then he tried to throw it. The ball dropped more or less at his feet.

Darina scooped him up, sat him on her lap and felt in the pocket of her jacket for one of the tiny boxes of raisins Jemima had given her.

Martin's attention was on the child, the deep pouches under his eyes prominent as he stared at him. 'I knew, of course, that she'd had him before she died.'

'Poor Sophie,' said Darina, feeling the solid round-ness of Rory, now for once still as he explored how to open the little box. 'Did you know she was pregnant?'

'I, well, yes I did,' he confessed, his eyes never leaving the boy. 'Though you could hardly tell, not even towards the end. She was so small and wore these loose clothes. It wasn't until . . .' His voice died away.

'Until you made love to her,' Darina said softly. Her panic had subsided now and she was beginning to feel the end of her quest was in sight.

Martin's hooded lids dropped over his eyes and he said nothing.

'Why don't you tell me from the beginning,' sug-gested Darina. Rory had now managed to open the box and was delicately fishing out the raisins one by one and popping them in his mouth. 'Did you find her some-where to live after she left Job and Nicola's?'

Martin stared at a discarded snack-bar wrapper on the dusty ground. His hands were loosely clasped between his legs and for the first time Darina noticed he wore a signet ring. There was a long pause. At last he heaved a great sigh and said, 'I suppose I knew it would all come out at some stage. I just hope Eleanor doesn't have to know.'

'Your wife?'

He nodded. 'Over the last year or so, things have been so much better between us.'

Darina wondered what his wife was like. All she could remember hearing about her was that she'd blamed Martin for the death of their son.

He raised his narrow shoulders, gave another big sigh then said, 'I was as surprised as everybody else when Sophie disappeared.'

'But you were in love with her,' Darina stated, now sure of her ground.

'It crept up on me,' he said in wonder. 'I didn't realize until I ran into her one evening in Ladbroke Grove, about four months after she'd disappeared. I'd gone out to get some wine, some friends had just rung and announced their arrival and we didn't have any. I was on my way back when she literally bumped into me. She'd been buying some food at a little supermarket that stays open late. A bag burst and oranges scattered on the pavement. I helped her pick them up then suddenly recognized her. It was such a wonderful surprise! And she seemed pleased to see me.' The depressed lines of his face lifted for a moment.

'She must have known you lived round there.' Rory finished eating his raisins and laid his head against Darina's chest. The feel of the weight against her breast was oddly satisfying, she tightened her grip around him slightly as he closed his eyes.

Martin nodded. 'When she was with Job and Nicola, I

took her to the Portobello Road market once. I thought it might amuse her. And then I drove her around North Kensington and showed her the Grand Union Canal. I also pointed out my street – but I didn't show her which was my house. I, well, I thought she might get the wrong idea. Anyway, as I gave her back the oranges, I asked her what she was doing and she suddenly panicked and got all upset. Thought I was going to tell her family.'

'What did you do?'

'Promised her I wouldn't and persuaded her to come and have a drink with me in a nearby pub.'

Darina had a sudden vision of his wife waiting at home, the friends arriving, and Martin sitting in the pub with Sophie and the wine.

'What did she tell you?'

Martin ran his hands down his well pressed trouser legs. 'She wasn't very coherent. She kept on asking me to promise I wouldn't tell anyone where she was. I swore I wouldn't and after a bit she calmed down. I tried to get her to tell me where she was living but she got all upset again, so I backed off. But I got her to agree to have lunch with me the following Saturday.'

'What about your wife?' Darina asked. 'Didn't she want to know what you were up to?' She couldn't imagine William suddenly taking off at lunchtime for a date with another girl. But then, she thought suddenly, how many Saturdays recently had he worked? If he'd taken someone out to lunch, she'd never know! It was an unsettling thought.

'That was when things were at their worst between us. When Eleanor returned from her mother's she told me she couldn't see we had any future. I'd persuaded her to stay and try for a bit longer. But it wasn't working.

I need hardly say when I got back that night, the frost practically sent me into cold storage. No, at that time Eleanor didn't care what I did.' He mulled that over for a little.

'So what happened next?'

'We met for lunch and Sophie seemed really happy to have someone to talk to.'

Rory was now asleep and Darina slightly shifted him into a more comfortable position on her lap, then studied Martin's lined face, noting the brown eyes and the long ears. Rory didn't look like him at all but, then, genes were funny things. Maybe they could skip a generation or two.

'Look, you don't want to know about Sophie and me, what you need is where she was living and who she was living with,' Martin said rapidly, turning towards her. 'You want to know who Rory's father is.'

Darina was startled. 'But aren't you his father?'

'Me?' Martin gave a short laugh. 'My dear, if only I was!'

Chapter Twenty-Two

'I had mumps just before I met Eleanor. Destroyed my ability to father children.'

'But,' stammered Darina, 'your son?' She floundered, the puzzle Sophie had left eluding her once more.

'Wasn't mine.' Martin stared at the ground again. 'That was half the trouble. After I'd recovered and the doctor had told me the worst, I was very upset. A mutual friend introduced Eleanor and I poured it all out on our first date. She was very sympathetic. Later she told me she was pregnant by some man she had no intention of marrying and asked if I'd like to be its father in every way other than biological. It seemed a gift from the gods. I mean, Eleanor was intelligent, attractive and everything I thought I wanted in a wife, and she could give me a child. We married a few weeks later. When Charles was born I was over the moon. Until that terrible accident.' He paused and twisted his hands together. 'That's not true, actually, things had started going wrong before that. I found out afterwards that Charles's real father had reappeared and Eleanor felt I didn't really match up to him. He mightn't have been husband material but he was sinfully attractive. That was her phrase, sinfully attractive. I, well, I was reliable. Until I allowed Charles to get run over.' He put his face in his hands, grinding the heels into his deepset eyes. 'God, I've relived those moments so often. If only we'd left home five minutes earlier, if only I hadn't gone back for my library tickets, if only I'd had a tighter grasp on his hand. But, there it was, we were on that particular piece of pavement at that particular moment in time. He saw a friend over the other side of the road, pulled free and ran straight under a speeding car. I shall hear the screech of those brakes in nightmares until the end of my life. And Eleanor told me I hadn't cared, that because Charles wasn't my son, I'd let him be run over. For months it was like living with an iceberg. Then her mother had the accident and Eleanor had to go to her; I thought it would give her a chance to get away and perhaps remember the good times we'd had together; instead she concentrated on all the bad.'

There was nothing Darina could say. She sat with Rory's warm weight against her and let Martin wrestle with his demons.

'Anyway,' he said heavily, 'that's all in the past now. But I wanted you to know why Sophie was like, well, a fine shower of rain on parched earth, if you can forgive a florid analogy.'

'I think it's rather good,' Darina said gently. She could see exactly how the gentle, loving, undemanding Sophie had been what tormented Martin had needed at that time.

'That first lunch we had, Sophie told me she was working in some record shop down Notting Hill Gate.' Right to the south of Notting Hill! Darina knew she would never have managed to work her way down there. 'And that she was living just round the corner from where we ran into each other. She told me,' there was remembered pain in his voice, 'she told me she was living with a young man who'd befriended her.'

'Befriended her?'

'She didn't tell me how then, just that he'd offered her somewhere to live. She wanted to know how things were going between Eleanor and me and I poured everything out. She was so warm, so sympathetic. As sympathetic as Eleanor had been when I first met her. By the end of lunch Sophie seemed quite relaxed and she gave me her telephone number. She said she was working the following weekend but perhaps we could have a drink one evening. And then Eleanor walked out saying she wanted to give her failed love affair another chance. After that, well, Sophie was the only bright spot in my life. I suggested she come round one Saturday night, said I'd cook for her.' He gave Darina a ghost of a smile. 'I'm not much good in the kitchen, I went to Marks and Sparks and bought everything ready made. They're very good,' he said anxiously, as though fearing she'd contradict him.

'I'm sure Sophie thought it was wonderful not having to cook,' Darina assured him. She remembered what Jemima had said about Sophie being half-starved. Had the only times she'd eaten been with Martin?

'When eventually I saw where she was living, I wondered how she could stick it.' He looked at Darina. 'Sophie stayed the night with me. She just asked if I'd like her to, as though it was the most natural thing in the world. And it was as if I'd been invited into a warm and brightly lit room after being condemned to hang around outside in the cold. I wanted her to move in with me but she said she couldn't leave Noah.'

'Noah?'

'The boy who'd befriended her. That was the night she told me what had happened after she'd left her brother's. We were in bed together and I think she felt safe in a way she hadn't for a long time.'

To be in bed with another woman's husband and to feel safe! What had Sophie been running away from? 'So why did she leave?'

Martin moved uncomfortably on the seat. 'She wouldn't tell me. "I couldn't stay, I couldn't," she kept saying. She got terribly upset. I held her and told her it didn't matter. She was so small and slight in my arms. Eleanor is quite tall,' he glanced at Darina, 'a little like you.'

Darina decided this was a compliment.

'Sophie said when she left Job and Nicola her only thought was that I might be able to help. She managed to get to Ladbroke Grove and then realized that she didn't know which my house was. She walked up and down my road, hoping I might come along. But then she remembered that I was Job's friend and would probably tell him where she was. She couldn't think of anyone she could trust, she said. She didn't have much money and was sure if she used her credit cards, her father would be able to trace her.'

'She wasn't altogether stupid, then,' Darina said. She tried to imagine how hopeless Sophie must have felt, alone and with nowhere to go.

'Sophie wasn't stupid,' Martin said with sudden passion. 'I told you that before. She was very sensitive and not very bright but she wasn't stupid.' He thought about this, then said again, 'No, not stupid. But that night she said she thought that life was no longer worth living. So she went and found her way to the canal. She was going to jump in. "I thought I wouldn't have to worry any more," she said and told me her mother had committed suicide. Apparently Sophie had always thought it was her fault. I think she felt committing suicide herself would somehow wipe out her sense of guilt.'

'Oh, poor girl!' Once again Darina tried to imagine what had happened to drive her to this desperate state. 'What happened to stop her?'

'She met Noah. Heaven only knows what he was doing there, probably buying drugs. He asked her if she'd got a light, typical of Noah.' Martin's voice was angry. 'Goes to buy a joint without having a match! When she said she hadn't any, he asked her what was wrong, said he could see something was and he'd like to help. Apparently they were the first friendly words she'd heard all day and made her burst into tears. Noah got the story out of her and, I'll say this for him, he got a grip on things. He took her to his hovel and looked after her. Gave her one of his joints, calmed her down, then found her something to eat. After that, she said, things didn't seem quite so awful and so she stayed with him.'

He made Sophie sound like an autumn leaf, blown by the wind, first one way, then another, entirely at the mercy of events.

'And she found a job.'

Martin nodded. 'Apparently it had been very difficult without any qualifications or experience but this shop needed part-time help. It was hard work being on her feet all the time but she liked being useful, she knew quite a lot about pop records and it was exciting earning money. I think most of it went on drugs for Noah, though. Food never seemed to feature much in her life.'

Poor little rich girl, Darina thought. 'When did you realize she was pregnant?' she asked.

Martin looked bleak. 'That first night I slept with her. I could remember exactly how Eleanor's body had looked and felt in the early stages.'

Darina glanced down at the sleeping Rory, at the curve of his fair eyelashes, the rosebud mouth. 'Was she sleeping with Noah as well?'

'Yes,' he said, his mouth drooping.

'My,' Darina commented.

'I know,' Martin said despairingly. 'She said we both needed her and it seemed natural.' That word again.

'Presumably if she was spending nights away, Noah knew about you?'

'She told him straight away, she said lies never got anyone anywhere.'

Had that been a reference to the way she'd been deceived over her parentage? 'Did you meet him?'

'Yes,' Martin said in a low voice. 'After she refused to move in with me, I insisted. I wanted to know who she was involved with.'

'What was he like?'

Martin shrugged helplessly. 'What can I say? He's a drop-out, a druggie. He lives for the moment and in total chaos. He has one of these charity housing flats, the rent's very low but even that he finds difficulty keeping up with. Sophie must have been a real godsend. There she was, working away and he just sat around smoking pot and snorting cocaine and no doubt trying anything else he could lay his hands on. Sophie said he earned money every now and then but it can't have been much.' He looked down at his hands, turning them around as though he'd never seen them before. 'I got angry with her when I realized she was pregnant. I hadn't met Noah then but she'd told me enough to know that he'd be a hopeless father. I said some pretty unforgivable things and she just sat in the middle of the bed, looking at the tiny curve of her stomach between her bony hips and wept. The tears just ran down her cheeks. So I held her and promised that everything would be all right.'

But everything hadn't been all right. 'What did you do?'

'I asked her to marry me!' Martin almost shouted out the words. Several people looked round but that was all. Darina could see what an ordinary group they must appear. A man and his wife and their child, probably fighting about some dreary domestic detail, or the fact that the man was out of work, for why else would he be sitting on a bench by the embankment on a weekday afternoon?

'I begged and pleaded with her. I told her my marriage was over, that Eleanor wasn't going to return. And she gave me this wistful little smile and said I might think I wanted to marry her but it wouldn't work. Then, quite suddenly, she cheered up and said I wasn't to worry, she'd manage things.'

How could he not have told Sophie's family? Darina wondered. Or at the very least helped her change her lifestyle. Then decided that Martin was someone who found it difficult to accept responsibility. 'According to Jemima, Sophie wasn't getting proper ante-natal care. Do you know if she was going to a clinic?'

Martin ran a hand impatiently through his thinning hair. 'She said she'd been to a doctor but he'd asked so many questions and wanted her to have a blood test. It seemed to worry her that. I tried to explain how it was all routine but she got upset, said giving birth was a completely natural process and that she'd got a book from the library! I didn't like to worry her and I thought there was plenty of time to get her used to the fact she needed medical attention, so I left it.'

'Didn't your wife, Eleanor, tell you how regularly she went to the clinic when she was having her baby?' asked Darina, amazed at his attitude.

'Well,' Martin ducked his head, avoiding her eyes, 'she kept all the details very private. She made it sound as though pregnancy was something men had nothing to do with. And I wasn't the father so I didn't think I had any right to pry. After all,' he added more strongly, 'I was working all day, how was I to know how often she went?'

Darina gave up.

'Anyway,' Martin continue, 'every time I asked how she was, Sophie said she was all right, everything was under control. I had to go away on business to the Far East for nearly a month. When I got back, I was horrified; her hands and feet were so swollen. I'd given her a ring and it was buried in flesh. I had to take her to a jeweller to have it cut off. I asked her what on earth she'd been doing and she burst into tears and told me unless I stopped going on at her, she'd leave. I was terrified I'd lose her again and I didn't know what to do.' He looked distracted. 'I was sure she needed a doctor. Eventually I took her back to Noah's. Then I contacted my own doctor and persuaded him to call on her with me the following night. But she wasn't there. Noah said he'd thought she was with me. The doctor said we'd wasted his time and went off in a huff. I didn't know what to do. I rang Noah the following day, still no news. He didn't even seem worried, said she'd come back when she was ready!' Martin's voice expressed his disgust at this attitude. 'Then, just as I was getting ready to phone the police and the hospitals, Job rang and said Sophie had died. I was devastated.' He buried his face in his hands again.

Darina held Rory tight and shivered.

Martin dropped his hands and sat back. He seemed exhausted. 'It was ages since I'd seen Job. They knew about Eleanor leaving, of course, and Nicola kept asking me round but I made excuses. I didn't feel I could face them, not when I knew where Sophie was.'

Darina said nothing. She found it almost impossible to understand how he could have failed the girl in the way he had.

'And did you tell Noah?' she asked, expecting to hear he hadn't.

'Yes, I went round there. Told him everything. Except, I said the baby had died. I couldn't stand the thought of someone like Noah being involved with Sophie's baby,' Martin burst out. Darina looked down at the happily sleeping Rory in her arms. 'Would you want him to have a drug addict for a father? Much better that he should think himself an orphan, brought up with all the advantages the Ealhams could give him.'

'They didn't do Sophie much good,' Darina told him ruefully.

Martin looked intently at her, his face more like a bloodhound's than ever. 'But aren't they a better alternative than some sleazy flat in Ladbroke Grove?'

'And you're sure Noah is Rory's father?'

He nodded vigorously. 'The timing fits. Job told me Rory was premature. And I knew Sophie, she couldn't have been sleeping with anyone else. No, Noah's his father, God help him.'

Darina felt depressed. She had the answer but it wasn't going to help. 'Couldn't Rory know who his father is and be protected from him at the same time?'

'What if Noah went to the courts and insisted on custody? You know what the law is like, it's giving all sorts of rights to the father these days.'

'Can I have Noah's last name and his address?'

A mulish look came over Martin's face and for a moment she thought he was going to refuse. She looked at him challengingly and, true to form, he caved in, brought out a small notebook and gave her the details.

Darina managed to find paper and pencil in her bag without waking Rory and wrote them down. Then she drew the buggy towards her and gently lowered the still-sleeping child in. 'When did your wife return?' she asked as she did up the straps.

'About a year ago,' he said. 'She just turned up, said it hadn't worked with the chap she'd gone off with, that she was sorry she'd been so rotten to me over Charlie's death and could we please try again.'

'You must have been very pleased.' What a wimp the man was, let anyone trample all over him!

'The best thing of all was she agreed to try artificial insemination. Now she's six months pregnant.' Martin's face was transformed, the depressed, hangdog look gone. 'I shall have a child after all.' He looked warily at her. 'You see why I'm so anxious Eleanor shouldn't hear anything about this?'

'You mean, you haven't told her about Sophie?' Darina was shocked.

'She thinks I was faithful while she was away,' he muttered.

'Well, I shan't tell her but these things have a way of getting out,' Darina said. 'Remember what Sophie said, lies never get you anywhere?'

He looked unconvinced.

Big drops of rain began to fall. 'Oh, dear,' Darina said, 'I'd better run.' She started pushing the buggy fast towards Westminster Bridge. Martin kept pace beside her. 'You promise you won't tell I knew where Sophie was and everything?' he repeated.

'If I can keep you out of it, I will,' she told him. The drops were turning into real rain and she started running.

Chapter Twenty-Three

Back home Rory demanded Darina's full attention.

She was giving him broccoli with minced ham in a cream sauce for supper. She reckoned she'd worked things out rather well. The ham was left over from the previous evening's supper and she'd worked out the baby food recipe while waiting for William to come home.

Which was as well because it proved no easy task to mince ham, make a white sauce and cook broccoli with Rory proclaiming how hungry he was. She gave him a bread stick, sat him on the kitchen floor with his toys and got down to preparing his evening meal.

It was the hardest cooking she'd ever done. Rory was everywhere. Opening kitchen cupboards, taking out bowls and plates and banging them together. Rubber bands linking handles together solved that one, much to Rory's disgust. The floor became a minefield, littered with the toys. If she turned her attention too whole-heartedly to what she was doing, Rory was out of the kitchen, through the hall and into the drawing room, with all its little knick-knacks. He proved astonishingly adept at opening doors and finally Darina had to lock the drawing-room door, which meant Rory went for the stairs instead. And every time she had to interrupt her cooking, it meant she had to wash her hands again before returning to the stove.

It didn't take long to convince Darina that the only way to produce food for Rory was while he slept. Gourmet convenience baby food suddenly seemed highly desirable.

Finally she was able to leave the prepared food in a cool place and take him up for a bath. That was fun.

She'd found a baby bubble bath in the supermarket the previous day and he splashed happily while she washed him, hair and all. Then dried him in a big, warm, fluffy towel, playing peek-a-boo. It was amazing how such simple games could give so much pleasure to them both! Then it was time for a clean nappy, the sleeping suit and a cardigan so he wouldn't get cold.

Finally Darina reheated a portion of the ham and broccoli in the microwave, then had to wait until it cooled sufficiently before she could anxiously offer up the first mouthful.

Rory looked at the loaded spoonful suspiciously, his head on one side. Then opened his mouth, accepted the portion, swallowed it – and opened up for more.

Darina glowed with success and put a big tick on the recipe, now spattered with grease and bits of broccoli.

How well, she wondered, would it take to mass production? The broccoli could have a tendency to go to mush but with careful cooking and folding in on a batch principle, it should work. But if it was made with a huge machine paddling it all together, she reckoned it might taste all right but the texture would be nothing. Who was going to win out over the production method – Val or Basil?

And if it was Val, with no preservatives, the

distribution would have to be handled very carefully. It would surely add to the cost. Still, wonderful for mothers to know they were giving their children food as pure as if they'd made it themselves. Darina could now understand the charms of fish fingers.

Rory finished the ham and Darina got out one of the fruit fromage frais without extra sugar she'd so carefully chosen, and fed that to Rory. Then she looked at the E numbers on the carton. Surely pure, plain yoghurt with some fruit puree added would be better for him? Something else for Val to produce, perhaps. Finally Darina heated up a bottle of milk and gave it into his eager hands while she gathered up the toys from the floor.

Boy, did babies take up time! Three hours had elapsed since they'd got back home from the embankment. And she was utterly exhausted. Jemima's claim that Rory spent so much time sleeping Darina would be able to do everything she wanted was nonsense. Darina wondered how much Jemima had had to do with him.

Then wondered why she hadn't heard from her. She'd expected a call Thursday evening. Then that there'd be a message on her answering machine when she'd returned after her meeting with Martin. Nothing. Her mobile hadn't rung either. Darina picked up the kitchen receiver and checked the line was working. Then she rang Jemima's mobile number, only to be told that the machine wasn't switched on. Well, it was a vote of confidence, showed she wasn't worried about her nephew, but it was odd, Darina thought.

By the time William got back, late as usual, Darina had got Rory asleep and, with the help of a glass of wine, gathered herself together. She braced herself as she heard the front door open, not sure she had the energy to deal with a husband who had been as difficult as William the previous evening.

'How's the lad?' was William's first question.

'Sleeping,' said Darina with heartfelt gratitude.

'I'll just go and check on him,' he said, putting down his briefcase and disappearing upstairs.

It was a little time before he came down and she saw he'd changed into jeans and a sweatshirt. She gave him a glass of wine as he sat down at the kitchen table, laid for their supper. 'We're having baby food,' she told him, summoning her reserves of cheerfulness. 'Gourmet variety – ham and broccoli.'

'Ham,' William said, then he looked at his drink. 'I think I'll have mineral water,' he said sliding his glass over to Darina. 'You drink this.' Then he pushed away his plate, 'I always said nursery food was my favourite but I think I'll give this a miss. Make myself a couple of boiled eggs.' He went over to the stove and put on a small saucepan of water on to heat.

Darina felt her temper begin to rise. Was he rejecting her food as well as her? 'William,' she started in a dangerous voice.

'I went to see your man this afternoon,' he said before she could get further.

'My man?'

'The homoeopathic doctor.'

Darina stared at him, not able to believe what she was hearing. 'Darling! How did you find the time?'

'It isn't my time you should be asking about, it's his. I felt so dreadful last night I thought anything was worth trying and rang as soon as I got into the station this morning. Only to hear that his first appointment was six weeks away! I gave the receptionist a great sob story about being responsible for the nation's safety and how I couldn't do that in my state of health and she wasn't moved at all.' He shook his head and lowered two eggs into the boiling water. 'But after lunch she rang and said the doctor had just had a cancellation and could I make it by three? I put everything off and went over.'

'My,' Darina said. This was extraordinary! And worrying, William must have been feeling really awful. 'What did he say?'

'He thinks your instinct is probably right, especially when I told him I'd had a full physical from the medics only last month and they'd given me a clean bill of health.'

'What did you tell him your symptoms were?'

'Extreme tiredness, headaches, a general feeling of not being able to cope and the leg rash.'

'Darling, I didn't realize it was as bad as that!'

'I didn't want you to,' he told her frankly.

'But we should share things. No wonder you've been so crabby! Promise me you'll let me know if it gets as bad again?'

He gave her one of his old smiles and Darina realized just how much she'd missed them. 'Promise,' he said.

'Did he test you and find out what you shouldn't be eating?'

'Ah,' he said, gazing at his watch. 'What he's done is to put me on something called an elimination diet. If I feel better after a few days, and he warned me I could feel worse before that happens, then I'm probably eating something my system finds difficult to cope with.'

'What do you have to cut out?'

'Quite a lot, I'm afraid. All preserved meats, like that ham, and sausages, which is going to be a serious deprivation; all dairy products, especially cheese. When the doctor discovered how much I like it, he said it could be a major source of the trouble. All smoked and shell fish, all cereals, yeast, some oils, all citrus fruit and tomatoes, coffee and tea, and, alas, alcohol. There could be one or two other things, I've got all the details in my briefcase.'

'That's a hell of a list,' Darina said slowly. 'Val only mentioned wheat and dairy products.'

'After my system's cleansed and I feel really good, we start adding ingredients back, one at a time, to see if I get a reaction. Eventually, we find out what it is that's causing the trouble.'

'And do you believe it's going to work?' Darina found it hard to accept that her normally sceptic husband was willingly submitting himself to this regime.

'If it's going to help me feel able to cope again, I don't mind what I do,' he said simply, took his eggs out of the water and brought them over to the table.

'You'd better give me the list and let me work out how to feed you.'

'And is there something I can make a packed lunch out of for tomorrow that won't contain any no-noes? If I'm passing up Rory's gourmet dinner tonight, I don't want to upset the regime tomorrow.'

'That means you're working again.' It wasn't a question.

'Afraid so. We've got to get this case wrapped up.'

Got to get the case wrapped up or got to get together with Sergeant James? And if the latter, what could Darina do about it?

*

313

The next morning Darina checked William's list of allowables. While he fed Rory, she cooked a breast of chicken in olive oil for his lunch then sliced and mixed it with a chopped ripe pear, runner beans and grilled red peppers, all tossed in a little vinaigrette dressing.

William checked what she was doing while spooning soggy cereal into Rory and eating two apples and a banana for his own breakfast. 'The doc suggested rice is good to start the day on,' he told her. 'If it's brown, of course. You eat that all up, boy. Grow up nice and strong, be an athlete.' He threw a punch at Rory's midriff, pulling it back before it connected. Rory thought that was a great joke and then grabbed at the spoon, showering William with milk and bits of cereal.

William took it back. 'We can't have that, what will the team think if I come in spattered with your breakfast?'

'The team?' wondered Darina. That was new. She decided to take advantage of the change in atmosphere.

'I forgot to tell you last night, I've discovered who his father is.'

William turned and stared at her. 'You have? Good work! Who is it?'

Darina told him of her conversation with Martin. 'All I've got to do now is get hold of this Noah Whitstable person and I can report to Jemima.' She glanced at the telephone. 'I'll have another go at her mobile this morning, she'll be so pleased.'

But would she be? Darina had to agree with Martin that Noah didn't sound an ideal dad for Rory.

'If he's still at that address. Sounds an unreliable sort

of person to me,' William commented, brushing down his suit.

'He's listed in this year's phone book, I checked when I got back last night. I have a feeling it's all going to fall into place now. Here's your lunch,' Darina handed over the plastic box together with an apple and a bottle of mineral water.

'Great, one way or another I'm going to get to the bottom of this food intolerance thing as well as the arson case.' He gave both Darina and Rory a kiss and left, leaving Darina hoping his optimism wasn't misplaced in either direction.

From then on she didn't have a moment to relax. There was Rory to keep amused while she cleared up, did the minimum of housework and then sat down with William's list to try and plan meals and getting to grips with thinking how a seemingly innocuous diet could slowly poison one over the years.

Then it was time for Rory's rest and for Darina to attack more gourmet baby food recipes. Working as fast as her catering experience had trained her, she prepared chicken with courgettes and corn, hoping Rory would like the colour of the corn as well as its sweetness; pork with potato, leek and grilled red peppers; smoked haddock with rice and carrot; and lamb with couscous and parsnip. When she'd finished, she stood looking at the results with satisfaction. They all tasted excellent and the textures were interesting. Darina also reckoned the balance of protein, fats and vitamins would be good, too. It just remained to see what Rory thought. She put the various bowls of mixtures to cool in a sink filled with ice cubes.

Before she went upstairs to collect Rory, she tried

Noah Whitstable's number. No reply. Then she rang Jemima's mobile again – the machine was still switched off. Had she forgotten to take a battery charger with her? It seemed unlikely, Jemima had always been wedded to the phone. Anyway, if she had, wouldn't she have rung on an ordinary phone to check on Rory?

Darina tried not to feel uneasy as she set off with Rory for a walk in Chelsea Hospital grounds. There could be any number of reasons why Jemima hadn't been in touch. She stopped worrying as heavy rain started again and she had to dash back.

Lunch was another triumph as Rory eagerly demolished the chicken and corn dish. Then Darina wondered if he would have eaten baked beans with exactly the same gusto. Did it really matter what you gave small children as long as the nutritional factors were right and they ate it? She wished Rory could talk, could tell her what he really thought. But he couldn't so she had to be content that he'd appeared to appreciate the dish. Until proved otherwise, she would remain convinced it was important to educate the palate from an early age.

She put Rory down for his nap then took the chance to try and call both Noah and Jemima. Still no joy. She caught up on her mail and tried to get down to some work but no sooner had she managed to get started than Rory woke and it was playtime.

Followed by bath time, supper time and, at last, bedtime. The previous night Darina had only been woken once. She hoped this meant that tonight Rory would sleep all the way through. She went downstairs, poured herself a drink, collapsed into a chair and wondered how mothers ever managed to cope.

Perhaps it was like trench warfare; you just got used

to it. Maybe after a while you couldn't imagine any other sort of life.

If it wasn't that Rory was such an enchanting child, so good-humoured and with such a wonderful smile, so openly loving, so intelligent and so obviously happy to be with her, Darina would have been desperate.

She had one more go on the telephone. And this time Noah's phone was answered by a female voice with an Australian accent. Noah, she said, was away for the weekend but would probably be back on Monday. Cheered by this, Darina dialled Jemima again. No luck there. She rang Blackboys. An answering machine. She left a message for Basil to ring when he got back.

Worry niggled away at Darina. Two days, Jemima had said, was all Darina had to look after Rory for. Two days were now up and Jemima hadn't been in contact.

'I don't understand it,' she said to William when he got back.

'She doesn't sound the most reliable of girls.'

Darina dished up wild mushroom risotto while he laid the table. 'She really seemed frightened on Thursday, said she was sure someone had tried to run her down.'

'Any evidence?' asked William calmly, arranging cutlery.

'Only what she said.'

'Hysterical, was she?'

'Not hysterical, exactly.' Darina brought over the dish of risotto. 'It was as though she couldn't bear to be where she was any longer than she absolutely had to. She practically pushed me and Rory out of the door. I'd have said she was genuinely frightened. Whether it was justified or not is, of course, a different matter. I still think it's odd that she isn't anxious about Rory.'

'Why? She knows he's being well looked after.' He paused then added, 'He's a great child, I only wish we could see more of him.'

Darina wasn't going to get involved in another discussion about starting a family. 'It's all ready,' she said. 'Is the table?'

The risotto was made with brown rice and was accompanied by salad. It was followed by a home-made mango sorbet that was as creamy as ice cream. 'Not bad,' said William. 'I don't mind following a diet if this is what I get.'

'Are you feeling any different?'

'Yes, worse,' he said cheerfully. 'I've got the most terrible headache. Withdrawal symptoms, I was warned.'

'Poor you. But I suppose you could look on it as encouraging, shows that something's happening.'

'Unless I'm just developing a propensity for migraines!'

'How's the case going?'

'Stickily,' he said, looking depressed. 'Nothing seems to be breaking for us. One or two interesting developments, though. Forensic think they've identified a heavy rolling pin amongst various bits of charred wood in the factory and Val Douglas's secretary says there was a new one, a sample sent in by a kitchen equipment company, sitting on her desk that night, waiting for a test run.'

'You mean that's what could have been used to kill the nightwatchman?'

'Well, knock him out anyway.'

'You mean he was left to die in the fire?'

William nodded unhappily, 'The autopsy says he died from asphyxiation not the wound in his head.'

'That's awful! Anything else?'

'I don't know but Maeve O'Connor, Rory's ex-nanny, rang us yesterday and said she had something to tell us and would drop by. But she hasn't. If only I'd been the one to speak to her! I'd have told her to remain where she was and sent a car. As it was, by the time I got the message, she'd gone out somewhere and we haven't been able to contact her again.'

'Do you think it could be important, whatever it is?'

William finished his glass of apple juice. 'Heaven knows! I'd have thought if it was, she'd have told us when Pat and I interviewed her but she's a funny little thing and was very upset about her father.'

'Probably still is. Give her a day or so and she'll be back in touch.'

'I just hope you're right.' William got up and started stacking the supper plates together.

Darina left William clearing up and had another go at ringing Jemima. Once again she got the message that the mobile was switched off. She tried Blackboys again. This time Jasper answered.

'Hi,' Darina said. 'Do you know where Jemima is?'

He didn't.

'Is your father there?'

'He's away until Tuesday, I think. What's up? Won't the son and heir do?' he added flippantly.

Darina nearly reminded him that Job was the heir. 'Not unless you want to take over Rory,' she said instead, then remembered that Jemima had said she couldn't trust Jasper with him.

'You mean, *you've* got Rory?' he said, astonished. 'I

thought Jemima had taken him with her. Dad will go berserk,' he added with a note of satisfaction in his voice.

'I'm quite able to look after Rory,' Darina said with dignity.

'Frustrated mothering instincts?'

'Nothing of the sort. He's the guinea-pig for Val's gourmet baby-food line.'

'Dad won't like that, either.' Jasper appeared to delight in needling her.

'Why ever not?'

'He's got some hot-shot experts working on it.'

'Is it his company or Val's?' Darina asked pointedly.

'Depends which one you talk to,' Jasper shot back. 'And we all know who holds the money bags. If you take my advice, you won't invest too much time working on any ideas you may have come up with.'

Darina felt dismay. Then wondered just how much Jasper knew about things anyway. As far as she knew, he had nothing to do with his father's business and certainly nothing to do with Val's. 'Thank you for your advice,' she said smoothly.

'No trouble,' he returned equally smoothly. 'Now, why don't I come and collect Rory from you?'

'I'm enjoying having him and he was given into my care by Jemima,' Darina said carefully. 'Do you know when she will be back?' she asked.

'I'm not my sister's keeper,' he said carelessly.

'So you don't know where she went?'

'No idea. Look, I'm the boy's uncle, I do think I should be looking after him.'

Darina thought about happy-go-lucky Jasper coping with food times, bedtimes, play times. 'I can't agree, Jasper,' she said firmly. 'And I know Basil would want him to stay here.' That seemed to take care of that. But her worry over Jemima's whereabouts remained. She couldn't forget how tense Jemima had been and her relief when she'd realized Darina was prepared to take care of Rory so she herself could get away. Get away from what or whom?

Darina spent an uneasy evening turning over possibilities as William worked on his case notes. It didn't seem either of them had come to any satisfactory conclusion before it was time for bed.

Once again Rory woke them during the night and this time it was William who went in and set the cassette player going. In the morning, Darina brought Rory and his bottle of milk into bed with them while William got breakfast. Hers was croissants and coffee, his was cold mushroom risotto and hot apple juice. 'I stirred it with a cinnamon stick,' he said proudly. 'Makes all the difference.'

'How's the headache?'

He groaned. 'Don't ask!'

There followed a pleasant hour with Darina and William fielding clocks, ornaments, books and pencils as Rory explored the bedside tables, finally allowing him to hang on to an antique paperweight of polished black stone. This Rory threw on to the duvet and then the floor with increasing enthusiasm.

'You look after him,' Darina said after a while, 'I'm getting up.'

Yesterday's rain hadn't let up, which meant they couldn't take Rory out. William played with him while Darina cooked lunch, changing her planned cauliflower cheese to accompany the half shoulder of lamb to cauliflower cooked with cumin. She slipped slivers of garlic underneath the meat skin and wondered what could replace the apricot crème caramel she'd planned for pudding. She couldn't even soak the dried apricots in orange juice for a compote. Pastry of any sort was out as well. As was chocolate. She sighed. Well, fruit was better for them anyway.

Just as she started feeding Rory his meal, the telephone rang. Darina snatched it up, convinced it had to be Jemima at last.

It was for William.

His face grew dark as he listened. 'I see,' he said at last. 'You've sent for the SOCO team and the pathologist, of course?'

The Scenes of Crime Officers were required for a wide range of felonies but a pathologist surely meant a fatality. Darina felt herself go cold.

William put down the phone. 'I'm sorry, darling, I've got to go. A body has been discovered by the lock gates, on the very edge of my patch, damn it!' He paused then said carefully, 'It's a woman, they think she's been in the river several days.'

Darina felt sick. 'A lock? It wouldn't be downstream of Blackboys by any chance?'

'Now look, darling, Blackboys is quite a way from where she's been found. There's absolutely no reason to think it's your friend, Jemima.'

'No, of course not,' Darina said without conviction.

Chapter Twenty-Four

Pat James had gone into the office on Sunday morning with a feeling of expectation. Being on call offered opportunities.

If she wasn't interrupted by any new criminal activity, she could work through the computer entries on the arson case and just maybe uncover a trail that would lead to the killer of the nightwatchman.

But no sooner had she flashed up the first entry than the door opened and in came the last person she wanted to see.

'All quiet on the manor front, then?' asked Terry in a horribly jocular way.

He was dressed in his usual uniform of jeans and a leather blouson, except that under the jacket was a T-shirt sporting a psychedelic print rather than his more normal open-necked checked shirt.

'Unable to keep away, then?' she retorted.

He strolled over to his desk. 'Left my Raybans.'

She looked at the greyness of the day outside. 'Of course, couldn't be expected to slay the girls without your Raybans,' she muttered to herself.

'You said something?' he asked pleasantly.

'Off somewhere exciting?' She matched his conversational tone.

'Just down the pub.' He put the glasses in the top pocket of his jacket and strolled over to where she sat. 'Anything interesting, sergeant?'

'Nothing that sticks out, sir.' She enjoyed calling him sir rather than the more intimate guv.

'Since I'm here, might as well have a coffee and run an eye over the case myself,' he said, shrugging his shoulders out of the jacket and draping it round a chair. 'Fancy one yourself?'

Pat sighed. It was obvious he was as keen to make the vital breakthrough as she was. And that the office was no longer her own. 'Just had one,' she said repressively. Did he think he could get round her by switching on the electric kettle?

Equipped with a cup of instant, Terry sat himself at another VDU and started tapping keys, whistling through his teeth is a way Pat found immensely provocative.

Just as she thought she couldn't stand it any longer, her phone rang.

She listened, then said, 'Right, I'm on my way,' put back the receiver and picked up her jacket.

'Trouble?' Terry looked up, his hazel eyes bright, his thin face alert.

'Lock-keeper's reported a body in the river,' Pat said reluctantly. The last thing she wanted was to be accompanied by Terry. 'No need for you to disturb yourself, sir.'

'I'm sure you're more than capable of handling the initial stages, sergeant,' Terry said, getting up and grabbing his jacket. 'But I think I'll come along for the ride.'

There was nothing she could do.

'Know the way?' he asked as she got into the car in furious silence.

Over the last couple of weeks she'd spent every one of the few precious spare moments she'd had in studying the area covered by the station.

'Yup,' she said shortly and started the engine.

'If you turn right at the lights, I'll show you a back route that's much quicker,' Terry said.

He would, he just would insist on showing off, she thought as she flicked the indicator switch and pulled into the centre of the road. But it was, she had to admit as she cruised along a residential street, a nifty little way. One that maybe she would have worked out if she'd taken a good look at the map before they'd started.

The lock normally attracted quite a few visitors on the weekend and the tourist season wasn't quite over. Despite the fact that it had only just stopped raining, there were a number of cars outside the pub that stood next to the lock-keeper's house and a crowd of people blocked the view of the river.

'Bloody voyeurs,' said Terry.

They worked their way through the crowd of people.

A constable had cordoned off an area of river bank next to the lock with blue and white crime-scene tape and was now trying to keep the curious back. More people crowded the decks, craning their necks, trying to see what was causing the hold up.

'DI Pitman and WDS James, constable,' said Terry, flashing his warrant card. 'Show us the rabbit.' Pat winced.

'It's here, sir,' the constable said stolidly and turned to lead them down the short stretch of grass between the tape and the river, but not before Pat had seen the expression on his middle-aged, craggy face. It made her forget Terry's crassness and try to turn her mind into a blank. This had to be a nasty one.

'By rights, she should have gone over the weir,' the constable said. 'But *Fun Days*, that boat there,' he indicated a powerful and expensive-looking cruiser drawn into the side of the river as though waiting for the lock, 'well, it got too far over, saw the weir and swung sharply over to this side. The body must have been coming down at the time. With all the rain we've had, the current's pretty strong.'

Yes, the river was flowing fast, past the willows lining both the banks that were edged with humbler houses than the mansions that lay further upriver but desirable all the same. For the river was like a private road, one that was sheltered from the dreariness and overcrowding of so much of the densely developed area it ran through as it gathered strength on its way into London and out to the sea.

Terry hid Pat's view of the body. The stillness of his shoulders, the rigidity of the set of his head, betrayed shock. Then he replaced his Raybans and stepped aside without a comment.

Forcing herself to take several slow, deep breaths, Pat looked at the corpse lying on the path beside an upturned boat. Then she gasped, closed her eyes and hung on to her sanity before opening them again slowly, aware of Terry's silent presence beside her.

This was not a body so much as a piece of mangled flesh. The screws of the boat had torn into the head and shoulders, mincing the features into nothingness, ripping off the ears, chewing up the shoulders. Blood streaked the loose fragments of skin and muscle and splinters of bare bone. There were no eyes, no nose, only a rictus for a mouth and cracked bones where once had been a jaw. Wet strands of dark hair adhered to what was left of the scalp but even they couldn't make the head look human. The lower arms and hands of the corpse, though, had been left untouched. Yet they also looked unnatural, bloated and blanched by immersion in the water.

Pat's stomach gave a sickening lurch. She counted slowly, thinking of nothing, and gradually it settled.

'Spoiled their Pimms, it did,' the constable said, with a jerk of his head towards the boat. 'The woman saw it first, apparently, and screamed at her husband to cut the engine. Which he did. Too late, of course. But, then, it would have been too late anyway. Reckon she's been dead several days.'

Pat could see into the cabin of the cruiser moored at the side of the river. A woman was crying helplessly, her arms wrapped around herself. The man stood staring out of the cabin's wide window, his hands jammed into his trouser pockets. Each of the figures looked intensely alone.

'Have you got their names, constable?' Terry asked. There was an oddly detached note to his voice as though, he, too, couldn't come to terms with the sight they'd been presented with.

'Yes, sir.'

'And sent for the SOCO team and the pathologist?'

'Yes, sir.'

'And no doubt the guvnor will be here soon?'

The sick feeling in Pat's stomach suddenly intensified as she realized that part of her resentment at Terry's presence had been because if he hadn't shown up, she would have had the pleasure of working with William alone, just the two of them. The two of them and the Soco squad, the pathologist, the uniform branch and probably the Superintendent as well. What a cosy little duo that would have been!

But they would have been a team within a team. Now Terry would be part of it, too.

'Haven't seen many worse sights than that,' Terry said casually to her. 'And I don't know many officers who could have taken it the way you've done.'

She wanted to make some flip remark back, instead tears threatened and she had to turn away for a moment. 'Line of duty, isn't that what it's about?' she muttered.

A police van drew up and several white-clad technicians came over carrying screens.

'Thank God,' said Terry. 'Now we can get a bit of privacy. Give us a shout if the pathologist or the chief arrives,' he told the constable.

By the time William arrived on the scene, Pat and Terry had interviewed the badly shocked couple on board *Fun Days* but learned little more that could be added to the constable's brief statement.

They negotiated the narrow plank that linked boat to shore and went to join their chief.

'Glad I haven't had my lunch,' was his brief comment. 'Don't suppose I'll have much of an appetite for the rest of today. Pity, Darina's preparing one of her specials, roast lamb with home-made red currant jelly. Ah well!' He gave them both a grin that said, ghastly as the job was, they had to retain a sense of proportion.

Suddenly Pat saw how ridiculous she was being. This was a man who hadn't been married much more than a year. Who'd been crazy about his wife ever since Pat had known him. What on earth had she been thinking of?

'Any sign of the pathologist yet?' William continued.

'He's another one being dragged away from some-one's speciality, guv,' Terry said with an answering grin. 'Lunching with the wife's relations, apparently. He said he'll be with us about three thirty, didn't think the delay would matter.'

'He's right, of course,' said William absently. He looked again at the pathetic remains. 'No sign of any identity, I suppose?'

Terry shook his head. 'The constable went through her pockets, but nothing.'

'Any record of a missing person who might fit the description?'

It had been Pat who had put together such details as were available: woman, about five foot eight inches tall, short brown hair, unmarried or at least wearing no rings, dressed in blue designer jeans, a silk shirt and a leather waistcoat. It wasn't much to go on but it at least suggested the dead woman had had a lifestyle of quality.

'No,' she said in a voice that sounded odd to her ears.

William looked at her sharply. 'You all right, sergeant?'

'Yup.' Pat pulled herself together. Terry's glee if she fell apart now was not to be borne.

'Better go and see if the lock-keeper can give us any guidance on where the body floated down from.'

There followed a long, long afternoon of frustrating activity.

The lock-keeper could only suggest that the body had been caught upriver by a tree root or reeds, then been dislodged by the increased current caused by the heavy rains. 'Can't have come far without someone seeing it, though,' had been his comment. 'The bad weather's cut down on the number of craft on the river but you'd have thought someone would 'ave seen 'er if she'd come far.'

Cold, wet and depressed, Pat and Terry finally finished their inquiries at the lock.

By eight o'clock the body had been inspected by the pathologist and removed. Post-mortem would be carried out the following morning. The SOCO technicians had finished their investigations. 'Nothing more they can do,' William told Pat and Terry. 'That's the devil with water, it washes so much away. But they're satisfied the incident occurred just as the *Fun Days* owners claim.'

He turned and looked upriver. Twilight had deepened into night and a fine rain was falling. Light splashed out from the pub and the lock-keeper's cottage and from the little houses by the river. Beyond, from where the corpse must have come, all was dark. 'How far is Blackboys?' William asked Terry.

'Blackboys?' Terry sounded disconcerted. 'I dunno, let's see, 'bout two miles, something like that, guv. You're not suggesting the corpse can have had anything to do with *Blackboys*?'

'Darina's worried about Jemima Ealham. She says the girl went away last Thursday for a couple of days and she hasn't been able to contact her since.'

Pat remembered the chic girl who'd accused the nanny of stealing her pearls. A little madam, she'd thought at the time. Someone used to luxury and getting her own way. 'The clothes could certainly be hers,' she said doubtfully. It was difficult to tie in that terrible piece of ripped flesh and bone with the self-possessed

Jemima Ealham but, she found, by no means impossible. 'The jeans are really expensive.' They'd had the make advertised on the metal buttons and she'd seen them, or an almost identical pair, featured in a fashion magazine.

'Might be an idea if the two of you paid a call on Blackboys. It's unlikely our unfortunate corpse is that of Jemima Ealham but we can't afford to ignore the possibility. I'll see you at the station later.'

'Waste of time, this, if you ask me,' Terry muttered to Pat as he followed her to the car. 'Why should anyone want to kill the silly bitch?'

Pat's feelings entirely, but she wasn't going to question William's judgement. 'Stranger things have happened,' she murmured, opening the car door and slipping into the driver's seat, glad to be out of the rain, now getting heavier by the minute.

She had to think as she switched on the engine how to get to Blackboys from where they were. But after a moment the route slipped into place in her mind and she started driving confidently.

No alternative suggestions as to the way came from Terry and they reached the drive of the big house in little more than fifteen minutes.

'It'd be less by river,' Terry said as they drew up.

It seemed as though all the lights had been turned on in the house. No curtains were drawn and rectangles of golden light beamed out of the big windows. Chandeliers could be seen in a couple of rooms. As Terry rang the doorbell, the insistent beat of rock music could be heard.

There was no response. 'Someone's in all right,' said

Terry; he grasped the big brass door knocker and beat authoritatively on it. Before he'd finished, the door was opened, almost causing him to stumble as the knocker was wrenched out of his hand.

There stood the handsome young man Pat had glimpsed on her last visit. Jasper, the son.

'Yes?' he enquired.

His fair hair was tousled, a cigarette held casually in his hand.

Terry and Pat flashed their warrant cards.

'My goodness,' said Jasper gaily, standing back from the door. 'The police again and on such a nasty night, too! Not to mention it being Sunday. Well, you'd better come in.'

The music was louder now, pouring down the stairs from somewhere up above as they walked into the brightly lit marble-floored hall. Pat wondered if some-one waited for Jasper's return.

Jasper took them into the library where Pat and William had interviewed Val Douglas. Here too, all the lights were on but the room was chilly. Pat wondered whether she would ever feel warm again.

Jasper made no move to light the fire that stood ready in the hearth but waved courteously towards the leather seating. 'And what can I do to help the processes of justice this evening?'

'Well, it's your sister, Jemima, we'd like to speak to, actually,' said Pat.

'Jemima? Oho, what's the dear girl been up to?'

'It's not that she's done anything,' Pat said patiently. Terry appeared to be happy to leave things to her for the moment. 'We'd just like to be reassured as to her whereabouts.'

'Reassured?' Jasper shot back. 'You make that sound very unsettling.' There'd been a subtle change in his attitude. The flip, self-confident young man was suddenly uncertain. He came and sat next to Pat. 'Why don't you level with me? What's with my sister?'

'The thing of it is,' Pat said slowly, 'Darina Lisle is worried that she hasn't been in touch and this afternoon the body of a woman answering to your sister's description was found just down river from here.'

His face grew quite pale. 'Jemima, drowned? Don't be absurd, of course she can't be drowned. She's just gone off for a few days. She's like that. Does things on the spur of the moment. She'll be back any time now.'

'Well, when she does reappear, could you please ask her to telephone us?' Terry said, getting to his feet.

Jasper stubbed out his cigarette. 'You bet!' Then he looked down at his feet. 'You wouldn't like me to have a look at this person, I suppose?' he said quietly. 'Just to make sure it isn't my sister?'

'I'm afraid identification isn't possible,' Pat said gently. 'The body has been very battered about the head.'

That got to him. He took another cigarette from a box on the desk, and lit it with hands that shook. After a deep drag he said, 'That's awful!'

Pat liked the uncertain youngster he now was much better than the cavalier young man who'd opened the door to them.

'Look, I'll try and track down Dad, he'll know what to do.'

'Let us know if you hear anything,' Pat repeated as they left.

She switched the heater full on as they drove away leaving a clearly shaken Jasper standing in the doorway.

'Fat lot of good that did,' grumbled Terry as they went down the drive. 'We're definitely no nearer identifying the poor bitch.'

'You know,' said Pat, changing down as they approached the wrought iron gates and the road, 'Jemima Ealham isn't the only missing girl we know of.'

Terry looked at her. 'You're thinking of that Irish bint? The nanny who stole the pearls?'

'Who was accused of stealing the pearls,' Pat corrected him. 'Yes. We had that message on Friday to say that she was coming in to tell us something but she's never appeared.'

'Probably found something better to do,' Terry said.

Pat turned out of the gates and increased her speed. 'The clothes on the corpse were far too good to be hers but why don't we drop by that hostel she's staying at and see what gives?'

Terry thought for a moment. Then said, 'Well, it's not far out of our way.'

At the hostel, they were told that Maeve O'Connor had gone out on Friday and hadn't been seen since. 'They don't always let us know if they're taking a trip somewhere,' a comfortable looking woman in her forties said. 'She's paid up until the end of next week.'

'Are her things in her room?' Pat asked.

'We'll go and see, shall we?'

The room was small and shared with another girl who received the police inquiries with profound disinterest. 'I dunno,' she said. 'Hardly spoke to her. There's things in that cupboard, though.' She pointed to one of a pair of narrow wardrobes that stood side by side between the beds.

Pat flipped through the few garments that were hanging there. 'These are very good quality,' she said.

'Yeah, she said the daughter of the house gave them to her, cast-offs, she said. I should be so lucky with cast-offs.'

Pat looked at a smart pair of trousers and silently agreed.

Chapter Twenty-Five

By the time William returned home on Sunday evening, Darina was at the end of her tether.

Rory had been fractious all day. It was as though he'd picked up the vibes from her. Only at lunchtime had he been amenable, wolfing down the smoked haddock with his usual ardour. But afterwards he hadn't wanted his rest. Even music had failed to calm him and at length Darina had taken him downstairs to play. But he'd thrown his toys around, demanding attention, then hitting at her. By the time supper and bedtime were reached, both of them were exhausted. Rory had finally fallen asleep sitting on the sofa beside her with his bottle of milk. She carried him up to his cot and settled him down with a sigh of thankfulness.

William rang from the station and said it had been impossible to identify the corpse. She asked for a description. 'I know it sounds as though it could be her,' William said hurriedly down the line, 'but there's nothing that says it is.'

Perfectly true but it didn't help. Nor did the fact that Jemima's mobile was still not switched on.

When William finally walked through the door, Darina rushed at him. 'I have no more information,' he said wearily.

She dragged her mind back from Jemima. 'You look exhausted,' she said. 'Have you had anything to eat? I've got some soup ready and there's cold lamb.'

'That'd be nice. Pat and Terry produced fish and chips. By the time I'd picked the flesh out of the batter, it wasn't enough to keep a kitten happy. One thing that might cheer you is that the nanny's gone missing as well and she also fits the dead woman's description. But, look, I've been thinking about what you said, Jemima being frightened and suggesting your investigation into Rory's background might have disturbed something.'

'She didn't exactly say that,' Darina said carefully.

'So tell me what she did say and who you've told you're looking for Rory's father.'

Darina felt as if her heart were made of lead. Surely nothing she'd done could have threatened Jemima? 'Job Ealham and his wife, the PR chap, Paul Robins, Job's friend Martin Price and Cynthia Beauchamp, an old friend of Basil's. I don't think any of them would have told anybody else, I stressed it was confidential. Look, I'll tell you everything we discussed but then you fill me in on what's going on with your fire investigation.' And I'll count the number of times you mention Pat James, she thought to herself.

At the end of their joint exchange of information, William admitted he couldn't identify any threat to Jemima and Darina hadn't heard one mention of the female sergeant. Was that a good or a bad sign? she wondered as they went up to bed.

She found it difficult to sleep.

In the morning William came up as Darina was heating Rory's milk. 'I'll let you know as soon as we find out anything, promise.'

'Aren't you having anything for breakfast? I did some rice for you last night and there's lots of fruit.'

William hesitated then said, 'It's the autopsy this morning.'

Darina stared at him, her face white. There was nothing that could be said.

After William had left, Darina took Rory back upstairs with her and sat him on her bed with his bottle while she tried Jemima's mobile again. Still switched off. While she dressed she tried to tell herself it meant nothing. She looked at Rory, holding his bottle in his chubby little hands, dragging greedily on the nipple, squinting at her to check on what she was doing. It seemed she could hardly remember a time when she didn't have a small boy to take care of.

What did he think of losing Maeve, his surrogate mother, and of being handed over to someone he hardly knew? Jemima was right, Darina told herself finishing dressing. He needs a proper father.

She scooped Rory up from the bed. 'You can have an egg,' she told him, going downstairs.

At nine o'clock, with Rory fed and dressed and playing with a car, she rang Noah again.

The same Australian voice answered. 'Yeah, he's here. It was you rang before, wasn't it? Half a mo and I'll get him for you.'

'Noah,' came another voice, male and soft.

Darina asked if it would be convenient if she came round that morning.

'Guess so,' the soft voice said. 'But what's it about?'

'Do you remember Sophie Ealham?'

'Sophie? Sure. Why do you want to talk about her?' She heard something at the back of his voice, a little slippy note as though he wasn't really comfortable with the thought of Sophie Ealham.

'I can't explain over the telephone, that's why I want to come round,' she told him.

Finally he agreed.

She put Rory in his car seat, confident he'd go to sleep once she started driving. He looked up at her with eager eyes. 'Da!' he said, waving his hands excitedly. 'Da, da, da!'

'Yes, we're going to take a little ride to meet your daddy,' she told him as she fastened the straps and seat belt.

That seemed a good idea to Rory, he clapped his hands together and gave her his big grin and for once he didn't go to sleep as she drove up towards Ladbroke Grove again.

Noah Whitstable's insignificant door was located between a newsagent's and a laundrette and was badly in need of a paint job. Darina rang the bell and waited with Rory in her arms.

After a little she heard footsteps coming downstairs, then the door opened and there was Noah Whitstable.

He was tall, with wheat fair hair and a pleasant, rather weak face. It was impossible to tell what colour his eyes were, so dilated were the pupils. He hadn't shaved and a fair stubble that had nothing of the designer about it covered his lower face. He was dressed in shabby jeans, the material on the knees so pale it was almost white, and a T-shirt with a washed-out design. Both shirt and jeans looked clean. His feet were bare, the big toes splayed as though unused to being confined in shoes. Standing a step up from the pavement level, he was sufficiently tall to be able to look down on Darina.

When he saw Rory, his face lit up. 'Hey, man,' he said, flicking a finger against the little cheek. 'Who've we got here, then?'

Well, at least he liked children.

'Can we come in?' Darina asked.

'Sure, come upstairs.' He turned and led the way up uncarpeted wooden treads.

The tiny landing offered a couple of doors, one of which stood open.

Because the room had very little furniture, it seemed larger than it was. A stove and sink were in one corner, a battered table with two chairs in another. A low table stood in front of two huge cushions covered with some sort of Indian material. A bronze joss-stick holder held two expired sticks. The faint smell of incense fought with cooking spices to create an atmosphere that was warm and slightly mysterious.

Sitting on one of the cushions was a small girl with spiky hair a lurid shade of lime, a broad face and lively eyes. There was a nasty looking bruise on her left cheek. She was wearing denim dungarees over a skimpy white T-shirt and flip-flops. Her toenails were painted lime green to match her hair. She jumped up when Darina entered and came across bouncing off her flip-flops like a little kangaroo.

'Hey, isn't that the most gorgeous tyke you ever saw?' said the Australian accent that had answered the phone. 'You're heaven, you are,' she told Rory. 'Isn't he heaven, Noah? Can I hold him?' She held out her arms and Rory gave her his big grin, chuckled, then buried his head in Darina's shoulder.

That acceptance of her as his protector made Darina

feel wonderful. 'He's a little shy,' she told the girl, 'let him get used to you.'

'What's his name?' She didn't seem at all upset as she gently stroked the thick fair hair.

'Rory, and I'm Darina.'

'I'm Laurel,' she said. 'Would you like something?'

'Coffee would be nice.'

'We don't drink coffee,' Laurel said cheerfully. 'Not good for the system. We've got roasted barley or camomile tea.'

Darina opted for the latter.

Noah moved over to the little kitchen area and busied himself with putting a kettle to heat on the gas. Darina was struck by how little equipment there was. No electric kettle, no gadgets on the small working surfaces, only a couple of cupboards to hold everything that preparing, cooking and eating food called for. There was, however, a small fridge.

'Rory's Sophie's baby, isn't he?' Noah said as he switched on the gas. 'I knew that frigging Martin was lying to me.' The viciousness in his voice took Darina by surprise. He banged a fist down on the edge of the sink, making her jump. 'Sodding bastard.' His accent, which had seemed well educated on the doorstep, now sounded rougher, nearer to south London than Knightsbridge.

'Noah,' said Laurel in a warning voice. 'He can't hurt you.'

The muscles under his T-shirt knotted as his hands clenched on to the sink's edge, making him look unexpectedly powerful. Then, just as suddenly as it had come, the violent mood passed. He opened the cupboard above the sink and took out three earthenware mugs. 'That sod was always jealous of Sophie and me.' He had a way of talking that jerked along, like a car that had grit in its petrol. He leant back against the sink. His jeans hung so loosely on his lean frame Darina wondered if they'd been bought from some street market or from a second-hand shop. Everything about the place said its inhabitants survived on very little money. Yet there was none of the squalor Martin had led her to expect. All was clean and neatly organized.

Darina folded herself down on to one of the cushions. 'If you didn't believe him, why didn't you find out what had happened for yourself?'

Noah scratched his head. 'Didn't seem I could.' No trace now of the emotion that had racked him.

'Didn't Sophie tell you anything about herself?'

Laurel sat beside Darina and started to play with Rory, running fingers up his jersey and on to his nose. He leant back against Darina and chuckled at her.

Noah busied himself with getting out herbal tea bags. He seemed all elbows and hands with his legs in almost constant motion. 'Sophie, well, she didn't talk 'bout her family.'

'Noah doesn't like to talk about his background.' Laurel lifted an uncomplaining Rory on to her lap. 'My father deserted us and my mum says the less she sees of us the better, me and my brothers have ruined her life, if it hadn't been for us, she could have gone off and done something, that's what she says,' she told Darina with great good humour. 'So I reckon if someone doesn't talk about their family it's usually with good reason. Makes sense to forget and all that. That right, Noah?'

He nodded and looked relieved to have been spoken for. The kettle boiled. He made the teas and brought

342

them over, placing Darina and Laurel's mugs on the low table.

Laurel clucked, opened a small drawer in the table, brought out raffia mats and put one under each of the mugs. 'He's hopeless,' she told Darina. 'Before I came here, you wouldn't believe what the place looked like.' She wrinkled her nose.

'Stuff it, Laurel,' Noah said amiably. 'Making me sound like some sort of berk.'

'Reckon you've always needed a woman to keep you straight,' she said without malice. 'Reckon without that Sophie girl you were getting in a right old mess until I came along.'

'How did you meet Sophie?' Darina asked, cautiously sipping the tea, then relaxing as she realized it was a good quality camomile, fragrant and soothing with no dusty aftertaste.

Noah went and leant against the windowsill, holding his mug in both hands. Yesterday's rain had gone and a watery sun was shining, making a halo of his fair hair. 'Met her by the canal,' he muttered into his tea.

'Martin says she tried to throw herself in it. Is that true?'

He ducked his head again. 'Maybe,' he murmured.

'Do you know why?'

He shrugged his shoulders. 'Like I said, she didn't like talking about her family.'

'So it was something to do with them?' Darina coaxed him.

Noah put his mug on the table, walked over to the other side of the room, inspected the poster of some pop group that hung on the wall, flicked at a small tear in one of its curling sides, then turned and leant against the wall. 'Dunno, really,' he said. 'I told her it was stupid to throw her life away. She said she didn't have a home so I said she could come here.'

Darina tried to picture a desperate Sophie, so desperate she'd wanted to end everything, being offered a lodging by this taciturn young man.

'So she came back with you that night?'

'Yeah, and, like, it seemed sort of all right.'

'You mean, she cleaned the place up,' Laurel said suddenly, glancing up from playing horsey-horsey with Rory. 'And cooked. Jammy for you,' she added approvingly.

'I wasn't no good at cooking,' Noah muttered.

'You liked her,' said Darina. 'And she liked you?'

'Yeah, well, as I said, it seemed sort of all right.'

Yes, Darina could see how to Sophie it must have done. Someone who placed no intellectual demands on her, who made her feel wanted and important, who'd told her it was stupid to throw her life away and then showed her something she could do with it.

'What did you think when she suddenly disappeared?' she asked.

Noah took a flat tin out of his back pocket and slid down the wall. He opened the tin, took out a pack of cigarette papers and some weed and started rolling what looked to Darina like a joint. He glanced up at her and his eyes were the dark pools she'd seen when he opened the door. 'Thought she'd legged it,' he said briefly.

'Had you had an argument?'

He looked down at his hands, skilfully rolling the paper round its shredded contents.

Darina waited.

Laurel was showing Rory how the bronze incense

holder could be rolled across the table and hauling him back from lunging after it.

Noah finished preparing his joint, found a match book in his pocket and lit it. He took a long drag, laid his head back against the wall and closed his eyes. Smoke eventually floated down his nose and the sweet, curious smell invaded the room. 'I couldn't stand that she didn't visit the clinic,' he said finally, his eyes still closed.

'You mean the ante-natal clinic?'

'Yeah! I mean, you're pregnant, right? So you want everything for the baby to be right, don't yer?'

'Why wouldn't Sophie go for check-ups?'

Noah took another drag then wrapped his arms around his knees, the dark emptiness of his eyes looking across the room at the window. 'Don't know,' he said. 'Just wouldn't. Said it was a natural process.'

'Did you try to get her to go?' Darina tried to imagine the two of them in this small flat, Sophie insisting she didn't need medical help and this drop-out but strangely sensible young man trying to persuade her she did. And Martin in the background, offering her glimpses of the sort of life she'd known before.

'Her ankles and wrists had no right to swell like that. I told her.' Noah was getting angry again. For a moment Darina thought he was going to hit the floor but instead he took an even deeper drag on his joint. 'So we had this row,' he said, his eyes closed again, his head once more back against the wall. 'I didn't mean to hit her but some-times, well, sometimes things get too much for me.'

Laurel was still holding Rory but she was looking at Noah, her expression watchful.

'I don't think I hurt her much. And she came back that night and the next. And I thought things was all right. Then she didn't and I reckoned I'd blown it after all and she'd gone to that other fellow.' His face looked bitter. 'Then Martin frigging Price comes round and tells me she's dead. And the baby.'

He looked at Darina, his expression curiously blank. 'Why'd he have to tell me that, eh? Why? Weren't it bad enough Soph had died?'

'Would you have been able to look after him?' she asked. 'A new born baby without a mother?'

'Why should I 'ave to look after 'im?'

Darina felt baffled. 'He's your son, isn't he?'

Laurel's head with its spiky green hair turned towards Noah. 'Hey, mate, you never told me you'd had a son!' She sounded injured.

'Why should I?' he ground out.

'I thought we'd told each other everything!' Laurel was dismayed.

'We have,' he said truculently. 'Don't you trust me?'

'What do you mean?'

'Are you going to believe what this, this woman says rather than me?'

'You mean . . .'

'Yeah. That boy *isn't* mine.'

Chapter Twenty-Six

'He isn't your child?' Darina felt as though she was in a lift which had suddenly dropped a great many floors. 'Are you sure?'

'Course I'm sure. She was pregnant when she came 'ere.'

'But,' said Darina. 'But,' she repeated. 'Jemima, that's Sophie's elder sister, she says that Rory was born at least six weeks premature and that means Sophie didn't become pregnant until, well, until she started living with you.'

Noah looked at her scornfully. 'So what makes you believe what this Jemima says?'

What, indeed? Had Jemima been deceiving her? Or had Jemima herself been deceived? She'd repeated what her father had told her.

Suddenly the whole landscape of Sophie's last year of life shifted for Darina and she realized that her investigation had got her nowhere. The truth about Rory's conception didn't lie here.

'Let me make sure I've got this right,' Darina said at last. 'Sophie told you she was pregnant when you first met her?'

'Yeah, she told me, oh, 'bout three weeks after we met. Didn't say much, just cried.'

'And even knowing she was pregnant, Sophie had wanted to kill herself?' Darina couldn't believe it. It went against everything she'd found out about the girl.

Noah took a deep drag on his cigarette and let the smoke emerge gently through his nose. 'That's what I said to her after she told me.' He looked around the small room. 'She'd been desperate before she come here, she said.'

Desperate? When she had two homes she could have gone to? Not to mention Lady Beauchamp's. But Tiggy was abroad and Cynthia Beauchamp would have undoubtedly told Basil Ealham his daughter was with her. Darina thought of the powerful, short-fused man who Sophie looked on as father. Was she really so terrified of him? But it had to be that relationship that lay at the heart of why she'd disappeared. A terrible possibility began to dawn on Darina.

Noah offered his cigarette to Laurel but she shook her head. 'Not while the boy's here, Noah,' she said, sounding shocked.

'The boy, yeah,' he said and carefully pinched the smouldering end of the joint, then placed the fag end in his tin box and returned it to his back trouser pocket. 'She didn't *know* she was pregnant, she was afraid she was,' he said, enunciating his words carefully, sounding once again well educated. 'Like I said, she wouldn't go to the doctor, not after that one time. Said everything was OK, said native women didn't need doctors. She seemed almost terrified.' He winced.

'Did she tell you who the father was?' Darina asked, holding her breath.

'Nah, she was too afraid,' he said in disgust. 'If I'd ever met him, he'd have known all about it.' He drummed the fingers of his right hand on his knee. 'I bopped that ponce Price one when he tried to interfere between us.' He laughed, a high unsteady whinny. 'Right prat he looked. Must've had a real shiner to show everyone!'

Martin hadn't said he'd had an actual set to with Noah. Had he been ashamed at being bested by a hippy? Or had there been some other reason for his reticence? Darina only had his word that he was sterile. She felt now that she couldn't trust anything anyone had told her.

'Did she ever tell you that she was illegitimate?'

'You kidding me?' Noah looked genuinely startled. He got up and moved jerkily over to the window and stood looking out, his right fingers beating an irregular pattern on his leg.

'She found out just before she left home to go and live with her brother and sister-in-law.'

'She never said nothing like that. Seems to me you been listening to the wrong people.' Noah appeared to lose interest.

Rory staggered across the room, opened the cupboard by the stove and started taking out cleaning stuff.

Noah let out a roar and kicked the door to. 'Bugger off,' he said to Rory, who started crying.

Laurel dashed across and picked him up. 'You bastard,' she said to Noah, 'pick on someone your own size.'

'Like you, eh,' he said and swung the back of his hand at her. But she ducked and scuttled out of range.

Noah looked at her, a tic flickering his left eyelid. For a moment Darina thought he was going to fling himself after Laurel. Instead, 'Gotta see someone,' he muttered, opened a jar at the back of the sink, removed some money and left the room.

'That's right, fuck off,' Laurel called after him. She went and looked in the jar and cursed. Then she brought a whimpering Rory back to the low table. 'Let's see what we can find here, shall we?' she said to him and reached beneath one of the cushions to drag out a magazine. 'Look at the pretty pictures.' She flicked over the pages. Rory plumped a finger down on a photograph of a horse and made a noise that might have been a whinny.

'Where's he gone?' Darina asked.

Laurel tossed her head, her face defiant. 'To get a fix. He's taken this week's rent and the housekeeping money, everything I earned last week. My next job doesn't start until Wednesday.'

'What do you do?'

'I'm a freelance butcher.'

'A butcher?' Darina was amazed, and then cross with herself for being amazed. Why shouldn't a girl be a butcher? 'Where did you train?'

'Back in Tazzy, Tasmania. I know I look little but I'm strong.' Laurel squared her shoulders as though to demonstrate.

'I'll believe you,' Darina said, looking at the bruise on her cheek.

'I didn't duck fast enough that time.' Laurel fingered the greeny-black contusion ruefully. 'Usually I can see them coming. Noah's a lovely guy. It's just his habit.'

'The drugs, you mean?'

'The pot calms him down but with the smack, well, you don't know what he'll do.'

'Does he work at all?'

'Oh, yeah, now and then. He's real intelligent, could

do anything.' Laurel said this with pride. 'He's always getting odd jobs around. Drove an old guy up to Newcastle on Saturday with overnight stay and train fare paid back. Course, he dossed down and hitched, doubled his pay.'

'So he should be able to pay the rent?'

Laurel shook her head regretfully. 'Owed too many people. And to think I was the one made him pay them back! Or some of them.'

'Noah's lucky to have you.'

Her face broke into a sad grin, 'You said it! He knows it too. When he's himself. And, like I said, then he's a lovely guy. We have some really great times together. It's just you can't trust what he says. He could win Olympic Gold in the lying game.'

Darina remembered how quickly Noah had turned from being a charmer to lashing out. 'Has he told you anything about Sophie?'

Rory picked up the magazine and flapped it experimentally. Darina rescued it and shoved it back beneath the cushion.

'Not much,' Laurel admitted. 'I didn't want to hear. I mean, what girl wants to be told about the previous love in her boyfriend's life?'

'So Noah loved Sophie?'

'Sure!'

'I thought maybe she just made him comfortable, earned the money and all that.'

'Like me, you mean?' Laurel said sardonically. 'Actually, he loves me in his own way, too. And I'm better for him than Sophie, I don't depend on him like she did. That sort of girl always needs a man in her life.'

Had Sophie? There'd always been one there,

sometimes more than one. First Jasper and her father, then her elder brother, then Noah and Martin. In the end, none of them had been able to help.

'My strength is that I can always leave and Noah knows it,' Laurel declared pugnaciously. 'I'm not hooked on him.'

Darina wondered how far that was true.

All the way back to her house, Darina thought about what Noah had said.

Sophie had suspected she was pregnant when she left Battersea. So what Basil had told Jemima was, at best, misleading. Rory wasn't a premature baby at all. The fact that he'd been so small was because Sophie hadn't been eating properly and had neglected herself. That chimed in with what Martin had said. Oh, if only Martin could have told her family where she was! Or at the very least bullied her into going to a doctor.

But according to Job, Sophie had left home because her father bullied her. Everyone Darina had spoken to had said how sensitive Sophie was and how she dissolved into tears whenever she thought she was being got at. Darina herself could remember how shy she was at five. Perhaps Martin had good reason for respecting her wishes.

How happy had Sophie been living with Noah? He seemed very unstable. Laurel said he could be great. Darina wondered just what 'great' meant. From what Noah said, Sophie had found someone even more dysfunctional than herself and discovered a role in looking after him. But Laurel claimed you couldn't rely on anything Noah told you and his sudden loss of control had been shocking. As shocking as Val's had been. How often did people lose their tempers with children? How often had Noah lost control with Sophie?

According to Martin, he'd offered her an escape route.

But then her family would have known where she was.

Was that the reason she hadn't gone to him? But what was it she'd said? That even though he thought he wanted to marry her it wouldn't work? Why not? Because she wasn't in love with him?

Sophie obviously had her own moral code. Darina thought that rather than being weak as everyone seemed to think, Sophie had had an amazing inner strength.

She'd been very upset on hearing Basil wasn't her father. Well, that was natural. Judging by Martin, 'natural' was a word that meant a lot to Sophie. She had found it natural to move in with her brother and sister-in-law when she didn't want to live at home any more. It was natural to give comfort when it was needed even if it involved sleeping with two men whilst bearing another man's child. It was not natural to move in with someone just to make your life more comfortable. What had been so unnatural she had had to move out of her brother's house?

Darina was very much afraid that she knew.

Stopped at traffic lights, Darina looked at Rory through the rear view mirror. He was chuckling to himself, then saw a dog in the car next door. 'Dog!' he shouted gleefully, 'dog!' He banged on the window pane. The dog barked at him and he laughed even more. Nothing shy or retiring there.

Much as she wanted to, Darina could see no resemblance to Noah or Martin or Paul Robins. But, thought Darina, she herself was nothing like her petite, chic mother.

Her mother! The lights went green and Darina shot away in a panic. She had completely forgotten that her mother was coming today. Might even have arrived!

Darina raced home through the traffic, her thoughts in a jumble. Likenesses and non-likenesses to parents, what she was going to do if her mother had arrived before she got home, and whether William had identified the body from the river. Her certainty that it was Jemima's had been constantly at the back of her mind, an aching tension that threatened to break through everything else.

But at least she reached home before her mother.

First thing was to check the answermachine. No messages. Darina felt relief. Fears could be dissipated, facts could not.

Clutching Rory by the hand, Darina found a couple of late roses in the tiny courtyard. She put them on her mother's dressing table in the back bedroom and thanked heaven she kept the beds made up, a house in Chelsea meant chums ringing up at any time for a night's lodging. She switched on the electric blanket and then put Rory in his cot.

Rory didn't like this.

Darina took him out of his cot and wondered whether pandering to his wishes was bad training for later. The doorbell rang, she put Rory back and ran downstairs, ignoring his screams of protest.

'Darling!' said Ann Stocks. She stood on the doorstep dressed in an elegant chocolate-brown suit with a silk blouse. The soft neckline flattered her neck and the cream lightened her pretty face. 'What on earth is that noise? I know it's a long time since I've seen you but you can't, surely, have managed to produce a child?' She tilted her face to receive Darina's kiss.

'I'm babysitting, Ma. Where's your car? Let me get your case.'

Ann's little BMW was not far away. Somehow she always managed to find parking near to where she wanted. Darina hefted a large suitcase out of the boot.

'I know what you're thinking, darling, but I really didn't know what to bring and when you've got the car, it doesn't matter, does it?' Ann retrieved a couple of jackets and a fur-collared coat from the back seat. 'Now tell me all about this child you're babysitting.'

'You'll love him,' Darina said, hauling the case back to the house. And I've got the most marvellous nursery food for us all to lunch on. However did you manage to get this in the car?

'The gardener, darling. Lunch sounds heavenly. Nursery food was always your father's favourite. Not that I was any good in the kitchen, as you know. Don't you think you should do something about that baby?'

But Rory's cries were lessening. 'He'll be asleep in a few minutes, he needs a rest. Do you want to go up to your room now?'

'Oh, I think a drink first, don't you? It's nearly twelve after all.'

In the short hour before Rory woke again, Darina got her mother a pre-lunch gin and tonic and heard all about what was happening with her bridge, the village feuds, the change of ownership in the local shop, the new restaurant that had just locally opened and the dreadful things a great friend had said to her.

Ann appeared in great form. Eighteen months earlier her second husband had died after a short but very happy marriage. Darina decided that she had now adapted once again to widowhood.

'Now, darling, tell me all about you. That's what I've come here to hear.' Ann sat back in the small armchair that was her favourite and looked about her. 'I'm so glad your tenants didn't do too much damage, this is such a pretty room. You know, if you didn't want to live here yourselves, you could let it for far more than they were paying. I don't care how nice they were, you were robbing yourself.'

Darina opened her mouth to say that she and William were very happy here themselves when the first cry came from upstairs.

Her mother fell instantly for Rory. 'What a delightful child,' she said.

Rory opened his big blue eyes and reached for her pearls. 'Gah!' he said, twisting the string.

'Naughty, naughty,' Ann said, laughing, and gently removed the pearls. 'Let's find something else for you to play with, shall we?' She reached into her lizard-skin handbag, detached the pearl and gold chain from her glasses and dandled that. Rory went for it in a big way. Darina looked on in astonishment. She had never seen her mother take any interest in babies before.

Soon they were all sitting down to minced lamb with parsnip and peas. 'Darling, he's gorgeous, just like you were as a baby.'

'I bet I wasn't as handsome,' said Darina.

'You were the most beautiful baby in the world. And

your father adored you. I was almost jealous!' Ann pouted prettily.

Darina knew there was no way even a baby could have displaced Ann in her husband's affections. 'I must have been a great trial,' she said. 'Babies seem very demanding.'

'I loved every minute of you. I don't suppose I was a very good mother, far too selfish, and you were so much more intelligent than me, but you were a joy.'

Ann sounded as though she meant it. Darina looked at her and thought how amazing life could be. Here she was, over thirty and it was the first time she felt truly loved by her mother.

Chapter Twenty-Seven

By the time William arrived at the morgue, everything was ready. The green-overalled pathologist was already examining the dreadful remains. Still dressed in her damp clothes, the unknown woman lay on a stainless steel table with a channel running round its edge. The smell of formalin mixed with decay with undertones of river debris floated towards William, the disturbing odours filling the pores of his skin.

Leaning against the wall beside the door, as though reluctant to move away from an escape route, was Terry Pitman, his thin face set into knife-like lines.

The pathologist nodded to his team and the police officers. 'Hope everyone had a good breakfast,' he said cheerfully. 'Bacon and eggs really sets a man up for the day.'

William could have told the last pathologist he'd worked with that he was a sadist and just to get on with the job but Peter Ross was an unknown quantity.

'All you cutters of cadavers are the same, not happy unless we're ready to puke,' he growled out. 'And you may well have your wish before this job's over.'

Ross looked at him as though for the first time. 'Not a pretty sight, is she?' he said jovially, adjusting the overhanging microphone. 'But you'll be OK, and Tel there never flinches.'

William saw Terry stir slightly and knew he had no more confidence in himself than William did.

'Right, we'll make a start,' said Peter Ross.

The curiously remote process of removing the layers of a dead person never failed to upset William.

Because he didn't know the identity of the victim, it should have been easier to watch but nibbling away at the edges of his consciousness was Darina's conviction that this was her friend, Jemima Ealham. But more likely was the chance that this was the body of Maeve O'Connor. Killed because she knew something she was going to tell police?

But maybe this wasn't murder. Maybe it was an accident or suicide. And maybe it wasn't either Jemima Ealham or Maeve O'Connor.

William's headache seemed worse than ever and he found it almost impossible to think straight.

The dry, disinterested voice of the pathologist had started to dictate his findings.

'Rigor mortis no longer present. Body has been in the water at least two days.' He turned over the woman's clenched hand. 'Cadaveric spasm of the right hand.' Then glanced at William and Terry and added, 'Often a drowning person will grab at whatever's to hand. You can find stones, water weeds, branches, all sorts of things when you undo the fingers.' Gently but firmly he was doing that as he spoke. 'Well, well, well,' he murmured. 'Look what we have here.' He beckoned to William, who came forward and was given a small circle of metal with a notched cross band. A moment's inspection revealed it to be a button.

Screwing up his eyes, William tried to read the lettering impressed into the metal. 'US Issue' he finally made out. Fishing out a small plastic evidence bag from his pocket, he slipped the button inside. It could mean something or nothing.

'Cadaveric spasm?' he asked.

'Usually a sure indication of death by drowning,' said the pathologist, watching his assistants take scrapings from under the fingernails of both hands. 'The victim panics, clutches at anything that can save him then movement is arrested by a sudden stopping of the heart. The shock of sudden immersion into cold water can lead to reflex cardiac arrest. Doesn't always happen, of course.'

'When it does, does it mean the victim doesn't breathe in water?' asked Terry, coming forward also.

'If it happens instantly, the classic signs of death by drowning are not present,' agreed Peter Ross. 'Then handfuls of pond weed or reeds can be indicators that the victim was alive when immersion took place.'

'But this isn't such an indicator,' murmured William, still inspecting the button.

'No. She almost certainly grabbed it just before death, though.'

'And it doesn't belong to any of her clothes?'

The pathologist examined the outer garments carefully. 'Not that I can see.'

William had a sudden vision of the dead woman struggling with an attacker, perhaps starting to lose consciousness and clutching at her assailant's coat, ripping off the button in the process. Would her attacker have realized it had gone?

The pathologist picked up the right hand again,

looked at it closely, then studied the left. 'Flesh swollen by immersion in water but we should be able to obtain fingerprints for you.'

The autopsy proceeded with the detailed examination of the clothed body, then the removal of the dead woman's garments. 'Pants intact without visible staining,' the dry voice said. 'Doesn't look as if any attack was sexual unless the assailant found himself with an unexpected corpse on his hands and decided to dump it as quickly and unobtrusively as possible.'

Finally the body lay naked on the examination table.

William wondered if it was his imagination or was the disturbingly complex aroma of the mortuary actually growing stronger? Or was it just the headache that seemed to be increasing in intensity? He allowed medical terms to float by him but found his attention became focused on the terribly bruised and damaged neck area. 'Any chance she could have been strangled before being dumped in the river?' he asked abruptly.

The pathologist paused with a sigh of heavy resignation. 'Now, now, chief inspector, you should know better than that.' Then he relented. 'This was the area I was about to turn to.' He turned his steely gaze on to the ruined neck. 'It's difficult to be certain, water immersion always plays the devil with blood, but if you want my expert opinion,' he paused meaningfully.

What else could he want, William thought with exasperation but said, 'I'd be most grateful.'

'Well, putting it in layman's terms and considering the boat injuries occurred a couple of days after immersion, I think the likelihood she was strangled is strong. I shall be most surprised if we find signs of anoxia in the air passages or lungs.'

'Which would only be there if the death was by drowning?'

'Quite, chief inspector.'

Well, a likelihood of death by strangulation wasn't hard evidence but at least it gave them something to work on. Photography of the wounds proceeded before the gut wrenching business of stripping what was left of the scalp from the remains of the skull before it was opened up with an electric saw.

At the end of the autopsy, William, his sensibilities anaesthetized by all he'd experienced, summed up the particular points he'd caught during the mentally bruising process. 'So, you found no signs of anoxia either in the air passages or the lungs and you consider death occurred before immersion in the river. And your expert opinion is that the victim was over twenty-five but no older than the early forties.'

The pathologist sucked his teeth for a moment. 'The skull and teeth are so badly damaged it's hard to be sure of either limit but it's a good guestimate,' he said finally. 'Sorry I can't narrow it any further.'

'And the victim has been in the water two to three days.'

'Certainly at least two days. Water slows up the disappearance of rigor mortis but, as I said at the beginning, the body shows no sign of it now. And not longer than four days, the decomposition gases had not begun to swell the body.'

William felt thankful for minute mercies.

'You'll get my full report as soon as it's been typed up. Good to meet you chief inspector, I look forward to our future collaboration.'

'Quite.' William found it impossible to sound enthusiastic.

'That age thing,' said Terry after he'd taken a deep breath of the clear air outside the mortuary. 'Twenty-five to forty means the nanny is well in the frame. She was twenty-seven.'

And Jemima Ealham was the same age as Darina, early thirties.

Back at the station CID room, Pat James was on the telephone. The moment William and Terry entered, she waved compulsively at them. 'Right,' she said to her caller. 'Right, got that. Look, the chief inspector has just returned to the office, I'll have a word with him and ring you back, OK?'

She put down the phone, her eyes snapping with excitement. 'You'll never guess who that was.' Then recollected herself. 'Sorry, guv. It was Paul Robins. He went to the airport to meet Val Douglas this morning from her international conference but she wasn't on the plane. When he got back to the office, the organizer had been on the line. Apparently Robins was their liaison chap. Val Douglas never turned up at the conference! They rang her home number all weekend but no answer. As soon as he'd had the call, Robins went over to her flat to see if she was ill. No sign of her. He rang Basil Ealham's offices. He's abroad and she hasn't been seen. He rang one of her daughters but she hasn't spoken to her since the middle of last week. So then he rang here to see if we knew of any accident.'

William and Terry looked at each other. 'How old would you say Mrs Douglas was?' William asked Pat.

'Thirty-eight, forty?'

'Within the frame, definitely, guv,' said Terry.

'Where is Robins now?'

'Still at Mrs Douglas's flat, he said he'd stay there until I rang him back.'

'Right, we'll take the clothes over and see if he can identify them and we'll have another look at her place. Sergeant, ring the mortuary, stop them sending the clothes to forensic's and then collect them and meet me at the Douglas flat.'

Pat reached for her coat.

'We need to check whether she showed up for her flight and instigate a house-to-house for any sightings of her that evening. Also to check with her secretary, see if she knows anything about her movements or can throw light on unexpected appointments or callers. You know what's needed, inspector.' William threw the words at Terry like a golfer hitting balls on a driving range.

'Right, guv, leave it to me.'

As he rang Val Douglas's bell, William saw the door of the next flat open a crack.

Paul Robins flung open Val's door, his face drawn. 'What do you think has happened?' he asked immediately. 'Val would never have just walked out on a conference like that.' He led the way into the living room, collapsed into one of the small armchairs and put his head in his hands. 'I'm distraught,' he said unnecessarily.

The room looked smaller and shabbier than it had the previous week. Because Val Douglas was no longer drawing the eye with her dynamism and dark good looks?

'Would you like a cup of tea?' William asked.

Paul shook his head violently. 'I couldn't drink a thing. It's the not knowing that's so awful. I promised to ring Sally the moment I knew anything.'

William looked at the telephone, a red light glowed on the answering machine. 'Have you checked the messages?'

Paul looked up. 'Oh my God, no! Why didn't I think of that?' He made to get up but William was before him.

'Hi, Mum! Sorry to have missed you,' said a fresh young female voice. 'Just wanted to wish you good luck with the conference. Look forward to hearing all about it when you get back.'

There were a number of clicks and then a Dutch accent asked if Mrs Douglas could contact the Conference Organizer as soon as possible and gave an international number. More clicks. A repeat of the same message. Then a call from the desk sergeant at a nearby police station that asked Mrs Douglas to contact them, they'd found what seemed to be a case of hers.

Almost before the message ended, William was dialling the number that had been given and talking to the duty sergeant.

'The case was found in a ditch in a back lane not far from the river yesterday afternoon,' William told Paul when he'd finished. 'Some honest soul thought it must have fallen off a roof rack and took it to their local station. The police opened it and found clothes, personal possessions and what seem to be Mrs Douglas's conference papers. They had her name and address on.'

'Oh, God,' groaned Paul. He levered himself up and

walked over to the window. 'What can have happened to her?'

The doorbell rang. William opened it to Pat, who carried several transparent plastic bags.

He took them into the living room. 'Would you please look at these, sir, and tell me if you recognize any of them?'

Paul looked nervously at the bags, then took the one containing the waistcoat, handling it as though it could be infectious. 'Where has it come from?'

'Have you seen it before?' William repeated patiently.

Paul gazed at the still damp leather through the plastic, turning the bag this way and that to get the best view.

Finally he said, 'I can't be sure but it's like one Val wears.'

Suddenly he thrust it back at William. 'What's happened to her? You know something, I'm sure you do. Why don't you tell me?'

William jerked his head at Pat, indicating the kitchen. She took the hint.

'Sit down, Mr Robins,' he said gently.

Paul slowly lowered himself into a chair.

William put the bags on a table and sat opposite him. 'The body of a woman was pulled out of the river yesterday. She was wearing those clothes,' he indicated the bags. 'With what you have told us and the discovery of Mrs Douglas's suitcase, it is beginning to look as though it could be her.'

Paul gazed at him. Sweat began to bead his brow. He tried to speak several times, finally he managed, 'You want me to identify her?'

'I'm sorry, that won't be possible. The body is damaged beyond recognition.'

'Beyond recognition?' Paul brought the words out slowly. Then, 'Basil!' he shouted. 'I knew it! He's done her in!'

'Why do you suggest that?'

'Because he couldn't stand being stood up! My God, the man's ego is higher than the Empire State.' Paul walked rapidly to the window and back again to stand in front of William, balancing on the balls of his feet like a boxer ready to launch the first blow. 'I'll do him! I will!'

Pat brought in a tray of tea. William hastily removed the garment bags so she could put it down on the table.

'How do you know Mrs Douglas broke off her engagement to Mr Ealham?' William asked.

Paul flung himself back into the armchair and ignored the tea Pat placed beside him. 'God,' he groaned. 'If only I'd been earlier!'

Pat gave William a cup then sat down with one herself. He looked at his tea, the delicate of aroma of Darjeeling reached his nostrils. William's head pounded with pain and he longed to sip the fragrant liquid. He reached for the cup. Then withdrew his hand. What was the point of only doing half the job? If he didn't feel any better in a couple of days, though, he was going to give up this stupid diet.

'OK,' said Paul. 'Here's the full story. Thursday evening I was desperate. Val hadn't responded to any of my calls and I was terrified she was going to announce her engagement to that man.'

'Why?' interposed William quietly.

'Why?' Paul looked at him startled. 'Ever since the fire everything about Val this last week has suggested

367

that she was deciding to marry Basil Ealham. Staying at Blackboys, working from his offices, closing me out of her life! But I thought she'd wait until she got back from Europe. I knew Basil was supposed to take her to the airport but I thought if I arrived early enough, I could persuade her to let me take her.'

'She told you Basil Ealham was taking her to the airport?' asked Pat, catching William's eye.

Paul nodded. Then seemed to realize something wasn't quite as he'd thought. 'You mean, he wasn't going to?'

'She told us he was catching a plane from Gatwick and hers went from Heathrow.'

Paul looked at William with bitter eyes. 'The bitch!' Then he frowned. 'But he collected her anyway.'

'You saw Basil Ealham pick up Mrs Douglas?' asked William carefully.

'I missed them by that,' Paul clicked his middle finger and thumb together. 'I should have been there in good time but, would you believe it, I had a puncture. I never have punctures! You wouldn't believe how fast I tried to mend it. But I didn't know where anything was and then the nuts were impossible to move, I had to stand on the spanner, can you believe that?' He was disgusted. 'And when I at last got here, it was to see Mr Mighty's Roller disappearing in the distance! I was gutted!' He flung himself back in the chair and raised his eyes to the ceiling.

'What time was this? asked William.

'Six twenty-two! I can tell you to the last minute, my eyes were on the clock all the way after I'd mended that puncture. I've never driven so fast through traffic before!'

Six twenty-two, thought William. He and Pat had left just before quarter to six. There'd been no trace of Basil's Rolls Royce then. Had he come back for Val Douglas?

'But there I was, watching them both drive away from me. I'd thought it was my last chance, swooping down, carrying her off and swaying her with my eloquence.' He fixed William with a wild eye. 'You don't know how eloquent I can be with Val. That's how . . . well, that's another part of the story.'

William made a mental note not to forget to follow this up. 'Are you sure it was Mr Ealham's Rolls Royce?'

Paul nodded vigorously. 'I wouldn't forget that number plate: BE1; Be First, what monumental cheek!'

'What did you do then?'

'Went back to my flat and got plastered. I haven't been that drunk since my college days.' He rubbed his forehead. 'I spent Friday in an alcoholic haze with the mother of all hangovers. I switched off the phone, locked the door and gave myself up to blinding self-pity.' He paused but neither William nor Pat said anything.

'Anyway, I finally pulled myself together and by this morning I'd returned to a state approaching normality. On my desk as I get in is a note of my office answer-machine messages from my secretary. The first one is from Val, obviously rung in before Basil arrived.'

Pat put down her cup of tea and reached for her notebook.

'She'd said she wanted me to know she'd finished with Basil and could I meet her at the airport on Monday. I knew her flight, of course, I'd done all the arranging, and I reckoned I could just make it in time. And I did, but she wasn't on the flight. At first I thought she'd changed it because I hadn't rung her in Holland. I tell you, marble-plinthed bronze horses weren't as high as the one Val could get on when she reckoned you'd failed her in any way.' He looked moodily at his trouser leg and flicked a piece of fluff away. 'I rang her here and left a message, it'll be on there if you play it to the end.' He flicked his gaze towards the answermachine. 'Then I went back to the office and my secretary tells me the Conference Organizer has been on the line asking if Val's all right and wanting to know why she never turned up. That's when I started to get really worried. I rang Sally, Blackboys and Basil's office and then came over here to see if she'd collapsed on the way to the airport and been brought back. But everything was just as you see it and no Val. It wasn't much of a hope anyway and by the time I rang you lot, I was out of my mind. And now you tell me she was in the river all the time!' He ended on a sort of wail.

Pat refilled his cup, put in two spoons of sugar and gave it a good stir. 'Drink that,' she commanded.

Paul raised the tea obediently to his lips. Then put it down again without drinking. 'It can't be her in the river.' He sounded as though hysteria would break out at any moment.

William said, 'When you were talking about how eloquent you could be with Mrs Douglas, you told us that that was how, then broke off and said that was another part of the story. What did you mean?'

'Eloquent?' Paul looked puzzled. 'Oh,' he added, his face clearing, 'I remember.' Then he paused and flicked again at his trousers. 'Look,' he said in a man-to-man manner, 'I'm going to level with you. I told your sergeant over here,' he glanced at Pat, 'Aherne wasn't blackmailing me. Well, he tried it on.'

William felt a sense of excitement. The case was beginning to unravel, he could sense it.

'The thing was, shortly after Aherne started working as nightwatchman, I called on Val one evening. I knew she wanted to make sure of Ealham's money, the company was going to go to the wall if someone didn't inject some cash and I was all for it, my money was involved as well. But she was distancing herself from me.'

'You mean you and she were an item before that?' interposed Pat.

'An item? You bet we were,' he said with sudden energy. 'We didn't broadcast it around, Val didn't think it would be good for business, but in private, we could have made all the headlines, that's how big an item we were.'

It sounded as though Val pushed the sexual button whenever she wanted something, William thought.

'Anyway, I was getting really frustrated. I rang and said I wanted her to check a press release. When I arrived I sent Aherne out to buy some cigarettes and gave him some money to have a drink at the same time. I thought that would get rid of him for at least half an hour or so. How was I to know he'd sneak back?' he complained, his voice a whine.

'You mean your eloquence got through to Mrs Douglas?' William asked.

Paul gave a reminiscent smile, 'And how!' Then distress washed over him again. 'But it was only that one evening. And then Aherne made me meet him in that wretched café and told me he was Ealham's spy. But that he wouldn't tell him what he'd seen as long as I

371

coughed up three hundred a week. Three hundred! Well, I tore him off a strip, I can tell you!'

'And did he back down?' William asked.

'Well, no.' Paul plucked at the crease in his trousers. 'I, well, I decided I'd pay him for a week or two and see how things went.'

'But you didn't make any payments,' William suggested calmly.

'Well, I was going to, but then there was the fire, you see.' Paul stumbled to a stop, looking miserable. 'I didn't have to tell you any of this,' he said aggressively.

'So why are you telling us?'

'Don't you see, Ealham distrusted Val, that's obvious. If he found out she'd been double-dealing, he would, well,' he shuddered graphically. 'The man's a monster. Only a monster would set a spy on the woman he loved!'

'We shall need you to give a statement at the station,' William said expressionlessly. 'We'll let you know when.'

'But what about Val, are you really saying she's dead?'

'I think it looks almost certain that she is,' William said slowly. 'Fingerprints from the corpse and from here should confirm it.'

'Oh God,' Paul said.

'I'd like the sergeant here to go with you to your home, Mr Robins, and look through your wardrobe.'

Paul swallowed nervously. 'Don't you need a search warrant for that?'

'We can always get one,' William assured him. 'Co-operation on your part, though, will greatly assist our inquiries.'

Another nervous swallow. 'In that case, I'll be happy.'

'The sergeant will be with you in a minute,' William said and took Pat outside. 'You know what we need?'

'To check whether any of his clothes have a button missing matching the one the victim was clutching. Also if they bear signs of having been near a river or damage sustained during a possible struggle.'

'And check for signs of spilt petrol as well. I don't like it that he claims she rang and said she'd broken with Basil Ealham when she told us it was nothing more than a tiff. Either she's an even more devious woman than we realized or he's setting up an alibi. Watch him like a hawk.'

Pat nodded. 'I wouldn't put anything past the Douglas woman, though, guv. She could just have been hedging all her bets.'

William nodded. 'We need some sort of evidence. Before you go, get a SOCO team over here, I want this place gone over with the same sort of care they'd give the love of their lives. I'll let them in. I'm going to have a word with whoever it is next door takes such a keen interest in their neighbour.' He went back into the living room and got Paul Robins's key off him.

A brass knob on the next door flat shone brilliantly at William as he rang the bell. There was a long pause. Then came the sound of shuffling feet. The door was slowly opened a crack and the same eye he'd seen the other night looked at him. 'Yes?' It was a croak more than a word.

William flashed his warrant card. 'DCI Pigram, I wonder if I could have a word?' It was impossible to know whether the owner of the eye was male or female.

A delighted cackle. 'That's what they say on *The Bill*!' The door closed and he heard the sound of a chain being drawn. The door opened again, wide this time. The peeping Tom was a woman. She looked in her seventies with a frizz of iron-grey hair, a deeply lined face, large, bright grey eyes, a hook of a nose, thin mouth, emaciated figure in an elegant emerald green two-piece, what must once have been sensational legs, and feet in slippers.

'I'll take another look at that warrant card, the way you flashed it at me it could be anything.' William handed it over and she carefully scrutinized the identifying photograph. Finally she handed it back and motioned him in. 'Molly Cummings. To what do I owe the pleasure, then, chief inspector?'

Her living room was the same size as Val Douglas's, furnished with what looked like the remnants of a more gracious life. There was a less than appetizing smell and William saw a foil dish of some supermarket cottage pie steaming gently on a table by the window. The aroma combined with the influence of the autopsy and his splitting headache to make him feel faintly sick.

'I'm sorry, I've interrupted your lunch.'

'No matter.' The woman picked up dish and fork, there was no plate. 'It can go back in the oven. Like a coffee, would you?'

William refused politely. She disappeared and he turned to look out of the window. It was screened with a net curtain. It was fine enough to conceal from her neighbours that Molly Cummings spent the day in an upright armchair monitoring their activities but coarse enough to offer a perfect view.

Molly Cummings reappeared and sat down. 'Pull up a seat and tell me what you want,' she ordered, waving her hand at another chair.

William obeyed, seating himself so he could see her full face. Her eyes were sharp and malicious, as was the slight smile on her face. She wore a wedding ring on her left hand.

'Mrs Cummings, I'm anxious to know whether you saw anything of your neighbour, Mrs Douglas, after my sergeant and I left here last Thursday evening.'

She looked down at her slippers, set her feet toes to toes. 'I'm a nosy old parker,' she said looking up again. 'As you know. A bit of a bitch too, I expect, but there's not much that's interesting in my life.'

William said nothing.

'Other people are my hobby. Take Mrs Douglas. Goes away for days on end. Has at least two steady boyfriends, which of them does she stay with, I wonder? Both tall and both fair headed but what a difference! She controls one and the other controls her. How much does each know about the other, eh?' Amused, sardonic, Molly Cummings was enjoying herself. 'And something's up. She hasn't been here since Thursday but the pet arrived at least an hour ago. And I don't suppose he's been sitting in there doing nothing, do you?'

'Mrs Cummings, did you see anything of Mrs Douglas Thursday evening?'

She looked a little piqued. 'I was leading up to that, young man. Quite an evening that was! First the macho man. And such a row they had! Always knew she was too wilful for that one. Then you and that woman arrive. Then everything's quiet for a little. But just as I settle with my supper, I hear her come out and the lift arrive. It pings as the doors open, you probably noticed.'

'Did you see her get in?'

She shook her head. 'Stayed in my chair.' William

could imagine her with fork poised. Wondering whether she'd reach the door in time to see anything, then deciding it wasn't worth a try.

'But I saw her come out down below. She was carrying a case.' Molly seemed delighted to have an audience for her nosiness. 'She sat down on the wall, as though waiting for someone. It's a very convenient height for sitting on, that wall. I sometimes take a little breather there on my way back from shopping.' William looked through the curtain. The wall was some two feet in height and finished off with a slight pillar either side of the path that led up to the flats.

'Did you see what the case looked like?'

'One of those smallish things on wheels with a handle, you see all the stewardesses using them in airports.' She looked impishly at him. 'Quite a traveller I was in the old days. If I had the cash I'd be off tomorrow even now.'

'I can believe it,' William assured her gravely. 'Did you see what colour it was?'

'No,' she said reluctantly.

'Never mind, you've given us a most helpful description. Now, you said she sat on the wall, what happened then?'

'She stayed there for about ten minutes and kept looking at her watch. Waiting for someone to collect her, I thought. And he's late. Then I saw a Rolls Royce draw up. He had to double park, no hope of a place after six o'clock here. The passenger window slid down and the driver bent forward, I could just see his fair head. Macho man, all right. He didn't always use the Rolls, sometimes it was a Volvo, but that night I reckoned he'd put his best foot forward. Because he had ground to make up, hadn't he? I mean, walking out like that and then being late collecting her.'

'And what time exactly was this?'

'Six fifteen. I know because I listened to the news headlines as I heated my fish pie.'

Six fifteen was about an hour after he and Pat had arrived. Plenty of time for Basil to have gone home, decide he'd take Val to the airport after all and get out his best car. It all fitted in with what Paul Robins had told them. 'And Mrs Douglas got in the Rolls?'

'Not at first she didn't.' Molly was making the most of her story. 'Came to the car, stuck her head through the window and stood there arguing with him.'

William looked at the distance between a car double parked in the road and this third floor window. 'How could you tell she was arguing?'

'What else would she have been doing?' Molly gave a cackle. 'And he must have sweet talked her because after a little she takes her head back, goes and picks up her case, puts it in the boot, then gets in and off the car glides.'

Something about this scenario struck William as odd. 'The driver didn't get out of the car at all? Didn't help her with her luggage?'

'Macho man doesn't have many manners.' Another cackle. 'And the car was beginning to cause a hold up.'

'Well, thank you, Mrs Cummings, you've been most helpful.'

'Just a minute, young man, don't you want to hear the rest?'

'Rest?'

'Two minutes after macho man whisks wilful lady off, a taxi arrives. Has to double park again. Driver gets out, walks up the path, waits around for a few minutes, then comes up to the third floor and rings Mrs Douglas's bell. I know she's not there so I think only fair if I tell him she's gone.' She gave William a malicious grin. 'Was he cross! Said he'd only been fifteen minutes late, and she should have waited for him. Can't wait when you've a plane to catch, I told him.'

'How did you know she had a plane to catch?'

'I didn't but he needed to realize you can't keep clients hanging about. In my day nobody kept me waiting.'

William would have bet money on it.

Molly Cummings had nothing else useful to add. William asked if she'd mind coming down to the station to make a statement.

'If you send a car for me.' She looked unexpectedly skittish.

William promised.

He let himself back into the Douglas flat, now empty, and played the telephone message tape right through. Paul Robins's call was there but nothing else of interest.

He put on a pair of plastic gloves and looked quickly through the desk. Nothing interesting came to light. He drew a blank in the bedroom as well. While he worked he mentally sifted through Molly Cummings' evidence.

A visit to Blackboys seemed called for. Robins had said Basil Ealham was still away. It would be interesting to see if Rolls Royce BE1 was there and if he could find any trace of a jacket with a missing metal button. And if young Jasper was home, William could reassure him that the corpse from the river now seemed highly unlikely to be his sister. Which reminded him. William took out his mobile and tried to call Darina. But all he got was the answermachine. Eventually the SOCO team arrived and William left them in possession.

The garage block at Blackboys was at the side of the house, set nicely back and shielded by massive shrubs.

William parked his car in front of the garage. Each of the four doors was open and he could see the Rolls Royce, its cream paint gleaming, its number plate bold. Beside it were two Volvos, one large family car, the other a smaller, sportier model. The fourth space was empty.

William went up to the house.

The door was opened by the housekeeper. William showed her his warrant card and asked to come in.

'Oh, it's not Jemima, is it? Her who you found in the river? Jasper told me,' she said as William raised an enquiring eyebrow.

'I'm happy to say it now looks as though the body we found was not Miss Ealham's.'

The look of relief on her face was heartwarming. 'Thank heavens, I must tell Mr Ealham immediately.' She moved in the direction of the library.

William went after her. 'I understood he was still away.'

'He came back this morning. Jasper rang him last night.' Mrs Starr moved again in the direction of the library. Once again William detained her. 'Can you tell me, please, do you recognize this button?' He fished the small plastic evidence bag out of his pocket.

She took and studied it. 'Why, that's off Mr Ealham's hunting waistcoat.'

'Hunting waistcoat?'

'Well, it's what he calls it.' She gave him an amused glance. 'More like a photographer's vest it is, lots of pockets. It usually hangs with the outdoor clothes, through here.' She took him through a door that opened on to a corridor. At the end a glass panelled door led into the garden. Beside it a row of hooks held a variety of jackets and coats. Mrs Starr shuffled amongst them and produced a khaki, many-pocketed safari type waistcoat.

William compared the buttons with the one in the plastic bag. It was a perfect match. He took hold of the garment. 'Thank you. Now I'll go and reassure Mr Ealham about his daughter,' he said.

Chapter Twenty-Eight

Darina drove to Blackboys with her mind in a turmoil. Beside her, her mother turned to play peek-a-boo with a delighted Rory, who for once showed no signs of falling asleep in the car.

The telephone had rung just as they were finishing lunch.

'Basil Ealham. I understand you have my grandson,' he said abruptly, no grace notes of greeting. 'Good of you to help but I'd like him returned now.' No would it be convenient, or can I come and collect him!

'Have you heard from Jemima?' Darina had to assume the fact he hadn't mentioned her disappearance yet must mean something.

'I gather she's taken off somewhere,' the autocratic voice said. 'She'll turn up, she always does.' The certainty in his voice was immensely comforting. But the Basils of this world always think they can order everything the way they want; until they discover some things are beyond even their power. 'You'll bring Rory back?' It was only just a question.

'Certainly,' said Darina. 'Once he's finished his lunch.' She didn't want Basil Ealham to think he could order her about the same way he did everyone else.

'Right.' Darina had been left with the tone buzzing in her ear.

'I've got to take Rory back,' she'd said to her mother. 'I'm sorry, you've only just arrived and I abandon you.'

'I'll come with you, darling. Help to keep baby amused.' Ann made a funny face at Rory and he screwed up his eyes and chortled with delight, the spoon he was trying to feed himself with waving in a highly dangerous manner.

'Are you sure?' asked Darina, dismayed. Everything told her this was not a good idea.

'I remember that house and Basil Ealham, I can't wait to see both again,' her mother insisted.

Darina faced facts. There was no way Lady Stocks was going to be deprived of this treat.

She pulled up in front of Blackboys and noted with relief that hers was the only car standing on the forecourt. She wasn't in the mood to cope with police, Val Douglas or anybody else today.

She opened the door for her mother then unfastened Rory from his seat. Remembering the amount of time it had taken the two of them to stack the car with all his bits and pieces, Darina decided Basil was going to help take them out.

Ann Stocks gazed up at the façade of the house. 'Oh, I do so remember this. Such a lovely place I thought, then I saw what they'd done to the inside.'

'I think you'll approve now, Ma.' Darina lifted Rory out of the car, carried him chattering excitedly to the front door and rang the bell.

Rory insisted on being put down.

The door was opened by a man in his mid-thirties.

Darina gazed at him in awe. This had to be the most

magnetic male she'd met in a long time. Dark hair flopped over a face that was too irregular to be called handsome but was nevertheless devastatingly attractive with its dark, dancing eyes, slightly crooked nose and wry mouth. He had a lean, contained body clad in well cut jeans, an equally well cut checked shirt and a puffa waistcoat. He could have stepped out of some American tobacco ad.

'Hi,' he said amiably.

Darina collected her scattered wits. 'Hi, I mean, hello. I've brought Rory back. I'm Darina Lisle and this is my mother, Lady Stocks.'

'Ann Stocks,' her mother said firmly with the smile that had been known to weaken the knees of the most intractable male. 'How nice to meet you, Mr, er?' She put her head on one side in pretty enquiry and proferred her hand.

How, Darina wondered in despair, had she managed to miss out on acquiring even some of her mother's brightly honed social graces?

He took her hand, 'Titus Masterson.' Then looked down at Rory, who had suddenly turned a little shy and stood clutching at Darina's hand. 'You must be Rory.'

Rory stuck his thumb in his mouth and nodded.

'Titus!' Darina said, light dawning. 'Is Jemima with you?'

He nodded. 'We've been snowboarding in the Trossachs.'

'I'm sorry?' It was all too much for Darina.

'Snowboarding, darling, such a healthy activity,' Ann Stocks said. 'Can we come in? Basil is expecting us.'

Titus stepped back with fluid grace. 'I've lost my

383

manners, I do apologize.' His accent had just a trace of the transatlantic.

In the big hall, Rory lost his shyness and suddenly took off in the direction of the library.

'Hey, son,' said Titus, going after him. 'I wouldn't go in there.'

Too late. Rory had already yanked on the door's handle and pushed it open. 'Dah!' he shouted, 'dah!' and ran across the room.

Titus, Darina and her mother all followed.

Basil was sitting behind his desk, his face a mask of anger. In front of him stood Jemima dressed in jeans, T-shirt and trainers, her short hair windswept, her thumbs stuck belligerently in her hip pockets.

'Oh, Jemima,' said Darina with heartfelt relief. 'I've been so worried about you.'

'You see!' Basil grated out as he bent down to lift an excited Rory on to his knee.

'I'm over thirty, a grown woman, I don't have to leave an itinerary every time I take off,' Jemima insisted.

'But you seemed so frightened,' Darina burst out. 'When I couldn't get hold of you, I didn't know what to think.'

Jemima looked slightly shamefaced. 'I did ham it up a bit. Titus had rung me, you see.' She glanced at him with a look that didn't seem able to pull itself free. 'And asked me to go away with him. I couldn't say no, he mightn't have asked me again. And I knew you wanted to develop the baby-food recipes so I thought you'd like looking after him. Were you really worried about me?'

Darina was very angry. 'I was. Particularly when that body was found . . .'

'Body?' Jemima asked. 'What do you mean, body?'

'The corpse of a woman was pulled from the river yesterday. For a while it seemed as though it might be yours,' William said, coming forward from where he'd been standing by a window. 'I rang you,' he said to Darina. 'But you must have left. There's a message on your answering machine.'

'William, how nice,' said his mother-in-law, giving him another of her full voltage smiles.

'I didn't see your car,' Darina said.

'It's by the garage, behind the shrubs,' he said. He seemed to be clutching some sort of khaki garment.

Jemima reached an arm back towards Titus with a smile the like of which Darina had never seen her give before. He slipped an arm round her shoulders.

'And how nice to see you again, Basil,' Ann Stocks said, moving on to offer him her hand. 'It's been a long time.'

He looked at her blankly for a moment then smiled. Darina was reminded of rhymes about tigers. 'Ann Lisle, how delightful.'

'Stocks, now. I was widowed and remarried.'

'Lucky man,' he said, holding her hand in his.

Ann twinkled at him. 'You always were a most charming man,' she said. 'Unfortunately, Geoffrey died also but not before we had a most happy time together.' She sat herself down on one of the sofas.

'What's happening?' Darina whispered to William. 'What are you doing here? It can't be official, surely?'

'Strangely enough, it is,' he said repressively. 'But my investigation appears to have been hijacked.' He moved over to the desk. 'Mr Ealham, can we continue our conversation somewhere quiet or would you prefer to come down to the station?' His voice was steel, his manner composed and Darina felt very proud of him. She went and sat beside her mother.

Basil removed his glasses from Rory's grasp. 'Carry on, chief inspector.'

William made no move and remained silent. Basil swept the others with a look that was hard to read. 'The body that wasn't Jemima's appears to be that of Val Douglas.'

Darina gasped. Jemima clutched at Titus's sleeve.

'And the police are accusing me of her murder.' Basil's voice was strained but steady.

'Dad!' Jemima screamed and ran to his side. 'Dad, they can't do that.'

Basil lowered Rory to the floor and ignored his daughter. 'You can have no evidence that will stand up in court,' he said to William.

'I have yet to accuse you of murder,' William said quietly. 'All I said was we have two witnesses who saw you and your car collect Mrs Douglas from her home on Thursday night. She has not been seen alive since.'

'You saw me leave her flat after she'd broken off our engagement. She can't have failed to tell you that. That was the last time I saw her.'

'Our witnesses say you came back later,' William said quietly.

Rory roared for attention, dancing up and down, and stretching up his arms to Basil.

Darina rose but was beaten by Jasper, who came into the library at high speed and dashed across the floor. 'There, there, little man! All is well, Jass is here.' He picked the boy up, swinging him high above his blond head. Rory's cries gave way to screams of delight.

Jasper lowered and held him against his chest, Rory still chortling. 'What a holy circle!' Jasper exclaimed. 'My sister returned from the grave, Rory delivered once more unto his loving family, dear Darina, the police, and who else?' He looked at Ann Stocks and Titus, his eyes black holes.

'I'm Darina's mother and this young man, I believe, belongs to your sister,' Ann said with all the aplomb of a society hostess.

'Jasper, sit down,' Basil said with weary authority. 'Everyone, sit down while I explain the facts of the matter to this impertinent inspector.'

Darina looked at William, who said nothing. She perched on an arm of a sofa by way of compromise.

Rory tugged at Jasper. He was lowered reluctantly to the floor, he then made a bee line for Darina. She felt as though she'd been given the biggest compliment of her life, sat on the sofa properly and gathered him up on her lap.

William looked very annoyed. Then he shrugged his shoulders and waited as Jemima and Titus also sat.

The only people left standing were William and Jasper, who leaned his wide shoulders against the bookshelves and radiated good humour.

'Now,' said Basil, with the authority of a chairman taking a board meeting. 'Before we had the pleasure of Jemima's arrival, inspector, you were suggesting I set fire to the premises of Eat Well Foods because I wanted to acquire the company free of debt. And that I clubbed the nightwatchman to death because I had engaged him to spy on Mrs Douglas and he was now trying to blackmail me. Do I have it aright?'

Ann Stocks stood up. 'Darling, I don't think this is

something we should be involved with, do you?' she said to her daughter. 'Why don't we leave it to the police and Basil's family?'

'Sit down.' Basil's voice was a whiplash. Any veneer of sophistication had been peeled away. 'I want you as witnesses. I want there to be no doubt, absolutely no doubt at all about this.'

Ann stared at him for a long moment. He stared back at her. Patrician dignity and charm of manner faced raw power. 'Well, if my presence can assist in any way,' she said gracefully and sat down again.

Basil turned to William, 'Well?' he barked.

'I suggested to you a scenario that required investigation,' William said, his voice rough but steady. 'Your interest in the firm is public knowledge. Your only alibi for that night was Mrs Douglas, who admitted she took a sleeping pill. We have received evidence that Mr Aherne was employed by you to spy on Mrs Douglas and you would have known about the spare rooms that could be converted into accommodation for him, thereby ensuring his constant presence at the factory.'

Basil sat very still. 'That is pure supposition. What is this evidence,' he gave a savage emphasis to the word, 'that I employed Gerry Aherne as a spy? You can have no proof, the man's dead.'

'Convenient for you, isn't it?' William said quietly. He stood easily, a picture of contained control, nicely contrasting with Basil's flamboyant style. But Darina could see the muscle that twitched at the side of his jaw and knew that he didn't feel nearly as assured as he looked.

'And can you tell me why I should want to murder Val? For God's sake, I was engaged to her!' For a fleeting second his face crumpled, then his expression regained its cool composure.

'An engagement she broke the night she was killed, sending you from her in a rage.'

Basil laughed. 'Rage? Is that what you call it? You haven't been around me long if you call that a rage. All right, I was pissed off, I'll give you that. Wouldn't you be? You've just given a woman a twenty thousand pound ring and she throws it back in your face. It allows you to be something less than sweetness and light, right? But she'd have come round. By the time I'd returned, she'd have forgotten all about, what was it she called it?' He turned his eyes to the ceiling, one hand negligently tapping the desk as he sought the right phrase. It was an impressive performance. 'Ah yes, my "sacrifice of quality to the gods of mammon". That was it.' He glared at them. 'She already knew where extravagant production methods were taking her.'

Suddenly he stabbed the air with his finger, pointing it at William, and thrust his face forward, his expression cold and mean. 'How did this witness,' a sardonic note lit the word, 'claim I collected Val from her flat?'

William took a step forward, he was losing patience, Darina could tell. 'She recognized the car and you driving it. Look . . .'

Darina knew he was going to insist the rest of the interview was conducted down at the station, where Basil wouldn't be able to play to an audience. Instead Basil interrupted him. 'And this was at what time?'

'About six twenty,' said William grimly.

'And what was the car that your so-called witness saw?'

'Your Rolls Royce, cream with registration number BE1.'

Jemima stirred. 'But, Dad.'

'Quiet, please,' Basil said. 'I'll deal with this.' He turned back to William. 'First I'll ask you how I could have been picking up Val at six twenty when that was just about the time I was checking into my flight at Gatwick? I imagine the airline's computer records will confirm that. If not, the valet service that collected my car on arrival will certainly be able to – AND confirm that it wasn't a Rolls Royce I was driving but a Volvo estate.'

He'd wanted this, Darina recognized. He'd wanted to humiliate William in front of them all. But if he thought this meant William would give up, he was badly mistaken.

'Sock it to them, Dad,' Jasper said. 'You tell 'em.' He smiled beatifically at his father.

'And we'll tell them that you and Val decided at your celebration dinner you couldn't take her to the airport,' Jemima said, looking belligerently at William from the safety of Titus's arm. 'The timing's were all wrong. She made a joke of it, said it was a fine fiancé that couldn't see his girl off to her conference.' She spoke steadily but her eyes were worried.

'You tell them, girl,' agreed Jasper. He thrust his hands into his pockets and started a tuneless humming. He had the happy, unthinking expression of someone who'd removed himself from day-to-day concerns and was inhabiting a world free from pain and sorrow and problems such as writing the great English novel, or even one that proved publishable, or coping with life without his father's backing. Darina realized he was stoned and an idea occurred to her. She slid Rory to the ground and whispered, 'Go see Uncle Jasper.'

The boy set off in his wayward walk, covering the short distance between them in a moment. He wrapped his arms around Jasper's legs and raised his face. 'Dah!' he said peremptorily. Jasper bent down and picked him up.

'Jasper, give Rory to me,' Basil commanded.

'He's fine with me, Dad,' Jasper said, in that same carefree tone.

Basil rose. His complacency had vanished. He strode over and took Rory from his son.

And now Darina was quite certain she was right. The resemblance was startling. And since they'd arrived at Blackboys, other details had clicked into place. Including the reason for Basil's wanting William to rehearse what evidence he had for accusing him of arson and two murders. And the answer was shocking.

'Did you know that Jemima asked me to investigate Rory's parentage?' she asked Basil conversationally as he returned to his desk with the boy.

William gave her the sort of look that should be patented under 'to kill'. She ignored it.

Basil's face darkened. 'What's this?' he rapped out at Jemima.

Some of her composure vanished but she faced her father. 'Dad, Rory has to have a proper parent. You wouldn't do anything about it so I had to.' Her look was pure challenge.

'There's no point,' Basil ground out. 'The trail's dead. I knew that at the time he was born.'

'What you knew,' Darina said calmly, 'was who Rory's father actually was.'

Jemima turned and stared at her. 'You mean, you've found out?'

When Darina said nothing, she moved urgently towards her. 'I hired you, you've got to tell me.'

Darina reached into her pocket and brought out Jemima's cheque. 'I'm returning this.' She handed the folded slip of paper to a disbelieving Jemima, then addressed Basil. It was one of the few times she appreciated her height. 'I can't really blame you, you wanted to protect both Rory and Jasper, didn't you?' She felt very, very sad. 'Over the last few years, it wasn't Jasper who looked after Sophie; it was Sophie, who everyone has kept telling me couldn't cope with life, who looked after him. Until his need for her became too much. Did she tell you why she had to leave home? Or did you assume like the rest of your family that you were asking too much of her?'

The colour had left Basil's face, leaving it an unhealthy grey. He hugged a half-asleep Rory to his chest. 'God damn you,' he grated.

'No!' shouted Jemima. 'I don't believe you.'

William looked at Darina with a dawning comprehension.

Jemima rushed at Jasper and grabbed his arms, shaking him. 'Tell me she's lying, Jass! You couldn't have done that, you couldn't!'

Titus went and pulled her away from her brother. 'Hush, angel, you've got me now, nothing matters any more.' She turned and buried her face in his chest.

Jasper clutched nervously at the bookshelves behind him and threw a glance of appeal at his father. 'Dad,' he started uncertainly.

'Shut up,' Basil said tersely.

'You've always protected Jasper,' Darina told Basil, flicking her hair back over her ears, watching his eyes move uneasily over her. 'After his mother died, you really tried to be there for him, and for Sophie, and they worshipped you. But I don't suppose Val understood your relationship, did she? Did you realize she distrusted him? And that he didn't like her any more than she did him? What was it you said to her on the phone when I was here for lunch that day? "You know Jasper never joins us"? Something like that. He couldn't stand the sight of her. And when you became engaged and had that family evening, he took that as a sign the comfortable life here with you and his son was over.'

Jasper was still leaning against the bookshelves but his insouciance had gone. Darina remembered the young boy she had shared that Italian holiday with, so anxious to entertain and be loved, so secure with Sophie, the one person who never asked him awkward questions, who never made a demand he couldn't fulfil. Behind her she could sense William's tense concentration.

'Dad?' Jasper pleaded uneasily. 'You tell them, Dad. We belong together. You, me and Rory. You loved Sophie, too. That Douglas bitch can't have meant anything to you. It was her business you were interested in, wasn't it? I thought, if she didn't have it, if it was burned down, then you'd lose interest. It wasn't my fault that chap suddenly appeared.'

They were all looking at him now, dawning horror on their faces as what he was saying gradually made sense to them. Except for Ann Stocks, whose expression was deeply puzzled.

'Jasper, shut up!' Basil said with every bit of his

considerable authority. He might as well have saved his breath.

'But then you went and got engaged!' Jasper sounded bewildered. 'Why did you do that? Sophie wouldn't have liked her and I couldn't have her looking after Rory, you must see that?' he said beseechingly. He and Basil might have been alone in the room for all the attention he paid to the others. 'When I turned up the other night, she didn't want to come with me at first. Said she was waiting for a taxi. But it didn't take long to persuade her I could take her to the airport instead. Or to drive down to the river and do what had to be done. She was easy meat!' Then his face suddenly crumpled. 'I miss Sophie! She told me it wasn't right to love her, but I had to, I had to!' He brought up his arm and wiped his eyes with his sleeve.

William held out the garment he'd been clutching. 'Is this yours?' he asked.

Jasper looked at it and smiled. 'The hunter's waistcoat,' he said. 'Dad says it's his and Jemima wears it but actually it's mine.' Automatically he slipped it on, the khaki twill settling neatly round his shoulders. He played with one of the metal buttons, then looked startled as it came off in his hand.

'Jasper Ealham,' said William, sounding very official, 'I'm arresting you for the murder of Gerry Aherne and Val Douglas. You do not have to say anything . . .'

Darina sighed as the caution unwound its formal phrases, but Jasper appeared incapable of taking anything in.

'I must ask you to accompany me to the station,' William ended.

Basil stood up. He'd aged twenty years since Darina

and Ann had entered the room. 'Can't you see he's in no fit state to be questioned?' he ground out.

Rory put his arms around his grandfather's neck and looked as though he was about to burst into tears. 'I must insist on my lawyer being present.' Basil reached for the telephone.

'Jasper!' shrieked Jemima, clutching at Titus. 'Say something! Tell them you didn't do it!'

Titus turned her so her head was buried in his chest and held her tightly.

Darina walked over to the desk and lifted Rory out of Basil's arms. 'We'll take him upstairs,' she said to her mother.

They left the library.

Chapter Twenty-Nine

As they started across the hall, Rory started to cry. Darina felt him warm and solid against her as they climbed the stairs. 'You can stay with him in the nursery while I get his things upstairs,' she told her mother. 'That is, if you don't mind?'

'It's such a relief to get out of there,' Ann said. 'That poor boy, did he really do all those dreadful things?'

Darina nodded, hefting the heavy child more comfortably on her hip, 'I think so. Once Sophie had died, Rory and Basil were his whole world. But Val threatened to destroy it.'

They reached the second floor and Darina opened the nursery door. Then nearly dropped Rory in surprise. 'Good heavens,' she said.

Maeve O'Connor stood there in a pair of smart jeans and a silk shirt.

She took the still crying boy from Darina, sat down in the rocking chair and hushed him. 'What's all the fuss that's going on downstairs?' she asked. 'Mrs Starr said there was a heap of people in the library and not to disturb them. So I came up here until they all left. Is Basil, Mr Ealham,' she corrected herself, 'by himself now?'

Darina shook her head. 'I'm afraid not.' She waved

her mother to a chair by the table in the window and took one of the others herself. 'Where've you been? The police thought you might be dead.'

'Stupid they are!' Maeve said contemptuously.

'Apparently you rang and said you had something to tell them, then disappeared.'

'I only went over to Ireland, to tell Mam about my da's death. I didn't want her to hear it from someone else. And to tell her about being accused of taking Miss High and Mighty's stinking pearls.' She rocked gently. Rory was calming down now. 'And Mam said to come back here and tell Mr Ealham it was nothing to do with me. And didn't he know it, anyway? The money he gave me!'

'I think it was Jasper put the pearls in your drawer,' Darina said.

Maeve didn't seem surprised at this suggestion. 'He was jealous of me and the boy. He wanted himself to be the only one in his life. He's strange that one, going out at all hours, and taking God knows what. Smoking a bit of pot's all right but he's into all sorts of other things too. He went out the other night in the wee small hours and came back looking as though he'd seen a whole host of ghosts.'

'Was that the night Mrs Douglas's factory was burned down?' asked Darina.

Maeve nodded and held Rory a little more closely. 'The boy woke in the night. I was holding him by the window and saw Jasper coming in round the back. Must have been after three. And I'd heard him come in earlier about eleven. Couldn't think where he'd been.'

'Is that what you were going to tell the police?'

'I didn't know what to do,' she suddenly burst out. 'I

397

knew it would make trouble for him – and that meant trouble for Basil, I mean Mr Ealham. I thought and thought about it, turned it round and round in me mind, I did. And finally I thought, I had to tell them. After all, Da died, didn't he? I thought Jasper must have been somewhere else entirely, but, then, he mightn't.' She stopped abruptly. Tears gathered in her eyes and silently ran down her face. Awkwardly she freed an arm from holding the boy and wiped them away.

'Did he?' she looked fiercely at Darina.

'I'm afraid it appears he did set fire to the factory,' she said quietly and went and took Rory from the girl.

'Ah, the bugger!' Maeve wrapped her arms around herself and rocked faster and faster.

'Jasper is Rory's father.'

'The Lord save us,' said Maeve in a whisper and Darina knew she was being serious. Maeve looked at Rory, now dropping off to sleep in Darina's lap. 'Mam said I should come back for his sake. No child should lose his mother, she said, and that's what I am to him, a mother. A child has an appetite for love, Mam says, that needs feeding as much as his tummy does.'

'We all need that,' Ann murmured. 'Well, darling, what about all that stuff in your car? Do you think this nice child can give us a hand?'

'I've been looking after Rory for the last few days,' Darina explained to Maeve. 'I've got his cot and a heap of things, plus a whole shelf of pots of convenience gourmet food that you can put in the freezer.'

Maeve looked at her dully, then rose. 'We'd better get them up, then.'

Twenty minutes later, with Darina and Maeve doing

the shifting while Ann held the sleeping boy, they had everything out of the car.

'So that's that,' said Darina as they placed Rory in the re-assembled cot. 'We'd better leave now. Good luck with Mr Ealham.'

'Oh, I know how to play him,' Maeve said. She seemed to have absorbed the shock of hearing about Jasper. She stood by the cot looking at Rory, her expression a mixture of love and streetwise savvy.

'I think we should say goodbye to Basil,' said Ann when they reached the hall. She knocked on the library door and entered.

It was more than Darina felt capable of but she followed her mother into the room.

William and Jasper had gone. Jemima was quietly crying on the sofa. Titus sat beside her, looking as though he'd rather be somewhere else. Basil was talking on the telephone.

He finished the call as Ann and Darina entered.

'Basil, I'm sorry, really I am,' Ann said. 'Don't blame Darina, though, she only did what she had to.'

He pulled a hand down his face, stretching the skin. He closed his eyes for a moment and stood up. For a second Darina thought he was going to lay into her, then he sighed deeply and said simply, 'I should have realized just how unstable Jasper was. If only Sophie had told me!'

'You didn't know?' Darina asked.

He glanced down at his hands. 'She said something that made me realize it was better to keep them apart, that was why I was happy for her to go to Job and Nicola. I thought a few months there would sort everything out. I didn't realize, though, how far it had gone. I told

399

Jasper better not to visit her. That I'd cut his allowance and turn him out if he didn't let her make her own life. I thought that'd mean he'd leave her alone. If only she'd told me! God, Val dead, I can't believe it. And Gerry Aherne.'

For the first time since she'd known him, Darina was able to feel a certain sympathy for Basil. He had bitter days ahead.

'Sophie knew how close you were to Jasper,' Jemima said angrily. 'He has always been able to do exactly what he wanted as far as you are concerned. When she first said she couldn't stay here, you should have kicked him out.'

He looked infinitely sad, 'But he was my son and she was, well, someone else's child.'

Jemima gasped and Darina realized that she had been in such a state the last time they'd met, she hadn't been able to tell her this. 'Not yours!' Jemima said to Basil. 'But you never said!' Then looked at him suspiciously. 'How did Jasper know?'

'He saw your mother and Sophie's father together one time. He was too young to understand then but later he put things together,' Basil said wearily. 'He asked me and I, well, I had to confirm it.'

'I still think you should have turned out Jasper instead of letting Sophie leave,' Jemima said mutinously, sitting on the sofa with her head held high. She rose and walked with swift, jerky steps towards the windows. 'I can't bear to think of it. Jasper going round there, forcing her to do what he wanted. Sophie must have been a soft touch, she would have hated to hurt him. And no wonder she couldn't tell anybody about it, it would have destroyed Jasper.' She swung round and confronted Basil again. 'Didn't you ask him if he'd been with her when she disappeared?'

Basil rubbed wearily at his face. 'Of course I did! And he told me.' He looked incredibly tired. 'He's always told me the truth. He said he'd visited her several times at Job's, twice when she was on her own and then hadn't been able to control himself. He said she cried every time but let him. And she never breathed a word to me.' He pulled his skin again, as though he had to find a new look to face the world. 'I tried everything to find her. When the man I'd hired couldn't find any trace of her and we heard she hadn't applied for benefit, I really did think she'd done away with herself. I didn't realize she was pregnant but when I saw Rory, I knew he must be Jasper's son. The only thing I could do for Sophie then was to give Rory a good home and hide the truth.' He looked hopelessly at Jemima. 'But you had to go and find it out.'

'You should have told me, Dad,' she said belligerently. 'It's no use trying to hide things like that.'

'Anyway, it wasn't Jemima who set fire to that factory and murdered your friend,' Titus chipped in. 'Come on, darling, let's get going.'

She turned to him in astonishment. 'Go? What do you mean? Surely you can see I can't leave Dad now?'

It seemed to Darina that Basil looked at his daughter with new eyes but Jemima's attention was all on Titus.

He shifted his feet a little uneasily, looked first at Jemima, then at her father. He seemed to be calculating various odds. Then, 'Well, I suppose we can stay for a while,' he said smoothly.

'A while? Dad's going to need me in the business, aren't you?' she said to Basil. 'You won't need to duplicate what I do any more. I'll be your right hand. And then I'll be your left as well.'

She looked very earnest. She went up and stood beside her father. 'We'll see Jasper through this, we'll be all right.'

Titus looked out of the window and Darina wondered if he was already thinking about the next Colorado River he'd go after.

'Jemima, we're going now but I'll be in touch,' she said. 'Believe me, if I'd known where this was going to lead, I'd never have started. Oh, just one thing, was it really true that you were nearly run over?'

Jemima looked slightly shamefaced, but only slightly. 'Well, it might have been a tiny bit of an exag-geration. I was desperate for you to take Rory, you see.' So she could go to Titus.

'Never, never do that again,' Darina said sternly.

'Oh, I won't,' her friend said blithely. 'Everything's going to be all right now. Dad's really going to need me.' She didn't even look towards the young man who stood gazing out of the window. But Basil held out his hand towards her.

'Now, darling,' said Ann when they were on their way back to Chelsea, 'I think you'd better tell me the whole story.'

'Poor little Rory,' she said when Darina had finished. 'What is to become of him?'

'Maybe Maeve will prove a steadying influence.'

'If Basil can keep his hands off her!' Ann said tartly.

'Mother! You saw what a state he's in.'

'That's not going to last long. The man's always

rutted like a stag. I remember a party your father and I went to at Blackboys, dreadful people and the food was too pretentious for words, some fashionable caterer had provided it, the champagne was excellent, though. Anyway, half-way through the evening Basil said he wanted to show me his prize orchids, took me into the conservatory and I practically had to fight him off. I made sure we didn't accept any more invitations.'

'You never told me that!'

'Well, darling, Jemima was your friend.'

'Was that before or after I went to Italy with them?'

'Oh, after, darling. I'd never have let you go otherwise. Anyway, it wouldn't surprise me if Basil had a lech for Sophie himself and that's why he wasn't sorry she wanted to leave home. Which I suppose could say something for him.'

If they hadn't reached home at that point, Darina would have argued about this. But by the time she'd found somewhere to park the car and they'd got in the house, she was beginning to wonder if her mother mightn't have a point.

'I think we need a cup of tea,' Darina said, going through to the kitchen.

'Oh, yes, how lovely. I'll get some cups out, shall I?'

Darina always used mugs but said nothing. There was something wrong with the kitchen and she tried to work out what it was as she filled the kettle.

'You'll miss that little boy,' her mother said, taking out the Spode porcelain tea set that had been her wedding present to them from the back of a cupboard. That was it – no Rory! It was all horribly neat, empty and quiet.

*

403

Darina expected William to be late. It was a surprise, therefore, when he walked in shortly after seven thirty as she and her mother were having a drink in the drawing room.

'Now I can say properly how pleased I am to see you,' said Ann, holding up her face for his kiss. 'You were splendid this afternoon.'

'I agree, darling,' said Darina, giving him a warm embrace. 'I'm sorry if I seemed to take over at one point, but it was all clear to me and I couldn't see any other way to get it over to you.'

'You were a good catalyst,' he said, his hand lingering on the back of her neck. 'Hey, isn't that Rory's?'

Darina looked where he was pointing; a small car had crashed into the skirting board. She picked up the toy and held it in her hand for a moment before placing it on a side table. She waited for William to say how quiet the house was without Rory.

'At least we'll be able to have a full night's sleep now,' he said cheerfully, sitting in his chair. 'As you're up, darling, can you get me a drink?'

Just about to pour William a whisky, Darina remembered his diet and gave him a glass of mineral water with ice instead. 'Have you finished interviewing Jasper already?'

'Haven't even started,' he said ruefully. 'The Ealham solicitor turned up immediately after we reached the station and insisted Jasper was seen by a doctor. Who gave him a sedative. Result, we won't be able to speak to him until tomorrow. Thanks,' he added, holding up the glass she'd given him in a mock salute.

'Are you going to be able to make a case against him?'

'We've got a SOCO team going through his quarters

and over the Rolls. Preliminary reports suggest they've found a pair of trainers with gravel in their soles that could match the gravel outside the broken factory window, and jeans and a sweatshirt splashed with petrol. There are female hairs in the Rolls that could be Val Douglas's, and Jasper's prints are all over it. Both of them had ample access to the car so it mightn't mean anything but for the fact that, according to the commissionaire at the Ealham offices, the Rolls had a complete valet clean last Thursday. Basil never used it at all that day, it was driven back to the house by an employee, who left it in the garage around five o'clock without, he said, a speck of dust on it. He even polished the steering wheel and car door as he got out. The only prints on the wheel are Jasper's, so the case is building up.'

'My, what a lot you've managed to achieve,' Darina said admiringly, then told him what Maeve had told her about seeing Jasper leaving and entering the house in the small hours of the morning the factory had been set on fire.

'Well,' William said, 'it's all circumstantial so far but we should be able to make it stick. However, I fear it may be a case of diminished responsibility.'

'Does that mean Broadmoor?' Ann asked.

William nodded. 'Probably.'

'Have you any doubts about his guilt?' Darina asked.

'What, after he more or less confessed everything to us all? Not that that would stick in a court of law. But, no, it all fits too neatly.'

'How is he?'

'Beginning to come down off his high.'

'Your team must be pleased the case is sewn up,

not to mention Superintendent Roger Marks,' Darina grinned at her husband, for once not resenting the influence the super had on his life.

'Cock-a-hoop. Two murders solved in one day. It's even put Operation Chippendale in the shade.'

'And will Sergeant Pat James become a permanent member of your team?' Darina found herself asking.

'That's up to Roger. I hope so, against all the odds and after a sticky start, she and Terry Pitman seem to have hit it off.' He seemed so pleased with this fact, Darina released a breath she hadn't realized she'd been holding.

'When did you put everything together?' William asked her curiously.

'Only very gradually, I'm afraid. Rory's resemblance to both Basil and Jasper is striking and at first I thought Basil was the father. This morning I met Noah Whitstable, an out-and-out no hoper who's just about managing at the moment because he's living with a very competent Australian girl. It was clear Sophie had looked after Noah just the way Laurel was doing now. Heaven only knows why, he knocks her about and is as likely to shout at her as thank her. She seems to like being needed. And I think it was the same with Sophie.

'Anyway, there we were in the library and Jasper came in, his eyes dilated just like Noah's, obviously under the influence of some drug, and I suddenly realized that he was probably as unreliable and maybe potentially violent as Noah and that Sophie could have slipped into a relationship with Noah because he reminded her so much of her brother. So then all sorts of things fell into place.

'You see, as I gradually learned more about Sophie, the thing that puzzled me was that everyone claimed she couldn't cope with pressure from Basil. But her sister-in-law told me she spoke regularly to him on the telephone and never seemed upset by any of their conversatons. It didn't seem to add up. If, however, she was happy for everyone to think that it was Basil she couldn't live with, but that the real reason was something else entirely, it all made some sort of sense.'

'She sounds quite a remarkable girl,' said Ann.

'I think she was. It was such a tragedy she couldn't bring herself to go to the doctor or the clinic when she was pregnant.'

'Why didn't she?'

'I think it was because she was afraid they would discover the baby she was carrying was Jasper's. He had told her blood tests could identify your father and she took that to mean if she had a blood test, the truth would out.'

'Even I know it's not as simple as that!' exclaimed Ann.

'Everyone was right that poor Sophie wasn't very intelligent, at least, not in that way,' Darina said sorrowfully.

'And you worked all that out without an ounce of solid evidence,' her husband said with grave admiration. 'Would that we could conduct our investigations like that.'

Darina threw a cushion at him. 'Well, now you and your team can beaver away at producing hard evidence to make a case. It's up to you to see that justice can be done.'

William ignored this. 'I say, that's the most wonderful smell. I do hope it's supper, I didn't get any lunch and I'm starving.'

'Roast lamb with red rice from the Camargue, broccoli and carrots, followed by pears poached with cinnamon and served with a sheep's milk and vanilla sauce thickened with cornflour. All allowed on your diet. How's the headache?' Darina asked anxiously.

William paused, as though he needed to think about it. 'Do you know,' he said in surprise, 'it's gone! I feel great, really, really great.' He gave her a beaming smile and rose. 'In fact, I'll have some more mineral water, I haven't felt this good in years.'

'What have you been doing?' asked Ann curiously. Then, after the diet had been explained to her, 'Heavens! Are you condemned to this extraordinary regime for the rest of your life?'

'No,' William assured her. 'Soon we'll be able to identify what's been causing the problem.'

'Well, that's a relief. I just hope you won't have to cut out anything you really like.'

'Probably cheese,' he said gloomily. 'But it's worth it if I can go on feeling like this.' He stretched his arms out, 'Anyone want to go dancing? I might just be able to keep going all night.'

'I've got other plans for tonight,' Darina said with a smile.